THE TREK EAST

THE TREK EAST

モルモン教と日本

Mormonism Meets Japan, 1901–1968

Shinji Takagi

Salt Lake City, 2016
Greg Kofford Books

Copyright © 2016 Shinji Takagi
Cover design copyright © 2016 Greg Kofford Books, Inc.
Cover design by Loyd Ericson
Cover image courtesy of D. Clayton Fairbourn.
Author photo courtesy of Richard Grant Herron.

Published in the USA.
All rights reserved. No part of this volume may be reproduced in any form without written permission from the publisher, Greg Kofford Books. The views expressed herein are the responsibility of the author and do not necessarily represent the position of Greg Kofford Books.

ISBN 978-1-58958-560-7 (paperback)
ISBN 978-1-58958-561-4 (hardcover)
Also available in ebook.

Greg Kofford Books
P.O. Box 1362
Draper, UT 84020
www.gregkofford.com

Library of Congress Control Number: 2016945073

To my fellow travelers on the Trek East:
Sue L.
Kenta B.
Emi R.
Naomi E.
Koji M.

Contents

Preface	xiii
A Note on Japanese Words	xvii

Chapter 1.
Mormonism's Trek East: An Introduction

1.1. Introduction	1
1.2. Mormonism Meets Japan	2
1.3. Key Issues from Early Mormon History in Japan	6
1.4. How this Book is Organized	11

Chapter 2.
Tomizo and Tokujiro: The First Japanese Mormons

2.1. Introduction	15
2.2. Tomizo Katsunuma	16
2.3. Tokujiro Sato	32
2.4. Conclusion	47

Appendix

2.1. Children of Tomizo and Tokujiro	48

Chapter 3.
Mormons in the Press: Japanese Reactions to the 1901 Arrival of Heber J. Grant and Company

3.1. Introduction	51
3.2. Japan at the Turn of the Twentieth Century	53
3.3. Reactions of the English-Language Press	57
3.4. Reactions in the Japanese Press	62
3.5. The Question of Polygamy	67
3.6. Hirobumi Ito and the Legal Prostitution Controversy	70
3.7. Constitutional and Legal Questions	74
3.8. The Osaka Controversy	76
3.9. A Voice of Reason: Eitaro Okano	79
3.10. Conclusion	81

Appendix

3.1. *Morumonshū* by Toru Uchida, January 1902	83

Chapter 4.
Monks, Nationalists, and the Emperor:
Understanding the Religious and Intellectual Climate of Meiji Japan

4.1.	Introduction	87
4.2.	Japan's Early Religious Roots	90
4.3.	The Rise of State Shinto	98
4.4.	Christian Evangelization and the Nationalist Reaction	105
4.5.	The Penumbra of Hope and Hostility	114
4.6.	Conclusion	118

Chapter 5.
Planting the Apple Tree: People, Places, and Publications, 1901–24

5.1.	Introduction	119
5.2.	Early Decisions and Events	120
5.3.	Early Friends and Converts	123
5.4.	Defining the Geographical Scope of Missionary Work	134
5.5.	Presenting the Message in Japanese	144
5.6.	Conclusion	158

Appendix

5.1.	Prominent Men Befriended by Early Mormon Missionaries	159

Chapter 6.
Proclaiming the Way in Japanese:
The 1909 Translation of the Book of Mormon

6.1.	Introduction	167
6.2.	The Choice of Style	170
6.3.	The Work of Revision	173
6.4.	The Literary Value	178
6.5.	The Manner of Translation	182
6.6.	Notable Words and Expressions	185
6.7.	The Question of Accuracy	188
6.8.	Conclusion	192

Appendices

6.1.	Major Differences between Classical and Contemporary Japanese	194
6.2.	Advertising the Publication of the Japanese Book of Mormon	195

Chapter 7.
The Japan Mission under Taisho Democracy: Failure or Forfeit?

7.1.	Introduction	203
7.2.	Taisho Democracy and the Japan Mission	204
7.3.	Mormonism's Measured Response and Its Aftermath	210

7.4. Understanding Why the Japan Mission Was Closed	218
7.5. Political and Religious Developments in Interwar Japan	230
7.6. The Withdrawal Decision in Light of Subsequent History	240
7.7. Conclusion	244

Chapter 8.
Mormonism's Transpacific Interlude:
Retreat and Regrouping, 1924–44

8.1. Introduction	247
8.2. Resuscitating the Dimming Light	248
8.3. The Ministry of Takeo Fujiwara, 1934–36	253
8.4. Mormonism and the Japanese Population of the American West	259
8.5. Mormon Missionary Work among the Japanese of Hawaii	270
8.6. Conclusion	284

Appendix
8.1. Mike Masaoka and the Japanese Americans during World War II	286

Chapter 9.
The Eagle and the Scattered Flock:
Early Mormon Activities in Occupied Japan, 1945–48

9.1. Introduction	291
9.2. Chaplain Nelson and the First Postwar Baptisms	294
9.3. The Conversion of Tatsui Sato	300
9.4. Edward L. Clissold and the Tokyo Saints	307
9.5. Russell N. Horiuchi and the Nara Sunday Group	311
9.6. Reestablishing the Church in Japan	315
9.7. Conclusion	321

Chapter 10.
Riding on the Eagle's Wings:
The Japanese Mission under American Occupation, 1948–52

10.1. Introduction	323
10.2. The Japanese Mission Begins Work	324
10.3. The Arrival of Missionaries	328
10.4. Clissold Completes His Mission	334
10.5. Geographical Expansion under Clissold and Mauss	338
10.6. Organizational Developments under Mauss	342
10.7. Conclusion	346

Appendices
10.1. Selected Area Beginnings by District	347
10.2. The Ichishima Land Deal	357

Chapter 11.
Enlarging the Borders: Modern Ecclesiastical Developments, 1952–68

11.1. Introduction	361
11.2. The Evolving Scope of Missionary Work	363
11.3. The Opening of Work in Okinawa and Korea	373
11.4. Securing Places of Worship	380
11.5. Developing Local Leadership	391
11.6. Conclusion	395

Chapter 12.
Leafs, Steeples, and Testimonies:
Building the Foundation for Future Growth, 1948–68

12.1. Introduction	397
12.2. The Translation of LDS Scriptures	399
12.3. Assessing the Quality of the 1957 Translation	404
12.4. Revamping the Approach to Missionary Work	409
12.5. The Building Program	413
12.6. Building the Testimonies of Japanese Mormons	422
12.7. Understanding the Postwar Growth of the LDS Church in Japan	431
12.8. Conclusion	438

Annexes

1. The Iwakura Mission in Salt Lake City	443
2. George Jarvis: Was He the First Mormon Missionary to Japan?	447
3. The Rise and Fall of Walter Murray Gibson	449
4. Notable Japanese Mormons from the Prewar Period	453
5. Mormon Mission Presidents, 1901–68	471
6. Selected Major Newspapers in Japan that Published Articles, Editorials, and Letters on Mormonism Between August and September 1901	473
7. Mormon Missionaries in the Japan Mission, 1901–24	477
8. Converts and Children of Record Baptized in Prewar Japan, 1902–39	479
9. Mormon Converts Baptized in Occupied Japan, 1946–52	483
10. Mormon Missionaries in the Japanese and Northern Far East Missions, 1948–68	495
11. Early American Labor Missionaries in Japan, 1962–69	521
12. Partial List of Locally Called Labor Missionaries in the Northern Far East Mission, 1962–68	523

Glossary of Mormon and Japanese Terms	527
Bibliography	531
Subject Index	555
Name Index	569

List of Tables

1.1. Population in Japan and the United States, 1900–60 — 9
5.1. Proselytizing Areas and Convert Baptisms in the Japan Mission, 1901–24 — 143
5.2. Mormon Tracts in Japanese, May 1903–December 1921 — 150
8.1. Characteristics of Japanese Population in Utah, 1890–1940 — 264
8.2. People of Japanese Ancestry in Hawaii, 1890–1940 — 271
8.3. Japanese/Central Pacific Mission in Hawaii, 1937–44 — 279
11.1. Full-Time Mormon Missionaries Who Arrived and Completed their Missions during May 1952–August 1968 — 365
11.2. Property Purchases by the LDS Church in Japan, 1948–65 — 381
12.1. LDS Church Constructed Buildings in Japan, 1948–67 — 418
12.2. Labor Inputs in the First Two Mormon Building Projects in Japan, December 1963 — 421
12.3. Net Migration in Selected Urban and Rural Prefectures in Japan, 1959–61 — 435

List of Figures

1.1. Full-Time Missionaries and Cumulative Baptisms in Japan, 1901–68 — 7
4.1. Yearly Numbers of Baptisms and Missionaries in the LDS Japan Mission, 1902–24 — 89
5.1. Principal Proselytizing Areas in the LDS Japan Mission, 1902–24 — 135
5.2. Areas in Japan where Mormon Missionaries Labored, 1902–24 — 138
7.1. Mormon Baptisms per Missionary per Year — 207
7.2. Average Experience of Mormon Missionaries in Japan, January 1902–July 1924 — 225
10.1. Number of Mormon Missionaries in Occupied Japan, June 1948–April 1952 — 332
11.1. Number of Full-Time Mormon Missionaries in Japan, May 1952–August 1968 — 364
11.2. The Arrival of Mormon Missionaries in the Japanese and Northern Far East Missions, 1952–68 — 366
11.3. Latter-Day Saint Districts with Proselytizing Areas in Japan, 1953 — 369
12.1. Japan's Real Gross Domestic Product (GDP) Growth and Nominal GDP in Major Industrial Countries, 1952–70 — 398
12.2. Per Capita Gross Domestic Product in Japan and the United States, 1952–70 — 399
12.3. Productivity of Full-Time Mormon Missionaries in Japan, 1948–68 — 410
12.4. Monthly Mormon Baptisms in Japan, January 1955–December 1964 — 413
12.5. Urbanization and Industrialization in Japan, 1940–70 — 432
12.6. Mormon Converts in Largest Metropolitan Areas in Japan, 1948–68 — 434
12.7. Gender Composition of Mormon Converts in Japan, 1948–68 — 436

Preface

The Trek East presents a historical analysis of the Mormon experience in Japan from 1901 to 1968. The book chronicles major events and ecclesiastical developments, recounts notable personalities, and discusses the historical contexts of key decisions regarding early Mormon history in Japan. To be sure, this is a topic upon which various accounts have already been written.[1] Unfortunately, what is written relies almost exclusively on missionary journals and other English-language sources. Also, much misinformation and misunderstanding has been perpetuated, and the quality of scholarship has been uneven. Reflecting the predominantly *descriptive* (as opposed to *analytical*) approach of the existing literature, moreover, few studies attempt to explain why certain things happened the way they did and to place the Mormon experience in a broader historical context; most give exclusive attention to what happened with little regard to the societal context that gives meaning. In writing this book, I have tried to elucidate important historical episodes against Japan's evolving economic, legal, political, religious, and social backgrounds by utilizing primary and secondary sources in the English and Japanese languages. The outcome is not the type of devotional history some Mormon readers may expect. From time to time, our story involves individuals whose judgments and decisions were conditioned by external circumstances and who took actions that turned out to be imperfect ex post. As always, it requires an eye of faith to see divine guidance in human affairs.

An event of nearly twenty-five years ago made me an accidental historian. A mutual friend, Ryuichi Inoue, introduced me to Bill McIntyre, who had a manuscript that needed to be translated from English to Japanese. I met Bill at a Tokyo café in May 1993 and agreed to offer help in translating his work in progress. Bill had the noble desire to tell the history of their church in their own country to Japanese Mormons, who had limited access to writings on Japanese Mormon history, which were available exclusively in English. Having some previous experience with translation work (though admittedly not in history), I assumed that I could complete the task rather quickly. How different the outcome has turned out to be! Not only did it take nearly three years to publish what became our joint

---

1. The most comprehensive of these are Murray L. Nichols, "History of the Japan Mission of the Church of Jesus Christ of Latter-day Saints, 1901–1924" (MA thesis, Brigham Young University, 1957) and Reid L. Neilson, *Early Mormon Missionary Activities in Japan, 1901–1924* (Salt Lake City: University of Utah Press, 2010). The former is a distinctively ecclesiastical treatment of the prewar mission while the latter focuses on missiology.

work,[2] but it has ultimately taken me the next quarter of a century to be able to free myself from the spell cast on that occasion.

I learned quickly that there was no such thing as translating an English text on Japanese history into Japanese (unless only well-known events and names are involved). Transliteration from English of Japanese proper nouns, such as geographical and personal names, requires knowing the actual places and people because there are multiple combinations of Chinese characters that would sound identical in Japanese. The scholar in me, moreover, kept questioning what was written in English and raising additional questions. Thus began a long process of research in order to identify the Chinese characters, solve puzzles to my satisfaction, and discover new facts hitherto unknown. Not only did I have access to the library of a major national research university as a professor of economics, but I also happened to have privileged access to a small library with a large collection of prewar reference works at the Ministry of Finance. From 1992 to 1994, I was commuting weekly from my university in Osaka to Tokyo, where I had an appointment at the government to direct a team of researchers. The library was just across the hall from my office. Ready access to the vintage materials certainly came in handy for my new Mormon history project at the opportune time.

The reader will note, from the personal interviews and correspondence that are cited herein, that most of the primary research for this book was conducted in the final years of the last century. I can only remember with gratitude the kindness and generosity of so many people who responded to my inquiries, by granting me interviews, replying to my letters, sending me copies of their treasured documents and photographs, and sharing their own personal histories (both diaries and biographical accounts) or those of their parents and grandparents. I have worked sporadically to complete this project by, at the suggestion of Armand Mauss, writing chapters as articles for publication in scholarly journals. Five of the eleven main chapters (Chapters 2, 3, 6, 9, 10) were previously published in *BYU Studies* (2000, 2001), the *Journal of Mormon History* (2002, 2003), and the *Journal of the Book of Mormon and Other Restoration Scripture* (2009). In preparing these for inclusion, however, I have suitably edited them, corrected any errors, and added new material in a number of places (most appendices were not part of the original articles). Another chapter (Chapter 4) was written in 2013 as I was preparing a short chapter for a collected volume edited by Patrick Mason and published by the University of Utah Press in 2016. In order to complete the book by writing the remaining five chapters, however, I needed to wait until the fall of 2014, when my life finally became free of pressing commitments in economics. Pleasantly, leaving academia has allowed me to claim my own personal time when I am not paid to work.

I owe heavy debts of gratitude to a number of people. I am especially grateful to Bill McIntyre, the coauthor of joint work whose content, including some photographs, I have liberally used as if my own; Armand Mauss, without whose

---

2. *Nihon Matsujitsu Seito Shi* (Kobe: Beehive Shuppan, 1996).

constant encouragement and professional advice this book probably would not have been written;³ and the late Wade Fillmore, who shared his insights and findings and whose passing in the summer of 2015 coincided with the beginning of an urge to complete the book. Ronald Barney, Randall Dixon, and Ronald Watt, formerly of the LDS church historical department, showed flexibility and sympathy for a foreign researcher making sporadic visits to Salt Lake City for at most two days at a time; Susan Thompson assisted me in July 1996 during my visit to the special collections library at Brigham Young University (and an unnamed student assistant made a photocopy of virtually the entire Alma O. Taylor journal); Greg Gubler, formerly of Brigham Young University–Hawaii, likewise facilitated my archival research during a one-day visit to Laie in February 1997; and Eric Walz of Brigham Young University–Idaho shared some of the findings from his research on Japanese immigrants in the United States. Conan Grames helped with last-minute research at the Church Historical Library in Salt Lake City, as did my nephew Seiji Funakoshi at libraries in Tokyo. Former Mormon leaders and missionaries, their descendants and families, and friends who provided valuable information and assistance in the course of this research are too numerous to mention by name.

In preparing the manuscript for publication, the late Wade Fillmore, Chris Fuller, Van Gessel, Conan Grames, Armand Mauss, and Norm Shumway provided comment and feedback at various stages. Anonymous peer reviewers provided critical comments on five chapters of the book when they were originally published as stand-alone pieces. Jonathan Giles read the first draft of the entire manuscript to provide critical comment and suggestions for improvement. Austin Smith read the final draft to catch any remaining errors and improve the clarity of exposition, and suggested additional material for inclusion from his repertoire of knowledge. Last but not least, I must express deep gratitude to my wife and our four children, who saw her husband and their father work intermittently on this project for so many years. A household full of jovial voices when the work started is now as still as a Zen temple. Aptly, the famed poet Basho said of the passing of time: "Days and months are transient guests for countless generations, and the years too are travelers that come and go."⁴ Rightly, it is to them that this book should belong.

Shinji Takagi
Arlington, Virginia
February 2016

---

3. I contacted Armand for the first time in July 1998 concerning his father Vinal G. Mauss, a prewar missionary to Japan and one of the first postwar mission presidents in Japan. It was later learned that he was a long-time family friend of my daughter-in-law. Armand was a guest at my son's wedding in the summer of 2005.

4. My own translation of the opening passage of Matsuo Basho, *Oku no Hosomichi*, 1702: "Tsukihi wa hakutai no kakaku ni shite, yukikau toshi mo mata tabibito nari." This has been translated by a number of highly competent people, but I am yet to find a translation that accurately captures the beauty and the "sound" of the original.

A Note on Japanese Words

Names: Except for historical figures (who died before the Meiji era), Japanese names are rendered in the Western style, with given name first and family name second. This appears to be a well-established practice in the literature on Japanese immigration to Hawaii, for example, where those with Japanese names cross national borders. In this book, moreover, those born in the United States occasionally have Japanese given and family names (e.g., Kenji Akagi, Kimiaki Sakata, and Tomiko Shirota). Confusion is best avoided by adopting the Western naming convention for all.

Macrons: A macron, indicating a long vowel, is used when a Japanese word is used as a foreign word. For example, Shinto and Showa are English words when they appear by themselves, so no macrons are used. When they appear in a Japanese sentence, for example as a reference in the bibliography, they are italicized in most cases and spelled as *Shintō* and *Shōwa*. Likewise, personal names and most geographical names (e.g., Kyoto, Osaka, and Tokyo) are considered to be English words. No macrons are used. Other proper nouns are generally treated as Japanese words but may not be italicized.

Japan's Main Islands with Selected Places of Historical Significance

Chapter 1

Mormonism's Trek East: An Introduction

1.1. Introduction

This volume presents a historical analysis of the experience of the Church of Jesus Christ of Latter-day Saints (hereafter referred to as the LDS Church) in Japan from 1901 to 1968. The year 1901 saw the establishment of the first Mormon mission in Japan, while 1968 represents the year in which, as the culmination of sustained growth in the 1960s, the church for the first time divided the mission into two separate entities covering northeastern and southwestern Japan. Mormon missionary work in the pre–World War II period was carried out in Japan from 1901 to 1924, when it was temporarily halted for lack of success (though some writers have attributed the closing to other reasons). Since its return to Japan in 1948, following the war's end, the church has had a continuous presence, this time with some visible success. According to the latest Japanese government statistics, the LDS Church is Japan's second largest Christian denomination (its membership exceeded only by the Roman Catholic Church), with 126,856 members meeting in 287 congregations in 2014.[1] It might be of some interest to investigate how Mormon pioneers in Japan laid the foundation for future growth.

This introductory chapter provides background information, in order to help readers anticipate what is ahead and to facilitate understanding for those who are not familiar with Mormonism or Japan (as such, knowledgeable readers may wish to skip this chapter and go directly to any of the succeeding chapters, each of which is presented as sufficiently self-contained). Section 1.2 presents a primer on Mormon and Japanese history relevant to our topic and explains the approach taken. Section 1.3 highlights some of the key issues that emerge from

---

1. In 2014, Roman Catholicism claimed 444,719 members, while the third largest, the United Church of Christ in Japan (*Nihon Kirisuto Kyōdan*), had 119,747 members; the Baptist denominations with a combined total of 42,230 members were a distant fourth. Bunkachō, ed., *Shūkyō Nenkan* (Tokyo: Bunkachō, 2015), 80–85. These numbers likely grossly overstate the true strength of each denomination as the rate of activity is rather low, but should accurately reflect the relative strengths of major national denominations. It should be noted that the Japanese government does not report the activities of the Jehovah's Witnesses as they are not nationally registered under the Religious Corporation Law.

early Mormon history in Japan that are addressed in the rest of the book. Section 1.4 describes the outline of the book by giving a summary of each chapter. For those readers unfamiliar with Mormonism or Japan, a glossary placed towards the end of the book provides the meanings of basic Mormon and Japanese terms the knowledge of which the rest of the book takes for granted.

1.2. Mormonism Meets Japan

The Church of Jesus Christ of Latter-day Saints was founded in 1830 by Joseph Smith in upstate New York. The doctrines taught by Smith included belief in the Bible, millennialism, continuous revelation, and the restoration of ancient biblical practices, such as church government led by prophets and apostles, temple ceremonies, and, at one time, even plural marriage (polygyny). Smith brought forth the Book of Mormon, which he claimed was the translation of ancient American scripture. The Bible, the Book of Mormon, the Doctrine and Covenants (a volume of revelations received by Smith and his successors), and the Pearl of Great Price (a volume of Smith's writings) constitute the "standard works" or the canon of Mormon scripture. Because of their belief in the Book of Mormon, church members are often called Mormons and sometimes referred to as Latter-day Saints or simply "Saints."

From the earliest days of the church's existence, the Mormons moved westward in search of a haven from persecution—first from New York to Ohio and then to Missouri. Expelled from Missouri in 1839 by the extermination order of Governor Lilburn Boggs (proclaimed in October 1838), they established a city in Illinois, which they called Nauvoo. Nauvoo would become the second largest city, after Chicago, in the state of Illinois, and where the saints found temporary peace and prosperity. This, however, was not to last very long. Persecution intensified following the martyrdom of Joseph Smith in June 1844 at the hands of a mob. In the middle of a harsh winter, in February 1846, the saints, under the leadership of Brigham Young, began to cross the icy Mississippi on a westward journey towards the Great Basin, then Mexican territory. By mid-May, nearly 12,000 people had crossed the river to the Iowa side; by autumn, Nauvoo was virtually empty.[2]

Mormonism's trek west was a decades-long process by which the Mormon pioneers traveled to the American West by wagons, handcarts, and railroad, transformed the arid desert into productive farmland, and built communities in which they could practice their religion freely. In July 1847, the first company of saints arrived in the Salt Lake Valley. Subsequently, literally tens of thousands of

---

2. James B. Allen and Glen M. Leonard, *The Story of the Latter-day Saints* (Salt Lake City: Deseret Book, 1976), 221; Leonard J. Arrington and Davis Bitton, *The Mormon Experience: A History of the Latter-day Saints* (New York: Alfred A. Knopf, 1979), 96.

Mormons, including converts from the British Isles and other parts of Europe,[3] gathered in the place they called Zion and built hundreds of communities in much of Nevada and Utah and parts of Arizona, California, Idaho, Oregon, and Wyoming.[4] Despite these achievements, however, lasting peace, let alone religious freedom, remained elusive. Following the Mexican–American War of 1846–48, the land they had claimed became a territory of the United States. As the practice of plural marriage became public,[5] especially following the completion of the transcontinental railroad in 1869, an open conflict ensued with the federal government.

Determined to crush the Mormons, the United States Congress passed a series of laws to terminate the practice of plural marriage,[6] including the Edmunds–Tucker Act of 1887 which, among other things, forced wives to testify against their husbands, dissolved the church as a legal entity, and confiscated all church property in excess of $50,000. When the United States Supreme Court ruled in May 1890 that the seizure of church property under the Edmunds–Tucker Act was constitutional, the LDS Church had no choice but to give up the practice of plural marriage. In October 1890 the fourth church president, Wilford Woodruff, issued an official statement (the "Manifesto") declaring the termination of plural marriage as a religious practice. This paved the way for the territory of Utah to gain statehood in 1896 and for the Mormons at long last to enjoy freedom from government harassment.[7]

In the meantime, on the other side of the Pacific, Japan was opening up its doors to the outside world just as the Mormons were making the desert in

---

3. From 1846 to 1887 more than 85,000 European converts traveled to Utah, many of whom were assisted by the church's Perpetual Emigration Fund. Arrington and Bitton, *Mormon Experience*, 136.

4. For the Mormon colonization of the Great Basin during the nineteenth century, see Leonard J. Arrington, *Great Basin Kingdom: Economic History of the Latter-Day Saints, 1830–1900* (Cambridge, Mass.: Harvard University Press, 1958).

5. Demographics, such as population growth and the average age difference between husbands and wives when they typically marry, would place an upper limit on the sustainable share of polygyny in a population, as the number of marriage-age women is finite and society cannot tolerate too many unmarried men. Davis Bitton and Val Lambson estimate mathematically that the reasonable, sustainable limits were 15–20 percent for men and 25–30 percent for women in nineteenth-century Utah. Davis Bitton and Val Lambson, "Demographic Limits of Nineteenth-Century Mormon Polygyny," *Brigham Young University Studies Quarterly* 51 (2012): 10.

6. The Morrill Anti-Bigamy Act of 1862 banned bigamy and limited church ownership in any territory of the United States, while the Edmunds Act of 1882 made polygamy a felony and unlawful cohabitation a misdemeanor as well as disfranchised polygamists and made them ineligible for public office. The Morrill Act was not enforced. Richard S. Van Wagoner, *Mormon Polygamy: A History* (Salt Lake City: Signature Books, 1986).

7. Edward Leo Lyman, *Political Deliverance: The Mormon Quest for Utah Statehood* (Urbana, Ill.: University of Illinois Press, 1986).

the valleys of the mountains "blossom as the rose."[8] The arrival in July 1853 of Commodore Perry of the United States Navy set in motion a series of events that led to the collapse of the Tokugawa regime and the restoration of direct imperial rule in 1868, in what is known as the Meiji Restoration. Early in the seventeenth century, the Tokugawa family, having received the title of *shōgun* (military general) from the emperor, had begun to rule Japan from its castle in Edo (present-day Tokyo), while the emperor remained in Kyoto as the symbol of residual authority but without any actual power. The inherent contradiction of the Tokugawa regime, namely, the system of rule by one dominant clan over competing ones, became evident when Japan was dragged into contact with foreign powers in the early nineteenth century. It was not possible for the Tokugawa family to assume the role of central government of a modern nation-state based on the revenue from its fiefs alone. Perry's visit only hastened the timing of what was inevitable.

The Meiji Restoration was orchestrated by the two rebel clans of Satsuma and Choshu in southern Japan. Filled with nationalistic fervor, these and other clans joined forces under the banner of *sonnō jōi* ("revere the emperor, expel the barbarians"), united in their determination to overthrow the shogunate for yielding to foreign pressure to open the country. Once in power, however, the new government of Emperor Meiji, seeing the technological and military superiority of the Western nations, recognized the futility of any attempt to expel the barbarians; instead, the government embarked upon a sustained program of modernization by importing new ideas and technologies from the West. The emperor's charter oath, promulgated on 6 April 1868, declared in part: "Evil practices of the past shall be abandoned ... Knowledge shall be sought all over the world."[9] His reign was named Meiji (lit. enlightened rule), the capital was formally moved from Kyoto (which means capital city) to Edo (renamed Tokyo, meaning eastern capital city), and an ambitious period of nation building was launched under the national slogan *fukoku kyōhei* ("enrich the state, strengthen the military").

Mormonism's "Trek East" thus took place against the backdrop of three forces of history that emerged in the second half of the nineteenth century. First, with the aspirations of Manifest Destiny achieved in conquering the western frontier, the United States was expanding its influence as a Pacific military and economic power. Second, Japan was opening up its borders after 220 years of national seclusion, allowing its enterprising young men (and even some women) to travel abroad, foreign missionaries to enter the country, and its citizens eventually to practice a religion of their choice. Third, the Church of Jesus Christ of Latter-day Saints, having solidified its base in the intermountain West and finally freed from government harassment, was beginning to think of going beyond the then-established missions. In the process, Mormon leaders noted the spectacular rise of Japan to the ranks of the modern nations of the world while remembering

---

8. Isaiah 35:1.

9. Kōdansha, *Japan: An Illustrated Encyclopedia* (Tokyo: Kōdansha, 1993), 177.

favorably the visit in early 1872 of a high-level government mission led by Prince Tomomi Iwakura to Salt Lake City.[10] These impressions were among the reasons for their decision, in 1901, to open Asia's first permanent mission in Japan, with Heber J. Grant, an apostle and future church president, assigned to the task.

To be sure, this was not the first time missionaries were sent to Asia or possibly even to Japan. In August 1852, Brigham Young, convinced by the 1848 revolutions in Europe that the second coming of Christ was imminent, called more than one hundred missionaries to various parts of the world, including Hindustan (India), Siam (Thailand), and China. The work did not last very long in any of these places in Asia, however. After struggling for some time, they all returned home.[11] The China missionaries, Hosea Stout, James Lewis, and Chapman Duncan, finding themselves in the middle of the Taiping Rebellion, headed back to Utah after only two months in Hong Kong. Departing on 22 June 1853, they traveled over the territorial waters of Japan on their return journey. Stout's journal entries for 1 July and 4 July state, respectively: "at dark we could discover fire in many places on the island which we suppose to be Japanese fishing boats"; "We are now in about 'Lat 30' and ... Japan ... is now in plain view."[12] They may well have been the first Mormons to pass through Japan—though George Jarvis, a British sailor who later settled in St. George, Utah, claimed that he had been the first missionary called to Japan. Even if the claim is true, any contemplated mission was to be a temporary one.[13]

If we compare our story to a dramatic performance, the stage where the play takes place is Japan except in Chapter 8, where we take a temporary departure to the other side of the Pacific. Following the temporary withdrawal of missionaries from Japan in 1924, the church continued work among the Japanese immigrant population in Hawaii and, to a lesser extent and in a less formal way, in the continental United States. Throughout the play, the main actor is the LDS Church collectively, occasionally joined by missionaries, Utah leaders, and Japanese members. We take a distinctively "macro" approach, by paying comparatively little attention to the personal experiences of individual missionaries and members (except in Chapter 2 where we present the biographical sketches of two pioneer members—but even here our emphasis remains on the historical context of their experiences). Instead, we pay considerably more attention to the

---

10. For details, see Annex 1 towards the end of this volume.

11. Reid L. Neilson and Laurie F. Maffly-Kipp, "Nineteenth-century Mormonism and the Pacific Basin Frontier: An Introduction," in *Proclamation to the People: Nineteenth-century Mormonism and the Pacific Basin Frontier*, ed. Laurie F. Maffly-Kipp and Reid L. Neilson (Salt Lake City: University of Utah Press, 2008), 10. "Minutes of Conference," *Deseret Evening News*, 18 September 1852, 4, gives the names of fourteen missionaries sent to Asia.

12. Juanita Brooks, ed., *On the Mormon Frontier: The Diary of Hosea Stout 1844–1861* (Salt Lake City: University of Utah Press, 1964), 485.

13. See Annex 2 towards the end of this volume for an analysis of this claim.

stage set, lighting, and props. We are particularly interested in the logic behind the script—why certain decisions were made and their historical contexts. The book is therefore as much about Japan as about Mormonism. The reader will observe, through the eyes of Mormonism, the economic, intellectual, legal, political, religious, and social aspects of Japan as the country evolved across history and Mormonism's Trek East continued in search of a haven yet to be found.

1.3. Key Issues from Early Mormon History in Japan

The era of Mormon history covered by this book consists of the prewar period (1901–24), what might be called the intervening period (1924–48), and the postwar period (1948–68), with the exceptions of Chapters 2 and 4, which touch upon events prior to the opening of the mission. The first period corresponds to the original Japan Mission, when eighty-eight full-time missionaries claimed 174 converts;[14] the third period is that of the Japanese Mission (renamed in 1955 as the Northern Far East Mission) when an estimated 1,142 missionaries claimed an estimated 9,570 converts (see Figure 1.1). During the second period, there was no formal church presence, except for short-lived attempts to restore limited church activity (see Chapter 8) and for the self-initiated efforts of American servicemen (see Chapter 9). In Hawaii, formal missionary work was briefly carried out among the Japanese immigrant population (see Chapter 8).

From 1901 to 1968, sixteen men served as mission presidents among the Japanese population of Japan and Hawaii.[15] Of these men, Hilton Robertson served three times, in prewar Japan, Hawaii, and postwar Japan. Edward Clissold served twice, in Hawaii and postwar Japan. Normally, seasoned leaders serve as Mormon mission presidents, but few fit this description in the prewar era. Except for Heber J. Grant, who was forty-six years old when he first arrived, the rest were relatively young men in their twenties or early thirties; two of them served as single men. These features of the prewar period were dictated by the need to call mission presidents from among the few who had served as missionaries and acquired language proficiency.

Mormon proselytizing missionaries serve under the supervision of mission presidents. Today, they are typically young men ("elders") and women ("sisters") in their late teens or early twenties, who come to serve at their own (or their families') expense for twenty-four and eighteen months, respectively. In the prewar period, however, some missionaries were married men who left their families at home, while in the immediate postwar period some were World War II veterans in their mid to late twenties. The terms of their service in Japan were variable and

---

14. This number includes five member children who were baptized at the age of eight or (in one instance) nine.

15. Annex 5 towards the end of this volume provides a chronological list of all Mormon mission presidents.

Figure 1.1. Full-Time Missionaries and Cumulative Baptisms in Japan, 1901–68

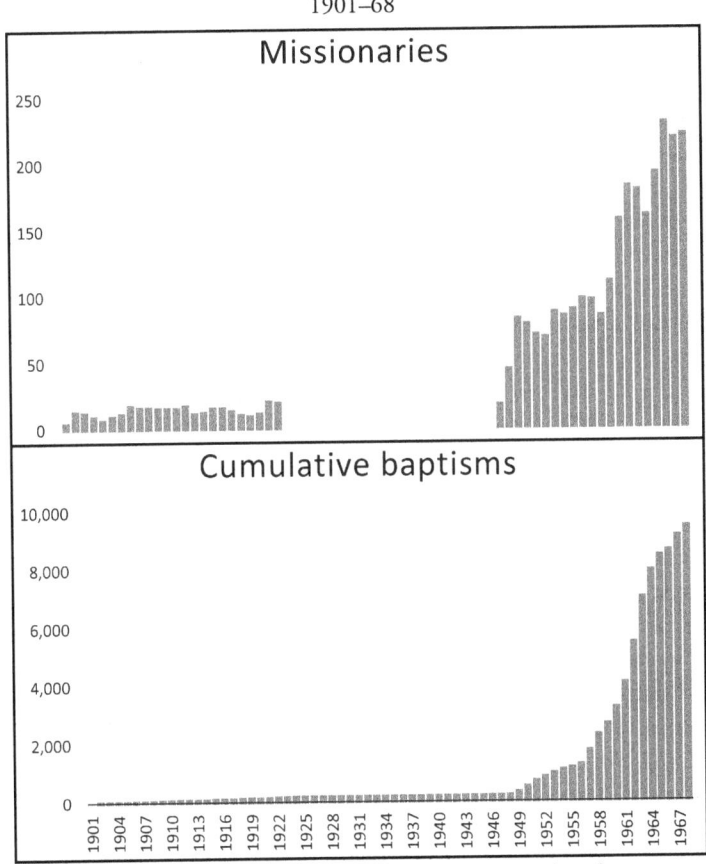

Excludes American military baptisms. Author's estimates based on various church records.

generally much longer. The prescribed term during much of the prewar period was four years. After World War II, the term of service was initially three years for men (and two years for women), but it was shortened to thirty months for men in 1959. This longer tenure in the field reflected the need to acquire proficiency in the Japanese language. The church had no systematized program of language training until early 1969, when the Language Training Mission in Hawaii was expanded to include instruction in Japanese.

Mormon missionaries, especially the early ones, were hampered not only by the lack of systematic language training but also by the lack of religious literature in the Japanese language. This book devotes some space to discussing how the early missionaries wrote their own tracts and translated them into Japanese (see Chapter 5). Many of the missionaries, because of their youth or farming background, had limited formal secular education. The fact that they could write their own tracts must reflect the effectiveness of the religious education they had received while growing up in Mormon communities. It also reflected the less "correlated" (i.e., coordinated) nature of the LDS Church in the first half of the twentieth century, when mission leaders enjoyed greater autonomy from Utah headquarters. It was well into the 1960s before the church began to centralize many of its ecclesiastical operations, including the preparation of manuals, missionary tracts, and curricular materials.[16] The history of the LDS Church in Japan is all the more interesting because the decisions, especially those in the prewar and immediate postwar periods, reflected the choices of individual missionaries far more than would have been the case during more recent decades.

This book devotes considerable space to the translation of the LDS scriptures, the Book of Mormon in particular. The Book of Mormon, described by Joseph Smith as the keystone of Mormonism, has been translated into Japanese three times, with translations published in 1909, 1957, and 1995. The 1909 translation is the topic of Chapter 6 (with additional discussion in Chapter 5) and the 1957 translation is discussed in Chapter 12. For each, not only the historical particulars of the translations but also the ultimate question of their quality and accuracy are addressed. The Doctrine and Covenants has also been translated three times, but the first translation, completed in 1914, was never published; the other two translations were made as part of the new translations of the three standard works, including the Pearl of Great Price, published in 1957 and 1995. The 1957 translation is a topic of discussion in Chapter 12.

A person becomes a Mormon convert when he or she is baptized by immersion, after which the "gift of the Holy Ghost" is conferred in a "confirmation" ceremony. The convert is expected to practice certain outward observances, including adherence to the Word of Wisdom (abstention from alcoholic drinks, coffee, tea, and tobacco), attendance at Sunday meetings, and, once matured in the faith, participation in temple ceremonies (such as baptism for deceased ancestors, an "endowment" in which covenants are made in anticipation of promised blessings, and a "sealing" for eternity of wife and husband or of children to parents). When the Mormon missionaries first arrived in Japan, the church had no temples outside Utah. The first temple constructed outside Utah was the Hawaii Temple (dedicated in 1919) in Laie, on the northern shore of Oahu. Few prewar converts gained sufficient knowledge to mature in the faith, but even if some did it would have been nearly impossible to travel to Hawaii, let alone to Utah, for temple worship. In all likelihood, only two Japanese converts partici-

---

16. How the "correlation movement" changed the basic nature of the Mormon subculture is discussed masterfully by Armand L. Mauss, *The Angel and the Beehive: The Mormon Struggle with Assimilation* (Urbana, Ill.: University of Illinois Press, 1994), especially 163–67.

Table 1.1. Population in Japan and the United States, 1900–60

	Japan (millions)	United States (millions)	Relative size of Japan (percent)
1900	44	76	57.9
1920	56	106	52.8
1940	72	132	54.5
1960	94	178	52.8

Excludes overseas possessions. Statistics Japan, www.stat.go.jp; United States Bureau of the Census, Statistical Abstract of the United States: 1970, ninety-first edition (Washington: United States Department of Commerce, 1970).

pated in temple ceremonies in the prewar period. Chapter 12 discusses how the church organized its first excursion to the Hawaii Temple in 1965 for its 150 or so Japanese members.

The church's general lack of commitment to prewar Japan is evident in the number of missionaries assigned to labor in the field: for a country of 45 to 55 million people (about half the population of the United States, see Table 1.1), the number averaged 12.5 and never exceeded twenty at any given time. From 1901 to 1924, the number of missionaries sent to Japan was less than 0.5 percent of the global total; no new missionaries were received in five of the twenty-four years.[17] While the number of converts was few, so was the number of missionaries. In order to make a fair comparison across time, a more robust measure of missionary success can be calculated by dividing the number of converts by the number of missionaries, which we call missionary productivity. It turns out that prewar productivity was lower than the productivity observed in the heyday, but not other parts, of the postwar period (see Chapters 4, 11, and 12).

Nor was missionary productivity uniform within the prewar period. Because the missionaries were delivering essentially the same message broadly in a similar style, an explanation of the variable receptivity must relate to the "demand" side. The prewar years were a turbulent period, when the confluence of indigenous and transplanted thoughts never found equilibrium. In such an environment, even a decade made a difference in terms of the public's receptivity to a foreign religious idea. Initial resistance to foreign ideas was followed by a more accommodating attitude; but when the accommodation was carried to the extreme, subdued in-

---

17. According to the LDS Church Almanac (www.ldschurchnewsarchive.com/almanac), the number of missionaries called on missions between 1901 and 1924 was 19,063. If each mission had received an equal allocation, the number of missionaries sent to Japan would have been about ten times the actual number. The number would have been much larger if allocation had been made in proportion to the population of the country.

digenous ideas erupted to the surface.[18] Mitigating the nationalistic undercurrent were the liberalizing forces of modernization, which found expression in demand for civil liberties. These topics are discussed in Chapter 4, while the question of how Japan's receptivity to the Mormon message changed is addressed in Chapter 7.

The number of missionaries was limited not just during the prewar era but also during the postwar era. While it is true that the number of missionaries serving in Japan at any given time was much larger in the postwar period, all of the country was under the jurisdiction of a single mission, which placed an upper limit on the number of missionaries. The number gradually increased from less than twenty to about eighty during the occupation period; it was only in the early 1960s that the number exceeded 100 for the first time (see Figure 1.1). The LDS Church had to wait until after the split of the mission in 1968 before it could double and then triple the number of missionaries to start penetrating virtually every corner of Japan. This meant that, throughout the period covered by this book, the church was faced with the question of how to allocate scarce resources across the country. It was often the case that the opening of a new area for missionary work required the closing of an existing area. Why certain areas were selected over others for missionary work receives extensive attention in Chapters 5, 10, and 11.

With so few convert baptisms, the Mormon proselytizing effort in prewar Japan is generally considered to have been a total failure. It thus comes as a surprise that what has emerged as the dominant explanation of the 1924 closure of the mission is political: the closing was due to the deterioration in the Japan–United States relationship associated with the prospective and actual passage in the United States Congress of an anti-Japanese immigration law. Chapter 7 reassesses the established view by weighing various factors of both long-term and short-term nature that may have contributed to the decision to close the mission. The chapter then assesses this decision in the light of subsequent Japanese history, including by considering counterfactually what might have happened to Mormon missionaries had they remained based on the experience of other Christian denominations.

Unlike some other Christian denominations, Mormon missionary work in prewar Japan did not involve the construction of schools or hospitals. In addition, as the LDS Church relies on lay priesthood for leadership, no seminary was established to train ministers. This in part explains why the church owned no property when it left in 1924 (though there was some talk of purchasing property for the mission home in the late 1910s).[19] It was only in 1948 that the

---

18. What made this possible was a feature of Japanese intellectual culture, which Masao Maruyama compared to an "octopus trap" that can simultaneously catch multiple octopi in separate compartments. Masao Maruyama, *Nihon no Shisō* (Tokyo: Iwanami Shoten, 1961), 129–48.

19. The Japan–United States Treaty of Commerce and Navigation, which had come into force in April 1911, allowed Americans to own residential and commercial buildings, but not land, in Japan.

church purchased its first property in Japan following the end of World War II (see Chapter 10). In the early years of the postwar mission, the church purchased a number of existing buildings—mostly large, vintage Japanese homes—to use as meetinghouses. With a phenomenal pickup in the number of convert baptisms, the church began to construct modern building facilities from 1962 on. Chapters 11 and 12 discuss, respectively, early property purchases and the labor missionary program under which member volunteers constructed buildings.

In sum, publication and translation work, missionary productivity, geographical scope, and physical infrastructure are some of the major building blocks of this book's analysis of Mormon missionary work in Japan. These and other themes, coupled with the "demand-side" analysis of the receptivity of Japanese soil, are contextualized against the background of larger societal developments that must have influenced the underlying decisions. These include international treaties, government policy, the enactment of laws, economic conditions, and social movements. No religious activity takes place in a vacuum. Early Mormon history in Japan was no exception. By trying to understand the economic, intellectual, legal, political, religious, and social contexts in which Mormon missionary work took place, this book attempts to present a more holistic interpretation of the Mormon experience than would be possible with an approach based solely on the Mormon side of the story. It is hoped that the reader will find his or her own answers to the ultimate questions: was Mormon missionary work a success or failure? And what explains the outcome?

1.4. How this Book is Organized

The rest of this book consists of eleven chapters. Two chapters (2 and 4) substantially cover the pre-mission period, four chapters (3, 5, 6, and 7) the prewar period, one chapter (8) the intervening period, and the last four chapters (9, 10, 11, and 12) the postwar period. Each chapter is sufficiently self-contained, allowing the reader to follow without knowing the content of the other chapters. Even so, the chapters are arranged roughly in chronological order. Given the topical focus of each chapter, some overlap in information is to be expected. To avoid overly duplicative writing, however, occasional use is made of cross-referencing when the reader can find additional, related information elsewhere in the book.

To anticipate what is ahead, a brief summary of each chapter follows:

Chapter 2 "Tomizo and Tokujiro: The First Japanese Mormons" reviews the lives of two men, Tomizo Katsunuma (1863–1950) and Tokujiro Sato (ca. 1851–1919), each of whom has a claim to being the first Mormon of Japanese ancestry. Both were born in Japan during the final days of the Edo period (which lasted from 1603 to 1868) and emigrated to what is now part of the United States. Their conversion to the Mormon faith, having taken place in Utah and Hawaii in the 1890s, predated by several years the establishment of the LDS Japan Mission in 1901. The chapter attempts to cast their lives against the economic, political, and social conditions of their day and to give recognition to their role as "pathbreakers" in Mormonism's Trek East.

Chapter 3 "Mormons in the Press: Japanese Reaction to the 1901 Arrival of Heber J. Grant and Company" presents a review and analysis of the press coverage in Japan of the arrival on 12 August 1901 of the first Mormon missionaries. The amount of press coverage given the Mormon missionaries during the next month was unprecedented, with major newspapers throughout the country devoting considerable space—often on front pages—to articles and editorials reporting or otherwise commenting on the arrival of this new Christian sect with unusual doctrines. The chapter considers why Mormonism received such a reception by delving into the social and intellectual conditions of Japan at the turn of the twentieth century.

Chapter 4 "Monks, Nationalists, and the Emperor: Understanding the Religious and Intellectual Climate of Meiji Japan" attempts to elucidate the "demand-side" of the Mormon message in the early twentieth century. The chapter reviews Japan's early religious roots, the arrival of Christianity and the role played by Buddhism in its suppression, the short-lived attempt by the Meiji government to promote Shinto as the state religion, Japan's second encounter with Christianity, and how, once the institutions of a modern state were in place, monks and nationalists conspired to attack Christianity. Towards the end of the nineteenth century, there emerged a state-imposed ideology centered on the emperor, whose nationalistic tendency was only mitigated by the liberalizing forces of industrialization and modernization. Such was the world that greeted the arrival of the Mormon missionaries.

Chapter 5 "Planting the Apple Tree: People, Places, and Publications, 1901–24" outlines the achievements of the Japan Mission from its opening in 1901 to its suspension in 1924. The chapter, after discussing early decisions and events, focuses on three dimensions of Mormon missionary work: (1) people, including collaborators, friends, investigators, and converts; (2) geographical areas where work was carried out; and (3) Japanese-language books and tracts produced to disseminate the Mormon faith. Among other things, the chapter reviews the notable individuals the missionaries befriended (including their place in Japanese history), offers an analysis of the type of people they attracted, attempts to explain why and how certain areas were selected for proselytizing work, and discusses how uniquely Mormon terms were translated from English to the Japanese language.

Chapter 6 "Proclaiming the Way in Japanese: The 1909 Translation of the Book of Mormon" presents an analysis of the first Japanese translation of this Mormon scripture. The chapter focuses on the merits of the translation itself, by discussing questions of style and quality. It examines the work of revision, emphasizing how native reviewers, including able literary critic and writer Choko Ikuta, perfected Alma O. Taylor's draft translation; and identifies several recurring patterns of departure from literalism, which make the translation sound natural, graceful, forceful, or complete in Japanese. It concludes by addressing the ultimate question of accuracy.

Chapter 7 "The Japan Mission under Taisho Democracy: Failure or Forfeit?" presents a historical analysis of the Mormon experience during a period known as Taisho Democracy. The Taisho period (1912–26) saw Japanese society become increasingly industrial and modern and forces of industrialization and modernization unleashing liberalistic aspirations in political thought and public consciousness. The chapter considers how these changes in the intellectual climate affected the Mormon proselytizing work. Despite the seeming signs of relative missionary success, the Mormon authorities closed the mission in 1924. The chapter considers what may have accounted for the withdrawal decision and assesses this decision in light of subsequent Japanese history.

Chapter 8 "Mormonism's Transpacific Interlude: Retreat and Regrouping, 1924–44" discusses major events and developments between 1924 and 1944, regarding the work of the LDS Church among people of Japanese ethnicity. The chapter, after summarizing how sixty or so Japanese Mormons initially maintained contact with each other following the closure of the mission, reviews the short-lived attempts to restore formal church activity. The chapter then shifts attention to the other side of the Pacific, where in the 1920s and 1930s an increasing number of Japanese were converted to Mormonism. The chapter first discusses the origin and pattern of Japanese immigration before describing how the church approached the people of Japanese ancestry in the continental United States and the Hawaiian Islands.

Chapter 9 "The Eagle and the Scattered Flock: Early Mormon Activities in Occupied Japan, 1945–48" reviews some of the events and personalities of major significance from the beginning of Allied occupation in September 1945 to the time the Japanese Mission was established in March 1948. During this mostly undocumented period of about thirty months, there was no organized church structure, so it was through the self-motivated, and often unauthorized, initiatives of American Mormon servicemen that the work of the LDS Church was carried out. This chapter uncovers and preserves important events as accurately as possible, restores some forgotten individuals to their rightful place in history, and places the early LDS church beginnings in the broader context of that singular period when changes in the structure of Japanese society were initiated by an occupying foreign power, of which the church was a part.

Chapter 10 "Riding on the Eagle's Wings: The Japanese Mission under American Occupation, 1948–52" reviews major ecclesiastical developments in the Japanese Mission from its establishment in March 1948 to the time the San Francisco Peace Treaty took effect in April 1952. By the time the LDS Church returned to Japan, the post-surrender transformation of Japan's political, economic, and social foundation had substantially been achieved. As a beneficiary of the American military presence, the church received military resources on a reimbursement basis; the missionaries received temporary accommodations at military member homes and installations, rode on military trains, used the military medical facilities for treatment, and otherwise enjoyed the status accorded by being citizens of the occupying powers. This chapter traces the mission's early beginnings within the broader historical context of that period, and presents historical analyses of why things happened the way they did when they did.

Chapter 11 "Enlarging the Borders: Modern Ecclesiastical Developments, 1952–68" reviews Mormonism's major ecclesiastical developments from the end of the occupation in April 1952 through the end of August 1968. The period saw the church experience real, sustained growth in Japan for the first time. The missionary force tripled, while the membership increased more than ten-fold. The church purchased properties and called local members to assume a greater leadership role. In July 1955, the Northern Far East Mission was created to take over the work previously performed by the Japanese Mission, with an expanded geographical responsibility. The chapter reviews the evolution of the full-time missionary force, the organization, termination, and consolidation of member branches and districts, the opening of work in Okinawa and Korea, the systematic purchases of properties, and the development of local leadership.

Finally, Chapter 12 "Leafs, Steeples, and Testimonies: Building the Foundation for Future Growth, 1948–68" reviews Mormonism's major postwar developments and activities designed to build the faith and testimonies of Japanese members. The period roughly corresponds to Japan's high growth period, when the country completed a reconstruction from the devastation of the war and transformed itself into an advanced industrial country. It was this rising economic prosperity that allowed the church in Japan to construct meetinghouses and an increasing number of Japanese Mormons to participate in mission-organized excursions to the Hawaii Temple. The chapter concludes by attempting to place the church's postwar growth against the background of major social and demographic changes taking place and showing how the church had grown to approximately 10,000 members in thirty-five branches organized into five districts.

These chapters are followed by twelve annexes and a glossary. The first three annexes provide supplementary information on important events or personalities that are referred to in the main text. Annex 4 gives short biographical information on ten Mormon converts in prewar Japan. Annex 5 is a list of all Mormon mission presidents who served in Japan or among the Japanese population of Hawaii from 1901 to 1968. Annex 6 is a detailed list of newspaper articles and editorials on Mormonism published in Japan during the months of August and September 1901. The remaining six annexes contain chronological or alphabetical lists of Mormon missionaries in Japan during 1901–24 and 1948–68, Japanese converts to Mormonism during 1902–24 and the occupation period of 1946–52, and American and Japanese labor missionaries who served during 1962–68. The glossary briefly explains the meanings of Mormon and Japanese terms the reader may encounter in the rest of this book.

Chapter 2

Tomizo and Tokujiro: The First Japanese Mormons

2.1. Introduction

This chapter reviews the lives of two men who were born in Japan during the final days of the Edo period (1603–1868), emigrated to what is now part of the United States, and joined the Church of Jesus Christ of Latter-day Saints in the 1890s. Their conversion to the Mormon faith predated by several years the establishment of the LDS Japan Mission in 1901.[1] Frequent contacts between the Japanese and the Mormons are well documented during the nineteenth century. Following the completion of the transcontinental railroad in 1869, Ogden, Utah, became an important railroad junction, where just about every Japanese traveler stopped on his way to much of the United States and Europe.[2] Some even stayed in Utah and its surrounding regions.[3] Contacts were also made in Hawaii, following the beginning of large-scale Japanese emigration in 1885.[4] It can be presumed that some of these Japanese affiliated themselves with the Mormons though the number was likely small.[5]

---

1. The formal name of the mission established in Japan in 1901 was the Japan Mission, though it is frequently referred to in the literature as the Japanese Mission. The missions established later in Hawaii (in 1937) and in postwar Japan (in 1948) are both officially called the Japanese Mission.
2. Given the frequency of transpacific and transatlantic passenger service and the timely railroad connections, the most convenient and often fastest way to travel from Japan to Europe was via the transcontinental railroad in the United States, even after the completion of the Suez Canal in 1869.
3. The United States Census of 1890 reported 2,039 Japanese residents, of whom about half were in California. From 1891 to 1900, 27,440 Japanese were admitted to the United States. Yuji Ichioka, *The Issei: The World of the First Generation Japanese Immigrants, 1885–1924* (New York: Free Press, 1988), 8, 51. See also Section 8.4 in Chapter 8.
4. During the initial ten years (1885–94) alone, almost 30,000 Japanese emigrated to Hawaii. Ichioka, *Issei*, 40. See also Section 8.5 in Chapter 8.
5. The first recorded contact was made at the Mormon school in Laie in the late 1880s, when several Japanese pupils were enrolled. Church membership records suggest that there was a baptism of a Japanese woman by the name of Miki in Maui. Andrew Jenson, comp., "The History of the Hawaiian Mission of The Church of Jesus Christ of Latter-day Saints," as quoted by Russel T. Clement and Sheng-Luen Tsai, "East Wind to Hawaii:

The rest of this chapter tells the stories of two such people, Tomizo Katsunuma (1863–1950) and Tokujiro Sato (ca. 1851–1919). Tomizo received the best education available in Japan, became a veterinarian, came to the United States in part to pursue further studies in veterinary science, and spent most of his life as a United States immigration officer, veterinarian, and prominent citizen in Hawaii. In contrast, Tokujiro had little formal education, came to Hawaii at a young age as a contractual immigrant worker, married a native Hawaiian, and earned his living as a carpenter, butcher, cook, and taro farmer. This chapter attempts to cast their lives against the economic, political, and social conditions of their day and to give recognition to their role as path-breakers in Mormonism's Trek East.

2.2. Tomizo Katsunuma

In 1937, Edward L. Clissold began his summary of notable events in the ministry of the LDS Church among the Japanese population of Hawaii with these words:[6]

> Any story of the Japanese members of the Church of Jesus Christ of Latter-day Saints in the Hawaiian Islands should begin with the arrival in Hawaii in 1898 of Dr. T. Katsunuma, a then recent graduate of the Utah State Agricultural College [sic], and a member of the Church holding the office of a priest in the Aaronic Priesthood.[7]

Tomizo Katsunuma was a prominent and respected man of some influence in the Japanese and non-Japanese communities of Hawaii during the first half of the twentieth century, when the Japanese constituted about 40 percent of the total population.[8]

Contributions and History of Chinese and Japanese Mormons in Hawaii," *Proceedings of the Second Annual Conference of the Mormon Pacific Historical Society* (1981).

6. A prominent Mormon in Oahu, Edward L. Clissold was particularly active in LDS affairs among the Japanese. At various times, he served as president of the Waikiki Branch, chairman of the Oahu District Council, counselor in the presidency and president of the Oahu Stake, president of the Japanese Mission (in Hawaii), and thrice president of the Hawaiian Temple. From 1948 to 1949, he served as the first president of the Japanese Mission (in Japan) following the conclusion of World War II (see Chapter 10). As the quoted summary of the beginning of work among the Japanese in Hawaii appears at the beginning of the president's reports concerning the newly created Japanese Mission (in Hawaii), Clissold was apparently writing at the request of the incoming mission president, Hilton A. Robertson, to summarize some of the notable events in the history of the church among the Japanese people of Hawaii up to that time. See Section 8.5 in Chapter 8.

7. Edward L. Clissold, "Missionary Work among the Japanese in the Hawaiian Islands." Central Pacific (Japanese) Mission, "Mission President's Reports, 1937–49" (Laie, Hawaii: University Archives, Brigham Young University–Hawaii, hereafter cited as BYU–Hawaii Archives). At the time Tomizo attended, the school was called the Agricultural College of Utah.

8. Stephan Thernstrom, ed., *Harvard Encyclopedia of American Ethnic Groups* (Cambridge, Massachusetts: Harvard University Press, 1980), 561–62.

Tomizo, who was a veterinarian by training and practice, worked for the United States government as an immigration inspector in Honolulu from 1898 to 1924. Because of this role and because he was responsible for initiating the emigration of Japanese to Hawaii from his home prefecture of Fukushima, he was honored as the Father of Immigrants. Among the Mormons of Hawaii, he was respected as one of the church's first members of Japanese ancestry.

2.2.1. Early Years in Japan

Tomizo Katsunuma was born on 6 October in the third year of Bunkyu (or 16 November 1863) in the castle town of Miharu, Banshu (now Fukushima Prefecture).[9] He was the third son (and fourth child) of Naochika Katogi,[10] a samurai of the Miharu domain, and his wife Yo (or Yoko).[11] After studying the Chinese classics at the domain school, he attended primary school where he was in the first graduating class under the new educational system of the Meiji period (1868–1912).[12] He then went on to study Chinese books and Western learning at a newly opened secondary school in Miharu until 1878, when at the age of fifteen he was enrolled at Sendai Foreign Language School in Sendai, where he studied English reading and writing.

---

9. Japan was on the lunar calendar until 2 December in the fifth year of Meiji (or 31 December 1872). For this reason, an attempt will be made throughout this chapter to list both the Japanese and Western (Gregorian) dates for important events and incidents within Japan through the end of 1872. Several different dates have appeared in various documents for Tomizo's birthday, including 6 October (Church membership records; Tsuyoshi Ebihara, *Katogi Yasuji no Jinsei Techō* [Yokohama, self-published, 1977]), 1 November (Kanji Takahashi, *Imin no Chichi Katsunuma Tomizō Sensei* [Honolulu: Bunkichi Suda, 1953]; Hatsutaro Yunojiri, *Katogi San Rōkyōdai* [Tokyo and Osaka: Denki-no-tomo, 1932]), 11 November (obituary in the *Hawaii Times*, 12 September 1950), and 18 November (obituary in the *Honolulu Advertiser*, 12 September 1950). It is likely that 6 October was the correct lunar date and that the November dates are wrong solar transformations. Unless otherwise noted, the biographical information in this section comes from Yunojiri, *Katogi San Rōkyōdai*; and Takahashi, *Katsunuma Tomizō Sensei*.

10. Naochika was born in Taira on 15 September in the fourth year of Tempo (1833) as the fourth son of Isota Katsunuma, a retainer of Tsushimamori Ando, the lord of the Iwaki-taira domain. For a long time, he was a teacher of Toda-school judo. At the persistent request of the lord of the neighboring Miharu domain, Naochika moved to Miharu and transferred the charge of the judo school to his most trusted disciple. At that time, according to the wishes of the Miharu domain, Naochika succeeded the old Katogi family and formally became the domain's judo teacher. As Naochika could not face the prospect of losing his Katsunuma name, Naochika asked the youngest son Tomizo to retain the Katsunuma name.

11. Yo was the daughter of Koroku Hanazawa, a retainer of the Iwaki-taira domain.

12. The Meiji period under the reign of Emperor Meiji began when the restoration of direct imperial rule was proclaimed in early 1868.

In 1880, Tomizo moved to Tokyo and entered the Preparatory School of the University of Tokyo in Hitotsubashi. There he completed three years of study in liberal arts,[13] but a lack of funds forced him to give up the idea of pursuing higher education. After returning home he first took a job for meager pay at a silk-reeling factory; he then worked as the principal of an elementary school in the village of Michiwatashi for a monthly wage of ¥10. When a secondary school was opened in the village of Tatsuta, he was appointed as a teacher of English.

This area of the country (Tamura County) was a breeding center for horses, and a need was felt to train a resident veterinarian with county funds. In 1885, Tomizo was requested by the county commissioner to attend the Tokyo School of Veterinary Science for a monthly allowance of ¥15. He subsequently transferred to the department of veterinary science at the Imperial College of Agriculture in Komaba and, upon graduation in 1888, was appointed assistant researcher at the school.[14]

2.2.2. Arrival in the United States

In the late 1880s, there was a sort of emigration fervor in Japan. In part, this reflected the depressed state of the economy. Following the Satsuma Rebellion (armed uprisings carried out by former samurai of the Satsuma domain) of 1877 and the inflationary consequence of financing the war, the Meiji government began to pursue a deflationary policy in the early 1880s under the leadership of Finance Minister Masayoshi Matsukata. The agrarian distress created by the deflationary policy of the 1880s was so severe that the government changed its previously cautious attitude towards emigration and instituted in 1885 a program of supervised emigration to Hawaii.[15] At the same time, the Chinese Exclusion Act of 1882, which halted the immigration of Chinese laborers, had created a

---

13. At that time, students completing the three-year course of study in liberal arts at the Preparatory School were offered admission to the University of Tokyo to study law, letters, and science. Because of this privilege, admission to the Preparatory School was extremely competitive and was based on an entrance examination covering many subjects. Tōkyō Daigaku, *Tōkyō Daigaku Hyakunen Shi*, vol. 1 (Tokyo: Tōkyō Daigaku Shuppankai, 1984), 551–600.

14. The Imperial College of Agriculture was founded in 1878 by the Ministry of Home Affairs and became part of the Imperial University (later Tokyo Imperial University) in 1890, when the University of Tokyo (with programs in law, letters, science, and medicine) was upgraded to become a comprehensive university with the addition of agriculture, engineering, and the Graduate School. Tōkyō Daigaku, *Hyakunen Shi*, 742–83.

15. A preliminary agreement with the Kingdom of Hawaii was signed in 1884, succeeded by the Immigration Convention of 1886. Robert Walker Irwin, businessman and Hawaiian consul general in Japan, played a key role in the negotiations. Gary Y. Okihiro, *Cane Fires: The Anti-Japanese Movement in Hawaii, 1865–1945* (Philadelphia: Temple University Press, 1991), 23.

demand for Japanese workers in the United States. In this atmosphere, Tomizo determined to look for a chance to emigrate.

The chance came rather quickly. Upon hearing that one of his elder brothers, Shigenori, was going to the United States to survey the electric power industry, Tomizo decided to go along. On 25 April 1889, the two brothers departed in a steamboat for America, leaving behind a Meiji Japan agitated over the establishment of the Imperial Diet. Tomizo was twenty-five years old and had been married to Mine Endo for less than a month, the wedding having taken place on 30 March.[16] According to his biographer, Mine nevertheless encouraged his decision, allowing her husband to move ahead in pursuit of his purpose and dream.[17]

On 10 May 1889, the two brothers arrived in San Francisco. After staying with Tomizo for several days, Shigenori traveled on the transcontinental railroad to observe electricity-related enterprises in the East and remained in the United States until January 1890.[18] Being left alone, Tomizo stayed in the vicinity of San Francisco, visiting ranches in the surrounding communities with the help of Sutemi Chinda, the Japanese consul in San Francisco.[19] He subsequently engaged in raising sheep and cattle at a large-scale ranch in Santa Rosa managed by a Japanese man named Nagasawa.[20]

In those days, there was an association of Japanese in San Francisco called the Patriotic League, whose principal members included the founder Yoshizo Kasuya (future speaker of the House of Representatives) and others who would also become prominent in Japanese politics. In the 1880s, Japan was swept by a nationwide popular political movement called the Freedom and Popular Rights Movement, in which certain dissatisfied elements of society were demanding a reform of the Meiji government along Western democratic lines. The government dealt forcefully with the movement, imprisoning many of its leaders and executing a few. The Patriotic League was initially organized in January 1888 by dissident leaders who had fled the country.[21] Whatever the circumstance, Tomizo was invited to join the league and participated in political discussions with his compatriots.

---

16. Mine was the eldest daughter of Tsuneshi Endo, senior clerk of the Tamura County government.

17. Takahashi, *Katsunuma Tomizō Sensei*, 6.

18. After returning to Japan, Shigenori Katogi became an engineer at Miyoshi Electric Factory (Japan's first manufacturer of electric devices, including generators and light bulbs) and, during his spare time, published a magazine called *Denki no Tomo* (lit: Friends of Electricity). He later became independent, established a company called Denyū-sha, and was engaged in business in the Ginza district of Tokyo.

19. Ebihara, *Katogi Yasuji*, 52. Chinda later served as Japan's ambassador to the United States.

20. Tomizo Katsunuma, *Kansho no Shiborikasu* (Honolulu: Katsunuma Kinen Shuppan Kōenkai, 1924), 113.

21. It is not clear how much of that political zeal remained once the Meiji Constitution (with a nominal democracy) was promulgated in 1889.

2.2.3. Encounter with the Mormons

Tomizo's introduction to Mormonism came as a direct consequence of his connection with the Patriotic League. In the early 1890s, members of the league established a business providing mail handling, remittance, translation, letter writing, and other services to Japanese immigrant workers.[22] The first subcontractor was a man by the name of Tadashichi Tanaka, who set up his office in 1891 in Nampa, Idaho, and staffed it with student laborers from San Francisco. As one of the student laborers supplied by the Patriotic League, Tomizo was Tanaka's right-hand man in the Idaho office. As Tanaka had earlier managed a house of ill repute in the railroad town of Ogden, Utah, it is possible that Tomizo first went to Utah in 1890 before moving to Nampa in 1891.[23]

Tomizo's business and other activities in the early 1890s must have taken him to places in Idaho, Utah, and other Western states and territories. In 1891, another brother, Shutaro, came to the United States to study dairy farming at the Agricultural College of Utah (now Utah State University) in Logan. During his studies, Shutaro made trips to Salt Lake City to conduct experiments in sericulture,[24] almost certainly accompanied by Tomizo. Although it is not known how Tomizo ended up in Logan (where he would be baptized into the LDS Church), it is likely that his departure from Idaho was triggered by Tanaka's dismissal as the field agent in spring 1893, on charges that wages withheld from the workers on the Oregon Short Line were mishandled.[25] The decision to relocate

---

22. A commercial firm called Nichibei Yōtatsusha (Japanese American Contracting Company) was established in 1892, and an agreement was signed with Hiroshima Emigration Company (formally known as Kaigai Tokō Kabushiki Kaisha) for the provision of immigrant labor. It is likely that the business itself was established much before 1892. Ichioka, *Issei*, 48–51.

23. Ichioka, *Issei*, 49–50. According to Takahashi, *Katsunuma Tomizō Sensei*, 7, Tanaka lived in Salt Lake City and, in 1890, invited Tomizo to come to manage his business of distributing everyday necessities to railroad workers and receiving orders from them. The designation of Salt Lake City as the place of Tanaka's residence is probably wrong, but if the year 1890 is right, Tomizo must have lived in Ogden, Utah, at least for a while. According to Ebihara, *Katogi Yasuji*, 239, when Shutaro Katogi, the elder brother of Tomizo, arrived in the United States in the fall of 1891, Tomizo was already in Idaho. Shutaro's specific purpose in coming to the United States was to acquire skills in dairy farming, but he had to study English for about eighteen months until April 1893. This latter date coincides with the dismissal of Tanaka as the labor contractor for the Oregon Short Line. See the paragraph immediately below.

24. Ebihara claims that Shutaro met Brigham Young on one of his visits to Salt Lake City. Ebihara, *Katogi Yasuji*, 239–40. Of course, this cannot be true as Young had been dead for over ten years, prompting one to question the authenticity of some of the historical events in his book.

25. Ichioka, *Issei*, 74.

in Logan may have been a joint decision with his brother. Shutaro stayed in the Idaho–Utah area from 1891 to about 1895.[26]

While in Logan, Tomizo first entered Brigham Young College, a Mormon academy, and completed a course in "theology," probably religious education. His enrollment at Brigham Young College may have been inspired by his desire to study Mormonism or may have been only a precursor (in terms of mastering the English language) to his studies in veterinary medicine at the Agricultural College. The registrar's office at Utah State University has records of Tomizo's enrollment for the academic years 1895 and 1896. It is not clear, therefore, if he actually graduated from a degree-granting program. According to his biographer, he completed the course of study in agriculture in three years, upon which he became an assistant for a Dr. Fischer, a German professor in veterinary science.[27]

During his Logan years, Tomizo naturally had frequent contacts with Mormons. Prominent among them was a wealthy Danish convert by the name of Carl Christian Amussen.[28] After retiring from his successful jewelry business in Salt Lake City, Amussen was living in a two-story, French-style villa in Logan, with "marble fireplaces, a great winding stairway in solid mahogany with turned balustrades, two grand porticos, one facing each street, a steam heating plant, and modern plumbing."[29] His initial contact with Tomizo was likely related to the fact that Amussen was a horseman who was proud of his white Arabian horses. It may be recalled that, even before coming to Logan, Tomizo was a veterinarian skilled in the handling of horses.

Amussen spent his winters in Santa Barbara or the Monterey Peninsula in California. During those winter months, according to the Amussen family historian, "he entrusted his house to a Japanese student by the name of Katsunuma. Before he left Logan, the Japanese friend had been converted to the Church, typifying and exemplifying the missionary zeal which characterized the entire life of Carl Christian Amussen from the time of his conversion until the day of his death."[30] Tomizo was baptized by Guy W. Thatcher and confirmed a member

---

26. During this time, the two brothers visited the Columbian Exposition (the so-called Chicago World Fair) of 1893 and New York City. In the summer of 1894, they traveled from Logan to Salt Lake City to visit His Imperial Highness Prince Yorihito, who was on his way home from France by way of the United States. Katsunuma, *Kansho no Shiborikasu*, 152. After leaving Logan, Shutaro spent a year in Wyoming learning cattle-raising techniques before going back to Japan in 1896. Upon his return, he attempted a large American-style dairy operation but failed. Ebihara, *Katogi Yasuji*, 240–41.

27. Yunojiri, *Katogi San Rōkyōdai*, 63.

28. Amussen was the father, with his third wife, Barbara McIsaac Smith, of Flora Amussen, who would become the wife of Ezra Taft Benson, the thirteenth president of the LDS Church.

29. David A. Burton, "Carl Christian Amussen" (paper prepared for the family reunion of the Ezra Taft Benson family, July 1978).

30. Ibid.

of the LDS Church by Joseph E. Lewis on 8 August 1895. He was subsequently ordained a deacon by R. M. Lewis on 25 January 1896.[31] It was also during his Logan years that Tomizo became a naturalized American citizen—citizenship was possibly granted in recognition of his service in the Utah National Guard—and in 1896 cast his first vote, for Democratic presidential candidate William Jennings Bryan.[32]

2.2.4. Relocation in Hawaii

In 1894, the Japanese government terminated its program of supervised emigration to Hawaii.[33] In response, there was a rise of private emigration companies that recruited laborers for profits. In 1898, for example, there were nine such companies, which shipped 12,293 laborers abroad, mostly to sugar plantations in Hawaii.[34] While in Utah, Tomizo was recruited by one of those companies, Hiroshima Emigration Company.[35] The company had enjoyed a long-standing relationship with the Patriotic League and hired some of the league members as executives. Prominent among them was Tsutau Sugawara, who had set up an office in Honolulu in 1895.[36] The recruitment of Tomizo may have been initiated more directly by Tatsusaburo Matsuoka, Tomizo's office mate in Nampa, who also became an executive of Hiroshima Emigration Company upon his return to

---

31. "Deceased Member Records, 1941–88," LDS Church Archives. No other Aaronic priesthood ordinations are recorded.

32. Although the generally accepted interpretation of naturalization laws at the time was that Japanese were ineligible for citizenship, the final interpretation was in the hands of local officials, and according to one estimate, as many as 460 Japanese were granted citizenship by local judges. This flexibility was abolished in 1922 when the Supreme Court ruled that naturalization was limited to "free white persons and to aliens of African nativity and to persons of African descent." Japanese remained as "aliens ineligible to citizenship" until the passage of the McCarran–Walter Immigration and Nationality Act in 1952. William K. Hosokawa, *Nisei: The Quiet Americans* (New York: William Morrow and Company, 1969), 89–91; and Yukiko Kimura, *Issei: Japanese Immigrants in Hawaii* (Honolulu: University of Hawaii Press, 1988), 40. Incidentally, the obituary on Tomizo published in the 12 September 1950 issue of the English-language *Honolulu Advertiser* states that he was granted citizenship because the judge thought he was a Caucasian.

33. The last ship carrying contractual immigrants under government supervision arrived in Honolulu on 28 June 1894. Under this program, a total of 29,139 individuals traveled from Japan to Hawaii between 1885 and 1894. Soen Yamashita, *Nippon Hawai Kōryū Shi* (Tokyo: Daitō Shuppansha, 1943), 19; also Okihiro, *Cane Fires*, 25–27.

34. Ichioka, *Issei*, 48.

35. What is called Hiroshima Emigration Company in Tomizo's biography here quoted was formally known as Kaigai Tokō Kabushiki Kaisha, which was incorporated in Hiroshima in 1893. Masaaki Kodama, "Imin Kaisha ni tsuite no Ichi Kōsatsu," *Geibi Chihō Shi Kenkyū* 127 (1980): 12–25.

36. Ichioka, *Issei*, 51–52.

Tomizo Katsunuma and family, circa 1915. Courtesy June Stageberg.

Japan in 1897. Accepting the company's offer, Tomizo left Utah for the Pacific and arrived in Honolulu on 15 January 1898.

Tomizo's involvement with Hiroshima Emigration Company was apparently brief because, in the early spring of the same year, he made his first trip home under contract with Kumamoto Emigration Company.[37] Until that time, most of the immigrants to Hawaii had come from the regions in western Japan, including Fukuoka, Hiroshima, Kumamoto, and Yamaguchi. Kumamoto Emigration Company was the first of the major emigration companies to pay attention to the Tohoku region, and the charge given to Tomizo was to recruit immigrants from that region, including from his home prefecture of Fukushima. Upon his return home, he gave stirring speeches in his Tohoku accent and inspired many to emigrate to Hawaii.[38] Tomizo returned to Hawaii on 26 July 1898, accompanied by a group of about a hundred Fukushima immigrants.[39]

Obviously, the highlight of his first trip home was the reunion with his wife, Mine, whom he had not seen for almost ten years. He had not even seen their

---

37. Kimura, *Issei*, 33. It was formally known as Kumamoto Imin Gōshi Kaisha.

38. According to Tomizo's own account, when he "returned home for the first time in the spring of the thirty-first year of Meiji, [he] became an agent of Kumamoto Emigration Company and recruited emigrants to Hawaii in the Tohoku region." *Nippu Jiji*, 13 January 1934. Author's translation of the Japanese original.

39. Kimura, *Issei*, 33.

son, Katsumi, who was born in Miharu following Tomizo's departure for the United States. For a few months in the first half of 1898, they lived in a detached room in the eastern part of the Endo house in their hometown of Miharu. Thus, Tomizo indisputably became the first Japanese Mormon to live in Japan.[40] Their union was not to be disrupted again by a long absence. Soon after the birth of the second child, Kiyomi (in January 1899), the family traveled to Hawaii to be with Tomizo.[41]

2.2.5. Life in Hawaii

Upon his permanent settlement in Hawaii, Tomizo became an immigration officer of the United States government. Given his earlier connections with Japanese emigration companies, his American citizenship and his ability to speak English (though not without a strong accent) must have been important factors in this appointment. Hawaii was being annexed to the United States at the time of his appointment (the process of annexation was completed in August 1898) and was to become a full territory in June 1900. With this changed status of Hawaii, the period of contractual immigration ended, and was succeeded by a period of free immigration. A flood of Japanese immigrants continued to come, and the United States government needed someone of Tomizo's background to handle their arrival, which averaged about sixty per ship.[42]

Whenever a group of Japanese immigrants arrived, Tomizo took a launch with customs officers to the ship, which was temporarily anchored awaiting their arrival.

---

40. He was not the first Mormon to live in Japan. In a journal entry on 14 August 1901, Alma O. Taylor, one of the first missionaries to Japan, wrote about visiting the widow of the late Mr. Ponseforte, who "had at one time lived in Salt Lake City and was a member of the Church." This man "apostasied before leaving the U.S." and "some twenty or twenty five years ago . . . came to Japan and married a Japanese woman." Alma O. Taylor, Journal, Special Collections, Harold B. Lee Library, Brigham Young University (hereafter cited as BYU Archives).

41. The claim of Kimura that the family traveled together (Kimura, *Issei*, 33) is obviously incorrect, as Kiyomi was born in Miharu. In an interview with the author, Kiyomi stated that Tomizo had called the family to Hawaii only after getting a permanent job as an immigration officer. Kiyomi Katsunuma Suzuki, interview by author, Honolulu, Oahu, 1 February 1997. Although the exact time cannot be ascertained, the family must have joined Tomizo relatively soon, as a picture taken in December 1900 shows Tomizo and Mine together and the couple's second son Takeo was born in Honolulu in February 1902.

42. Takahashi, *Katsunuma Tomizō Sensei*, 13. From July 1894 to 1908 (when the Japan–United States Gentlemen's Agreement, which severely restricted the entry of Japanese laborers, came into force), a total of 108,534 contractual or free immigrants traveled from Japan to Hawaii under private (nongovernmental) schemes. From 1908 to 1924 (when the general provisions of the Johnson–Reed Immigration Act came into force), a total of 62,277 immigrants (many of whom were "picture brides") traveled to Hawaii by invitation only. Yamashita, *Hawai Kōryū Shi*, 19, 339–40.

The team would then make a preliminary check of passengers as the ship was being docked along the pier. Things would generally move smoothly for the first-class passengers. Immigrants and other third-class passengers would be housed in the Immigration Department in order to go through the necessary inspection. Tomizo worked in this capacity until 30 June 1924, the day before the general provisions of the Johnson–Reed Immigration Act took effect, ending the immigration of Japanese nationals to the United States (see Section 7.3.3 in Chapter 7).

During that period, hardly a single Japanese immigrant landed in Hawaii without being inspected by Tomizo. Because of that status, he was well respected in the Japanese community, and many, including those who arrived as "picture brides" (women whose marriages to resident immigrants were arranged across the Pacific through the exchange of photographs), came seeking his advice even on personal matters.[43] He was called "Doctor Katsunuma" or sometimes simply "Doctor" in the Japanese community, not because he had a doctorate (which he did not), but out of respect for his professional training in veterinary medicine, which he continued to practice and which he continued to regard as his true vocation in life.[44]

He was known for his sharp wit, humor, and jovial personality. According to the historian Yukiko Kimura, he was "unconventional, unpretentious, and had an open and direct way of doing things. . . . Japanese residents of Hawaii, rural and urban, accepted him with affection and respect because of these characteristics."[45] Yasutaro Soga, a friend and a prominent figure in the Japanese community of Hawaii, wrote:

> Dr. Katsunuma, who was always called *Rōkō* among us and "Dr. Party" among the people,[46] was a popular figure in the society circles of Honolulu. This was true not only among us the Japanese, but also among the white, Chinese, Kanaka (native Hawaiian), and Portuguese peoples. Regardless of race, religion, social status, or age, he would talk to any acquaintance he might meet on the streets of Honolulu with the same familiarity. Whenever I was with him, his conversation with an acquaintance would become so long that I was sometimes distressed. . . . Like myself, he did not drink much. At parties, however, he was famous for his Japanese limerick, which went something like "it is human to have facial pits, horses don't have them." At Rotary Club socials and other functions, he would make people burst into laughter by imitating a cock crow or a horse laughter. In this manner, Dr. Katsunuma was a unique personality among us, his associates in Hawaii.[47]

---

43. Kimura, *Issei*, 40.
44. A story is told that, when His Imperial Highness Prince Sadachika made a visit to Honolulu on his way back from the United States, one of the fine horses on board given as a gift to the imperial family fell sick. Tomizo was called and successfully treated the sick horse. Takahashi, *Katsunuma Tomizō Sensei*, 16; and Katsunuma, *Kansho no Shiborikasu*, 232.
45. Kimura, *Issei*, 42.
46. *Rōkō* is an honorific title used to address an elderly person.
47. Takahashi, *Katsunuma Tomizō Sensei*, preface; author's translation of the Japanese original.

Arriving immigrants were sometimes dumbfounded by the words that came out of Tomizo's mouth, which were spoken with a Tohoku accent and were full of humor and wit. Towards the immigrants from Fukushima Prefecture, his paternalistic feelings were sometimes manifested violently, particularly when he was young. His biographer cites an eyewitness account:

> [The man] was a Matsumoto or something like that from Adachi County. When we arrived at Honolulu harbor, Mr. Katsunuma told us to gather together, so we all went upon the deck. This man came up considerably late. He was wearing an unlined summer kimono with splashed patterns, and walked up pattering his wooden clogs of medium height, with a tobacco case hanging down from his waist. Even we could tell that he was in trouble. Furious with anger, Mr. Katsunuma ran up to that man, kicked him with his shoe, and trampled on him two or three times when he fell, yelling, "Where do you think you are? You are a disgrace to Fukushima."

The biographer interpreted Tomizo's behavior as reflecting "his constant passion for the improvement of younger immigrants."[48]

2.2.6. A Community Leader

With no propensity for smoking or drinking, Tomizo enjoyed reading and writing as a favorite pastime. In 1907, when the old and deteriorating Japanese consulate building (purchased by the first consul in 1886) was put on sale, Tomizo purchased the building, moved it to Metcalf Street, and, upon renovation, called it *Bashōan* after his pen name, Basho.[49] He was often found reading a book in a wisteria chair on the veranda of the house. His writings reveal that he was an avid reader, knowledgeable about many things, both East and West, old and new.[50] For example, he wrote on such diverse subjects as the Japanese beetle, tattoos, and the contemporary Japanese haiku poet Meisetsu Naito.

Writing almost became his profession. With the printing press and movable types that he had shipped from his brother in Tokyo, he upgraded the *Yamato Shinbun* (a mimeographed newspaper with which he was associated from the earliest days) to a printed daily paper. In 1906, Yasutaro Soga (originally of Tokyo) was invited to become the president and editor-in-chief, and the title was changed to *Nippu Jiji* (later the name would change again, to *Hawaii Times*). Tomizo supported the newspaper company by serving as vice president and by frequently writing columns that enjoyed wide readership and commanded considerable influence among the Japanese-reading public. Tomizo obviously loved the newspaper business because he was engaged in it until just before his death. In describing Tomizo's writing style, Soga expressed himself in these words:

---

48. Takahashi, *Katsunuma Tomizō Sensei*, 13–14; author's translation of the Japanese original.
49. *Bashō*, in this configuration of Chinese characters, literally means "horse laughter," no doubt intended as a pun for the great seventeenth-century haiku poet Matsuo Basho.
50. See, for example, Katsunuma, *Kansho no Shiborikasu*.

[Dr. Katsunuma] had an inquisitive mind, had passion for newspapers, and had a first class style of his own when it came to writing. His "Tohoku" accent even manifested itself in writing. Because 'e' and 'i' were reversed, we were always troubled.[51]

A collection of Tomizo's essays that appeared regularly in the Sunday columns of the *Nippu Jiji* from April 1922 to June 1924 was later published as a book under the title of *Kansho no Shiborikasu* (Strained Lees of Sugarcane), with 10,000 copies printed by Nippu Jiji Company. This 300-page book not only is revealing of Tomizo's witty character but is also a great source of information on the social history of Japanese immigrants in Hawaii.

Tomizo often acted as an arbitrator in public or private disputes. In 1900, when a number of Chinese workers were killed in a major collision, the Japanese offenders were sentenced to death. Tomizo resolutely stood up in their defense and eventually succeeded in reducing the sentence. From this time on, Tomizo became a great advocate of the Japanese community in Hawaii. In 1909, Tomizo and his newspaper repeatedly demanded that the working conditions of Japanese plantation workers be improved, and supported the four-month-long strike that involved 7,000 workers from all major Oahu plantations.[52] When an incident of serious consequence occurred in the Japanese community, Tomizo was often called to intervene and find a peaceful settlement.[53]

For many years, Tomizo was a confidant of Japanese consuls stationed in Honolulu. When preparation was being made for the festivities of the first emperor's birthday (to be held on 3 November 1900) after Hawaii had become a United States territory, the consul recognized the need to be sensitive and requested that Tomizo become a member of the planning committee. Tomizo was also a charter (and the first non-Caucasian) member of the Rotary Club of Honolulu. He was involved in many community functions and activities, including the management of the Japanese hospital; the 26 March 1922 reunion of the first group of Japanese immigrants (called *gan-nen-mono*) and their descendants;[54] and the festivities held on 8 February 1935, in celebration of the fiftieth anniversary of

---

51. Takahashi, *Katsunuma Tomizō Sensei*, preface; author's translation of the Japanese original.

52. The early twentieth century saw increasing resistance to oppressive working conditions on plantations by Japanese and other immigrant workers. The issue in 1909 for the Japanese laborers was the demand their "Higher Wages Association" made to the Hawaiian Sugar Planters' Association for full equality with the Portuguese and Puerto Rican laborers (who were paid $22.50 per month as opposed to $18.00 for the Japanese). Instead of negotiating with the Higher Wages Association, the planters let "the press conduct the debate and [denied] the association the dignity of a response or recognition." The *Nippu Jiji* was among the several Japanese dailies that supported the Japanese laborers and saw six of their men arrested and imprisoned on conspiracy charges. See Okihiro, *Cane Fires*, 41–81 (especially 47–53).

53. Takahashi, *Katsunuma Tomizō Sensei*, 16–17.

54. For *gan-nen-mono*, see Section 2.3 below on Tokujiro Sato. On this occasion, all four surviving members of the first group were present. If Tokujiro had lived a few more

the commencement of the government-supervised program of emigration. He had a close association with both Christian and Buddhist leaders of the Japanese community, and Japanese dignitaries visiting Hawaii often called on him.

As a leader of the Japanese community in Hawaii, Tomizo twice represented the community in attending the imperial coronation ceremonies in Japan. The first time was in September 1915 when Tomizo made his third trip home,[55] leading a group of about fifty people. Before traveling west to Kyoto to attend the coronation of Emperor Taisho, the group was invited by Shigenobu Okuma, then prime minister of Japan, to his residence in Tokyo, where Tomizo is said to have "mystified Marquis Okuma by giving a formal reply which was both relevant and witty."[56] The second occasion was in 1928, when he made his fourth and last trip home to attend the coronation of Emperor Showa (or Hirohito), which was held on 13 November.

2.2.7. Early Association with the LDS Church

Writing in 1937, Clissold explained that when Tomizo had first arrived in Hawaii almost forty years earlier, he "attended services regularly at Auwaiolimu (in Honolulu) for several months. As the services were held entirely in Hawaiian, however, he became discouraged and for many years attended church only at conference time. During these periods of inactivity, he continued to claim membership and never hesitated to admit that he was a Mormon."[57] The festivities of the fiftieth anniversary celebration of the Hawaiian Mission, which were held in December 1900, might have been one of those occasions when Tomizo attended church. A picture taken on that occasion features Tomizo with George Q. Cannon, one of the first Mormon missionaries to Hawaii, who returned to represent the LDS Church's First Presidency.[58]

According to Clissold, Tomizo also met with Heber J. Grant, then a member of the Quorum of the Twelve Apostles:

---

years, there would have been a meeting of Tomizo and Tokujiro, the main characters of our story. Katsunuma, *Kansho no Shiborikasu*, 1–4.

55. The second trip was made in 1904, during which Tomizo visited the mission home in Tokyo. See Section 2.2.7 immediately below.

56. Takahashi, *Katsunuma Tomizō Sensei*, 18; author's translation of the Japanese original.

57. Clissold, "Missionary Work." Writing about the Japanese Mission in Hawaii in 1939, Mormon apostle John A. Widtsoe used almost identical sentences to describe Tomizo, indicating that he relied on Clissold for the information. John A. Widtsoe, "The Japanese Mission in Action," *Improvement Era* 42 (1939): 88–89, 125.

58. Clement and Tsai, "East Wind to Hawaii"; R. Lanier Britsch, *Moramona: The Mormons in Hawaii* (Laie, Hawaii: Institute for Polynesian Studies, Brigham Young University–Hawaii, 1989), 114–16.

In this picture, Tomizo stands next to wife Mine (to his right) and George Q. Cannon of the LDS Church First Presidency (to his left), December 1900. Courtesy June Stageberg.

> When President Heber J. Grant passed through Hawaii on his way to preside over the Japanese Mission, Dr. Katsunuma met him and offered his services as missionary. For some reason he was not called to the mission field and continued to live in Hawaii.[59]

The statement that Grant passed through Hawaii on his way to Japan is obviously incorrect, as the *Empress of India*, which carried the first missionaries to Japan in August 1901, did not visit Honolulu.[60] The timing of Tomizo's meeting with Grant must have been in March 1902, when the Mormon apostle visited the Hawaiian Mission on his way back from Japan to attend the April general conference in Salt Lake City.[61]

Apparently, Heber J. Grant and his companions knew about Tomizo from the earliest days of their mission in Japan. It is possible that they had heard about him from George Q. Cannon while they were still in Utah. Alma O. Taylor, one of the first missionaries to Japan, writes that, on 19 August 1901, they received

---

59. Clissold, "Missionary Work."

60. *Empress of India* was a steamship of the Canadian Pacific fleet, which did not include a stop in Honolulu in its transpacific passenger service between Vancouver and Yokohama.

61. In a letter addressed to President Samuel E. Woolley of the Hawaiian Mission, dated 21 April 1902, Horace Ensign, secretary of the Japan Mission in Tokyo, acknowledged the receipt of money and writes: "We trust that the time spent with our beloved President, Apostle Grant, was profitable." Japan Mission, "Letterpress Copybooks, 1901–23," LDS Church Archives.

at their boarding house in Yokohama a man by the name of Ushida, "who at one time went to school for about four months in the L.D.S. College . . . and was well acquainted with Thomaz [sic] Katsunuma who now lives in Honolulu, H.I. and is a member of the Church." On the same day, the missionaries received a letter from "Mr. Katogi the Brother of T. Katsunuma . . . [who] had been in Salt Lake City and appreciated the kindness of the Mormons in helping him in the raising of silk."[62] Shutaro Katogi, who must have learned of the arrival of the Mormon missionaries by reading newspaper accounts,[63] invited Grant to come to see him in Tokyo and offered assistance to the church. On 25 August, the editors of the Tokyo newspaper *Shakai Shinpō* came to interview the missionaries in Yokohama, as recorded in Taylor's journal:

> They brought with them a letter of introduction from Mr. Katogi with whom Bro. Grant had become acquainted while in Tokio a few days ago. . . . These gentlemen told us that . . . if we would go to Tokio that they wanted to call a large meeting and give us the opportunity of addressing through an interpreter, the Japanese people. They also said that the proprietor of their paper Mr. Oda told them that he would take great delight in introducing us to the people of his country. They also were the bearers of a message from Mr. Matsuoka, . . . telling us that he would furnish us a house without charging rent if we would only come to Tokio.[64]

During his second trip home in 1904, Tomizo himself sought out and visited the mission home in Tokyo. Taylor describes the visit:

> Learned upon returning to headquarters that Bro. Katsunuma from Hawaii had visited Prest. E[nsign] on Monday the 4th [of April 1904]. Bro. Katsunuma is the first Japanese to join the Church in all the world. He was converted in Utah many years ago. He has become an American citizen and is now in the civil service at Hawaii. He having received a month's furlough, is in Japan visiting friends & relatives. He sought "Mormons" out the first thing and seemed pleased with what they had accomplished & were doing. He was glad to see some Latter-day Saint Hymns in his native language and gave the sect. of the Mission ¥[yen] 10.00 towards further translation.[65]

---

62. Taylor, Journal, 19 August 1901.

63. See Chapter 3 for an analysis of the press coverage of the arrival of the first Mormon missionaries in Japan.

64. Taylor, Journal, 25 August 1901.

65. Taylor, Journal, 9 April 1904. ¥10 was exactly $5 when converted at the gold parity (both Japan and the United States were on the gold standard at that time). It would be more than ¥30,000 (about $300) when converted to current yen in purchasing power terms. This was a considerable sum, given the much lower level of wages then. Author's estimates based on the Japan Long-Term Economic Statistics Database, Institute of Economic Research, Hitotsubashi University, Tokyo.

2.2.8. A Japanese Mormon in Hawaii

During the early years in Hawaii, in addition to the language difficulty, his wife's attitude toward religion may have played a part in Tomizo's general inactivity in the LDS Church. She became a staunch Methodist and did not think much of the Mormons.[66] The rest of the family apparently attended the Methodist Church. As English increasingly became a dominant language in Hawaii, however, Tomizo must have become a more active participant in Mormon services. In a Sunday newspaper column published on 6 November 1921, he talks about the visit of an English professor from Utah and mentions that they became acquainted with each other because of their church association.[67] Certainly by the mid to late 1920s, Tomizo was fully active in the church. The Diamond Jubilee of the LDS Hawaiian Mission, celebrated on 12 December 1925, may have been what triggered his return to full church activity.[68]

In the early 1930s, Tomizo became instrumental in the organization of a Japanese Sunday school in the Kalihi (Honolulu) Branch in May 1934 and the subsequent establishment of the Japanese Mission in Hawaii (see Section 8.5.2 in Chapter 8). In the critical meeting of key individuals held in the Hawaiian mission home on 6 April 1934, Tomizo was present, along with Castle H. Murphy (mission president) and Edward L. Clissold, and offered the opening prayer.[69] In connection with the First Presidency visit in Hawaii in the summer of 1935, J. Reuben Clark Jr. writes that "among the Japanese Saints in Honolulu [was] . . . Dr. Tomizo Katsunuma, who at one time attended college in Utah."[70] In Clark's account, Tomizo was undoubtedly a member of the group of Japanese saints who "gave to President Grant and his group a delicious dinner and afterward a delightful entertainment of song, dance, instrumental music and recitation."[71]

Writing in 1939 about the 1937 establishment of the Japanese Mission in Hawaii, Mormon apostle John A. Widtsoe mentions Tomizo as one of the seventeen church members of Japanese ancestry found by Hilton A. Robertson, the incoming mission president.[72] Following the mission's establishment, on 1 October

---

66. Suzuki, interview.

67. Katsunuma, *Kansho no Shiborikasu*, 8–9.

68. In October of that year, Barbara Amussen, the widowed wife of Carl Christian Amussen, arrived in the Hawaiian Mission on a special short-term mission and was assigned as a companion to her daughter Flora. The author of an Ezra Taft Benson biography claims that Barbara and Flora, learning that Tomizo, "a Japanese gardener whom Carl Amussen had converted in Logan," had "slipped into inactivity," fellowshipped him back into activity. Sheri L. Dew, *Ezra Taft Benson: A Biography* (Salt Lake City: Deseret Book, 1987), 86–87.

69. Clissold, "Missionary Work."

70. J. Reuben Clark Jr., "The Outpost in Mid-Pacific," *Improvement Era* 38 (1935): 533.

71. Ibid.

72. In his *Improvement Era* article, Widtsoe erroneously writes that the Japanese Mission in Hawaii was organized in February 1936. Work began in February 1937 when Robertson arrived. Widtsoe, "Japanese Mission," 88.

1939, Tomizo was ordained an elder by Robertson.[73] Widtsoe describes Tomizo as "a student of Brigham Young College and the Utah State Agricultural College [sic], and the first Japanese baptized into the Church" and as "active in the service of the mission in Honolulu."[74] He goes on to say that there was "much friendliness among the Japanese for our work" and that the "Japanese daily, *Nippu Jiji* of Honolulu, under the able leadership of Mr. Yasutaro Soga . . . made frequent timely references to the work of the Latter-day Saints among the Japanese." This is to be expected. Soga was one of Tomizo's closest friends, and Tomizo himself was involved in the editorial work of the *Nippu Jiji*.

After retiring from civil service in 1924, Tomizo returned to his real vocation as a veterinarian and continued the pleasant pastime of writing. He spent his retirement quietly until the summer of 1950, when he was hospitalized at Kuakini Hospital. He gradually weakened because of advancing age and, on 11 September, closed his colorful life of almost eighty-seven years. His wife Mine and other close relatives were at his bedside. The funeral was solemnly held on 13 September at the large Mormon tabernacle on Beretania Street, with Edward L. Clissold conducting. The tabernacle was filled with flowers, and many dignitaries were in attendance. The memorial addresses were given by Yasutaro Soga and Chomatsu Tsukiyama (president of the Senate). It was said to be the largest funeral held there in many years, with no room left even to stand.[75] An obituary appeared in the English-language *Honolulu Advertiser*, under the large headline "Dr. Katsunuma, First Japanese Mormon, Dies."[76]

2.3. Tokujiro Sato

Tokujiro Sato, also known in Hawaii as Toko, Toku, or Sasaki,[77] is another person who has a claim to being the first Japanese Mormon. Unlike Tomizo Katsunuma, very little is known, let alone written, about him. The contrast with Tomizo goes beyond the availability of reliable information. In all likelihood, Tokujiro was a person of humble means and little education.

2.3.1. An Eyewitness Account

The best place to begin is an eyewitness account that describes the 1919 encounter of Tokujiro or Toko with Elias Wesley Smith, the son of the late LDS

---

73. "Deceased Member Records, 1941–88."
74. Widtsoe, "Japanese Mission," 88, 125.
75. "Bashōan Tomizo Katsunuma Dies," *Hawaii Times* (Japanese), 12 September 1950, 3; Yasutaro Soga, "Memories of the Late Dr. Tomizo Katsunuma," *Hawaii Times* (Japanese), 16 September 1950.
76. "Dr. Katsunuma, First Japanese Mormon, Dies," *Honolulu Advertiser*, 12 September 1950.
77. Yasuo Baron Goto, *Children of Gan-nen-mono: The First-Year Men* (Honolulu: Bishop Museum Press, 1968).

Church president Joseph F. Smith and then president of the Hawaiian Mission (though most dates and other factual details are incorrect):

> During my recent visit, through the different conferences on the Islands of Maui and Hawaii, I had the privilege of meeting the first Japanese convert to the Church of Jesus Christ of Latter-day Saints, who is now living at Kukuihaele, Hawaii. We held an interesting meeting in his home and spent the night there.
>
> Becoming interested in Brother Toko, I learned that he was born in Tokio, Japan, in the year 1849. At the age of seventeen he worked his way to Hawaii, arriving here in 1866. In 1879 he married a Hawaiian by the name of Kalala, and they have happily passed their ruby anniversary. He joined the Church in 1892, and has been and is still a faithful member.
>
> He related to me many interesting incidents that took place here many years ago, among which was the Walter Murray Gibson trouble, and how he witnessed Gibson's unlawful rise to power, and his dishonorable failure. . . . Brother Toko is now seventy years of age, hale and hearty, and able to work six days a week raising kalo (a Hawaiian vegetable used in making poi) for the market. In this way he earns an honest living. He has a large family of bright children.[78]

Smith's statement is valuable as a starting reference, not because it is entirely correct (which it is not), but because it raises so many questions. For one thing, the arrival date of 1866 means that Tokujiro left Japan when the country was still under Tokugawa rule. Could he have left then? Very likely the dates of both his birth and arrival, if not anything else, are incorrect.[79] Even if those dates are taken at face value, one wonders how someone who arrived in Hawaii in 1866 and joined the LDS Church in 1892 could witness the Walter Murray Gibson trouble of 1861–64, if the statement refers to Gibson's unlawful administration of Lanai, the gathering place for the Hawaiian Mormons.[80] Maybe Smith was putting his own words into Tokujiro's mouth, when Tokujiro was thinking of something else.

Smith's statement, however, convincingly demonstrates that in Kukuihaele on the island of Hawaii there was a Japanese man who claimed to have arrived in Hawaii long before the government-supervised program of emigration began in 1885 and whom a Mormon leader regarded as belonging to the church, a man having been baptized before the opening of missionary work in Japan in 1901. Furthermore, Smith's encounter with Tokujiro is entirely plausible. Smith arrived in Honolulu on 25 June 1919, replacing Samuel Edwin Woolley, who had served

---

78. E. Wesley Smith, "The First Japanese Convert to the Church," *Improvement Era* 23 (1919): 177.

79. Unfortunately, some Mormon writers have taken the wrong dates at face value. See, for example, Clement and Tsai, "East Wind to Hawaii"; and Sharlene B. C. L. Furuto, "Japanese Saints in Hawaii and Japan: Values and Implications for Baptism," *Proceedings of the Eleventh Annual Conference of the Mormon Pacific Historical Society* (1990): 1–15.

80. After missionaries were removed in 1857, Walter Murray Gibson appointed himself leader of the LDS Church in Hawaii and seized its property. See Annex 3 towards the end of this volume for further details.

as mission president for twenty-four years from 1895 to 1919.⁸¹ Thus, the new president needed to quickly acquaint himself with the conditions prevailing in various parts of the islands. Because Smith was born in Laie during his father's exile (1885–87) and had himself filled a mission to Hawaii from 1907 to 1910,⁸² he spoke Hawaiian fluently, as did Tokujiro (albeit with a Japanese accent). So the two undoubtedly conducted the conversation in that language, sometime between 25 June and 22 October 1919 (when the report was filed).⁸³

2.3.2. Gan-nen-mono

As previously mentioned, organized immigration of Japanese workers to Hawaii did not begin until early 1885, when the Japanese government initiated a supervised program of emigration under a provisional agreement with the Kingdom of Hawaii. The first group of 948 Japanese immigrants arrived in Hawaii aboard the *City of Tokio* on 8 February 1885, to work mostly on sugar plantations. Tokujiro Sato's arrival in Hawaii predates the first group of government immigrants by almost twenty years, because he came in 1868 (not 1866, as stated by E. Wesley Smith) as a member of the only group of immigrants who left Japan before the commencement of government emigration.⁸⁴ As the year 1868

Tokujiro Sato, at his home in Kukuihaele, Hawaii, circa 1919. Courtesy Clara Toshiko Taise.

---

81. Britsch, *Moramona*. Smith is credited for moving the headquarters of the mission from Laie to Honolulu.

82. Joseph F. Smith, second counselor in the First Presidency since 1880, had come to Hawaii to escape the harassment of federal government marshals associated with the practice of polygamy and remained in Laie from February 1885 to June 1887. In late June, he left Hawaii for Utah upon hearing of the ill health of John Taylor, who subsequently died in July 1887. R. Lanier Britsch, *Unto the Islands of the Sea: A History of the Latter-day Saints in the Pacific* (Salt Lake City: Deseret Book, 1986), 141–43.

83. This fact convincingly refutes the family oral tradition that Tokujiro died on 11 November 1918.

84. In addition, about a dozen Japanese are said to have come to Hawaii as individual immigrants prior to 1885. The information on *gan-nen-mono* comes from Soen Yamashita, *Gan-nen-mono no Omokage* (Tokyo: Nihon Hawai Kyōkai, 1968); supplemented by Roy M. Shinsato, "The Gannen Mono: Great Expectations of the Earliest Japanese Immigrants of Hawaii," *Hawaii Historical Review* 1 (1965): 180–94; Yamashita, *Hawai*

was the first year of Meiji,[85] this group came to be called collectively "first year men" or *gan-nen-mono* in Japanese.

With declining population,[86] and following the emergence of sugar, pineapple, and other agricultural industries, Hawaii was anxious, at least from the early 1850s, to receive foreign workers to cover the shortfall of labor.[87] Desiring to secure Japanese workers and knowing Japan was opening to international intercourse in the late 1850s, the Hawaiian authorities approached the Tokugawa shogunate about the matter in 1865 by appointing Eugene M. Van Reed, a Dutch-American businessman living in Yokohama, as Hawaii's consul in Japan.[88] No formal agreement could be secured because the shogunate objected not only to the idea of emigration itself but also to a businessman acting in a diplomatic capacity. On 22 April 1868,[89] however, Van Reed was finally successful in obtaining the permission of the shogunate to recruit up to 350 Japanese immigrants to work on sugar plantations in Hawaii for three years.

Van Reed contracted with Japanese agents to recruit immigrant workers on the streets of Edo (present-day Tokyo) and Yokohama. Those recruited were mainly city dwellers, who had little experience in farming. Perhaps about half were vagabonds, coolies, gamblers, drunkards, and other troublemakers who crowded the urban streets of Japan during that period of great political and social unrest. Some were the second and third sons of small merchant houses, struggling in the economic depression of the time. Others were carpenters, plasterers, and other construction workers who had been employed in the rapidly developing open treaty port of Yokohama. An overwhelming majority of them were young, over two-thirds of them being in their late teens and twenties.

Their contract was for three years (counting from the date of arrival in Hawaii), during which time they would be required to work twenty-six days a month for $4.00 (or $3.00 in the case of women). Transportation, food, lodging, and medical care would be provided by the employers, free of charge. Those

---

Kōryū Shi; Hiroshi Shimaoka, *Hawai Imin No Rekishi* (Tokyo: Tosho Kankōkai, 1978); United Japanese Society of Hawaii, ed., *Hawai Nihonjin Imin Shi,* second edition with a supplement (Honolulu: Hawai Hōchi, 1977).

85. The new era of Meiji was declared on 8 September of the fourth year of Keio (according to the lunar calendar), or 23 October 1968, and made retroactive to 1 January of that (lunar) year.

86. The population of Hawaii, which stood at 130,313 in the 1832 census, declined to 84,165 in 1850, and then to 69,000 in 1860. Shinsato, "Gannen Mono," 181.

87. The initial importation of Chinese workers began in 1852, followed by, among others, Polynesians (1859), Japanese (1868), Portuguese and Micronesians (1878), Puerto Ricans (1900), and Koreans (1903). Yamashita, *Hawai Kōryū Shi,* 20.

88. Masaji Marumoto, "'First Year' Immigrants to Hawaii and Eugene Van Reed," in *East across the Pacific: Historical and Sociological Studies of Japanese Immigration and Assimilation,* ed. Hilary Conroy and T. Scott Miyakawa (Santa Barbara, California: ABC-Clio, 1972), 7–17.

89. Or 31 March, according to the lunar calendar.

recruited accepted these terms, thinking that they would be rich when they returned home in three years. Uneducated as they were, they had no idea what *Hawaii* meant, let alone where the place was located. They called the place *tenjiku*, the ancient name for India, or simply a faraway place.

The fourth year of Keio (1868) was the year during which political power was transferred from the Tokugawa shogunate to the new imperial government of Emperor Meiji. The transfer of power was far from peaceful. Early in the year, following the declaration of imperial rule at the imperial palace in Kyoto, a civil war broke out. Strengthened by their victories in earlier battles, the imperial (now government) forces were marching towards Edo just about the time the immigrants were being recruited on the streets. Unfortunately for Van Reed and his party of immigrants, the Meiji government took over the political control of the port of Yokohama on 9 May 1868,[90] just when the chartered British ship *Scioto* was about to leave with the immigrants on board.[91] On 6 May,[92] the immigrants had already begun boarding, upon the satisfactory completion of a medical examination.[93]

The new authorities stationed in Yokohama disapproved the shogunate's earlier agreement to allow its subjects to emigrate to Hawaii as contractual workers. Van Reed protested, saying that it would be a breach of diplomatic protocol not to honor the international agreement of a previous regime. On their part, the Meiji authorities argued that Hawaii was not a commercial treaty partner. Furthermore, they did not think that the terms of the contract were satisfactory and objected to the credentials of Van Reed as Hawaiian consul. They were also aware of the prevailing public opinion that the immigrant workers would be made slaves once they reached Hawaii.

Seeing the intransigence of the Japanese authorities, Van Reed turned to a last resort measure. On 17 May 1868,[94] with customs clearance from the British (but not Japanese) authorities,[95] he allowed the *Scioto*, carrying 150 Japanese

---

90. Or 17 April, according to the lunar calendar.

91. Although the ship was built in 1849 at Brunswick, Maine, and was owned by George F. Lovett of Boston, it flew the British flag, having been registered in Gibraltar under British law. Goto, *Children of Gan-nen-mono*.

92. Or 14 April, according to the lunar calendar.

93. Because of the generally poor health of the people, only 141 people out of some 400 applicants passed the medical examination. Because the ship left in a hurry, the quota of 350 immigrants was not used up. Nine of the rejected applicants smuggled onto the ship, making the total 150. Yamashita, *Gan-nen-mono*, 30–31.

94. Or 25 April, according to the lunar calendar.

95. Under the terms of the Ansei commercial treaties, Western powers, including Britain, France, Hollands, Russia, and the United States, were given extraterritorial privileges in Japan.

immigrants (144 men and six women), to leave Yokohama harbor.[96] As the ship slowly moved out to the open sea, there was much rejoicing among the passengers because they were finally freed from the lingering fear that they would be arrested and punished by the government authorities. The immigrants had generally been ignorant of the intricacy of either politics or diplomacy but understood only that their departure was in question and their lives were possibly in danger.

The ship arrived in Honolulu on 19 June. On the following day, the 149 immigrants (one had died at sea) were allowed to go ashore. While on board, all the men, except for two who would do so later, had had their characteristic topknots chopped off as a token of gratitude for having survived the voyage across rough seas and also possibly as a symbol of their severance from their old world. After two weeks of vacation in Honolulu, the immigrants were assigned to different employers, who were required to pay $70 per immigrant to the Hawaiian government and to make an advance of $10 in cash to each immigrant, which would then be deducted from monthly wages.

In the meantime, the unauthorized departure of the *Scioto* had become a diplomatic embarrassment for the new government. To restore national dignity, the government tried in vain to work with the resident diplomatic community to explore ways of punishing Van Reed and to secure the return of the immigrants. Just at that time, complaints of mistreatment, poor diet, and other hardships began to surface among the immigrants in Hawaii. For one thing, the immigrants were city dwellers unaccustomed to a rural lifestyle, let alone farming. Besides, their working conditions were severe, as they were made to work twelve straight hours a day under the heat of the sun. There were at least two natural deaths and one suicide. There were also complaints of inadequate pay, particularly when half the wages were withheld for deferred payment upon their return home. These and other problems were undoubtedly compounded by language difficulties. The plight of the Japanese immigrants reached the Japanese consul in San Francisco, and several letters arrived from Tomisaburo Makino, the leader of the immigrants in Hawaii, requesting the Japanese government to intervene on their behalf.

In consequence, the Japanese government dispatched twenty-five-year-old Kagenori Ueno as special envoy to Hawaii. Traveling by way of San Francisco, Ambassador Ueno arrived in Honolulu on 27 December 1869,[97] and immediately began to investigate the situation and to negotiate with the Hawaiian authorities.[98] Ueno proposed two alternatives. One was that all immigrants be returned to Japan immediately at the expense of the Japanese government. The

---

96. An alternative figure for the number of immigrants, 153, is widely accepted among Japanese historians. The ship's American physician, David J. Lee, reported the figure of 148. Goto, *Children of Gan-nen-mono*. Okihiro, *Cane Fires*, 20, gives 149. Based on admittedly secondary evidence presented by various authors, the present author is satisfied that the most reasonable figure is 150.

97. Or 25 November, according to the lunar calendar.

98. Shinsato, "Gannen Mono," 186.

other was that only those wishing to return immediately be returned at the expense of the Japanese government but the remainder be returned at the end of the three-year contract period at the expense of the Hawaiian government. On 10 January 1870,[99] the Hawaiian government accepted the second of the two proposals, subject to the condition that the agreement was "limited by the general law of all nations and of this country [and] by the fact that should any desire to remain the Hawaiian Government has no authority to compel them to go."[100] In the event, forty-two immigrants returned to Japan, and the rest (including two women) remained.[101] The working conditions and general treatment of the remaining immigrants improved, so no more serious complaints were reported during the rest of the initial contract period.

2.3.3. Life in Japan

Because the unauthorized departure of the *Scioto* in 1868 was a major diplomatic incident, there exist several government and semiofficial records that detail the names, ages, and, in some cases, occupations of the immigrants. The trouble is that much discrepancy exists across different records, owing not only to poor record keeping but more importantly to the fact that the immigrants (with the exception of four or possibly five) were commoners without surnames. Tokugawa society allowed only limited social mobility, with a clear distinction between the ruling class and the commoners. Various classes of samurai (warriors turned domain officials) were part of the ruling class, while the commoners included *chōnin* (townspeople) and *hyakushō* (farmers; broadly village people engaged in various economic activities); as a general rule, occupations were passed from father to son. To use a surname was a privilege reserved for samurai, some landed farmers, and favored townspeople, including artisans and merchants of wealth and distinction. Surnames were recorded for only four of the 150 *gan-nen-mono*, and the rest frequently changed their names after arriving in Hawaii, making it difficult to trace individual immigrants through time.

The various records show that there were two immigrants by the name of Tokujiro (with no surname). The statement of E. Wesley Smith, however, establishes that the Tokujiro we seek is listed as eighteen years old when he boarded the ship, the other Tokujiro being listed as twenty-seven years old.[102] In the old

---

99. Or 10 December of the second year of Meiji, according to the lunar calendar.
100. As quoted in Shinsato, "Gannen Mono," 186–87.
101. When the initial three-year contract period ended, twelve more immigrants (including one born in Hawaii) returned to Japan at the Hawaiian government's expense, about forty moved to the continental United States, and about fifty remained in Hawaii as *gan-nen-mono*. Because one of the two remaining women left for Japan, only one woman ultimately remained in Hawaii.
102. Yamashita, *Gan-nen-mono*, 70–71.

Japanese way of counting age,[103] this means that he was born during the fourth year of Kaei (or the twelve-month period from 1 February 1851 to 29 January 1852, and not 1849 as Smith claims) and that he was sixteen or seventeen years old in terms of Western counting when he came to Hawaii, depending on the exact date of his birth.[104] It is almost certain that Tokujiro was not of the samurai class, despite the claim of the family oral history to the contrary.[105] For one thing, he did not have a surname, or at least it is not recorded that he did. For another, Tatami-machi (or Tatami-cho), which is believed to have been his place of residence,[106] was in the Kyobashi section of Edo,[107] a small area southeast of Edo Castle, and was where artisans specializing in the making of *tatami* (mat extensively used in the furnishing of Japanese-style houses) were concentrated. Given the definite demarcation that existed between the sections for samurai and townspeople, no samurai could have possibly lived in that part of town.[108]

By the time he left home at the age of sixteen or seventeen, Tokujiro may well have already been an accomplished *tatami* maker in his own right. Family oral history has it that he was skilled in carpentry and helped build houses in the Waipio Valley on the northeastern coast of the island of Hawaii.[109] That he was a skilled carpenter cannot be disputed, as the house that he had built for himself stood for over one hundred years.[110] These carpentry skills could have been ac-

---

103. In the old Japanese system, a child is one year old when he or she is born, and a year is added on each New Year's Day.

104. Hence, Tokujiro was around sixty-eight years old (not seventy years old) when he met E. Wesley Smith in 1919.

105. The oral history, as summarized in Joelle Segawa Kane, "Gan-nen-mono," states that Tokujiro was "a samurai of the *Hatamoto* class, which was the rank of the loyal guards of the Tokugawa Shogun." It is virtually impossible to conceive of such a person of distinction wanting to go to Hawaii as a contractual immigration worker.

106. Yamashita, *Gan-nen-mono*, 73. This fact is corroborated by the family portrait of Tokujiro, on which it is stated (most likely by Tokujiro himself) that he is from Tatami-machi, Kyobashi-ku, Tokyo.

107. The Kyobashi section of Edo is now part of several large city blocks located in Kyobashi 3-chome, Chuo-ku, Tokyo, a short distance southeast of the Yaesu entrance of Tokyo station. Tōkyō-shi, *Tōkyō-shi Chōmei Enkaku Shi*, vol. 1 (Tokyo: Tokyo-shi, 1938), 60–61.

108. Two additional facts from the Hawaii period add strength to our conjecture that Tokujiro was not of the samurai class. First, later in Hawaii, Tokujiro was engaged in the butchery business, considered to be the most despicable occupation in Tokugawa Japan. Second, before settling on Sato, he chose two surnames, Sato and Sasaki, as if he did not know which one to keep.

109. Albert Sato Toko, interview by author, Kamuela, Hawaii, 12 June 1999. Toko is a grandson of Tokujiro.

110. The house was still standing when the author visited the place in 1999. In an interview with the author, Leslie Lactaoen, the then current occupant of the house, testified of the solid construction of the house, which had stood the test of time. Leslie P. and Renee Lactaoen, interview by author, Kukuihaele, Hawaii, 12 June 1999.

quired as part of his apprenticeship in *tatami* making, which involves mastering the use of carpentry tools. His supposed samurai status, undoubtedly of his own or his family's concoction, may be traced to the possible contractual relationship that his shop maintained with one of the *hatamoto* (Tokugawa retainer) families. Tatami-machi was linked by a bridge over the outer moat to the cluster of large *hatamoto* houses, which faced the inner moat of the castle. *Tatami* makers were placed in that precise location for the very purpose of serving the needs of those households and even the Tokugawa household itself.

In 1868, the town that Tokujiro was leaving behind was in the state of economic and social chaos. With the opening of Japan to international trade in the late 1850s, the relative prices of basic commodities began to change, resulting in a sharp redistribution of wealth. With trade came a rise in the relative prices of exportables such as silk and tea, while those of importables such as sugar and cotton fell. The wholesale merchants of Edo were particularly hard hit, as the flow of commodities was diverted to Yokohama and new merchants emerged to exploit the business opportunities created by the opening of trade. To make matters worse, the Tokugawa shogunate began to stockpile rice and other essential commodities in preparation for the impending showdown with the anti-shogunate forces. With shortage and inflation, poverty was rampant.[111] The Keio period (1865–68) was a period of great social unrest, during which there were at least five major riots in Edo.

In spring 1868, it was under these economic and social conditions that the townspeople of Edo heard that the imperial forces were coming to destroy the city. In the end, Edo Castle was handed over to the imperial forces in a peaceful settlement on 3 May,[112] and the city was spared from being burned, but the people in general were not fully informed of these developments. For some time, the streets remained filled with people carrying household effects in their attempt to flee the city. For Tokujiro and the other newly recruited immigrants from Edo, the call for laborers to work in Hawaii was not only an opportunity for life in a new land but also an opportunity to escape from economic depression and possible death in the old land. This sense of terror and urgency to escape is captured by the following quote from the (not-so-reliable) family oral history of Tokujiro:

> Tokujiro and thirteen other [sic] of his fellow samurai [were told that] if they were caught by the Imperial forces they would be beheaded. Seeing that they could not escape death if they remained in Japan, their leader suggested them to find a way to run

---

111. According to an incomplete survey conducted in the fourth year of Keio (1868), there were about 74,000 people in Edo who were considered destitute. Of this figure, about 2,000 were in the Kyobashi area. Another source states that there were about 300,000 people in poverty in the second year of Meiji (1869). Hiromichi Ishizuka, *Tōkyō no Shakai Keizai Shi* (Tokyo: Kinokuniya Shoten, 1977), 21–24.

112. Or 11 April, according to the lunar calendar.

away to some far away country. Until Tokujiro and his fellow guards could find a way to escape they had to stay in hiding to prevent being captured by the Imperial forces.[113]

What is remarkable about this story, which Tokujiro must have told his family members in one form or another, is its seeming resemblance to the well-known story of a group of immigrants from Edo called *Imado-gumi,* headed by Komekichi Sakuma. The Imado-gumi group of twenty-five immigrants left the street of Imado in the Asakusa section of Edo on 7 May for their thirty-mile journey towards Yokohama.[114] Heading south, they walked through the chaotic downtown streets of Edo and came to Takanawa, when they saw a large army of government soldiers marching into town. Terrified, they suddenly stopped and hid themselves in a grove of trees upon a hill in Shinagawa and remained there until the last of the soldiers was seen walking up north to the central part of Edo.[115] Other than the samurai reference, the resemblance between the two stories is so striking that one wonders whether Tokujiro was a member of Imado-gumi, with Komekichi being the leader. Or perhaps, the Imado-gumi story is only representative of a similar scene experienced by all of the forty or so immigrants from Edo.

2.3.4. Life in Hawaii

The records filed by the *gan-nen-mono* chief Makino indicate that, when the time came to allocate the 148 immigrants (excluding one infant) among different employers, fifty-one were sent to Oahu, seventy-one to Maui (of this, fifty-one went to Haiku Sugar Company alone), twenty-two to Kauai, and four to Lanai (under the employ of W. M. Gibson).[116] E. Wesley Smith's statement that Tokujiro witnessed the Walter Murray Gibson trouble may well mean, if taken literally, that he was one of the four immigrants assigned to Lanai in the employ of Gibson. By 1868, the Gibson trouble had been long over, but Gibson still lived in Lanai. We know from a different source that, of the four assigned to Lanai, three (including a married couple) returned home in connection with the visit of Ambassador Ueno in early 1870.[117] The fourth immigrant assigned to Lanai might have been Tokujiro.

Alternatively, Tokujiro could have been sent to Maui. After all, almost half the people were sent there. Lanai, particularly the valley of Palawai, where Gibson likely lived, was only a short distance from Lahaina, Maui, across the channel. As Lanai lacked most amenities of life, Gibson must have frequented Maui to

---

113. Kane, "Gen-nen-mono."
114. Or 15 April, according to the lunar calendar.
115. Yamashita, *Gan-nen-mono,* 16–18.
116. Okihiro, *Cane Firres,* 21; Yamashita, *Gan-nen-mono,* 38–39. There are different accounts of their allocation.
117. Makino's report filed on 29 January 1870. Yamashita, *Hawai Kōryū Shi,* 217–19.

purchase basic supplies. Even in Maui, Tokujiro and others could easily have had opportunities to see Gibson from time to time. In fact, the family oral history states that Tokujiro was first sent to Maui. Yet again, it is also possible that he first went to Lanai but moved to Maui in conjunction with the promise of the Hawaiian government, made with Ambassador Ueno, to improve the working conditions of the Japanese immigrants. He would not have stayed in Lanai if the conditions there had been so bad that three out of the four initial immigrants decided to leave.[118]

Interestingly, the list of *gan-nen-mono* filed on 21 May 1871 by Makino with the Hawaiian government designates "Toku Jilo" as desiring to go to the United States after the conclusion of the initial three-year contract period.[119] In early 1871, in response to an inquiry by Makino, the Japanese government authorized the remaining 100 or so immigrants to return home, remain in Hawaii, or go to the United States without penalty. Judging from what we know about his later life experiences as well as his generally limited ability to speak English, it is almost certain that Tokujiro did not go to the United States when the contract was fulfilled in June 1871. As he was prepared to leave whatever place he was in, he may well have left for the island of Hawaii at that time.

It may have been around the time of the enactment in Japan of the Household Register Law in 1871 that Tokujiro took the surname Sato. Initially, when he arrived in Hawaii, he chose to be called Toku or Toko. Shortening of Japanese names to adapt to the Hawaiian manner of speech was a common practice in those days.[120] When the time came to pick a surname, he could have easily adopted the name chosen by his family in Tokyo. When we recognize that he claimed that he was from Tatachi-machi, Kyobashi-ku, Tokyo, and that the Kyobashi section of Tokyo became a city ward (*ku*) only in November 1878,[121] we can be reasonably sure that he maintained some contact with his family at least until sometime after that date. Alternatively, the fact that he also used the surname Sasaki at least for a while may indicate that he chose the name Sasaki first, only to find out later that his family back in Japan had adopted a different name.

Tokujiro's presumed years in Maui were followed by a permanent move to the island of Hawaii. According to one source, Tokujiro went to Waipio on the northeastern coast to work as a butcher and to farm taro.[122] Another source sug-

---

118. In a personal interview, one of the descendants of Tokujiro told the author that Tokujiro might have fathered children in Maui.

119. Shinsato, "Gannen Mono," 192–93.

120. As another example, the *gan-nen-mono* leader Tomisaburo Makino (Makino being his samurai surname) chose to be called Tomi Saburo, as if Saburo was his surname. Sometimes, he signed his name T. Saburo. Yamashita, *Gan-nen-mono*, 66.

121. Kyōbashi Kyōkai, comp., *Kyōbashi Hanshō Ki* (Tokyo: Kyōbashi Kyōkai, 1912), 7.

122. Jiro Nakano, "Sentaro Kawashima: Japanese Settlers of Waipio Valley," *Hawaii Herald*, 20 June 1986 14–15.

gests that he lived in Pahoa, on the east coast south of Hilo.[123] Yet again, the family oral history states that he went to Waimea (on the highland about ten miles south of Waipio) to work for Samuel Parker at his ranch as a carpenter and a cook and that the two developed a friendship that lasted a lifetime.[124] Samuel Parker (1852–1920) was the flamboyant grandson of John Palmer Parker (1790–1868), who jumped ship in Hawaii, befriended King Kamehameha I, and built a large and prosperous ranch on the Waimea plain. Wherever Tokujiro lived or worked in early years, he finally ended up in Kukuihaele (about five miles south of Waipio along the Pacific coast), where he built his own home and spent his final years. Information is so scant that we cannot possibly reconstruct the sequence of his life in Hawaii. One thing we know for sure is that his entire life on the island of Hawaii was spent in a relatively small region connecting (roughly from north to south) Waipio, Kukuihaele, Waimea, and Pahoa. His life in these locations may have been overlapping and not necessarily sequential.

Sometime after arriving on the island of Hawaii, Tokujiro married Kalala Keliihananui Kamekona, a Hawaiian with mixed Irish and Chinese lineage. According to family sources, Kalala Keliihananui Kamekona was the daughter of Kamekona (from the Waipio Valley) and Kaiahua (from the neighboring Waimanu Valley).[125] She is said to have been born in Mana or Waipio circa 1851, but this date cannot be correct because it would make her fifty-five or fifty-six years old when the last child, Kaniela, was born in February 1907. According to Smith's 1919 account, Tokujiro and Kalala were married in 1879 and had "happily passed their ruby anniversary." The reference to the ruby anniversary must be Smith's creation because it is difficult (though not impossible) to believe that she did not have children for almost ten years after marriage (until the latter half of the 1880s) when she was fertile enough to give birth to ten children during her lifetime.[126] These considerations seem to suggest that Tokujiro's marriage to Kalala took place in the middle of the 1880s and that Tokujiro was then in his early thirties and Kalala in her early twenties (having been born around 1862).

Kalala's possible birthplace of Mana is interesting because, in all likelihood, it refers to Mana Hale (in Hawaiian, House of the Spirit), the house built by John Palmer Parker outside of Waimea on the lower slope of 13,796-foot-high Mauna Kea. Undoubtedly, *Mana* later began to mean the whole compound of the Parker home or even the whole community of ranchers, workers, and their families working on Parker Ranch.[127] Samuel Parker and his royal wife, Harriet Panana Napela, had a lavish lifestyle, alternating their residence between Mana

---

123. Okihiro, *Cane Fires*, 23.
124. Kane, "Gan-nen-mono," 4.
125. Kamekona family records, provided by Noelani Kamekona, Pearl City, Hawaii.
126. This statement should be qualified by the possibility that the unnamed child who died in infancy had been the first child and was born much earlier.
127. The headquarters of Parker Ranch moved in 1879, when John Parker II, the son of Jon Palmer Parker and the uncle of Samuel, moved to a more central location in

Tokujiro Sato and Hawaiian wife Kalala, circa late 1880s. Courtesy Clara Toshiko Taise.

and the king's palace in Honolulu. They were part of Hawaii's high society and regularly entertained "world travelers and socialites." Their parties are said to have "rivalled even those of King Kalakaua, a close friend of theirs."[128] Kalakaua was on the throne from 1874 to 1891. During 1878–87, the king's close confidant and advisor was Walter Murray Gibson, who, after being excommunicated from the LDS Church in 1864, tried his hand in Hawaiian politics and served as the premier and minister of foreign affairs before being forced to flee the country for a life of exile in California. No doubt Gibson was one of those distinguished guests at Parker's home in Mana, and Tokujiro had plenty of opportunities in his capacity as the family chef to get to know Gibson. In this light, Tokujiro's presumed witness of Gibson's rise and fall takes on a new meaning.

Given Tokujiro's work and Kalala's family connection in Mana, it is possible that the two met and were married in Mana. Tokujiro may have obtained work as a cook at Parker Ranch because of his previous experience as a butcher in Waipio. Alternatively, his Parker Ranch job may have been his first in Hawaii. In any case, after being married, the couple must have spent much of their married life in Waipio,[129] where Tokujiro raised taro, built homes as a carpenter, and

---

Waimea. Samuel continued to live in Mana. Parker Ranch Foundation Trust, "Parker Ranch Historic Homes" (Kamuela, Hawaii: Parker Ranch Visitor's Center, not dated).

128. Jackie Kido, "Hawaii's Ranching Dynasty: Parker Ranch," *Spirit of Hawaii* (July 1997): 10.

129. The predominant population of Waipio consisted of Hawaiians and Chinese, with a few Japanese. There were no plantations, but rice was cultivated on its fertile soil. Toko, interview.

after 1885, when Japanese immigrants began to arrive in Hawaii, helped them with the Hawaiian language and Hawaiian culture. A story is told of Sentaro Kawashima, a young Japanese immigrant, who was taught by Tokujiro to speak Hawaiian and English, farm taro, and make poi and *okolehau* (homemade Hawaiian whiskey).[130] Tokujiro had become fluent in the Hawaiian language, so he was sometimes asked by a court of law to act as an interpreter.[131] Such an assignment was not unusual for the *gan-nen-mono* who stayed in the Hawaiian Islands, because, with very few or even no other Japanese around, they had to assimilate into Hawaiian society.

It is said that when Tokujiro moved to Kukuihaele and built a house for his own family he carried lumber from the Waipio Valley on an ox wagon.[132] Kukuihaele is only a short distance from Waipio, but it is located at least a few hundred feet above the valley. To carry the lumber up the steep hill must have been a strenuous and arduous task, a task that cannot possibly be carried out by someone in his old age. Thus, when the house was built in Kukuihaele, he was perhaps in his late thirties or early forties (in other words, the house was probably built sometime during the 1890s). It is almost certain that the house was built by 1901, because Tokujiro was there when Kawashima arrived at the Kukuihaele plantation during that year.[133] In Kukuihaele, Tokujiro raised taro (as he had done or possibly continued to do in Waipio) on an irrigated farm adjacent to the back of his house. The farm was about half an acre in size and stretched out on a moderate slope overlooking the Pacific Ocean. For a time, the couple had a store, selling *poi* or taro and beef. The beef might have been procured through his old connection with Samuel Parker, indicating that Tokujiro's association with him was a long one.[134]

---

130. Nakano, "Japanese Settlers," 14.

131. Toko, interview; Clara Toshiko Taise, interview by author, Naalehu, Hawaii, 7 February 1999.

132. Lactaoen, interview.

133. According to Nakano, "Japanese Settlers," 14, Tokujiro told Kawashima to quit the plantation and to farm taro in Waipio and served as a go-between in arranging a marriage with a Hawaiian woman named Kainoa. Apparently, Tokujiro maintained two residences, one each in Waipio and Kukuihaele, through the early years of the twentieth century.

134. In an interview with the author, Albert Sato Toko, a grandson of Tokujiro, recalled a story told by his father John to the effect that he (John) had one day left school to go to see his father in a mountain home. As John Toko was born in 1892, this story must mean that Tokujiro still worked at Parker's mountain compound in the 1900s. Albert also speculated that, as Tokujiro and Kalala were thus physically separated during periods of substantial length, Kalala was unfaithful and gave birth to children of other men.

2.3.5. Association with the LDS Church

According to E. Wesley Smith's statement, Tokujiro supposedly joined the LDS Church in 1892 and had been and was still a faithful member of the church when they met in 1919. Tokujiro may well have joined the church, but there is no record to support the claim that his baptism took place in 1892. It is difficult to have faith in the validity of that date, when every other date in Smith's statement has turned out to be incorrect. Moreover, the descendants of Tokujiro generally are skeptical of the claim that he was a member of the LDS Church, though they do not deny the possibility.[135] A handful of church records do exist, however, to establish his association, if not affiliation, with the church.

The membership records for the Waipio Branch in the Northern Hawaii District do list Tokujiro (as Toko Sr. born circa 1845), though no baptism information is given. His wife, Kalala, is also listed (as Clara Toko baptized in Mana), although no date is given for either birth or baptism. The children's baptisms, when they did occur, are more accurately recorded. The records show that at least six of the nine children were baptized: Mary Melelaulani and Hana on 7 December 1902; John (listed as Toko Jr.) on 9 December 1902; Pula on 6 March 1904; Willard Matsu (Kanuka) on 16 November 1913; and Kaniela on 17 April 1919. No records exist, however, for the other three children, Ohumukini, Emily, and Fukui.[136]

Given the very fact that membership records exist for Tokujiro, that almost all of his children were baptized, and that the visiting mission authority considered him a faithful member, the weight of the evidence seems to suggest that Tokujiro was a baptized member of the LDS Church.[137] Considering that, when the first three of the children were baptized in December 1902, the oldest child (Mary) was fifteen years old, there is a reasonable basis for believing that Tokujiro was baptized prior to 29 August 1895, her eighth birthday (which in the LDS Church is the age of accountability when one becomes eligible for baptism). Otherwise, Tokujiro and Mary would have been baptized at the same time. On the other hand, to believe that he was baptized after Mary is difficult (though not impossible) because then the baptism would have more likely been recorded, given the better record-keeping practice in later years. It may be that Tokujiro was

---

135. Taise, interview; Toko, interview.

136. See Appendix 2.1 for the list of children in order of birth. According to Kaniela, the youngest son, as told by his daughter, all the children of Tokujiro were baptized as children except for Fukui. Subsequently, Fukui too joined the LDS Church, as he married an active Hawaiian Latter-day Saint.

137. As an interesting sidelight, Sentaro Kawashima, Tokujiro's student in taro farming and the Hawaiian way of life, joined the LDS Church on 7 March 1927, and was ordained an elder on 24 October 1929. He is said to have remained a well-respected and stalwart member of the church until his death on 17 October 1956. Nakano, "Japanese Settlers"; Deceased member records.

baptized along with his eldest daughter Ohumukini, whose baptism information is not available but who is also considered to have been a member.[138]

The Tokujiro Sato family was far from being the typical Mormon family of contemporary America. Their religious understanding and practice were constrained both by the cultural settings of the day and by the different expectations that the church had of its members. The descendants remember Kalala as fond of drinking *okolehau* and as being "cranky" most of the time, possibly because of her drinking habit.[139] In his later years, perhaps with the increasing population of Japanese, Tokujiro came to emphasize his Japanese identity. Although he exclusively spoke Hawaiian to his children, he spoke Japanese to some of the grandchildren as they developed proficiency in that language; he also apparently encouraged at least one of his daughters to marry a Japanese man and gave up one of his sons for adoption to a Japanese family.[140]

Tokujiro died in his home shortly after his meeting with E. Wesley Smith in 1919,[141] and after a funeral held presumably at an LDS meetinghouse, he was buried in a cemetery located on the Pacific shore.[142] For one reason or another, none of the children took the name Sato, although John and John's son Albert carried it as their middle name. After all, Sato was a name foreign to Tokujiro. John took the name Toko, Willard (who was given up for adoption) carried the name Yamamoto, and the two youngest sons decided to use their mother's honored Hawaiian name of Kamekona. Whatever shortcomings Tokujiro and Kalala might have had as Mormon parents, a host of practicing Latter-day Saints are found among their descendants, particularly those who have come through the Ohumukini, Fukui, and Kaniela lines. His grave no longer exists because it was washed away in a tidal wave, but the legacy of hard work and perseverance that he exhibited throughout his life continues among them.

2.4. Conclusion

Tomizo Katsunuma and Tokujiro Sato each have a legitimate claim to being the first Japanese Mormon. Both happened to be at the crossroads of major historical transformations making their conversion to Mormonism possible. First, with the western frontiers secured, the United States was becoming a Pacific military and economic power, eventually annexing the peaceful and independent kingdom of Hawaii. Second, following the opening of the country to international intercourse, Japan itself was rapidly developing into a modern nation-state,

---

138. Noelani Vera Kamekona, interview by author, Pearl City, Oahu, 7 February 1999.
139. Taise, interview; Toko, interview.
140. Taise, interview.
141. Kaniela's best recollection held that Tokujiro had died in Kukuihaele on 11 November 1918. This date cannot be correct, because he was alive when E. Wesley Smith came to see him in 1919.
142. Kamekona, interview.

and a host of adventurous Japanese were venturing out of the country to explore opportunities abroad. Finally, against these major transpacific political developments in the background, the Mormons were trying to solidify their base in the Intermountain West and were beginning to engage in an aggressive proselytizing program in the Pacific. Without the changes created by these currents in the surrounding power and opportunity structures, neither Tomizo nor Tokujiro would have been freed from the shackles of tradition to embrace a new religion in a new land and to be Mormon pioneers of Japanese ancestry.

Some may challenge the use of the term "pioneer" to describe these early Japanese Mormons, at least in the usual sense in which the term is understood. After all, they never walked the plains for a thousand miles. They were never harassed or molested for their religious beliefs. They never helped, at least in a major way, the institutional establishment of the LDS Church in their communities, let alone in their native land. They held no leadership positions in the church to speak of. In some ways, they were marginal affiliates of Mormonism. Perhaps they can more appropriately be called "path-breakers," a special type of pioneers separated from the binding root of a certain cultural tradition and serving as a bridge between the real pioneers (who are to come) and their old world.[143] Indeed, neither Tomizo nor Tokujiro may have been stalwart converts in the full sense of the word, but path-breakers they were—even pioneers in their internal struggle to reconcile the tenets of Mormonism with the demands of Japanese culture, the same struggle that has continued to this day among their fellow Mormons of Japanese ancestry.

APPENDIX 2.1. CHILDREN OF TOMIZO AND TOKUJIRO

CHILDREN OF TOMIZO AND MINE[144]

>   Katsumi, son, born on 12 May 1890, Miharu, Fukushima.
>   Kiyomi, daughter, born on 24 January 1899, Miharu, Fukushima.
>   Takeo, son, born on 20 February 1902, Honolulu.
>   Yasuko, daughter, born on 13 May 1904, Honolulu.
>   Yoshiko, daughter, born on 8 September 1906, Tokyo.
>   Woodrow, son, born on 9 March 1913, Honolulu.

---

143. Armand L. Mauss, letter to author, 7 August 1999; Armand L. Mauss, e-mail to author, 21 October 1999.

144. Yunojiri, *Katogi San Rōkyōdai*, 67. Katsumi's reported birthday, more than a full year after the departure of Tomizo for the United States on 25 April 1889, could be an error.

Children of Tokujiro and Kalala[145]

Ohumukini, daughter, birthdate unknown, Hawaii.
Mary Melelaulani, daughter, born in 1887, Hawaii.
Hana, daughter, born in 1889, Waipio, Hawaii.
John, son, born in 1892, Waipio, Hawaii.
Pula, son, born in 1895, Waipio, Hawaii.
Emily, daughter, birthdate unknown, Hawaii.
Fukui, son, born in 1901, Hawaii.
Willard Matsu (Kanuka), son, born in 1904, Waipio, Hawaii.
Kaniela (Daniel), son, born in 1907, Waipio, Hawaii.

---

145. Family sources, supplemented by Goto, *Children of Gan-nen-mono*; membership records for the Waipio Branch of the Northern Hawaii District, LDS Church Archives. The years of birth are only approximate. In addition, there was another child who died in infancy.

Chapter 3

Mormons in the Press: Japanese Reactions to the 1901 Arrival of Heber J. Grant and Company

3.1. Introduction

This chapter presents a review and analysis of the press coverage in Japan of the arrival on Monday, 12 August 1901 of Heber J. Grant, a member of the Council of the Twelve Apostles of the Church of Jesus Christ of Latter-day Saints. Accompanied by Horace S. Ensign, Louis A. Kelsch, and Alma O. Taylor, Grant arrived in Tokyo Bay aboard the *Empress of India*, a steamship operated by Canadian Pacific Railway Company.[1] Their intention was to organize in Japan the first permanent mission of the church in Asia. This "quartet,"[2] after passing quarantine, took a steam launch for the Grand Hotel in Yokohama's foreign settlement.[3] When the four missionaries checked in at the elegant hotel, which professed to be the "largest and most complete hotel in the Far East," "second to none either in Europe or America,"[4] they obviously had no conception of the extensive coverage they would receive in the Japanese press.

The amount of press coverage given the Mormon missionaries during the next month or so was unprecedented and has not been surpassed in the subsequent history of the LDS Church in Japan. More than a dozen newspapers in the capital city of Tokyo, two nationally influential newspapers in the dominant commercial city of Osaka, and no less than twenty major regional newspapers throughout the country devoted considerable space—often on front pages—to

---

1. At that time, the Canadian Pacific fleet consisted of three ships— the *Empress of China*, the *Empress of India*, and the *Empress of Japan*—and connected Vancouver and Hong Kong, via Victoria, Yokohama, Kobe, Nagasaki, and Shanghai. See the newspaper advertisement that frequently appeared in those days, for example, the *Japan Times*, 8 August 1901.

2. The expression "quartet" was first used by Augusta, the plural wife of Heber J. Grant, in a letter addressed to her husband in Japan. Alma O. Taylor, Journal, 25 December 1901, BYU Archives.

3. Currently, on this location stands the Yokohama Doll Museum.

4. See the newspaper advertisement that frequently appeared in those days, for example, the *Japan Times*, 8 August 1901. See also Heber J. Grant, "A Japanese Journal," comp. Gordon A. Madsen, 12 August 1901, Americana Collection, Harold B. Lee Library, Brigham Young University.

The Grand Hotel in Yokohama's Foreign Settlement. Courtesy Yokohama Archives.

articles and editorials reporting or otherwise commenting on the arrival of this new Christian sect with unusual doctrines.[5] From 13 August, the day after the missionaries' arrival, to 10 September, not a day went by without something about Mormonism being printed somewhere in Japan; during this time, no less than 160 articles, editorials, and letters appeared in the Japanese press.[6] The scope of this massive newspaper coverage was reinforced by articles about the missionaries' arrival that were published in two of the most influential national magazines, the *Chūō Kōron* (Central Review) and the *Taiyō* (Sun).[7]

---

5. Frederick R. Brady, "The Japanese Reaction to Mormonism and the Translation of Mormon Scripture into Japanese" (MA thesis, Sophia University, 1979); and Murray L. Nichols, "History of the Japan Mission of the Church of Jesus Christ of Latter-day Saints, 1901–1924" (MA thesis, Brigham Young University, 1957). The present chapter expands the scope of analysis in these earlier studies and offers a socio-historical explanation for the newspaper coverage of the first Mormon missionaries.

6. See Annex 6 towards the end of the volume for lists of articles and editorials organized by date and by place of publication.

7. A brief editorial and a brief communication, respectively, appeared in the September issue (dated 1 September) and the October issue (dated 1 October) of the *Chūō Kōron*, and a two-page article by a religious commentator was published in the 5 September issue of the *Taiyō*. Along with the *Nihonjin* (The Japanese), the *Chūō Kōron* and the *Taiyō* were considered to be the three leading national magazines of the period. Taketoshi Nishida, *Meiji Jidai no Shinbun to Zasshi* (Tokyo: Shibundō, 1961), 262. Nothing was written on Mormonism in the *Nihonjin* during the months of August and September.

The chapter considers why the Mormon missionaries received such a reception in Japan. This analysis reveals far more about the social and intellectual conditions of Japan at the turn of the twentieth century than about Mormonism per se; it gives a glimpse into the society in which Mormons were about to proselytize. The chapter (1) shows that the press spread knowledge throughout Japanese society of this important event in the history of the LDS Church;[8] and (2) provides the historical and social context within which Mormon missionary work began in Japan. In particular, the unusual degree to which Mormonism was discussed in the Japanese press was related to the nature and role of the resident foreign press, the competitive nature of the newspaper industry (especially in Tokyo and Osaka) with a propensity towards sensationalism, and, most importantly, Japan's own internal conflict regarding its social institutions.

3.2. Japan at the Turn of the Twentieth Century

Following many years of political difficulties associated with the practice of polygyny, the Latter-day Saints in the United States had finally received some relief in part as a result of the Manifesto of 1890 and the granting of statehood to Utah in 1896.[9] Perhaps for these and other reasons, Mormon leaders could now afford to devote more attention and resources to missionary work outside the then established missions.[10] The leaders noted the spectacular rise of Japan to the ranks of the more "progressive" nations of the world, propelled as it was by the

---

8. Although no hard figure is available, it can be reasonably assumed that no less than half of Japan's 44 million people were literate at the beginning of the twentieth century. This conjecture is based on the following two pieces of indirect evidence. First, by the end of the Tokugawa period, Japan already had a highly literate society which "compared favourably . . . with some contemporary European countries." Practically every samurai was literate, as were "the majority of town-dwellers with a settled occupation" and "a good proportion of the farmers of middling status." In 1868 somewhat more than 40 percent of boys and about 10 percent of girls were receiving some kind of formal education, meaning that at least 25 percent of the population were literate. R. P. Dore, *Education in Tokugawa Japan* (Berkeley and Los Angeles: University of California Press, 1965), 2–3, 254, 291; Shunsuke Tsurumi, *An Intellectual History of Wartime Japan 1931–1945* (London and New York: Routledge & Kegan Paul, 1986), 7. Second, in 1902, thirty years after a government-directed program of school building began in 1872, the rate of primary school enrollment was 90 percent, and less than 20 percent of draft-age males were illiterate. Takenori Inoki, *Gakkō to Kōjō: Nihon no Jinteki Shihon* (Tokyo: Yomiuri Shinbunsha, 1996), 25–27.

9. In the so-called Manifesto of 1890, LDS Church president Wilford Woodruff declared that the church was "not teaching polygamy or plural marriage, nor permitting any person to enter into its practice." The proclamation was accepted by the membership of the church in a general conference held on 6 October.

10. For a general overview of the LDS Church at the end of the nineteenth century, see James B. Allen and Glen M. Leonard, *The Story of the Latter-day Saints* (Salt Lake City: Deseret Book, 1976), 435–65.

promulgation of a written constitution in 1889 with guaranteed religious freedom and parliamentary representation, the defeat of China in the Sino-Japanese War of 1894–95, and the subsequent adoption of the gold standard in 1897.[11] In fact, upon the announcement of his mission call at the April 1901 general conference, Heber J. Grant commented on his very positive impression: "The Japanese are a wonderfully progressive people. . . . Of the Oriental races they are without doubt the most enterprising and intelligent. . . . Some authorities say that when it comes to absorbing knowledge they eclipse any people in the world today."[12] Some Mormons, including Grant, were even led to believe that the Japanese were a chosen race, who had inherited the blood of Israel through the Book of Mormon prophet Lehi.[13]

Perhaps little appreciated by the Mormon leadership at the time was a legal development of major significance to prospective missionary work in Japan. In 1894, the Japanese government agreed to revise the series of commercial treaties, collectively known as the Ansei treaties, which the Tokugawa shogunate had signed with eleven Western nations in the late 1850s and the early 1860s.[14] The Ansei treaties not only allowed the signatory countries access to major ports and commercial cities for trading purposes,[15] but also gave their nationals the right to be tried in a consular court according to their own laws.[16] In exchange for these

---

11. For a general overview of nineteenth-century Japanese history, see W. G. Beasley, *The Modern History of Japan* (London: Weidenfeld and Nicolson, 1963).

12. "Opening of the Mission in Japan," *Deseret Evening News*, 6 April 1901, 9.

13. Heidi Harris claims that the concept of "believing blood" in relation to the hierarchy of Asian races reached its zenith in 1901. Heidi Harris, "Changing Racial Perceptions of the Japanese: LDS Rhetoric between 1901 and 1930," 23 August 2010, available at: www.patheos.com/blogs/oneeternalround. For the doctrinal origin of the view, see Armand L. Mauss, *All Abraham's Children: Changing Mormon Conceptions of Race and Lineage* (Urbana and Chicago: University of Illinois Press, 2003), 1–40.

14. The earlier treaties signed with the United States (the Kanagawa Treaty negotiated by Commodore Matthew C. Perry), Britain, Holland, and Russia during 1854–55 were not commercial treaties. They only obliged Japan to open Hakodate, Nagasaki, and Shimoda for the provision of coal, food, and water; to allow consuls to be stationed; and to grant most favored nation status and the right for their nationals to be tried in a consular court. In these (as well as Ansei) treaties, the slight individual differences in terms that might have existed across treaties were immaterial because the best terms were to be applied to all countries because of the most favored nation status clause. Shigeru Yamamoto, *Jōyaku Kaisei Shi* (Tokyo: Takayama Shoin, 1943), 27–55.

15. The major ports were Hakodate, Hyogo, Kanagawa, Nagasaki, Niigata, and Shimoda. Shimoda was to be closed six months after the opening of Kanagawa. The commercial cities were Edo (present-day Tokyo) and Osaka.

16. For example, Article VI of the Treaty of Amity and Commerce signed between the United States and Japan in 1858 stated in part: "Americans committing offenses against Japanese shall be tried in American consular courts, and when guilty shall be punished according to American law."

extraterritorial privileges, the Ansei treaties and the associated domestic statutes limited foreigners' freedom of access within Japan. In principle, foreigners were not allowed to travel in Japan without explicit permission and were required to live in designated foreign settlements established in the treaty ports and cities, most notably Yokohama, Kobe, and Tokyo.[17] The foreign settlements were restricted areas, in which the Japanese government strictly controlled entrance by Japanese and exit by foreigners.

Attempts to change the Ansei treaties began a few years after the imperial government took over the governance of Japan from the Tokugawa shogunate in 1868.[18] The new government of Emperor Meiji commenced the seemingly fruitless effort of renegotiating with the foreign powers the terms of what it had started calling the Unequal Treaties because of the system of extraterritoriality enjoyed by the foreigners in Japan. The revision of the fifteen Ansei treaties remained the single most important objective of Japanese foreign policy during the subsequent quarter of a century.[19] The termination of extraterritoriality, even a modification of it, was opposed by the treaty port communities.[20] They generally took a hostile and condescending attitude towards the natives and wanted to maintain their privileges and freedom from Japanese law. On the other hand, Protestant missionaries were in favor of a modification. They were eager to proselytize in the interior without resorting to subterfuge or fearing harassment from the police.[21]

The system of extraterritoriality was beset with problems and was not a sustainable arrangement in any case.[22] First, in some countries, such as the United States, the constitutionality of consular courts was questioned. Second, there was

---

17. Yokohama was opened in lieu of Kanagawa, and Kobe in lieu of Hyogo. Edo was renamed Tokyo in 1868.

18. Eleven of the treaties were inherited from the Tokugawa regime, and four additional ones were signed after the Meiji Restoration.

19. How the system of extraterritoriality worked in Japan and how the government attempted to revise the Unequal Treaties are discussed in Francis Clifford Jones, *Extraterritoriality in Japan and the Diplomatic Relations Resulting in Its Abolition 1853–1899* (New Haven: Yale University Press, 1931). Several diplomatic attempts at treaty revision are given in Ian Nish, *Japanese Foreign Policy 1869–1942: Kasumigaseki to Miyakezaka* (London and Boston: Routledge & Kegan Paul, 1977).

20. James Edward Hoare, *The Japanese Treaty Ports, 1868–1899: A Study of the Foreign Settlements* (PhD diss., University of London, 1970), 213.

21. Fearing the reactions of the Western diplomatic community, the government's attitude toward the work of Christian missionaries in the interior was equivocal. For example, local officials would display open opposition, which might then be overruled by the central government. Moreover, the intensity with which restrictions on Christian missionary activities were enforced differed from period to period and from place to place. Charles W. Iglehart, *A Century of Protestant Christianity in Japan* (Rutland, Vermont and Tokyo: Charles E. Tuttle, 1959), 60.

22. Hoare, *Japanese Treaty Ports*, 157–59, 165–70; see Jones, *Extraterritoriality in Japan*, 47–70 on how the British and other consular courts operated.

a lack of experienced officers to administer justice. Third, the appeals process was so costly that many (mostly Japanese) were effectively deprived of justice. For example, those tried in consular courts had to file an appeal with a higher court located in foreign countries, such as Shanghai (Britain) or Saigon (France). Some serious crimes such as murder could not be tried in Japan in the first place. Fourth, some countries did not maintain consuls in Japan. Fifth, problems occurred when jurisdictions overlapped (as would happen when a case involved a Frenchman and a Dutchman).[23] For these and other reasons, extraterritoriality in Japan was becoming increasingly unworkable by the late 1880s.[24] Thus, the treaty powers were prepared to make concessions in return for commercial advantages, such as access to the Japanese market. In part to ease the apprehension of the foreign powers, the Japanese government took a series of measures to reform its legal system along Western lines, including its criminal, commercial, and civil codes.

After multiple attempts, Japan finally secured an arrangement in 1894 with the British government that would abolish extraterritoriality in exchange for allowing foreign merchants to have access to Japan outside the treaty ports and cities. With the decisive British agreement in hand, the Meiji government succeeded in convincing the other countries to sign similar agreements. The revised treaties came into force for all fifteen treaty powers in the summer of 1899 amid some domestic furor over the prospect of allowing foreigners, especially Christian missionaries, to move freely among the populace.[25]

Heber J. Grant and his associates arrived in Yokohama just two years after the foreign settlement there had been legally abolished and foreigners could live and travel in Japan as they pleased. This is not to say that missionary work could not have been conducted in Japan prior to 1899. In fact, several mainstream Christian denominations had already been established in Japan and had met with some success (see Section 4.4.1 in Chapter 4).[26] Even so, their method of prosely-

---

23. Such a problem occurred in 1868 when a British ship collided with an American steamer off the Japanese coast. Frequent cases involved a seaman from one country whose ship belonged to another. Jones, *Extraterritoriality in Japan*, 28, 59–60.

24. Hoare, *Japanese Treaty Ports*, 212.

25. The revised treaties came into force on 17 July 1899 for thirteen of the fifteen treaty powers and on 4 August for the remaining two, namely, Austria and France. For Germany, the revised treaty came into force on 17 July, but the right to a consular trial was retained until 3 August. Yamamoto, *Jōyaku Kaisei Shi*, 621.

26. It is estimated that, at the turn of the twentieth century, there were about 130,000 Christians in Japan (against the population of 44,000,000), including some 54,000 Roman Catholic and 30,000 Orthodox members. Otis Cary, *A History of Christianity in Japan: Roman Catholic and Greek Orthodox Missions* (New York: Fleming H. Revell, 1909), 355, 423; and Otis Cary, *A History of Christianity in Japan: Protestant Missions* (New York: Fleming H. Revell, 1909), 296. Among the many Protestant denominations that had come to Japan by far the most prominent were the Anglican–Episcopal, Baptist, Congregational, Methodist, and Presbyterian–Reformed churches, which were collectively called the "Big Five." Iglehart, *Protestant Christianity*, 80–82.

tizing was not the kind the Mormons generally employed. Mainstream churches had established their bases of operation in the foreign settlements, notably in Yokohama, Tokyo, and Osaka,[27] and had reached the Japanese by building mission schools, where religion could be mixed with secular instruction. Christianity was also spread by foreign teachers employed in Japanese schools; these teachers were given somewhat greater freedom of movement within the country. Most of the notable early Christian converts of the Meiji period were social elites who were influenced by Christian teachers while studying at some of the country's most prestigious institutions of secondary or higher education. Given the limited financial and human resources of the LDS Church in the second half of the nineteenth century, building schools in Japan probably would not have been possible.

3.3. Reactions of the English-Language Press

When Grant and his associates arrived two years after the segregation of foreigners had been lifted, Yokohama possessed a thriving foreign community along the harbor in the original settlement as well as in a newer settlement upon a hill overlooking the harbor. To meet the needs of the foreign community, estimated at between 2,000 and 2,400 in number,[28] Yokohama maintained several foreign-language newspapers, including the *Japan Advertiser*, the *Japan Herald*, and the *Japan Mail*.[29] Of these, the *Japan Advertiser* (founded in 1890) was the only notable newspaper under American management. Unfortunately, because all of these newspapers had a circulation of at most only several hundred, no known copies from this period exist in any Japanese public library. Thus, for information regarding the foreign press in Japan, we must rely on newspaper clippings in Alma O. Taylor's scrapbook, references in his diaries, and some weekly mail editions that have been kept in major libraries overseas.[30]

---

27. With the completion of the railroad connecting Kobe and Osaka in 1874, most merchants in Osaka moved to Kobe. In Tokyo, foreigners were permitted to live outside the settlement. Thus, virtually all the residents of the Tokyo and Osaka settlements ended up being Christian missionaries. Akio Hotta and Tadashi Nishiguchi, eds., *Ōsaka Kawaguchi Kyoryūchi no Kenkyū* (Kyoto: Shibunkaku Shuppan, 1995), 43, 55; Hoare, *Japanese Treaty Ports*, 43–44.

28. Hachiro Ebihara, *Nihon Ōji Shinbun Zasshi Shi* (Tokyo: Taiseidō, 1934), 73.

29. The *Japan Herald*, initially under British management, was founded in 1861 and continued to exist until the outbreak of World War I in September 1914, when the Japanese government ordered the paper to close down because its owner then was a German. The *Japan Mail* was founded in the 1870s. In 1918 it was absorbed by the *Japan Times* of Tokyo. Ebihara, *Ōji Shinbun Zasshi*, 18–20, 81, 210–12.

30. Many daily newspapers printed special weekly mail editions, containing a digest of local news, for consumption in foreign countries. The British Library has maintained copies of these mail editions of the *Japan Mail* and the *Kobe Chronicle*. The microfilms are maintained by major Japanese libraries. The relevant newspaper clippings from Taylor's scrapbook are reproduced in chapter four of Brady, "Japanese Reaction." See also Nichols,

The Bluff Settlement in Yokohama. Courtesy Yokohama Archives.

The English-language press in Yokohama reacted immediately to the arrival of the Mormon missionaries. By this time, the Protestant missionaries, who were an important component of the foreign community in Yokohama, had already been informed by their headquarters that the Mormons would shortly be arriving in Japan. The elders' arrival on 12 August was reported in the *Japan Advertiser* on the following day, with a comment that they would "find the native apparel better than their wares."[31] The paper was at that time under the editorship of a Unitarian missionary by the name of Arthur M. Knapp (editor, 1899–1902).[32] The *Advertiser*'s rather unkind reaction may have exaggerated any lack of civility on the part of the Unitarian missionary, for Elder Grant wrote the following in his journal a few days later:

> I got a letter to the editor of the *Advertiser*, Mr. Napp [sic], and called on him. He received us very kindly and promised us fair treatment at the hands of his paper. He published the address to the Japanese people and wrote an editorial that we need

---

"History of the Japan Mission." Both Brady and Nichols erroneously refer to *Japan Advertiser* as *Yokohama Advertiser*, because the latter is how Taylor called it.

31. As quoted in Taylor, Journal, 13 August 1901. We do not know what else was said in the article, but Taylor thought of it as "a beginning of the ill feeling which we found had been created by the efforts of wicked men who claimed to be members of Christianity."

32. According to the 27 August issue of the *Yamato Shinbun*, Knapp is reported to have traveled on the same ship as the Mormon missionaries and heard Grant say that he would take a Japanese woman as a plural wife. Of course, this cannot possibly be true, calling into question the credibility of the very story that Knapp and Grant traveled together across the Pacific.

not look for much success in this land but said we would be kindly received by the Japanese people.³³

The significance of the *Japan Advertiser*'s reaction lies not so much in its message as in the fact that it was the first to report the arrival of the Mormon missionaries and consequently gave rise to a proliferation of newspaper reports, articles, and editorials on Mormonism during the following month.

At that time, both in terms of influence and readership, the *Japan Mail* and the *Japan Herald* were much more important in Yokohama and elsewhere in Japan.³⁴ Of the two, the *Herald* was more hospitable to the Mormons. On 14 August, Grant visited the office of the *Herald* and received a warm reception. The editor said that he would like to write a story about the Mormon missionaries and agreed to publish an 800-word official statement that Grant had prepared. As the editor had promised, the next day's *Japan Herald* carried the entire transcript, unedited, of Grant's "Address to the Great and Progressive Nation of Japan," which in part reads:

> In company with my associates sent to you from the headquarters of the Church of Jesus Christ of Latter-day Saints in Salt Lake City, Utah, an Apostle and minister of the Most High God, I salute you and invite you to consider the important message we bear. We do not come to you for the purpose of trying to deprive you of any truth in which you believe, or any light that you have been privileged to enjoy. We bring you greater light, more truth and advanced knowledge, which we offer you freely.³⁵

An account of the interview with Grant was published on the same day (15 August). After quoting the thirteen Articles of Faith in their entirety, the account explained the missionary program of the LDS Church (in which some 1,600 missionaries worked without remuneration), the proper name of the church (with *Mormons* being a nickname), its belief in the Book of Mormon, the termination of polygamy with President Wilford Woodruff's Manifesto, and the secular accomplishments of Utah Mormons. Grant wrote in his journal: "The Herald report of my interview is very fair indeed and the next day after its publication I called and thanked Mr. Harrison for it."³⁶ At that time, J. H. Brooke was

---

33. Grant, Journal, 12–18 August. The 20 August issue of the *Japan Times* suggests that the *Japan Advertiser* apparently argued against allowing the Mormon missionaries to preach in Japan.

34. After the publication of the *Japan Herald* and the *Japan Mail* ceased, the *Japan Advertiser* became a very influential English-language newspaper in Japan. Ebihara, *Ōji Shinbun Zasshi*, 151, 204; Hoare, *Japanese Treaty Ports*, appendix.

35. According to Preston Nibley, a church historian, this address was prepared by University of Utah professor and future Mormon apostle James E. Talmage. Murray L. Nichols, letter to author, 26 August 1996. The entire piece is reprinted in the 26 September 1901 issue of *the Latter-Day Saints' Millennial Star*, published in Liverpool by the LDS European Mission, 625–27.

36. Grant, Journal, 12–18 August 1901.

both the owner and the editor of the *Japan Herald*;[37] Harrison may have been his subordinate. The elders' cordial relationship with Harrison appears to have lasted for a long time, as Taylor intimated in his journal on 2 February 1902: "In the evening [we] entertained at supper Mr. Harrison the editor of the Japan Herald."

The *Japan Mail*, on the other hand, was not so hospitable and took a consistently hostile position towards the Mormons. For example, it accused the Mormons of believing in polygamy and thereby degrading women, of coming to Japan "in the guise of Christianity" to carry men to "the days of Lot and Abraham," and of being "corruptors of morality" and "enemies of pure happiness"; it equated plural marriage with concubinage; it belittled the letters to the editor written by Grant; and it reprinted a rather lengthy anti-Mormon article entitled, "The Mormon Menace," written by a non-Mormon resident of Utah.[38] At that time, the *Mail* was both owned and edited by Captain F. Brinkley, a retired British army officer who was connected somehow with the Japanese government.[39] As will be explained more fully below, the *Mail*'s anti-Mormon stance reflected its Protestant missionary clientele. The *Mail*'s stance may also have been a reflection of its usual anti-American sentiment, which was quite strong in the foreign settlement community at that time.[40] On 17 August, the *Mail* called the *Herald* the "champion of the Mormon Mission" because of its favorable views of the Mormons. In response, that evening the *Herald* called the *Mail*'s editor "an amateur journalist." The *Mail* asserted that the Mormons should not be allowed to remain in Japan to preach, a position echoed by the Japanese-managed *Japan Times* of Tokyo in its 20 August editorial.[41]

---

37. J. H. Brooke owned the paper from 1870 to 1902 and edited it from 1893 to 1902. Hoare, *Japanese Treaty Ports*, 339.

38. "Mr. Grant's Explanation," *Japan Mail*, 6 September 1901; "The Mormon Controversy," *Japan Mail*, 7 September 1901.

39. Brinkley was owner and editor from 1881 to 1912. Hoare, "Japanese Treaty Ports," 337. The *Mail*'s rivals accused Brinkley of being in Japanese pay, to which he admitted only that the Japanese government had a number of subscriptions to the *Mail*. According to Hoare, *Japanese Treaty Ports*, 337–38, the paper did tend to give the Japanese view, though it could be critical of the Japanese when British interests were involved. The views expressed in the *Mail* on the Mormon missionaries, however, should not be taken to reflect the views of the Japanese government, which at least initially did not have a position on the matter.

40. Hoare, *Japanese Treaty Ports*, 327.

41. *Japan Mail*, 17 August 1901; *Japan Herald*, 17 August 1901; "The Mormons," *Japan Times*, 20 August 1901, 2. The *Japan Times* was founded in 1897 by a group of prominent Japanese in Tokyo. In 1918 it absorbed the financially troubled *Japan Mail* and, for a time, changed its name to the *Japan Times and Mail*. Ebihara, *Ōji Shinbun Zasshi*, 165–69.

From the vantage point of faraway Kobe, another large foreign settlement immediately west of Osaka, some 350 miles southwest of Tokyo,[42] the editor of the *Kobe Chronicle* wrote this perspective on the press war in Yokohama:[43]

> [The] arrival of a Salt Lake City Apostle with a number of elders has aroused some attention in Japan, though it seems to have caused far more stir among the foreign newspapers than among the Japanese, who naturally regard the establishment of one more sect in Japan with more or less indifference. As was to be expected, the missionaries already established in this country are not pleased at such an encroachment on their preserves. . . . A Yokohama foreign journal which may be taken as representing the missionaries even went so far as to advocate that the preaching of these missionaries should be officially forbidden.

The editor then went on to criticize the *Japan Times*:

> It is not very surprising, perhaps, that such intolerance should be advocated by a foreign journal in touch with missionaries already established in the country, but we certainly were surprised to find the Japan Times, published in Tokyo and edited by a Japanese, taking up the same attitude a day or two later, and urging that the teaching of Mormon doctrines should be prohibited in this country.

Predicting that the Mormons "will find [that] their efforts at proselytisation in Japan will be received with stolid indifference," the *Chronicle* editor concluded by calling for religious tolerance:

> It is to be hoped that religious intolerance is not one of the innovations from the West which is to be introduced into Japan. . . . [We] hope that the Government will not be misled by the efforts of rival propagandists into a departure from the attitude of tolerance which has been so honourable a feature of the Meiji era, and in which Japan has set such a fine example to Christendom.[44]

Strictly on rational grounds, the editor, probably an American named Robert Young, was not fond of Christianity. Thus, his opposition to Christianity in general was translated into his fair treatment of the Mormon missionaries who were being ill-treated by their Protestant counterparts.[45]

The more substantive problem with the foreign press in Yokohama was the lack of professionalism, compounded by the small size of the foreign community

---

42. Kobe was opened as a foreign settlement in 1868, some nine years after the opening of Yokohama. In 1901, it had about 1,000 foreign residents, in contrast to over 2,000 in Yokohama. Ebihara, *Ōji Shinbun Zasshi*, 77. These figures exclude Chinese residents. With Chinese included, the population of foreign residents was about 5,000 in Yokohama and 2,000 in Kobe. Hoare, *Japanese Treaty Ports*, 47.

43. The *Kobe Chronicle*, founded by Robert Young in 1890, was renamed the *Japan Chronicle* later in 1901 and remained as one of the most influential foreign language newspapers in Japan throughout the pre–World War II period. The editorial office later moved to Tokyo. In the early twentieth century, it had the largest circulation of any English-language newspaper in Japan, followed by the *Japan Herald*. Ebihara, *Ōji Shinbun Zasshi*, 149, 203–4.

44. "Mormon Missions," *Kobe Chronicle*, weekly edition, 21 August 1901, 226.

45. Ebihara, *Ōji Shinbun Zasshi*, 204.

itself. According to the historian James Hoare, the "invective of the Yokohama papers became notorious not only in Japan but far outside the country. The lack of real news often meant that editors had little better to fill their papers with than personal attacks on their rivals. The smallness of the foreign communities meant that no such attacks could be ignored and so the cycle went on."[46] Moreover, the smallness of the foreign communities also meant that the newspapers depended heavily on subscribers for operating funds. Consequently, maintaining an impartial view on issues was difficult, and "switches in editorial policy, even under the same editor, were . . . a marked feature" of what has been called "treaty port journalism."[47] The controversy with which the Mormon missionaries were accosted by the Yokohama foreign press was a product of treaty port journalism, the very type of newspaper controversy the elders were later counseled by their church's First Presidency to avoid.[48]

3.4. Reactions in the Japanese Press

Despite the *Kobe Chronicle*'s claim that the Mormons had been met with "indifference," the Mormon elders also received wide, though by no means universal, coverage in the Japanese press. Likely, the Japanese press obtained the news of the arrival of Mormon missionaries from the 13 August issue of the *Japan Advertiser* or the *Japan Herald*.[49] The *Jiji Shinpō* of Tokyo quickly responded on 14 August by noting their arrival. The *Yamato Shinbun* (also of Tokyo) published a similar report the following day. At the turn of the twentieth century, Tokyo had over a dozen competing newspapers, among which the *Yorozu Chōhō* had the largest circulation (at close to 100,000),[50] followed by such papers as the *Chūō Shinbun*, the *Hōchi Shinbun*, and the *Niroku Shinpō*.[51] The *Kokumin Shinbun*, the *Miyako Shinbun*, and the *Tokyo Asahi Shinbun* were also important. Though with a circulation of only about 10,000, the *Jiji Shinpō* was still considered to be

---

46. Hoare, *Japanese Treaty Ports*, 340.
47. Ibid., 339.
48. After the fact, towards the end of the year, the missionaries were told in a letter from the First Presidency to avoid newspaper controversy. Ronald W. Walker, "Strangers in a Strange Land: Heber J. Grant and the Opening of the Japanese Mission," *Journal of Mormon History* 13 (1986–87): 29.
49. The 15 August issue of the *Japan Herald* states that it had "a few days ago" chronicled the arrival of Heber J. Grant.
50. During the period under consideration, the *Yorozu Chōhō* did not publish an article of its own on the Mormon missionaries. On 21–22 August, however, it quoted on its front pages the thrust of the editorials published in the *Japan Times*, the *Jiji Shinpō*, the *Mainichi Shinbun*, and the *Osaka Asahi Shinbun* on Mormonism.
51. Hideo Ono, *Nihon Shinbun Hattatsu Shi* (Tokyo: Itsuki Shobō, 1982), 252–53.

a first-rate newspaper and highly influential because its readership was concentrated in the business community.[52]

Beginning on 16 August, the story of the elders' arrival was picked up by a number of regional newspapers throughout the country. Probably the news was obtained from the wire services or from the papers' Tokyo correspondents, who could communicate via telephone or telegraph, which had connected most major points of the country by that time.[53] The *Kobe Yūshin Nippō*, the *Niigata Shinbun* and the *Tōhoku Nippō* (both in Niigata), and the *Shizuoka Minyū Shinbun* were the first regional papers to report the news. They were followed by the *Hokkoku Shinbun* (Kanazawa), the *Kyoto Hinode Shinbun*, and the *Osaka Asahi Shinbun* on 17 August. Subsequently, reports, articles, and editorials relating to the Mormon missionaries and their message were published extensively in many of the country's major newspapers, including the *Ryūkyū Shinpō* of Naha, Okinawa.

In Tokyo, correspondents of the *Jiji Shinpō* and the *Niroku Shinpō* both reported accounts of interviews with the Mormon missionaries. On 16 August, the *Jiji* devoted the top two-thirds of page four to an interview with Grant held at the Grand Hotel. The interview summarized Grant's business career and explained the history and beliefs of the Mormons, including their persecution, industry, and practice of polygamy. This interview was picked up by the *Kyoto Hinode Shinbun* on 18 August and by the influential *Kahoku Shinpō* (Sendai), which published it in two parts on 18 and 20 August. Another interview, conducted by the *Niroku Shinpō*'s reporter, was published in five parts on 17–19, 21 and 23 August, again summarizing the history and beliefs of Mormonism. The *Niroku* also published on 19–20 August a cartoon depicting the four Mormon missionaries and, more significantly, the entire English-language text of Grant's "Address to the Great and Progressive Nation of Japan," with a Japanese translation. All in all, at least fifteen Tokyo-based newspapers reported, in one form or another, the arrival of the Mormon missionaries during the months of August and September 1901.[54]

---

52. Ono, *Nihon Shinbun*, 226–40. In 1936, the *Jiji Shinpō* was merged with the *Tokyo Nichinichi Shinbun*, which was then under the ownership of the *Osaka Mainichi Shinbun*.

53. There were wire services by the late 1880s, providing national and international news to local newspapers. Tsūshinshashi Kankōkai, *Tsūshinsha Shi* (Tokyo: Tsūshinshashi Kankōkai, 1948), 21–23.

54. This number includes the *Kokumin Shinbun*, the English-language *Japan Times*, and the *Shakai Sinpō*, in addition to the twelve Japanese-language newspapers listed in Annex 6. Brady, "Japanese Reaction," chapter five, provides, without much commentary or analysis, a chronological listing of Mormon-related articles and editorials in seven Tokyo-based newspapers. Brady's translation is less than accurate, particularly when fine nuances, subtleties, and sarcasms are involved or when meaning must be understood within a particular social and historical context. Some translated texts are outright misinterpretations or mistranslations (e.g., the important *Mainichi* editorial of 21 August 1901, on pages 130–31).

Tokyo's *Jiji Shinpō*, 16 August 1901, page 4.

Extensive commentary, including an exposition on Mormon history and doctrines, was also found in the *Kobe Yūshin Nippō* (16 August), the *Yamato Shinbun* (17–22, 24–27 August), the *Osaka Asahi Shinbun* (19 August), the *Osaka Mainichi Shinbun* (21, 23–24 August), the *Moji Shinpō* (22 August), the *Kyōchū Nippō* of Kofu (24, 27–28 August), and the *Tokyo Mainichi Shinbun* (5–6, 8 September). The *Kyōchū Nippō* series was a verbatim copy of the *Osaka Mainichi* series. Except for the *Osaka Asahi* article—which presented the thirteen Articles of Faith (see discussion below) and discussed in a factual manner the nature of the Book of Mormon, the proper name of the church, the place of secular pursuits in Mormon religious life, and the reasons for the practice and termination of polygamy—all the rest were anti-Mormon in tone.

For example, all but *Yamato* referred to the Spaulding theory as a credible explanation for the origin of the Book of Mormon.[55] Other frequently referenced topics included claims about fraudulent banking practices in Kirtland, the immoral and questionable character of Joseph Smith, the political ambition of the LDS Church to establish an independent kingdom, the founding of a secret society to protect Joseph Smith's life, the execution of oaths to demand absolute

---

55. The Spaulding theory postulates that Joseph Smith relied on the book manuscript of a Congregationalist preacher named Solomon Spaulding in producing the Book of Mormon. Paul C. Gutjahr, *The Book of Mormon: A Biography* (Princeton, New Jersey: Princeton University Press, 2012), 47–51.

obedience to authority, the Mountain Meadows Massacre,⁵⁶ and other usual fares of anti-Mormon literature. The *Mainichi* (Tokyo) called the Mormon religion "superstitious," "dubious," "unworthy of an educated person's attention," and its teachings "incompatible with civilization."⁵⁷

One religious newspaper gave particularly extensive coverage to the Mormons. The *Kyōgaku Hōchi* of Kyoto published at least twenty-nine articles on Mormon themes between 18 August and 24 September. Founded by a Buddhist priest in 1897, the *Kyōgaku Hōchi* was informally affiliated with *Jōdo Shinshū* (True Pure Land) Buddhism.⁵⁸ Significantly, it was read not only by Kyoto's citizenry but also by subscribing temples and other religious institutions throughout the country.

The newspapers contained translations of Mormon terms and texts that remained in the Japanese Mormon vocabulary for years. Of particular significance was the 19 August issue of the *Osaka Asahi*, in which the thirteen Articles of Faith and the expression Latter-day Saints were translated into Japanese. In the choice of words and sentence structure, the translation of the Articles of Faith is almost identical to the one the LDS Church would subsequently adopt, indicating the possibility that the church translator read the *Osaka Asahi* translation. The translation of the phrase "Latter-day Saints" (*Batsujitsu* or *Matsujitsu Seito*) is also the same as the one which was subsequently to be used by the church.⁵⁹ The *Osaka Asahi*'s translation of the Articles of Faith was reprinted in the 26 August issue of the *Yamato Shinbun* and the 29 August issue of the *Ryūkyū Shinpō*. In the 18 August issue of the *Yamato Shinbun*, the expression "Book of Mormon" was translated as *Morumon Kei* (or *Kyō*), the same wording that would be used by the LDS Church for over ninety years.

---

56. A massacre of overland immigrants from Arkansas and Missouri occurred in September 1857 against the backdrop of fear and hysteria created by the impending invasion of Utah by a federal military expedition. There were rumors that this company was a reconnoitering party in advance of the main federal army, while some members of the company made profane, provocative boasts that they had killed or molested the Mormons in Missouri. Regardless, some 120 persons were killed by a combined force of Mormon militia and Indians. The complicity of the LDS Church in this atrocity has been debated by scholars. Leonard J. Arrington and Davis Bitton, *The Mormon Experience: A History of the Latter-day Saints*, New York: Alfred A. Knopf, 1979, 166–70; Juanita Brooks, *The Mountain Meadows Massacre* (Norman, Oklahoma: University of Oklahoma Press, 1970); Ronald W. Walker, Richard E. Turley Jr., and Glen M. Leonard, *Massacre at Mountain Meadows: An American Tragedy* (New York: Oxford University Press, 2008).

57. Here as well as in all subsequent instances, the English translations of the original Japanese sentences and expressions are the author's own.

58. Its name was changed to the *Chūgai Nippō* in January 1902. Ruikotsu Matani, *Ningen Ruikotsu* (Kyoto: Chūgai Nippōsha, 1968), 202–5. Currently, the *Chūgai Nippō* is published two to three times a week and entirely devoted to reporting news of religious significance.

59. The expression *Batsujitsu* (or *Matsujitsu*) *Seito* was also used by the *Tokyo Mainichi Shinbun* in its front-page, three-part article published on 5 and 7–8 September.

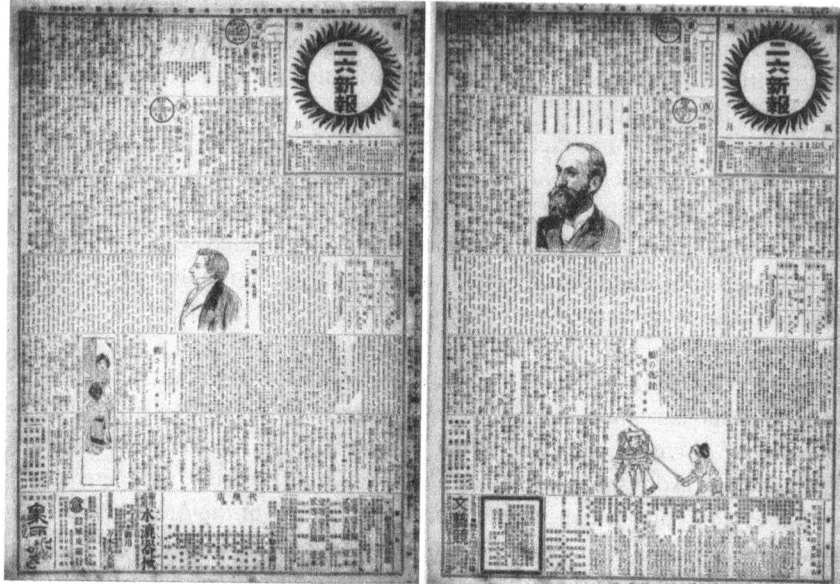

Tokyo's *Niroku Shinpō*, on 19–20 August 1901, published the entire English-language text of Grant's "Address to the Great and Progressive Nation of Japan," with a Japanese translation, on its front pages.

Next to the arrival of the Mormon missionaries, the most widely reported event was the refusal of a Yokohama boardinghouse keeper—an ex-Protestant missionary named Staniland—to admit them. This event was described in Alma O. Taylor's journal entry for 13 August 1901 as follows:

> During this afternoon we had been hunting for a place to board which would be cheaper than at the hotel and at one place to which Bro[ther] Kelsch, Bro[ther] Grant and Bro[ther] Ensign were directed they found suitable rooms but when they were about to accept them, the landlord said: "we had been expecting some Mormon preachers from Utah." The Brethren said that they were the ones and had just arrived the day before on the steamer Empress of India. "Oh!" said he, "I cannot take you under any consideration.["] After talking with him a few moments during which they asked him if he would not like to hear the other side of Mormonism, he said that he did not and would not have anything to do with them or their money, so they left him and sought elsewhere for accommodations.[60]

This incident was first reported by an English-language newspaper. The *Japan Mail* covered the event on 16 August in a condescending manner by saying that the paper was "given to understand that the Mormon elders who recently arrived in Japan are not staying at Beverly House, No. 2, Bluff," to which the *Japan Herald* sharply reacted in its evening edition. The *Herald* accused the "tenant of

---

60. Taylor, Journal, 13 August 1901.

the premises in question" for appearing "to glory in his indefensible conduct" by reporting the incident to "the all too complaisant Mail," and concluded that "to save trouble to future applicants for rooms, advertisements emanating from No. 2, Bluff, should be worded after this fashion: "Lodging to let, but only to persons deemed by the letter, to hold correct opinions. . . . Particulars to be had on the premises, at No. 2, also at the Japan Mail office." The Associated Press carried the news with a commentary that the Mormon missionaries had received "a sample of the lack of Catholicity which characterises Christian workers in the Orient, and of the sectarian feeling which vitiates their work."[61]

Starting 19 August, the boardinghouse incident was picked up by Japanese newspapers in Tokyo, Kyoto, Nagoya, Osaka, Fukuoka, Moji, and Naha.[62] For some reason, the story became distorted by the Japanese press to the effect that Staniland had admitted the missionaries but his wife, finding that they were Mormons, kicked them out. Some editorials, such as those in the *Mainichi* (Tokyo) on 21 August and in the *Jiji* on 25 August, capitalized on this version, arguing that the sexual immorality of Japanese men was reinforced by the blind obedience of Japanese women, who should be more like American women. Undergirding the reaction of the *Mainichi* and other papers to the Staniland incident was the anti-prostitution movement, a major social force at that time, as well as the conflict in Japanese society over the proper role of women.[63]

3.5. The Question of Polygamy

The Mormon missionaries, representing a religion whose recent history included belief in and practice of polygyny, arrived during a time of national debate over legalized prostitution and monogamy. From the mid-1880s on, Christians led a movement to abolish the system of licensed prostitution in Japan, in part responding to a similar movement in leading countries of the world.[64] Earlier, in 1872, the Meiji government had abolished the system of licensed prostitution that involved slavery by issuing the Anti-Slavery Law and the Prostitute Liberalization Law. The following year, however, yielding to pressure from brothel owners, the government allowed prostitutes to engage in the profession of their own free will and brothel owners to offer facilities to such prostitutes.[65]

---

61. See "Our Elders in Japan," *Deseret Evening News*, 5 September 1901, 4.

62. The *Hōchi Shinbun*, the *Niroku Shinpō*, and the *Yomiuri Shinbun* (all of Tokyo) reported the event on 19 August; the *Chūkyō Shinpō* (Nagoya), the *Kyōgaku Hōchi*, and the *Osaka Asahi* on 21 August; the *Kyūshū Nippō* (Fukuoka) and the *Moji Shinpō* on 22 August; and the *Ryūkyū Shinpō* on 1 September.

63. Ono, *Nihon Shinbun*, 257. The *Mainichi Shinbun* changed its name to the *Tokyo Mainichi* in 1906.

64. Tamio Takemura, *Haishō Undō* (Tokyo: Chūō Kōronsha, 1982), 4–5. For instance, licensed prostitution was abolished in Britain in 1886.

65. Takemura, *Haishō Undō*, 2–7.

The anti-prostitution movement regained momentum in 1885, when a women's magazine called *Jogaku Zasshi* was inaugurated and began campaigning against licensed prostitution. In December 1886, the Tokyo Women's Temperance Union was founded with the broader objective of promoting the liberalization of women and a charter that included (1) promoting the establishment of a wholesome association between husband and wife, (2) improving the status of women in the family, (3) abolishing prostitution, and (4) establishing the system of monogamy. Three years later, it filed a petition with the government, stating that the prevalent practice of concubinage was adultery. Also, in 1890, a move toward consolidation began. Local anti-prostitution organizations joined together to establish the National Anti-Prostitution League, and in 1893 the Tokyo Women's Temperance Union and other Christian women's organizations throughout the country formed the Japan Women's Christian Temperance Union (*Nihon Kirisutokyō Fujin Kyōfū Kai*).[66] By the late 1890s, the anti-prostitution movement was a major national movement and a significant social force.[67]

In this social movement, a significant role was played by the *Mainichi* of Tokyo and the Salvation Army, which had arrived in Japan in 1895. The *Mainichi*, an anti-prostitution newspaper, set up a daily column in which it reported the names of prostitutes who left the profession.[68] The Salvation Army, on its part, preached against the evils of prostitution in the 1 August 1900 issue of its magazine *Toki no Koe* (War Cry), calling for licensed prostitutes to leave the profession and offering assistance and asylum to those who responded to the call.[69] On 5 August, as a group of Salvation Army volunteers were walking through the red light districts of Tokyo with copies of the magazine, they were attacked by mobs

---

66. Ibid., 19–21; Kaneko Yoshimi, *Baishō no Shakaishi* (Tokyo: Yūzankaku Shuppan, 1984), 45–47.

67. There were important legal developments as well. In February 1900, the Supreme Court ruled in a landmark case that a prostitute was not bound by any contract that required her to work to pay off her debt. The case involved an indentured prostitute in Hakodate, Hokkaido, by the name of Futa Sakai, who had borrowed money from the owner of a brothel and agreed to work for him for thirty months but soon desired to quit. Although the rulings of both the district court and the appeal court were against Futa, the Supreme Court overruled, stating that, although the financial contract was valid, the labor contract was void as it violated the Prostitute Liberalization Law of 1872. In response to the Supreme Court ruling, on 2 October 1900, the Ministry of Home Affairs established a formal procedure stipulating that (1) no one under the age of eighteen could be a prostitute, (2) one must be registered at the police to be a prostitute, (3) cancellation of the registration could be done either in writing or verbally, and (4) cancellation could not be challenged by anyone. Takemura, *Haishō Undō*, 22–23; Yoshimi, *Baishō no Shakaishi*, 103–4.

68. Ibid., 93.

69. Takemura, *Haishō Undō*, 21–24; "Jorōshū ni Yoseru Fumi," *Toki no Koe*, 1 August 1900, 1.

hired by brothel owners. This incident was reported in newspapers throughout the country.[70]

Thus, the Mormon missionaries arrived in Japan at a time when Japanese society was debating the evils of its social institutions that subjugated women, including licensed prostitution and, more broadly, the marital relationship between husband and wife. In this light, it is easy to understand why almost all of the editorials on Mormon themes published in Japanese newspapers at that time discussed the Japanese practice of concubinage in the context of Mormon polygamy. For example, in a two-part, front-page editorial published on 16–17 August, the *Yamato Shinbun* made a far-fetched suggestion that the people of nobility (who frequently practiced concubinage) should all become Mormons and that the commoners be forbidden to become Mormons.[71] This way, the editorial argued, the evil practice of concubinage could be eliminated in Japan. On 21 August, the *Mainichi Shinbun* wrote a front-page editorial entitled "Foreign Mormonism and Domestic Mormonism," arguing that Japan's elite society did not have the moral qualification to reject Mormonism and that the practice of concubinage should be abolished. Other editorials were even introspective. For example, on 24 August, the *Kyoto Hinode Shinbun* published an editorial stating that prohibiting the preaching of Mormonism by legal means would be futile unless the system of monogamy was firmly established first. Otherwise, a "type of Mormonism" would continue to flourish in Japan.

Heber J. Grant fought the perception that the Mormons had come to preach polygamy. In his interviews with the Japanese press as well as in his letters to the editors of the *Japan Mail* and the *Japan Herald*, he vehemently denied any suggestion that the Mormon missionaries had come to preach polygamy, referring to the Manifesto of 1890. He was not entirely persuasive. For one thing, he simultaneously made rather laudatory remarks about polygamy, including the logic behind the Mormon practice of polygamy, phrases such as "beautiful" polygamist families, and comments about the social and biological virtues of such a practice. Perhaps more importantly, Grant admitted that he himself was a polygamist.[72]

---

70. The newspapers included the *Jiji* (6 August), the *Mainichi* (7 August), and the *Tokyo Asahi* (8 August). Takemura, *Haishō Undō*, 24; Yoshimi, *Baishō no Shakaishi*, 101–2.

71. The *Yamato Shinbun* was generally believed to be a nationalistic paper. Nishida, *Meiji Jidai*, 238–40.

72. As an interesting sidelight, the Mormon quartet included not one but two polygamists. Despite Grant's claim (made in the 16 August issue of the *Jiji Shinpō*) that the other two married elders were monogamists, Louis Kelsch, too, was in fact a polygamist. Kelsch, born in 1856 in Bavaria, Germany, was raised as a Catholic, emigrated to Nebraska in 1866 at the age of ten, and joined the LDS Church while visiting Salt Lake City in 1876. He served Mormon missions in several areas, including the Southern States, the Northwestern States, the Eastern States, England, and Germany. When he was called to Japan, he was president of the Northern States Mission. It was while he was serving in that capacity that he was asked by church president Lorenzo Snow to live the law of plural marriage, and with the permission of his first wife,

Probably for these and other reasons, many newspaper articles continued to claim that the Mormons still believed in polygamy, while fully acknowledging the official termination of the practice in the Manifesto.

The image of the LDS Church as a polygamist institution lingered for years. In October 1901, Kajiko Yajima, president of the Japan Women's Christian Temperance Union, and Chiseko Seda, president of the Tokyo Women's Temperance Union, filed with the Home Ministry a petition to ban the preaching of Mormonism on the grounds that the Mormons still believed in polygamy and that there were still polygamists in Utah.[73] As late as March 1907, Alma O. Taylor, then president of the Japan Mission, felt compelled to write for the *Jiji Shinpō* an article stating that there was "no fear of polygamy."[74] Likewise, Elbert D. Thomas, who succeeded Taylor as president, devoted considerable space to the topic of polygamy in an article published in the May 1911 issue of the *Seikō* (Success), a monthly magazine.[75]

3.6. Hirobumi Ito and the Legal Prostitution Controversy

The Mormon elders carried at least one letter of introduction to Hirobumi Ito (1841–1909), perhaps the single most important political leader of the Meiji period and one of the founding fathers of modern Japan.[76] The letter was written

---

Rosalia Atwood, married Mary Lyerla. Dorothy K. Zitting and Barbara O. Kelsch, "The Life Story of Ludwig Koelsch (Louis A. Kelsch), 1856–1917" (self-published, 1984), 47.

73. *Kyōgaku Hōchi*, 10 October 1901. The whole text of the petition was reprinted in the 25 October issue.

74. *Jiji Shinpō*, 29 March 1907, 8.

75. Elbert D. Thomas, "Netsuretsunaru Morumonkyō no Kyōri," *Seikō* 20 (May 1911): 185–92.

76. Hirobumi Ito was born in the Choshu domain (now Yamaguchi Prefecture) and was sent clandestinely by the domain (which was one of the major forces opposing the Tokugawa shogunate) to study in England. Following the Meiji Restoration, he was appointed to various government positions, including junior councilor (in charge of foreign affairs), director of the tax division, vice-minister and then minister of public works, and minister of home affairs, before becoming in 1885 the first prime minister under the modern cabinet system. He would serve as prime minister three more times, finally resigning from the position in June 1901, shortly before the Mormon missionaries arrived. In 1906, Ito became the first Japanese resident general in Korea and, in 1907, forced the Korean emperor to abdicate and established a full Japanese protectorate over Korea that paved the way for eventual annexation. Following his resignation as resident general in 1909, he was assassinated in Harbin, Manchuria, by a Korean nationalist. Ito was largely responsible for establishing modern political institutions in Japan, most notably the Constitution of the Empire of Japan (the so-called Meiji Constitution), which was promulgated on 11 February 1889. He also helped draft the Peerage Act of July 1884, in which five hereditary titles for the nobility were established on the basis of the European system, namely, prince (*kōshaku*), marquis (*kōshaku*, with a different character for *kō*), count (*hakushaku*), viscount (*shishaku*), and baron (*danshaku*). In this

by Angus M. Cannon, the younger brother of George Q. Cannon (who had been an apostle and a counselor in the First Presidency until his death in April 1901) and manager of the *Deseret News* office during 1867–74.[77] Cannon's association with Ito resulted from the visits Ito made to the United States in 1870 as part of his responsibility at the Ministry of Finance to study the United States monetary system and in 1872 as a member of the mission led by Prince Tomomi Iwakura, junior prime minister, to begin exploratory negotiations for treaty revision with the treaty powers and to study their modern institutions.[78]

Cannon spoke of Ito in the following manner:

I have known Count [*sic*] Ito, now Prime Minister Ito, for a good many years. I met him first in the spring of 1871 [*sic*] at Ogden and traveled with him over the Union Pacific as far as Omaha. . . . [He] was a bright, earnest and interesting character who absorbed information as a sponge does water. His people and their advancement seemed to be his particular pride and ambition. . . . [He] exhibited a lively interest in the Mormon people, the origin of their faith, and the struggles through which they passed. He asked me for a detailed statement of their history. I gave it to him and he listened most attentively during the two days and a half that we were fellow travelers and expressed a desire to learn more of them. After we separated I wrote home to my brother, President George Q. Cannon . . . to forward him a full list of books containing the principles of "Mormonism." I heard nothing further of Count Ito until, I think, in 1873 [*sic*] when I met him again, this time in Salt Lake City. I recognized him at once and his recognition of me was just as prompt. With him were a number of Japanese gentlemen and one of our own officials from Washington. The latter marveled at the familiarity that Ito showed concerning our faith and people, adding that his knowledge seemed much more extensive in this particular than that of most Americans. Ito had now been promoted to the position of head of the board of public works, a very important office in Japan. I met him a third time in Ogden later. He was then homeward bound from Washington, having been entrusted with

---

system, individuals with non-aristocratic backgrounds could be awarded hereditary titles for distinguished service to the nation. Ito himself (who was of a low-ranking samurai background) was appointed count in 1884, was promoted to the rank of marquis in 1895, and eventually rose to the highest rank of prince in 1907.

77. Angus Munn Cannon was born in Liverpool, England, on 17 May 1834. He was the business manager and later director and vice-president of the *Deseret News*. In the LDS Church, he presided over the Salt Lake Stake from 1876 to 1904, when the stake was divided into the Ensign, Liberty, Pioneer, and Salt Lake Stakes. He was then called as the patriarch of the new Salt Lake Stake and served in that capacity until his death on 7 June 1915. Donald Q. Cannon, "Angus M. Cannon: Pioneer, President, Patriarch," in *Supporting Saints: Life Stories of Nineteenth-Century Mormons*, ed. Donald Q. Cannon and David J. Whittaker (Provo, Utah: Religious Studies Center, Brigham Young University, 1985), 369–401; and Andrew Jenson, *Latter-day Saint Biographical Encyclopedia*, vol. 1 (Salt Lake City: Andrew Jenson History Company, 1901), 292–95.

78. On the very first leg of its journey through the United States and several European countries, the Iwakura Mission became stranded by snow and lodged in Salt Lake City for over two weeks. See Annex 1 towards the end of this volume for details.

important dispatches to the emperor. . . . He gave me the most urgent kind of an invitation to visit him in his own home should I ever have occasion to go to Japan.[79]

One thing Grant had not been informed of was the fact that Hirobumi Ito was known in Japan as a womanizer and an advocate of licensed prostitution.[80] In 1896, in an interview with the Tokyo correspondent of the *London Daily News*, Ito stated that he supported licensed prostitution as a realistic way of controlling vice and protecting the public. A summary of this interview was published in the September 1896 issue of the *Fujin Shinpō*, the monthly magazine of the Tokyo Women's Temperance Union, and Ito's position on prostitution became widely known in Japanese society.[81] Thus, the 24 August 1901 issue of the *Yonezawa Shinbun* called Ito "a Mormon in deed" and a "good representative of Mormonism in the Orient." The 27 August issue of the *Yamato Shinbun*, referring to Grant's letter of introduction to Ito, stated that Ito was the "overlord of the sexual world, and the supreme ruler of carnal desire." The fact that Grant had a letter of introduction to Ito sent a wrong and unintended signal to the Japanese public.

Apparently, Grant had every intention of meeting Ito upon his arrival in Japan. His intentions were implied in a short *Deseret Evening News* article under the headline "Arrive at Yokohama, Apostle Grant and Companions Now in the Mikado's Empire":

> President Snow received a cablegram today from Apostle Heber J. Grant announcing that he and his companions arrived safely at Yokohama last midnight. The cablegram merely stated the fact, giving no further particulars but those who are familiar with his plans say that Apostle Grant will first call on the highest government officials including the mikado himself, and will lose no time in getting the work started in Japan.[82]

The Japanese press was more explicit. The 16 August issue of the *Jiji Shinpō* quoted Grant as saying that he would visit Ito with a letter of introduction. On the same day, the *Shizuoka Minyū Shinbun* speculated that Ito might be the first person to be baptized by the Mormons.[83]

It is virtually certain that Grant was unsuccessful in meeting Ito. According to the 21 August entry of the journal of the Japan Mission, "President Grant went to Tokyo again, not having been successful in meeting the parties yester-

---

79. "Opening of a Mission in Japan," *Deseret Evening News*, 6 April 1901, 1.
80. Yoshimi, *Baishō no Shakaishi*, 52.
81. "Itō Kō no Danwa," *Fujin Shinpō* 20 (15 September 1896): 30–31.
82. *Deseret Evening News*, 13 August 1901, 2. *Mikado* is an English word for the Japanese emperor.
83. Some newspapers, such as the *Tokyo Asahi* (17 August), had the heading "A Mormon Elder Shakes Hands with Marquis Ito." The Japanese verb "shake" in its infinitive form, as it typically appears in a newspaper heading, may indicate a future intention, not necessarily an accomplished fact.

Mormons in the Press

On this front page of Tokyo's *Niroku Shinpō*, on 19 August 1901, a cartoon depicts distinguished Japanese gentlemen, including Hirobumi Ito, worshipping the four Mormon elders as "Mormon bodhisattvas," alluding to their practice of concubinage.

day for whom he has letters."[84] On 19 January 1902, Alma O. Taylor wrote in his journal, "Another [of the Japanese students who visited us was] the nephew of Marquis Ito to whom we have letters of introduction from Bro[ther] Angus Cannon, who . . . had met the Marquis a number of times." The fact that the missionaries still possessed the letters from Angus Cannon suggests that as of January

---

84. Grant was in Tokyo on 20–21 August, 27 August, and 2–3 September. If it took place at all, the meeting between Grant and Ito could not have been held much later. From 6 to 15 September, Grant made a tour of Japan, travelling through Lake Biwa, Suruga Bay, Kanazawa, Toyama, Naoetsu, and Karuizawa. On Ito's part, he left for the United States on 18 September to meet President Theodore Roosevelt (who had just assumed office at the death of President William McKinley Jr.) and to receive an honorary doctorate from Yale University (in its bicentennial commemoration on 23 October). He then made a tour of Europe and did not return to Japan until February of the following year. Minoru Toyoda, *Shodai Sōri Itō Hirobumi*, vol. 2 (Tokyo: Kōdansha, 1987), 256–64. As to the whereabouts of Ito in August, although he was spending his summer in the northern Sea of Japan coast, he was in his villa in Oiso on the Pacific coast on 8 August and 25 August (according to the daily reports published in the *Tokyo Nichinichi Shinbun*, which was controlled by the ruling Choshu faction of the government with Ito at the top). This means that Ito was in Tokyo at least twice during 8–25 August. But as Grant was not successful in meeting the people he had the letters of introduction to on 21 August, the only possible day on which he could have met Ito was 22 August (if he was in Tokyo again on that day). Nishida, *Meiji Jidai*, 167.

1902 the letters had not yet been given to Ito. A more definitive statement comes from the 19 October 1909 journal entry of Taylor:

> After dinner we were favored with a call from Mr. Akimoto a Japanese who has been engaged in beet raising in Idaho for a long time. . . . A friend of his who is a high official in the government told him that when Apostle Grant and his companions came to Japan, Marquis (now Prince) Ito proposed welcoming officially, by public reception, the Mormon missionaries. All Buddhist and Shinto sects approved the suggestion but the Christians (?) were unanimous in their opposition and said they could not accept an invitation to such a reception. This manifestation of ill will caused the Marquis to withdraw his proposal.[85]

If this story is true, it establishes that Ito was willing to see Grant but did not.

3.7. Constitutional and Legal Questions

Another topic frequently treated in the newspapers concerned the limits of religious freedom guaranteed by the Meiji Constitution. Chapter 3, Article 28 of the constitution reads: "Japanese subjects shall, within limits not prejudicial to peace and order, and not antagonistic to their duties as subjects, enjoy freedom of religious belief."[86] The key expression is "peace and order," which can restrict the exercise of religious freedom. Many newspaper articles and editorials used this restriction to argue that the government should prohibit the preaching of Mormonism. The first newspaper to take this line of reasoning was the *Japan Mail*, which argued in its 17 August issue that the Mormons should be officially forbidden to preach in Japan because their teaching threatened peace and order.

---

85. The man is Masanori Akimoto, a member of the 1894 entering class at Keio Gijuku (an elite private academy in Tokyo), who was the manager of Japanese laborers at the LDS Church-owned Utah–Idaho Sugar Company. See Eric Walz, e-mail to author, 11 December 1998. Keio Gijuku began its college division in 1890, with fifty-nine students in economics, law, and literature, offering three years of instruction. It is not surprising that a person of that background knew some prominent government figures. Fukuzawa Kenkyū Centā, *Keiō Gijuku Nyūshachō*, vol. 4 (Tokyo: Keiō Gijuku, 1986), 345; and Keiō Gijuku, *Keiō Gijuku Hyakunenshi*, vol. 2 (Tokyo: Keiō Gijuku, 1960), 52. The Utah–Idaho Sugar Company employed immigrant workers, including Japanese, because "thinning" beets to create living space was "stoop labor," which most American farmers would not perform. Leonard J. Arrington, *Beet Sugar in the West: A History of the Utah–Idaho Sugar Company, 1891–1966* (Seattle: University of Washington Press, 1966), 23, 71–73. Akimoto arrived in the United States in 1897, worked on a farm in California for three years, helped organize a labor recruiting company later to be known as Nichibei Kangyōsha (Japanese American Industrial Company) in 1900, and in 1903 moved to Idaho Falls to supervise the farm section of the agency before becoming assistant supervisor over farm laborers for the Utah–Idaho Sugar Company. Eric Walz, *Nikkei in the Interior West: Japanese Immigration and Community Building 1882–1945* (Tucson, Arizona: University of Arizona Press, 2012), 51.

86. "Constitution of the Empire of Japan, 1889," in *Japan: An Illustrated Encyclopedia* (Tokyo: Kōdansha, 1993), 233.

Over subsequent days, this position was adopted by Japanese newspapers, including the *Chūgoku*, *Hinode*, *Moji Shinpō*, *Kyūshū Shinbun*, and *Yonezawa Shinbun*.[87]

These arguments may have some validity as a Home Ministry ordinance stipulated that a religious organization must file an application before it could be authorized to preach. On 24 August, the *Osaka Asahi* and the *Tokyo Asahi* (both under the same management) became the first newspapers to take a look at this issue, noting that the Mormons had not yet filed an application with the authorities. Possibly in response to this *Asahi* report, which was picked up by the *Japan Herald* in the evening, Grant decided to go to Tokyo on 27 August to consult with the Home Ministry about securing a permit to preach and to distribute tracts in Japan.[88] He returned again to Tokyo on 2–3 September, in order to "attend to some business with the Home Department."[89]

As Grant discovered, the procedure to secure a permit was quite simple, requiring only that an application be filed with the local authorities, in this case, with the Kanagawa prefectural government. The press closely followed the actions of the Mormon missionaries in this matter. Between 25 August and 29 August, the newspapers frequently made references to the possible decisions of the authorities.[90] Curiously, the only thing which the Ito-affiliated *Tokyo Nichinichi* reported during August was the fact that, as of 28 August, the Mormons had not filed an application. The *Tokyo Nichinichi* may have considered it wise to distance itself from the controversy surrounding the possible relationship between Ito and the Mormon missionaries.

Grant and his companions continued their attempts to meet the legal requirements. On 6 September, they visited the chief of the Kanagawa police department to determine the requirements of the law. The chief told them that he would consult with the governor before informing them of the particulars. This incident was noted in the 10 September issue of the *Kyōgaku Hōchi*.[91] In the event, on 17 September, application was made to the governor to preach the gospel. On 20 September, the missionaries received a communication from the governor's office, requesting them to reappear and answer questions regarding their intentions. On 21 September, when they called again at the governor's office, they were told that they "did not have to make such an extensive application as [they] had done in order to get permission to preach and establish a mission, and that there were some points which the law required that had not been mentioned in the application." These developments were reported in the 21 September issue

---

87. The dates on which these newspapers picked up this position were 20 August for the *Chūgoku* and the *Hinode*; 21 August for the *Moji Shinpō*; 22 August for the *Kyūshū Shinbun*; and 23 August for the *Yonezawa Shinbun*.

88. Japan Mission, "Historical Records and Minutes," 27 August 1901, LDS Church Archives.

89. Japan Mission, "Historical Records," 2–3 September 1901.

90. Some of the newspapers dealing with this issue were the *Hinode*, the *Kobe Yūshin*, the *Kyōchū Nippō*, the *Kyūshū Nichinichi*, the *Yamanashi Nichinichi*, and the *Yonezawa Shinbun*.

91. Taylor, Journal, 6 September 1901; Grant, Journal, 6 September 1901.

of the *Tokyo Nichinichi*, the 23 and 24 September issues of the *Kyōgaku Hōchi*, and possibly other newspapers, as well as the October issue of the nationally influential *Chūō Kōron* magazine.[92] On 5 October, after a few more attempts, the missionaries completed the bureaucratic formalities.[93]

3.8. The Osaka Controversy

Some editorials took definite positions for or against the idea of allowing the Mormon missionaries to preach in Japan, with the Japanese press being roughly split between antagonists and defenders. The antagonists were led by the influential *Jiji Shinpō*, which on 20 August argued that Mormonism was a "perverse" religion and should be banned in Japan "as in the United States." On 23 August, the *Chūō Shinbun* likewise argued that Mormonism should be banned in Japan as the Mormons had not truthfully given up the practice of polygamy. These articles were followed by the 27 August issue of the *Kyūshū Nippō*, which supported the idea of banning Mormonism for being against Japan's morals.[94]

There were defenders of Mormonism as well. On 21 August, the day after the *Jiji* published its devastating editorial, the *Shizuoka Minyū Shinbun* defended the right of the Mormons as a Christian sect to preach in Japan, saying that the mysterious stories associated with Mormonism were not unusual in any religion. On 25 August, the *Dokuritsu Shinbun*, noting the earnestness of the Mormon missionaries in traveling thousands of miles to come to a country with a totally different culture, stated that complacent Japanese religionists could learn much from Mormonism. The *Chūkyō Shinpō* of 27 August devoted part of its front page to appeal to those who were advocating the idea of banning Mormonism, saying that the Mormon missionaries could not be so stupid as to preach the illegal practice of polygamy. It went on to say that what should be feared was not foreign Mormonism but domestic Mormonism, namely, the evil of concubinage practiced by wealthy Japanese gentlemen.

The most spectacular debate took place in the commercial city of Osaka between its nationally influential *Osaka Asahi* and *Osaka Mainichi*, which fiercely competed with each other and were often known to take opposite positions on issues that came up. The debate began on 20 August 1901, when the *Asahi* devoted

---

92. Taylor, Journal, 20–21 September 1901; Japan Mission, "Historical Records," 17 and 20–21 September 1901.

93. Taylor, Journal, 5 October 1901.

94. Among the national magazines, the article published in the 5 September issue of the *Taiyō* argued against allowing the Mormons to preach in Japan, while the editorial in the September issue of the *Chūō Kōron* supported the prerogative of the Mormons to do so, saying that there were some Shinto and Buddhist sects that should be banned first. The editorial then went on to say that, compared with the dubious character of these sects, Mormonism was even "respectable." Gakujin Tatsuyama, "Morumonshū Kitaru," *Taiyō* 7 (September 1901): 57–58; "Morumonshū," *Chūō Kōron* 16 (September 1901): 64.

two front-page columns to an editorial entitled "Mormon Missionaries Arrive," which read in part:

> Mormonism is distinguished by its practice of polygamy. Although it professes to uphold Christian teachings, it is despised by other Christians. . . . Several years ago, the United States government enacted a law to prohibit [polygamy], but the practice has not yet disappeared. Its teachings still approve [polygamy], and the state of Utah, in which the headquarters is located, is a stain in the United States of America. Now, the missionaries of a religion which is considered perverse, feared, and despised by the people of America and Europe have come to Japan and set out to preach.

The writer then went on to say that he objected to Mormonism because the polygamy it promoted could "degrade the public morals of Japan." As Japanese society was just beginning to recognize the evil of concubinage and public opinion was rising against such practice, he continued, allowing a polygamist religion to be preached might "rekindle" the dying practice. He recognized the constitutional freedom of religion but argued that religious freedom was guaranteed only insofar as religious practice did not violate the law. Inasmuch as polygamy was prohibited by law, it was constitutional to prohibit the preaching of Mormonism in Japan. "Hence," he wrote, "Mormonism is a perverse religion that disrupts social ethics and endangers public peace. It is thus appropriate from the standpoint of national policy to prohibit it today and to cut off the penetration of the vicious practice before it spreads."

The *Mainichi* immediately responded to the editorial. On 21 August, it devoted two front-page columns to an editorial entitled "What in the World Should Prevent Them?" After noting the wide coverage the Mormon missionaries had received in the Western-language newspapers in Yokohama and others in Tokyo and Osaka, the editor stated:

> I believe that there is no need to prohibit the preaching of Mormonism. . . . Inasmuch as it recently made a public declaration that it would give up polygamy, by the order of the United States government, there should be no fear that it will dare to break the law of the land even in Japan. Moreover, although our ancient custom may allow concubines to be kept, it does not permit the stupid act of having several legal wives. How could the teaching of the Mormon sect by itself make a difference?

The editor then explained the existence of many religions in Japan by saying, "It is because the Japanese people are broad-minded and do not show a particular dislike for any of them. Why should the Mormon sect be the only exception?" Although the editor noted the Mormon "tactics" of resorting to supernatural phenomena, he brushed them away by saying that Mormonism was not different from any other Christian, Buddhist, or Shintoist religion in this regard. He did not necessarily compliment Mormonism because he called it a foolish religion. He simply argued that education, and not legal sanction, should be used to make sure that such a religion not be accepted by the ignorant populace. As to the right of the Mormon missionaries to preach, his position was clear:

Constitutionally, Japan upholds the freedom of religion. As long as it is not prejudicial to public peace, any religion is permissible, be it Buddhism or Christianity. Among the ignorant public, even Renmonkyō and Tenrikyō are allowed to exist.[95] Then, what in the world should prevent the coming of Mormonism?

The impact of this debate should not be underestimated for at least three reasons. First, Osaka was (and, to a lesser extent, still is) an important economic center of Japan, the principal city of the historic Kansai region extending from Kyoto to Kobe. During the pre–World War II period, the economic might of Osaka was unmatched by any city, including Tokyo, in terms of manufacturing and finance. Second, the *Osaka Asahi* and the *Osaka Mainichi* were both newspapers of national significance. Their influence went beyond the fact that they were both read widely within the greater Kansai region. In 1888, the *Osaka Asahi* had expanded to the Tokyo market by purchasing the *Mezamashi Shinbun* and changing the name to the *Tokyo Asahi Shinbun*.[96] Although in 1901 the *Osaka Mainichi* did not have an explicit Tokyo presence, its management and editorial board included nationally prominent figures. Third, the Osaka newspapers were the first in Japan to assume a modern corporate form of management and, as such, quickly expanded their scale of operations, aided by their efficient sales and advertisement departments.[97] In 1897, for example, the *Osaka Asahi* had begun to subscribe to the Reuter wire service. In response, also in 1897, the *Osaka Mainichi* appointed Takashi (Kei) Hara, a prominent diplomat and future prime minister, to become the editor-in-chief (and, later, president of the company).[98] Hara used his diplomatic connections to appoint foreign correspondents in various parts of the world. At the turn of the twentieth century, the *Asahi* had a readership of about 120,000, while the *Mainichi* claimed 100,000.[99]

---

95. Renmonkyō (founded in 1868) and Tenrikyō (1838) were both Shinto-derived new religious traditions that advocated belief in supernatural phenomena. While Renmonkyō ceased to exist in the Taisho period, Tenrikyō remains a thriving sect with more than a million members.

96. Nishida, *Meiji Jidai*, 157; Hideo Ono, *Shinbun no Rekishi*, enlarged edition (Tokyo: Tōkyōdō Shuppan, 1970), 50. The separate names were kept until 1940, when the *Asahi Shinbun* became the common name for both *Asahi* papers.

97. The process towards a corporate form of management was completed when they legally became joint stock companies in 1918 (in the case of the *Mainichi*) and 1919 (the *Asahi*).

98. In 1900, Hara left the company to join the political party founded by Hirobumi Ito. He later served in the cabinets of three prime ministers (including Ito) and as prime minister from 1918 to 1921, when he was assassinated.

99. At that time, the *Osaka Asahi* and the *Yorozu Chōhō* (of Tokyo) were called the two giants, representing western and eastern Japan, respectively, each claiming about 120,000 subscribers. Ono, *Shinbun no Rekishi*, 66–67; and Ono, *Nihon Shinbun*, 316.

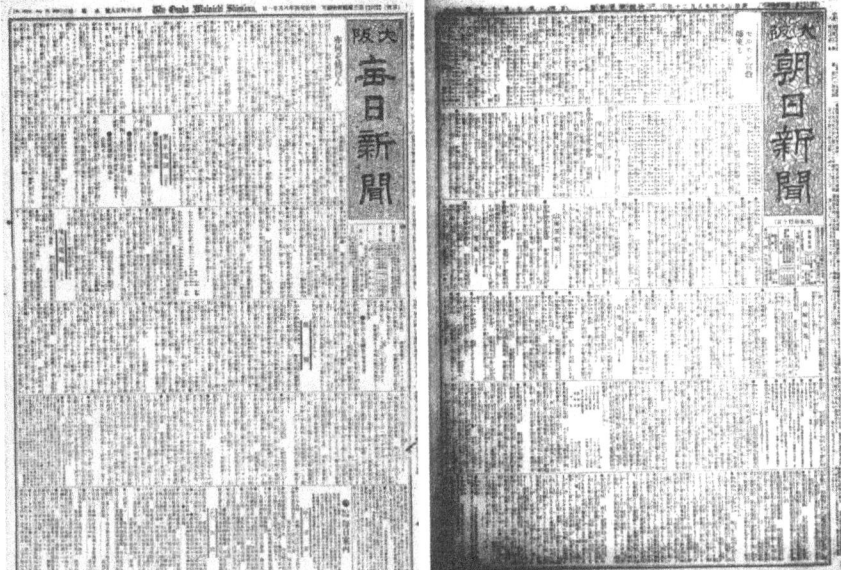

On 20–21 August 1901, two leading newspapers in Osaka, *Asahi* (pictured on the right) and *Mainichi*, devoted the first columns of their front pages to editorials arguing against and for allowing Mormons to preach in Japan.

3.9. A Voice of Reason: Eitaro Okano

One member of the press who was particularly helpful to the Mormon cause was Eitaro Okano, a prominent journalist and the English-language editor of the *Niroku Shinpō*.[100] The *Niroku Shinpō* promoted social justice and, as such, naturally defended the rights of prostitutes to leave the confinement of forced servitude.[101] The *Niroku* also had a tendency towards sensationalism and gained in readership after 1900. By the end of 1903, it had the largest circulation in Tokyo, with a peak readership of about 150,000.[102] Okano first visited the missionaries

---

100. Okano was one of three leading English-language reporters. Nishida, *Meiji Jidai*, 240. One of the other two was Eigo Fukai, of the *Kokumin Shinbun*, who later became governor of the Bank of Japan. According to the calling card pasted in Taylor's scrapbook, Okano had apparently been educated in the United States, with an LL.B., a Litt. B. and a doctorate in "public speaking." Alma O. Taylor, "Scrapbook, 1901–24," LDS Church Archives.

101. Nishida, *Meiji Jidai*, 241.

102. Nishida, *Meiji Jidai*, 176, 237; Ono, *Shinbun no Rekishi*, 64–65. The *Niroku Shinpō* was originally founded in 1893 but went out of circulation in 1895. It was started again in 1900 and began to compete with the *Yorozu Chōhō* for the same type of readers. By 1903 it surpassed the *Yorozu* in the number of readers.

on 14 August 1901, when they were still at the Grand Hotel.[103] Taylor's journal entry on that day states: "In the evening a Japanese editor of the largest Japanese newspaper in Japan published at Tokyo came from Tokyo to interview us." It has already been mentioned that, as a result, the *Niroku* published a five-part article based on that interview plus the full text of Grant's address to the people of Japan.

Apparently, the relationship between Okano and the missionaries became even more cordial. On 23 August, Taylor recorded:

> We found two representatives from the "Niroku Shimpo" newspaper published in Tokio. These gentlemen had called to learn more concerning our doctrines than what [they had] published already. . . . They had come to learn particularly of the difference in doctrine between our Faith and the beliefs of other Christians.

It was also Okano who arranged and assisted Grant's initial meeting with the Home Ministry official in charge of the religion bureau.[104] It is possible that his association with the missionaries continued for some time.

Okano's greatest defense of Mormonism was the editorial he published on 22 August.[105] Amid the frenzy caused by the voices of the influential *Jiji* and *Osaka Asahi* calling on 20 August for the authorities to prohibit the preaching of Mormonism, Okano defended the rights of the Mormons while encouraging the readers to look at the positive aspects of Mormonism. He began by reminding the readers of the finiteness of human wisdom, so that only the unlearned are "proud of the low level of our present civilization and are satisfied with the shallow state of our present knowledge." He then went on to say:

> It may be that what a majority calls good is evil and what a majority calls evil is good. . . . I am not advocating an unnecessarily skeptic view. . . . I am only a man who cannot blindly follow the opinion of a majority . . . Mormons have come. They have come for the first time since the opening of Japan. I welcome them. We must first find out [what they believe]. During the sixty some years since the establishment of their religion, they have withstood extreme opposition and persecution and now claim the membership of 300,000. . . . They virtually control the entire state of Utah, which has come to be called the most prosperous region in the United States. This is a fact. In [Mormonism], there must be something that is appealing. . . . Four missionaries have come across the vast ocean to enter Japan, which has been influenced by the civilization of Christian nations of the West for a long time. We must say that they are brave. As we hear, they are supporting themselves with their own funds. Their spirits are to be admired. I cannot bear mistreating them with a bitter face. I will instead welcome them with a smile of good will, and desire to listen to their doctrines.

---

103. Taylor, "Scrapbook." The scrapbook also shows that, on the previous day, the missionaries had met another reporter, Rihei Onishi of the *Jiji Shinpō*.

104. Grant, Journal, 3 September 1901.

105. In principle, Japanese newspaper editorials are unsigned.

Undoubtedly, Okano's 23 August visit to the missionaries was a fulfillment of his own public declaration. His was indeed a voice of reason amid the hysteria of the day.[106]

3.10. Conclusion

From mid-August to mid-September 1901, at least forty newspapers throughout Japan devoted considerable space to articles and editorials on issues surrounding the arrival of Mormon missionaries. When we recognize that there were only about one hundred respectable newspapers in Japan at that time and that the arrival of the Mormon missionaries was also covered by two of the leading national magazines,[107] we realize that the extent of the press coverage was massive indeed.

To be sure, the extensive press coverage was initially triggered by the generally hostile resident foreign press, which received much of its subscription revenue from the Protestant missionary community. Fuel was added by the culture of the treaty-port newspapers, which were managed by amateur journalists who took delight in petty arguments among themselves. The resident foreign press was frequently used as a source of foreign news; as such, the foreign language newspapers in Japan at that time exerted greater influence than the number of subscribers might have indicated. The foreign press's story of the arrival of Mormon missionaries was quickly picked up by the Japanese press. The ensuing fervor with which the subject of Mormonism was treated in the Japanese press was undoubtedly related to the tendency of Japanese newspapers towards sensationalism (designed to outrival their competitors, especially in Tokyo and Osaka) as well as to the sheer curiosity of the Japanese public concerning the Mormon practice of polygamy.

On a more fundamental level, the zeal with which the arrival of the Mormon missionaries was covered emanated from Japanese society's own internal conflict regarding the morality of its own marital and related social institutions, which was a major social issue dividing the country at the turn of the twentieth century. In this respect, the reaction of Japanese society to the arrival of the Mormon missionaries, as reflected in its press coverage, provides a means of understanding the fabric and dynamics of that society. Against the dominant sentiment calling the authorities to ban the preaching of Mormonism, there were voices of reason and fairness, which indicated the (increasingly) pluralistic nature of Japanese society.

In terms of proselytizing work, the impact of the extensive press coverage was likely more positive than negative, if there was any effect at all. For one thing, the

---

106. Okano's generous attitude toward the Mormons was ridiculed by the author of an article published in the 5 September 1901 issue of the *Taiyō*, 57–58.

107. At the end of 1896, there were eighty-seven respectable newspapers in Japan outside of Kyoto, Okinawa, Osaka, and Tokyo. Nishida, *Meiji Jidai*, 251.

Japanese elite, if not the public in general, was by then quite tolerant of religious diversity and probably did not care in one way or another what the Mormons believed or practiced. Hence, whatever the negative message the press coverage might have contained, it was more than offset by the positive benefit of mere publicity. As a result of this publicity, the Mormon missionaries received offers of speaking opportunities, letters, and visitors.[108] Although these did not immediately result in convert baptisms, the missionaries did, as a result, meet in late August with Tatsutaro Hiroi, who agreed to serve as their translator, interpreter, and Japanese teacher (see Section 5.3.1 in Chapter 5).[109]

The press coverage led to the publication in the October 1901 issue of a major national magazine of an article on Mormonism entitled "Morumonkyō to Ramakyō (Mormonism and Lamaism)" by prominent writer Goro Takahashi.[110] Takahashi, implicitly referring to the warm welcome the Tokyoites gave in July to Akya-Hutuktu, a spiritual leader from Peking's Yonghe Temple (popularly known as "Lama Temple"), criticized the self-contradiction between their acceptance of Lamaism (a branch of Buddhism that developed in Tibet, in which polyandry is practiced) and their rejection of Mormonism. He then noted that the Mormons had terminated the practice of polygyny "when Utah became a state," while quoting a passage from the Book of Mormon (Jacob 3:27–28) to affirm that polygyny was not central to Mormonism in any case but had been practiced under special circumstances.[111]

This defense of Mormonism was soon followed, in January 1902, by the publication of a major treatise on Mormonism entitled *Morumonshū* (The Mormon Sect), in which the author, a Buddhist priest by the name of Toru Uchida, attempted to present what he called an "objective" summary of Mormonism's history and doctrines (see Appendix 3.1). All in all, the press was thus instrumental, not only in arousing interest in the Mormon message at least among the reading public, but also in making sure that the news of the arrival of Mormonism in Japan penetrated every region and sounded in virtually every ear.

---

108. Taylor, Journal, 25 August 1901, mentions the offer of a speaking engagement in a large public hall in Tokyo.

109. In his journal entry on 18 August 1901, Taylor spoke of "a majority" of the visitors the missionaries received as "fraudulent and absolutely devoid of desire to assist us," while the "expression of friendship" came from "their pockets rather than their hearts." See Nichols, "History of the Japan Mission," 17–19.

110. Goro Takahashi, "Morumonkyō to Ramakyō," *Taiyō* 7 (5 October 1901): 21–25. Goro Takahashi (1856–1935) was a nationally recognized scholar who had been a member of the joint Protestant committee that translated the Bible into Japanese in the 1870s and 1880s. See Section 5.3 in Chapter 5 for Takahashi's biographical sketch.

111. Jacob 2:27–28 in part reads: "For there shall not any man among you have save it be one wife; and concubines he shall have none . . . whoredoms are an abomination before me; thus saith the Lord of Hosts." Takahashi had evidently read much of the Book of Mormon.

APPENDIX 3.1. *MORUMONSHŪ* BY TORU UCHIDA, JANUARY 1902

Toru Uchida published a 100-page booklet entitled *Morumonshū* in January 1902 from Bunmeisha, a Tokyo publisher focused on religious (mostly Buddhist) topics.[112] The Mormon elders were immediately made aware of this book from their Japanese language teacher Tatsutaro Hiroi, who purchased a copy.[113] The inside cover of the book states that the book was printed in December 1901 and lists Kōkyōshoin as the primary distributor. Kōkyōshoin was a Kyoto publisher of books on *Jōdo Shinshū* topics.[114] This is not surprising in view of the fact that Uchida was an ordained priest of the (Nishi) Honganji sect of *Jōdo Shinshū* Buddhism. Uchida would rise to prominence as an intellectual leader of Japan's war-time Buddhism during the 1930s and 1940s, affiliated with the Proselytizing Research Institute (*Fukyō Kenkyūsho*) of the Nishi Honganji Temple. Under the priestly name Koyu, he frequently contributed articles to the monthly periodical *Kyōkai Ichiran*.

Toru Uchida (1876–1960) was born into a priestly family in Saga Prefecture.[115] He taught English (and possibly philosophy and Buddhism) at Tokyo's Buddhist academies, including Tetsugakukan, following his graduation from Tokyo Imperial University in 1900, with a bachelor's degree in philosophy.[116] In 1905, he published a compilation of English writings on the life and teachings of the Buddha as instructional material for use by students in Buddhist

---

112. Frederick R. Brady, "Two Meiji Scholars Introduce the Mormons to Japan," *Brigham Young University Studies* 23 (1983): 167–78, erroneously pronounces Uchida's first name as Yu and speculates that he was a Christian. This author does not share Brady's characterization of the book as "a wealth of misinformation" based on "careless scholarship, prejudiced sources, or both." As noted below, there are indeed pieces of misinformation, but one cannot fault Uchida for accessing both Mormon and non-Mormon sources. Neither does this author agree with Brady's assertion (and the tone with which it is made) that "Uchida's translations of Mormon terms are at great variance with the terms used by the Church in Japan today; some are from the Protestant lexicon and others are merely translated badly." The terminology in current use by the LDS Church (where most words are indeed borrowed from the Protestant lexicon) cannot be the standard by which Uchida's translation or writing is to be judged.

113. Taylor, Journal, 29 January 1902, notes: "It is not a criticism of our claims but rather a brief outline of our history. The Lord is moving on the hearts of some to write that which will help to place the truth before the people of this land."

114. Kyoto Furitsu Toshokan, "Toshokan Kyoto," No. 40, 15 January 2003, 2.

115. He would return to Saga following the end of World War II to become the head priest of his family temple until his death in 1960. Kawasoemachi-shi Hensan Iinkai, *Kawasoemachi Shi* (Saga: Sagashi Kyōiku Iinkai, 1979), 945; Konen Tsunemitsu, *Nihon Bukkyō Tobei Shi* (Tokyo: Bukkyō Shuppankyoku, 1964), 477.

116. Teikoku Daigaku Shusshinroku Hensansho, *Teidai Shusshin Roku* (Tokyo, 1922); Gakushikai, *Kaiin Shimei Roku* (Tokyo, 1955).

schools.[117] *Jōdo Shinshū*, especially its (Nishi) Honganji branch, had from the beginning of the Meiji era been the vanguard of defending the country against the spread of Christianity. In 1899, the Nishi Honganji Temple sent two missionaries to San Francisco, which led to the founding of what would become the Buddhist Churches of America.[118] Uchida himself went to San Francisco as a missionary (*kaikyōshi*) in 1905 and remained there for eighteen years until 1923;[119] he was a frequent contributor to the Buddhist Mission's monthly Japanese-language periodical *Beikoku Bukkyō* (Buddhism in America).[120] In 1915, he co-organized an International Buddhist Congress in San Francisco and carried a copy of its resolution on the need to restore peace in Europe to United States president Woodrow Wilson.[121]

This background may explain why Uchida felt compelled to write a book on Mormonism soon after or even possibly before the arrival of the missionaries. The Nishi Honganji Temple had known of the arrival of Mormon missionaries ahead of time, either from its contact with the Japanese consul in San Francisco or from the press reports from Salt Lake City (for example, it was reported in the *Jōdo Shinshū*-affiliated *Kyōgaku Hōchi* in July 1901).[122] His apparent command of Mormon theology and practice must reflect his access to the Nishi Honganji Temple's reservoir of Mormon and non-Mormon sources of information, including up-to-date intelligence gathered by the Buddhist Mission in San Francisco.

The book consists of eight chapters covering the origin, history, scriptures, doctrines, and church organization of Mormonism, the conflicts of the LDS Church with the federal government, and the church's contemporary scene. The book is a bit repetitious as it treats similar topics more than once in different chapters. In some sense, part of this is unavoidable. For example, the origin of the Book of Mormon is intimately connected both with the history and with the scriptures of the church. Uchida generally translates the English term Book of Mormon as *Morumon no Sho*, which is the term in contemporary use by the LDS

---

117. Toru Uchida, comp., *The Light of Truth (The Life and Teachings of Buddha)* (Tokyo: Morie Honten, 1905).

118. Their arrival on 2 September 1899 is regarded as the founding date for the Buddhist Churches of America. William K. Hosokawa, *Nisei: The Quiet Americans* (New York: William Morrow and Company, 1969), 130–31.

119. Tsunemitsu, *Bukkyō Tobei Shi*, 269.

120. *Beikoku Bukkyō*, monthly, published by the Buddhist Mission, San Francisco. As far as this author can ascertain, Uchida's first editorial appeared in its February 1909 issue.

121. The conference was held in early August in connection with the Panama–Pacific International Exposition (whose purpose was to celebrate the completion of the Panama Canal). Three leaders of the conference, including Uchida, presented a copy of the resolution to Wilson on 23 August, asking him to make efforts to restore peace in Europe. *Tokyo Asahi Shinbun*, 22 September 1915. See also Tsunemitsu, *Bukkyō Tobei Shi*, 51–88, 476.

122. See "Morumonshū no Nihon Fukyō," *Kyōgaku Hōchi*, 23 July 1901, 1, which cited an American newspaper for the information.

Church in Japan. His use of Christian terminology sometimes betrays his identity as a non-believer. For instance, he uses the neutral word *kyūseishu* (instead of the Christian counterpart *sukuinushi*) for savior and *sōi* (where *sō* typically means Buddhist monk and *i* means status) for priesthood. The Japanese word for Mormonism that he uses (*Morumonshū*) also gives the flavor of Buddhist writing. None of the Japanese terms he used to translate major Mormon-specific terms correspond to the terminology subsequently adopted by the LDS Church in the early twentieth century.

Uchida begins by noting that the LDS Church was about to start missionary work in Japan, and states that the purpose of the book is to explain the church as objectively as possible; he further states that his intention is to refrain from making subjective judgment on its veracity, ethical value, or practical benefits. For the most part, he follows through with his promise, but his bias shows up from time to time. For example, while admitting that the accusatory remarks about young Joseph come from his enemies, Uchida nonetheless comments that they were proved correct by Smith's subsequent life (p. 10). It is worth emphasizing that Uchida's bias may be against Christianity more generally. He is no fan of Christianity. He even appears fair toward the Mormons when he discusses the persecution they received from the hands of those who professed to be Christians (p. 35).

Part of what appears to be his bias against the Mormons may reflect the source of information. No references are provided; neither does a bibliography appear at the end (writers in early twentieth century Japan were not held to the contemporary standards of citation and attribution). But judging from some of what he writes, it is clear that almost all the information came from non-Mormon sources. For example, the angel who gave the plates to Joseph Smith is spelled (and transliterated) as Mormoni, the son of Mormon who was the "last" prophet on the American continent; as commanded by an angel, Joseph Smith, as John the Baptist of the New World, baptized and conferred the Aaronic priesthood on Oliver Cowdery (pp. 20–21); Joseph's parents were dishonest people who had been accused of theft; Smith appealed to the authority of revelation because he lacked learning and eloquence (pp. 21–22).

Innocuous errors are not a few, e.g., Nauvoo receiving a special charter from the federal government (p. 44); Ohio being the place of the New Jerusalem (pp. 23, 35). But none of these are serious. More vicious to the Mormon faith is a rather long discussion of the Spaulding theory of the origin of the Book of Mormon (pp. 58–61). Though Uchida states that he simply listed both sides of the story, leaving the reader free to decide for himself (p. 61), he essentially concludes that the origin of the Book of Mormon can be explained by the Spaulding theory, with Joseph Smith having become acquainted in 1829 with Sidney Rigdon who possessed the Spaulding manuscript (p. 23). The book also covers the standard fares of anti-Mormon literature, such as the failure of the Kirtland "bank" (pp. 25–26); the establishment of the Danite vigilante force (p. 26); the temple endowment as a religious drama depicting God, Satan, Adam, and Eve (pp. 71–72); and a massacre of 150 [sic] people at Mountain Meadows, instigated by local Mormon leader John Lee (p. 81).

Uchida's knowledge of Christianity becomes evident when he contrasts Mormonism with Protestant Christianity. He says that Mormons believe in the Trinity though, unlike Protestant sects, their God is anthropomorphic; in believing that God and Christ are separate, they are like the Arians; in noting that the Holy Ghost has no personality, he says that the Mormons are like the Macedonians (pp. 62–63). He appears familiar with the Bible, but does not quote from the Protestant translation of the Bible.

As might be expected, the most repeated theme is polygamy, which Uchida calls the strangest doctrine, barbaric, and the greatest mark of Mormonism (pp. 91–94). Being forbidden by a passage in the Book of Mormon, the practice of polygamy was not made public until 1852 (pp. 68–69). He recounts the Mormon's conflicts with the federal government over polygamy, and how the LDS Church was "forced" to give up polygamy by external pressure. When the church banned the practice of polygamy, some members broke away to form a new sect (p. 70). Uchida claims that the church has not really given up its doctrine of polygamy, and it is still practiced among the members (pp. 84–85). In his concluding remarks, however, he argues that the strength of Mormonism comes from the cohesion created by external opposition to polygamy, along with religious zeal and the well-disciplined church organization (pp. 91–94).

For the most part, one must acknowledge that the book is factual and fair. Uchida reviews the thirteen Articles of Faith one by one (pp. 63–68); explains the various offices of the priesthood (pp. 73–75); talks about the cooperative spirit among the Mormons, who are "more hard working than members of other denominations" (p. 47); and how they have prospered in Utah (pp. 86–88). Uchida gives considerable biographical information on Brigham Young, calling him "a great man" who was steady in disposition, strong willed, and possessed of wisdom and common sense (pp. 43–44). The book is also detailed and up-to-date (though one cannot ascertain the accuracy of specific facts or numbers). For example, the construction of the Great Salt Lake Temple cost the LDS Church $4 million over forty years, while the cost of building the Tabernacle was $300,000; the church collects more than $1 million each year in tithes offering, just to quote a few passages.

Chapter 4

Monks, Nationalists, and the Emperor: Understanding the Religious and Intellectual Climate of Meiji Japan

4.1. Introduction

This chapter discusses the religious and intellectual climate of Meiji Japan in order to understand the "demand-side" of the Mormon message in the early twentieth century. Over the past two centuries, Mormon missionaries have carried roughly the same message with them throughout the world, but the reception has varied widely from one place or period to another. While the existing literature on missiology, Mormon foreign missions in particular, has focused on the American missionaries and their message, it is only half the story of how American religious ideas are received in various settings around the globe. It is therefore appropriate that we should first analyze the religious, intellectual, and socio-political context in which prewar missionary work began in the first decade of the 1900s before reviewing Mormonism's early achievements in the following chapters.

The Japan Mission of the Church of Jesus Christ of Latter-day Saints operated from August 1901 to July 1924. During the twenty-three-year period of the mission's existence, a total of eighty-eight American missionaries, including mission presidents and their wives, labored in Japan to claim 174 baptisms (113 males and sixty-one females).[1] Two of these missionaries are counted twice—Joseph H. Stimpson and Lloyd O. Ivie, who first served as single men and then returned as married mission presidents. The eighty-six missionaries collectively gave approximately 3,465 months of service, equivalent to what 158 missionaries would provide if each spent twenty-two months in the field. The average tenure in Japan

---

1. Andrew Jenson, compl., "History of the Japan Mission," 1934, Japanese Mission, "Historical Records and Minutes," LDS Church Archives. Some of the men left their wives at home to serve in Japan, including Justus B. Seely of Ephraim, Utah, and Ezra L. Anderson of Salem, Idaho. Charles L. Schmalz, "The Church in Japan 1905–1908, One Man's Mission," September 1994, 2; Heber Grant Ivins, Journal, 3 June 1912, Special Collections, J. Willard Marriott Library, University of Utah. See Annex 7 for a list of all prewar Mormon missionaries to Japan and Annex 8 for a list of all prewar Mormon converts in Japan.

Elders Ensign, Taylor, Grant, and Kelsch (from left to right) stand on the spot in Yokohama where the land of Japan was dedicated to the preaching of the gospel on 1 September 1901. Photo taken on 19 February 1902. Courtesy LDS Church Archives.

was 39.4 months, with nine missionaries spending more than five years.[2] Dividing the number of convert baptisms by the number of missionaries (Figure 4.1),[3] we obtain the annual average productivity of 0.58, meaning that 7.6 baptisms were produced by 13.3 missionaries during an average year.

With so few convert baptisms, the Mormon proselytizing effort in prewar Japan is generally considered to have been a total failure. Heber J. Grant, upon returning from his term as the mission's inaugural president, stated at the October 1903 general conference of the church: "I regret I am not able to tell you that we have done something wonderful over in Japan."[4] Gordon B. Hinckley, writing in 1964, characterized it as "a work of devotion and disappointment probably without parallel in the history of the missions of the Church." He then noted: "In a single month in 1963 there came into the Church as many as the total baptized from 1901 to 1924."[5] It is true that the number of converts was minuscule, but so was the number of missionaries. For a country of 45–55 million people (slightly more than half the population of the United States), the number averaged 12.5

---

2. Stimpson served in Japan for a combined total of eleven years and six months, while Alma O. Taylor remained in Japan for eight years and seven months, except for a brief trip he made to the Asian continent toward the conclusion of his mission.

3. The number of missionaries is calculated from preceding end-year figures.

4. Church of Jesus Christ of Latter-day Saints, *Conference Report*, October 1903.

5. Gordon B. Hinckley, "The Church in the Orient," *Improvement Era* 67 (1963): 167–70.

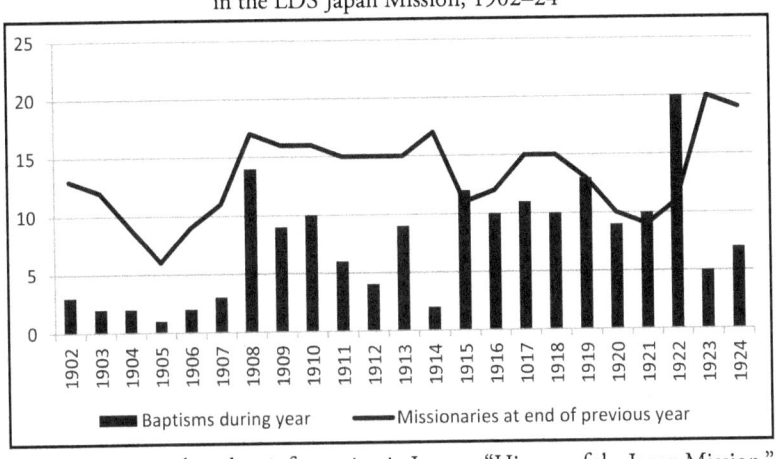

Figure 4.1. Yearly Numbers of Baptisms and Missionaries in the LDS Japan Mission, 1902–24

Author's estimates based on information in Jenson, "History of the Japan Mission."

(based on end-month figures), including the childbearing wives of missionaries. At no time did the number exceed twenty; there were occasional stretches of time when the number was in the single-digits. The number of missionaries who served in Japan from 1901 to 1924 was less than 0.5 percent of the total number the church dispatched around the world. The annual productivity of 0.58, a figure independent of the amount of inputs, does not look unusually low to contemporary observers of the LDS Church in Japan.[6]

Reid Neilson argues that the Mormon achievement was lackluster, compared to the experience of American Protestants, who he claimed were more successful because their approach and practices, with an emphasis on education work, were more adapted to Japanese society.[7] Although Protestantism gained tens of thousands of Japanese converts during the prewar period, the height of its success,

---

6. Publicly available LDS Church data do not provide a breakdown of converts and missionaries by country. According to the 2011 *Church Almanac*, church membership in Japan increased by 637 from end-2010 to end-2011, including births, deaths, and net move-ins. At the time of the Great East Japan Earthquake in 2011, the church announced that 638 missionaries were serving in Japan at the time ("LDS Church to Move Japan Missionaries out of Tsunami Area," KSL News, 15 March 2011, available at www.ksl.com/?nid=148&sid=14743094). This means that the annual productivity of missionary work in 2011 was certainly less than one.

7. In contrast, the Mormons "merely imposed or translated their message" almost exclusively through "personal contacting." Reid L. Neilson, *Early Mormon Missionary Activities in Japan, 1901–1924* (Salt Lake City: University of Utah Press, 2010), 84, 90. Such a view may be too simplistic given the diverse approaches and experiences evinced by the American Protestants, not to mention Christians more generally.

coming in the 1880s, did not coincide with the LDS Japan Mission. The prewar years were a turbulent period in Japanese history,[8] when Japan was suddenly exposed to a cascade of new ideas from the outside world, and the confluence of indigenous and transplanted thoughts never seemed to find equilibrium. In such an environment, a decade could make a difference in terms of the public's receptivity to a foreign religious idea.[9] A fair assessment of the prewar Mormon experience requires understanding the evolving religious and intellectual climate of Meiji Japan without treating it as a static, homogeneous entity.

The rest of this chapter reviews Japan's early religious roots, the arrival of Christianity and the role played by Buddhism in its suppression, the short-lived attempt by the Meiji government to elevate Shinto as the state religion, Japan's second encounter with Christianity, and how, once the institutions of a modern state were fully in place, monks and nationalists conspired to attack Christianity.[10] This chapter shows that initial resistance to foreign ideas was typically followed by a more accommodating attitude; but when the accommodation was carried to the extreme, subdued indigenous ideas erupted to the surface. Political and economic forces were additional influences in the marketplace of ideas. There emerged a state-imposed ideology centered on the emperor, which would become increasingly binding upon the public. Mitigating this conservative trend were the liberalizing forces of industrialization and modernization, which found expression in greater pluralism, religious tolerance, and democratic aspirations. Such was the world that greeted the arrival of Mormon missionaries in 1901.

4.2. Japan's Early Religious Roots

4.2.1. Shinto-Buddhist Syncretism

Shinto, the supposed native religion of Japan, is believed to have emerged broadly in the current form during the ninth century when, following the introduction of Buddhism, diverse indigenous religious beliefs and practices respond-

---

8. The period began with the opening up of the country in the late 1850s, following about 220 years of self-imposed national seclusion. The country subsequently experienced a revolution in 1868, by which the Tokugawa family's right to rule was abrogated and restored to the emperor (posthumously named Meiji); major wars with China (1894–95) and Russia (1904–05), in which Japan defeated both; an annexation by force of Korea in 1910; and the transformation of a feudal, agrarian society into an industrial and military power capable of waging a sustained war with United States.

9. Such a possibility is suggested by the experience of the LDS Church in Japan during the immediate post-World War II period. How the initial enthusiastic reaction to the Mormon message was quickly followed by widespread apathy is documented in Chapters 10 and 12.

10. For an introductory review of Japanese religious history and major religious traditions, see H. Byron Earhart, *Japanese Religion: Unity and Diversity*, fourth edition (Belmont, California: Wadsworth/Thomson, 2004).

ed to the need to develop a systematic form. In the process, Shinto adopted from China the Confucian and Daoist criticisms of Buddhism. The word Shinto itself was borrowed from China to create an identity of its own.[11] Over time, fusing of Shinto and Buddhism took place within the framework of Buddhist metaphysics. As Shinto underwent philosophical and ethical rationalization under Buddhist influence, Buddhism took on elements of ancestral worship, which was alien to itself.[12] For more than a millennium Shinto–Buddhist syncretism (*shinbutsu shūgō*) was an integral feature of Japanese religious life.

The original elements of Shinto were magical and animistic: numerous objects of awe in natural phenomena were recognized as deities (*kami*). Shinto was liturgical and amoral: what mattered was to please *kami* through public acts of worship, to reap temporal blessings. Shinto was geographic: a particular *kami* resided in a particular locality. To this extent, it was also polytheistic. As a localized religion, Shinto was ritualistically connected with communal life, and the authority to rule had mythical and religious overtones. As the development of agriculture created kinship groups, *kami* began to take on human character; they became the tutelary deities of clans and the communities they ruled. The progressive control of local clans by the imperial court was effected by the acceptance of the supremacy of the national over the local religious rites. The people gave the first harvest to the court in exchange for the bestowal of divine favor.[13]

After Buddhism reached Japan in the early sixth century, the social elites faced a dilemma. Buddhism's appeal was irresistible. Shinto, possessing no concept of afterlife or individual sin, was not meeting their spiritual needs. On the other hand, as the ruler–priests of their communities, how could they convert to a new faith without upsetting the social order? From the eighth to the ninth century, stories are recorded of local deities in various parts of Japan speaking through mediums that their suffering was too great and that they were converting to Buddhism, in a self-scripted drama played out for public display. As *kami* converted to Buddhism, so did the community leaders, and a number of Buddhist temples (called *jingūji*, lit. "shrine–temples") were built in the precincts of Shinto shrines ostensibly to ease the suffering of the gods. The court authorized the *jingūji* in order to retain the local clans' loyalty and thereby the tax revenue.[14] Syncretism was the inevitable consequence of ruler–priests embracing a foreign religion.

---

11. Masao Takatori, *Shintō no Seiritsu* (Tokyo: Heibonsha, 1993), 154, 244, 305; Minoru Sonoda, ed., *Shintō: Nihon no Minzoku Shūkyō* (Tokyo: Kōbundō, 1988), 3–4.

12. Takatori, *Shintō*, 16; Robert N. Bellah, *Tokugawa Religion* (Glencoe, Illinois: Free Press, 1957), 64–66.

13. Akio Yoshie, *Shinbutsu Shūgō* (Tokyo: Iwanami Shoten, 1996), 66–67; Yoshiro Tamura, *Japanese Buddhism: A Cultural History* (Tokyo: Kōsei Publishing, 2000), 24; Helen Hardacre, *Shinto and the State 1868–1988* (Princeton, New Jersey: Princeton University Press, 1989), 10.

14. Yoshie, *Shinbutsu Shūgō*, 11–25, 55–58, 70–75; Sonoda, *Shintō*, 142.

A fine example of syncretism, the Hōzanji Temple in Nara (built in 1678) is seen protected by a Shinto deity. The torii gate marks the entrance to the Shinto part of the compound on the left.

Buddhism began to spread beyond the ruling class, following the introduction in the early ninth century of the esoteric tradition.[15] Esoteric Buddhism emphasized magic and mysticism as tools of obtaining individual salvation, precisely the elements the public was accustomed to practicing in folk Shinto. It was also accommodative, allowing *kami* to be interpreted as diverse manifestations of the supreme Buddha. This view, called the *honji suijaku* theory,[16] emerged from the late tenth century and by the early fourteenth century engulfed the Japanese religious scene. The supremacy of Buddhism over Shinto was evident.[17] The title *gongen*, "provisional manifestation" (i.e., manifestations of particular Buddhist deities), was attached to the names of many Shinto deities, and temple–shrines—the opposite of the earlier shrine–temples—were constructed on the grounds of major Buddhist temples, where a *kami* protecting the temple was worshiped.[18]

---

15. In esoteric Buddhism, the secret treasury of teachings could only be transmitted directly, from teacher's mind to disciple's. Tamura, *Japanese Buddhism*, 67–68.

16. While *honji* means the purest, original form of divinity, *suijaku* means phenomenal appearances. Thus, the *honji suijaku* theory explains the relationship between Shinto and Buddhism in terms of *kami* being the protectors and phenomenal appearances of Buddhist divinities that represent the original form of divinity. Hardacre, *Shinto and the State*, 14.

17. The most important Shinto deity, *Amaterasu*, the Goddess of the Sun, became linked to *Dainichi Nyorai*, the Japanese version of *Vairocana*, the Cosmic Buddha.

18. Yoshie, *Shinbutsu Shūgō*, 76–78, 167–69, 178, 184; Tamura, *Japanese Buddhism*, 87.

4.2.2. The Arrival of Christianity

When Francis Xavier and his Jesuit companions arrived in Kagoshima in 1549, Japan was in a period of "Warring States." In the twelfth century, the court-based aristocracy had lost the monopoly of power, causing provincial military governors to emerge. In the fifteenth century, the military governors were superseded by feudal lords (*daimyō*) who increasingly relied on the feudalistic lord–vassal relationship in the exercise of power. Daimyo domains became virtually autonomous principalities, and competing daimyo fought to expand territorial control. The emperor (*tennō*) remained in Kyoto as the symbol of residual sovereignty but without political power. Early Catholic work coincided with the process by which three daimyo, Oda Nobunaga (1534–82), Toyotomi Hideyoshi (1536–98), and Tokugawa Ieyasu (1542–1616), successively beat their rivals into submission and unified the country. The process was completed by Ieyasu, who legitimized his hegemony with the imperial conferral of the title *shōgun*.

During Nobunaga's life Christianity spread rapidly across Japan. At the close of 1581, Otis Cary estimates that there were 150,000 Christians, many of whom were nobles and the majority on the island of Kyushu (the number would increase to an estimated 300,000 or 1.2–1.5 percent of the population at the beginning of the seventeenth century).[19] This was made possible by the advocacy Christianity received from powerful daimyo. Nobunaga in particular welcomed Christianity as an instrument of weakening the Buddhist establishment, which was at the height of its influence.[20] Several Kyushu daimyo, keen to reap commercial benefits, welcomed the priests who had the patronage of Portuguese merchants. The preaching was reinforced by works of charity; the Jesuits built schools, hospitals, and leprosaria, as well as seminaries to train local priesthood.

---

19. This number (300,000) appears to be widely accepted. See, for example, Earhart, *Japanese Religion*, 135. Otis Cary's estimate, at 900,000 (or about 4 percent of the population), is considerably larger. Otis Cary, *A History of Christianity in Japan, Volume 1: Roman Catholic and Orthodox Missions* (New York: Fleming H. Revell, 1909), 83, 91–92. The population share of 4 percent may more accurately reflect the Christian strength in western Japan, Kyushu in particular, where the Christians, including daimyo and other leading figures, were concentrated.

20. With ubiquitous civil unrest, some influential temples had amassed their own militias and used force to defend their properties and to assert their political will. New Buddhist leaders had also captivated a large segment of the population with their versions of Buddhism, which were centered on faith in the saving grace of the Buddha. The most successful was the Pure Land School, whose founders taught that Amida and his retinue of bodhisattvas would come to welcome believers and escort them to the Pure Land of heaven; and that, instead of relying on futile human effort, one must depend upon the power of Amida by reciting a mantra to attain rebirth in the Pure Land. *Jōdo Shinshū*, the dominant offshoot of the Pure Land School, became so powerful that it often mobilized peasants and townspeople to put up armed resistance to the authority of daimyo, including Nobunaga. Tamura, *Japanese Buddhism*, 81–82.

By the time of Hideyoshi's ascendance, the Buddhist establishment was securely under control, presenting little need to check Buddhist ambitions. Hideyoshi instead offered support to Buddhism, while adopting harsh measures against Christianity. In 1587, he ordered the missionaries to leave the country. He then became alarmed by the aggressive activities of Franciscan priests after their arrival in 1592. While the Jesuits had acted circumspectly in order not to provoke the suspicion or anger of Hideyoshi, the Franciscans worked with the utmost zeal in religious propaganda. In 1597 twenty-six missionaries and Japanese associates were taken to Nagasaki to be crucified as martyrs. Hideyoshi issued an edict forbidding any daimyo to become a Christian. Despite these measures, the missionary work continued nearly unmolested. Thousands of converts, including many of high rank, were made between the edict of 1587 and the death of Hideyoshi in 1598.[21]

Ieyasu decisively defeated the Toyotomi forces in the Battle of Sekigahara in 1600 and in 1603 established the Tokugawa shogunate in Edo, present-day Tokyo, from which he ruled some 250 daimyo domains. Initially, his attitude toward Christianity was ambivalent. The new shogun showed no inclination to either repeal or enforce Hideyoshi's edicts against Christianity; he even gave financial aid to missionaries. The missionaries soon came out of their hiding places. The churches that had been destroyed were rebuilt in western Kyushu; the houses of the Jesuits were re-established in Kyoto and Osaka. In the two years, 1598–99, the number of baptisms amounted to 70,000. While Ieyasu viewed Catholic allegiance to God or the pope as offensive, he saw potential commercial gains from tolerating Christianity.[22]

A change in Ieyasu's attitude toward Christianity became apparent in 1612 when his attempts to establish trade with Mexico had proven futile. He banned Christianity in all domains under direct Tokugawa control and among the direct Tokugawa vassals. Two years later, in 1614, Ieyasu ordered daimyo to send to Nagasaki all the missionaries living in their domains, to destroy the churches, and to force the Christians to renounce their religion. The authorities responded with a cruelty and rigor unparalleled in Japanese history.[23] Contributing to Ieyasu's changed attitude was the arrival of traders from Protestant countries at the turn of the seventeenth century; the economic rivalry between the Catholic and the Protestant nations made the Tokugawa shogunate suspicious of the motives behind the Catholic activities.[24]

The death of Ieyasu in 1616 brought no relief to the Christian cause. His son Hidetaka was more determined to suppress Christianity, and the personal tem-

---

21. Cary, *Christianity in Japan*, vol. 1, 118, 121–31; Tamura, *Japanese Buddhism*, 142–43; Anesaki, *Japanese Religion*, 245.
22. Cary, *Christianity in Japan*, vol. 1, 135–38.
23. Ibid., 176–78; Anesaki, *Japanese Religion*, 250–51.
24. Japan commenced trade with the Dutch in 1609 and with England in 1613. Hiroto Saegusa and Hiroo Torii, *Nihon Shūkyō Shisō Shi* (Tokyo: Mikasa Shobō, 1938), 210–11.

perament of the third shogun Iemitsu, grandson of Ieyasu, hastened the inevitable. In 1635, the shogunate ordered daimyo to extirpate Christianity from their domains.[25] The persecution and suppression of Christianity went hand in hand with the progressively tightening control of foreign trade and foreign travel. In 1616 foreign trade was restricted to Nagasaki and Hirado; in 1624, the Spanish were expelled from Japan; in 1636 the Portuguese were confined to Deshima, a small man-made island off the port of Nagasaki. In 1635 an edict was issued to prohibit any Japanese from traveling abroad or from returning home once away.

The final nail in the coffin of the Christian cause was the Shimabara Rebellion of 1637–38, a peasant uprising on the island of Kyushu against the harsh taxation of their crops. The peasants, numbering over 30,000, put up a fierce fight against Tokugawa's samurai fighters for four months, which took the shogunate more than 120,000 soldiers to subdue; over 1,000 were killed and nearly 7,000 wounded among the Tokugawa forces. Because the leader named Amakusa Shiro was a former Christian, as were many of the uprising peasants, the central authorities rightly or wrongly saw in the gravity of the incident a Christian cause and renewed their determination to crack down on any remaining residue of Christianity.[26]

In 1638, the shogunate strengthened the suppression of Christianity by offering large monetary rewards for anyone who identified clandestine Christians and promising to pardon the informants. To eradicate Christianity once and for all, in 1639, the Tokugawa authorities declared a policy of national seclusion, permitting few foreigners to enter and no Japanese to leave the country. The Portuguese, suspected of having encouraged the revolt, were ordered to leave the country and forbidden to return. In 1640, the Office of Religious Inquisitor was instituted. In 1641, the Dutch concession was restricted to Deshima in Nagasaki harbor.[27] Except for limited commercial or diplomatic intercourse with the Chinese, Dutch, and Koreans, Japan would be closed to the outside world for the next 220 years.

4.2.3. Tokugawa Buddhism

It was Buddhism that the Tokugawa shogunate turned to as an instrument of enforcing the suppression of Christianity. As early as 1614 a Christian who renounced his religion was required to become a parishioner (*danka*) of a Buddhist

---

25. Fumio Tamamuro, "Bakuhan Taisei to Bukkyō," in *Ronshū Nihon Bukkyō Shi*, vol. 7, ed. F. Tamamuro (Tokyo: Yūzankaku, 1986), 4–6; Cary, *Christianity in Japan*, vol. 1, 190, 215–17; Anesaki, *Japanese Religion*, 251–53.

26. An alternative interpretation is that although the Tokugawa authorities understood it as a conventional peasant revolt against the harsh taxation, they characterized it as a religious revolt in order to create a pretext for eradicating Christianity through force and by fostering a fear of Christianity among the people. Tamamuro, "Bakuhan Taisei," 8–15; Fumio Tamamuro, *Sōshiki to Danka* (Tokyo: Yoshikawa Kōbunsha, 1999), 53–60.

27. Tamamuro, *Sōshiki to Danka*, 60–66; Cary, *Christianity in Japan*, vol. 1, 229.

temple and to obtain a certificate (*terauke-shōmon* or *ukebumi*) from the temple.[28] The practice of temple registration (*terauke*) first appeared in targeted locations, such as Kyoto and Nagasaki, where a concentration of Christians was suspected. From the mid-1630s, the *terauke* system was applied more widely across the country, with registries prepared on a village or town basis.[29] The system became firmly established following the Shimabara Rebellion. The shogunate required all Japanese to undergo temple registration and to submit thereafter to an annual scrutiny of religious beliefs by Buddhist monks, making all Japanese, including Shinto priests, Buddhists by law.[30]

The eradication of Christianity was meant to be total. Not even a reference to it was permitted in books, and its very name might have been lost were it not written so prominently on the public proclamation boards of every town: "The evil sect of Christianity is strictly prohibited."[31] Those found practicing Christianity, and their families and close relatives, were tortured, imprisoned, and in some cases put to death. From 1687 separate registries for former Christians were created, a practice that continued until the Meiji era, to trace those with any former ties to Christianity. When they died, their corpses needed to be examined by an official, whose clearance was required before they could be buried (in a separate location!). They were subjected to a religious persecution and prejudice that would last 200 years. Fear of Christianity was thus implanted in the deepest conscience of the public.[32]

The *terauke* system was part of a larger system of religious control. In 1615, the shogunate had broken up large Buddhist sects into smaller ones, to place them under better control. Over the subsequent years, the shogunate organized Buddhist sects into a hierarchical structure, from the head temple (typically, but not always, located in Kyoto) down to local temples in what was called the *honmatsu* system. The head temple served as a seminary to train the priesthood for that sect, controlled the appointment of priests, was responsible for temple assets, and maintained a liaison office in Edo. The presiding priest was appointed by the ruling shogun, and at his recommendation, given purple robes and an official title by the emperor. Shinto shrines were also placed under the shogunate's control, but the imperial court was given charge of the ordination of priests and the prescription of Shinto rites.[33]

---

28. Tamamuro, *Sōshiki to Danka*, 6–22.
29. Fumio Tamamuro and Junko Oguri, "Bakuhan Taiseika no Bukkyō," in *Edo Bukkyō*, ed. H. Nakamura, K. Kasahara, and H. Kaneoka (Tokyo: Kōsei Shuppansha, 1972), 28–29; Yoshio Yasumaru, "Rekishi no nakadeno Kattō to Mosaku," in *Kindaika to Dentō*, ed. Y. Yasumaru (Tokyo: Shūjunsha, 1986), 21.
30. Tamamuro, *Sōshiki to Danka*, 60–66, 130–62.
31. Cary, *Christianity in Japan*, vol. 1, 241.
32. Tamamuro, "Bakuhan Taisei," 28–35; Tamamuro, *Sōshiki to Danka*, 130–68.
33. Tamamuro, *Sōshiki to Danka*, 69–72; Takeo Yamamoto, "Jinja eno Minzoku Shinkō," in *Edo Bukkyō*, ed. H. Nakamura, K. Kasahara, and H. Kaneoka (Tokyo: Kōsei Shuppansha, 1972), 232.

This system, by creating a demand for temple affiliation, led to an unprecedented surge in temple construction; temples that had been no more than small huts swelled into grandiose structures.[34] For an ordinary citizen, the system for the first time provided an opportunity to be part of Buddhist rituals, to which only privileged people had access previously. The fear of being labeled as a Christian was so strong that Buddhist monks had enormous leverage over the people, especially those on the Christian registries. The system thus became a hotbed of corruption. Monks, for example, would charge an exorbitant fee for a funeral or solicit funds for the erection of a new worship hall. Local monks could be engaged in outright acts of extortion, by demanding monetary or sexual favors. Buddhist priesthood, with its social status and a lavish lifestyle, became an attractive occupation for aspiring men with no religious inclinations. Priesthood offices and temple ranks were often sold as commodities.[35]

From 1671, a standard template for religious registries cemented every person to his temple. Regardless of what he actually believed, he had no freedom to choose his own temple; at birth the place of his funeral was known with virtual certainty. As Buddhism's grip on the people tightened, their hearts departed. Buddhism, though part of everybody's life, was not meeting their spiritual needs, creating room for new religious traditions to emerge outside the official realm.[36] Worship of the Shinto *Inari* god, for example, became a fad from time to time. The public received traveling monks in hope of obtaining divine favor.[37] True religious seekers went underground to practice new religions that would occasionally arise. Whenever these practices surfaced, the authorities attempted to suppress them with vigor. Worship at Shinto shrines was another way of releasing their religious sentiment. An increasing number of people made pilgrimages to the Grand Shrine of Ise in central Japan.[38]

---

34. Tamamuro and Oguri, "Bakuhan Taiseika no Bukkyō," 34.

35. Not a few monks, lacking sufficient knowledge of Buddhist texts, hired specialists when occasion required a sermon to be preached, and followed a written script to perform a religious rite. The *honmatsu* system served as a mechanism for siphoning assets from the bottom, for example, to cover the expenses of ornate ordination ceremonies or building grandiose worship halls at the central or regional head temples. The large temples with beautiful gardens one now enjoys visiting in Kyoto are a reminder of how effective this system of extortion worked over the two centuries of state patronage. Tamamuro, "Bakuhan Taisei," 38–40; Tamamuro, *Sōshiki to Danka*, 72–98, 195–223; Tamamuro and Oguri, "Bakuhan Taiseika no Bukkyō," 26.

36. Tamamuro, "Bakuhan Taisei," 26–27; Tamamuro and Oguri, "Bakuhan Taiseika no Bukkyō," 10.

37. Noboru Miyata, "Hayari Shinbutsu to Zokushinkō," in *Edo Bukkyō*, ed. H. Nakamura, K. Kasahara, and H. Kaneoka (Tokyo: Kōsei Shuppansha, 1972), 187–91, 216.

38. Junko Oguri and Tetsuya Ohama, "Chika Shinkō: Sono Genryū to Jittai," in *Edo Bukkyō*, ed. H. Nakamura, K. Kasahara, and H. Kaneoka (Tokyo: Kōsei Shuppansha, 1972), 92–110; Yasumaru, "Kattō to Mosaku," 28–29.

4.3. The Rise of State Shinto

4.3.1. Nativist Thoughts

Buddhism, having become an instrument of state control, lost its ideological influence. Its status as the country's governing ideology was thus given to Confucianism, which was more suitable as a basis for defining feudal relationships.[39] The corruption of Buddhism, evident as early as the 1660s, gave rise to the systematic development of anti-Buddhist ideology among Confucian scholars. Some enlightened daimyo, under Confucian influence, attempted to weaken the hold of Buddhism over the people, for example, by transferring the responsibility for creating family registries from temples to government officials or by reducing the number of temples within their domains. Though these efforts were short-lived, criticism of Buddhism became widespread across the whole spectrum of society.[40]

Shinto came under the greater influence of Confucianism during the Edo period. Under the *terauke* system, Shinto priests and their families were required to be parishioners of a Buddhist temple, subjugating Shinto shrines to Buddhist temples in the syncretistic tradition. But under the framework of Confucianism, Shinto–Confucian syncretism emerged, which emphasized such ethical virtues as filial piety, loyalty, and honesty. Called *bushidō*, this helped justify the privileged position of samurai in society, though they were no longer needed as warriors; the bushido ethics appealed first to the samurai class, but the influence spread to other segments of society. At the cult center of Ise, Buddhist elements were removed, leaving Confucian elements alone, as Confucian scholars tried to indigenize Confucian philosophy.[41]

A sustained period of relative peace encouraged scholarly learning, especially studies of the Japanese classics, broadly known as National Learning (*kokugaku*). The Mito School, based on meticulous historical research, proved that there had been a time when the emperor ruled personally, showing in great detail the features of that era and the events that brought about its demise. The end result was to undermine the legitimacy of the shogunate and to create a nostalgic feeling in favor of returning to the days of direct imperial rule. In a nativist reaction to the Confucian domination of national thought, the eighteenth century saw the rise of *Fukkō* Shinto, which emphasized the importance of ancestor worship and claimed the moral and racial superiority of the Japanese.

Shintoists in this tradition became fierce critics of Buddhism and attempted to remove Buddhist and Confucian elements from the practice of Shinto.[42] They

---

39. Saegusa and Torii, *Shūkyō Shisō*, 198, 204.
40. Tamamuro, *Sōshiki to Danka*, 100–28; Tamamuro and Oguri, "Bakuhan Taiseika no Bukkyō," 38.
41. Yamamoto, "Minzoku Shinkō," 232–35.
42. Bellah, *Tokugawa Religion*, 102–3; Yamamoto, "Minzoku Shinkō," 238–40.

were characterized by irrational religious fervor and establishment of personal deities; they strove to return to the thought and consciousness of the ancients before the country became "polluted" by contact with foreign culture and religion. *Fukkō* Shinto turned into a nativist sociopolitical movement towards the end of the Edo period. The slogan *sonnō* (revere the emperor) typified their emphasis on the emperor, while the term *kokutai* (national structure) expressed the uniqueness of their concept of the state.[43]

4.3.2. Shinto as the State Religion

The arrival in 1853 of Commodore Matthew Calbraith Perry of the United States Navy off the coast of Japan set in motion a series of events that would culminate in the country's opening and the end of 250 years of feudal rule by the Tokugawa family. In 1854, Japan signed a Treaty of Peace and Amity (the Treaty of Kanagawa) with the United States, agreeing to open the remote ports of Hakodate and Shimoda to American ships for provisioning. In July 1859, the Treaty of Amity and Commerce (the Harris Treaty), signed a year earlier, came into force, opening the ports of Kanagawa and Nagasaki immediately and, over the coming years, the ports of Hyogo and Niigata as well as the cities of Edo and Osaka, to foreigners for commercial purposes. The Tokugawa shogunate signed similar treaties with Britain, France, Holland, and Russia. These are collectively known as the Ansei treaties.

The opening of Japan, conceded under threat of force, created a vehement anti-Tokugawa reaction, especially among the powerful daimyo of western Japan. Coupled with the nativist political philosophy of National Learning, they gravitated around the slogan *sonnō jōi* or "revere the emperor, expel the barbarians," rallied around the throne, and set out to overthrow the shogunate. With the decisive victory over the Tokugawa forces, in early 1868, the rebel domains of Satsuma and Choshu (with additional contingents from others) restored the throne to political power, moved his residence from Kyoto to Edo, which was renamed Tokyo (lit. East Kyoto), and called the new period of his reign Meiji (lit. enlightened rule). This ended the long historical separation of reigning sovereign and ruling authority that had existed since the twelfth century.

Once in power, the new Meiji government appealed to the imperial throne to legitimize the revolution, and upheld the Shinto concept of national structure. In 1868, the government proclaimed the unity of religion and politics (*saisei itchi*) and restored the ancient office of chief national priest (*jingi kan*) and placed it over the civil bureaucracy. Over the coming years, it issued a series of ordinances to establish Shinto as the state religion and to remove Buddhist influences from it (*shinbutsu bunri*). From 1871 to 1872, the government confiscated land from Buddhist temples, abrogated the right of self-rule, and abolished the temple

---

43. Saegusa and Torii, *Shūkyō Shisō*, 235; Hardacre, *Shinto and the State*, 16–17.

registration system. By 1871 all Buddhist rituals at the imperial court had been abolished.[44] In 1873, the government prohibited the requirements of celibacy, tonsure, and vegetarianism for Buddhist priesthood. These and other related measures terminated, at the stroke of a pen, the Shinto–Buddhist syncretism that had been part of Japan's religious scene for more than a millennium.[45]

Invigorated, Shinto fanatics took to the streets, destroying Buddhist temples and removing or burning religious artifacts. The plundering represented the frustration of Shinto priests who had been subjugated by Buddhist monks for hundreds of years. The physical and psychological damage to Buddhism was substantial. From 1871 to 1876, the number of Buddhist temples declined from an estimated 465,049 to 71,962 and the number of monks from 75,925 in 1872 to 19,490 in 1876.[46] The acts of vandalism were spontaneous and by no means officially sanctioned. In desperate need of support from influential and wealthy temples, especially the powerful *Jōdo Shinshū* sects of Pure Land Buddhism, the authorities repeatedly asserted that the government had no intention to ban Buddhism, with their desire only to elevate the public's respect for the ancestors.[47]

A new system of religion was in the making, in Shinto's clothing.[48] In 1871, the government brought all shrines under the umbrella of the Ise Shrine by ranking them according to a single hierarchy, while abolishing a number of minor shrines of dubious character; it ordered magic and other superstitious practices to be removed. The Shinto of Meiji Japan needed to be a modern religion capable of stacking up against the Christianity of the West. The Shinto deities connected with the imperial court were elevated. The Grand Shrine of Ise, which enshrines *Amaterasu* the Sun Goddess, the legendary ancestor of the emperor, was naturally placed at the top.[49] Additional grand shrines were built to enshrine past

---

44. During the Edo period, for example, funeral rites for the imperial family were performed by Buddhist priests. Yoshio Yasumaru, *Kamigami no Meiji Ishin* (Tokyo: Iwanami Shoten, 1979), 64–66.

45. Yasumaru, *Kamigami*, 51–52; Yoshio Yasumaru, "Tennōseika no Minshū to Shūkyō," *Nihon Rekishi*, vol. 16 (Tokyo: Iwanami Shoten, 1976), 325–27; Sonoda, *Shintō*, 34–35; Shigeyoshi Murakami, *Nihon Hyakunen no Shūkyō* (Tokyo: Kōdansha, 1968), 37–38; Eishun Ikeda, "Kindaiteki Kaimei Shisō to Bukkyō," *Ronshū Nihon Bukkyō Shi*, vol. 8, ed. E. Ikeda (Tokyo: Yūzankan Shuppan, 1987), 11.

46. Winston Davis, *Japanese Religion and Society: Paradigms of Structure and Change* (Albany, New York: State University of New York Press, 1992), 160–61; Yasumaru, *Kamigami*, 117, Table 1.

47. Ibid., 79–80.

48. Yasumaru, "Minshū to Shūkyō," 334; Hardacre, *Shinto and the State*, 4.

49. Within Ise, the centuries-old relative standings of the Inner Shrine (enshrining *Amaterasu*) and the Outer Shrine (enshrining *Toyouke*, the god of agriculture and industry) were reversed in favor of the Inner Shrine. During the Edo period, the Inner Shrine was relatively unimportant as, at the level of folk religion, *Amaterasu* did not represent the progenitor of the imperial family. Yasumaru, *Kamigami*, 8.

Monks, Nationalists, and the Emperor

emperors (it was discovered that the first emperor had no shrine!).⁵⁰ In 1869, the Shōkonsha Shrine (renamed Yasukuni in 1879) was established to honor the war dead. Yasukuni would cement the consciousness of the public to the destiny of the nation at each succeeding war.⁵¹

Between 1870 and 1884, the Shinto leaders tried to establish a state religion through a Great Promulgation Campaign (*taikyō senpu undō*), in which they preached a "Great Teaching" consisting of: (1) reverence for the gods and patriotism; (2) promulgation of the heavenly Reason and the Way of Humanity; and (3) reverence for the Throne and obedience to the authorities.⁵² In 1872, they established an ecclesiastical board (*kyōbushō*), in place of the now defunct office of chief national priest, as a way to involve Buddhist monks as National Evangelists (*kyōdōshoku*).⁵³ In 1873, a Great Teaching Institute (*Daikyōin*) was established to train National Evangelists.⁵⁴ The Great Teaching had no basis in popular thought and the idea was so vague even to the evangelists themselves that chapbooks on what to preach had to be created. Not knowing exactly what to say, they expounded the virtues of paying taxes, and of complying with compulsory education, conscription, and the solar calendar.⁵⁵

The attempts to create a national religion out of Shinto were not successful. Influential Buddhist leaders, such as Mokurai Shimaji, had never bought into the Great Promulgation Campaign and lobbied the government to abolish the ecclesiastical board.⁵⁶ In 1875, four *Jōdo Shinshū* sects left the board, and in 1877 the board itself was dissolved. At this stage, Buddhists were no longer bound by the Great Teaching and were free to preach what they wanted. In 1882 the government separated Shinto ceremonial rites from religion, formalizing the separation of Sect Shinto (denominational branches of Shinto) from Shrine Shinto. The system of licensed National Evangelists would continue until 1884, when Sect Shinto and Buddhism became totally freed from state control. Shrine Shinto, in-

---

50. Most importantly, the shrine for Emperor Jimmu, the first legendary emperor of Japan, was built at Kashihara in Nara Prefecture in 1890.
51. Hardacre, *Shinto and the State*, 92–93.
52. Anesaki, *Japanese Religion*, 334–36.
53. While all Shinto priests became National Evangelists, Buddhist monks were required to take a test to qualify. Once qualified, they were not allowed to mix Buddhist teachings as they gave their sermons and were placed under the supervision of Shinto priests. Evangelists could teach nothing but the three principles. In the process, Buddhism traded its independence for the prestige of a connection with the state. Masashi Sakurai, *Kinsei Nihon Shūkyō Shisō Shi* (Fukuoka: Tonshindo, 1944), 21–28.
54. Susumu Shimazono, *Kokka Shintō to Nihonjin* (Tokyo: Iwanami Shoten, 2010), 13–14; Yasumaru, *Kamigami*, 182–84.
55. Hardacre, *Shinto and the State*, 42–44; Murakami, *Hyakunen no Shūkyō*, 56–58.
56. Sakurai, *Shūkyō Shisō Shi*, 29.

cluding the ceremonies at the court and the communal Shinto cult, was regarded as a civic institution and remained under state control.[57]

4.3.3. Clandestine Christian Work

In July 1859, the Ansei treaties came into force, giving the nationals of the five foreign powers the right to free exercise of their religion, as well as the right to build churches, within the restricted foreign settlements.[58] Although the ban on Christianity remained in place for the Japanese public, the first sets of missionaries arrived in quick succession, to take up residence in Nagasaki and Yokohama.[59] In the early 1860s, there were thus missionaries in Japan from the Roman Catholic Church (represented by the Society of Foreign Missions of Paris) and the (Russian) Orthodox Church,[60] as well as the Congregational, Dutch Reformed, Episcopal, and Presbyterian churches on the Protestant side.

In early 1865, following the construction of an edifice dedicated to the Twenty-Six Martyrs (see Section 4.2.2) on a prominent hill in Nagasaki's foreign settlement, a group of women came forward from a nearby village, identifying themselves as Christians. By the middle of the year, the Catholic missionaries had learned of such Christian communities in twenty or more places.[61] As the Tokugawa regime was collapsing, the hidden Christians became more open in confessing their faith. The official reluctance to treat them harshly may have been motivated by the shogunate's desire to gain support from the resident French

---

57. Anesaki, *Japanese Religion*, 336.

58. For example, Article VIII of the Treaty of Amity and Commerce, signed between the United States and Japan, stated in part: "Americans in Japan shall be allowed the free exercise of their religion, and for this purpose shall have the right to erect suitable places of worship. . . . The Americans and Japanese shall not do anything that may be calculated to excite religious animosity. The Government of Japan has already abolished the practice of trampling on religious emblems."

59. Cary, *Christianity in Japan*, vol. 1, 45–50.

60. The presence of the Orthodox Church would for the most part be limited to northern Japan, by virtue of the fact that work began with a Russian Orthodox chaplain attached to the Russian consulate in the treaty port city of Hakodate, Hokkaido. In the late 1860s, Hakodate became one of the last strongholds of samurai still loyal to the shogun, including those from the Sendai domain. To such men Christianity held a special appeal and offered a ray of hope for their future as well as for the future of their country. Near the close of 1871 several men from Sendai were baptized in Hakodate, and the work spread to the city of Sendai on the main island of Honshu. With the help of his samurai converts, Pere Nicolai almost single-handedly built the Orthodox Church into a community of nearly 9,000 believers by 1883. At the end of 1907, the Orthodox Church had 30,166 members, 265 chapels or preaching stations, and 175 buildings. Cary, *Christianity in Japan*, vol. 1, 375–423.

61. In 1892 the Vicar Apostolic of Southern Japan estimated that about 50,000 descendants of the ancient Christians had been discovered and that only about a half of them had formally joined the Catholic Church. Cary, *Christianity in Japan*, vol. 1, 281–93.

Ōura Tenshudō, a Catholic cathedral built in 1865 and refurbished in 1879, is dedicated to the Twenty-Six Martyrs. This is where a group of crypto-Christians came forward to confess their faith to Father Petitjean in 1865.

minister in Tokyo, in their struggle against the revolutionary forces. Soon persecution commenced, with the arrest of hidden Christians.[62]

In early 1868, the new Meiji government took power. Although the emperor's inaugural charter oath proclaimed that "[e]vil practices of the past shall be abandoned" and "[k]nowledge shall be sought all over the world," these evidently did not apply to Christianity. Just as the government was restoring the ancient religious order, it was reaffirming the long-standing Tokugawa ban on Christianity. The proscription sign-boards prohibiting Christianity were posted anew at prominent places throughout the country. In fact, the elevation of Shinto was meant in part as a guard against the real threat of Christianity, now that a number of hidden Christians had come out of hiding.[63]

The Meiji government not only refused to release those hidden Christians seized by the Tokugawa authorities, but in early 1870 deported and incarcerated over 3,000 of them across some thirty provinces. Around 600 people had died and many apostatized by the time they were freed and repatriated in 1873.[64] The work of Catholic missionaries proceeded in remote areas of Nagasaki. During 1871–72, nearly 700 children and 1,600 adults were baptized; by the time the persecution ended, the Catholic missionaries had established ties with 15,000

---

62. Ibid., 296–306.
63. Yasumaru, *Kamigami*, 69.
64. Marius B. Jansen, *The Making of Modern Japan* (Cambridge, Massachusetts and London: The Belknap Press of Harvard University Press, 2000), 463.

people, and knew that there were many thousands more who had inherited the faith of the ancient Christians.⁶⁵ The religion, however, had become highly corrupted over the 250 years of isolation, with syncretic elements of Shinto and Buddhism.⁶⁶ Many hidden Christians found it difficult to revert back to Catholicism, an alien religion.⁶⁷

Protestantism was for the most part represented by American missionaries.⁶⁸ They came with a zeal born of the Second Great Awakening, which had begun in America and spread to Britain in the early nineteenth century.⁶⁹ Having come from an English-speaking country, they saw teaching English as a way of getting around the restrictions on proselytizing activities. Some established small schools, often at their homes, to teach additional subjects. Given the absence of Japanese-language literature, the missionaries initially relied on the Chinese books brought from China, because educated people were able to read Chinese (and this defined the type of people they could reach); the Chinese translation of William Alexander Parsons Martin's *Evidences of Christianity* (1855) was especially popular. Buddhist monks were occasional students, eager to expose what

---

65. Cary, *Christianity in Japan*, vol. 1, 332–34.

66. Field research done in the 1990s in Ikitsukishima, off the coast of Nagasaki, reveals that a clandestine church organization, with a "father" figure on top, had operated for centuries, while preserving through oral transmission the performance of baptisms, prayers, and sacraments. The prayers retained the original wording of the *orations* (liturgical prayers) found in the sixteenth century *Book of Prayers* to a remarkable extent, though they sound more Japanese than Latin. Raw fish (*sashimi*) and rice wine (*sake*) substituted for bread and wine in the sacrament of Holy Communion, disguised more as a community dinner. Two funerals were performed for the same person almost simultaneously, one by a Buddhist monk and another in a separate room designed to cancel the validity of the Buddhist mantra. During the Edo period, Buddhist monks were apparently complicit in the preservation of crypto-Christianity, so long as the believers complied with their duties as temple parishioners. Kentaro Miyazaki, *Kakure Kirishitan no Shinkō Sekai* (Tokyo: Tōkyō Daigaku Shuppankai, 1996), 76–106, 159–60.

67. In Ikitsukishima, conversion to Catholicism was particularly slow and highly incomplete. It is estimated that only sixteen of the about 2,000 households existing in 1912 belonged to the Catholic Church. Miyazaki, *Kakure Kirishitan*, 25–26. In 1903, the Society of Foreign Missions of Paris reported that hidden Christians were more difficult to convert than pagans. Cary, *Christianity in Japan*, vol. 1, 364.

68. Having come from Puritan America and its colonies in the American Midwest, these men and women brought a specific kind of faith, which emphasized personal conversion, implicit faith in the Bible, moral rigor, and a sense of mission. John F. Howes, "Japanese Christians and American Missionaries," in *Changing Japanese Attitudes Toward Modernization*, ed. Marius B. Jansen (Princeton, New Jersey: Princeton University Press, 1965), 340–45.

69. Hiroaki Matsuzawa, "Kirisutokyō to Chishikijin," *Nihon Rekishi*, vol. 16 (Tokyo: Iwanami Shoten, 1976), 286.

they thought was an evil religion. In 1868 they published an exposé entitled "Tales of Nagasaki: The Story of the Evil Doctrine."[70]

Some were drawn to the Christian message because they considered Christianity, Protestantism in particular, as the spiritual basis of the great Western powers. It was from among these people that Protestantism claimed their first fruits. The first recorded baptism occurred in Yokohama in 1864, and the second took place in Nagasaki in 1866; there would be an estimated eight more Protestant baptisms through early 1872.[71] These were brave men who embraced a foreign religion in defiance of the law. Especially after the Meiji government started to persecute the Urakami Christians, they fully knew what might befall them if their conversion were made known. In March 1870 the persecution of Protestantism began, involving the arrest of converts and those who assisted the missionaries, though not always in a consistent manner.[72]

4.4. Christian Evangelization and the Nationalist Reaction

4.4.1. The Spread of Christianity

The Urakami Incident became the single greatest diplomatic challenge faced by the new Meiji government. From December 1871 to September 1873, the government dispatched a high-level delegation headed by Prince Tomomi Iwakura (the Iwakura Mission) to conduct an exploratory renegotiation with the foreign powers concerning a possible removal of extraterritoriality (giving foreign nationals the right to a consular trial) from the Ansei treaties.[73] The Iwakura Mission received protest and reproach wherever they visited over the treatment of the Urakami Christians. In each capital, the mission was told in no uncertain terms that a revision of the treaty would not be possible as long as Christians were not allowed to practice their religion freely.[74] These views, as communicated home, started the process towards effectively ending the ban on Christianity.

Soon the Urakami exiles were receiving more lenient treatment, and in March 1872 they were released. Then, in February 1873, the government repa-

---

70. Hamish Ion, *American Missionaries, Christian Oyatoi, and Japan, 1859–73* (Vancouver: University of British Columbia Press, 2009), 26–27.

71. Ion, *American Missionaries*, 3, 47; Otis Cary, *A History of Christianity in Japan, Volume 2: Protestant Missions* (New York: Fleming H. Revell, 1909), 55–56; Charles W. Iglehart, *A Century of Protestant Christianity in Japan* (Rutland, Vermont and Tokyo: Charles E. Tuttle, 1959), 41.

72. Masashi Sakurai, *Meiji Shūkyō Undō Shi* (Tokyo: Moriyama Shoten, 1932), 84–86.

73. See Annex 1 towards the end of this volume.

74. For the English translation of a substantial portion of the official mission records, see Kunitake Kume, *Japan Rising: The Iwakura Embassy to the USA and Europe 1871–1873* (Cambridge and New York: Cambridge University Press, 2009).

triated almost 2,000 of them to their homes in Nagasaki,[75] and caused the notice boards against Christianity to be removed from public view. The Christian community rejoiced greatly, thinking that the ban had been lifted,[76] but the official explanation was measured: there was no need for the notice boards because the contents were widely known. Sporadic harassment of Christians continued, but mostly by local officials.[77] After a year or two of equivocation, between 1874 and 1876, an official policy of condonation was in place. The government took no legal action to lift the ban, but the Japanese people felt safe to embrace Christianity and the foreign missionaries likewise to spread their message more openly.[78] In March 1876, the government's decision to designate Sunday as a weekly holiday (effective from April) further boosted the Christian cause.[79]

As the Catholic Church focused almost all of its attention to claiming the hidden Christians in the villages of Nagasaki,[80] the task of evangelizing the Japanese nation fell upon the shoulders of Protestantism. By this time, an interdenominational committee had been formed (in October 1872) to commence the translation of the New Testament into Japanese. Although the committee swelled in size as the work began in 1874, the translation was principally done by Samuel Robbins Brown, James Curtis Hepburn, and D. C. Greene. Three Japanese, Takayoshi Matsuyama, Masatsuna Okubo, and Goro Takahashi, assisted. The translation of the Old Testament began in 1876 but was soon interrupted; the work restarted in earnest in 1882. The Japanese translations of the New and Old Testaments were completed in 1880 and 1887, respectively (the first official Catholic translation from the Vulgate of the New Testament, by Belgian missionary Émile Reguet, came out only in 1910).[81]

With centuries of anti-Christian indoctrination, one should not expect a mere change in policy to have altered overnight the public's receptivity to Christianity. Foreigners were also not allowed to travel freely in the interior in

---

75. Cary, *Christianity in Japan*, vol. 1, 311–33.

76. Ion, *American Missionaries*, 121–22.

77. Government documents suggest that saving the costs of maintaining the boards was an important part of this decision. Responding to an inquiry from the British minister, in November 1873, the Japanese Foreign Ministry stated that the ban on Christianity remained in force. Eiichi Suzue, "Kirishitan Kinsei Kōsatsu Tekkyo Fukokugo no Kinkyō Seisaku," *Kirisutokyō Shigaku* 53 (July 1999): 88, 90–93.

78. Suzue, "Kinkyō Seisaku," 97–99.

79. Up to this time, the first, sixth, eleventh, twenty-first, and twenty-sixth days of each month had been designated as regular official holidays. Hideteru Yamamoto, ed., *Nihon Kirisuto Kyōkai Shi* (Tokyo: Nihon Kirisuto Kyōkai, 1928), 50–51.

80. In 1909, there were 62,694 Catholics in Japan, of which 44,931 were in Nagasaki. Cary, *Christianity in Japan*, vol. 1, 371.

81. Ion, *American Missionaries*, 82–83; Hideo Kishimoto, ed., *Meiji Bunka Shi*, vol. 6 (Shūkyō) (Tokyo: Hara Shobō, 1979), 312–14. In the meantime, an unofficial Catholic translation of the four Gospels, by Goro Takahashi on behalf of the archbishop of Tokyo, was published in 1895 (Matthew and Mark) and in 1897 (Luke and John).

any case, hindering any evangelical work. Thus, the Christian message was first preached by missionaries and laymen who were employed by public schools. Enterprising young people gathered about them to study secular subjects mixed with Christianity. The authorities' attitude was equivocal. They were never friendly, but they knew the diplomatic repercussions of mistreatment. Not infrequently local government officials would openly oppose Christian undertakings, though sometimes they were overruled by Tokyo. Work in the interior was made easier only from 1894, when the agreement reached with the foreign powers to revise the treaties prompted the authorities to apply leniency in issuing passports without waiting for the stipulated five year period to elapse.[82]

In the 1870s the people became disillusioned with what the Meiji Restoration had delivered. Farmers became impoverished as their sons were conscripted and their agricultural land taxed; a number of peasant riots ensued between 1871 and 1874. The samurai class lost the means of livelihood. Except for those from the winning side of the revolution, they had no station in society. It was against this background that Western knowledge entered Japan like a flood, among which was the idea that all men were created equal. In 1874, the proposal for a popularly elected parliament ignited a movement that would engulf the whole country. The *genrō* (the inner circle of elder statesmen from former Satsuma and Choshu domains) who effectively ran the government attempted in vain to suppress what came to be known as the Freedom and Popular Rights Movement. To appease the public, in 1881, the government promised to establish a parliament within ten years.[83]

The government then set out to build modern institutions, including legal codes and a constitution, in part to receive recognition as a civilized nation worthy of equality with the Western powers. From around 1883, the Meiji government embarked upon an aggressive policy of Westernization. Starting with the court circles, prominent persons began to wear Western clothes and to adopt the Western style of living; Western culture, in arts, drama, literature, and music, was readily adopted; and a whole new vocabulary was coming into the Japanese language. The word "freedom" was flooding the country, adopted as the names of consumer goods, public bath houses, and restaurants.[84] In 1885, 99,000 English-language books were imported into Japan; in 1886, the number increased to 204,000.[85]

The wave of Westernization was a great boost to the Protestant cause. Christian churches were crowded even with those who cared little for religion, and became a sort of fashionable place where the enlightened men and women would meet.[86] From 1882 to 1889 the adult membership in Protestant churches

---

82. Iglehart, *Protestant Christianity*, 48–49, 60, 91.
83. Toru Miyagawa and Kazuo Hijikata, *Jiyū Minken Shisō to Nihon no Roman Shugi* (Tokyo: Aoki Shoten, 1971), 14–15, 19, 35.
84. Miyagawa and Hijikata, *Jiyū Minken Shisō*, 106–9; Iglehart, *Protestant Christianity*, 67.
85. Sakurai, *Shūkyō Shisō Shi*, 237.
86. Anesaki, *Japanese Religion*, 356.

increased from a little over 4,000 to nearly 30,000.[87] From 1859 to 1873, only six Protestant denominations had come to Japan; from 1873 to 1879, nineteen additional ones arrived.[88] In 1882, there were nine Christian schools for men with 454 students and fifteen schools for women with 566 students. In 1888, there were fifteen men's schools with 2,709 students and thirty-nine women's schools with 3,663 students; because the government gave limited educational opportunities to women, Christian education was a significant part of women's education.[89] During the same year, nearly 7,000 people were baptized.[90]

The success of Protestantism in the 1880s was a self-sustaining process, led by Japanese Christian leaders. Most of the 1,000 or so Japanese who had become Protestants during the 1870s were highly educated intellectuals of the samurai class.[91] Many came from the domains that had backed the Tokugawa shogunate, and found their opportunities limited in the new society. By learning about the West from the foreigners they hoped to improve their station, and also to work out the spiritual resurrection of the nation.[92] Others had been influenced by great Christian teachers, such as William Smith Clark of the Massachusetts Agricultural College who came to Japan to set up the Sapporo Agricultural College. Some had studied abroad and returned to Japan by this time.

Christian intellectuals, through their writings, helped in the evangelization of Japan. In the early 1880s, they began to publish several influential national periodicals, such as the *Jogaku Zasshi*, *Kokumin no Tomo*, and *Rikugō Zasshi*.[93] The Christian cause was further helped by the freedom of burial granted by the government in 1884. Up to this time, the 1872 directive had stipulated that funerals could only be performed by Buddhist monks or Shinto priests.[94] During the 1880s, evangelical work spread among the agricultural population. Those who embraced Christianity were neither the large landlords closely connected with the religious order nor the peasants whose sustenance was dependent on the communities. Many Christian farmers became pioneers in introducing new crops and succeeded in cultivation of tea, dairy farming, and sericulture; some became agri-business owners, including in brewing and spinning.[95]

---

87. Ion, *American Missionaries*, 300.
88. Yamamoto, *Kirisuto Kyōkai*, 174.
89. Women constituted more than two-thirds of foreign missionaries during the Meiji period. Misako Kunihara and Rui Kohiyama, "Nihon Joshi Kirisutokyō Kyōikukai no Sōsetsu to Katsudō," *Kirisutokyō Gakkō Kyōiku Dōmei Hyakunenshi Kiyō* 7 (June 2009): 19–20.
90. Sakurai, *Shūkyō Shisō Shi*, 237.
91. In 1877, there were about 700 Protestants in Japan. Murakami, *Hyakunen no Shūkyō*, 62–63.
92. Howes, "Japanese Christians," 346–47; Anesaki, *Japanese Religion*, 337–38; Matsuzawa, "Kirisutokyō to Chishikijin," 288.
93. Ibid., 293; Kishimoto, *Meiji Bunka Shi*, 317.
94. Yamamoto, *Kirisuto Kyōkai*, 48, 398.
95. Eiichi Kudo, *Meijiki no Kirisutokyō* (Tokyo: Kyōbunkan, 1979), 45–49.

4.4.2. The Nationalist Reaction

Then, the pendulum swung back. The Westernization of the 1880s had awakened the sense of Japanese identity. Nationalistic undercurrents, which had sat dormant, gradually came to the surface and fought back the onslaught of Christianity.[96] Non-Christian and anti-Christian thoughts had also come to Japan: John Stuart Mill was followed by Charles Darwin and Herbert Spencer, causing the people to realize that not all civilization was Christian. A division appeared within the Christian movement itself, with the arrival of missionaries from progressive groups that held a relativistic and evolutionary view of religion: Wilfried Spinner of the General Evangelical Protestant Missionary Society in 1885; Arthur May Knapp of the American Unitarian Association in 1887; and George L. Perin of the Universalist General Convention in 1890.[97] As the Christian cause began to suffer, the number of adult baptisms, which in 1888 had been about 7,000, would decline to less than 3,000 annually toward the end of the 1890s.[98]

In 1888, the leading nationalist reactionaries at the Imperial University got together to publish what would become an influential periodical called *Nipponjin* (The Japanese). Buddhists, and also Shintoists, saw in this an opportunity to assert their positions and began to criticize Christianity as an enemy of the nation. Their attacks upon Christianity, partly making use of the newly borrowed ideological weapons from the West, were based more on political and social than religious reasons. Buddhists launched a movement to promote and protect Buddhism under the rubric of "revering the emperor and protecting the nation (*sonnō gokoku*)." The Great Alliance to Revere the Emperor and Serve the Buddha (*Sonnō Hōbutsu Daidōdan*), founded in 1889, was representative of this new Buddhist activity. The blow to Christianity was effective and many dubious converts renounced their faith.[99]

This marked the comeback on the national scene of Buddhism, which had been badly damaged by the anti-Buddhist movement of the 1870s. The persecution had transformed Japanese Buddhism into a supporter of the military and

---

96. Masao Maruyama argues that Japan had no indigenous ideology to serve as a synthesizer of imported ideas. As a result, a number of competing ideas coexisted peacefully in national consciousness even when they were mutually contradictory. At a time of crisis, however, the traditional ideologies would surface violently and attempt to expel the others. Masao Maruyama, *Nihon no Shisō* (Tokyo: Iwanami Shoten, 1961), 2–66, 145.

97. The General Evangelical Protestant Missionary Society represented the liberal Protestantism of Germany and Switzerland, which accepted higher criticism and took an accommodating view of non-Christian religions. The Unitarians disavowed any missionary activity and defined their aim only as fraternization with the non-Christian world; they received broad acceptance in Japan among the educated class, including Buddhist scholars. Norihisa Suzuki, *Meiji Shūkyō Shichō no Kenkyū* (Tokyo: Tōkyō Daigaku Shuppankai, 1979), 25–70.

98. Iglehart, *Protestant Christianity*, 91–93.

99. Kishimoto, *Meiji Bunka Shi*, 351; Anesaki, *Japanese Religion*, 360–61; Tamura, *Japanese Buddhism*, 162.

political policies of the Meiji state, by claiming that the *Dharma* was virtually coextensive with the law of the land.[100] When the Freedom and Popular Rights Movement was crushed, Buddhist thinkers abandoned the liberal cause and decided to align themselves with the nationalist forces and to offer their expertise in attacking Christianity.[101] The early 1880s already saw a proliferation of books written by Buddhist monks attacking Christianity, some based on Western philosophy and modern scientific evidence. The conclusion that many Christian doctrines contradicted scientific truth while Buddhism's truth was confirmed by science heartened Japanese Buddhists, who had been troubled by the cultural association of Christianity with modern civilization.[102]

The policy of Westernization formally ended with the promulgation in 1889 of the Constitution of the Empire of Japan. With it, the fluid period of nation building was over, and reversion to things Japanese began.[103] Christians welcomed the constitution wholeheartedly, as guaranteeing the freedom of religion, but little did they understand that the freedom was a qualified one. Article 28 stated: "Japanese subjects shall, within limits not prejudicial to peace and order, and not antagonistic to their duties as subjects, enjoy freedom of religious belief." As imperial subjects, they were to accept the fundamental premise of the constitution, namely: "The Empire of Japan shall be reigned over and governed by a line of Emperors unbroken for ages eternal" (Article 1); and "The Emperor is sacred and inviolable" (Article 3).[104] How to reconcile faith in God with acceptance of the divinity of the emperor would haunt Japanese Christians during the rest of the prewar period.

Nationalism erupted violently on the very day that the Meiji Constitution was promulgated. On 11 February 1889, Arinori Mori, the education minister and a widely recognized advocate of Westernization, was fatally wounded by a nationalist with Shinto leanings. Various nationalist organizations were formed in the early 1890s. Even Yukichi Fukuzawa, a leading proponent of Western learning and liberalism of the early Meiji era, joined the nationalist cause.[105]

---

100. A slogan that played a decisive role in Buddhist teachings was *shinzoku-nitai*, the Pure Land doctrine that religious truth can be divided into absolute and relative. *Jōdo Shinshū* identified the absolute truth with the Dharma, and the relative with civil law, so that *shinzoku-nitai* was understood as a call for an undivided obedience to established religious and political institutions. Davis, *Japanese Religion*, 158.

101. Tamura, *Japanese Buddhism*, 170.

102. For example, Enryo Inoue, a *Jōdo Shinshū* monk educated at the anti-Christian Imperial University, was the most prominent critic of Christianity during the 1880s. He applied Western philosophy to argue that Buddhism, but not Christianity, was more consistent with modern philosophy and that it could be employed to promote Japan's modernization; Buddhism's spiritualism was also more compatible with the theory of evolution. Yasumaru, "Kattō to Mosaku," 52–56; Hiromichi Serikawa, *Kindaika no Bukkyō Shisō* (Tokyo: Daitō Shuppansha, 1989), 34–66; Tamura, *Japanese Buddhism*, 162–63.

103. Miyagawa and Hijikata, *Jiyū Minken Shisō*, 111–12.

104. Kōdansha, *Japan: An Illustrated Encyclopedia* (Tokyo: Kōdansha, 1993), 233.

105. Kishimoto, *Meiji Bunka Shi*, 355–56; Sakurai, *Shūkyō Shisō Shi*, 250.

Advancing the cause was the Imperial Rescript on Education, which Emperor Meiji proclaimed on 30 October 1890, nearly coinciding with the effective date of the constitution on 29 November. Stipulating what the imperial subjects should believe, and thus defining the limits of the freedom guaranteed by the constitution, the 315-character text upheld Japan's unique national structure and exhorted all subjects to work courageously towards maintaining the prosperity of the imperial throne.[106] The Ministry of Education distributed a certified copy of the rescript to every school in Japan.

In July 1891, in connection with the Imperial Rescript on Education, the Ministry of Education issued an order requiring students to assemble on national holidays to read the rescript and to bow before the portrait of the emperor (and often the empress), commonly called *goshin-ei* but officially known as *oshashin* (lit. honorable photograph). The certified copy of the rescript and the portrait were to be housed in a secure building, and students were expected to bow as they walked past the building each morning and afternoon. They were expected to study and memorize the text of the rescript. In this manner, a form of emperor worship was to become a daily activity.[107] State Shinto was once again raising its ugly head.

---

106. The full text of the official English translation of the imperial rescript is as follows:

Know ye, Our subjects:

Our Imperial Ancestors have founded Our Empire on a basis broad and everlasting and have deeply and firmly implanted virtue; Our subjects ever united in loyalty and filial piety have from generation to generation illustrated the beauty thereof. This is the glory of the fundamental character of Our Empire, and herein also lies the source of Our education. Ye, Our subjects, be filial to your parents, affectionate to your brothers and sisters; as husbands and wives be harmonious, as friends true; bear yourselves in modesty and moderation; extend your benevolence to all; pursue learning and cultivate arts, and thereby develop intellectual faculties and perfect moral powers; furthermore advance public good and promote common interests; always respect the Constitution and observe the laws; should emergency arise, offer yourselves courageously to the State; and thus guard and maintain the prosperity of Our Imperial Throne coeval with heaven and earth. So shall ye not only be Our good and faithful subjects, but render illustrious the best traditions of your forefathers.

The Way here set forth is indeed the teaching bequeathed by Our Imperial Ancestors, to be observed alike by Their Descendants and the subjects, infallible for all ages and true in all places. It is Our wish to lay it to heart in all reverence, in common with you, Our subjects, that we may all thus attain to the same virtue.

Department of Education, *The Imperial Rescript on Education Translated into Chinese, English, French and German* (Tokyo: Department of Education, 1909).

107. The portraits were not given widely to private schools until the 1910s. Some Christian schools managed to wait until the 1930s to receive them. Hideo Sato, ed., *Kyōiku: Goshin-ei to Kyōiku Chokugo*, vol. 1 (Tokyo: Misuzu Shobō, 1994), 6–9, 16–20, 39–40; Sakurai, *Shūkyō Shisō Shi*, 259.

It did not take State Shinto very long to claim its first Christian victim. On 9 January 1891, just two months after the rescript was proclaimed, a special commemorative meeting was called at the prestigious First Higher School in Tokyo to celebrate the receipt of a certified copy. As requested, Kanzo Uchimura, a leading Christian thinker educated at the Sapporo Agricultural College and Amherst, went before the rescript but failed to bow deeply.[108] Uchimura's action was a target of immediate criticism at the school by the faculty and the students. As the incident was reported prominently in the press, there was an outburst of public outcry, leading eventually to Uchimura's resignation from the most prestigious of the national higher schools.[109]

The Uchimura scandal and other related incidents gave ammunition to the nationalist critics of Christianity. In January and February 1893, Imperial University professor Tetsujiro Inoue, among them, highlighted the fundamental inconsistency of Christianity with the foundational principle of nationalism in the Meiji Constitution. Christians and their advocates on their part defended Christianity, with Goro Takahashi providing the harshest rebuttal.[110] The public debate raged for some time, involving eminent scholars on both sides.[111] Whatever the outcome, it was evident that nationalism had defeated Christianity. Even Takahashi, while

---

108. Uchimura, in a letter dated 6 March 1891, told American friend D. C. Bell: "On the 9th of Jan. there was in the High Middle School where I taught, a ceremony to acknowledge the Imperial Precept [sic] on Education. After the address of the President and reading of the said Precept, the professors and students were asked to go up to the platform one by one, and bow to the Imperial signature affixed to the Precept, in the manner as we used to bow before our ancestral relics as prescribed in Buddhist and Shinto ceremonies. I was not at all prepared to meet such a strange ceremony, for the thing was the new invention of the president of the school. As I was the third in turn to go up and bow, I had scarcely time to think upon the matter. So, hesitating in doubt, I took a safer course for my Christian conscience, and in the august presence of sixty professors . . . and over one thousand students, I took my stand and did *not* bow! It was an awful moment for me, for I instantly apprehended the result of my conduct. The anti-Christian sentiment which was and still is strong in the school . . . found a just cause (as they suppose) for bringing forth against me accusations of insult against the nation and its Head, and through me against the Christians in general. . . . My personal affair gradually passed into the general question of the Relation of Christianity to the Nation and the Imperial Court." Sato, *Kyōiku*, 161–62.

109. Kishimoto, *Meiji Bunka Shi*, 354–55.

110. Takahashi attacked Inoue's every display of learning with his own display of masterful scholarship in Western and Oriental thought. He asked Inoue, for example, if Christianity was inconsistent with the imperial rescript, what about Buddhism? Was not Buddhism an otherworldly religion that advocates forsaking parental and filial duties? To claim that Christianity is anarchism was to confuse morality, religion, and politics. The series of articles Takahashi wrote from March to June 1893 were compiled as Goro Takahashi, *Hai Gitetsugaku Ron* (Tokyo: Minyūsha, 1893).

111. Masao Maruyama observes how primitive this debate was. It involved no substantive analysis of the logical, moral, and other merits of each position. Instead, it focused on whether a Japanese person could be a Christian. According to Maruyama, the debate had

attacking the criticism of Christianity, implicitly accepted the imperial rescript as an embodiment of ethical conduct for all Japanese. In the March 1893 issue of the *Kyōiku Jiron*, Uchimura, in defending his conduct, accepted the imperial rescript and argued that the emperor would be more pleased with obeisance in practice than obeisance in ceremony.[112] Christians too became nationalists.

Following the Uchimura Incident, the enrollment in Christian schools declined drastically. For example, the number of students at eight major Christian secondary schools declined from more than 2,000 in 1888 to around 1,000 in 1892, influenced also by the strengthening of public education.[113] Harassment of Christian students at public schools became more frequent. In 1892, the governor of Kumamoto Prefecture ordered a Christian school to dismiss a teacher who was reported in the press to have described the mission of the school as teaching cosmopolitanism (as opposed to nationalism). Elsewhere in the same prefecture, encouraged by the governor's anti-Christian stance, the principal of a school expelled a student for reading the Bible.[114] These incidents indicate how, in the 1890s, the Imperial Rescript on Education excited local educational and political officials to attack Christianity.

The Christian cause suffered another setback in August 1899, when the government issued an order prohibiting religious education and ceremonies in accredited schools.[115] With the strong urging of foreign missions, most Christian schools continued to offer religious education at the risk of being downgraded to non-regular schools, which carried the penalty that their students would not enjoy exemption from conscription and graduates eligibility for academic advancement. Doshisha and other established Christian academies chose to become secular institutions. Compulsory primary education could not be offered by non-accredited schools, so some Christian schools were forced to close.[116] To be sure, the religious education order was not targeted specifically at Christian schools, but at all religious schools. Its intent was to elevate the status of State Shinto, as embodied in the imperial rescript, by removing from the public domain of education any religious elements alien to it.[117]

---

not advanced from the late Edo period or even from the early seventeenth century. Masao Maruyama, *Nihon no Shisō* (Tokyo: Iwanami Shoten, 1961), 7.

112. Sato, *Kyōiku*, 165–69; Kishimoto, *Meiji Bunka Shi*, 356–59.

113. Akio Dohi, "Kindai Tennōsei to Kirisutokyō," in *Kindai Tennōsei no Keisei to Kirisutokyō*, ed. Tomisaka Kirisutokyō Sentā (Tokyo: Shinkyō Shuppansha, 1996), 289–90.

114. As this incident was reported by the press, it became a national issue, prompting national Christian leaders to take up the issue with the government. The student was eventually allowed to return to school. Dohi, "Kindai Tennōsei," 304–14.

115. Monbushō Kunrei, no. 12, 3 August 1899.

116. Kazuo Ishida, "Shūkyō Kyōiku Kinshi no Shirei nitsuite," *Seisen Joshi Daigaku Kiyō* 8 (1961): 41–43.

117. Religious schools were thus allowed to operate only within the parameters set by the imperial rescript. Ishida, "Shukyō Kyōiku Kinshi," 66–68.

4.5. The Penumbra of Hope and Hostility

4.5.1. Emerging Culture of Tolerance and Pluralism

As the twentieth century dawned, there was a ray of hope: industrialization was beginning to unleash liberalizing forces in thought and mores. The Sino–Japanese War of 1894–95 had already brought the first wave of industrialization, with large industrial plants popping up across the country. Military spending continued to increase even after the conclusion of the war, as Japan came into direct confrontation with Russian influence on the Asian continent. The industrial revolution was completed during the first decade of the twentieth century, expanding manufacturing in such industrial sectors as chemicals, cotton spinning, machinery, shipbuilding, and steel. As factories in the cities absorbed migrants from rural communities, the plight of workers became a social issue, and labor disputes frequent.[118] Socialism emerged through the mediation of Christianity, which offered universalistic perspectives on social justice.[119]

Economic and social changes were nurturing a culture of intellectual tolerance and pluralism. Moderation of the government's attitude toward Christian education was evident in the 1900s. In order to meet the industry's increasing demand for engineers and managers, the government became encouraging towards the efforts of Christian churches to provide secondary and higher education. The Ministry of Education was applying the 1899 ban on religious education more leniently, by exempting students of Christian schools from conscription and giving their graduates eligibility for academic advancement; it also allowed Christian schools to provide religious education in the dormitories.[120] A number of Christian academies established post-secondary divisions from 1903 to 1912.[121] The Roman Catholic Church appeared on the national scene when, responding to the request of a papal envoy, the government endorsed the idea of a Catholic university in Japan. Following preparatory work that began in 1906, Tokyo's Sophia University was established in 1913 as Japan's first Jesuit institution.[122]

---

118. Yujiro Nakamura, *Meiji Kokka no Aki to Shisō no Ketsujitsu* (Tokyo: Aoki Shoten, 1971), 19–26; Murakami, *Hyakunen no Shūkyō*, 72.

119. The headquarters of the first socialist movement in Japan was provided by the Unitarian Association in 1898. Nakamura, *Meiji Kokka no Aki*, 38–42; Iglehart, *Protestant Christianity*, 104–5. Later, Unitarianism emerged as a strong supporter of the labor movement and socialism. Universalist Choko Ikuta, a teacher at Narumi Eigo Jogakkō headed by Universalist preacher Shigetaro Akashi, would assist in the 1909 translation of the Book of Mormon into Japanese. Suzuki, *Meiji Shūkyō Shichō*, 62, 77. See Section 6.2 in Chapter 6.

120. See Ishida, "Shūkyō Kyōiku Kinshi," 46–47.

121. Haruki Onishi, "Kirisutokyō Daigaku Setsuritsu Undō to Kyōiku Dōmei," *Kirisutokyō Gakkō Kyōiku Dōmei Hyakunenshi Kiyō* 1 (June 2003), 38–39.

122. Yu Gao, "Kindai Nihon niokeru Kokka to Misshon Skūru," *Tokyo Daigaku Daigakuin Kyōikugaku Kiyō* 50 (2010), 35–43.

Monks, Nationalists, and the Emperor

Contributing to the broader acceptance of Christianity was its successful rebranding as a nationalistic religion. Just as the persecution of the 1870s had caused Buddhism to become nationalistic, Christianity was made nationalistic through the process of "Japanization" that followed the traumatic experience of the early 1890s. The Japanese Christian leaders tried to prove Christianity's usefulness by supporting the Sino–Japanese War, during which Protestant churches dispatched five chaplains to Manchuria, engaged in relief efforts, and provided assistance to the families of the war dead. This was repeated on a larger scale, a decade later, during the Russo–Japanese War.[123] Just as Buddhism had proved its usefulness by offering to defend the country from the ideological onslaught of Christianity, Christianity was now proving that its followers could be loyal subjects of the emperor. A more conformist form of Christianity was in the making as it sought acceptance and recognition.[124]

The national leadership of Protestantism in Japan was firmly in local hands. In an attempt to remove the stigma of dependence on the West, churches in the 1890s had sought to become self-sustaining by refusing to accept assistance from abroad. Tension inevitably arose between the local leaders and the foreign missionaries, who could only think of the Japanese as perennial children.[125] In reality, the missionaries from rural America were no match for the intellectual prowess of national Japanese leaders. It was they who guided the Christian cause through the difficult period of persecution. As Christians became involved in social causes, they received greater acceptance. The Salvation Army even received support from the imperial family and the national business community, as it championed the anti-prostitution movement and advocated the rights of the working class. The public gradually began to associate Christianity with works of mercy.[126]

This successful rebranding led to a resurgence of Christianity. The 1900s was a decade of active Christian proselytizing. The majority of the religious seekers came from students attending national universities and higher schools in urban areas. With the psychological impact of modernization and war, the young students became introspective and, in the process of soul searching and self-reflection, attracted to the Christian message. American missionaries, cognizant of this, began to establish Young Men's Christian Associations (YMCAs) adjacent to national schools, which had earlier been a bastion of anti-Christian thought. Some of those who were converted to Christianity at the turn of the twentieth century would later occupy positions of influence within the Japanese establishment and as financial supporters of the Christian cause.[127] But this was no longer the Christianity of the nineteenth century; it was a Christianity clothed in the robes of nationalism.

Buddhism was also changing. It was no longer the religion preoccupied with attacking Christianity. In 1899, an Association of Buddhist Puritans (*Bukkyō Seito*

---

123. Dohi, "Kindai Tennōsei," 319–30; Iglehart, *Protestant Christianity*, 101, 118–119.
124. Ibid., 133.
125. Ibid., 95–97.
126. Ibid., 106–7; Murakami, *Hyakunen no Shūkyō*, 77–79; Sakurai, *Shūkyō Shisō Shi*, 305–7.
127. Matsuzawa, "Kirisutokyō to Chishikijin," 311–14; Kudo, *Meijiki no Kirisutokyō*, 24–27.

Dōshikai) was established by a group of young Buddhists, who were critical of the corruption, formalism, and hypocrisy of the established Buddhist sects, especially of their complicity in allowing imperial state ideology to indoctrinate the public. The Buddhist reformers interacted actively with Christians on an equal footing and encouraged Christian contributions to their periodical *Shin Bukkyō* (New Buddhism). The group enjoyed an especially close relationship with the Japanese Unitarians.[128] Contributing to this ecumenical atmosphere was an earlier participation of Japanese Buddhist leaders in the World's Parliament of Religions held in Chicago in 1893.[129] Buddhists also joined the Christians in social causes.[130]

4.5.2. The Religious Climate at the Turn of the Twentieth Century

The key to understanding the prewar Mormon experience is to recognize the fundamental duality of Japan's religious and intellectual climate. On the one hand, the national campaign of indoctrination in State Shinto had begun, while the anti-Christian campaign of the nationalist–Buddhist alliance had successfully run its course. This exerted an increasingly binding influence on the public's conscience, and defined the outer parameters of what Mormonism could achieve. To be sure, nationalism per se did not pose the problem. It was the idea that being a Christian was somehow incompatible with the duties of an imperial subject. That such a view permeated Japanese society is evident from the following entry in the missionary journal of Alma O. Taylor about Japanese member Hachiro Mori:

> Yesterday a letter came from [Brother Mori]. He requested to have his name taken off the Church records. The reason for such a request is that . . . he has fallen into error on doctrine getting the strange thought that no one can be a Christian and still be loyal to Japan. This letter . . . came as a thunder bolt from a clear sky for all during the past year, Bro. Mori has written very fine spirited letters and paid his tithes regularly and honestly.[131]

On the other hand, there was a new societal tendency toward openness and pluralism, brought on by the liberalizing forces of industrialization and modernization. Coupled with Christianity's successful rebranding, this led to its wider social acceptance and a promotion of broader religious ecumenism. Although few had the intellectual and spiritual fortitude to embrace the Mormon message, along with all that it entailed, the missionaries had no lack of listeners or friends.

---

128. Tamura, *Japanese Buddhism*, 171; Yasumaru, "Minshū to Shūkyō," 342–43.
129. The Japanese Buddhist delegation included four representatives (one each from the *Jōdo Shinshū, Rinzai, Shingon,* and *Tendai* sects) and Zenshiro Noguchi as interpreter, joined in the United Stated by Kinzo Hirai. Hirai, who assisted the Mormon missionaries in securing the use of Kinkikan, a Buddhist lecture hall, would later introduce Noguchi as a potential reviewer of the draft Japanese translation of the Book of Mormon. Suzuki, *Meiji Shūkyō Shichō*, 218–19; see also Section 5.3 in Chapter 5 and Section 6.3 in Chapter 6.
130. Murakami, *Hyakunen no Shūkyō*, 72–74.
131. Alma O. Taylor, Journal, 5 January 1909, BYU Archives.

A large group of children gather at the farewell party for a departing missionary, Kofu, January 1910. Courtesy D. Clayton Fairbourn.

The first public meeting in Tokyo, arranged through the assistance of a Buddhist monk in April 1903, drew an audience of about 500 persons (see Section 5.3.3 in Chapter 5). Likewise, the first Sunday schools in Tokyo (November 1903), Sendai (August 1905), and Morioka (January 1908) had the attendance of 89, 58 and 26 persons, respectively; in 1910, the Christmas program in the relatively small city of Kofu was attended by over 1,200 persons. The official mission report for the year 1906 stated that 156 families had investigated the LDS Church during the year when there were only eleven missionaries.[132] Upon returning home in 1910, Alma O. Taylor remained upbeat, stating that the "work in Japan has been, is, and . . . will be fruitful," and that, given "the power and blessing and support of heaven" clearly manifested, it would be "almost an insult to our Father to think . . . that the missionaries in Japan are accomplishing nothing."[133]

The rise of nationalism has been noted by previous LDS authors as a challenge the Mormon cause faced in prewar Japan. Gordon B. Hinckley, for example, explained that Japan, having defeated China and Russia, "was caught up in a wave of ultra-nationalism [which] found expression in feelings against the West and a return to ancestral religions."[134] Such a view is only partially correct. The rise of nationalism was a reaction to the influx of foreign ideas, and the shackle was a new state-sponsored ideology centered on the emperor, not ancestral religions. More importantly, the restricting forces of nationalism were

---

132. Jenson, "History of the Japan Mission."
133. Alma O. Taylor, "Japan, the Ideal Mission Field," *Improvement Era* 13 (1910): 781, 783.
134. Hinckley, "The Church in the Orient," 169.

counterbalanced by the liberalizing forces of industrialization and modernization. This duality solves the apparent contradiction between the scanty fruits the LDS Church claimed (albeit with scanty evangelical efforts) and the general acceptance of the missionaries by the public. The balance between the two was delicate and would evolve over the period of the Japan Mission's existence.

4.6. Conclusion

From a religious and intellectual standpoint, the Mormons appear to have arrived in Japan at the worst possible moment. Christianity had flourished, but its fortunes were now in decline. State Shinto had been established, with the Imperial Rescript on Education serving as the tool of national indoctrination. The nationalist–Buddhist alliance was in ascendancy, having succeeded in portraying Christianity as unpatriotic and incompatible with the national structure. Buddhism, which had earlier been discredited as a corrupt religion, was proving its usefulness to the country's spiritual aspirations. Handicapped also by lack of preparation in language and culture, the Mormon missionaries faced the challenge posed by the hostility of the soil.

From a legal standpoint, the missionaries could not have come much earlier. The Meiji Constitution had come into force only in 1890, guaranteeing religious freedom. Likewise, the revised treaties with the Western powers established only in 1899 the right of foreign nationals to move freely in the interior. Though the government had unilaterally lifted most travel restrictions in the mid-1890s when the treaties were signed, it would have been difficult for Mormon missionaries to proselytize outside the foreign settlements had they come much earlier. The timing was thus virtually forced upon them if an evangelization of Japan was to be attempted during the prewar period, unless they were willing to expend resources to build schools.

The Mormon cause was not doomed to failure, however. The liberalizing forces of industrialization and modernization were beginning to counter the suffocating grip of State Shinto. Nationalistic currents remained alive in the national consciousness, but there was a tendency toward intellectual tolerance and pluralism. Though the religious and intellectual climate defined the broad contour of what the Mormons could achieve, the Mormon missionaries could find a niche for their message in the cacophony of competing ideas. The balance between the restraining forces of state indoctrination and the tendency towards religious tolerance and intellectual pluralism was a delicate one. As will be observed in the following chapters, the balance would evolve over the period of the Japan Mission's existence, in responding to political and social developments, and as the national program of indoctrination progressed. This duality defined the religious and intellectual climate of Japan in which the Mormons were about to launch missionary work.

Chapter 5

Planting the Apple Tree: People, Places, and Publications, 1901–24

5.1. Introduction

This chapter outlines the achievements of the Japan Mission of the Church of Jesus Christ of Latter-day Saints,[1] from its opening in 1901 to its suspension in 1924. The chapter, after discussing early decisions and events, focuses on three dimensions of Mormon missionary work: (1) people, including collaborators, friends, investigators, and converts; (2) geographical areas where work was carried out; and (3) Japanese-language books and tracts produced to disseminate the Mormon message. Among other things, the chapter reviews the notable individuals the missionaries befriended (including their place in Japanese history), offers an analysis of the type of people they attracted, attempts to explain why and how certain areas were selected for proselytizing work, and discusses how uniquely Mormon terms were translated from English to the Japanese language.

The LDS Japan Mission was presided over by eight men: Heber J. Grant (August 1901–September 1903); Horace S. Ensign (September 1903–July 1905); Alma O. Taylor (July 1905–January 1910); Elbert D. Thomas (January 1910–October 1912); Heber Grant Ivins (October 1912–March 1915); Joseph H. Stimpson (March 1915–February 1921); Lloyd O. Ivie (February 1921–January 1924); and Hilton A. Robertson (January–August 1924). Except for Grant, who was forty-six years old when he first arrived in Japan, the rest were relatively young men. Three of them were in their twenties and four of them in their early thirties when they served as mission president. Except for Taylor and Ivins, they were married men and accompanied by their wives during at least part of their service in Japan.

---

1. The formal name of the Mormon mission established in Japan in 1901 was the Japan Mission, although it was frequently referred to as the Japanese Mission. The missions established later in Hawaii (in 1937) and in postwar Japan (in 1948) were both officially called the Japanese Mission.

Over the twenty-three-year existence of the mission, eighty-eight missionaries converted 174 Japanese men and women to Mormonism.[2] While it would be of interest to explore the personal experiences, religious or otherwise, of these missionaries and converts, this is not the approach we take in this chapter. Rather, we take an explicitly "macro" approach, focusing on the tangible achievements of the mission collectively, in the three areas noted above. What is arguably the most notable achievement of the mission, the 1909 publication of a Japanese translation of the Book of Mormon, will receive only cursory coverage in the chapter, as it is the dedicated topic of a separate chapter (see Chapter 6). A detailed analysis of how and why the mission was closed is also presented in a separate chapter (see Chapter 7).

5.2. Early Decisions and Events

On 12 August 1901, Heber J. Grant and three associates, Horace S. Ensign, Louis A. Kelsch, and Alma O. Taylor, arrived in Japan to open the first permanent Mormon mission in Asia. They sojourned in Yokohama's foreign settlement for nearly two months; on 1 September, Grant dedicated the land of Japan for the preaching of the gospel. It was then formally decided, on 30 September 1901, that they should relocate to Tokyo, the capital of Japan, just twenty-five miles north. With arrangements at the Metropole Hotel having been made (for ¥80 per month per person), on 18 October 1901, the four elders moved to the Tsukiji district of Tokyo. Tsukiji had been Tokyo's foreign settlement (Tokyo, along with Osaka, had been one of the two "open cities"), but few foreign merchants had actually lived there. Instead, Tsukiji had become a center of Christian activity (as had Osaka's Kawaguchi district).[3] The Metropole Hotel, the former residence of a United States minister to Japan, had opened for business in 1890.[4]

The wisdom of moving to Tokyo had been debated among the Mormon missionaries for some time. Taylor's journal entry of 28 August gives as benefits of moving to Tokyo "fewer foreigners, a higher class of natives, a more religious sentiment, and by far better instructors in the language and much cheaper living."[5] Their intention was to study the language for about a year while observing the

---

2. This number includes five member children who were baptized at the age of eight or (in one instance) nine. See Annex 7 for a list of all prewar Mormon missionaries sent to Japan, and Annex 8 for a list of all prewar Mormon converts in Japan.

3. The area of the former Tsukiji foreign settlement changed its name to Akashi-cho, and is now part of the Chuo ward of Tokyo. St. Luke's International Hospital stands nearby. Tōkyō-to Chūō Kuyakusho, ed., *Chūō-ku Shi* (Tokyo: Tōkyō-to Chūō Kuyakusho, 1958), 107–11, 124.

4. In January 1907, the Metropole Hotel merged with the Imperial Hotel to become its Tsukiji branch. Teikoku Hoteru, *Teikoku Hoteru Hyakunenshi* (Tokyo: Teikoku Hoteru, 1990), 132–34.

5. Alma O. Taylor, Journal, 28 August 1901, BYU Archives.

conditions to see if it would be appropriate to send for their wives (in the case of three married men) and to request more missionaries.[6] In Yokohama, the elders did find a Japanese teacher, whom they called "a laborer," but one wonders how a laborer could be a Japanese language teacher. It is possible that, in Yokohama with a sizable foreign population, many whose work catered toward foreigners had some command of English regardless of their occupation. Clearly the missionaries thought what they could find in Yokohama inadequate. Finding it nearly impossible to find a suitable house in Tokyo, they decided to live in a hotel as the only practical option. Grant and Kelsch remained in Tsukiji (except for a temporary relocation to the "Central Hotel"),[7] while on 5 December 1901 Ensign and Taylor moved into a Japanese hotel or boarding house in the Surugadai area of Kanda (for ¥40 per month per person).[8]

During the early months the Mormon missionaries benefited from the publicity they had received in the press (see Chapter 3). The curiosity the press had aroused led a number of people, including some prominent ones, to visit them. Among their early visitors was Hajime Nakazawa, a professed Shinto priest, who would become one of the first two converts the missionaries made within a few short months. On 8 March 1902, on the shore of Omori in Tokyo Bay, Nakazawa was baptized, confirmed, and ordained an elder. This event was symbolic indeed. Nakazawa was presumably affiliated with a religious sect whose roots went back to the ancient indigenous religion of Japan,[9] and the name *Hajime* signifies "beginning" or "first." Two days later, on 10 March 1902, Saburo Kikuchi was likewise baptized, confirmed, and ordained an elder. Kikuchi was a Christian preacher who was holding street meetings in Ueno Park and other locations.[10] The timing of these baptisms was in part dictated by the impending departure of Grant for the United States, ostensibly to attend the April 1902 general conference and to bring additional missionaries, along with his wife and daughter, from Utah.

---

6. Ronald W. Walker, "Strangers in a Stranger Land: Heber J. Grant and the Opening of the Japanese Mission," *Journal of Mormon History* 13 (1986–87): 25.

7. The Central Hotel must refer to the Chūōkan, which was located at 20 Gorobeicho. Tōkyō-shi, ed., *Tōkyō Annai*, vol. 1 (Tokyo: Shōkabō, 1907), 259. This is now part of or in the vicinity of the Yaesuguchi section of Tokyo's central railroad station.

8. Andrew Jenson, comp., "History of the Japan Mission," 1934, Japan Mission, "Historical Records and Minutes," LDS Church Archives. Taylor, Journal, 9 October 1906. Taylor's journal indicates that he spent at least part of his stay in Kanda at the Kirinkan, which was located at 9 Fukurocho. Tōkyō-shi, *Tōkyō Annai*, 257. It is just south of the current Ochanomizu station on the Japan Railway Chuo Line.

9. Judging from the circumstances surrounding his contact with the LDS Church, it does not seem appropriate to consider him a ceremonial priest of a Shinto shrine. More likely, he held a pastoral office in a religious organization based in part on Shinto principles. In Japanese religious terminology, such Shinto offshoot groups are collectively called Sect Shinto (of which there were thirteen sects during the Meiji period), as opposed to Shrine Shinto.

10. It appears that after his conversion to Mormonism he started supporting himself by selling medicine. He never became an active participant in Mormon activities.

Despite these two early baptisms, the Mormon missionaries arrived in Japan ill prepared. The first years were especially challenging. Unlike the experience of Mormon missionaries in the British Isles in the nineteenth century, they experienced no mass conversion of local people.[11] As will be shown below in the choice of geographical areas for missionary work (see Section 5.4), many decisions appeared haphazard. Taylor, writing in 1936, remembered Grant once telling him in Japan that "he never once felt sure . . . that any given decision or plan was right," and noted that the missionaries "were left to the painful course of proof by trial."[12] Grant was discouraged after two years, feeling that he "was not accomplishing anything." He then "went out into the woods and got down on [his] knees, and told the Lord that whenever He was through with [him in Japan] . . . [he] would be very glad and thankful if He would call [him] home and send [him] to Europe to preside over the European missions." A few days after that a cable arrived: "Come home on the first boat."[13] On 8 September 1903, he left Yokohama, with wife Augusta and daughter Mary, for San Francisco. After spending four months at home, he left to preside over the European Mission from 1 January 1904 to 5 December 1906.

While Grant was an accomplished businessman and an apostle who saw himself as equal to the best in Japan, he had no previous experience with missionary work. This appeared to be a source of tension with the younger missionaries, who were eager to go out among the people to learn their language and customs in the long-established Mormon tradition. In the middle of November 1901, Grant finally yielded as Ensign and Taylor became increasingly restive and even demanding.[14] But it was only after the response to an inquiry was received from the First Presidency (encouraging them to work among the people) that, in December 1901, Ensign and Taylor finally moved out of their Western surroundings into Japanese life.

With the benefit of hindsight, Taylor accepted in 1936 that lack of prior missionary experience had in fact uniquely qualified Grant, as the Japan Mission "needed a man unhampered by the precedents and prejudices of remote experience." As a result, the way Grant first organized work was different from "what first missionaries had done and current missionaries were doing in other lands," in that he used

---

11. The first seven Mormon missionaries arrived in the British Isles in July 1837. More than 1,500 converts were made within two years; there were 8,245 Mormons by June 1842. Daniel H. Ludlow, ed., *Encyclopedia of Mormonism* (New York: Macmillan, 1992): "British Isles, the Church in."

12. Alma O. Taylor, "Memories of Far-off Japan: President Grant's First Foreign Mission 1901 to 1903," *Improvement Era* 39 (1936): 691.

13. Heber J. Grant, "Greetings across the Sea," *Improvement Era* 40 (1937): 405. In early May, Grant had written a letter to Anthon H. Lund, a newly called counselor in the First Presidency, hinting of his availability to succeed Francis M. Lyman as head of the European Mission. Walker, "Strangers," 35–36.

14. Ibid., 28.

"the best hostelries" as his early headquarters. "This gave harmonious background to his towering personality and impressive address. . . . He and his companion did not realize it at the time, but this . . . policy discredited those who had glibly prophesied that the 'Mormon' Elders would promptly become mendicant priests among the lower classes. Their fine quarters and gentlemanly position made it compatible for the editors of the leading newspapers and magazines to come clamoring for interviews with the 'Mormon' Apostle." Taylor "who stayed on in Japan longer after President Grant came home, discovered through the years so many benefits of President Grant's policies and activities in the early months of the mission."[15]

5.3. Early Friends and Converts

The Mormon missionaries found friends and collaborators among the people who responded to the publicity about Mormonism, and sought out the best talent to help their work. The early fruits of this effort were found among Japanese Christians and young students. Among the converts, men outnumbered women by two to one throughout the period, reflecting their higher level of education and greater social participation in prewar Japan. Additional persons of prominence the Mormon missionaries befriended are discussed in Appendix 5.1.

5.3.1. Tatsutaro Hiroi (1875–1952)

Tatsutaro Hiroi was the Mormon missionaries' Japanese language teacher and also acted as the LDS Church's first translator in Japan.[16] Not yet a prominent man when the missionaries met him, Hiroi was well-connected in Japan's intellectual circles and would claim some prominence as a professor of English and comparative religion at Toyo University. Hiroi is now known in Japan as the father of the animal welfare movement, particularly credited for being instrumental in the founding in 1902 of the Society for the Prevention of Cruelty to Animals (*Dōbutsu Gyakutai Bōshi Kai*).[17]

Hiroi's association with the Mormons lasted a long time. In late 1903, the missionaries went to "the Law School at Kanda to speak before the English Society," of which Hiroi was the president. In late 1909, Mormon missionaries went to a lecture on Mormonism held at a Unitarian hall and met Hiroi after

---

15. Taylor, "Memories of Far-off Japan," 690–91.
16. Much of the biographical information on Hiroi in this section comes from Shinichi Yoshinaga, comp., "Kindai Nihon ni okeru Chishikijin Shūkyō Undō no Gensetsu Kūkan" (Maizuru, Kyoto: Maizuru Kōtō Senmon Gakkō, 2012), 371–72.
17. In 1899 he contributed articles advocating animal welfare to two of the leading national magazines *Taiyō* and *Chūō Kōron*. Tatsutaro Hiroi, "Dare ka Gyūba no tame ni Namida wo Sosogu mono zo," *Taiyō* 5 (1899): no. 17, 174–76 and no. 18, 171–75; Tatsutaro Hiroi, "Dōbutsu Hogo Ron," *Chūō Kōron* 14 (December 1899): 7–14.

the meeting.[18] In 1919, he visited Grant during a visit to the United States. In November 1949, he wrote a postcard to Murray Nichols, then a full-time missionary in Osaka, about this meeting:

> I am 75 but healthy and ambitious still. When I was in Washington, D.C. in 1919... President Grant called at my hotel twice. He was a guest of Senator Smoot of Utah. He was a splendid gentleman, estimated me more than I was worth.[19]

Hiroi then commented on his friendship with Mormon servicemen and urged Nichols to fill the vacuum created by the war with "your gospel."

Tatsutaro Hiroi was born in Yanagawa, Fukuoka Prefecture. He studied at a Methodist academy and was baptized as a Christian in 1892. As he came to question the divinity of Christ, he transferred to the German Protestant Seminary (*Doitsu Shinkyō Shingakkō*) of the Evangelical Church (*Fukyū Fukuin Kyōkai*). Founded by the German Evangelical Protestant Mission in 1885, the church introduced higher criticism to Japan; it recognized the Bible not as the word of God but as a religious record of men. Upon graduation in 1897, Hiroi became an ordained minister in the church. In 1899, however, he criticized the Evangelical Church for racial prejudice, resigned from the ministry, and left Tokyo for Fukui Prefecture to teach school.[20] Through his involvement in the animal rights movement, he became acquainted with prominent liberal Christians and "New Buddhists" who associated themselves with the Unitarian Association. Undoubtedly, it was through this connection that, in 1903, he obtained a teaching position in English and comparative religion at Tetsugakukan, a Buddhist academy (renamed as Toyo University in 1906). He also held teaching positions at other schools.

Hiroi's desire to help the Mormons may have come out of his increasing affinity with the Unitarian Association, which he would formally join in 1904.[21] The Unitarians in Japan, consisting of liberal Christians and progressive Buddhists, espoused ecumenicalism and met to discuss religion in a socializing setting; the Unitarian Association was more like a club for intellectuals than a church. It is also possible that, given his interest in promoting the animal welfare movement, he considered being a secondary school teacher in Fukui as inconvenient. Work as a Japanese teacher for the newly arrived Mormon missionaries was a way to relocate to Tokyo.[22] Hiroi visited the Mormon missionaries at least twice in late

---

18. Taylor, Journal, 13 December 1903; 7 November 1909.

19. As quoted in Murray L. Nichols, "History of the Japan Mission of the Church of Jesus Christ of Latter-day Saints, 1901–1924" (MA thesis, Brigham Young University, 1957), 18; Alma O. Taylor, letter to Heber J. Grant, 27 January 1920, LDS Church Archives. Nichols does not recall how Hiroi learned of his address. Murray L. Nichols, letter to author, 18 January 1996.

20. Tetsuji Iseda, "Meijiki Dōbutsu Aigo Undō no Dōkizuke wa Ikanaru Mono de atta ka," *Shakai to Rinri* 20 (2006): 142.

21. How he was converted to Unitarianism is explained in Tatsutaro Hiroi, "Nyūkai no Ji," *Rikugō Zasshi* 284 (1904): 120–31.

22. Iseda, "Meijiki Dōbutsu Aigo Undō," 139–53.

August 1901 while they were still in Yokohama. Taylor called him "undoubtedly a well educated man" who spoke English well and a school teacher in "a little town in the southern [sic] part of the country."²³

Whatever the reason, in mid-September, Hiroi agreed to become a language teacher. When Grant returned from his week-long trip in the interior, a letter from Hiroi was waiting for him, expressing his interest in working as a Japanese language teacher and a translator. Grant noted in his diary for 16–17 September:

> We all prayed very earnestly for the Lord to send us some man who could aid us in our work. When I got home and found that Mr. Hiroi was willing to come I felt that he was just the man.²⁴

On 4 October 1901, Grant wrote to Hiroi at Fukui Secondary School:

> You may rest assured that we will employ you for at least four or five months. If we wish to employ you for a longer period we will notify you, and if not, we will give you the sixty days requested in which to look for another position.²⁵

His teaching obligations kept him from relocating to Tokyo until mid-November 1901,²⁶ so in the meantime he introduced Rev. Aoki, his former associate in the German Evangelical Protestant ministry, to serve as an interim teacher.²⁷ Hiroi came to teach the language to the Mormon missionaries nearly every day from mid-November to mid-May 1902.

His association with the Mormons did not change his religious views. In the January 1903 issue of the *Rikugō Zasshi,* Hiroi discussed the divinity of Christ and the nature of God from a progressive Christian perspective and referred to the Mormon belief in a personal God as bigotry.²⁸ Hiroi remained on the faculty of Toyo University until his retirement in 1945. From 1899 to 1912, he contributed thirty-two articles to the *Rikugō Zasshi,* a Unitarian magazine, on such topics as Christianity, protection of animals, socialism, and religion in general. In 1917, his treatise on the history and doctrines of Christianity was included in a major volume on three major religions, Buddhism, Christianity, and Shinto, compiled by a Buddhist scholar.²⁹ In 1920, in a letter addressed to Grant, Taylor

---

23. Taylor, Journal, 25 August 1901; 28 August 1901.
24. Heber J. Grant, "A Japanese Journal," not dated, Americana Collection, Harold B. Lee Library, Brigham Young University.
25. Heber J. Grant, letter to Tatsutaro Hirai, 4 October 1901, Japan Mission, "Letterpress Copybooks, 1901–1923," LDS Church Archives.
26. Taylor, Journal, 30 October 1901; 16 November 1901.
27. Taylor, Journal, 30 October 1901.
28. Tatsutaro Hiroi, "Shingaku jō no Miketsu Mondai," *Rikugō Zasshi* 265 (1903): 17–29.
29. Tatsutaro Hiroi, "Kirisutokyō Kōyō," in *San Dai Shūkyō,* ed. Beiho Takashima (Tokyo: Heigo Shuppansha, 1917), part 2: 1–58. The piece on Buddhism was written by Mokurai Shimaji, a *Jōdo Shinshū* priest who was one of the foremost leaders of Meiji Buddhism.

called Hiroi "a grafter . . . [but] bright in the use of English," to which Grant replied: "I agree with your opinion of Hiroi."[30]

5.3.2. Goro Takahashi (1856–1935)

Goro Takahashi, perhaps one of the greatest minds of prewar Japan, was a language and religious scholar,[31] who in December 1901 published an article in the *Taiyō*, a leading national magazine, entitled "Morumonkyō to Ramakyō (Mormonism and Lamaism)," to defend Mormonism (see Section 3.10 in Chapter 3).[32] The Mormon missionaries learned of the article when it was translated into Japanese by their teacher and interpreter Tatsutaro Hiroi. On this occasion, Taylor described Takahashi as "the man who fought strongly for the Christians some years ago and who is looked upon as one of the strongest minds in the kingdom." Upon receiving an invitation from Grant, Takahashi came to see the missionaries at the Metropole Hotel on 11 December 1901. Two days later, a letter was received from him, proposing to write a book in defense of Mormonism, which would be entitled *Morumonkyō to Morumonkyōto* (Mormonism and Mormons) and published in late August or early September 1902. This was not the first time Takahashi offered to help the missionaries. Takahashi had earlier written to them while they were still in Yokohama, inquiring whether they needed any literature translated into Japanese and offering his services.[33]

Goro Takahashi was born in 1856 in Echigo (present-day Niigata Prefecture) into the family of a village official. In 1868, Takahashi left home to pursue education in Buddhist theology, Chinese classics, and National Learning. He moved to Tokyo to pursue Western studies, became a student of Dutch Reformed missionary Samuel Robbins Brown, and mastered the English, German, and French languages. When the joint Protestant translation of the Bible began in 1874, Takahashi participated in the efforts as assistant to Brown. It was during this time that Takahashi developed additional proficiency in Greek, Latin, and Hebrew. This was not to be his last work of translating the Bible. Befriended by Catholic missionary Michel Steichen, Takahashi helped him translate the four Gospels

---

30. Taylor, letter to Grant; and Heber J. Grant, letter to Alma O. Taylor, 14 March 1920. LDS Church Archives.

31. Much of the biographical information on Takahashi in this section comes from Shōwa Joshi Daigaku Kindai Bungaku Kenkyū Shitsu, *Kindai Bungaku Kenkyū Sōsho*, vol. 39 (Tokyo: Shōwa Joshi Daigaku Kindai Bungaku Kenkyū Shitsu, 1975), 247–315; Susumu Odagiri, ed., *Nihon Kindai Bungaku Daijiten*, vol. 2 (Tokyo: Kōdansha, 1977), 279–80.

32. Goro Takahashi, "Morumonkyō to Ramakyō," *Taiyō* 7 (October 1901): 21–25.

33. Taylor, Journal, 11 December 1901.

into Japanese from the Vulgate, which were published in two volumes in 1895 (Matthew and Mark) and 1897 (Luke and John).[34]

Following the Uchimura Incident (see Section 4.4.2 in Chapter 4), when Imperial University professor Tetsujiro Inoue published his scathing criticism of Christianity "Kyōiku to Shūkyō to no Shōtotsu" (Conflict between Education and Religion) in 1893 from the standpoint of nationalism, Takahashi attacked Inoue's logic and character by publishing "Nise Tetsugakusha no Daibenron" (Pompous Argument of a False Philosopher) in an issue of the *Kokumin no Tomo*. Takahashi provided the harshest rebuttal of the nationalist attack on Christianity during the national debate that ensued. Takahashi attacked Inoue's every display of learning with his own display of masterful scholarship in Western and Oriental thought. He asked Inoue, for example, if Christianity was inconsistent with the imperial rescript, what about Buddhism? Was not Buddhist an otherworldly religion that advocates forsaking parental and filial duties? To claim that Christianity is anarchism was to confuse morality, religion, and politics. The series of articles Takahashi wrote from March to June 1893 were compiled as a book.[35]

Takahashi was a prolific writer of religious, philosophical, and literary topics, authoring over 600 books and articles during his lifetime. His first books were *Shintō Shinron* (New Theory of Shinto) and *Bukkyō Shinron* (New Theory of Buddhism), both published in 1880. When the Christian monthly *Rikugō Zasshi* (the Cosmos) was inaugurated in 1880, Takahashi became a frequent and regular contributor.[36] He shifted his writings primarily to the national magazine *Kokumin no Tomo*, when it started in 1887, and contributed articles on literature and philosophy. He taught languages and literature at a number of secondary and tertiary schools throughout his life. He devoted his later years to translating Western classics, while teaching English literature at Komazawa University. His many translations include Lord Byron's *Childe Harold's Pilgrimage* (1898), Johann Wolfgang von Goethe's *Faust* (the first part only, 1904), and Plutarch's *Parallel Lives* (four volumes, 1914 and 1915), as well as various writings of Francis Bacon, Thomas Carlyle, Ralph Waldo Emerson, Michel de Montaigne, and Lucius Seneca.

Takahashi has frequently been referred to as a Christian writer, but this appellation should be carefully considered. He was baptized as a Christian while he

---

34. Goro Takahashi, trans., *Sei Fukuinsho, Jō* (Tokyo: Tenshu Kōkyōkai, 1895); Goro Takahashi, trans., *Sei Fukuinsho, Ge* (Tokyo: Tenshu Kōkyōkai, 1897).

35. Goro Takahashi, *Hai Gitetsugaku Ron* (Tokyo: Minyūsha, 1893).

36. Takahashi contributed eighty-nine articles to the *Rikugō Zasshi* between 1880 and 1899. The *Rikugō Zasshi* (1880–1921), though a Christian magazine, exerted strong intellectual influence on Japanese society. From around 1890, the magazine was edited by a group of Unitarians (it absorbed the Unitarian periodical *Shūkyō* in 1898). Norihisa Suzuki, "Kaisetsu," *Fukkokuban Rikugō Zasshi*, vol. 12 (Tokyo: Fuji Shuppan, 1988), 9–12.

was studying English with Brown.[37] He frequently wrote articles for a Christian magazine. As noted, during the trial decade of the 1890s for Christianity, Takahashi defended the Christian cause against the onslaught of criticism from Buddhists and nationalists. Certainly, he held a strong interest in Christianity, but it is probably safe to say that he was habitually interested in all religions. His later years were devoted to a study of spiritualism. He frequently wrote on non-Christian religious topics and at the end of his life started translating the Quran into Japanese, but was not able to complete before he died. Soon after he finished writing the promised book on Mormonism, he began writing a book on three holy men—Confucius, Gotama Buddha, and Jesus Christ, which was published in 1903.[38] So his commitment to Christianity was equivocal.

Takahashi became a frequent visitor, making a weekly visit typically on Sundays, and developing close friendship with the Mormon missionaries. To assist Takahashi in the preparation of the book, Grant provided him with Mormon sources of information, including: *Autobiography* by Parley P. Pratt; *The Bible and Polygamy* by Orson Pratt; *History of Joseph Smith by His Mother* by Lucy Mack Smith; *Key to the Science of Theology* by Parley P. Pratt; *Missouri Persecution* by B. H. Roberts; *My Reasons for Leaving the Church of England and Joining the Church of Jesus Christ of Latter-day Saints* by Robert Moseley Bryce Thomas; *A New Witness for God* by B. H. Roberts; and *Voice of Warning* by Parley P. Pratt. It is evident from the book he published, *Morumonkyō to Morumonkyōto*, that Takahashi had read at least a significant portion of the Book of Mormon. Grant advanced Takahashi about ¥400 ($200) for a hundred copies of the proposed book. Takahashi's relationship with the Mormons suffered in December 1903 when he learned that the first convert Hajime Nakazawa, caught in an act of theft at the mission home, had been excommunicated.[39] Takahashi wrote the missionaries a letter accusing them of lack of charity toward someone who had lost his job in the Shinto priesthood as a result of becoming a Mormon.

5.3.3. Kinzo Hirai (1859–1916)

Kinzo Hirai was a language scholar and an ordained Zen priest, who helped with translating early Mormon tracts into Japanese.[40] He was also helpful in assisting the Mormon missionaries during the translation of the Book of

---

37. Nihon Kirisuto Kyōdan Shuppan Kyoku, *Kirisutokyō Jinmei Jiten* (Tokyo: Nihon Kirisuto Kyōdan Shuppan Kyoku, 1986), 844.
38. Goro Takahashi, *Sekai Sansei Ron* (Tokyo: Maekawa Bun-ei-kaku, 1903).
39. This incident was reported in the 19 December 1903 issue of the *Tokyo Nichinichi Shinbun*, 5.
40. Much of the biographical information on Hirai in this section comes from Shinichi Yoshinaga, comp., "Hirai Kinzo ni okeru Meiji Bukkyō no Kokusaika ni kansuru Shūkyōshi-Bunkashi-teki Kenkyū" (Maizuru, Kyoto: Maizuru Kōtō Senmon Gakkō, 2007), 7–26.

Mormon.⁴¹ The first critic of Taylor's draft translation of the Book of Mormon was his younger brother, Hirogoro Hirai. In April 1903, when the Japan Mission was about to send missionaries to the interior of the country, the missionaries wanted to mark the event by holding a large public meeting in Tokyo, in part to "remind the public that the 'Mormons' were still in Japan."⁴² The YMCA initially agreed to allow the Mormons to use its hall but withdrew the offer the next day.⁴³ The missionaries, then, turned to Hirai for help:

> Through the assistance of Mr. Hirai we were able to procure the hall known as the "Kinkikwan" located in the Nishikimachi district of Kanda for the purpose of holding a meeting there on the night of the 18th.⁴⁴

Grant reported that about 500 persons were present and sat on the floor listening to Frederick A. Caine and Taylor speak in Japanese and Ensign and Grant in English for over two hours.⁴⁵ Copies of an English tract prepared for this occasion (of which Taylor's speech was a translation) were distributed after the meeting;⁴⁶ five thousand copies of the Japanese translation were delivered to the mission home on 14 May 1903.

Kinzo Hirai was born in Kyoto in 1859. He pursued his early studies at German and English language schools. Outraged by the way he saw foreigners treating Japanese people, he became a nationalist and an advocate of Buddhism and, from 1877, made his name as an eloquent critic of Christianity. In 1885, he established a private academy called Oriental Hall in Kyoto; this was meant to be the Buddhist counterpart to Christianity's *Dōshisha*, also located in Kyoto. In 1889, he was ordained a priest in the *Rinzai* Zen School of Buddhism. In 1892, he left for the United States to preach Buddhism and, in the following year, joined the Japanese Buddhist delegation attending the World's Parliament of Religions, held in Chicago in connection with the Columbian Exposition,

---

41. Taylor spelled Hirai's given name Kinza, as did Hirai himself. This follows the historical convention of using phonetic Japanese letters on the basis of how words were presumably pronounced during the Heian period. Consistency in the use of phonetic Japanese letters requires that the name be spelled Kinzo in this volume.

42. Horace S. Ensign, "The Japanese Mission," *The Latter-day Saints' Millennial Star* 66 (1904): 337–40.

43. Upon receiving a letter withdrawing the offer, Grant sent a letter asking them to state the reasons. Heber J. Grant, letter to N. Sumi, 9 April 1903, Japan Mission, "Letterpress Copybooks, 1901–1923," LDS Church Archives.

44. Taylor, Journal, 9–22 April 1903. The Kinkikan would become the principal venue of Japan's labor movement activity from the latter part of the 1900s. Tōkyō-to Chiyoda Kuyakusho, ed., *Chiyoda-ku Shi* (Tokyo: Tōkyō-to Chiyoda Kuyakusho, 1960).

45. Joseph and Marie Featherstone recorded that about six hundred people had been present, most of whom were English-speaking students. Joseph F. and Marie S. Featherstone, Journal, 18 April 1903, in possession of Dean R. Featherstone, Bountiful, Utah.

46. "Introducing the Gospel in Japan," *Improvement Era* 6, (1903): 708–14; "Activity in Japan Mission," *The Latter-day Saints' Millennial Star* (1903), 363–66.

where he spoke criticizing the hypocrisy of Christianity as seen in the actions of the Western powers toward Japan.[47] It was during his two-year stay in the United States that his religious outlook became more ecumenical.

An ecumenical speech Hirai delivered at a Unitarian gathering in Kyoto in August 1899 incited an outrage from the Buddhist establishment. This prompted him to move to Tokyo, where he actively participated in the activities of the Unitarian movement. Through this connection, he obtained a teaching position at the secondary division of Tokyo Higher Normal School. In 1901 he became an English teacher at Tokyo Senmon Gakkō (renamed Waseda University in 1902) and a year later assumed a faculty position at Tokyo Language School (present-day Tokyo University of Foreign Studies) where he would remain as a professor until 1910.[48]

Somehow the Mormon missionaries became aware of his speech in Chicago while they were still in Salt Lake City. At the urging of Heber J. Grant, Hirai's speech at the World's Parliament of Religions was reprinted in the 29 June 1901 issue of the *Deseret Evening News*.[49] They must have contacted Hirai soon after their arrival in Tokyo. Recalling Hirai in a letter to Grant in 1920, Taylor said of him: "Mr. Hirai was one of the most splendid characters I have ever met. He was a good and unselfish friend to me when in Japan. He was of noble spirit and the personification of simplicity in living. He was a polished scholar and a true knight of Yamato. Since coming home I have had a letter from his daughter announcing his death."[50] Hirai's relationship with the Mormons continued even after Elbert D. Thomas took over as mission president.[51] Following his death, mission president Joseph H. Stimpson visited the family on behalf of Alma O. Taylor.[52]

5.3.4. Literary Figures Who Aided the Work

The LDS Church sought the best talent to assist the translation of hymns and the Book of Mormon, which were published, respectively, in 1905 and 1909. Two noted poets were hired to arrange thirteen hymns: Kosaburo (or Suimei) Kawai (1874–1965) and Takeki Owada (1857–1910). Kawai, a native of Osaka, began publishing poetry at the age of eighteen; he was elected to the Japan Arts Academy

---

47. John H. Barrows, ed., *The World's Parliament of Religions*, vol. 1 (Chicago: Parliament, 1893).
48. Konen Tsunemitsu, *Nihon Bukkyō Tobei Shi* (Tokyo: Bukkyō Shuppankyoku, 1964), 368–75; Yoshinaga, "Hirai Kinzo ni okeru Meiji Bukkyō," 19–20.
49. Grant read the speech on 20 June 1901 before the missionaries' departure from Utah. Impressed, he used his influence to have it printed "in the Deseret News." Japan Mission, "Historical Records and Minutes," 20 June 1901, LDS Church Archives.
50. Taylor, letter to Grant.
51. Thomas had attended the World's Parliament of Religions in Chicago, where he was impressed by Hirai's speech. Elbert D. Thomas, "Elbert D. Thomas," in *Thirteen Americans: Their Spiritual Autobiographies*, ed. Louis Finkelstein (New York: Harper & Brothers, 1953), 133.
52. Joseph H. Stimpson, Journal, 3 August 1916, BYU Archives.

in 1937 for his contribution to the development in Japan of colloquial, prosaic poetry. Owada, born in Uwajima in present-day Ehime Prefecture, taught literature at the University of Tokyo and Tokyo Higher Normal School before becoming a full-time poet in 1891; he is remembered in Japan as the author of many railroad and military songs.[53] In the translation of the Book of Mormon, the church was successful in securing the services of Choko Ikuta (1882–1936), a rising star in the literary circles who was destined to become a prolific critic, novelist, playwright, and translator, including Friedrich Nietzsche's *Also Sprach Zarathustra* (see Section 6.3 in Chapter 6 for more biographical information on Ikuta).

5.3.5. Early Investigators and Converts

The Mormon missionaries in prewar Japan predominantly attracted students who were pursuing upper secondary or higher education, employees of the public sector, and, among the less educated, those who were already Christians. For example, the second convert, Saburo Kikuchi, was a street preacher of Christianity. The third convert, Yoshiro Oyama, was employed in the foreign department of the post office, which was part of the Teishinshō (Ministry of Communications), a government agency. Tatsusaburo Nanbu, the only person baptized in Morioka (in August 1911), was employed by the Iwate prefectural government.[54] The first female convert, Tsune Nachie, who was baptized while employed as a maid and cook at the mission home, was a member of the Church of England (*Seikō Kai* or the Anglican–Episcopal Church of Japan). Outside Tokyo, the first convert in Kofu (in July 1908), Muraji Yoneyama, was a Methodist.[55]

These characteristics of early Mormon converts are consistent with what has been observed in other cultural contexts among various religious traditions. The empirical literature on the economics and sociology of religion has found, for example, that those who switch religions tend to choose religions similar to theirs and that religious switching tends to occur early in their life cycles. In terms of rational choice theory, these tendencies can broadly be explained in terms of religious human capital.[56] To enjoy the benefits of a particular religion requires human capital

---

53. The railroad songs (*testudō shōka*), numbering more than three hundred, were written from the perspective of a traveler who visits every part of Japan by train.

54. Ivins, Journal, 12 February 1913.

55. Takeo Fujiwara, "The Official Report from the Japan Mission of the Church of Jesus Christ of Latter-day Saints, 1 January–30 April 1935," 28 April 1935, LDS Church Archives.

56. The basic framework of analysis is to postulate an individual (or a household) who maximizes an intertemporal utility function defined in terms of secular and expected afterlife consumption, where secular consumption is a standard household commodity that depends on time inputs and purchased goods, and afterlife consumption depends on religious activities that in turn depend on time inputs, purchased goods, and religious human capital. See Laurence R. Iannaccone, "Introduction to the Economics of Religion," *Journal of Economic Literature* 36 (1998): 1479–82.

specific to that religion, such as knowledge of doctrines and rituals or attachment to that religious culture. Thus, the cost of conversion to Mormonism is expected to be lower for someone who is already a Christian and can therefore use part of the same religious human capital; and a younger person is likely to possess a smaller stock of capital (which is acquired through "on-the-job training"), so the return from the existing stock of capital, or the cost of giving up the current religion, is smaller. In the case of a younger person, moreover, the benefit of switching to a new religion will be enjoyed over a longer period, making its expected net present value greater.[57]

In prewar Japan, education appeared to play a particularly important role in enabling conversion to Mormonism. The intellectual life of Japan at the turn of the twentieth century reflected the influences of two opposing forces: rising nationalism in the form of a state-sponsored cult and advancing modernization (see Section 4.5 in Chapter 4). With the Imperial Rescript on Education, national indoctrination in State Shinto had begun in the 1890s for those receiving compulsory education. The sociologist Peter Berger argued, in the context of Western Christian history, that the "secularization" driven by the "dynamic of industrial capitalism" freed modern man from the "domination of religious institutions and symbols." While such secularization promoted general irreligiosity, it also allowed "individualization" of religion. In a secularized sphere, religion thus became a matter of the choice or preference of the individual.[58] In this Bergerian framework, one can consider the role of post-compulsory education in prewar Japan as that of liberalizing individuals from the legitimizing requirements of society in religious choice. Those receiving secondary and higher education were more likely to regard switching to a Christian sect as socially acceptable behavior (Section 7.2.2 in Chapter 7 further discusses the role of advanced education in the conversion process). Berger observed that secularization affected different groups of society differently, with the impact stronger on classes directly connected with the modern sector.[59] This observation correlates well with the role of education in the secularization of prewar Japan.

Indeed, by far the largest share of the early investigators and converts came from Tokyo's sizable student population. Kenzo Kato (baptized on 11 October 1903) was a student of law. In July 1905, the missionaries met Katsumi Tokoyo,[60] who would become a friend and helper. He was then a student at the Imperial University and later became an employee of the Bank of Formosa (Taiwan), a government institution.[61] Yasubeiye Chiba (baptized on 29 August 1906), who helped with copy-

---

57. Rodney Stark and Roger Finke, *Acts of Faith: Explaining the Human Side of Religion* (Berkeley and Los Angeles: University of California Press, 2000), 114–25; also Iannaccone, "Economics of Religion," 1479–82.
58. Peter L. Berger, *The Sacred Canopy: Elements of a Sociological Theory of Religion* (Garden City, New York: Doubleday, 1967), 105–53 (especially 107–9, 131–34).
59. Ibid., 108.
60. Taylor, Journal, 10 July 1905.
61. Kōyūchōsakai, ed., *Teikoku Daigaku Shusshin Meikan* (Tokyo: Kōyūchōsakai, 1932).

ing the Book of Mormon translation, was a student at a normal school.[62] Hachiro Mori, who was the "private secretary of the minister of finance," was Tokoyo's friend and later became a scribe for the Book of Mormon translation.[63] He was baptized on 23 November 1907. Takeshiro Sakuraba (baptized on 24 February 1910), who also became a scribe for the Book of Mormon translation, was a student at "the Methodist College" and later became a secondary school teacher.[64]

Japan's prewar system of education was a complex, multi-track system; it also frequently changed over time. For those wishing to go beyond primary education, however, its essential features can be summarized as follows.[65] The first six years of primary education were followed by (1) two or three years of higher primary school (*kōtō shōgakkō*), (2) five years of secondary education (*chūgakkō*) for boys, or (3) four or five years of secondary education (*kōtō jogakkō*) for girls.[66] Higher education was available for graduates of *chūgakkō* (and *kōtō jogakkō* in exceptional cases) in the form of higher school (*kōtō gakkō*) or *senmon gakkō*.[67] In prewar Japan, those who received secondary education were considered educated. As the number of schools was limited, many left homes at the age of twelve or thirteen to attend secondary school in larger cities; by graduation, they had turned seventeen. Those in higher schools or *senmon gakkō*, often living away from home, were elites already in their late teens. Students thus matured and became independent earlier than would be the case today, as they progressed through the educational system rather quickly. This is the segment of the population among which the Mormon missionaries had greater success.[68]

---

62. Chiba later became an elementary school teacher.

63. Taylor, Journal, 3 September 1906; 20 October 1906. He later became a secondary school teacher and relocated to Korea in early 1908 after becoming employed with "a tobacco company," which was a government-owned enterprise. Taylor, Journal, 20 September 1907; 15 February 1908.

64. Daniel P. Woodland, Journal, 1 May 1908, in possession of John W. Welch, Provo, Utah; Alma O. Taylor, "Japan, the Ideal Mission Field," *Improvement Era* 13 (1910): 781. Sakuraba was a 1909 graduate of Aoyama Gakuin and later changed his surname to Takahashi. Aoyama Gakuin, *Aoyama Gakuin Ichiran* (Tokyo: Aoyama Gakuin, 1926), 133.

65. Hiroshi Imai, "Meiji Ishin to Kyōiku," in *Kyōiku no Seido to Rekishi*, ed. Yoshiyuki Hirooka (Kyoto: Mineruva Shobō, 2007), 120–31; Hiroshi Imai, "Kindai Kokka no Seiritsu to Kyōiku," in *Kyōiku no Seido*, 132–42.

66. The length of compulsory education was raised from three or four years to six years in 1907.

67. In 1903 the Ministry of Education allowed *senmon gakkō* to be called universities (*daigaku*) although private universities could not legally exist until 1919. At the top of the educational hierarchy were imperial universities (*teikoku daigaku*).

68. At the time of baptism, about 70 percent of the converts were between sixteen and twenty-five years of age; the average age was 22.9. The number of those forty-one years old or above was in the single digits (about 5 percent).

This large semi-Western house in Yoyogi, Tokyo served as the LDS mission home from 1902 to 1908. Courtesy LDS Church Archives.

In his journal, Alma Taylor often mentions his contacts as attending a *senmon gakkō* or "the normal school."[69] Taylor's frequent encounters with normal school students reflected the locations of his living quarters. Tokyo had two normal schools at that time. One of them, Tōkyō Kōtō Shihan Gakkō (Tokyo Higher Normal School, a predecessor of the present-day University of Tsukuba), was located in Kanda, where Taylor was staying temporarily in 1902. This school offered four-year advanced teacher's education to graduates of secondary schools ages seventeen or above. The other school, Tōkyō-fu Shihan Gakkō (Tokyo Prefectural Normal School, a predecessor, along with other units, of present-day Tokyo Gakugei University), was in Aoyama near the mission home when it was in Sendagaya. This school offered four-year teacher's education to graduates of higher primary schools or equivalents ages fifteen or above. It was parallel to the upper secondary and lower higher school grades.

5.4. Defining the Geographical Scope of Missionary Work

5.4.1. Overview

For the Mormon missionaries, the first eighteen months in Japan was a period of preparation. The missionaries remained as boarders in hotels or boarding houses, first in Yokohama and then in Tokyo, to study the language. Missionary

---

69. In May 1902, Taylor met T. Matsuda, a student "at the Senmon Gakkō."

Figure 5.1. Principal Proselytizing Areas
in the LDS Japan Mission, 1902–24[1]

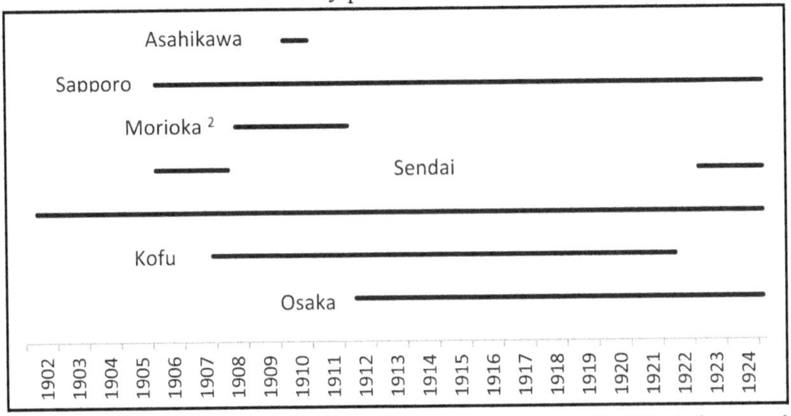

Asahikawa	—
Sapporo	————————————————————
Morioka[2]	———
Sendai	—— ———————————— —
Kofu	————————————
Osaka	————————

1902 1903 1904 1905 1906 1907 1908 1909 1910 1911 1912 1913 1914 1915 1916 1917 1918 1919 1920 1921 1922 1923 1924

[1] Includes only those areas where at least one convert was made. [2] Excludes several months of proselytizing work that resumed for a few months in 1913 and between 1922 and 1923. Author's estimates based on Jenson, "History of the Japan Mission."

work, if any, was confined to a small area in or around Tokyo. A mission home was located only in anticipation of Grant's return from the United States, with wife Augusta, daughter Mary, Horace Ensign's wife, and six additional missionaries, on 17 July 1902. The arrival of women made it imperative that a house should be secured to maintain family life. On 24 July 1902, the main group of missionaries moved into a large house they located in Yoyogi (16 Kasumigaoka Machi) in the then western outskirts of Tokyo.[70] It was of semi-Western construction, consisting of Western and Japanese rooms.[71] After a temporary relocation to a "strictly Japanese house" in Sendagaya from November 1908 to May 1909,[72] the mission found a large Western house with servant quarters in Ichigaya (81 Yakuojimae Machi).[73] The mission home would remain there until July 1922, when it moved, for the last time, to Yodobashi (87 Tsunohazu) just west of Shinjuku station.[74]

During the twenty-three-year period of the mission's existence, a total of eighty-eight American missionaries labored in Japan, but for a country of 45–55

---

70. The location is near the past and future site of the National Stadium.

71. A proposed major renovation of the house by the landlord necessitated the move. Taylor, Journal, 1 November 1908.

72. It appears that this was intended to be a temporary move, pending the completion of an innovation of a more permanent facility. Taylor, Journal, 19 November 1908.

73. Taylor, Journal, 24 March 1909; 26 March 1909; 29 April 1909; 1 May 1909. The features of this house are described in Alma O. Taylor, "A Few Words from Japan," *Improvement Era* 12 (1909): 782–88.

74. Jenson, "History of the Japan Mission." This was outside the Tokyo city limit at that time.

million people (about half the population of the United States), the number only averaged 12.5 at any given time. The small workforce permitted the mission to proselytize only in a handful of locations; the missionaries stayed long enough to produce one or more baptisms only in seven cities (Figure 5.1). Generally, the church had only enough resources to maintain four areas for activity. From May 1912 (when the structure became more or less stable) to its close in July/August 1924, the mission consisted of four conferences: Kofu (which in 1922 was replaced by Sendai), Osaka, Sapporo, and Tokyo.

Tokyo was the only area where missionary work was performed continually until the close of the mission. Occasionally, multiple preaching stations were maintained in Tokyo and its surrounding cities and towns. In early 1902, for example, Ensign and Taylor lived in Kanda, while Grant and Kelsch remained in Tsukiji. After the first mission home was located, single elders lived elsewhere in the city. Taylor, for quite some time, worked in the city of Chiba east of Tokyo;[75] he then worked in Negishi in northern Tokyo. He would typically return to the headquarters for the Sabbath or as circumstances required. Missionary work was also carried out in Asagaya and Nakano, which are now busy residential cities in western Tokyo but were back then relatively unspoiled farming communities.[76] From November 1907 to September 1908, the Japan Mission maintained another house in Yochomachi, Okubo in Tokyo's Ushigome district. Located not far from the mission home, this was generally referred to in mission records as the Yochomachi Branch (but sometimes was called "field house").

5.4.2. Opening the First Areas for Missionary Work

Work outside Tokyo began in April 1903 when Joseph Featherstone and Sandford Hedges were sent to Chiba (22 April): Frederick Caine and Horace Ensign to Nagano (23 April); and Erastus Jarvis and John Stoker to Naoetsu (also 23 April). Here, Chiba referred to, not the city, but the Boso Peninsula in Chiba Prefecture. The Chiba elders initially went to Nago but found living quarters in Funakata. Missionary work was carried out in Boso, including in such little towns and villages as Funakata, Hojo, and Nago, which are now subdivisions of the city of Tateyama. On 2 May, Featherstone and Hedges returned to the headquarters and gave a "very favorable" report of their work in Boso. On the basis of this report, on 9 June, Featherstone returned to Boso accompanied by wife Marie. They arrived in Nago and stayed at the Yamadaya (a Japanese-style hotel) until they found and moved into a house in Hojo on 9 July.[77] The Featherstones'

---

75. Taylor began his work in Chiba on 14 September 1903.

76. Jarvis was first sent to Nakano in January 1904, when work in Nagano and Naoetsu was terminated (see below). Work spread from there to Asagaya.

77. Featherstone, Journal, 2 May, 9 June, and 9 July 1903.

Mormon missionaries and friends on a ferry in Tokyo Bay, circa 1902. From right to left: Taylor, Ensign, Nakazawa, Hiroi, Kikuchi, Grant, and Kelsch. Courtesy BYU Archives.

made good friends and were successful in attracting a relatively large number of people to their meetings.[78]

One can only speculate why mission president Grant opened the small fishing communities of Boso, of all places, for missionary work. Two reasons can be offered. First, there was a convenient ferry service from Tokyo to Hojo, on the other side of Tokyo Bay. Second, Grant evidently liked the rustic atmosphere of the area as a retreat from the suffocating noise and pollution of Tokyo. The special collections library of Brigham Young University has a picture of Grant, his three Mormon associates, Japanese interpreter Tatsutaro Hiroi, and the first two Japanese converts Hajime Nakazawa and Saburo Kikuchi on a boat, presumably bound for or returning from Boso. Grant had known the area from early in his mission and thought of it as a special place, judging from the fact that his family spent part of the early summer of 1903 there.[79] On 14 September 1903, Caine

---

78. An evening meeting on 2 August 1903 was attended by about a hundred people; they had about 150 people on 5 August and about 200 on 9 August. On 22 July 1903, they went to a lecture by a Japanese missionary of the Church of England. At the close of the meeting, Joseph was invited to speak. Marie records: "He arose and talked for ten minutes with great ease." Featherstone, Journal, 22 July, 2 August, 5 August, and 9 August 1903.

79. It appears that Boso remained a summer retreat for the mission president's family. Joseph Stimpson's wife and child spent part of the summer months there in 1917. Stimpson, Journal, 23 June 1917.

Figure 5.2. Areas in Japan where Mormon Missionaries Labored, 1902–24

and Jarvis were sent to Hojo, which the mission president thought would provide a place of convalescence for Jarvis.[80]

To understand why the first sets of missionaries were sent to Naoetsu on the Sea of Japan coast and Nagano in the interior, one must know the trip Grant had made in September 1901 (when the missionaries were still in Yokohama) with an American businessman by the name of Walter S. Stone and "his Japanese man Mr. Sato." Grant describes this trip as a tour of "about one thousand miles" in west central Japan.[81] Leaving in the evening of 6 September 1901, the company traveled west to Nagoya, then headed north from Maibara to Tsuruga Bay on the Sea of Japan coast, and arrived at Kanazawa in the afternoon of the next

---

80. Jarvis was suffering from a mental illness at this time. Jenson, "History of the Japan Mission," 21 December 1904.
81. Grant, "A Japanese Journal."

day. Grant was in Toyama on 9 September, Niigata on 11 September, Naoetsu on 12 September, Karuizawa on 13 September, and back in Tokyo and Yokohama on 15 September. The American businessman's purpose for the trip was to purchase silk from the silk producing regions of the country,[82] so Grant did not stop at any of the major cities along the more developed Pacific coast. This likely explains why Grant selected the first areas of missionary work from among the cities on the Sea of Japan and in the interior (see Figure 5.2).

While traveling the Shinano region of the country, which reminded him of Cache and Utah Valleys (except that "the mountains were green to their summits in place of being rugged and barren as is generally the case with ours"), Grant remarked:

The three-story Matsubakan was a popular inn located near Naoetsu station. It went out of business during the depression years of the early 1930s. Courtesy BYU Archives.

> I would sooner live in this valley and do our missionary work from here than in any place that I have yet seen and if I am not impressed to remain in Tokyo shall be tempted to make some place in it our headquarters . . . I would give almost anything within my power if I could go through this valley and preach to the people in their own language. I have been delighted and pleased with all that I have seen today and someday I hope and pray that I can come to this place and preach the Gospel of our Lord and Master Jesus Christ to the people residing in it.[83]

Naoetsu (pop. about 11,000) was the terminus on a train line coming out of Tokyo. At the turn of the twentieth century, it took about twelve hours to travel from Tokyo's Ueno station to Naoetsu. A separate line was completed in 1900 connecting Naoetsu and Niigata. Although there was another line coming from Osaka on the west to Toyama on the Sea of Japan coast, however, the construction of a rail link between Naoetsu and Toyama was not yet complete. The northern tip of the Japan Alps reaches that part of the coastal area, with steep cliffs lining the coast for several miles, especially near Itoigawa. Civil engineering techniques were not sufficiently developed to allow the construction of a tunnel until after 1911 (the rail link was completed in 1913). Because it was the terminus for five

---

82. Alma O. Taylor journal, 6 September 1901.
83. Grant, "A Japanese Journal."

daily trains to and from Tokyo, Naoetsu was an important transportation hub, with several inns competing for customers near the station.[84]

Naoetsu was also the site of a refinery being built by a subsidiary of Standard Oil. Grant was aware of this, as he noted in his diary for 12 September 1901, pointing out the financial size of the company, a fact that interested Grant because of his extensive business experience:

> [At] Naoetsu is the headquarters of the Japan company that is really a branch of the Standard Oil Co. of U.S. The capital is ten million yen or $5,000,000 of our money. The name is the International Oil Co.[85]

This was Asia's largest refinery at the time, with the monthly production of 450,000 liters of petroleum. The manager was a former American diplomat by the name of Edwin Dun, who was assisted by over twenty American engineers. The plant was sold to Japanese interests in 1907.[86]

Nagano and Naoetsu proved to be too small to sustain two sets of missionaries. On 14 September 1903, the two areas were combined, and Hedges and Stoker were made responsible for both places; following the conference held in early January 1904, they did not return to the area. On 20 January 1922, Nagano was reopened when Kofu was closed, but work lasted only ten months, until 17 November of the same year.

5.4.3. Locating Permanent Fields of Labor

The second round of geographical expansion occurred in July 1905, when missionaries were sent to Sapporo (pop. 70,000) on the northern island of Hokkaido and Sendai (pop. 100,000) in the northern portion of the main island of Honshu. On 10 July 1905, John Chadwick, Justus Seely, and John Stoker left for Hokkaido, while William Fairbourn and Sanford Hedges left for Sendai. The Hokkaido missionaries were not certain when they left where they would locate their headquarters. Their first destination was Iwanai, which they reached on 15 July. From 15 August to 3 September, Stoker made an extensive survey of towns on the island, while his companions remained in Iwanai. As Stoker felt that Sapporo was the most promising site, the group moved from Iwanai to Sapporo on 14 September.[87] They reported to the mission home in Tokyo: "after seeing the most important towns, cities, and villages of the Island . . . Sapporo . . . is the

---

84. Yorinori Miyagawa, *Naoetsu Hanshō Ki* (Naoetsu: Muro Shobō, 1900), 4–5; Joetsu Kyōdo Kenkyū Kai, ed, *Shashinshū: Meiji-Taishō-Shōwa Takada Naoetsu* (Tokyo: Tosho Kankōkai, 1979), 88; Naoetsu no Rekishi Henshū Iinkai, ed, *Naoetsu no Rekishi* (Naoetsu: Naoetsu Kyōiku Iinkai, 1971), 90–91, 120–21.
85. Grant, "A Japanese Journal."
86. Naoetsu no Rekishi Henshū Iinkai, *Naoetsu*, 26–27, 65–67, 217.
87. Schmalz, "The Church in Japan," 4.

best place to operate the headquarters of the mission."[88] Though Sapporo was the prefectural capital, it was only the third largest city on the island of Hokkaido. It was also less accessible than the gateway city of Hakodate whose population was not only larger but also more rapidly growing. Even so, Sapporo would prove to be fertile ground for missionary work, especially given its size. The first Sunday school was held on 8 October 1905, with twenty-seven children.[89]

In order to identify additional fields of labor, mission presidents Alma O. Taylor and Elbert D. Thomas made at least three exploratory trips around the country. A curious feature of these trips—and the selection process more generally—is that these leaders did not think it obvious to send missionaries to large cities with convenient rail connections to Tokyo, such as Nagoya and Osaka.[90] Osaka would eventually be opened (following some trial and error), but Taylor's, if not Thomas's, preference seemed to be for mid-size provincial capitals. The first of these trips was made from 8 to 18 January 1907, when Taylor made a tour of central Japan. Heading west, he visited such places as Kawagoe, Kofu, Tatsuno, Iida, Nakatsu, and Nagoya; on the way back, he visited Okazaki, Toyohashi, Hamamatsu, Shizuoka, and Numazu. Taylor was not impressed with Nagoya, where he spent only three hours, while he recorded his impression of Shizuoka as "the best place outside of Tokyo that I have seen."[91] Then, from 1 to 16 October of the same year, Taylor traveled to northern Japan in connection with a visit to the proselytizing areas of Sendai and Sapporo. Leaving Sendai, Taylor visited Morioka on the way to Sapporo; while in Sapporo, he traveled north to Asahikawa. On his return journey, he visited Odate, Akita, Yamagata, and Fukushima before reaching Tokyo.[92] The last of the trips was made by Thomas in March 1911, when he made a tour of southern and western Japan, which included Hiroshima, Kobe, Nagoya, and Osaka on the main island of Honshu, Matsuyama on the island of Shikoku, and Kagoshima and Nagasaki on the island of Kyushu.

It was in response to Taylor's first trip that the small provincial city of Kofu (pop. 50,000) was opened. On 7 February 1907, William Fairbourn and Joseph Stimpson left for Kofu, accompanied by John Stoker who was to assist in starting the work. Sunday school was first held on 31 March. Following his second trip, on 23 October 1907, Taylor decided to open Morioka (pop. 40,000) but this required the closing of Sendai. James Anderson and John Chadwick arrived in Morioka at the beginning of November, with the Sunday school organized in early January 1908. It appears that, with a marginal increase in the number of missionaries, Taylor felt that more areas could be opened around this time.

---

88. Taylor, Journal, 8 September 1905.

89. Schmalz, "The Church in Japan," 6.

90. A Tokyo convert by the name of Kentaro Yokoi (baptized on 13 February 1917) soon moved to Nagoya. On 17 May 1917, mission president Stimpson paid him a visit in Nagoya and administered the sacrament to him.

91. Taylor, Journal, 8–18 January 1907.

92. Ibid., 1–16 October 1907.

Sapporo Sunday school, circa. 1910. Courtesy Aiko Horiuchi.

During the first week of July 1909, Sapporo elder Joseph Preston Cutler, accompanied by Robert Barton who had just arrived in Japan, opened the city of Asahikawa (pop. 45,000) to the north; on 22 June 1909, Walter Steed and Elliot Taylor left for the city of Shizuoka (pop. 60,000), a city with which Alma O. Taylor had been favorably impressed. With a reduction in the number of missionaries, however, these cities could not be maintained. Shizuoka was closed in February 1910, followed by the closing of Asahikawa in July 1910.

In September 1911, six months after Elbert Thomas completed his tour of southern Japan, Osaka (pop. 1.2 million) was opened for missionary work, but this required the closing of Morioka (on 29 August 1911).[93] On 11 September, Roland Emmett, James Miller, and James Scowcroft left Tokyo for their new assignment. Osaka was Japan's second largest city, located about 350 miles southwest of Tokyo. A dominant commercial city, the economic importance of Osaka in some areas surpassed that of Tokyo. Osaka's port city, Kobe, boasted a sizable foreign community. It is indeed curious why it took the Mormon missionaries ten years to open Osaka. Like Sapporo, Osaka too would prove to be a productive area for missionary work. The opening of Osaka defined the geographical scope of Mormon proselytizing work in prewar Japan. On 29 May 1912, the Japan Mission was formally divided into four conferences: Kofu, with Joseph Stimpson as president; Osaka, with Jay C. Jensen; Sapporo, with William Ellis; and Tokyo, with Robert Barton.[94] This structure would remain intact for more than ten years, until January 1922.

Toward the end of the Japan Mission, mission president Lloyd Ivie made frequent changes in what may have been a frantic attempt to produce results. On 20 January 1922, Kofu was closed "temporarily." This precipitated a series of experimental reallocations of missionaries, none of which lasted very long.

---

93. Ivins, Journal, 29 August 1911.
94. At this time, fields were renamed as conferences, and presiding elders as presidents. Ivins, Journal, 30 May 1912.

Table 5.1. Proselytizing Areas and Convert Baptisms in the Japan Mission, 1901–24

Areas (*principal areas)	Population (1,000s), 1908	Population (1,000s), 1918	Duration of proselytizing work (months)	Number of convert baptisms	Average annual convert baptisms
Tokyo*	2,186	2,347	October 1901– June 1924 (271 months)	63	2.8
Sapporo*	70	95	July 1905– June 1924 (203 months)	37	2.2
Sendai	98	123	July 1905– November 1907; July 1922– June 1924 (51 months)	2	0.5
Kofu*	50	58	February 1907– January 1922 (179 months)	37	2.5
Morioka[1]	36	48	November 1907– August 1911 (45 months)	1	0.3
Asahikawa	40	69	July 1909– July 1910 (12 months)	1	1.0
Osaka*	1,227	1,642	September 1911– June 1924 (153 months)	33	2.6

Includes only those areas where at least one convert was made. [1] Excludes several months of proselytizing work that resumed between 1922 and 1923. Author's estimates based on Jenson, "History of the Japan Mission"; Japanese government, *Nihon Teikoku Jinkō Tōkei*, 1908 and 1918.

First, the Kofu elders were transferred to Nagano, but the work lasted only ten months, until 17 November 1922. Second, on 13 February 1922, missionary work began in Mito, with Orlando Fowler and Howard Jensen transferred from Sapporo,[95] but this left the Sapporo conference without missionaries. Following the missionary conference held in Tokyo on 1 May, the work in Mito ceased as Fowler and Jensen were called to Sendai (work was again carried out in Mito

---

95. Ivie dedicated Mito for the preaching of the gospel on 19 February. James Alden Richins, "The Life Story of Orlando Fowler, 1902–1923," June 1999, 18.

from 9 March to 28 April 1923).⁹⁶ Third, work in Sendai commenced again when Fowler and Jensen arrived on 13 May 1922, but they left for Sapporo at the end of the month.⁹⁷ On 11 July 1922, the newly arrived couple Wallace and Louese Browning was appointed to labor in Sendai. Finally, work was also restarted in Morioka but only briefly (until 21 April 1923). At its closing in the summer of 1924, the Japan Mission, with a total of fourteen missionaries, operated four conferences: Osaka, Sapporo, Sendai, and Tokyo.

Comparing annual average baptisms across proselytizing areas, we find no evidence that the average number was significantly lower in Kofu or Sapporo than in Osaka or Tokyo (Table 5.1). On the contrary, productivity was similar across the four cities. Likely, the missionary workforce was too small to experience diminishing marginal returns in any area where missionaries stayed for any extended period of time. The difference in productivity is more pronounced when we compare these cities to those where the missionaries did not stay very long. The duration of missionary work cannot be the only determining factor, but these numbers seem to suggest that the type of religious climate was similar between large metropolitan cities and medium-sized provincial capitals. What appears to be lack of planning and logic in the selection of cities probably did not, after all, affect the total number of baptisms achieved by the Mormon missionaries in the prewar period.

5.5. Presenting the Message in Japanese

5.5.1. Morumonkyō to Morumonkyōto *by Goro Takahashi*

The book Goro Takahashi wrote in defense of Mormonism, *Morumonkyō to Morumonkyōto*, was published in late August or early September 1902. The Mormon missionaries hoped that they could use the book as a proselytizing tool until such time as their own tracts became available. Takahashi, judging from the public's reaction to the press coverage of Mormonism, may have hoped that he could make easy money by writing this book. If so, he was disappointed. When the book failed to sell, Grant agreed to buy most of the 700-volume run. The book appeared on a list of mission publications printed at the end of every successive tract. Perhaps to cut the number of copies in stock, in March 1906, the

---

96. Fowler returned to Mito on 9 March 1923, accompanied by Rulon Esplin. They left Mito for Tokyo on 28 April 1923. Richins, "Orlando Fowler," 27–28. The mission journal entry for 27 April 1923 states that the elders working in Mito "for the past 6 weeks" had returned to Tokyo.

97. When they arrived in Sapporo on 1 June, the missionaries remarked that "the saints [had] done fine by carrying on the work while [they] were absent and they [were] glad to think that they could do it and meet with success." As quoted on p. 22 of Richins, "Orlando Fowler."

missionaries distributed 350 copies of the book to the House of Peers, including eight copies to the officers of the House.[98]

The 257-page book consists of ten chapters. While it amply displays Takahashi's intellectual prowess and encyclopedic knowledge, it is rather eccentric in organization and coverage: Chapter 3 alone is 80 pages, and 70 pages of them (or about a third of the whole book) are devoted to ancient American civilization. As Takahashi had promised, the book is apologetic of Mormonism. The preface expresses the author's hope that he will have demonstrated by the end of the book that Joseph Smith and Brigham Young were extraordinary individuals, heroes of the nineteenth century. Takahashi occasionally uses the Chinese word for the Christian god (*tentei*) instead of *kami*, which is a Shinto deity albeit an established word for the Christian god.

Takahashi starts out sensationally by raising Mormonism as the greatest question under heaven (Chapter 1). "Why is it so? It is because the Mormons are a prosperous people even though they have been repeatedly persecuted by fellow Americans who profess belief in Christianity." "Now that the ill fame of Joseph Smith has faded, the Mormons are commanding respect from many in the United States." Takahashi then gives an outline of Mormonism, including a review of the thirteen Articles of Faith (wherein is summarized "pure or primitive Christianity") as well as the family and personal background of Joseph Smith (Chapter 2). He reviews the origin of the Book of Mormon, the nature of reformed Egyptian characters, and the story line of the book, followed by an extensive (60-page) treatise on the languages and legends of the Aztec and Maya civilizations based on his reading of the latest scholarly literature (Chapter 3). His knowledge of linguistics and world languages is impressive. He definitively refutes the Spaulding theory of the origin of the Book of Mormon as a fabrication by Joseph's enemies (Chapter 4).[99]

The next four chapters cover the history of the church, from its establishment through the termination of the practice of polygamy. Takahashi talks about the persecutions of the Mormons, temporary prosperity in Nauvoo, the martyrdom of Joseph Smith (Chapter 5), the church's exodus to the West, and arrival in Salt Lake Valley (Chapter 6). As notable events in Utah, Takahashi mentions the miracle of seagulls and how the Great Basin compares to the land of Palestine.[100] He discusses the Mormons' struggles with the federal government, while acknowledging their

---

98. Taylor, Journal, 21 March 1906; 24 March 1906.

99. The Spaulding theory postulates that Joseph Smith relied on the book manuscript of a Congregationalist preacher named Solomon Spaulding in producing the Book of Mormon. Paul C. Gutjahr, *The Book of Mormon: A Biography* (Princeton, New Jersey: Princeton University Press, 2012), 47–51.

100. The seagull miracle refers to the providential appearance of seagulls in Salt Lake Valley when, in the early summer months of 1848, hordes of crickets moved upon the land to eat up the first crop of the new settlers. The seagulls began to devour the crickets, "sweeping them up as they went along." Leonard J. Arrington, *Great Basin Kingdom:*

patriotism shown in the volunteer service of a Mormon battalion of 500 soldiers during the Mexican–American War (Chapter 7). Polygamy is explained in the context of the Mormon doctrine on celestial marriage; verses of the Doctrine and Covenants are translated to elucidate this doctrine. The Mormons had been persecuted well before the doctrine of polygamy was made public. Now that the practice of polygamy had ceased in order to avoid conflict with federal law, Takahashi argues that the Mormons would not want to come all the way to Japan to preach something they no longer practice. He compares attacking the Mormons for polygamy to shooting an arrow where there is no target (Chapter 8).

The last two chapters are about the LDS Church's contemporary scene. Chapter 9 discusses the Mormons' social organization and their cooperative attitudes; how laziness is frowned upon, with the Mormons considering themselves as the stewards of earthly possessions. Among the topics discussed are the law of consecration, tithing, and the establishment of ZCMI.[101] Chapter 10 elaborates on the church's success and prosperity in the contemporary world. Takahashi explains the church organization (with fifty stakes, seventeen missions, and 1,700 full-time missionaries), how religious success is accompanied by temporal prosperity; and farmlands and factories of Utah. He completes the book by stating that the Mormons are a sincere and upright people, though whether their doctrines have come from revelation remains to be proven (pp. 256–57).

Takahashi's favorable position toward the Mormons is evident throughout the book. He calls the Smith family devout people (p. 30); states that Joseph Smith was an honest believer in the experience he had (p. 33); and says that Joseph was by nature devout (p. 43). He brushes away attacks against Joseph Smith's money-digging career, because use of a mining rod was a common practice in the early nineteenth century; he was in any case a young boy doing what he was told by his employer (pp. 60–61). Though some of the witnesses to the golden plates, from which the Book of Mormon was translated, left the church, none had repudiated their testimonies (p. 65). Though more information has been coming out recently concerning the ancient civilizations of America, Takahashi further points out, Smith, as young as he was, knew nothing of it and made a bold declaration by writing of such history (pp. 104–6). Takahashi even justifies the presumed establishment of the infamous Danite vigilante force by the Mormons as a legitimate force of self-defense (pp. 214–15). Takahashi defends polygamy as practiced among different peoples throughout history, including among the Japanese as concubinage (pp. 221–25).

Takahashi's knowledge of Christianity and Japanese religions is utilized to the fullest. He compares Joseph's theophany to that of the Apostle Paul on the

---

Economic History of the Latter-Day Saints, 1830–1900 (Cambridge, Massachusetts: Harvard University Press, 1958), 49–50.

101. Zion's Cooperative Mercantile Institution (ZCMI), founded in 1868 by Brigham Young and opened for business in 1869, was a large retail establishment in Utah. Arrington, *Great Basin Kingdom*, 298–302.

way to Damascus (p. 38) and challenges other Christian denominations to explain why revelation has ceased in this age (p. 40). Referring to the different ways in which the Prophet Moroni was recorded to have quoted from the English Bible, Takahashi noted that Joseph Smith, while a literal believer in the Bible, recognized that there were errors in biblical translations, thus challenging great theologians of the world when he was merely sixteen or seventeen years old (pp. 52–53). If Jesus had appeared to the Apostle Paul, it is not unreasonable to claim that Peter and John appeared to Joseph Smith (p. 173). Takahashi justifies the mysterious origin of the Book of Mormon by comparing it to that of *Dainichi Kyō*, a sacred sutra of esoteric Buddhism (p. 70–72); he justifies the supernatural experience of Smith by comparing him to Nichiren, the founding priest of the *Nichiren* sect of Japanese Buddhism (pp. 72–73).

5.5.2. Producing Tracts to Carry the Message

A tract is a useful instrument of proselytizing in any situation, but in the case of Mormon missionary work in Japan it was indispensable, given the limited ability of the missionaries to speak the Japanese language. The first tract, "Batsujitsu Seito Iesu Kirisuto Kyōkai ni kansuru Kinkyū Rinkoku," which was a translation of the English tract distributed at the inaugural meeting ("An Announcement concerning the Church of Jesus Christ of Latter-day Saints"), was published in May 1903, a few weeks after the first sets of missionaries were sent outside of Tokyo. This was translated by Alma O. Taylor and completed with the help of Japanese convert Yoshiro Oyama and Goro Takahashi.[102] From August 1903 to December 1921, thirteen additional tracts were produced by the Japan Mission, excluding three that were parts of an existing tract published separately (Table 5.2).[103]

Notably, many of these tracts were prepared in English by the missionaries themselves and were subsequently translated into Japanese with help from their Japanese friends. For example, the second tract "Ikeru Makoto no Kami (The True and Living God)" was written in English by Alma O. Taylor and its translation was completed with the help of Kinzo Hirai.[104] The ninth tract "Tasai Shugi no Osore Nashi (No Fears of Polygamy)," also prepared by Taylor, was meant to be included as an appendix in the Japanese translation of *A Brief History* (see Section 5.5.3 immediately below). This was translated by Hirogoro Hirai, a

---

102. Taylor, Journal, 20 March–8 April 1903. The English text of this tract is reprinted in the 4 June 1903 issue of *the Latter-day Saints' Millennial Star*, 363–66; and the July 1903 issue of the *Improvement Era*, 708–14.

103. "Kami wa Imasuka (Is There a God)," published in September 1904, consisted of four essays written by four authors. Three of these, "Bijutsuka (The Artist)," "Chikyū no Kanyōnaru Daikikanshu (The Great Architect of Earth)," and "Rippōsha (The Law Giver)," were published separately in June 1907 for distribution at meetings; 750 copies of each were printed.

104. Taylor, Journal, 8 July 1903.

brother of Kinzo and teacher of English at Waseda University (see Section 6.3 in Chapter 6).[105]

Four tracts were translations of English-language material produced elsewhere. Two of these were prepared by James E. Talmage, at the request of the Japan Mission. Talmage (a member of the Council of the Twelve Apostles, 1911–33) was then a professor of geology at the University of Utah and considered a leading intellectual in the church. The first of these "Hito wa Kami no Keitō wo Yūsu (In the Lineage of the Gods)" was requested by Horace Ensign before he left Japan, translated by Alma Taylor, and completed with the help of Kinzo Hirai.[106] The other one was "Banbutsu no Shu (Lord of All)," translated by James Anderson.

The third tract from outside the mission to be translated was "Wa ga Eikoku Kyōkai wo Satte Batsujitsu Seito Iesu Kirisuto Kyōkai ni Ireru Riyū (My Reasons for Leaving the Church of England and Joining the Church of Jesus Christ of Latter-Day Saints)" by Robert Moseley Bryce Thomas (1887). As noted earlier, a significant portion of the people who were attracted to Mormonism were Christians. Clearly, the need for such a tract was felt in order to explain in Japanese how Mormonism differed from other branches of Christianity. The need probably was not so strong, but strong enough to justify the second printing of 2,000 copies in March 1911.

The last tract to be published by the church (in December 1921) was also a translation. Titled "Shinmin no Tokuchō (Characteristics of the Citizens of God)," it was the translation of a sermon given by Nephi Jensen, who was then president of the Canadian Mission. The six-page tract attempts to dispel the negative perception the public may have held of the Mormons by demonstrating, either by quantitative evidence or by appealing to statements of prominent men, that the Mormons excelled in economic prosperity, educational attainment among the youth, ethical standards, health, and spirituality.

The pace of tract production drastically declined after 1909. The church published only three additional tracts, including "Shinmin no Tokuchō" just mentioned above (which was to be the last tract), "Sukui no Michi (Way of Salvation)," and "Atarashii Hikari (New Light)." Published in February 1913, "Sukui no Michi" was a sermon by Elbert Thomas, covering such topics as premortal existence, free agency, the resurrection of Jesus Christ, the restoration of the divine church, repentance, and baptism (this would be included in a volume of his sermons entitled *Tō Shi Sekkyō Shū*, see Section 5.5.3 immediately below). Prepared by Lloyd Ivie and published in May 1921, "Atarashii Hikari" was a brief (five pages) outline of the Mormon message, designed to invite those who received a copy to investigate the church. Any of these later tracts were probably not necessary, given the supply of existing tracts and, more importantly, as the

---

105. Taylor, Journal, 25 March 1907; 28 March 1907; 15 April 1907.
106. Taylor, Journal, 12 May 1906; 7 June 1906.

Book of Mormon and other book-length materials were available by this time in the Japanese language.

5.5.3. Books and Hymnals

During its twenty-three-year existence, the LDS Japan Mission published four books and two hymnals.[107] The first book was *Batsujitsu Seito Iesu Kirisuto Kyōkai Ryakushi*, a translation of *A Brief History of the Church of Jesus Christ of Latter-day Saints* (first published in 1893) by Edward H. Anderson. The book, published in August 1907, took John Stoker three years to complete. Stoker received help from a Mr. Yoshida in Tokyo, Mr. Okafuji, a teacher in the normal school in Sapporo, and Professor Kintaro Oshima of the Sapporo Agricultural College, whom Taylor befriended on a ferry crossing the Tsugaru Strait from Aomori to Hakodate in April 1906. Oshima became friendly to the Mormon missionaries because he knew of future Mormon apostle John A. Widtsoe as both of them had pursued doctoral studies at the University of Göttingen in Germany under the same teacher.[108] The book contains two appendices not part of the original book, one on the Mormon stance on polygamy (a reprint of the April 1907 tract by Alma O. Taylor) and the other on the history of missionary work in Japan. The main text covers the period from Joseph Smith through Joseph F. Smith, indicating that the translation was based on a later edition of the 1893 classic.

Second, concurrently with the translation of the Book of Mormon, Frederick Caine prepared a 92-page book *Morumon Kei to wa Nanzoya* (What is the Book of Mormon?), the publication of which was timed to coincide with the publication, in October 1909, of the Japanese translation of the Book of Mormon (see Section 5.5.4 immediately below). The book explains the origin and outline of the book, rebuffs various criticisms of the book, tells how some of the prophecies in the book have been fulfilled, and argues how recent archeological discoveries in Central America support the claims the book makes of its truthfulness.

Third, in December 1914, a collection of Elbert D. Thomas's sermons in Japanese was published by Lloyd Ivie in Kofu on behalf of the mission as *To Shi Sekkyō Shū* (Sermons of Mr. Thomas). Apparently, the idea originated at the end of October 1912, immediately following Thomas's departure, when it was

---

107. In addition, the church published an English-language book written by H. Grant Ivins. Entitled *A Life of Christ for Japanese Students*, the thirty-nine-chapter book was published in August 1914. It was used to teach Japanese students a biblical account of Christ in English (based on the sequence of events given by Frederic W. Farrar, *The Life of Christ*, 1874). An appendix to the book contained the words of sixty-six songs taken from the hymnal for classroom use. The second edition was published in October 1916. On this occasion, Ivins, now back in Salt Lake City, added a set of questions for each chapter.

108. Taylor, Journal, 10 April 1906; 23 July 1906; 22 October 2006. Widtsoe (apostle, 1921–53) then held academic positions at Utah's institutions of higher education. Eventually, he would serve as president of the University of Utah.

Table 5.2. Mormon Tracts in Japanese, May 1903–December 1921

	Date of first publication	Title [English title or equivalent]	Author [Translator]	Number of copies printed through 15 June 1912
1	May 1903	Batsujitsu Seito Iesu Kirisuto Kyōkai ni kansuru Kinkyū Rinkoku [a translation of the English tract "An Announcement concerning the Church of Jesus Christ of Latter-day Saints," published by the Japan Mission in 1902]	Heber Jeddy Grant [Alma O. Taylor]	JPN:19,000 ENG: 1,000
2	August 1903	Ikeru Makoto no Kami [The True and Living God]	Alma Owen Taylor	51,000
3	September 1904	Kami wa Imasuka [Is There a God][a]	Alma Owen Taylor, compiler	9,000
4	March 1905	Wa ga Eikoku Kyōkai wo Satte Batsujitsu Seito Iesu Kirisuto Kyōkai ni Ireru Riyū [a translation of "My Reasons for Leaving the Church of England and Joining the Church of Jesus Christ of Latter-Day Saints" (1887)]	Robert Moseley Bryce Thomas [Fred A. Caine]	3,000
5	April 1905	Kitō no Hitsuyō [Necessity of Prayer]	Sanford Wells Hedges	3,000
6	June 1905	Batsujitsu Seito [The Latter-day Saints], meant to replace the first tract	Sanford Wells Hedges	75,000
7	March 1906	Iesu Kirisuto no Ryakuden oyobi Shimei [The Life and Mission of Jesus Christ]	Joseph Frederick Featherstone	15,000
8	June 1906	Hito wa Kami no Keitō wo Yūsu [a translation of "In the Lineage of the Gods"]	James Edward Talmage [Alma O. Taylor]	25,000
9	April 1907	Tasai Shugi no Osore Nashi [No Fears of Polygamy][b]	Alma Owen Taylor [Hirogoro Hirai]	2,000
10	May 1908	Shinkō [Faith]	John William Stoker	30,000
11	March 1909	Banbutsu no Shu [a translation of "Lord of All"][c]	James Edward Talmage [James Anderson]	2,000
12	February 1913	Sukui no Michi [Way of Salvation][d]	Elbert D. Thomas	n.a.
13	May 1921	Atarashii Hikari [New Light]	Lloyd O. Ivie	n.a.
14	December 1921	Shinmin no Tokuchō [a translation of "Characteristics of the Citizens of God"]	Nephi Jensen [Lloyd O. Ivie]	n.a.

a. Compilation of four short essays by Mormon authors, one of which is Taylor's own contribution. The other contributors are Walter J. Sloan, James X. Allen, and James E. Talmage. Three of these were published separately in June 1907 for distribution at meetings.

b. This was included as an appendix to the translation of *A Brief History of the Church* published in August 1907.

c. The tract contains an appendix on polygamy, which is a reprint of the April 1907 tract by Alma O. Taylor. The original article appeared in the August 1908 issue of the *Improvement Era*, with a footnote stating that it was prepared for publication in Japan. From March 1911, this was incorporated as part of "Kami wa Imasuka."

d. Based on Thomas's sermon. This was included as a chapter in *To Shi Sekkyō Shū*, a collection of Thomas' sermons published in December 1914.

Heber Grant Ivins, "List of Tracts in the Japan Mission, 1912," LDS Church Archives; archived copies of all tracts.

decided to publish one of his sermons as a tract ("Sukui no Michi," published in February 1913, Chapter 23 in the book). In January 1913, it evolved into a book of sermons.[109] The book has twenty-eight chapters (or sermons), covering such wide topics as Central American civilization, faith and science, Joseph Smith, the law of tithing, obedience to civil authority, repentance and baptism, and even blacks and the priesthood. A number of passages from the Doctrine and Covenants are quoted, indicating that Japanese members were familiar with them though the book itself was not yet published in Japanese. The book of sermons was used as a Sunday school textbook for some time.

Fourth, *Shinshō Kōgi*, a translation of *The Articles of Faith* by James E. Talmage, was published in June 1915. The 450-page volume was a compilation of ten installments that had been published separately from May 1913 onward, possibly allowing the Japanese members to benefit from the book as soon as a portion was translated. The translation was made by church member Takeshiro Takahashi,[110] who was a teacher at Kogyokusha, a highly regarded private academy in Tokyo offering secondary instruction. The work of translation, which began in late 1911, was completed in December 1913. Mission president Heber Grant Ivins was closely involved in correcting the translation, from April 1913.[111] For this reason, the book lists Ivins and Takahashi as co-translators. Takahashi was paid a modest fee for the translation as well as for correcting the proofs.

In the prewar period, the LDS Church published two hymnbooks. The first one, *Batsujitsu Seito Sanbika* (English title: Psalmody of the Japan Mission of the Church of Jesus Christ of Latter-day Saints), was compiled by Frederick A. Caine and Horace S. Ensign and was published in June 1905. A smaller booklet by the same title but containing the words only was published a month later, in July. The hymnbook includes sixty-six songs taken from various English LDS hymnbooks, including the *L.D.S. Hymnbook*, the *Sunday School Song Book*, and the *Children's Friend*. The verses were translated from late 1903 to early 1905 in several installments and were used in church services as they became available; the accompanying melodies were composed by Ensign, an accomplished musi-

---

109. Ivins, Journal, 24 January 1913 and 24 December 1914.

110. Takahashi was baptized on 24 February 1910 as Takeshiro Sakuraba and ordained to the office of priest on 8 December 1912. A 1909 graduate of Aoyama Gakuin, a Methodist academy, he was twenty-four years old when the translation work began in earnest. Earlier, he had served as scribe for the Book of Mormon translation. He married Ai Takahashi in 1910 and took on her surname. It appears that, in the summer of 1915, Takahashi moved to Odate, Akita Prefecture, to become an English teacher at Odate Secondary School. Odate Chūgakkō, *Akita Kenritsu Odate Chūgakkō Yōran* (Odate, Akita: Odate Chūgakkō, 1917). His name does not appear in the school directory beyond 1921 or thereabouts. He may have moved to Taiwan at some point during the interwar period as there was a teacher by the name of Takeshiro Takahashi (from Akita Prefecture) at a secondary school in Taipei in 1942 (http:who.ith.sinica.edu.tw/mpView.action, accessed December 2015).

111. Ivins, Journal, 17 December 1913; 23 April 1914.

cian who had been a soloist and assistant conductor (under Evan Stephens) with the Mormon Tabernacle Choir.[112] As the English verses were faithfully translated, a new melody needed to be composed for each song. Mr. Y. Iwano, a friend of the mission, arranged most of the songs into Japanese verse. Kosaburo (or Suimei) Kawai (1874–1965), a noted poet, arranged ten hymns, while Takeki Owada (1857–1910), another noted poet and Japanese literature scholar, arranged three. Hajime Nakazawa, the first Mormon convert in Japan, arranged one.[113]

The second hymnbook, also titled *Batsujitsu Seito Sanbika* (English title: The Songs of Zion), was published in December 1915 (followed by the publication of a smaller and less expensive booklet without the music in March 1916).[114] The new songbook included 220 hymns taken from the *Songs of Zion* and the *Deseret Sunday School Song Book*. This time, the music of the original English hymns was retained, and the verses were translated in such a way that the Japanese verses fit the tune. Joseph H. Stimpson, in the preface, explained why the earlier hymnal needed to be replaced: "With all due respect to the composer, these tunes proved to be imperfect from a musical standpoint and the songs were so long that much of the force of the words was lost."

The work was initiated by Ivins in early 1914, with the help of church member Tomomitsu Noguchi (baptized in Tokyo on 16 April 1913) who subsequently moved to Sapporo. In June 1914, Ivins found help from church investigator Tomigoro Takagi (who would be baptized on 1 June 1915) and also occasionally from a man by the name of Izawa.[115] By September 150 songs had been translated from English to Japanese, and Ivins asked Toshichi Yamane, a colleague of Takeshiro Takahashi at Kogyokusha, to correct the translation.[116] These were combined with seventy additional songs, which were translated by Lloyd Ivie (with help from Koshun Shiono) and rendered into Japanese verses by Yamane.[117]

---

112. *The Encyclopedia of Mormonism*, under "Mormon Tabernacle Choir."
113. Taylor, Journal, 29 May 1905.
114. The smaller hymnbook contains two songs that are not found in the complete hymnal. One is a farewell song written by Tsune Nachie (to be sung to the tune of God Be with You till We Meet Again) and the Japanese national anthem *Kimi ga Yo*.
115. Ivins, Journal, 7 February and 14 July 1914; Tomigoro Takagi, "Atarashii Sanbika wo Utaimashō," *Seito no Michi* 5 (1961): 380–81; and Tomigoro Takagi, "Nihon Dendōbu no Kaiko," *Seito no Michi* 2 (September 1958): 25.
116. Yamane was paid ¥75.00 for the work. Ivins, Journal, 10 September 1914.
117. Ivie, Journal, 5 December 1914; 3 April 1915. Toshiko Yanagida, "Takahashi Nikichi to Takagi Tomigoro," 15 March 1993, handwritten note in possession of author. Koshun Shiono was apparently a writer of some fame. In 1893, he had published a book on the Soma family scandal, involving Tomotane Soma, former lord of the Sōma-Nakamura domain (in the eastern part of what is now Fukushima Prefecture), who suffered from mental illness. In 1883, his former retainer Takekiyo Nishigori accused the family of illegally incarcerating Tomotane; following Tomotane's death in 1892, Nishigori accused the family of poisoning him to death. See Koshun Shiono, *Tenka no Daigimon Sōmake Dokusatsu Jiken* (Tokyo: Takajima Kiyoshichi, 1893).

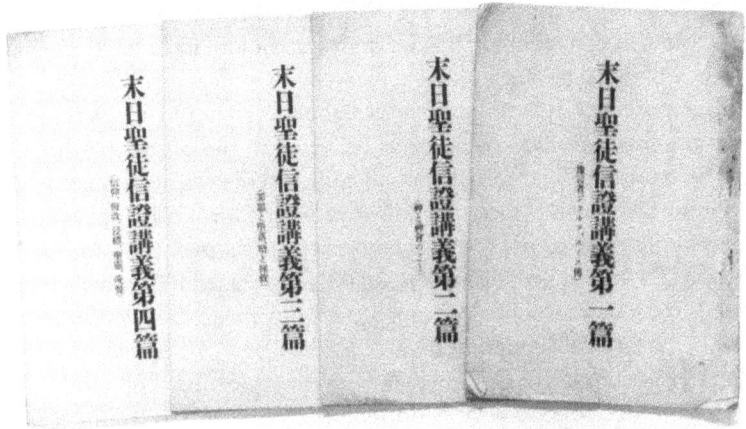

Shinshō Kōgi, a translation of *The Articles of Faith* by Talmage, was published in ten installments from May 1913. The consolidated volume was published in June 1915. Courtesy Bill McIntyre.

This songbook was to be used by Japanese Mormons until 1961 when some of the old hymns were revised and new hymns added by Tomigoro Takagi and his daughter, Toshiko Yanagida (see Section 12.5.1 in Chapter 12).

5.5.4. Translating Mormon Scriptures

In addition to the Bible, the LDS Church recognizes three other "standard works," namely, the Book of Mormon, the Doctrine and Covenants, and the Pearl of Great Price. Although one would expect the translation of these books of scripture to be high on the missionary work agenda, one must also acknowledge that it would be a laborious task to translate what is considered to be sacred religious writings into a foreign language in an accurate and befitting manner. Because no thought was given to asking a non-Mormon scholar to undertake the translation, someone (in this case, Alma O. Taylor) needed to gain sufficient proficiency in the language to begin the process. This explains why it took the Japan Mission eight years, until October 1909, to publish the Book of Mormon in Japanese. The translation of the Doctrine and Covenants started soon after, in April 1910, but it was never published before the mission closed. No attempt was made to translate the Pearl of Great Price. Prewar Japanese members and investigators thus remained severely handicapped in acquiring knowledge of many important Mormon teachings.

The translation of the Book of Mormon into Japanese was made by Taylor, with the assistance of Frederick A. Caine, from July 1904 to March 1908 (see Chapter 6 for a more complete discussion of the 1909 translation of the Book of Mormon). Three men served as scribes for the translation, Hachiro Mori (who, according to Taylor, wrote "over three fourths of it"), Yasubeiye Chiba, and Takeshiro Sakuraba;[118] Hiroyuki Namekawa helped with proofreading.[119] The criticism and correction of Taylor's draft translation, including changing the style from colloquial to classical, were made by three Japanese scholars, including Hirogoro Hirai, Choko Ikuta, and Kosaburo Kawai. On 11 October 1909, the first installment (1,000 copies) was delivered to the church by the printer. In early December 1909, specially bound copies were presented to the emperor, the empress, the crown prince, the crown princess, thirty titled men who were members of the Privy Council, and members of the cabinet. In connection with the October 1909 publication, the Japan Mission staged a massive advertising campaign to promote the book through the print media (see Appendix 6.2 in Chapter 6). Sales were disappointing.

The translation of the Doctrine and Covenants started soon after the publication of the Japanese Book of Mormon. The work of translation, by a Kofu member named Joji Shirai, took about four years to complete. Shirai had joined the LDS Church on 18 February 1908, his thirty-first birthday. He was a teacher at Kofu Municipal Commercial School, which was offering a five-year course of secondary vocational education.[120] Daniel P. Woodland recorded soon after his baptism: "Mr. Shirai is a professor who speaks fine English."[121]

On 17 April 1910, Shirai was set apart by mission president Elbert D. Thomas for this task; he was to begin with Section 107 before continuing to Sections 20, 89, and 119. According to the mission record for 28 July 1913, with the first three "divisions" having been received, mission president Heber Grant Ivins and church member Morisaburo Sato were "going over them."[122] On 29 December 1913, Shirai brought the translation up to Section 84, for which he was paid ¥83.10 (or $41.55 at the gold parity). Shirai was paid ¥17.20 ($8.60) on 15 May 1914, which may mean that the work was complete. On 10 July 1914, Ivins wrote a letter to the First Presidency asking if he should start preparing for the Doctrine and Covenants to be published in Japanese.[123] Years later, Lloyd Ivie stated that the church had never permitted the publication, saying that the time was not "ripe." More than forty years later, in September 1956, it was Ivie's understanding that the translation "was in the hands of the First Presidency."[124]

---

118. Taylor, Journal, 27 January 1908.
119. Ibid., 11 February 1909.
120. *Kanpō*, No. 8711, 3 July 1912.
121. Woodland, Journal, 4 September 1908.
122. Jensen, "History of the Japan Mission." Shirai also translated the preface to the songbook in September 1915. Stimpson, Journal, 10 and 18 September 1915.
123. Ivins, Journal, 29 December 1913; 15 May 1914; 10 July 1914.
124. In a letter to Murray Nichols dated September 1956, Lloyd Ivie stated that the completed translation had been kept carefully "in the inlaid cabinet in the Mission Home" and that, in 1921, he had requested the church to grant permission to publish it. As quoted in Nichols, "History of the Japan Mission," 40.

5.5.5. Translation of Mormon Terminology

By the turn of the twentieth century, the Japanese words for common biblical and other Christian terms had been established, thanks to the Protestant translation of the Old and New Testaments in the 1880s. These included such words as *ai* (love or charity), *akashi* (testimony), *ansokunichi* (Sabbath), *chōrō* (elder), *danjiki* (fast), *fukuin* (gospel), *gizensha* (hypocrite), *gūzō* (idol), *ihōjin* (Gentile), *imashime* (commandment), *kuiaratame* (repentance), *kyōkai* (church), *madoi* or *yūwaku* (temptation), *megumi* (grace), *okugi* (mystery), *sabaki* (judgment), *seirei* (Holy Ghost), *seito* (saint), *shinkō* (faith), *shito* (apostle), *shu* (Lord), *sugikoshi* (Passover), *sukui* (salvation), *sukuinushi* (savior), *tamamono* (gift), *torinashi* (intercession), *tsumi* (sin), and *yogensha* (prophet). For some other biblical terms, the adopted Chinese characters were established but their pronunciation evolved over time. Examples are: *kotonaru waza* (later changed to *kiseki*) for miracle, *makoto* (*shinri*) for truth, *okite* (*rippō*) for law, and *ten no tsukai* (*tenshi*) for angel. The translation of some terms remained somewhat fluid, including *kagirinaki inochi* (later to be replaced by *eien no seimei*) for eternal life, *saishi no osa* (*daisaishi*) for high priest, and *yomigaeri* (*fukkatsu*) for resurrection. Subsequent to the Protestant translation of the Bible, additional biblical translations were attempted, and the rising number of Christians found better ways of expressing some Christian concepts. The Japanese language itself was changing, but it is fair to say that the Mormon missionaries did not face the question of how to translate major biblical terms or Christian concepts.

This was not the case with a number of religious and ecclesiastical terms specific to the LDS Church. The most significant ones were the English terms *Latter-day Saints* and *Book of Mormon*. From early on, the Chinese characters for *Latter-day Saints* were quickly established, but it was somehow decided to pronounce them as *batsujitsu seito*, instead of *matsujitsu seito* as they would be pronounced in the postwar period. They were pronounced as *batsujitsu seito*, certainly by 1903, as shown by the pronunciation marks in the first missionary tract published in 1903. The practice could have started much earlier. Likewise, the Chinese character for *book* (in the Book of Mormon) was also quickly established, but the pronunciation of the character changed, from *kyō* to *kei*, around the time of the publication of the Japanese translation of the Book of Mormon in 1909. In his book (see Section 5.5.1 below), Goro Takahashi pronounced the term as *Morumon Kyō*, as did all successive authors or translators of Mormon literature through the translation of Edward H. Anderson's *A Brief History of the Church of Jesus Christ of Latter-day Saints* in August 1907. One finds that the pronunciation mark in the tract *Batsujitsu Seito*, first published in 1905, was *Morumon Kyō*, while it was *Morumon Kei* in the seventh printing of the same tract published in 1911.

One can only speculate why the unusual pronunciation was chosen for *batsujitsu seito* (Latter-day Saints) and why the pronunciation was changed from *Morumon Kyō* to *Morumon Kei* for the Book of Mormon. This requires knowledge of how Chinese characters were introduced to Japan. From the fifth to the eighteenth century, Japan incorporated Chinese characters into the phonetic system of its language. Along with the rise and fall of Chinese dynasties, the geographical area of primary cultural contact shifted, and so did the way the characters were originally pronounced in Chinese. During the fifth to the sixth centuries, for example, Japan adopted the way the characters were pronounced in the lower reaches of the Changjiang (Yangtze) River. As adapted to Japanese phonetics, this system of pronunciation is called *go-on* (lit. *Wu*-sound). This was followed in the eight and early ninth centuries by the adoption of the way the characters were pronounced in the area around Chang'an (present-day Xi'an). This system of pronunciation is called *kan-on* (lit. *Han*-sound).[125] The Japanese word Chinese characters, *kanji*, literally means *Han* (*Kan* in Japanese) characters.

A possible solution to the puzzle may be found in the fact that while the pronunciation system in Japan was largely changed from *go-on* to *kan-on* this transformation did not affect Buddhist terms. Since the Chinese pronunciation from which *kan-on* was derived was brought back to Japan by government missions to the Sui and Tang dynasties, arguably at the height of Chinese civilization, the *kan-on* system began to command legitimacy. The *kan-on* system further solidified its position following an A.D. 792 imperial edict promoting its use. On the other hand, the *go-on* system had by this time been firmly established in the reading of Buddhist sutras, as the original pronunciation from which it was derived had come to Japan with Buddhism itself. Thus, a dual system of reading Chinese characters developed in Japan,[126] with *go-on* mainly reserved for Buddhist terms and *kan-on* for most everything else, including in government and scholarly writing. For example, the same Chinese character for beauty is pronounced as *mi* in *go-on* and *bi* in *kan-on*; the character for male is *nan* in *go-on* and *dan* in *kan-on*; the character for female is *nyo* in *go-on* and *jo* in *kan-on*; and so forth.

It is then reasonable to assume that the unusual reading for Latter-day Saints and the switch from one reading to another for the Book of Mormon must reflect the desire of the Mormon missionaries to avoid Buddhist-sounding words, undoubtedly at the advice of natives knowledgeable about these issues: *batsu* and *kei* are *kan*-reading, while *matsu* and *kyō* are *go*-reading. For the word "latter-day," to pronounce it as *matsujitsu* would sound too much like the Buddhist concept of *mappō* (*matsu* and *ma* are the same character), a period of time in world history when *Dharma* is decayed. For the word "book," whereas the *go-on* reading of *kyō* denotes a Buddhist sutra, the *kan-on* reading of *kei* denotes a Confucian book of scripture, which connotes a sense of rationality and philosophical thinking. Even when the Book of Mormon was pronounced as *Morumon Kyō* in early publications, the word scripture was always read as *keiten*, not *kyōten*.

---

125. Tadashi Kamata and Torataro Yoneyama, *Dai Kango Rin* (Tokyo: Taishūkan Shoten, 1992), 851.

126. There are two other, minor systems of pronunciation called *sō-on* and *tō-on*.

The translation of many other uniquely Mormon terms was made only as circumstances necessitated. Many of these relate to the ecclesiastical organization of the church (such as the Mormon office of patriarch; geographical units such as ward and stake) or to deeper doctrines (such as celestial, terrestrial, and telestial kingdoms; exaltation). There was no urgency to translate these terms as long as the church organization was rudimentary and the missionaries focused on the basic message. It was more urgent to translate the sacrament prayers and the Articles of Faith. The sacrament prayers were first translated by Tatsutaro Hiroi in the spring of 1902; another translation was made about a year later by Goro Takahashi. In May 1904, Alma Taylor used these translations to create another, which was accepted by everyone in the mission.[127] The Articles of Faith too were translated early, likely by Goro Takahashi, as they appear in his book on Mormonism published in 1903 (see Section 5.5.1). Some adjustments were made to the translation, as can be verified by comparing the translations produced by Alma Taylor and John Stoker.[128]

To trace how and when some other Mormon terms were translated, the Japanese word *dendōbu* for Mormon mission (as in the Japan Mission) was likely coined by Goro Takahashi, as it appeared in his book; likewise, Takahashi adopted the word *kanchō* for church president.[129] The word *kanchō* denotes the head of a large Buddhist sect. Later on, the LDS Church instead would increasingly use the word *daikanchō* (*dai* means grand) for church president presumably because leaders thought that the head of the LDS Church must be more important than the head of a Buddhist sect. The word *shukufukushi* (patriarch) appeared by 1903 and *seisanshiki* (the ordinance of sacrament) and *shinken* (priesthood) by 1905.[130]

It was with the 1907 translation of Edward H. Anderson's *A Brief History of the Church of Jesus Christ of Latter-day Saints* that significant progress was made in establishing the Japanese translation of a large number of Mormon theological and ecclesiastical terms. By the time *To Shi Sekkyō Shū* (Sermons of Mr. Thomas) was published in late 1914, most terms appear to have been more or less established. This was certainly the case by the time the 1915 translation of James E. Talmage's *Articles of Faith* was published. The translation of *A Brief History*, for instance, coined such words as: *fukuinjidai* (dispensation), *shinkai* (godhead), *sutēkibu* (stake), and *teiinkai* (quorum). Likewise, *To Shi Sekkyō Shū* as well as the

---

127. Taylor, Journal, 22 May 1904.

128. For example, from *fukuinshi* to *shukufukushi* (for patriarch), from *kunkai* or *shikihō* to *gishiki* (for ordinance), and from *shiha* to *shizoku* (for tribe), but these adjustments were few and minor.

129. Most of the other uniquely Mormon terms Takahashi used did not enjoy currency in the prewar LDS Church in Japan. Some of these show his brilliance as a translator, and the contemporary church could benefit from using them, such as *enman no fukuin* (fulness of the gospel) and *kanrisuru shihainin* (steward in the context of stewardship).

130. Goro Takahashi had earlier translated the word priesthood as *kyōshoku* (lit. ministerial office) or *seishoku* (lit. holy office), whereas *shinken* literally means "God's authority."

translation of *The Articles of Faith* provided additional terms, including *daishuku-fukushi* (the Patriarch), *fujokyōkai* (Relief Society), *hoshi no sakae* (telestial glory), *saisho no chii* (first estate), *wādobu* (ward), and *yonin* (foreordination); it replaced the previously coined word for dispensation, *fukuinjidai*, with *shinken no jidai*. Some of these words, but not all, are in current use in the LDS Church.

5.6. Conclusion

The Japan Mission of the Church of Jesus Christ of Latter-day Saints operated from August 1901 to August 1924. In launching the work, Heber J. Grant, the first mission president, "started at the top." The missionaries lodged at first-class, Western hotels in Tokyo during most of the early months, studied the language by hiring a teacher, and received and sought out prominent men, some of whom became early collaborators; it was only after the missionary force was augmented nearly a year later that they moved into a large semi-Western house, which was used as the mission headquarters. Proselytizing work outside Tokyo started only in the spring of 1903. The selection of areas was haphazard and displayed what appeared to be a personal dislike by mission leaders for larger cities. Once the first few areas were selected, a new area could only be opened by closing one of the existing ones, as the missionary force remained limited. During most of its existence, the mission could support no more than four "conferences"—e.g., Kofu, Osaka, Sapporo, and Tokyo from 1911 to 1922. Whether or not thought was given to opening additional areas is a moot question, as there were no additional missionaries to send to new areas.

Two types of people were attracted to Mormonism: young students and older Christians. Given the limited language ability of the Mormon missionaries, and the fact that the investigators were from among the more literate population, the LDS Church would have benefited from more rapidly producing more Japanese-language literature. It took more than eight years to publish a Japanese translation of the Book of Mormon, the keystone of the Mormon religion. Another work of Mormon scripture, the Doctrine and Covenants, was never published though translated several years later. It is possible that the church would have had greater success in developing local leadership and strengthening the faith of Japanese converts in the Mormon message if more written material had been available to feed the flock. The Mormon proselytizing work in prewar Japan proved inconsequential for a country of fifty million people, slightly more than half the population of the United States. The perception that the Japan Mission was a total failure persists, but if there was a failure, it was largely the failure of the church to provide sufficient resources to make it successful.

Appendix 5.1. Prominent Men Befriended by Early Mormon Missionaries

Given the policy of starting "at the top," Grant and his associates met Japan's prominent men and even some historical figures. In 1902, Taylor wrote: "we have met and made friends with many prominent men . . . whose acquaintance would have been denied us, were it not that we followed the inspiration that directed us to make our home, at first, among the highest class."[131] Some of these people are discussed in this appendix.

1. Shiro Ichiki (1828–1903)

Heber J. Grant and his companions met Shiro Ichiki through the mediation of Tatsutaro Hiroi.[132] Ichiki was born in Kagoshima (Satsuma domain) into a samurai family. A student of gunnery, Ichiki was put in charge of producing firearms and guns, and negotiated with the foreign powers a purchase of military ships and other weapons, as Satsuma prepared for a showdown with the Tokugawa forces. In 1869, he led a military campaign to subdue the remaining Tokugawa soldiers who had fled to the northern island of Hokkaido. During the last sixteen years of his life, he compiled an official history of the Shimadzu family, the ruler of Satsuma. In addition, as part of an autobiography, he wrote an eye witness account of many important events during the last days of the Edo period leading up to the Meiji Restoration.[133]

His association with the Shimadzu family meant that Ichiki had access to the ruling class of Japanese society—virtually all of the key decision makers of the Meiji government (known as *genrō* or elder statesmen) had come from the Satsuma and Choshu domains. The Mormon missionaries were invited to his house on 13 February 1902. It is possible that Ichiki's interest in Mormonism arose from his knowledge of the Iwakura Mission's visit to Salt Lake City in 1872.[134] As a former samurai from Satsuma (on top of being the official chronicler of the history of the Shimadzu family), he was closely associated with Toshimichi Okubo, a former Satsuma samurai who participated in the Iwakura Mission as vice ambassador extraordinary. Being close to the inner circle of the government, moreover, Ichiki may also have been familiar with what Charles Le Gendre, French–American

---

131. Alma O. Taylor, "Some Features of Japanese Life," *Improvement Era* 5 (1902): 450.

132. Dai-Nippon Jinmei Jisho Kankō Kai, ed., *Dai-Nippon Jinmei Jisho*, vol. 1 (Tokyo: Kōdansha, 1937), 240; Kunihiko Shimonaka, comp., *Nihon Jinmei Daijiten*, vol. 1 (Tokyo: Heibonsha, 1979), 286; Nihon Rekishi Gakkai, comp., *Meiji Ishin Jinmei Jiten* (Tokyo: Yoshikawa Kōbun Kan, 1981), 91.

133. Shiro Ichiki, "Ichiki Shirō Jijoden," in *Kagoshima-ken Shiryō: Chūgikō Shiryō*, vol. 7, ed. by Kagoshima-ken Ishin Shiryō Hensan Sho (Kagoshima: Kagoshima-ken, 1980), 901–1037.

134. See Annex 1 towards the end of the volume for details.

advisor to the government, had earlier said about the Mormons.[135] In 1875, Le Gendre submitted a formal recommendation to Finance Minister Shigenobu Okuma that the Japanese government invite Mormon men, who were "mentally vigorous, forbearing, and skilled," to take Japanese wives, give them a "paradise" in Japan they had not yet found in the United States, and use them to colonize the island of Hokkaido.[136]

Taylor's journal entry on 14 February records the event of the previous day:

> Mr. S. Ichiki . . . has figured prominently in many of the wars in Japan especially during the troubles of the Meiji restoration. . . . To me our host is the man of the greatest character that we have yet met in Japan. He impressed me as being absolutely without hypocrisy and one who was not ashamed of his opinions and spoke them boldly whether to the high or the low.

In the meeting, Ichiki offered the Mormon missionaries an opportunity to "deliver an address on our teachings before a literary organization composed of newspaper editors and members of the House of Commons, in the hope that some of the prominent speakers and writers would be able to assist us in correcting the wrong impressions of our cause."[137] Ichiki visited the missionaries at the Metropole Hotel a few times, including at a farewell party for Grant who was returning to Utah to attend the April 1902 general conference.[138] In the end, nothing came out of their association with Shiro Ichiki.

2. TORANOSUKE MIYAZAKI (1872–1929)

Toranosuke Miyazaki was a religious fanatic who sought an audience with the Mormon missionaries on several occasions from 1901 to 1907. Taylor's scrapbook notes that Miyazaki visited the elders at the Metropole Hotel on 22 October 1901.[139] Taylor records on 12 May 1905:

---

135. Charles William Le Gendre (1830–99) was born in France, emigrated to the United States, and became a naturalized American citizen. Upon arriving from China in 1872, he remained in Japan until 1889, serving as advisor to different branches of the Japanese government. He published a book on the political and social conditions of Japan. General Le Gendre, *Progressive Japan, A Study of the Political and Social Needs of the Empire* (New York and Yokohama: C. Levy, 1878). Hiroshi Takeuchi, ed., *Rainichi Seiyōjinmei Jiten* (Tokyo: Nichigai Associates, 1983), 493.

136. Charles Le Gendre, "Ezochi Kaitaku ni Kansuru Ikensho," 18 July 1875, Waseda Daigaku Shakai Kagaku Kenkyūsho, compiler, *Ōkuma Bunsho*, vol. 2, Tokyo, 1959, 9–27. For an English-language account, see Sandra C. Caruthers, "Anodyne for Expansion: Meiji Japan, the Mormons, and Charles LeGendre," *Pacific Historical Review* 38 (May 1969): 129–39.

137. Taylor, Journal, 14 February 1902. See also Walker, "Strangers," 29.

138. Taylor, Journal, 16 February 1902; 23 February 1902; 9 March 1902.

139. Alma O. Taylor, "Scrapbook," LDS Church Archives.

Among [the visitors] was a man named Miyazaki who claims to be "The Christ." Some time ago this man was an inmate of a mental hospital.... This man first called on the "Mormons" about 3 1/2 years ago when we were living in the Metropole Hotel.... He seems to be quite fascinated with the claims we made at that time to have prophets in our church. This seemed to give him a desire for fame in the religious world.

Miyazaki called Taylor again as late as March 1907, this time to beg for money.[140]

Not much biographical information is known about Miyazaki, but he was a well-known religious figure from the late Meiji to the Taisho period. Miyazaki was the founder of a new religious movement known as *Shinsei Kyōdan*. In 1904, he published a book entitled *Waga Shin Fukuin*,[141] in which he proclaimed himself to be the greatest prophet in history—even greater than Jesus Christ and Buddha Shakyamuni. He taught that both Buddhism and Christianity had become corrupt; God was within us, so all that man needed to do was to recognize the divinity within him; once that realization was achieved, man's body became spiritualized; then even lusts became holy. Miyazaki speaks of the Mormon practice of polygyny, stating that polygyny in which the parties practiced spiritual love was superior to monogamy without such love; though Christianity professes monogamy, it allows a believer to remarry after the wife is dead, which amounts to polygyny. When accompanied by love, the union between husband and wife would be eternal. It is possible that some of these ideas were gleaned from Miyazaki's conversation with Heber J. Grant.[142] Miyazaki's book of "scripture" was translated by Goro Takahashi into English and published in 1910 as *My New Gospel*.[143]

Miyazaki was often seen preaching his gospel on the streets of Tokyo, so much so that he evidently became a household name for his eccentricity. Two of Japan's greatest modern writers, Ryunosuke Akutagawa and Ogai Mori, wrote about Miyazaki in their essays.[144] Akutagawa, for example, wrote how he was disturbed by a loud unsolicited sermon on his way to the funeral of an acquaintance, thinking whoever was doing this was irreverent. The annoyance was erased, however, as soon as he learned that the noise was coming from Miyazaki. It is not clear how large the membership of Miyazaki's religious movement was. In September 1914, when mission president H. Grant Ivins and missionary Arthur

---

140. Taylor, Journal, 12 March 1907.

141. Toranosuke Miyazaki, *Waga Shin Fukuin* (Tokyo: Maekawa Bun-ei-kaku, 1904).

142. H. Grant Ivins explicitly stated that Miyazaki had "obtained some of his ideas from the teachings of our church but he [had] made many of those ideas almost unrecognizable." Ivins, Journal, 27 December 1911.

143. Toranosuke Miyazaki, *My New Gospel*, trans. Goro Takahashi (Tokyo: New Gospel Society Publishing House, 1910).

144. Ryunosuke Akutagawa, "Sōgi Ki," 1916, in *Rashōmon, Hana, Imogayu* (Tokyo: Kadokawa Shoten, 1950); Ogai Mori, "Kanzan Jittoku Engi," 1916, in *Abe Ichizoku, Maihime* (Tokyo: Shinchōsha, 1968).

Cutler visited Miyazaki in his home, there were only two followers.[145] In 1925, a book was published by the Kobe branch of *Shinsei Kyōdan*, indicating that the number of followers might have increased somewhat and some of them were found outside Tokyo.[146]

3. INAZO NITOBE (1862–1933)

In the summer of 1903, Heber J. Grant met Inazo Nitobe at least twice, if not more, to discuss, among other things, Utah's sugar beet industry.[147] At that time, Nitobe was a senior official of the Japanese colonial government in Taiwan responsible for promoting the island's sugar industry, a position he held from February 1901 to January 1903. He occasionally returned to Tokyo where his American wife resided. During the early summer months of 1902, Nitobe was in Tokyo on his way to the United States and Europe on an assignment from the colonial government.[148] The LDS Japan Mission journal entry for 18 July 1903 records:

> Mr. and Mrs. Nitobe called in the evening. We found them very agreeable people and were glad to meet them. Mr. Nitobe is the author of a little book on Japan, entitled "Bushido," a copy of which was presented to Pres Grant some months ago by Captain Kakeki.[149]

The circumstances that led to their meeting are not known. It is possible that the association began as a friendship between their wives as American women of comparable age living in Tokyo. It could also be that Nitobe, learning of Grant's experience with the Utah Sugar Company,[150] contacted him. Although we know nothing about him, Captain Kakeki may have acted as the intermediary between the two.

---

145. Ivins, Journal, 13 September 1914.
146. Toranosuke Miyazaki, *Shinsei Kigen* (Kobe: Shinsei Kyōdan Kobe Shibu, 1925).
147. Much of the biographical information on Nitobe in this section comes from the following sources: George Oshiro, *Nitobe Inazō: Kokusai Shugi no Kaitakusha* (Tokyo: Chūō Daigaku Shuppanbu, 1992); Kingo Miyabe, "Shōden," Inazo Nitobe, *Nitobe Inazō Zenshū*, vol. 1 (Tokyo: Kyōbunkan, 1969), 427–45; Sharlie C. Ushioda, "Man of Two Worlds: An Inquiry into the Value System of Inazo Nitobe (1862–1933)," *East across the Pacific: Historical and Sociological Studies of Japanese Immigration and Assimilation*, ed. Hilary Conroy and T. Scott Miyakawa (Santa Barara, California: American Bibliographical Center–Clio Press, 1972), 187–210.
148. Nitobe, *Nitobe Inazō Zenshū*, vol. 1, 450.
149. The Japan Mission journal entry of 23 June 1903 records: "Pres Grant and wife called on Mr. Nitobe but he was not home and his wife was not well so they did not see either. In the evening Pres Grant called again and met Dr. Nitobe and had a long conversation on the beet sugar industry of Utah. He is interested in the agriculture of Japan and is a very influential man." Japan Mission, Historical Records and Minutes, 23 June 1903 and 18 July 1903.
150. In 1889, the Utah Sugar Company was incorporated in Salt Lake City, with implicit LDS Church support. Leading authorities of the church, including Wilford

Inazo Nitobe would become one of the most internationally known Japanese of the prewar period; his portrait was on the front cover of 5,000-yen currency notes issued by the Bank of Japan from November 1984 to April 2007. Born in 1862 into a high-ranking samurai family of the Nanbu (or Morioka) domain, he entered the Sapporo Agricultural College in 1877. The school maintained a Christian atmosphere due to its founding provost William S. Clark (1876–77) and several other American teachers, and Nitobe became a Christian along with a number of his classmates.[151] Upon graduation he worked for the Hokkaido Development Commission from 1881 to 1883, studied English literature and economics at the University of Tokyo from 1983 to 1984, and moved to the United States to study economics, history, and literature at the Johns Hopkins University in Baltimore from 1884 to 1887. It was during this period that he joined the Society of Friends (Quakers) and met his future wife Mary Patterson Elkinton, a Philadelphia Quaker.

Upon appointment to a faculty position at his alma mater in Sapporo in 1887, he was given a government order to go to Germany to pursue doctoral studies in agricultural economics. The Meiji government had adopted Germany as a model to emulate, so most government-funded students went to Germany to study during the Meiji period. In 1890, Nitobe obtained a doctor of philosophy degree from the University of Halle and returned to the United States to marry Mary Elkinton in 1891 before assuming his teaching duties in Sapporo. The next thirty years saw Nitobe in various positions of influence, including faculty positions at Kyoto and Tokyo Imperial Universities and president of the First Higher School and of Tokyo Women's Christian College. In 1920, he was appointed under-secretary-general of the League of Nations, a post he held until 1927. In 1926, he was appointed by the emperor to the House of Peers, the upper house of the Imperial Diet (where members served for life).

Woodruff and George Q. Cannon of the First Presidency, were among the shareholders. The church assisted the drive for funds to build a factory in Lehi, Utah, including by appointing Heber J. Grant as financial agent. During the first season, the company contracted with 556 farmers to grow 1,800 acres of beets, while the company itself operated 146 acres to grow beets. The first pound of sugar was made on 15 October 1891, proving to sceptics that sugar could be made from beets. Leonard J. Arrington, *Beet Sugar in the West: A History of the Utah-Idaho Sugar Company, 1891–1966* (Seattle and London: University of Washington Press, 1966), 6–7, 10, 13, 22–23. While in Japan, Grant remained chairman of the Utah Sugar Company. See Walker, "Strangers," 24.

151. Clark called himself president of the college, which might have been his understanding (see, for example, his inaugural address on 14 August 1876, as reprinted in the introduction to Sapporo Nōgakkō Gakugei Kai, comp., *Sapporo Nōgakkō* [Tokyo: Shōkabō, 1898]). In fact, Hirotake Chosho, an official with the Hokkaido Development Commission, served as the founding president (p. 27). Clark came to Sapporo on leave from the Massachusetts Agricultural College, where he was president from 1867 to 1879. Out of the second entering class of twenty-two students, seven, including Nitobe, were baptized in 1878 as Christians. Oshiro, *Nitobe Inazō*, 18.

He is best known for his book *Bushido: The Soul of Japan*, which he wrote in English and published in early 1900 through the Leeds and Biddle Company, a small Philadelphia publisher. It became a national bestseller in England following the Russo–Japanese War. It is reported that President Theodore Roosevelt read the book and distributed dozens of copies to his friends.[152] From October 1911 to June 1912, Nitobe gave nearly 170 lectures on Japan at a number of universities and other venues in the United States at the invitation of the Carnegie Endowment for International Peace. Of these lectures, the ones he delivered at six universities over a four-week period each were published as *The Japanese Nation: Its Land, Its People, and Its Life* in 1912 from G. P. Putnam's Sons in New York.[153] Some of the essays and lectures he prepared while he was in Europe as under-secretary-general of the League of Nations in Geneva were published as *Japanese Traits and Foreign Influences* in 1927 from Kegan Paul, Trench, Trubner & Co., London.[154]

Nitobe's apparent interest in Utah's sugar beet industry reflects two possible motives, which are not mutually exclusive. First, his immediate concern was undoubtedly about developing Taiwan's sugar cane industry. Taiwan had become Japan's first overseas colony in 1895 under the terms of the Treaty of Shimonoseki. Nitobe was appointed as a senior officer in charge of industrial promotion in the Japanese colonial government of Taiwan. He was asked to make plans to promote the sugar industry in Taiwan, which he prepared and submitted as a report in September 1901.[155] As a result of this recommendation, the production of sugar in Taiwan trebled in a few years, allowing Japan to become self-sufficient in sugar.[156] In the report he submitted to the colonial government, Nitobe devoted several pages to a comparison of sugar cane (grown in tropical climate) and sugar beets (grown in temperate climate) in terms of capital requirements, sugar content per unit of land, and labor input, concluding that it made more economic sense to produce sugar cane in Taiwan than to produce sugar beets in Hokkaido.[157]

Second, Nitobe may also have had enduring interest in Hokkaido's sugar beet industry. When he was about to join the Hokkaido Development Commission

---

152. The author's preface to the tenth edition published in 1905 by G. P. Putnam's Sons, New York.

153. Inazo Nitobe, *The Japanese Nation: Its Land, Its People, and Its Life, with Special Consideration to Its Relations with the United States* (New York: G. P. Putnam's Sons, 1912). These lectures were given at the universities of Brown, Columbia, Johns Hopkins, Virginia, Illinois, and Minnesota. Miyabe, "Shōden," 439, states that Nitobe gave 166 lectures across the United States.

154. Inazo Nitobe, *Japanese Traits and Foreign Influences* (London: Kegan Paul, Trench, Trubner & Co. Ltd, 1927).

155. Inazo Nitobe, "Tōgyō Kairyō Ikensho," September 1901. Ntobe, *Nitobe Inazō Zenshū*, vol. 4, 169–226.

156. Oshiro, *Nitobe Inazō*, 86.

157. Nitobe, "Tōgyō Kairyō Ikensho," 176–92.

in 1881 upon graduation from the Sapporo Agricultural College, he was asked by the provost what he would like to accomplish. In response, Nitobe gave him two priorities. The first was "opening up" (that is, development of additional farmland in Hokkaido) and the second was "crops (sugar beets)."[158] In Hokkaido, an experimental cultivation of sugar beets began in 1871, and the first sugar beet factory was built by the national government in 1880. The factory was sold to private hands in 1887; another private sugar company was formed in 1888. Both of these firms went out of business by 1901, however, owing to a shortage of crops and technological problems. It was not until 1919 that a sharp rise in the prices of sugar created a condition for the resumption of the sugar industry in Hokkaido.[159] It is possible at the time that Nitobe was considering how to revive sugar beet production there.

4. Kanzo Uchimura (1861–1930)

In September 1905, Alma O. Taylor went to see Kanzo Uchimura at his house. His journal entry for 13 September, recording this visit, described him as someone who believed the Bible but "does not belong to any one sect," who was "a gifted man in literary lines," and who was "held by some as the most able writer in Japan." Uchimura was probably the most prominent Japanese Christian of his time and the main character of the infamous Uchimura Incident of January 1891. His failure in a ceremony to bow deeply enough before the portrait of the emperor, while a teacher at the prestigious First Higher School in Tokyo, led to a national debate on whether a Christian could be a loyal subject of the emperor. The outcome of this was a diminished Christian cause in Japan against the rising tide of nationalism (see Section 4.4 in Chapter 4).

Kanzo Uchimura was born in 1861 into a samurai family of the Takasaki domain while the family was residing on an assignment in Edo. He was a classmate of Inazo Nitobe at the Sapporo Agricultural College, where he, too, became a Christian in 1878. Upon graduation in 1881, he worked for the Hokkaido Development Commission. It was during this time that, in 1882, he became one of the organizers of the Sapporo Independent Church and subsequently resigned from his position at the commission. In 1884, Uchimura went to the United States and was enrolled as a junior at Amherst College. While at Amherst, his Christian faith was firmly established thanks to the influence and advice of college president Julius Hawley Seelye. In 1888, Uchimura returned to Japan after studying at Hartford Theological Seminary for a year. He taught biology, English, geography, history at several schools, including the First Higher School, but most

---

158. Miyabe, "Shōden," 431.

159. Hokkaidō-chō Keizaibu, *Hokkaidō Nōgyō Gaiyō* (Sapporo: Hokkaidō-chō Keizaibu, 1935), 54; Nihon Tensai Seitō Kabushiki Kaisha, *Nihon Tensai Seitō Shichijūnen Shōshi* (Tokyo: Nihon Tensai Seitō Kabushiki Kaisha, 1989), 18.

of the rest of his life was spent in writing, lecturing, and Christian activities as a nondenominationalist.[160]

He was both a Christian and a patriot (he said that he served two J's—Jesus and Japan). He became a respected and influential writer because of his sense of justice and also because he did not hesitate to criticize openly when he saw injustice. In 1898, he founded a magazine called *Tokyo Dokuritsu Zasshi* to criticize the arrogance, corruption, and hypocrisy of politicians as well as businessmen, educators, and the nobility, especially the ruling elites dominated by people from the former Satsuma and Choshu domains. He sought to make out of Japan a country in which God's justice, love, and truth would be realized. An autobiography of his conversion to Christianity, which is a Japanese translation of the English original written in 1893 but published in 1906, is widely read today in Japan.[161] The book has been translated into Danish, French, German, and Swedish.[162]

---

160. Saburo Ouchi, "Nenpu," in Kanzo Uchimura, *Yo wa Ikanishite Kirisuto Shinto to Narishika* (Tokyo: Kōdansha, 1971), 252–61.

161. Kanzo Uchimura, *The Diary of a Japanese Convert* (Chicago: Fleming H. Ravell, 1906). The version published in Japan in the same year was entitled, *How I Became a Christian: Out of My Diary* (Tokyo: Keiseisha, 1906).

162. Saburo Ouchi, "Kaisetsu," Uchimura, *Kirisuto Shinto*, 236–51.

Chapter 6

Proclaiming the Way in Japanese: The 1909 Translation of the Book of Mormon

6.1. Introduction

This chapter presents an analysis of the first Japanese translation of the Book of Mormon, described by Joseph Smith as being the keystone of the Church of Jesus Christ of Latter-day Saints.[1] Several authors have discussed how Alma O. Taylor, with the assistance of Frederick A. Caine, initiated, continued, and finished the work of translation between July 1904 and March 1908, before the book was published in October 1909.[2] As interesting as these details may be, a historical evaluation of the 1909 translation can only be based on the merits of the translation itself. Thus, the chapter begins where the previous authors have left off by discussing, among other aspects, the style, quality, and accuracy of the translation. In making this evaluation, we primarily focus on how important ideas (with potential doctrinal implications or impact on religious behavior) are expressed and preserved.

This is not a linguistic exercise. This chapter does not, for example, discuss the semantic or syntactic issues of correspondence in meaning between words, whether sentence structure (e.g., passive or active voice construction, word order, and the like) is preserved or changed, or how sentence length compares between

---

1. Technical notes: the analysis of this chapter uses the 1979 LDS edition of the Book of Mormon as the source text to assess the 1909 Japanese translation (though the translators used the "sixth electrotype edition published at Liverpool"). Alma O. Taylor, letter addressed to Anthon Lund, 15 November 1904. Alma O. Taylor Papers, LDS Church Archives.

2. An overview is provided in Murray L. Nichols, "History of the Japan Mission of the Church of Jesus Christ of Latter-day Saints, 1901–1924" (MA thesis, Brigham Young University, 1957). See also Van C. Gessel, "Languages of the Lord: The Japanese Translations of the Book of Mormon"; and Sarah Cox Smith, "Translator or Translated? The Portrayal of the Church of Jesus Christ of Latter-day Saints in Print in Meiji Japan," in *Taking the Gospel to the Japanese, 1901 to 2001*, ed. Reid L. Neilson and Van C. Gessel, 127–45 and 233–6, respectively (Provo, Utah: Brigham Young University Press, 2006).

the source and target languages.³ Nor does it attempt to frame its discussion in terms of modern translation theory.⁴ In a fundamental sense, translation encompasses all forms of communication between two individuals. In written communication, for example, one first translates thought into coded graphic marks; the other person then translates those marks back into a mental text.⁵ But the written text may not convey the same message to the reader because words could carry different shades of meaning even in the same language, depending on the historical and cultural experience of the individual. Modern translation theory has thus become a discourse on language, mind, culture, and semiotics. At least for now, meandering into these territories does not seem helpful to the task at hand.

Admittedly, the assessment of the 1909 translation ultimately involves subjective judgment. In order to introduce as much objectivity as possible, we appeal to two widely accepted rules of good translation to frame the discussion: (1) the translated text must sound *natural* in the target language (called "transparency," or idiomatic translation, in the literature); and (2) it must be *faithful* to the original ("fidelity," or faithful translation). These sometimes conflicting requirements of transparency and fidelity have been debated for over two millennia in the theory and practice of interlingual translation, at least since Cicero and Horace in the first century B.C.⁶

The ultimate quality that interlingual translation strives to achieve is *equivalence*. Broadly, there are two approaches.⁷ First, literal translation attempts to transform the original text into the target language word for word. In practice, this is not fully possible because the rules of grammar and syntax differ between languages, so that *literal* translation may more appropriately be called *literalist* translation. For example, the Japanese idiomatic sentence describing a person whose physical predisposition does not easily permit partaking of very hot substance ("*boku wa nekojita da*") may be translated into English word for word as "I am a cat tongue." This of course is nonsensical. We must at least render it as "I have a cat tongue," or to better relay the meaning, "I have a tongue overly sensitive to heat." Second, free translation renders the original text sense by sense, for example, by rendering the above sentence as "I cannot eat or drink very hot things" or "I easily burn my mouth." There is no single correct translation. The

---

3. Such a linguistic assessment of the 1957 Japanese translation of the Book of Mormon is offered by Jiro Numano, "The Japanese Translation of the Book of Mormon: A Study in the Theory and Practice of Translation" (MA thesis, Brigham Young University, 1976). See Section 12.2.3 in Chapter 12.

4. Critical reviews of modern translation theory are offered by George Steiner, *After Babel: Aspects of Language and Translation* (London: Oxford University Press, 1975); and Willis Barnstone, *The Poetics of Translation: History, Theory, Practice* (New Haven: Yale University Press, 1993).

5. Barnstone, *Poetics of Translation*, 20.

6. Steiner, *After Babel*, 236.

7. Barnstone, *Poetics of Translation*, 23, 39.

art of translation is to determine the optimal mix of transparency and fidelity to achieve reasonable equivalence.

Practical applications are subtle, however. For example, one author suggests translating the English sentence "His rudeness was more than her sensitivity could tolerate" into Japanese as "*kare no burei na gendō wa sensai na kanojo ni wa totemo taerarenai mono de atta*," a literal retranslation of which might be "His rude language and conduct was something the sensitive woman could not tolerate." The same author further notes the occasional need to change words or parts of speech, suggesting that the English sentence "The nature of history would alter" be translated as "*rekishi ga henshitsu suru de arō*" (history would change in character), where *henshitsu* is a verb that can mean "to change in quality." These examples show that good literary writing in Japanese generally avoids use of abstract nouns, especially as subjects, to sound natural.[8]

Elaborating on the concept of fidelity, another author notes that the German sentence "*Dein Zagen zögert den Tod heran*" (from *Faust* by Johann Wolfgang von Goethe) has alternatively been translated by three competent translators into English in the following ways: "Thy irresolution lingers death hitherwards"; "Thy shrinking slowly hastens the blows"; and "My shrinking only brings Death more near."[9] If fidelity allows such variations between German and English, two relatively close languages, one would expect scope for even greater variations between English and Japanese. Fidelity, however, does mean that the translator must refrain from "showing his own self" in the work (except perhaps in the translation of poetry), that he should say neither more nor less than the original, and that his role is not to provide commentary or explanation.[10]

In the realm of religious translation, there may be another aspect to the concept of fidelity. When words of authority are involved, translation may need to be more *literal* or *literalist* even at the risk of making the translated text sound unnatural. Sidney Sperry characterized the English of the Book of Mormon as "translation English," "that type of English that would be produced by a translator who frequently follows the original too closely, the syntax of which is thus made plain in the English dress." He then cites as examples "hear the words of me" (Jacob 5:2) for "hear my words"; and "stealing away the hearts of the people" (Mosiah 27:9) for "deceiving the people."[11] Royal Skousen, noting that many of the changes made in succeeding editions of the Book of Mormon had been to "remove grammatical uses that are nonstandard in modern English," argued that

---

8. These examples come from Yoshifumi Saito, *Honyaku no Sahō* (Tokyo: Tōkyō Daigaku Shuppankai, 2007), 17, 24, and 34.

9. This example comes from Toyoichiro Nogami, *Honyaku Ron* (Tokyo: Iwanami Shoten, 1932), 7–8. The book was published as part of a multivolume compendium of scholarly works on Japanese and Western literature in the celebrated *Iwanami Kōza* series.

10. Nogami, *Honyaku Ron*, 4–5.

11. Sidney B. Sperry, "The Book of Mormon as Translation English," *Journal of Book of Mormon Studies* 4 (1995): 214–16.

Joseph Smith made a literal translation of a non-English text.¹² It is possible that, in the trade-off involving religious translation, greater weight needs to be given to fidelity, even to the point of being as literal as reasonably possible.¹³

The rest of this chapter begins by discussing the question Alma Taylor faced as to whether the translation should use a style based on the grammar of contemporary spoken Japanese or that based on the grammar of classical Japanese, which was more widely used at the time. The chapter then examines the work of revision, emphasizing how native reviewers, including able literary critic and writer Choko Ikuta, perfected Taylor's draft translation, before identifying several recurring patterns of departure from literalism, which make the translation sound natural, graceful, forceful, or complete in Japanese. The chapter will conclude by highlighting examples of notable words and expressions that give a special flavor to the 1909 translation and by addressing the ultimate question of accuracy. Finally, appendices highlight the major differences between classical and contemporary Japanese and summarize the Mormon missionaries' campaign to advertise the 1909 Japanese translation of the Book of Mormon.

6.2. The Choice of Style

It was important for Taylor's translation to be reviewed by "some native scholar" because he knew "[his] Japanese was all too imperfect to produce a translation worthy of the approval and respectful consideration of the public."¹⁴ The search for a reviewer began in earnest in June 1907 even before the work of translation was fully complete. Up to this time, Taylor had assumed that his translation would be corrected, revised, and perfected by a native reviewer in the style he had used—the style of the colloquial language he had learned to speak. As he soon learned, written Japanese was at the time in the process of significant change, and the choice of style in which to render the translation was no simple matter.

The style in which educated people wrote Japanese from around the eighth century through the early twentieth century is called *bungotai* (lit. "written language style"). Although *bungotai* in turn encompasses several distinct literary traditions, it shares a common set of grammatical rules established during the Heian period (794–1192), when Japanese literature flourished and great works, including the *Tale of Genji*, were created (see Appendix 6.1 for a simple comparison between the two styles). Because the Japanese of the Heian period was a great literary language, it should come as no surprise that the grammar (and to some

---

12. Royal Skousen, "The Original Language of the Book of Mormon: Upstate New York Dialect, King James English, or Hebrew?" *Journal of Book of Mormon Studies* 3 (1994): 29.

13. This is the position the LDS Church took in 1991 when it initiated the work of translating the Book of Mormon into contemporary Japanese.

14. Alma O. Taylor, "The History of the Japanese Translation of the Book of Mormon," not dated, BYU Archives.

extent the vocabulary) of the period became the standard of written Japanese over subsequent generations.

In the thirteenth century, the spoken language began to undergo transformation as the central players in Japanese society changed from the court nobles to the samurai warriors. The character of warrior life dictated the nature of the changes that took place—toward simplification. Spoken Japanese lost two vowels and a number of auxiliary verbs (which in Japanese define the functions of both verbs and adjectives in a sentence); the rules of verb conjugations also changed. Coupled with significant vocabulary changes, the difference between spoken and written Japanese by the middle of the nineteenth century was so great that an illiterate person would have hardly understood a sentence if it was read to him.

The significant divergence between spoken and written language became a major public issue at the beginning of the Meiji period (1868–1912), when the government set out to transform Japan into a modern nation. Some felt that *bungotai* was not an appropriate literary style for a modern state as the conventions were far too removed from the experience of ordinary people and hence too difficult for them to master.[15] Modernization requires a literate population because a new way of organizing society can only be facilitated through education. Universal education was instituted quickly, but the question remained as to the "language" of instruction, and out of this grew a national movement to "unify spoken and written language" (*gembunitchi* in Japanese).

The need some felt to unify spoken and written language as the prerequisite for a modern state was not unique to Japan but was shared by other countries, including China. Even European countries had confronted the same issue several centuries earlier. It was only in the fourteenth century that major literary works finally began to appear in the vernacular (as opposed to Latin), such as Dante's *Divina Commedia* and Chaucer's *Canterbury Tales*. Establishing the grammar of spoken language as the basis for writing requires the genius of a great writer. Writing, even in the colloquial style, entails greater elements of formality; it requires a great writer to develop rules of good writing. When Taylor completed the translation of the Book of Mormon, such rules were finally being established in Japanese, thanks to the efforts of modern writers, who all sought a language closer to their usual mode of communication.[16]

The question Taylor had to deal with was similar to what the Protestant missionaries had faced some thirty years earlier. In translating the Bible into

---

15. Nanette Twine, *Language and the Modern State: The Reform of Written Japanese* (New York: Routledge, 1991), 8.

16. There were three main schools whose writers contributed to the development of colloquial-style writing. Psychological realism attempted an "impartial description of man and his environment"; the *Shaseibun* school attempted to "portray places, people, and events in the objective manner of an artist"; and the Naturalist school believed that the only subject novelists could write on "with total lack of fabrication was themselves." Twine, *Language and the Modern State*, 25, 155–56.

Japanese, most foreign representatives of the Protestant missions felt that the translation should be rendered in contemporary style in order to make it accessible to a wide audience. On the other hand, their Japanese collaborators considered that the dignity of Chinese-heavy classical style would be more appropriate for an authoritative religious text. In the end, the latter position prevailed, in part because the rules of good writing in the colloquial style were not yet developed. The first joint Protestant translations of the New Testament (completed in 1880) and the Old Testament (in 1887) were rendered in classical style, though as a concession to the foreign missionaries the use of Chinese was light.[17]

The situation in the first decade of the 1900s was different in two conflicting respects. Following the publication of the Protestant translation of the Bible, the *gembunitchi* movement actually waned. This was due, in part, to the establishment of universal education, which raised the literacy level of the public. As a result, some newspapers, which had earlier used conversational style, reverted to classical style.[18] Instead, classical style developed into a modern style of its own called *futsūbun* (lit. "ordinary or common writing"). *Futsūbun*, while still based on classical grammar, used the colloquial vocabulary and accommodated elements of Western languages in translation style.[19] After about 1897 it was in wide use in newspapers, textbooks, and government business.

On the other hand, the *gembunitchi* movement received a renewed momentum at the beginning of the twentieth century. In 1904 the national government adopted the policy of introducing contemporary style material in language textbooks. Certain features of spoken Japanese, which make it sound repetitious and monotonous when committed to writing, needed to be overcome in the contemporary style. The modern novelists introduced new auxiliary verbs to accommodate variation, crispness, occasional change in tone, and room for the individuality of the writer to play out. Thus, Taylor in fact faced a viable choice—between the classical style of the *futsūbun* variety and the contemporary style just being established.[20]

Taylor records that many of the Japanese he sought advice from insisted that the "pure literary style" should be used. But he continued to believe that contemporary style was the most appropriate for the Book of Mormon:

> My writings have all been in what is called "gembunitchi." . . . This being nearer the form of every day speech, I had decided that, for general interpretation by all classes,

---

17. Norihisa Suzuki, *Seisho no Nihongo* (Tokyo: Iwanami Shoten, 2006), 99–100.

18. Masahide Yamamoto, *Gembunitchi no Rekishi Kōsatsu* (Tokyo: Ōfūsha, 1971), 46–49.

19. Masahide Yamamoto, *Kindai Buntai Hassei no Shiteki Kenkyū* (Tokyo: Iwanami Shoten, 1965), 2–7.

20. While 78 percent of novels were written in contemporary style in 1905, the percentage rose to 98 percent in 1907 and further to 100 percent in 1908. Outside the field of literature, the proportion of *futsūbun* remained high, as much as 54 percent in a representative magazine in 1907, though it declined to less than 10 percent in 1917. Yamamoto, *Kindai Buntai Hassei*, 51. See also Twine, *Language and the Modern State*, 188–93.

"gembunitchi" was the proper style for the Book of Mormon translation. Nor was this decision made without investigation, consultation and earnest reflection. I sought to adopt the style best calculated to serve the purposes of the Lord. And again, "gembunitchi" was in the line of my studies in Japanese, and I felt I would do better in it than in any other style.

Determined that the style should remain contemporary, Taylor started to "secure the services of a good critic" in that style.[21]

6.3. The Work of Revision

Taylor first approached Kinzo Hirai because their "experiences with this gentleman in the past had proved his integrity and ability."[22] Hirai was a language scholar and an ordained Zen priest, who had attended the World's Parliament of Religions held in Chicago in 1893 as a member of the Japanese Buddhist delegation and given a speech entitled, "The Real Position of Japanese toward Christianity."[23] From the turn of the twentieth century, he participated in the ecumenical activities of the Unitarian movement and taught English at several institutions of secondary and higher education.[24] In April 1903, the Mormon missionaries were able to secure the use of a meeting place to hold their first public meeting in Japan through the help offered by Hirai. Taylor had since maintained regular contact with him (see Section 5.3.3 in Chapter 5).

Kinzo Hirai, a Zen priest and language scholar, was helpful to the Mormons. Courtesy National Diet Library.

Hirai gave serious consideration to Taylor's request but concluded that he himself could not help. Instead, he introduced Taylor to his associate Zenshiro Noguchi (1864–?), who lived in Kobe some 400 miles southwest. Noguchi's association with Kinzo Hirai went back at least to the mid-1880s, when Noguch served as the headmaster of Oriental Hall, a Kyoto Buddhist academy, which Hirai himself had founded in 1885. In 1888, Noguchi traveled to Ceylon and India on behalf of leading Japanese Buddhists and escorted Henry Steel

---

21. Taylor, "The History."
22. Ibid.
23. John H. Barrows, ed., *The World's Parliament of Religions*, vol. 1 (Chicago: Parliament, 1893).
24. Konen Tsunemitsu, *Nihon Bukkyō Tobei Shi* (Tokyo: Bukkyō Shuppankyoku, 1964), 368–75. Shinichi Yoshinaga, comp., "Hirai Kinzo ni okeru Meiji Bukkyō no Kokusaika ni kansuru Shūkyōshi-Bunkashi-teki Kenkyū" (Maizuru, Kyoto: Maizuru Kōtō Senmon Gakkō, 2007), 7–30.

Olcott, an American Buddhist and president of the Theosophical Society, to Japan. In 1893, Noguchi accompanied the Japanese Buddhist delegation to Chicago as an interpreter;[25] in the same year, he published an English translation of *Shukyō Tetsugaku Gaikotsu* (Tokyo: Hozōkan, 1892), a classic work by *Jōdo Shinshū* priest and philosopher Manshi Tokunaga, as *The Skeleton of a Philosophy of Religion*.[26] Like Hirai, Noguchi became active in the Unitarian movement in Tokyo at the turn of the twentieth century. It appears that Noguchi was a salaried worker when Taylor visited him in July 1907.[27] Taylor left him with a sample of his translation for him to look over, along with a copy of the English Book of Mormon.[28]

Zenshiro Noguchi of Kobe corrected a portion of Taylor's draft translation of the Book of Mormon. Courtesy National Diet Library.

Taylor then visited Sendai, some 200 miles north of Tokyo, to see Genta Suzuki, a Methodist and a friend to the Mormon missionaries. Suzuki (1865–1945) had studied at Central College (now Central Methodist University) in Fayette, Missouri, where he received a bachelor of arts degree in 1894.[29] After returning to Japan, he became an English teacher at Kansei Gakuin, a Methodist academy in Kobe, and in April 1899 accepted an invitation from his brother-in-law to become the chief editor of the regionally influential *Kahoku Shinpō* in his hometown. Suzuki was responsible for English-language columns and wrote occasional articles on international affairs. He had also published translations of English-language novels.[30] Again, Taylor left him with a sample of his translation, along with a copy of the English Book of Mormon.[31]

Taylor corresponded with both men for some time, asking each to correct his translation of the first chapter of the First Book of Nephi in contemporary style.

---

25. Barrows, *World's Parliament*, 440–43.

26. Yoshinaga, "Hirai Kinzo ni okeru Meiji Bukkyō," 10. Tokunaga later changed his name to Kiyozawa.

27. Tsunemitsu, *Bukkyō Tobei Shi*, 375–79.

28. Taylor, Journal, 20 July 1907. Taylor was not impressed with Noguchi's character and his smoking and drinking habit, noting: "He does not impress me as a duplicate character to Mr. Hirai the difference all being in favor of the latter."

29. Joy Dodson, Missouri United Methodist Archives, Central Methodist College, e-mail to author, 5 June 1998.

30. Kahoku Shinpōsha, *Kahoku Shinpō no Hachijūnen* (Sendai: Kahoku Shinpōsha, 1977), 30–31. See also Kazuo Ichiriki, letter to author, 26 December 1997.

31. Taylor, Journal, 25–26 July 1907. Taylor was impressed with Suzuki's "personality" and believed that "he is as clean a man, morally speaking, as any I have approached."

The correction Taylor received from Suzuki, however, was in classical style (upon Taylor's insistence, Suzuki would produce another correction in contemporary style);[32] the correction received from Noguchi was made only in classical style, at the receipt of which Taylor wrote back asking him why.[33] As Taylor understood, the message from both men was that "all efforts at putting force and dignity into the translation as it stood in 'gembunitchi' had proved unsuccessful," indicating how difficult it was to use the contemporary style in a manner that deserved "public praise" because the rules of writing were not yet definite. "Consultation, prayer, inquiry and thought anew" on the choice of style helped determine the change.[34]

Genta Suzuki, editor of the *Kahoku Shinpō* in Sendai, was the second person to correct Taylor's translation. Courtesy Shichiro Suzuki.

After deciding to adopt the classical style, Taylor had no need to look for a critic outside of Tokyo. He thus signed a contract with Hirogoro Hirai (1866–?), Kinzo Hirai's younger brother and a teacher of English at Waseda University. In 1882, Hirogoro had graduated from Kyoto Prefectural Normal School and then studied at an English language school. In 1890, he published a Japanese translation of *John Milton: An Essay* by Thomas Babington Macaulay as *Miruton Ron* (Kyoto: Bunkōdō); in 1903, he published a Japanese translation of the utopian novel *Looking Backward* by Edward Bellamy as *Hyakunen go no Shakai* (Tokyo: Keiseisha). From 1903 to 1908, he taught English at Waseda's vocational and secondary divisions.[35] Earlier in the year, Hirogoro had helped translate Taylor's article on the Mormon practice of polygamy (published in the 19 March issue of the *Jiji*) as well as an appendix on the same topic Taylor had prepared for inclusion in the Japanese translation of *A Brief History of the Church* (see Sections 5.7.3 and 5.7.4 in Chapter 5).[36]

The contract was signed with Hirogoro on 2 September 1907. It stated that Hirai would devote all his time to the "criticism" of Taylor's Japanese translation of the Book of Mormon for ¥125 ($62.50 at the gold parity) per month. In March 1908, however, when Hirai had completed the work through the third chapter of the Third Book of Nephi, a presumed scandal involving Hirai was

---

32. Taylor, Journal, 30 July 1907; 6 August 1907; 13 August 1907.
33. Taylor, Journal, 13 August 1907; 15 August 1907.
34. Taylor, "The History."
35. Yoshinaga, "Hirai Kinzo ni okeru Meiji Bukkyō," 8, 29.
36. Taylor, Journal, 19 March 1907; 20 March 1907; 28 March 1907; 15 April 1907.

reported in the press.[37] Though Taylor became persuaded that the accusation was groundless and Hirai not guilty, his investigation of the matter revealed that Hirai had not severed his relationship with Waseda University, as prescribed in the contract, but he had "played sick to them," which "made him a liar to me."[38] The contract was revoked on 31 March 1908.

Anxious to get "one of the best writers in Japan," Taylor approached two gifted authors of national fame: Kinnosuke (or Soseki) Natsume and Yujiro (or Shoyo) Tsubouchi.[39] Both men declined the request, but Natsume recommended Hiroharu Ikuta, "a recent graduate of the Imperial University and author of several books which had been well received in literary circles."[40] Hiroharu (Koji) Ikuta (1882–1936), better known in Japan by his pen name Choko Ikuta, was a prolific literary critic, novelist, playwright, and translator of prewar Japan. He became active in literary circles while attending school and, according to the *Nihon Kindai Bungaku Daijiten* (Dictionary of Modern Japanese Literature), he became acquainted with Natsume in the winter of 1905.[41] In November 1907 he published a book entitled *Bungaku Nyūmon* (An Introduction to Literature) with a foreword by Natsume; in March 1908 he published an article on Natsume in the monthly *Chūō Kōron* (Central Review). In terms of literary skill, he was more than qualified to act as a reviewer for Taylor's translation.

Ikuta was qualified in three other important respects. First, he was thoroughly familiar with the language of the Bible. Ikuta had been an avid reader of the Bible while attending secondary school in Osaka. In the fall of 1898, he became affiliated with the Universalists, though his interest in Christianity began to wane as he developed interest in European philosophies and social ideas (he died a Buddhist). Second, Ikuta was a highly competent translator in his own right as he

---

37. The 16 March 1908 issue of the *Yorozu Chōhō* reported under a prominent heading that a married teacher of English at Waseda University by the name of Hirogoro Hirai had fallen in love with and took custody of a prostitute (thus liberating her from servitude in a brothel). A reporter from the *Miyako Shinbun* investigated this presumed incident, however, and demonstrated in a series of three articles beginning on 27 March 1908 that the accusation was groundless.

38. Taylor, "The History." In January 1908, the contract had been modified to allow Hirai to teach three hours on Wednesdays and Fridays at Waseda University. Taylor, Journal, 9 January 1908; 11 January 1908; 14 January 1908.

39. Soseki Natsume (1867–1916) and Shoyo Tsubouchi (1859–1935) were both major figures in the modernization of Japanese literature. Natsume, who began his career as a scholar of English literature, became one of the greatest novelists of modern Japan by writing several works of lasting influence, beginning with *I Am a Cat* (a satire on life in Meiji Japan seen through the eyes of a cat). Tsubouchi not only wrote plays and novels but also translated major Western literary works into Japanese, including the complete works of Shakespeare.

40. Taylor, "The History."

41. Nihon Kindai Bungakukan, ed., *Nihon Kindai Bungaku Daijiten*, vol. 1 (Tokyo: Kōdansha, 1977), 79–80.

would soon be recognized for his translations of Western literary and philosophical works. Early in his career, he produced the first Japanese translation of Friedrich Nietzsche's *Also Sprach Zarathustra*, which he published in January 1911 (his translation work, from May 1909 through 1910, began shortly after completing the work of revising Taylor's translation). Third, Ikuta had a special respect for the language of the Bible in classical style. In the preface to his second translation of *Also Sprach Zarathustra*, first published in 1921, Ikuta noted that the classical style was the only way to express the simplicity and clarity, and the grace and dignity, of the original work in the German language. In the preface to the 1935 reprint Ikuta added that, in translating *Also Sprach Zarathustra*, he had used the style of the Meiji translation of the Bible, just as Nietzsche was reported to have used the style of the German translation of the Bible by Martin Luther.[42]

Choko Ikuta and wife Fujio. Ikuta rendered Taylor's draft translation in classical style. Courtesy Natsuki Ikuta.

Finding Ikuta willing to undertake the assignment, Taylor left him with "two volumes of the manuscript as already corrected by Mr. Hirai" and requested that he make any necessary corrections. Ikuta's ability and reputation are well indicated by the following reaction of three literary experts, including Shoyo Tsubouchi, whom Taylor asked to comment on the corrections Ikuta had made without revealing their connection:

> The opinions of all three were that the changes, in most cases, were improvements. Then in a manner not calculated to betray myself, I asked about Mr. Ikuta, his ability and reputation. The answers were all complimentary to him. . . . I then asked if they thought that Mr. Ikuta was capable of producing a better work than the translation they had just been reading. The reply was that the translation as it was didn't need to be changed, but that a man of Mr. Ikuta's ability might be able to improve it just a little.[43]

On 29 July 1908, Ikuta signed a contract to devote at least five hours a day to the work except Sundays. He then worked on rendering Taylor's translation into classical Japanese, from August through early April of the following year, at the rate of ¥100 ($50 at the gold parity) per month. Ikuta both reworked the revision made by Hirai (through the third chapter of the Third Book of Nephi, roughly seventy-eight percent of the text) and worked on the rest of the book on

---

42. Friedrich W. Nietzsche, *Also Sprach Zarathustra*, trans. Choko Ikuta (Tokyo: Nippon Hyōronsha, 1935), 1–6.

43. Taylor, "The History."

his own, changing from contemporary to classical style, with Taylor fully engaged in checking and approving all the changes.⁴⁴ Thinking it wise that two reviewers look at each portion of his translation, Taylor went to see Kosaburo (or Matahei) Kawai, a noted writer and poet better known in Japan by his pen name Suimei, who had earlier helped translate Latter-day Saint hymns (see Section 5.7.4 in Chapter 5).⁴⁵ Taylor asked him to read over the portion Ikuta had revised alone. Kawai completed his work in a little over a month, from early May to early June 1909, likely producing only a few substantive changes.⁴⁶

6.4. The Literary Value

The 1909 Japanese translation of the Book of Mormon is a great literary achievement. The beauty and grace of the language used, for example, in translating Mosiah 3:19 (that begins with "For the natural man is an enemy to God") must be evident to many who are able to read it, perhaps much more so than the two subsequent translations published by the LDS Church in 1957 and 1995. The final language of the 1909 translation must heavily reflect the hands of Hirogoro Hirai and, to a greater extent, Choko Ikuta, who worked on Taylor's entire draft translation. To be sure, the work of translation was a collective effort, making it difficult to ascribe too much of the final product to any single individual. Neither Caine nor Taylor stood idly by while Hirai or Ikuta perfected the language. A handwritten note prepared by one of them reads:

> Beginning with chapter 28 of II Nephi . . . I note that the use of difficult words increases very materially. I shall be entirely disappointed if after the hard labor of both of us, the translation is marked with so many hard words that it will be hard for the ordinary people to understand it. I do therefore hope that the necessity to use difficult words in some places in order to express the true meaning will not be a justification for the use of difficult words and phrases where there is no absolute necessity for them.⁴⁷

It appears that the final language was friendlier to the average reader than Hirai or Ikuta perhaps would have produced on his own.

---

44. Taylor found it much more pleasant to work with Ikuta than with Hirai: "There is all the difference in the world between Mr. Ikuta and Hirai in the manner of questions about translation. Hirai was quick tempered, angered often, said nasty things and often made our discussions very unpleasant. Mr. Ikuta is a gentleman. He is quick and frank in acknowledging his errors. He gives respectful ear to my side of the questions discussed and thus we get along well and rapidly." Taylor, Journal, 27 August 1908.

45. Taylor, Journal, 29 May 1905.

46. Taylor accommodated Kawai's suggestions in a single meeting on 8 June 1909. Taylor, "The History." Given Kawai's background, his knowledge of English was probably limited.

47. "Observations on Translation," not dated. "Alma O. Taylor Papers, 1904–1935," LDS Church Archives.

There are a number of isolated instances of beauty and grace, such as Mosiah 3:19 noted above. But identifying such individual instances would be a highly subjective and random exercise. After all, how a particular phrase, sentence, or sequence of sentences sounds is a matter of personal taste or preference. In order to make as objective an analysis as possible, recurring uses of certain literary devices, expressions, or principles will be identified below in characterizing the overall literary value of the 1909 translation.

6.4.1. Smoothing out awkward expressions

The use of refined language contributes to the literary quality of the 1909 translation, which gives little indication that it was translated from a foreign language. The following example illustrates how a seemingly awkward expression in the English original was made smooth in Japanese:

> The eye hath never seen, neither hath the ear heard, before, so great and marvelous things as we saw and heard Jesus speak unto the Father; And no tongue can speak, neither can there be written by any man, neither can the hearts of men conceive so great and marvelous things as we both saw and heard Jesus speak. (3 Nephi 17:16–17)

> 1909 Japanese translation: warera no mi mata kikishi iesu ga tenpu ni inori tamaeru tokoro no kotoba wa, me ni imada kore wo mizu, mimi ni imada kore wo kikazu, kuchi ni ii uru mono mo naku, fude nite shirushi uru mono mo naku, mata ningen no kokoro no sōzō shi gataki hodo fushigi nishite katsu ōinari.

> Literal English equivalent:[48] (the words we saw and heard Jesus [use to] pray to Heavenly Father are so marvelous and so great that the eye has not yet seen, the ear has not yet heard, there is none who can utter with his mouth, there is none who can record with a pen, and the hearts of men cannot conceive them.)

The smoothness of the translation comes with the loss of what some Mormon scholars regard as Hebraic syntax (e.g., 1 Nephi 1:16; 1 Nephi 22:26; Mosiah 3:1–3; Mosiah 3:18–19; Mosiah 5:10–12; Mosiah 15:2–4; Alma 13:19).[49] Of course, it is simply not possible to preserve the original order of words and phrases, Hebraic or otherwise, but another factor influencing the outcome is the tendency to use varied translations for parallel expressions in the 1909 translation (e.g., use of two separate words to translate "remember" in Mosiah 5:11–12).

---

48. In this and subsequent examples, retranslations into English ("back-translation") are offered only as an aid to an English-speaking reader. These back-translations are literal in the sense of preserving word-for-word correspondence where feasible. These may not be the best translations. When equivalence is established, the source text is the best back-translation of the translated text.

49. See, for example, John W. Welch, "Chiasmus in the Book of Mormon," *Brigham Young University Studies* 10 (1969): 69–84; Kevin L. Barney, "Poetic Diction and Parallel Word Pairs in the Book of Mormon," *Journal of Book of Mormon Studies* 4 (1995): 15–81; and James T. Duke, "The Literary Structure and Doctrinal Significance of Alma 13:1–9," *Journal of Book of Mormon Studies* 5 (1996): 103–18.

6.4.2. Deletions and Additions

To make the translation sound less awkward, the following phrases were not translated at all: "either on the one hand or on the other" (1 Nephi 14:7); "And so it is on the other hand" (Alma 41:6)—translated simply as "but"; "yea, the word came unto them that it must be fulfilled" (3 Nephi 1:25); and "being on a parallel" (3 Nephi 26:5). On the other hand, some words and phrases were added, presumably to make the translation sound complete. For example, in paraphrasing 1 Nephi 18:2 (which describes how Nephi constructed a ship), the 1909 translation adds details that do not exist in the original: "Ware wa tenshu no oshie tamaishi hōhō nite fune wo tsukurishi yue, sono fune wa hito no tsukuru mono ni kotonarishi nari" (Because I built the ship according to the method that the Lord had taught me, the ship was different from what men would build). The translation of 4 Nephi 1:14 (which notes that "many of that generation" had passed away) is followed by the addition of a clause that does not exist in the original: "sono kōnin mo taterare tariki" ([but] their successors were also put in place). An even greater departure from literalism is found in Mormon 5:14–15, where the translation of three ideas placed in a complex manner is facilitated by using numbers "daiichi wa" (first), "daini wa" (second), and "daisan wa" (third).

6.4.3. Specific and Concrete Language

The language of the translation reflects the consistent application of a certain set of rules. An obvious pattern is to use specific or concrete language. Anybody who is familiar with the English original is immediately struck with the 1909 translation's tendency to replace an expression involving the English preposition *of* with a verb or verbal expression in Japanese. Thus, the "covenant people of the Lord" (1 Nephi 15:14) is translated as "tenshu no seiyaku wo ukeshi tami" (the people who received the covenant of the Lord). The conversion is not mechanical but involves serious thinking. Thus, the "true fold of God" (1 Nephi 15:15) is "makoto no kami ni shitagau mure" (the flock that follows the true God), and not the "true flock that follows God." Likewise, the "revelations of God" when "looked unto" (Mormon 8:33) are "kami no atae tamaishi keishi" (the revelations that God gave) in the past tense, while those revelations when denied (Mormon 9:7) become "kami yori sazukaru keishi" (the revelations you receive from God) in the present.

6.4.4. Active or Direct Style

The use of an active or direct style is a general rule of good writing in any language, and it was a feature of the 1909 translation even when it does not correspond to the English original. For example, "the blindness of their minds, and the stiffness of their necks" (Jarom 1:3) was translated as "kokoro kuraku, iji tsuyoki" (their hearts are dark, and their pride is strong). For "the blood of Christ atoneth for their sins" (Mosiah 3:16), we have "kirisuto wa onchi nite sono tsumi wo aganai tamau nari" (Christ atones for their sins by his blood). A related feature is the choice of simpler construction. Thus, "out of obscurity and out of darkness" (1 Nephi 22:12) is simplified as "kakuretaru kuraki kyōgai yori" (out of a hidden and dark state). The following is a more compelling example:

> Ye shall have mercy restored unto you again; ye shall have justice restored unto you again; ye shall have a righteous judgment restored unto you again; and ye shall have good rewarded unto you again. (Alma 41:14)
>
> Sono mukui wo uku beshi. Sunawachi airen to seigi to tadashiki saiban to zen to wa nanji ni kaifuku seraru beshi.
>
> (Ye shall be rewarded, that is, ye shall have mercy, justice, a righteous judgment, and good restored unto you).

In this and other similar examples (e.g., 3 Nephi 19:34; Ether 6:10), the construction is made so smooth in Japanese that any trace of Hebraism-like features is lost.

6.4.5. Literary Expressions

A number of literary or expressive phrases are found throughout the translation. For example, "had become . . . grossly wicked" (Helaman 6:2) and "began to grow exceedingly wicked" (6:16) are translated respectively as "hanahadashiki jaaku ni nagaretari" (lapsed into gross wickedness) and "hanahada jaaku ni katamukeri" (degenerated greatly into wickedness). To introduce symmetry in expression between speaking and writing, "no tongue can speak, neither can there be written by any man" (3 Nephi 17:17) becomes "kuchi ni ii uru mono mo naku, fude nite shirushi uru mono mo naku" (there is none who can utter with a mouth, neither is there anyone who can record with a pen). It is not simply "a dew before the sun" (Mormon 4:18) that is swept off but "asahi ni terasaruru tsuyu" (a dew lighted up by the morning sun). A "God of truth" (Ether 3:12) is really "makoto no michitaru kami" (a God full of truth).

6.4.6. Contrasting Words and Negative Expressions

Occasional use of contrasting words is another literary device. Thus, *asahimo* (a flaxen string) is used to translate the "flaxen cord" the devil uses to lead the people, but *nawa* (ropes) is the cords he uses to bind them (2 Nephi 26:22). If it is an "infant" that dies but does not perish, the counterpart who drinks damnation must be *otona* (an adult), though "men" is the original word (Mosiah 3:18). Use of negative expressions (including double negatives) to affirm positive ideas is a characteristic of classical Japanese. For example, "one eternal round" (1 Nephi 10:19) is translated as "eien ni kotonaru koto nashi" (not variable for ever); and "all things are given them which are expedient unto man" (2 Nephi

2:27) becomes "ōyoso sono tame to naru mono wa hitotsu toshite ataerarezaru koto nashi" (there is not a thing that is beneficial unto them that is not given). To "be remembered" (Moroni 6:4) is "wasurete naozari ni suru koto naku" (not to be forgotten or neglected).

6.5. The Manner of Translation

Supplementing words, paraphrasing, and attempting to interpret or explain (even when not necessary to produce a good idiomatic translation) are among the departures from literalism that characterize the 1909 translation. These features may well have reflected Taylor's desire to make the translation as understandable as possible to all classes of people. In one instance, Taylor asked the First Presidency if he could translate the expression "the Spirit of Christ" as *seirei* (the Holy Ghost), saying that the original term might suggest Christ's own spirit to the Japanese. The First Presidency counseled Taylor against it, arguing that the "same difficulty in grasping the meaning of these terms" would be met with by readers of the scriptures in any language:

> Religion, art and science each coin new words or give a peculiar shade of meaning to familiar words, and gradually these get established in the language. The same is the case with words used in the Japanese Bible. It may be hard for those who have not studied that sacred volume to comprehend the writer's meaning, but repeated readings of such terms will gradually make the meaning as clear to the Japanese mind as they are to one who understands English but has not made the scriptures his study.[50]

The First Presidency, however, approved certain explanatory words to be inserted in brackets in order to make the meaning "clearer to the reader" (for example, "Jesus" following "the Son of Man" or the "Lamb"; "three" before the words "beloved disciples" in Mormon 8:10; and "the emblem of" before "the flesh and blood" in Moroni 4:1).[51]

6.5.1. Supplementing Words and Phrases

In some cases, adding words or phrases may be absolutely necessary to express the meaning of a foreign sentence correctly in Japanese. In other cases, it may be helpful to the reader but not necessary for communicating the meaning. For example, the translation renders "to stir them up in the ways of remembrance" (1 Nephi 2:24) as "tenshu wo omoi okosashimen tame" (to make them remember the Lord). Likewise, "the life of my servant shall be in my hand" (3 Nephi 21:10)

---

50. First Presidency of the Church of Jesus Christ of Latter-day Saints, letter to Alma O. Taylor, 4 January 1908. "Alma O. Taylor Papers, 1904–35," LDS Church Archives.

51. First Presidency of the Church of Jesus Christ of Latter-day Saints, letter to Alma O. Taylor, 3 March 1908. "Alma O. Taylor Papers," LDS Church Archives.

is rendered as "sono hitori naru waga shimobe no inochi wa waga te no uchi ni mamoraru beki" (the life of my servant shall be protected in my hand).

Most cases of adding words and phrases appear to be meant only for literary purposes. For example, "May God raise you from death by the power of the resurrection, and also from everlasting death by the power of the atonement" (2 Nephi 10:25) is translated as "kami ga fukkatsu no chikara wo mote nanjira wo haka no ichiji no shi yori yomigaerase, zaikadaishoku no chikara wo mote nanjira wo eien no shi yori yomigaerase tamau" (May God raise you from the temporary death of the grave by the power of the resurrection, and raise you from everlasting death by the power of the atonement). Here, "haka no ichiji no" (temporary . . . of the grave) is added to the first occurrence of the word "death" in contrast to "everlasting death."

In some cases, the translators exercised outright poetic license, perhaps to be complete. For example, "[they] scourged his skin with faggots" (Mosiah 17:13) is translated as "takigi wo moyashite shi ni itarashimuru made sono hada wo yaki keri" ([they] put fire on faggots and burnt his skin unto death). Likewise, "[Alma] could not rest, and he also went forth" (Alma 43:1) is rendered as "yasumu koto wo ezareba, mata michi wo noben tame ide yukinu" ([Alma] could not rest, and he also went out to preach the word).

6.5.2. Paraphrasing

Paraphrasing is another device that could be necessary in some cases to convey the meaning correctly; in other cases, it is used only for literary purposes. For example, "come to the knowledge of the true Messiah" (1 Nephi 10:14) is translated as "shin no messha wo mitomuru ni itaru" (come to acknowledge the true Messiah), and "this corruption" (2 Nephi 9:7) as "kono kutsuru mi" (this body that will corrupt). Likewise, "{all men shall} have passed from this first death unto life" (2 Nephi 9:15) is rendered as "kono daiichi no shi yori fukkatsu sureba" (have been resurrected from this first death);[52] and "the will of the Son being swallowed up in the will of the Father" (Mosiah 15:7) becomes "ko no mune wa sudeni chichi no mune ni mattaku fukushi tareba nari" (the will of the Son has already been totally subjected to the will of the Father). Paraphrasing often involves the replacement of abstract nouns, as in some of these examples.

6.5.3. Interpretation

Translation by necessity involves interpretation. But the need for interpretation is even greater for the Book of Mormon because the meanings of some passages are not straightforward, especially when they involve deep religious messages or novel ideas. For example, if one is to translate "through the fulness of the

---

52. Curly brackets indicate phrases that appear in the original text and are significant in giving meaning to the phrase but are not relevant to the translation.

Gentiles" (1 Nephi 15:13) word for word into Japanese, one would have "ihōjin no kanzen naru koto ni yori" (by the completeness of the Gentiles), which makes absolutely no sense. The 1909 translation tries to interpret the passage by rendering it as "ihōjin ga kanzen naru fukuin wo ukuru ni yori" (as the Gentiles accept the perfect gospel). Likewise, "the severity of the Lord" (Omni 1:22) is translated interpretively as "sono kibishiki onbatsu" (his severe punishment); "repenting nigh unto death" (Mosiah 27:28) as "shisen bakari no itami mote kuiaratame" (repenting with the pain that nearly caused him to die); "a more excellent way" (Ether 12:11) as "mōse no rippō ni masareru michi" (a way that is superior to the law of Moses); and "in plain humility" (Ether 12:39) as "yono tsune no furi to ware to onaji kotoba to wo mote" (in an ordinary manner and with the same language as mine). The following involves a more delicate act of interpretation:

> I [come . . . to] do the will, both of the Father and of the Son—of the Father because of me, and of the Son because of my flesh. (3 Nephi 1:14)
>
> Ware wa waga reikon no kankei ni yori chichi no mune wo okonai, waga nikutai no kankei ni yori ko no mune wo okonau.
>
> (I do the will of the Father on account of the spirit, and do the will of the Son on account of the flesh)

In this example, interpretation seems to define the meaning more precisely.

6.5.4. Explanatory

There are instances where the interpretation becomes explanatory. For example, the 1909 translation renders "nor repent of the thing which thou hast done" (Mosiah 4:22) as "sono zaisan wo oshimite hodokosazaru tsumi wo mo kuiaratamezu" (not repent of the sin of being unwilling to part with your possessions and not imparting them); and "look to God and live" (Alma 37:47) as "kami ni tayorite eien no seimei wo ukeyo" (rely upon God and receive eternal life). Likewise, "the law is fulfilled" (3 Nephi 12:19) is translated as "furuki rippō wa mohaya sono mokuteki wo tasshite kōyō naki mono to nari tareba" (the old law has now fulfilled its purpose and become of no effect); "ye shall not resist evil" (3 Nephi 12:39) as "aku wo motte aku wo fusegu koto nakare" (ye shall not resist evil with evil); and "this is the law and the prophets" (3 Nephi 15:10) as "waga meirei wo mamoru wa, sunawachi rippō to yogenshara no kotoba ni kanau koto nari" (to keep my commandments complies with the law and the words of the prophets). The following might be one of the best examples:

> [They] have their reward. (3 Nephi 13:5)
>
> Karera wa makotoni sono okonai ni sōō suru mukui wo uku.
>
> (They will indeed receive a reward befitting their conduct.)

These cases could give the impression that the translation is like commentary on a passage of scripture (though only to someone familiar with the English original).

6.6. Notable Words and Expressions

There are some interesting choices of words and expressions in the 1909 Japanese translation of the Book of Mormon. Here, we focus on four such examples, namely, the frequent use of the Japanese word for "the way," how the English word "soul" is translated, the translation for "the Lord," and the way in which the English word "vineyard" is translated.

6.6.1. The Way

The Japanese word *michi* (*dào* in Chinese) is one of the favorite, multipurpose words of the 1909 translation. The word denotes "way" (in the sense of "path" or "road"), but it also has a variety of meanings, such as "logic," "means," "process," "reason," "religious teaching," "sense," and "vocation." *Michi* is most frequently used to translate the term "word" as in "the word of God" or "the word of the Lord," whereas *kotoba* would have been a more literal translation. Thus, "the word of God" missionaries were preaching in Alma 23:1 is translated as "kami no michi" (the way of God), as was "the word" the people were ready to hear in Alma 32:6.

The first Japanese translation of the Book of Mormon, *Morumon Kei*, was published in October 1909. Courtesy Bill McIntyre.

The use of *michi* for "word" in part follows the Chinese translation of John 1:1 where *dào* was used for the Greek word *logos* (the 1880 Japanese translation of the Bible also used the Chinese character *dào* for logos, but made it read *kotoba* thereby giving a dual meaning). Curiously, the 1909 translation of the Book of Mormon more frequently uses *mikotoba* (the holy word) when "the word of God" in the original is used in the sense of *logos*.[53] Thus, "the rod of iron" (1 Nephi 11:25) is "kami no mikotoba" (the holy word of God), and "the word of God," which is quick and powerful (Helaman 3:29), is also translated as "kami no mikotoba" (see also 4 Nephi 1:30).

Michi is also the principal word used to translate expressions such as "the plan of salvation" and "the plan of redemption." Thus "the great plan of happiness" (Alma 42:8) is translated as "hito ni kōfuku wo esasen to suru ōinaru michi" (the great way of having men obtain happiness). Likewise, for "the great and eternal plan of deliverance from death" (2 Nephi 11:5), we have "hitobito wo shi yori aganai sukuu tokoshie no ōinaru michi" (the eternal and great way of redeeming and saving people from death). *Michi* is used even when a counterpart does not appear in the original. Thus, the sentence "[Nephi and Lehi] began

---

53. Leslie A. Taylor, "The Word of God," *Journal of Book of Mormon Studies* 12 (2003): 52–63.

to grow up unto the Lord" (Helaman 3:21) is translated as "seichō shi yuku mama ni tenshu wo osore kashikomu michi wo manaberi" ([they] learned the way of fearing and respecting the Lord as they grew up). And "that thing which they do believe" with steadfastness (Helaman 15:10) is translated simply as "sono shinzuru michi" (the way of their belief).

6.6.2. Soul

Mormon theology (Doctrine and Covenants 88:15) gives a special meaning to the word "soul" as a compound made up of the body and the spirit, but this is not always the sense in which the word is used in the Book of Mormon. The Hebrew counterpart *nephesh* appears over 780 times in the Old Testament and has been translated not only as "soul" but also variously as "appetite," "creature," "desire," "emotion," "life," "living being," "mind," "passion," "person," or "self." Some biblical commentaries suggest that *nephesh* can be translated as "self" or even more simply as "I" or "me."[54] Newer English translations tend to translate *nephesh* much less frequently as "soul." For example, the New Revised Standard Version (1989) has "I loathe my life" for the verse translated in the King James Version as "My soul is weary of my life" (Job 10:1).

As might be expected, in the 1909 Japanese translation, the English word "soul" is translated variously as *hito* (man or person) (e.g., 2 Nephi 9:13; Alma 39:17), *kokoro* (heart) (e.g., 1 Nephi 1:15), and *reikon* (spirit) (e.g., 1 Nephi 15:31; Alma 40:18). Sometimes, it is not translated at all. For instance, the sentence "the final state of the souls of men is to dwell in the kingdom of God" (1 Nephi 15:35) is translated as "hito wa tsui ni kami no mikuni ni sumu" (men will eventually live in the kingdom of God). Likewise, "the enemy of my soul" (2 Nephi 4:28) is simply "waga teki" (my enemy), and "the welfare of your souls" (Jacob 2:3) is "nanjira no tokoshie no kōfuku" (your eternal happiness). Only rarely is "soul" translated according to the definition given in the Doctrine and Covenants (Mosiah 2:21; Helaman 8:28), for example:

[If] ye should serve him with all your whole souls . . . (Moriah 2:21)

Tamashii no chikara to mi no chikara to wo tsukushite tsukau tomo . . .

(If ye should serve him with all of the power of your spirits and of your bodies . . .)

6.6.3. The Lord

"The Lord" is typically rendered in the 1909 Japanese translation as *tenshu*, a new word that the Western missionaries working in China had created by combining two Chinese characters meaning "heaven" and "lord." This Chinese word

---

54. W. E. Vine, Merrill F. Unger, and William White Jr., *An Expository Dictionary of Biblical Words* (Nashville: Nelson, 1984), 388–89.

(*tiānzhǔ* in pinyin) was one of several words used to translate God (or its Latin equivalent *Deus*), and was sanctioned by the Roman Catholic Church in the early eighteenth century. In the nineteenth century, however, some Protestant missionaries began to use two existing words, *shēn* (*kami* in Japanese) and *shàngdì* (*jōtei* in Japanese).[55] Though they never reached agreement, the American Bible Society published a Chinese translation of the Bible in the mid-nineteenth century, with *kami* (*shēn*) for God. These developments explain why in Japan the Catholics and the Protestants adopted two different words for God (but *shàngdì* was never adopted in Japanese).[56]

It should be noted that the choice of *tenshu* in the 1909 Book of Mormon translation applies not to "God" but to "the Lord." Van C. Gessel discusses how Taylor came to believe that *tenshu* would more closely carry the meaning of the scriptural word 'Lord' "than the simple *shu*, which is used in referring to earthly lords."[57] In the 1909 translation of the Book of Mormon, however, there is a fine distinction between *tenshu* and *shu*: the former is used more generally with reference to the Lord, while the latter is sometimes used when the Lord speaks or appears to an individual (e.g., 3 Nephi 1:12).

In preserving Taylor's choice of the word *tenshu* for "the Lord," Ikuta must have been familiar with the controversy among the Protestants in Japan over the biblical choice of the word *kami* for God. From the latter part of the nineteenth century, some Protestant missionaries even began to insist that *tenshu*, used in the Roman Catholic Church, was a better term for "God" because the connotations of *kami* (a polytheistic spiritual entity residing in a particular location) were so ingrained in the language of Shinto that the use of the term was preventing the Japanese from coming to a proper understanding of God. Some influential Protestant publications called for a new translation of the Bible, in part to do away with the word *kami* for "God."[58]

6.6.4. Vineyard

A vineyard is a tract of land where grapes are grown, for which the Japanese word is *budōen* (lit. grape-garden). The allegory of the tame and wild olive trees, in Chapter 5 of the Book of Jacob in the Book of Mormon, takes place in the Lord's vineyard, which is understood to be "the world." The 1909 translation does not use the word *budōen* but instead uses *jumokuen* (lit. tree-garden). The thinking must be that a plot of land where both grapes and olives are grown cannot be just a vineyard. The same logic is repeated by the 1957 translation (where

---

55. The first word refers to an invisible being or a spirit, while the second means the ruler on high, the supreme ruler, or the emperor. Suzuki, *Seisho no Nihongo*, 35–37.
56. Suzuki, *Seisho no Nihongo*, 6, 27–28, 39–40.
57. As quoted in Gessel, "Languages of the Lord," 252.
58. Suzuki, *Seisho no Nihongo*, 41, 115–16.

the word *jumokuen* is retained) and by the 1995 translation where the word *kajuen* (lit. orchard) is used. In all these cases, the word *budōen* should have been used because the vineyard means the Lord's vineyard.

6.7. The Question of Accuracy

Accuracy has been a buzzword for linguistic and theological purity in most analyses of biblical translation.[59] In the realm of religion, inaccurate translation not only fails to achieve a satisfactory degree of equivalence but also could give a wrong idea and potentially jeopardize the reader. By the ultimate standard of accuracy, the 1909 translation earns high marks in this author's assessment. Even in a number of passages where the current 1995 translation is judged to be imperfect, incorrect, or questionable (e.g., 2 Nephi 2:10; Mosiah 1:2; Alma 36:9; Alma 43:46; Alma 60:10; Helaman 4:26; Helaman 16:12; 3 Nephi 29:9; Moroni 1:3),[60] the 1909 translation renders them correctly and skillfully (though the reverse could also be true in other passages—see below). But accuracy can be a relative concept, especially in translation, where there is a whole spectrum of correctness or incorrectness.

Though problems of accuracy are few, three types of imperfections can be identified in the 1909 translation: (1) debatable translations; (2) questionable translations; and (3) outright mistranslations.

6.7.1. Debatable Translations

Debatable translation involves imperfect equivalence when near perfect equivalence is technically feasible. These cases generally entail the use of a particular word for the original when a better word is available. For example, in Mosiah 7:31, the 1909 translation adopts the word *maneku* (to bring about) for "reap" (used in contrast to "sow") when a closely corresponding word is available in Japanese (*karu*). In some cases, the original words are not translated at all even though they have good Japanese counterparts, e.g., the "end" in the "end of its creation" (2 Nephi 2:12) or the "nature" in the "nature of that righteousness" (Helaman 13:38).

6.7.2. Questionable Translations

Questionable translation entails a greater deviation from the original than debatable translation, but it retains more ambiguity than outright mistranslation to allow disagreement. At least twenty-two such cases can be identified in

---

59. Barnstone, *Poetics of Translation*, 62–63.
60. The LDS Church corrected at least three of the more obvious errors in 2009, but others remain. The 2009 correction introduced a grammatical error where none had previously existed (in Alma 42:25).

the 1909 translation (though there could be more). Many of them are passages that are very difficult to interpret, but the problem would not have existed if the translation had been more literal, leaving the interpretation of a difficult or ambiguous passage to the reader. The following two examples should suffice to make this point:[61]

> [God] shall consecrate thine afflictions for thy gain (2 Nephi 2:2)
>
> Kami wa nanji no nameshi kannan shinku yori nanji no rieki wo shōzeshime tamawan
>
> (God shall cause thy gain to come out of the afflictions you experience)
>
> {And others will he pacify, and} lull them away into carnal security (2 Nephi 28:21)
>
> kore wo azamukite nikuyoku ni fukerashimuru
>
> (deceive them and cause them to indulge in carnal desires)

On the other hand, the following passage is not so difficult, but it appears that interpretation was carried too far:

> {If their works are evil} they shall be restored unto them for evil (Alma 41:4)
>
> Sono okonai wa so ga akunin naru wo shōsu beshi
>
> (Their works will testify that they are evil people)

Other cases of questionable translation entail the choice of words that give a different shade of meaning than that suggested by the original. These are questionable only because they have doctrinal implications or potential impact on religious behavior; otherwise, they could be brushed off as an inevitable but inconsequential outcome of translation. For example, the 1909 translation renders "turn away {from your sins}" (2 Nephi 9:45) as *kuiaratamete* (repent of); "are reconciled {unto God}" (2 Nephi 10:24) as *shitagai taru* (follow); "feasting upon {the word of Christ}" (2 Nephi 31:20) as *ajiwai* (taste); "{faith is} dormant" (Alma 32:34) as *muyō* (useless); and "lay hold upon {the word of God}" (Helaman 3:29) as *uke ireru* (accept).

Some cases border on mistranslation. For example:

> {I trust that} . . . ye look forward for the remission of your sins, with an everlasting faith, which is to come (Alma 7:6)
>
> Eien usezaru shinkō mote kitaru beki koto wo shinji nagara tsumi no yurushi wo ubeki toki wo yoki suru
>
> (Ye look forward to the time when ye receive the remission of your sins with a faith in things to come that does not perish forever)
>
> There was a punishment affixed, and a just law given, which brought remorse of conscience unto man (Alma 42:18)

---

61. The other cases in this category are 2 Nephi 3:17 and Mosiah 2:34.

Yo no hajime ni wa batsu sadamerare, tadashiki rippō taterareshi ga, kono rippō no tame hito wa hajimete ryōshin ni togamerarete kuyuru ni itareri

(A punishment was affixed and a just law given at the beginning of the world. Because of this law, man for the first time felt the pangs of conscience unto repentance)

The inadequacy of translation in a few passages has only been highlighted recently in light of new research on the Book of Mormon, concerning the "brightness" of possibly wooden swords (Alma 24:12 and other similar verses).[62] The remaining cases involve inappropriate words (i.e., 2 Nephi 2:22; Alma 13:3; Alma 31:35; Helaman 10:7),[63] failure to translate the English preposition "in" properly (i.e., Helaman 13:38; Moroni 9:25),[64] or simple interpretational errors (i.e., 3 Nephi 26:9; Ether 1:35).[65]

The following translation is either masterful or incorrect, depending on one's doctrinal perspective:

It is by grace that we are saved, after all we can do (2 Nephi 25:23)

Hito wa ikabakari tsutome hagemu tomo, sono sukuwaruru wa hitoeni kami no megumi ni yoru

(No matter how hard man may work, it is solely dependent upon God's grace that man is saved)

If "after all we can do" is a condition for being saved, this must be construed as a mistranslation. This translation, on the other hand, renders "after all" as "in spite of," highlighting thereby the power of God's grace.

6.7.3. Outright Mistranslations

Outright mistranslations are rare; only nine can be identified. Four involve interpretational errors and are not serious. Two of them (2 Nephi 26:11; Ether 2:15) translate "always" as *eikyū* or *eien ni* (forever) when rendering the idea that the Spirit "will not always strive with man." The substitution of "forever" for "al-

---

62. Matthew Roper, "Eyewitness Descriptions of Mesoamerican Swords," *Journal of Book of Mormon Studies* 5 (1996): 150–58. The way "brightness" is translated in these verses (*hikari wo hanatsu*—to emit light) leaves little alternative but to assume the swords to be metallic.

63. To transgress is translated as "*tsumi wo okasu* (to sin)" and "preparatory redemption" as "prepared redemption"; "souls are precious" is rendered as "*reikon* (spirits) are precious"; and to "have power among this people" is translated as "to have authority and power to work among this people."

64. Seeking happiness in doing iniquity is translated as "seeking happiness while doing iniquity," while being faithful in Christ is rendered as "being faithful to Christ."

65. To "try their faith" is translated as to "test whether their faith is strong"; "confounding the language of people" and "confounding the people" are translated synonymously (i.e., they cease to understand each other), but confounding a group of people can also mean scattering or dispersing them. See Hugh Nibley, *Lehi in the Desert and the World of the Jaredites* (Salt Lake City: Deseret Book, 1952), 172–73.

ways" seems to give too much focus on the eternal consequence of our actions, as opposed to the need to keep our actions righteous here and now. The translation of Helaman 14:9 "{Prepare} the way of the Lord" as "tenshu no kudari tamau michi" (the way through which the Lord will descend [from heaven]) is insightful but seems too restrictive. Surely, preparing the way of the Lord also includes the spiritual and mental preparation of the individual. Finally, whereas the original in Mormon 9:32 asserts that the record is written in "reformed Egyptian" characters, "according to our knowledge," the translation gives "warera wa warera no iwayuru hentai ejiputo moji wo manabishi tokoro no chishiki nite kono kiroku wo tsukurinu" (we made this record according to our knowledge of [or our knowledge obtained from learning] so-called reformed Egyptian characters).

The other cases are more substantive because they misinterpret the intended words of the prophets. Three of the cases involve failing to translate the conjunction "if" in the sense of "whether" (2 Nephi 33:11; Ether 4:10; Ether 5:6). For example:

And if they are not the words of Christ, judge ye (2 Nephi 33:11)

Nanjira kore wo kirisuto no mikotoba ni arazu to omou tomo

(Even if you may think that they are not the words of Christ)

In these cases, the reader who reads the Japanese translation would fail to respond to the challenge of a prophet to judge the validity of his words or authority.

The remaining two cases (2 Nephi 25:12; Mosiah 15:3) are even more serious as they involve possible doctrinal misrepresentations, as indicated below:

The Only Begotten of the Father, yea, even the Father of heaven and of earth (2 Nephi 25:12)

Tenchi no chichi no umi tamau hitorigo

(The Only Child begotten of the Father of heaven and earth)

In Mormon theology, the Son, albeit a separate personage, also plays the role of the Father (as in the sense of creator of the world or giver of salvation). This translation leaves no room for understanding that the "Father of heaven and of earth" could refer to Christ, and not to his father.

The Father, because he was conceived by the power of God; and the Son, because of the flesh (Mosiah 15:3)

Kami no michikara nite sono reikon no umare tamaishi kankei ni yori chichi nari. Nikutai wo mochi tamau kankei ni yori ko nari

(The Father, because his spirit was conceived by the power of God, and the Son, because he has a body)

Here, the translators are questionably contrasting "he" with "the flesh," thereby substituting "the spirit" for the first expression.

As serious as these errors may be, these are the only cases that can be identified of outright mistranslation that possibly involve possible doctrinal misrepresentation. The 1909 translation is substantially accurate and should convey broadly the same information to religious seekers, as would the English original.

6.8. Conclusion

The 1909 Japanese translation of the Book of Mormon is a great literary achievement. Commentary by some previous authors may have created the false sense that the translation was somehow rendered in an archaic language few understood. This is far from the case. It was a modern translation in every sense of the word by the standards of the early twentieth century. Though it was rendered in classical style, its classical style was of the *futsūbun* variety, which had been developed to accommodate the needs of an increasingly modernizing society and was at the time widely used.

In terms of the beauty and force of the language, the 1909 translation far surpasses the 1957 and 1995 translations (though perhaps not in terms of fidelity). The language in part reflects the skill with which Hirogoro Hirai and Choko Ikuta perfected Taylor's draft translation. The 1909 translation consistently uses specific and concrete language and an active and direct style, and employs a number of literary expressions and devices. To sound more natural, it supplements words and phrases as well as paraphrasing the original expressions even when not required to produce good idiomatic translation. These characteristics may also have reflected Taylor's desire to make the language as accessible as possible to the average reader. For the most part the translation is accurate, but the characteristic departure from literalism is a possible weakness that needs to be recognized as a work of religious translation.

The analysis of this chapter has paid relatively little attention to the choice of theological words, a topic that Gessel discusses in depth.[66] This reflects the view that the choice of words to express foreign concepts is not fundamental to the process of interlingual translation. If, for example, there is no equivalent word in Japanese for a certain concept, what is required is to create one (as was frequently done in Meiji Japan). This is a question of definition. If there are religious words the average Japanese reader is not familiar with, it is a question of education. Substantially the same issues of definition and education exist when an English-speaking teacher of a technical subject explains new concepts to an English-speaking novice.[67] The assignment of words is essentially a simple case of literal information transfer, conceptually the most straightforward aspect of translation.[68]

Selecting Japanese words for religious and philosophical terms was not central to Taylor's translation work in any case. The task of assigning existing words

---

66. Gessel, "Languages of the Lord."
67. These claims are based on the author's experience with teaching economics, a technical discipline of Anglo-Saxon origin, to American and Japanese university students.
68. Barnstone, *Poetics of Translation*, 26.

or inventing new words for most abstract Western concepts had largely been completed by the turn of the twentieth century. The first joint Protestant translation of the Bible, completed in the 1880s, had established the Japanese words for most fundamental Christian words.[69] The LDS Church had also published a number of tracts in the first decade of the 1900s in which the Japanese words for some uniquely Mormon terms were identified (see Section 5.5.5 in Chapter 5).

It is difficult to assess the choice of classical style. Should the LDS Church have waited until the written colloquial style was firmly established before attempting to translate the Book of Mormon? If so, how long? Until the early 1920s when the print media fully embraced contemporary style, or until after the end of World War II when official government documents began to be expressed in contemporary style?[70] One thing is clear. Writing in contemporary style with grace and dignity would have been a difficult task even in the 1950s. The public outcry over the colloquial style translations of the New Testament (published in 1954) and the Old Testament (in 1955) was so great that church translator Tatsui Sato, in making the second Japanese translation of the Book of Mormon, gave up the idea of rendering it entirely in contemporary style.[71] In fact, the church waited until 1995 to make a full colloquial style translation available to contemporary Japanese readers who might have limited familiarity with classical grammar.

In view of all this, Taylor's ultimate choice of classical style for the 1909 translation may well have been the right one. As a result, a writer of Choko Ikuta's ability could apply his literary skills in perfecting the translation. Though Ikuta may have had the final touch, Taylor, with the assistance of Caine, produced the initial translation and was fully involved in the finalization process, thus giving the LDS Church the ownership of the work that it deserves. Because of these individuals' efforts, Japanese-speaking Latter-day Saints can enjoy the privilege of reading the Book of Mormon from time to time in the language of the *Tale of Genji*, though with a modern vocabulary. Indeed, the way was proclaimed in the language of Japanese poetry—the beautiful language of their ancestors.[72]

---

69. Suzuki, Norihisa, *Seisho no Nihongo*, 94–95, 97.

70. Yamamoto, *Gembunitchi no Rekishi Kōsatsu*, 19, 37, 39–40, 57–58.

71. Suzuki, *Seisho no Nihongo*, 128–31. Sato used a mixture of contemporary and classical style by retaining the former style for informal parts (such as narratives and sermons), while using the latter for supplications to and utterances of God. Tatsui Sato, "Shinyaku Morumon Kei nitsuite," *Seito no Michi* 1 (July 1957): 4–5. See also Section 12.2.1 in Chapter 12.

72. Classical Japanese is still the principal medium of poetry, especially in *waka* and *haiku*. Even in the contemporary church, hymns are sung in classical Japanese. In the current edition of the Japanese LDS hymnbook all but five of the 200 hymns are written in classical style; of the five hymns that are written in contemporary style, four are children's songs.

Appendix 6.1. Major Differences between Classical and Contemporary Japanese

Other than the vocabulary, there are at least three notable differences between classical and contemporary Japanese, namely: (1) how certain verbs and adjectives conjugate; (2) auxiliary verbs; and (3) certain personal pronouns.

How Verbs and Adjectives Conjugate

Certain verbs and adjectives conjugate differently, so that they have different ending forms. For example:

Contemporary: ukeru (to receive)
Classical: uku

Contemporary: sugiru (to pass)
Classical: sugu

Contemporary: ikiru [mono] (a living [person])
Classical: ikeru [mono]

Contemporary: kaite (to write)
Classical: kakite

Contemporary: yonde (to call)
Classical: yobite

Contemporary: utsukushii [hito] (beautiful [person])
Classical: utsukushiki [hito]

Contemporary: nagai (long)
Classical: nagashi

These differences are not unlike the difference between *comes* and *cometh*, *are* and *art*, or *spoke* and *spake* in English.

Auxiliary Verbs

Another critical difference between classical and contemporary Japanese concerns auxiliary verbs, which determine the function of a verb (or an adjective) in a sentence. For example, one forms the past tense of a verb by adding *ta* in contemporary Japanese, while one adds either *ki* or *keru* (with slightly different nuances) in classical Japanese. Thus, *shiru* (to know) becomes:

Contemporary: shitta (knew)
Classical: shiriki or shirikeri

To negate a sentence, the auxiliary verb *nai* is affixed to a verb in contemporary Japanese, while *zu* is added in classical Japanese. For example:

Contemporary: nakanai (not to cry)
Classical: nakazu

As the Japanese language evolved over centuries, it lost many of the auxiliary verbs that classical Japanese used. For example, classical Japanese had an auxiliary verb (*nu*) that indicated completed action or present perfect tense. In contemporary Japanese, past tense (with the auxiliary verb *ta*) is substituted for present perfect tense, by adding an appropriate timing indicator (such as *just now*). Thus, for *nageku* (to lament), we have:

Contemporary: nageita (lamented)
Classical: nagekinu (have lamented)

Because auxiliary verbs usually come at the end of a sentence, they often set the tone of the whole sentence, and the pattern of their use in a collection of sentences determines the style or personality of writing.

Personal Pronouns

First and second person pronouns are different. For *I* and *you*, respectively, we have:

Contemporary: watashi or watakushi
Classical: ware or wa

Contemporary: anata
Classical: nanji, nare, or na

These are not unlike the difference between *you* and *thou* in English. The personal pronouns, however, are not fundamental to classical Japanese, because they are recognizable in contemporary Japanese though scarcely used.

Appendix 6.2. Advertising the Publication of the Japanese Book of Mormon

In anticipation of, and subsequent to, the publication of the Japanese translation of the Book of Mormon on 10 October 1909, the LDS Church engaged in an extensive national campaign to advertise the book through the print media. The first advertisements appeared ahead of the publication in two national magazines, the *Taiyō* (Sun) and the *Chūō Kōron* (Central Review).[73] These two magazines, along with the *Nihon oyobi Nihonjin* (Japan and the Japanese), were by far the most influential publications during the latter part of the Meiji period,

---

73. Ikuta's help was solicited in the preparation of these advertisements. Taylor, Journal, 20 September 1909 records: "[I] went to Mr. Ikuta's and got the manuscripts for advertisements in the Taiyō and Chuō [*sic*] Kōron Magazines. I took them to the advertising agency."

perhaps not unlike *Time* or *Newsweek* in contemporary American society.[74] In a 27 September 1909 letter, Alma O. Taylor wrote to the First Presidency: "Two of the leading magazines in Japan will contain in their Oct 1st number, one full page advertisement each, in which I promise the book to the public on Oct 10th and the printer says he will fulfill my promise."[75] Each of these magazines carried a full-page advertisement (with a slight variation from each other), announcing that "*Morumon Kei*," which is "A Great Book of Scripture, A New Testifier of God," would be published on the tenth of "this month." As with all subsequent newspaper and magazine advertisements, the name of the church did not appear, with the publisher simply stated as "the Japan Mission."

On 10 October, the day of the publication, it was Tokyo's prestigious *Jiji Shinpō* that took on the task of advertising. Though the circulation (estimated at 50,000 to 70,000) was modest, the *Jiji* ranked with the *Tokyo Asahi Shinbun* (with an estimated readership of 80,000 to 90,000) as the most influential, especially among the intellectuals.[76] The 10 October advertisement was followed by three additional advertisements on three subsequent days (11–13 October), which repeated the same theme with considerable variations. On the fourth and final day, the advertisement carried a detailed full-column explanatory note (written across the full width of a page) on the origin, nature, and content of the Book of Mormon.[77] After the *Jiji* advertisements ended, on 14 October, the *Yorozu Chōhō* began carrying its own set of four advertisements. The *Yorozu* was Tokyo's large circulation newspaper (with an estimated readership of about 150,000) popular especially among the younger people.[78] The *Yorozu*'s advertisements had a different format from the *Jiji*'s, although the second advertisement (carried on 15 October) was identical to the *Jiji*'s last one except that it did not include the detailed explanatory note on the Book of Mormon.

From 16 October through the end of the month, a number of newspapers throughout the country carried four-day advertisements, including Tokyo's influential *Asahi*. In the 27 September letter to the First Presidency, Taylor explained that he had "arranged for 4 one column advertisements in 20 of the influential

---

74. Taketoshi Nishida, *Meiji Jidai no Shinbun to Zasshi* (Tokyo: Shibundō, 1961), 262–63.

75. Alma O. Taylor, letter to the First Presidency, 27 September 1909. Japan Mission, "Letterpress Copybooks, 1901–1923," LDS Church Archives.

76. In Tokyo, at the end of the Meiji period, the *Hōchi* claimed by far the largest readership amounting to about 200,000, followed by the *Yamato* and the *Yorozu Chōhō* (about 150,000 each). The *Hōchi*, however, was mostly read by the lower income and less educated people. Nishida, *Meiji Jidai no Shinbun to Zasshi*, 272; and Hideo Ono, *Nihon Shinbun Hattatsu Shi* (Tokyo: Itsuki Shobō, 1982), 76.

77. Writing in Japanese newspapers runs from right to left, and from top to bottom; a column therefore is in reality a row.

78. Ono, *Nihon Shinbun Hattatsu Shi*, 76.

papers and 4 half column advertisements in 10 of the less influential papers."[79] This author has been able to identify twenty one of the thirty papers with which Taylor said he would place advertisements (see the list of newspapers and magazines at the end of this appendix). The advertisements had three different formats, which all shared similar language but displayed variations from day to day. Two of the three formats had a total of four column-equivalent space over four days (though with two different allocations), thus corresponding to what Taylor called "the influential papers"; the other format had one half column a day for a total of two column-equivalent advertising space over four days. In addition, Taylor's scrapbook includes a 23 October bilingual (English–Japanese) advertisement, which might have been published in the now-defunct *Japan Advertiser*.[80]

In 1911, two years after the publication of the Book of Mormon advertisements, some 118 newspapers existed outside of Kyoto, Okinawa, Osaka, and Tokyo, making the likely total in all of Japan close to, but not exceeding, 150 papers.[81] This means that about 20 percent of all respectable newspapers in Japan were involved in advertising the Book of Mormon translation. In terms of impact, this was more than sufficient. The list included three of Tokyo's leading papers and virtually all of the regionally influential ones, such as the *Fukuoka Nichinichi Shinbun* (Fukuoka), the *Hiroshima Kibi Nichinichi Shinbun* (Hiroshima), the *Hokkai Taimusu* (Sapporo), the *Kahoku Shinpō* (Sendai), the *Kobe Yūshin Nippō* (Kobe), the *Kyoto Hinode Shinbun* (Kyoto), the *Osaka Asahi Shinbun* (Osaka), and the *Shin-Aichi* (Nagoya).[82] The decision to publish newspaper advertisements in three less populous cities, Kofu, Morioka, and Shizuoka, was related to the fact that they were three of the six cities (along with Asahikawa, Sapporo, and Tokyo) where the missionaries were laboring at that time. The decision to advertise the book in Tsu, a city some 45 miles south of Nagoya, may well have something to do with the religious significance of the region that included Ujiyamada (present-day Ise) where Shinto's Grand Shine, with a divinity school, is located.

Concurrently, at least eight additional magazines of national prominence, including the two most important Christian publications, the *Gokyō* and

---

79. Taylor, letter to the First Presidency, 27 September 1909.
80. This advertisement could not be located in the archived issues of the *Japan Times*, the only English-language newspaper of continuous existence in Japan.
81. Nishida, *Meiji Jidai no Shinbun to Zasshi*, 251.
82. Some of these regional newspapers raised their prominence following the Russo–Japanese War. The *Fukuoka Nichinichi Shinbun*, originally established in 1877, merged with the *Kyushu Nippō* to form the *Nishinippon Shinbun* in 1942. The *Hokkai Taimusu* was formed in September 1901 by the merger of three competing newspapers in Sapporo; in 1942, it became the core part of the newly established *Hokkaido Shinbun*, which was formed by the amalgamation of all the newspapers throughout Hokkaido. In 1942, the *Shin-Aichi*, originally established in 1888, merged with the *Nagoya Shinbun* (renamed from the *Chūkyō Shinpō* in 1906) to form the *Chūbu Nihon Shinbun*. Ono, *Nihon Shinbun Hattatsu Shi*, 357–58.

the *Rikugō Zasshi*, carried advertisements during the months of October and November. In the 27 September letter to the First Presidency, Taylor noted that one "more prominent magazine" would "contain a full page advertisement in its November number."[83] He may well be referring to the *Taiheiyō* (the Pacific) or the *Shinjin* because the other magazines were either Christian in background or specifically addressed to women or educators.[84] With four-day advertisements in thirty newspapers throughout the country and full-page advertisements in at least ten national magazines, Taylor was confident that "every man and woman in Japan who [read] the leading papers and magazines [had] had the Book of Mormon's advertisement placed before their eyes."[85]

As a result of this extensive advertisement campaign, two Christian publications issued editorials on what they considered to be an alarming development. First, in the 30 October 1909 issue of the *Gokyō*, a weekly publication of the Methodist Church, an editorial entitled "Mormonism" stated that sixteen Mormon missionaries were currently proselytizing in Asahikawa, Kofu, Morioka, Sapporo, Shizuoka, and Tokyo, and that the public was being made aware of Mormonism as a result of the grandiose advertisements of the Japanese translation of the Book of Mormon. It explains the basic story of the Book of Mormon, argues that it was a creation of Solomon Spaulding,[86] and attacks the Mormons for adhering to the principle (if not the practice) of polygamy, which would harm the good morals of society. Second, the 4 November 1909 issue of the *Kirisutokyō Sekai* (Christian World) likewise published an editorial entitled "What is the Value of the Book of Mormon?" The editorial argued that the Book of Mormon was a fiction created by Solomon Spaulding, that Joseph Smith had introduced polygamy to cover up his immorality, and that Mormonism was not a Christian sect, warning the public against reading the book simply out of the curiosity caused by the advertisements.

Despite Taylor's hope to "attract attention" and have the public "inquire for the book so that the book store's present indifference [might] be changed to fair sized orders," the sale of the book was disappointingly slow. In the 13 November

---

83. Taylor, letter to the First Presidency, 27 September 1909.

84. The *Shinjin* was being edited by the same people as the *Shinjokai* (New Women's World). On 21 October 1909, the editors returned the advertisement for the *Shinjokai*, saying that they were "afraid that the feelings of the women will be wrought up against them if the word 'Mormon' is published in large type in their magazine." They accepted the advertisement for the *Shinjin* as they were "not afraid of hurting the feelings of the men." Taylor, Journal, 21 October 1909.

85. Alma O. Taylor, letter to the First Presidency, 13 November 1909, LDS Church Archives.

86. The Spaulding theory postulates that Joseph Smith relied on the book manuscript of a Congregationalist preacher named Solomon Spaulding in producing the Book of Mormon. Paul C. Gutjahr, *The Book of Mormon: A Biography* (Princeton, New Jersey: Princeton University Press, 2012), 47–51.

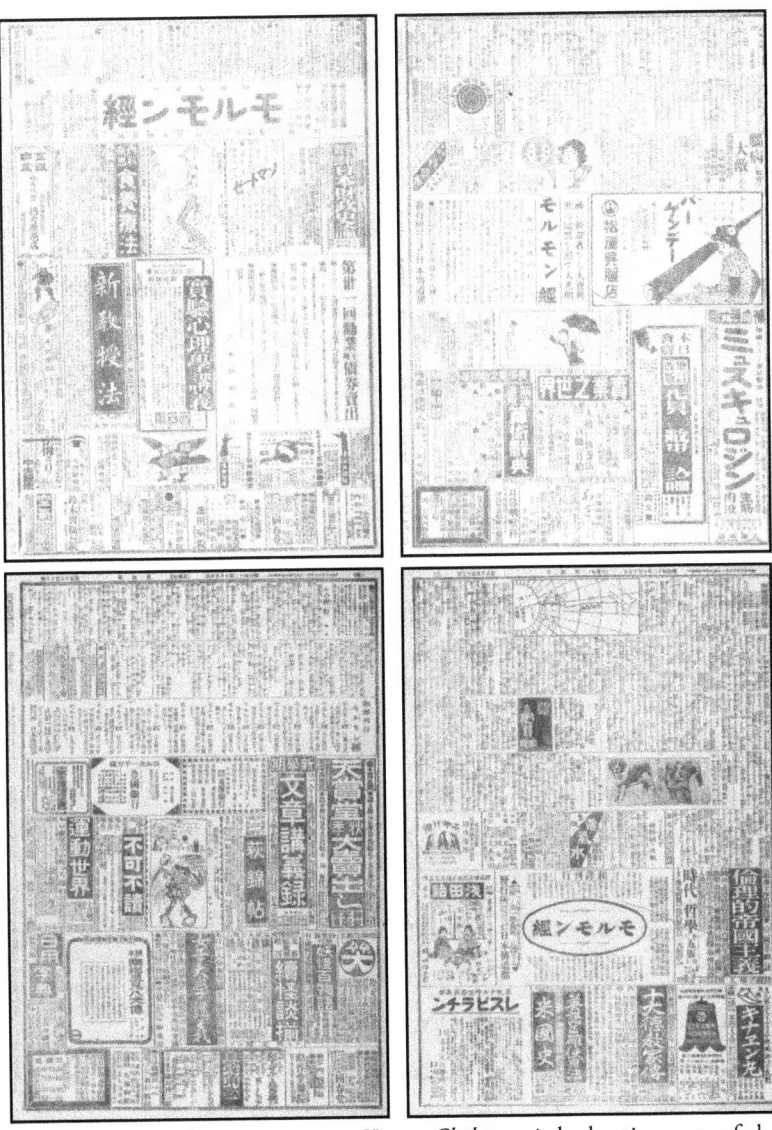

Tokyo's large circulation newspaper *Yorozu Chōhō* carried advertisements of the Book of Mormon on 14–15 and 17–18 October 1909. They are identified by the four Japanese phonetic letters モルモン written either from top to bottom or right to left.

1909 letter to the First Presidency, Taylor noted that 650 copies had been sold during the month since the publication of the translation.[87] But, at least, the Japanese public was offered a fair chance to read the book; in addition, eighty specially bound leather copies were given to the Japanese elites, including members of the imperial family and high government officials.

A Partial List of Book of Mormon Advertisements in October and November 1909

Newspapers (with three formats, as indicated by *, **, and ***):

(1) *Tokyo: *Jiji Shinpō*, 10–13 October.

(2) **Tokyo: *Yorozu Chōhō*, 14–15, 17–18 October.

(3) **Utsunomiya: *Shimotsuke Shinbun*, 16–17, 19–20 October.

(4) ***Tsu: *Ise Shinbun*, 17–20 October.

(5) ***Kofu: *Yamanashi Nichinichi Shinbun*, 17, 21–23 October.

(6) **Kyoto: *Kyoto Hinode Shinbun*, 17, 19–21 October.

(7) ***Morioka: *Iwate Nippō*, 17, 19–21 October.

(8) **Nagano: *Shinano Mainichi Shinbun*, 17–20 October.

(9) *Osaka: *Osaka Asahi Shinbun*, 17–20 October.

(10) *Sendai: *Kahoku Shinpō*, 17–20 October.

(11) *Tokyo: *Tokyo Asahi Shinbun*, 18–21 October.

(12) **Akita: *Akita Sakigake Shinpō*, 19–22 October.

(13) ***Hiroshima: *Hiroshima Kibi Nichinichi Shinbun*, 19–22 October.

(14) **Kanazawa: *Hokkoku Shinbun*, 19–22 October.

(15) *Kobe: *Kobe Yūshin Nippō*, 19–22 October.

(16) ***Kumamoto: *Kyushu Nichinichi Shinbun*, 19–22 October.

(17) *Nagoya: *Shin-Aichi*, 19–22 October.

(18) **Okayama: *Sanyō Shinpō*, 19–22 October.

(19) **Shizuoka: *Shizuoka Minyū Shinbun*, 19, 21–22, 24 October.

(20) *Fukuoka: *Fukuoka Nichinichi Shinbun*, 20, 23–24, 27 October.

(21) **Sapporo: *Hokkai Taimusu*, 22–25 October.

---

87. Taylor, letter to the First Presidency, 13 November 1909.

Magazines:

(1) *Taiyō*, monthly, 1 October.
(2) *Chūō Kōron*, monthly, October.
(3) *Kirisutokyō Sekai*, weekly, 21 and 28 October.
(4) *Gokyō*, weekly, 23 and 30 October.
(5) *Fujin Gahō*, monthly, 1 November.
(6) *Jogaku Sekai*, monthly, 1 November.
(7) *Rikugō Zasshi*, monthly, 1 November.
(8) *Taiheiyō*, twice monthly, 1 November.
(9) *Kyōiku Jikkenkai*, monthly, 5 November.
(10) *Shinjin*, monthly, November.

Chapter 7

The Japan Mission under Taisho Democracy: Failure or Forfeit?

7.1. Introduction

This chapter presents a historical analysis of the Japan Mission of the Church of Jesus Christ of Latter-day Saints during the latter part of its existence. The Taisho period (1912–26) saw Japanese society become increasingly industrial and modern, with a highly developed transportation infrastructure. In 1901, when the mission was established, there were only 4,400 miles of railroad; twenty three years later, in 1924, when the mission closed, this had nearly tripled to 12,000 miles. The volume of passenger traffic increased by 23.0 times and the volume of freight traffic by 6.3 times over this period.[1] During the Taisho period, an express train covered the distance from Tokyo to Kobe (about 600 miles) in nine hours, whereas it took nearly twenty hours at the end of the nineteenth century. Trucks were being used in place of animal-driven carts; buses and taxis, along with street cars, were replacing man-pulled *jinrikisha* as the principal means of local transportation in major cities.[2] Transportation was only one of the many visible changes. City skylines were another, with high-rise commercial buildings beginning to appear from the late 1910s in larger cities.[3]

Underlying these changes was the steady pace of economic development, industrialization, and urbanization. Real GDP, for example, nearly doubled from 1901 to 1924 (the size of GDP in 1938 was more than three times the size in 1901); industrial production grew by 3.3 times and agricultural production by 4.6 over the same period. The industrial base was diversifying, with the produc-

---

1. Japanese Government, Bureau of Statistics, *Nihon no Chōki Tōkei Keiretsu*, accessed 24 November 2015, www.stat.go.jp, Tables 12-7 and 12-8.

2. Naramoto Tatsuya, ed., *Zusetsu Nihon Shomin Seikatsu Shi, vol. 7: Meiji Jidai* (Tokyo: Kawada Shobō Shinsha, 1962), 58, 63, 66, 71; Kota Kodama, ed., *Zusetsu Nihon Bunka Shi Taikei, vol. 11: Meiji Jidai* (Tokyo: Shōgakukan, 1956), 102.

3. Tatsuya Naramoto, ed., *Zusetsu Nihon Shomin Seikatsu Shi, vol. 8: Taishō Shōwa* (Tokyo: Kawada Shobō Shinsha, 1962), 52–53, 55–56; Kota Kodama, ed., *Zusetsu Nihon Bunka Shi Taikei, vol. 11: Taishō Shōwa Jidai* (Tokyo: Shōgakukan, 1957), 328–30.

tion of steel expanding by 57 times and that of machinery by 19 times.[4] As the manufacturing and services sectors expanded, there was a continuous migration of workers from agriculture (rural areas) to cities against the background of increasing agricultural productivity. According to the first national census of 1920, the employment share was 55.4 percent for the primary sector (mostly agriculture), 19.4 percent for the secondary sector (manufacturing and mining), and 24.8 percent for the tertiary sector (services), with 0.4 percent unaccounted for.[5] The population share of cities with more than 10,000 inhabitants increased from 18.4 percent in 1903 to 32.4 percent in 1925.[6]

These forces of industrialization and modernization unleashed liberal aspirations in political thought and public consciousness, which found expression in demand for civil liberties and political participation. Japanese society was more open, more tolerant of religious diversity, and more accommodating of foreign ideas. This chapter, after characterizing the intellectual climate of the Taisho period, considers how these changes affected Mormon proselytizing work. Despite the seeming signs of greater missionary success, at least compared to the earlier period, the Mormon authorities in Utah closed the Japan Mission in 1924 by withdrawing the missionaries. The decision coincided with both a natural disaster that hit the Kanto area centered on Tokyo—the Great Kanto Earthquake—and a rising tide of anti-American sentiment associated with the passage in the United States of an immigration law discriminatory toward the Japanese. The chapter considers to what extent these temporary factors contributed to the withdrawal decision and how we can place that decision in the broader context of subsequent Japanese history. (Annex 4 towards the end of this volume provides the biographical sketches of ten notable Japanese converts from the prewar period.)

7.2. Taisho Democracy and the Japan Mission

7.2.1. Taisho Democracy

Chapter 4 noted the dualism of prewar Japan, wherein reactionary and progressive tendencies coexisted. From the end of the Meiji era, the balance be-

---

4. Kazushi Ohkawa, Nobukiyo Takamatsu, and Yuzo Yamamoto, *National Income*, vol.1 of *Estimates of Long-Term Economic Statistics of Japan Since 1868*, ed. by Kazushi Ohkawa, Miyohei Shinohara, and Mataji Umemura (Tokyo: Tōyō Keizai Shinpōsha, 1974), Tables 9, 10, 17, 18, 23.

5. Takafusa Nakamura, *Meiji-Taishō-ki no Keizai* (Tokyo: Tōkyō Daigaku Shuppankai, 1985), 104, 155–56, 183, 187, 191. With urbanization, an increasing number of men began to wear Western clothes. In the final years of Taisho, for example, about a third of men in the Ginza district of Tokyo were wearing Western clothes (while the share of women wearing Western clothes was less than 1 percent).

6. Tetsuya Hashimoto, "Toshika to Minshū Undō," in *Nihon Rekishi*, vol. 17 (Tokyo: Iwanami Shoten, 1976), 130–31.

tween the two was clearly tipping in favor of the latter, thereby stretching out the space within which Mormonism could possibly thrive. The societal trend toward openness and pluralism became progressively stronger, especially following the 1912 death of Emperor Meiji, which bestowed the throne on his sickly son (posthumously named Taisho). Freed from the spell of a charismatic leader, Japanese society experienced a rise of individualism and academic freedom, and a remarkable pluralism emerged in politics and thought. For example, there was a view, originally advanced by Tatsukichi Minobe in 1911, that the emperor was an "organ of the state," which effectively denied his divinity and inviolability. The idea of *minponshugi* (lit. "government for the people"), advocated in 1916 by Sakuzo Yoshino as a form of democracy in which sovereignty rested with the emperor, received a large following.[7] There was a call for universal suffrage, which strengthened after the end of World War I. To placate the public, in September 1918, the remaining Meiji elder statesman (*genrō*) turned to the political parties to install a cabinet headed by Kei (or Takashi) Hara, a commoner and head of the *Seiyūkai*, a conservative party originally founded in 1900 by Hirobumi Ito.[8]

What historians call Taisho Democracy, in the narrow sense, refers to the period of 1918 through 1932, during which party cabinets elected by the people (as opposed to those selected by the *genrō*) ran the government. In a broader sense, it is a symbolic designation for the new currents of cosmopolitanism, discontent, and reform that found expression in the years during and after World War I. Japan was more open to the world, and foreign culture and practices were easily imported. The Japanese had ready access to inexpensive editions of translations of virtually all of the major works of European philosophy.[9] Unlike the Westernization of the 1880s, however, Japanese society did not simply import basic ideas; it now had the maturity to absorb contemporaneous thoughts with all their contexts.[10]

"Culture" was the buzzword of the era.[11] During this period, popular culture developed, with weekly magazines, movies and cartoons, and restaurants and cafes appearing on the scene. Between 1918 and 1932, the number of journals registered under the Newspaper Law rose from 3,123 to 11,118. Farmers in rural areas began to drink beer and soda. High-rise buildings in urban centers offered a great display of domestic and imported goods; urban pleasures multiplied and diversified; private railroads connected suburban areas and carried their inhabitants

---

7. Osamu Kuno and Shunsuke Tsurumi, *Gendai Nihon no Shisō* (Tokyo: Iwanami Shoten, 1956), 151–60; Marius B. Jansen, *The Making of Modern Japan* (Cambridge, Massachusetts and London: The Belknap Press of Harvard University Press, 2000), 537; Keizo Ikimatsu, *Taishōki no Shisō to Bunka* (Tokyo: Aoki Shoten, 1971), 55.

8. Up to this time, prime ministers had been selected from among the *genrō*.

9. Jansen, *Modern Japan*, 537, 550, 574.

10. Ikimatsu, *Taishōki no Shisō*, 14.

11. Toru Miyagawa and Kazuo Hijikata, *Jiyū Minken Shisō to Nihon no Roman Shugi* (Tokyo: Aoki Shoten, 1971), 109–10.

to places of employment and shopping. By 1930, Japan had thirty universities with about 40,000 students; almost 90 percent of adult Japanese had at least six years of elementary education.[12]

Japanese society's new cosmopolitanism engendered greater tolerance of Christianity. From the 1910s through the mid-1920s, the government regularly invited representatives of Christianity, along with those from Buddhism and Sect Shinto, for consultation, thus recognizing Christianity as one of the country's three principal religions.[13] To one of these meetings in 1911, even the LDS Church was invited as a representative of Christianity.[14] In September 1912, Christian representatives were among those who attended the Shinto funeral rites for Emperor Meiji; in October 1915, fifteen Christians were decorated with imperial honors in connection with the coronation of Emperor Taisho. On this occasion, Japanese Christians throughout the country showed no hesitation in displaying their patriotism.[15] As Buddhists increased their involvement in social and charitable causes, the cooperation between the Buddhists and the Christians also increased.[16]

Japan was an urbanized, industrial society. It was no longer a country that could be dominated by a small handful of influential individuals in high office. New occupations and professions emerged, and literacy spread through public education. The public's demand for political participation and social reforms sometimes went wild; there were increasingly violent student, labor, and socialist movements. By and large, however, the party leaders in government steered a moderate course in domestic and international affairs. Throughout the 1920s, they cautiously accommodated the demands of anti-establishment groups, while placing Japan squarely in the prevailing international currents of cooperation, pacifism, and disarmament.

7.2.2. Intellectual Currents and the Mormon Cause

Reflecting these societal changes, especially the national mood of religious tolerance and pluralism, the Taisho period saw a marked increase in the productivity of the LDS Japan Mission. While the annual number of baptisms per mis-

---

12. Jansen, *Modern Japan*, 541, 570–73.
13. Charles W. Iglehart, *A Century of Protestant Christianity in Japan* (Rutland, Vermont and Tokyo: Charles E. Tuttle, 1959), 185–86; Akio Dohi, "Kindai Tennōsei to Kirisutokyō," in *Taishō Demokurashī, Tennōsei, Kirisutokyō*, ed. Tomisaka Kirisutokyō Sentā (Tokyo: Shinkyō Shuppansha, 2001), 297–301.
14. Elbert D. Thomas, "Elbert D. Thomas," in *Thirteen Americans: Their Spiritual Autobiographies*, ed. Louis Finkelstein (New York: Harper & Brothers, 1953), 149.
15. Dohi, "Kindai Tennōsei," 303–4; Katsuhito Kurahashi, "Taishō Demokurashī to Kagawa Toyohiko," in *Taishō Demokurashī, Tennōsei, Kirisutokyō*, ed. Tomisaka Kirisutokyō Sentā (Tokyo: Shinkyō Shuppansha, 2001), 262.
16. Masashi Sakurai, *Kinsei Nihon Shūkyō Shisō Shi* (Fukuoka: Tonshindō, 1944), 406–7.

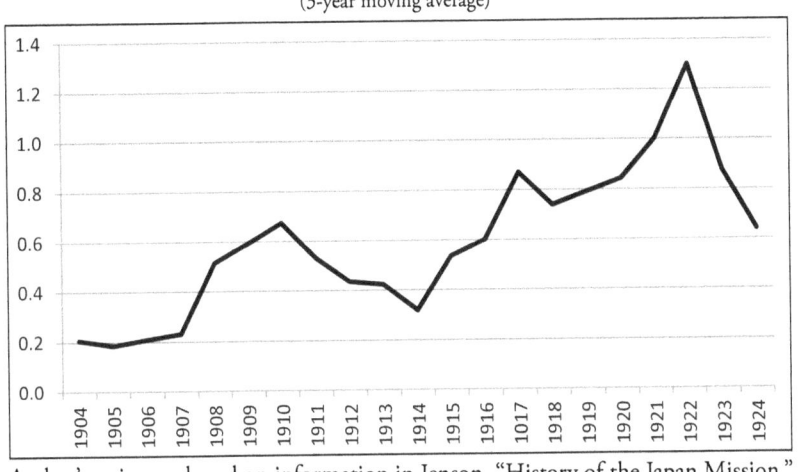

Figure 7.1. Mormon Baptisms per Missionary per Year
(3-year moving average)

Author's estimates based on information in Jenson, "History of the Japan Mission."

sionary averaged 0.36 per year during 1902–12, the number rose to 0.79 from 1913 through 24; the difference is statistically significant at the 5 percent level. When we smooth out the year-to-year volatility in baptisms by taking a three-year moving average, the increasing productivity of the Japan Mission during the Taisho period, especially from 1915 to 1922, becomes clearer (Figure 7.1). In fact, the average productivity of 1.02 baptisms per missionary per year observed from 1915 through 1922 exceeded what would be the productivity of LDS missionary work in Japan in the early twenty-first century.

What was the thought pattern of those who were attracted to Mormonism? The role of education in the individualization of religious choice was noted earlier (see Section 5.3.5). Japanese intellectual historians Osamu Kuno and Shunsuke Tsurumi explain this individualization process within the context of the nationalism of prewar Japan, which they characterize as a system rather than a thought. Based on the Meiji Constitution and the Imperial Rescript on Education, Japanese nationalism can be summarized as "the emperor's people, the emperor's country." The emperor (*tennō*), embodying both political and spiritual authority, enacted laws and issued rescripts on education and other spiritual pursuits. His subjects, on their part, were expected not only to obey the laws but also to incorporate the principles of his rescripts into their daily living.[17]

The operation of the system was dualistic. On the one hand, every child was taught from early childhood—through primary and secondary education (as well as in military training)—that the emperor was absolute and divine. The divinity of the emperor was so well inculcated that the concept virtually became second nature

---

17. Kuno and Tsurumi, *Gendai Nihon*, 126–31.

to the Japanese people. On the other hand, those in the ruling class knew that the authority of the emperor was symbolic and nominal; he was an organ of the state. This knowledge was a secret reserved to the ruling class as they progressed through the country's prestigious institutions of secondary and higher education. Kuno and Tsurumi call what was taught in public—the interpretation that viewed the emperor's authority as absolute—as the exoteric cult (*kenkyō*); alternatively, they call the elitist view of the imperial system—the interpretation that viewed the emperor's authority as limited by the constitution—as the esoteric cult (*mikkyō*). The national myth was propagated in primary and military schools, while the European world view was taught in higher schools and universities.[18]

When one accepts this characterization of how Japanese were taught to think, one would expect a predominant portion of Mormon investigators and converts to have come from among those who were receiving (or had received) higher education.[19] In contrast, the cost of converting to Mormonism must have been prohibitively high for those with little education. Tomigoro Takagi, writing in 1958 about his experience as an investigator in the early 1910s, recalled attending church meetings in Tokyo with such individuals as Toichi Kaneko (future Tokyo city council member), Ryosaku Takizawa (future attorney at law), Yoshiro Kikuchi (future member of the House of Representatives), and two daughters of Hogetsu Shimamura (noted literary critic, playwright, novelist, and poet of the prewar period).[20] Some ten years later, Koshi Nakagawa (baptized 11 July 1922) was a student in the faculty of economics at Keio University, from which he would graduate in 1924.[21]

Elsewhere in the mission, in Osaka, Go Inouye (baptized 21 October 1917) was a civil servant in the city government and was proficient in English.[22] Koichi Iwatsu (baptized 6 October 1918) was a higher school teacher; Muneharu Teranishi (baptized 31 August 1919) was a chemist and the manager of a man-

---

18. Kuno and Tsurumi, *Gendai Nihon*, 131–33; Shunsuke Tsurumi, *An Intellectual History of Wartime Japan 1931–1945* (London and New York: Routledge & Kegan Paul, 1986), 24–25, 28–29.

19. Another potential source of Christian converts would have been those who were dissatisfied with the existing social order, especially among the poor and uneducated. Some non-mainline churches, such as the Plymouth Brethren and the Watchtower, evidently obtained their converts from among this class of people. For the Mormons to reach them, however, would have required native missionaries who were skilled in the language and socially more accepted. Yoshimitsu Kasahara, "Kojin Kirisutosha no Teikō," in *Senjika Teikō no Kenkyū, vol. II: Kirisutosha Jiyūshugisha no Baai*, ed. Dōshisha Daigaku Jinbun Kagaku Kenkyū Sho (Tokyo: Misuzu Shobō, 1969), 44–45.

20. Tomigoro Takagi, "Nihon Dendōbu no Kaiko," *Seito no Michi* 2 (September 1958): 24.

21. *Shuro* 1 (February 1925): 18. When Nakagawa met Robertson in 1939, he was office manager for the "Far Eastern Asia Alcoholic Motor Fuel Co." Robertson, Journal, 8 May 1939.

22. Go Inouye, "Testimony of a Japanese Member of the Church," *Improvement Era* 21 (1918): 815–17.

ufacturing plant; Ichitaro Ohashi (baptized 8 June 1921) was a self-employed businessman, manufacturing cans for Tiger Shoe Polish; and Susumu Hisada (baptized 10 September 1922) was a dentist. Mr. Hosoi, a frequent investigator, was the manager of a bank and had been a professor at Osaka Higher Commercial School (present-day Osaka City University). Another frequent visitor was Miss Seki, the daughter of Hajime Seki who served as vice mayor (1914–23) and the mayor (1923–35) of the city of Osaka.[23] Somewhat later, Sapporo's Tadashi Yamashita (baptized 21 October 1921) was in the brokerage business and evidently making a good living.[24]

Young students at prestigious schools, who passed competitive entrance examinations, may have particularly been attracted to American missionaries, if not the Mormon message itself. They had already been chosen as the future leaders of Japan, and now faced several years of school.[25] To approach these students, the Mormon missionaries played baseball and basketball with Japanese secondary school and college teams, including Keio, Rikkyo (St. Paul), Seijo, and Waseda, just to name a few. Their contacts became more ecumenical during the Taisho period when it appears that Mormons were more readily accepted by other expatriates in Japan. They played baseball as members of the Tokyo Americans made up of diplomats, teachers, and ministers and missionaries from other denominations, and played baseball and basketball in tournaments hosted by the YMCA.[26] H. Grant Ivins, who played almost continuously for the team from 2011 to 2015, was the captain for two years and the manager for one.[27] Mormon missionaries in Japan were engaged in athletic activities with various school teams until the very end of the mission's existence.

Mormon mission leaders were generally upbeat about the state and prospect of missionary work in Japan. Concerning Sapporo, for example, mission president Joseph H. Stimpson described the conditions in July 1916 as being "in splendid shape" and the "spirit of the saints" in August 1920 as "very pleasing to me as they seemed enthused about the work."[28] In March 1921, mission president Lloyd O. Ivie reported that the conditions in Kofu and Osaka were "generally well,"[29] and as late as September 1923 called the branch in Sapporo "very promising and flourishing."[30] In Tokyo, the "regular" Christmas program in 1916 was attended by

---

23. Robertson, Autobiography, 22, 23 and 27 April 1939.
24. Robertson, Journal, 2 May 1939.
25. Tsurumi, *Wartime Japan*, 8.
26. Thomas, "Elbert D. Thomas," 148–49; James Alden Richins, "The Life Story of Orlando Fowler, 1902–1923," June 1999, 12, 20, 25–26.
27. When he was in Morioka, he played with a Japanese team. Heber Grant Ivins, Journal, Special Collections, Willard J. Marriott Library, University of Utah, 2 April 1911 and 2 June 1914.
28. Jenson, "History of the Japan Mission"; Joseph H. Stimpson, Journal, BYU Archives, 12 August 1920.
29. Jenson, "History of the Japan Mission," 3 March 1921.
30. Jenson, "History of the Japan Mission," 13 September 1923.

over 200 persons and the one in 1923 by eighty-nine people, most of whom were adults.[31] Stimpson reported to the First Presidency in March 1920: "The work here is progressing. . . . The prospects for the year are very good."[32]

The work was felt to be going so successfully that Stimpson in November 1918 recommended to the First Presidency that "now [was] the best time to undertake the building of a church and permanent headquarters in Tokyo for the Japan Mission."[33] At this time, the Japan–United States Treaty of Commerce and Navigation, which had come into force in April 1911, gave Americans in Japan the right to "own or lease and occupy" residential and commercial buildings and to "lease land for residential and commercial purposes" on the same terms as Japanese citizens.[34] The timing of this request appears to have been dictated by an issue with the landlord. The response from the First Presidency was encouraging. Regarding a house Stimpson had located in early 1919, the First Presidency in April approved the purchase if the property included "the adjoining area facing the street" and told Stimpson to "continue to look for suitable prices."[35] This implies that the church had every intention to stay in Japan as of early 1919. At that time, however, no purchase was made, presumably because a new arrangement was secured with the landlord to continue to rent the current house.[36]

7.3. Mormonism's Measured Response and Its Aftermath

7.3.1. David O. McKay's Tour of Japan, 1920–21

This rather positive assessment of the LDS Church in Taisho Japan is corroborated by the repeated pleas of mission leaders for more missionaries. Frustrated with the lack of missionaries, mission president Joseph Stimpson wrote to Mormon apostle David O. McKay in March 1920: "We have so few missionar-

---

31. Jenson, "History of the Japan Mission."

32. Joseph H. Stimpson, letter to the First Presidency, 18 March 1920, Japan Mission, "Letterpress Copybooks, 1901–1923," LDS Church Archives.

33. Joseph H. Stimpson, letters to the First Presidency, 28 November 1918 and 31 March 1919, Japan Mission, "Letterpress Copybooks, 1901–1923," LDS Church Archives.

34. It was only in November 1926 that the revised Foreign Land Ownership Law allowed foreigners in Japan the right to own land unconditionally. The original law, enacted in 1910, had already allowed foreigners in Japan to own land, but an imperial order required to put it into force was never issued. Tokushiro Ohata, "Nihon ni okeru Gaikokujin Taigū no Hensen (2)," *Ajia Kenkyū* 15 (July 1968): 67–69, 75.

35. First Presidency of the Church of Jesus Christ of Latter-day Saints, letter to Joseph H. Stimpson, 14 April 1919, LDS Church Archives.

36. In March 1919, Stimpson informed the First Presidency that the landlord had allowed them to stay for 130 yen a month in rent. Joseph H. Stimpson, letter to the First Presidency, 31 March 1919. Japan Mission, "Letterpress Copybooks, 1901–1923," LDS Church Archives.

Mormon apostle David O. McKay (left), with Hugh J. Cannon, Salt Lake Liberty Stake president, during their visit to Japan, December 1920–January 1921. Courtesy LDS Church Archives.

ies here . . . that the devil has to look elsewhere for a workshop."[37] As a result, at a meeting of the First Presidency and the Twelve held on 14 October 1920, McKay was assigned to visit Japan. This was to be part of a round-the-world tour that included a trip to China. On the following day, Hugh J. Cannon, the son of George Q. Cannon and then president of the Liberty Stake in Salt Lake City, was asked to accompany McKay.[38] They left Salt Lake City after being set apart for their work on 2 December 1920 and receiving information on Japan from Frederick Caine in Idaho who had previously served in the Japan Mission.

The two men left Vancouver, B.C. on 7 December 1920 aboard the *Empress of Japan* and arrived in Yokohama on 23 December. Christmas Day was spent at the Tokyo mission home:

> Christmas eve . . . found four little groups of the true followers of the Master fully prepared to do honor to the occasion. These were the branches of the Church of Jesus Christ located at Osaka, Tokyo, Kofu and Sapporo. It was Brother Cannon's pleasure

---

37. As quoted in Murray L. Nichols, "History of the Japan Mission of the LDS Church 1901–1924" (MA thesis, Brigham Young University, 1957), 69.

38. Hugh J. Cannon (1870–1931) was born on 19 January 1870 in Salt Lake City. While serving as mission president in Germany, in February 1904, Cannon was made president of the newly created Liberty Stake. Returning to Salt Lake City some months later, Cannon held that office for twenty years, from 1904 to 1923. Cannon later served as managing editor of the *Improvement Era* and a member of the General Board of Young Men's Mutual Improvement Association, the position he held at the time of his death on 6 October 1931. Bryant S. Hinckley, "Hugh J. Cannon," *Improvement Era* 31 (1928): 453–56; Bryant S. Hinckley, "Hugh J. Cannon," *Improvement Era* 35 (1931): 2–3. Also, see Andrew Jenson, *Latter-Day Saint Biographical Encyclopedia*, vol. 4 (Salt Lake City: Andrew Jensen Memorial Association, 1936).

and mine to be participants in the festivities at Tokyo. . . . I was conscious of a very keen regret: viz., that, excepting the members of the Church, it appeared that neither parents nor children had participated in the entertainment because of any sympathy for the Gospel. They had come either for amusement or gifts or both.[39]

The rest of their stay was spent traveling across the country to observe the conditions of the country and the church. On 26 December 1920, McKay and Cannon, accompanied by Stimpson, traveled to Kofu to participate in Sunday worship. On 28 December, they traveled from Nikko (where they spent a holiday) for Sapporo. When they arrived in Aomori the next day, the sea was so rough and weather so stormy that they decided to head back to Tokyo without crossing the Tsugaru Strait, with McKay feeling that "we might be snowed in and unable to return on time."[40] They arrived back in Tokyo on 30 December 1920. After an all-mission missionary conference held on 2–3 January 1921, the Mormon leaders left for their final destination of their Japan visit, Osaka, and then on to Shimonoseki for passage to Pusan, Korea and to Peking.[41] From there they would head to Hawaii in mid-January after visiting Nagasaki, Kobe, Osaka, Kyoto, Tokyo, and Yokohama en route.

Stimpson sensed that the visiting authority appeared "well pleased with the people" and heard him say that "the work ought to be pushed." McKay compared the shortage of manpower relative to the mission's potential to "trying to run a sixty horsepower machine with a one horsepower motor, and that out of repair."[42] McKay wrote to his close friend on the Council of the Twelve Apostles, Orson F. Whitney, on the way to Hawaii about his impression of the people he had met in Japan:

> They are a virile, home-loving, progressive people, whom, it seems to me, we ought to be able to lead to an understanding of the Gospel; and I sincerely hope you will exert your good influence toward the strengthening of the important mission.[43]

---

39. David O. McKay, "Christmas in Tokyo," *Juvenile Instructor* 56 (1921): 113–15.

40. Stimpson, Journal, 29 December 1920; Hugh J. Cannon, *David O. McKay Around the World: An Apostolic Mission* (Provo, Utah: Spring Creek, 2005), 28.

41. After arriving in Peking on the evening of 8 January 1921, the two men found a spot in the Forbidden City, where on the following day McKay dedicated the "Chinese Realm" for the preaching of the gospel. Hugh Jenne Cannon, "Around-the-world travels of David O. McKay and Hugh J. Cannon," LDS Church Archives; Hugh J. Cannon, "The Land of China Dedicated," *Juvenile Instructor* 56 (1921): 115–17; Francis M. Gibbons, *David O. McKay: Apostle to the World, Prophet of God* (Salt Lake City: Deseret Book Company, 1986), 106–9.

42. Missionary annual reports for 1921, as quoted in Reid L. Neilson, *Early Mormon Missionary Activities in Japan, 1901–1924* (Salt Lake City: University of Utah Press, 2010), 130–32; J. Christopher Conkling, "The Dark Ages: The L.D.S. Church and Japan from 1924 to 1948," unpublished, Brigham Young University, December 1973, 3.

43. McKay's hope that Whitney would exert his influence may indicate the general reluctance of the church leadership to give any more resources to the Japan Mission. David O. McKay, letter to Orson F. Whitney, 1 February 1921, LDS Church Archives.

McKay recommended to the headquarters that married couples be called to Japan to provide stability to younger missionaries in each area. Subsequently, additional missionaries, including couples, were sent to Japan, but the number, which reached the all-time peak of twenty by the end of 1922, was not sustained.

7.3.2. Labor of Hilton and Hazel Robertson in Osaka

Hilton and Hazel Robertson, one of the four couples called to serve in Japan following the McKay visit, exemplify the experience of the LDS Church under Taisho Democracy.[44] Following their brief assignment in Sapporo, the Robertsons arrived in Osaka on 15 September 1921. On their first Sunday (18 September), Hilton observed forty-four people in

Missionaries and members at the Osaka church building, 5401 Shinpoincho, Tennoji, in the early 1920s. The man in kimono is Tsuruichi Katsura. Courtesy LDS Church Archives.

attendance at Sunday school. In 1921 and 1922, Sunday morning attendance fluctuated between twenty and fifty-five; attendance was somewhat smaller at evening meetings, ranging between twenty and forty. Even the Great Kanto Earthquake of 1 September 1923, which primarily affected Tokyo and its surrounding area (see Section 7.3.3 immediately below), had little impact on church attendance in Osaka. About a week later, on 9 September, there were thirteen present at sacrament meeting besides the missionaries, and about twenty at "night meeting." On 18 November 1923, Robertson recorded: "The Sacrament Meeting was about as usual but our night meeting was full, many new investigators present." The Christmas program in 1921 saw 125 people present, including members, investigators, and friends.[45]

Even though the Robertsons never developed proficiency in the Japanese language, Hilton's journal entries are full of optimism about the progress of the work. Part of this may reflect the maturity of some Osaka members who bore part of the burden of the work. Soon after the Robertsons' arrival, on 27 November 1921,

---

44. Hilton Robertson and Hazel Metcalf were married on 5 June 1912 in the Salt Lake Temple. They received a mission call on 18 March 1921 and landed in Japan on 6 June 1921. Robertson, Autobiography.
45. Robertson, Autobiography, 25 December 1921.

Japanese members Hisaichi Hamada and Tsuruichi Katsura were ordained elders. Of the work rendered by these men, Robertson remarked in a August 1922 journal entry: "At night I took charge of the Street Meeting. Elders Katsura and Hamada were the speakers. They both gave splendid talks to about two hundred people."[46]

Hilton Robertson thought of himself as having great success in Osaka, seeing "a spirit of harmony and love existing here among the saints as well as the missionaries."[47] Hilton's ministry in Osaka ended in January 1924, when he assumed the presidency of the Japan Mission.[48] At the farewell party held in the Robertsons' honor on 14 January, the "house was full there being about seventy five present including saints, investigators and friends." On the next day, a large number of people ("between 75 & 100") came to Osaka station to bid them farewell.[49] During the Robertsons' time in Osaka, missionary work was briefly carried out on a limited basis in the town of Ono, about 20 miles northwest of Kobe, where Hilton was employed as a part-time school teacher. This arrangement appeared to continue for some time, as Elwood L. Christensen took over Hilton's place after January 1924.

7.3.3. Dark Clouds Gather

From 1923 to 1924, missionary work in Japan suffered a temporary setback, owing first to a natural disaster in September 1923 and then a deteriorating diplomatic relationship between Japan and the United States in early 1924.

Earthquake in September 1923. A magnitude-7.9 earthquake hit the Kanto region of Japan shortly before noon on 1 September 1923, devastating Tokyo, Yokohama, Chiba, and their surrounding areas.[50] Because the earthquake occurred around lunch time, when some people were using charcoal for cooking, the direct damage was compounded by fire. About 109,000 buildings collapsed while another 212,000 burned down. According to the latest estimates by Japan's National Astronomical Observatory, more than 105,000 people lost their lives. About 90 percent of these deaths were due to the direct and indirect consequences of fire. Because about 60 percent of residential dwellings were damaged, if not destroyed, the authorities created some 160 evacuation centers at Buddhist temples, Shinto shrines, and schools. There was a mass exodus of people from

---

46. Ibid., 8 August and 18 November 1922.

47. Ibid., 17 September 1922.

48. The First Presidency notified Ivie of the appointment of Robertson to succeed him as early as August 1923, but Ivie did not inform Robertson of this change until 17 November 1923. Robertson, Autobiography, 17 November 1923.

49. Ibid., 14–15 January 1924.

50. Kokuritsu Tenmon Dai, comp., *Rika Nenpyō*, vol. 88 (Tokyo: Maruzen Shuppan, 2014), 746–47.

Tokyo and Yokohama into the suburbs as well as to areas outside the Kanto region. The material damage from the earthquake is estimated to have been ¥4.6 billion, about 30 percent of gross national product.[51]

At this time, there were only four missionaries at the mission home in Tokyo. Just prior to the earthquake, from 21 to 28 August 1923, a missionary conference of the Japan Mission had been held in Sapporo. Mission president Ivie and his family had not yet returned to Tokyo. Upon learning what had happened, the missionaries from the other conferences came to join the Tokyo missionaries in identifying the conditions of the local members in the Tokyo area. Everyone was found safe ("not one received even a scratch") though one had lost her home.[52] Nami Suzuki and her family started living in a small house located on the church property in Shinjuku.[53]

The Japanese immigration issue in the United States. The Johnson–Reed Act (officially called the Immigration Act of 1924), which included the National Origins Act and the Asian Exclusion Act, was enacted on 26 May 1924 in the United States. The law, while in most cases limiting the annual number of immigrants who could be admitted from any country to 2 percent of the number of people from that country living in the United States in 1890, placed an outright ban on the entry of any alien who by virtue of race or nationality was ineligible for citizenship. This meant that those Asians who were not previously prevented from immigrating, the Japanese in particular, could no longer be admitted to the United States as immigrants. This was a violation of the 1907 Gentlemen's Agreement between Japan and the United States,[54] so the Japanese government protested. According to the Office of the Historian, United States Department of State, the United States Congress considered preserving the racial composition of the country more important than promoting good ties with Japan.[55] The bulk of the law took effect on 1 July 1924, followed by the exclusion portion of the law (without which a nominal quota of 146 immigrants would have been granted to Japanese) on 1 March 1925, seven months after all Mormon missionaries left Japan.

---

51. Nakamura, *Meiji-Taishō-ki no Keizai*, 159.

52. The experience of these missionaries is told in Ernest B. Woodward, "Thrilling Experience of Four 'Mormon' Missionaries in the Tokyo Disaster," *Improvement Era* 27 (December 1923): 126–33.

53. Robertson, Autobiography, 194.

54. In view of the increasing anti-Japanese agitation in California, the United States and Japan reached the so-called Gentlemen's Agreement by which Japan restricted emigration by not issuing passports to prospective emigrants except the close kin and picture brides of those already in the United States and its territories. Yukiko Kimura, *Issei: Japanese Immigrants in Hawaii* (Honolulu: University of Hawaii Press, 1988), 15.

55. "The Immigration Act of 1924," Office of the Historian, United States Department of State, accessed 24 November 2015, https://history.state.gov/milestone/1921-1936/immigration-act.

Japanese sentiment against the United States had been deteriorating as the passage of the immigration act became imminent. On 16 April 1924, mission president Robertson wondered if it would be a sensible thing to suspend tracting "until the feeling of revenge has died down among the people."[56] Robertson recorded that during the week of 23 April "a plain clothes man from the police office called to see if we had been molested or disturbed in any way by radicals." Following the passage of the act, the missionaries were requested on 30 May to "remove our sign board at the end of the street . . . so there will be nothing to direct the people our way." On 28 June 1924, two posters that read *Beijin Haiseki* (Expel the Americans) were found on the mission home door.

7.3.4. Closing of the Mission

Despite the relative success its few missionaries were enjoying, even with this temporary setback, in June 1924, the Church of Jesus Christ of Latter-day Saints made a decision to close the Japan Mission "temporarily." On 26 June, a telegram dated the ninth of June was received in Tokyo from the First Presidency: "Have decided to withdraw all missionaries from Japan temporarily. Cabling you twelve thousand Yen for that purpose. If more needed cable us. Arrange return immediately."[57]

This came as no surprise to Hilton Robertson, as he had received previously on 13 June a letter from the Yokohama Specie Bank notifying him of the receipt of 12,000 yen. On the following day (14 June), he saw in the *Japan Times* a small front-page dispatch from Salt Lake City, under the heading "Latter Day Saints Find No Work Here,"[58] stating that "Because the field has been found unfertile, the Mormon missionaries will be immediately withdrawn from Japan."[59] On 16 June, Robertson wrote letters to all the missionaries in the field, informing them of the situation and asking them to "press the sale of books in order that we might leave the publications in Japan."[60] On 23 June, he started making arrangements to secure passage for the missionaries; on 26 June, just before the telegram arrived, he had sent a letter to William and Sylvia Glover in Sapporo releasing them to return home.[61] Whatever the reason, the arrival of the telegram was delayed by more than two weeks. On 28 June, a formal letter dated 10 June was received

---

56. Robertson, Autobiography, 16 April 1924.
57. Ibid., 26 June 1924.
58. The 12 June 1924 issue of the *Deseret Evening News* had a short column under the heading "Japanese Mission of Church Closed," announcing that the "decision was reached principally because of the 'almost negligible results of missionary efforts' in that country."
59. Of this, Hilton Robertson wrote in his journal: "we were some what [sic] excited at news we read in the paper about the mission being closed." Robertson, Autobiography, 15 June 1924.
60. Robertson, Autobiography, 16 June 1924.
61. Ibid., 26 June 1924.

The Japan Mission under Taisho Democracy 217

from the First Presidency, telling Robertson to dispose of all church property and to close the mission.

The announcement to close the mission was a surprise to most missionaries,[62] but the decision was a long time coming. The First Presidency in their 12 June 1924 statement noted that "the matter of the temporary closing of the mission and the withdrawal of the missionaries who are laboring there, [had] long been under consideration by the Presidency and the Council of Twelve."[63] Indeed, for several years rumors had circulated among some missionaries and their families in Utah that the mission might be closed.[64] No new missionaries had been called to Japan after June 1923. Robertson had been corresponding with the First Presidency since he took office at the beginning of 1924. In a letter addressed to Robertson on 22 February 1924, Heber J. Grant foreshadowed what might be forthcoming by noting the scanty fruits of missionary labors in Japan.[65] Robertson had a premonition but the timing was a surprise:

> I expect a great change to take place in the future in this mission. The mission will automatically remove itself from this country in another year or there will be some new missionaries come over. I don't expect the mission to close immediately; not for a year at least.[66]

The progression from inquiry to decision involved some vacillation. When Robertson in early February 1924 informed the First Presidency that the mission was practically out of publications, "excepting Books of Mormon, Song Books and a few tracts," suggesting that a new printing of several publications be made "at considerable expense" to the church, he received a reply authorizing him to "publish a new Edition to the Articles of Faith by James E. Talmage, also another edition to the History of the Church, both in the Japanese language."[67] In this same letter, the First Presidency also informed Robertson that "although the work in this land had never been promising . . . they did not feel that the mission should be closed down. They felt our people had a responsibility in warning and

---

62. In 1978, Christensen, recalling the event, said: "It came as a shock and a surprise. In fact, I couldn't believe it." Elwood L. Christensen, interview by R. Lanier Britsch, 1978, James Moyle Oral History Program, LDS Church Archives, 15.

63. The full text is reprinted in the 10 July 1924 issue of *The Latter-day Saints' Millennial Star*, 441.

64. Vinal G. Mauss, interviews by R. Lanier Britsch, 1975, James Moyle Oral History Program, LDS Church Archives, 9. Even during Stimpson's era (1915–21), reports were received regularly from missionaries that the church authorities were thinking about closing the mission. Lanier R. Britsch, "The Closing of the Early Japan Mission," *Brigham Young University Studies* 15 (1975): 181–82. McKay's visit to Japan was made in part to evaluate the future of the mission.

65. Britsch, "Closing," 172.

66. Japan Mission, "Minutes," LDS Church Archives, 19 May 1924.

67. Ibid., 4 February 1924.

teaching this people and it still remained a question to them whether or not they would be justified in going into other fields."⁶⁸

Following the announcement of the mission's closing, four individuals were baptized into the LDS Church during the months of June and July, including two in Sapporo and one each in Sendai and Tokyo. On 2 August 1924, Robertson left for Osaka to give the members instructions and encouragement and to see friends, and boarded a ship from Kobe to return home. At a stopover in Yokohama, he was joined by the rest of the remaining missionaries. By this time, Wallace and Louese Browning, William and Sylvia Glover, and Milton Taylor had already departed for home. The remaining group of eight missionaries, including Elwood and Arva Christensen, Rulon Esplin, Vinal Mauss, Lewis Moore, Hilton and Hazel Robertson, and Earnest Woodward, left Japan on 7 August 1924 homeward bound.

7.4. Understanding Why the Japan Mission Was Closed

In order to understand why the Japan Mission was closed in 1924, one must make a clear distinction between "structural" or permanent factors that are applicable to the entire duration of the mission, on the one hand, and "temporary" factors that are specific to the period immediately preceding the closing of the mission, on the other.⁶⁹ To be sure, the mission was confronted with the Great Kanto Earthquake in September 1923 and the rising anti-American sentiment associated with the passage of the Johnson–Reed Act. These added to other factors that were causing church activity in Tokyo to collapse.⁷⁰ A permanent decision, however, could not have been made for temporary reasons. The First Presidency, in a letter dated 10 June 1924, clearly stated that they were not "particularly alarmed over the situation in Japan." They believed that the current problems would soon subside.⁷¹ In what follows, we will first consider four structural factors before considering six temporary factors, including the impacts of the earthquake and the Johnson–Reed Act, which may have determined the *timing* of the withdrawal decision, if not the decision itself.

---

68. Robertson, Autobiography, 4 April 1924.

69. Some of these issues, as well as additional ones, are discussed by Britsch, "Closing"; and Neilson, *Mormon Missionary Activities*, 120–42.

70. For example, Hilton Robertson who was visiting Tokyo from Osaka recorded on 12 August 1923: "The Tokyo Branch is surely run down. They don't seem to have any spirit. The attendance is low and the saints are showing very little if any interest in the work." After arriving in Tokyo as mission president, he recorded on 27 January 1924: "There were only six present at Sunday School and no saints at all at Sacrament Meeting so we held the same in English." Robertson, Autobiography, 14 August 1923 and 27 January 1924.

71. Britsch, "Closing," 188.

7.4.1. "Structural" Factors Contributing to the Withdrawal Decision

Infertility of the soil. The First Presidency, in a letter addressed to Hilton Robertson on 22 February 1924, questioned the wisdom of continuing the mission by stating:

> When we stop to think that over twenty years of hard labor have been performed in Japan, it certainly looks as though the Lord would justify us if we saw fit to close that mission. . . . We do not wish to lose one soul in Japan, but if the same amount of labor in some other country was performed the chances are we would have many many times as many converts.[72]

Over the period from 1901 to 1924, the average number of converts a missionary made in Japan was 0.58 per year, with a peak of 1.82 in 1922. In contrast, a comparable figure for the Swiss–German Mission, which was the church's highest baptizing mission in the early 1920s, was 16.6 during the period 1919–24. In terms of the absolute number of baptisms for 1921, the Japan Mission (at ten baptisms) came in second to the last place among the twenty-five missions of the church.[73]

The fact that only about 170 people had joined the church was probably the single most important reason why the Mormon authorities closed the mission. The First Presidency, in the 10 June 1924 letter, stated that "from the standpoint of converts" success had been "so limited that, at least for the present, under existing circumstances, it will be better to withdraw."[74] The authorities, in their assessment, were focusing on outputs without looking at the inputs. For a country of 45–55 million people (slightly more than half the population of the United States), the number of missionaries in the mission averaged 12.5 (at no time did the number exceed twenty), and the total number amounted to less than 0.5 percent of all the missionaries called by the church from 1901 to 1924. To be sure, productivity was much lower than productivity in some other missions, but the numbers for 1919 through 1922 were comparable to productivity in postwar Japan (1948–56) when more than seventy missionaries were serving, and was higher than that observed in the early twenty-first century. Certainly there would have been many more convert baptisms if the church had made more missionaries available.

---

72. As quoted in Britsch, "Closing," 171–72.

73. The last place was the Armenian Mission, with three baptisms recorded for the year. If the Japan Mission had had the same number of missionaries as the Swiss–German Mission (ninety missionaries at the end of 1920), however, the same productivity observed for the nine missionaries serving in Japan would have produced 100 baptisms, placing it in eighteenth place (or eleventh place outside the United States) in the church. This would have been almost the same as the Australian and Norwegian Missions (with 102 baptisms each), more than the French (sixty-two) and Swedish (fifty-four) Missions, and slightly below the Canadian Mission (121). Gilbert W. Scharffs, *Mormonism in Germany: A History of the Church of Jesus Christ of Latter-day Saints in Germany between 1840 and 1970* (Salt Lake City: Deseret Book Company, 1970), Table 4 (on page 60) and Table 5 (page 62).

74. Britsch, "Closing," 188.

Even so, any hope that the opening of the Japan Mission would "prove the key to the entrance of the Gospel in the Orient," with the "Jews" of Asia carrying missionary work to their "Gentile" Chinese neighbors, was dashed by the initial lack of a miraculous success in Japan. Heidi Harris, building on the seminal work of American sociologist Armand Mauss, argues that the concept of "believing blood" in relation to the hierarchy of Asian races reached its zenith in 1901.[75] "Believing blood" was a dominant Mormon theological construct from the nineteenth to the twentieth century, which postulated that only those with direct biological lineage to the ancient House of Israel had the capacity to accept the gospel. According to Mauss, the idea grew out of the synthesis of a particular interpretation of LDS scripture (which linked the early Mormons to ancient Israel, particularly the tribe of Ephraim) with British Israelism (a view that the British Isles were inhabited by descendants of Israel) and Anglo-Saxon triumphalism (a view that glorified the Anglo-Saxon heritage). It was largely this idea that directed the first Mormon missionary efforts to the British Isles, where most of the Mormons traced their ancestry.[76]

Mauss further argues that a religious idea ("believing blood") not only determined human behavior (the establishment of a mission) but was also in turn influenced by the success of missionary work. Thus, as the work spread and met with success, the boundary of believing blood expanded—to Germany, the Nordic countries, and even Polynesian and other Pacific Island peoples.[77] In the case of Japan, it appears that a religious idea was invented as a justification for doing missionary work. By the end of the nineteenth century, the spectacular rise of Japan as a modern nation had somehow convinced Mormon leaders that the Japanese people possessed the blood of Israel through Lehi.[78] That Heber J. Grant had such a view is shown by his dedicatory prayer offered in Yokohama on 1 September 1901. On this occasion he stated his feeling that "the blood of Lehi and Nephi had been transmitted unto the people of this land, many of whom have the features and manners of the American Indians."[79]

Such a view of the Japanese people, however, faded quickly among the American Mormons. Responsible for this was not only the Mormon missionaries' failure to claim the fruits expected of a chosen race but also the racial prejudice that emerged in Utah and elsewhere in the United States with a rise in the Japanese immigration population. Instead, by the late 1910s, a view had

---

75. Heidi Harris, "Changing Racial Perceptions of the Japanese: LDS Rhetoric between 1901 and 1930," 23 August 2010, accessed 24 November 2015, www.patheos.com/blogs/oneeternalround.

76. Armand L. Mauss, *All Abraham's Children: Changing Mormon Conceptions of Race and Lineage* (Urbana and Chicago: University of Illinois Press, 2003), 1–40.

77. Mauss, *All Abraham's Children*, 10.

78. Harris, "Changing Racial Perceptions."

79. Alma O. Taylor, Journal, 1 September 1901, BYU Archives; Mauss, *All Abraham's Children*, 34.

developed within Mormon theology that the Mongolian race, to which they included the Japanese, descended from Japheth, Noah's son.[80] The Japheth theory was then used to explain Asian propensity toward paganism and the perceived failure of the Japan Mission (though some continued to embrace the believing blood theory).[81] It is possible that what appeared to be a half-hearted Mormon effort in Japan reflected their leaders' disillusionment with what the country had turned out to be as well as their uneasiness with continuing the work in such infertile soil. Any efforts in Japan were marginalized. Perhaps trapped in a vicious cycle of fewer resources and less success, they were unwilling to add missionaries without more productive results and without knowing when or how to pull out.

Language difficulty. From the vantage point of a prewar Japanese convert, Takeo Fujiwara wrote in 1933:

> This closing was probably due to the fact that the missionaries could not make themselves understood to the Japanese people. . . The Japanese people are very reasonable and quick to learn if the Gospel can be explained to them.[82]

It does not take Fujiwara to know that Japanese was a difficult language for American missionaries to acquire, especially when there was no systematic course of instruction. Some missionaries, such as Alma O. Taylor, Frederick A. Caine, Elbert D. Thomas, Joseph H. Stimpson, and Lloyd O. Ivie, developed a high degree of proficiency in Japanese, but the mastery of the language required many years, necessitating a long tenure in the field (see below).

Long service. During the period 1901–24, a total of eighty-eight Mormon missionaries served in Japan. The average term of service was 39.4 months. Of the eighty-eight, twenty-two went home early for various reasons;[83] for fourteen of them, the term of service was cut short by the closing of the mission in 1924; Stimpson's term as mission president was unusually long (seventy-one months), while Ivie's term as mission president was cut short for family reasons (twenty-five months).

---

80. Harris, "Changing Racial Perceptions." This is an example of human experience creating a new religious idea. In the period following the end of World War II, the relative success of missionary work throughout the world has diminished the relevance of any racial group favored above another. For the most part, Mormonism has now embraced the Pauline idea that all those who accept the gospel become Abraham's children (Romans 9:6–8; Galatians 3:7–9, 27–29). Mauss, *All Abraham's Children*, 32.

81. In the April 1926 general conference, Lloyd O. Ivie, former president of the Japan Mission, expressed his belief that "there is the blood of Israel among that people" and remarked that "there will be a great work done" among them. *Conference Report*, April 1926, 94–96.

82. Takeo Fujiwara, "Relationship between Shinto and Mormonism," *Improvement Era* 36 (1933): 654–55, 675–76.

83. Nine were released for misconduct; six for illness; and seven for other reasons, including death in one case.

When these people are removed, the average term of service becomes 50.7 months or a little over four years. While the average masks the considerable variation in the early years (for example, Taylor served for 103 months, Caine ninety-two months, and Stimpson sixty-seven months), four years became the officially stated term of service during the time of mission president Elbert D. Thomas.[84] All of the missionaries called after May 1912 served almost exactly forty-eight months.[85]

Prior to 1910, the term was not set when a missionary was called, which created uncertainty and stress. Upon leaving the mission in 1910, mission president Alma O. Taylor wrote:

> Five, six, seven or eight years, perhaps, sounds long and cruel to some people, but I do not believe that any strong, broad, loyal Latter-day Saint, who knows and keeps the first two greatest commandments, would allow years of sacrifice to be a consideration in answering a call of God to Japan.[86]

For many, that was a tall order to fill. The parents and bishop of John L Chadwick (who arrived in Japan on 1 June 1905) requested that the missionary be released after three years, just like any other missionary. In April 1908, Taylor responded to Bishop James Wood in North Ogden:

> You do not seem to understand that three years in this mission is only equivalent to a year or a year and a half in other missions. The fact that Elder Chadwick has been here for three years shows nothing to us who understand what it means to be a missionary in Japan.[87]

The parents stopped sending him support money in July 1908, so Chadwick was released on 16 September 1908. At least to some families, it was a special challenge to send their sons or daughters on missions to Japan.

Lack of strategic planning. As far as one can ascertain, there was little strategic planning from the beginning to the end of the Japan Mission's existence; most decisions appear to have been made haphazardly, both at the local and general headquarters levels. While this may be a corollary of the Mormon leaders' early disillusionment with Japan, a number of consequences followed from this. First, there was no systematic program of developing local leadership, which limited the menu of options when the mission was closed. Second, the church was never fully committed to Japan, thereby limiting the number of missionaries, not allowing properties to be purchased, and never specifying what resources would be provided to Japanese members to strengthen their faith and theologi-

---

84. First Presidency, letter to Elbert D. Thomas, 14 February 1910, as quoted in Nichols, "Japan Mission," 75.

85. Orlando Fowler, for example, received a mission call in 1921 for "four years." Richins, "Orlando Fowler," 5.

86. Alma O. Taylor, "Japan, the Ideal Mission Field," *Improvement Era* 13 (1910): 784.

87. As quoted by Charles L. Schmalz, "The Church in Japan 1905–1908, One Man's Mission," September 1994, 11; also Nichols, "Japan Mission," 74.

cal knowledge (it took eight years to publish the Book of Mormon in Japanese; the Doctrine and Covenants was translated but never published). In the words of Lanier Britsch, "leaders of the Church felt ambivalent toward Japan. It was almost as though they had a policy of succeeding first and sending missionaries later. Requests for more missionaries were frequent from the various mission presidents, but they were seldom granted."[88]

Not that no one was thinking strategically. For example, H. Grant Ivins, the son of Mormon apostle Anthony W. Ivins who served as mission president during the last three years of his mission, thought that the church would benefit from having a married missionary serve for fifteen to twenty years. This would be necessary, he thought, to allow the missionary to "obtain a thorough knowledge of Japanese, of the customs and manner of thought of the people, and to be able to guide efficiently the young missionaries." Ivins put these thoughts in a letter to the First Presidency on 22 December 1913, offering his services if "difficulty were experienced in finding someone willing to undertake such a work." As he anxiously waited for a reply, he expressed in his diary:

> If I should be appointed to the work I suggested, it would mean a life away from all I love, a life of no associations that are pleasant, and comparative poverty at forty. But what I should be able to accomplish should overbalance all such inconveniences.[89]

It is possible that the appointment of Joseph H. Stimpson to return to Japan as a married man to succeed him was a partial response to Ivins' suggestion. Likewise, David O. McKay's idea in 1921 of sending a married couple to each area reflected strategic thinking, but this came too late and was never fully followed through.

7.4.2. "Temporary" Factors Determining the Timing of the Withdrawal Decision

Personal disposition of Lloyd O. Ivie. The near collapse of church activity in Tokyo, which preceded the Great Kanto Earthquake, appears to have been caused primarily by the personal disposition of mission president Lloyd O. Ivie. Although, given Ivie's position, the whole mission was inevitably affected in one way or another, the problem was largely confined to Tokyo, with the work generally prospering in Osaka and Sapporo, if not in Kofu.[90] Ivie was undiplomatic in character and created relationship problems with his missionaries and the members.[91] Orlando Fowler recorded an event that happened on 8 October 1922:

---

88. Britsch, "Closing," 179.
89. Ivins, Journal, 22 December 1913.
90. Robertson recorded on 30 January 1924: "the way . . . Tokyo has been operating it is only a waste of time and money for missionaries to be here. And unless we can change the situation here it should be closed down at least in Tokyo and people in some other part be given an opportunity."
91. Britsch, "Closing," 185; Christensen Oral History, 14.

In the afternoon Bro. and Sis. Glover came out and we were talking about bad spirit among the missionaries and the Saints and the Pres. when Ivie and his wife walked in on us. She said we heard everything, Gee but they looked angry.[92]

He may also have had an issue with handling power and authority. After he was informed of his release in August 1923, he held on to the office until February 1924. His successor, Hilton Robertson, was only informed of his appointment in November 1923—not by Ivie, but because Hilton discovered his name mentioned as a mission president in a Salt Lake City newspaper.[93] In transferring the mission property to his successor in February 1924, Ivie refused to sign the "mission account report."[94]

In all fairness to Ivie, there was a health issue with his wife and later with his new-born child, on top of what appeared to be a marital problem. Distance also made it difficult to receive guidance or moral support from his supervisors in Utah. Vinal G. Mauss recalled in 1975:

> Brother Ivie . . . had obstacles. His married life was not pleasant for him, I'm sure. He had difficulties there. He kept those difficulties to himself, but it was quite evident that he had problems there. . . . [T]he problems of home life there were not conducive to this missionary couple. . . . He didn't have the confidence of most of his missionaries. A number of his missionaries were older elders. Some of them probably close to his age.[95]

Whatever the reason, Ivie was not effective as a leader, maintaining little contact with his missionaries. On 5 February 1923, for example, Hilton Robertson received the first letter in six weeks from him.[96] In February 1924, Robertson learned that there were practically no publications left and that there was an overdraft of 1,368 yen, for which Ivie had used the building fund contributed by members to cover.[97] Right before closing the mission, in June 1924, Robertson and Milton Taylor spent an evening working on children's records to "bring[ing] them up to date as there had been nothing done with them since Pres. Stimpson's time."[98]

---

92. As quoted in Richins, "Orlando Fowler," 25.

93. Robertson recorded on 17 November 1923: "Received a word today that I had been appointed President of the Mission sometime in August, but until today Pres. Ivie had never notified me of the change. I saw from reports in the paper that I as President of the Japanese Mission had not reported the disaster to the First Presidency. When I saw such reports I wrote to find out what was the reason of me being refered [sic] to as the one in charge of the Mission." Robertson, Autobiography, 170.

94. Robertson managed to get Ivie's signature aboard the ship just before departure. Robertson, Autobiography, 7 February 1924.

95. Mauss Oral History, 5.

96. Robertson, Autobiography, 5 February 1923.

97. Ibid., 4 February 1924.

98. Ibid., 16 June 1924.

The Japan Mission under Taisho Democracy

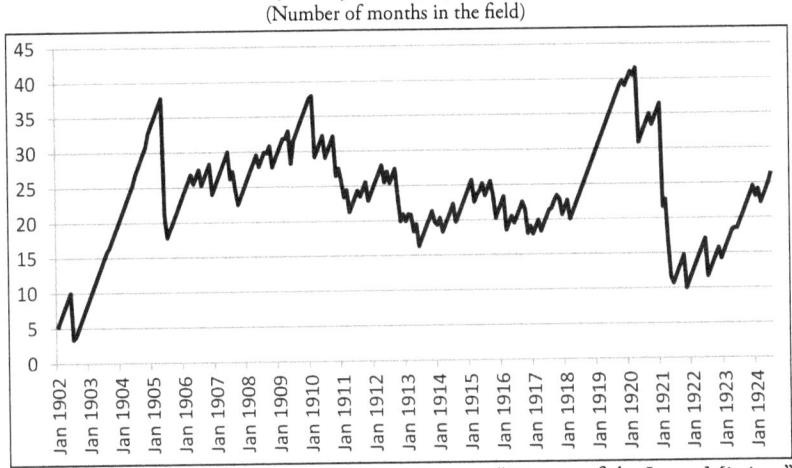

Figure 7.2. Average Experience of Mormon Missionaries in Japan, January 1902–July 1924 (Number of months in the field)

Author's estimates based on information in Jenson, "History of the Japan Mission."

Location of the new mission home. In July 1922, the mission home moved to a new location in Yodobashi (87 Tsunohazu) near the western side of Shinjuku station. This turned out to be an undesirable location in terms of access and visibility. In January 1924, Hilton Robertson and Earnest Woodward set out to rectify this situation by checking out to see if it would be possible to get the old building back.

> Brother Woodward and I went to see about rerenting the former building occupied by the church at Ushigome but found it had been rent [sic] and was being used for a hospital. It is closer in and the saints and investigators like it much better.[99]

In May 1924, when the missionaries were advised by police to remove the sign board at the end of the street, they thought that there was "nothing to direct the people our way now. This makes our location much less desirable and it was bad enough before."[100] It is possible that the location of the mission home contributed to disappointing church attendance in Tokyo.

Precipitous fall in the number of experienced missionaries. The lack of strategic planning made it impossible to maintain a minimum level of language proficiency within the mission. The small missionary force compounded the lack of strategic planning when a certain number of missionaries returned home early for a variety of reasons, creating a vacuum of language skill among the remaining missionaries. This is what happened from January to June 1921 when the average tenure of missionaries in the field declined precipitously from 36.4 months to

---

99. Ibid., 29 January 1924.
100. Ibid., 30 May 1924.

10.7 months; in November and December of the same year, the average tenure was again below one year (Figure 7.2). On 1 November 1921, mission president Ivie noted that, with the departure of so many experienced missionaries, "we have none besides myself who can be considered capable of handling the language."[101] This became a hindrance to reopening work in Kofu, which was closed in January 1922. Ivie and Wallace Browning visited Kofu in August 1922 and "had a very enjoyable time with the Saints and friends there, but decided not to open that field at that time because it would take someone well skilled in the Japanese language to ever make Kofu go."[102]

Economic difficulties at home. The decade of the 1920s in the United States, which historians call the "roaring twenties," is a period in which wages grew, new industries emerged, and a new type of pop culture began to flourish with the arrival of automobiles and the radio. Real gross national product increased by 4.2 percent per year from 1920 to 1929. This prosperity, however, was not shared by all sectors. Following the end of World War I, during which American agriculture supplied much of the food demand in Europe, agricultural prices began to fall precipitously as production recovered in Europe. Agricultural commodity prices fell by 40 percent from 1919 to 1921; real average net income per farm fell by more than 70 percent from 1920 to 1921. As the Federal Reserve raised interest rates in order to curtail the inflationary pressure built up during the war, many farmers struggled to service the debt accumulated during the farm boom of the 1910s. There was a surge in farm foreclosures during the 1920s and (with the onset of the Great Depression) well into the 1930s.[103]

While the initial fall in agricultural prices was caused by a temporary factor associated with the end of hostilities in Europe, the stagnation of the agricultural sector continued throughout the 1920s. In part, this was due to the tremendous transformation of the American economy, which required the resources employed in agriculture to be reallocated to other industries. With rising agricultural productivity, an incentive needed to be created for agricultural workers to move out. Falling agricultural prices and incomes were part of the working of this economic law.[104] As a result of these temporary and permanent factors, farm prices declined by more than 30 percent, agricultural wages by 25 percent, and farm income by

---

101. Jenson, "History of the Japan Mission," 1 November 1921.

102. Ibid., 11 August 1922.

103. W. Elliot Brownlee, *Dynamics of Ascent: A History of the American Economy*, second edition (New York: Alfred A. Knopf, 1979), 384–99; Jason Henderson, Brent Gloy, and Michael Boehlje, "Agriculture's Boom–Bust Cycles: Is This Time Different?" *Federal Reserve Bank of Kansas City Economic Review* (Fourth Quarter, 2011): 84–85, 90–93; Gene Smiley, "The U.S. Economy in the 1920s," EH.Net Encyclopedia of Economic and Business History (under "Economy, US, 1920"), accessed 17 January 2016, https://eh.net/encyclopedia-2/.

104. Smiley, "The U.S. Economy."

more than 20 percent, from 1920 to 1924. Over the same period, the total value of farm land and other properties declined by nearly 30 percent.[105]

The economy of Utah was especially hard hit by these developments. Part of the plight of Utah farmers may have been aggravated by the high cost of geographical mobility, which limited their ability to move out of Utah to take advantage of economic opportunities available elsewhere in the country.[106] Regardless, the agricultural depression of the 1920s adversely affected the ease with which Mormons could support their missionaries, especially those serving in Japan, where the term was unusually long. In January 1924, for example, mission president Hilton Robertson received a letter from William Davies of Ogden, Utah, stating that his father could no longer keep him in the field and "asking that he return home."[107] Assuming that the monthly cost of supporting a missionary in Japan was $25 in 1923,[108] this would translate to about $340 in 2015 if mechanically reflated by the consumer price index published by the United States Bureau of Labor Statistics; $25 in 1923 was about 50–75 percent of the average monthly farm wage in the United States.[109] There is a pitfall in comparing monetary values across time, but whatever the merit of such an exercise, it is clear that $25 was no small amount for families at home particularly during the economic difficulties of the 1920s.

On the leaders' part, the economic hardships the members were experiencing may have further diminished their willingness to pay for the additional administrative cost of operating what appeared to be an unproductive mission. Church headquarters was sometimes late in sending money to the mission, and the mission president was evidently under instruction to keep the expenses down. In August 1922, Ivie wrote to Salt Lake stating that "we had received no money from you since about the middle of June, July bills came in, and still none came. . . . We got down to our last penny;[110] and "I am doing my best to keep the expenses down even to incurring a slight criticism from some of the brethern [sic]."[111] Clearly, the church was experiencing a fall in tithing revenue as the income of its members declined.

---

105. United States Department of Commerce, *Historical Statistics of the United States 1789–1945* (Washington: United States Department of Commerce, 1949), series E. 1–5, 61–71, 88–104.

106. This point was forcefully made by the economic historian Elliot Brownlee to explain the plight of farmers in the Great Plains, the southeastern cotton belt, southern Appalachia, and the northern Great Lakes region in the 1920s. Brownlee, *Dynamics of Ascent*, 398–99

107. Robertson, Autobiography, 29 January 1924.

108. This conjecture is based on the diary of Orlando Fowler, which states that he received $25 from home in March 1923. Richins, "Orlando Fowler," 4. See also Ivins, Journal, 3 August 1915. Obviously, the total cost of supporting a missionary for the church (total expenditures divided by the number of missionaries) was higher. Neilson, *Mormon Missionary Activities*, 129, gives an estimate of $40.

109. The average monthly farm wage in 1923 was $37.24 with board and $48.25 without board. *Historical Statistics of the United States*, series D. 172–76.

110. Lloyd O. Ivie, letter to the First Presidency, 9 August 1922, LDS Church Archives.

111. Lloyd O. Ivie, letter to Arthur Winter, 26 August 1922, LDS Church Archives.

Economic difficulties prompted church president Heber J. Grant to conserve church finances by trimming expenditures. He used his contacts with national business and political leaders to keep key Utah and church-owned enterprises afloat. Over this period, the LDS Church either closed down or transferred to state ownership several institutions of higher learning, including Weber College in Ogden (1922); Brigham Young College in Logan (1926); and Dixie College in St. George (1933).[112] Around the time the Japan Mission was closed, the church was also considering closing the Tongan Mission, despite the fact that it had more than a thousand members.[113] The closing of the Japan Mission may well have been part of this broader restructuring of church finances. Interestingly, John A. Widtsoe, who became an apostle in March 1921, attributed the closing of the mission to "political and economic upheavals."[114] Since there was no major economic upheaval in Japan, he must have been referring to the one in Utah.

The Great Kanto Earthquake of September 1923. The near collapse of church activity in Tokyo preceded the Great Kanto Earthquake of September 1923, so the earthquake cannot be the main reason for the poor church attendance. Vinal Mauss thought years later that the earthquake had had no "major effect as far as the closing of the mission was concerned."[115] Even so, the earthquake did cause missionary work in Tokyo to be suspended for some time and must have further contributed to the stagnation of church activity there. It is also possible that the natural disaster caused the church authorities in Utah to recognize the risk of keeping a mission in a foreign country so far away and encouraged them to reassess the prospects of continuing the work.[116]

The passage of the Johnson–Reed Act. Much has been made of the intensifying anti-American sentiment in Japan associated with the impending and actual passage of the Johnson–Reed Act in May 1924. For example, some Mormon historians, arguing that the passage of this law was more serious than the earthquake, observed:

> When the Oriental Exclusion Law went into effect on 1 July 1924, the day was observed throughout Japan as a day of mourning and humiliation. Some scholars date the rise of ultranationalism in Japan from this event in 1924. The exclusion law had the effect of turning public sentiment against all proselytizing work. The day of humiliation, 1 July, came after President Grant's telegram arrived in Tokyo. The anti-American protests of that day firmed up in the minds of our missionaries the futility of remaining in Japan.[117]

---

112. *Encyclopedia of Mormonism*, vol. 1, Academies; vol. 2, History of the Church.
113. Britsch, "Closing," 188.
114. John A. Widtsoe, "The Japanese Mission in Action," *Improvement Era* 42 (1939): 88–89, 125.
115. Mauss Oral History, 10–11.
116. Britsch, "Closing," 186.
117. James R. Moss, et al., *The International Church* (Provo, Utah: Brigham Young University Press, 1982). These authors are incorrect in asserting that the exclusion law went

In any event, the hysteria, such as it was, was a temporary phenomenon. First, church attendance was considerably up by May 1924, as Robertson observed on the 18th: "There [were] forty five present at S.S. . . . Our largest meeting was held at night with an attendance of 45 investigators and saints present."[118] Second, the anti-American sentiment was likely not held widely throughout Japan. Murray Nichols, based on his interview with Robertson, states: "in Osaka anti-American feeling was much less severe and missionary work continued to go forward until the last."[119] Third, Japan's fascination with things American—from major league baseball to Hollywood movies—would flourish during the rest of the Taisho era and into the early years of the reign of Emperor Showa (1926–89) (see Section 7.5.1 below). Gilbert Bowles, the head of the Society of Friends mission in Japan, wrote to the Philadelphia headquarters in late September or early October 1924:

> So far we have met with nothing but kindness from the Japanese people—though deep in their hearts lies ever the sense of the great injury which they believe their best friend (the American people) has done them. Only jingoes and inexperienced people talk in terms of war. . . . But outwardly the people are just the same. It seemed perfectly natural for my neighbour on the train to take a pear from his basket and after peeling it offer it to me.[120]

In fact, missionary work by other Christian denominations went on as usual. Certainly, no major denomination left Japan; some new ones even arrived.[121] The resolution of the July 1924 meeting of the Southern Baptist Mission in Japan noted "the courtesy and kindness accorded us as Americans by the Japanese people in the face of their strong feeling of resentment."[122] In September 1926, the Watchtower Bible and Tract Society sent Junzo Akashi, who had joined the soci-

---

into effect on 1 July 1924. The exclusion portion of the law took effect on 1 March 1925.

118. Robertson, Autobiography, 18 May 1924. Christopher Conkling refers to an article published in the *Yamato* "only two weeks" after the last missionaries departed for America, which ascribed "the declining interest in the immigration issue to a trait peculiar to the Japanese, whose irritable and touchy temper soon subsides with the lapse of time." Conkling, "Dark Ages." This author has not been able to verify that a magazine or newspaper by that title was being published anywhere in Japan during 1924.

119. Nichols, "Japan Mission."

120. *Monthly Bulletin of the Mission Board of the Religious Society of Friends of Philadelphia and Vicinity* 1 (September 1924), as quoted by Tetsuko Toda, "Misshon Bōdo to Hainichi Imin Hō," *Yamanachi Kenritsu Joshi Tanki Daigaku Kiyō* 38 (2005): 26.

121. At least twenty-nine new Christian mission organizations, including seven from the United States, arrived in Japan between 1925 and 1938. These included the Society of St. John the Evangelist (1933), Christian Evangelistic Church (1935), and Orthodox Presbyterian Church (1938). Opus Dei arrived in 1928. David Reid, "Internationalization in Japanese Religion," in *Religion in Japanese Culture: Where Living Traditions Meet a Changing World*, ed. Noriyoshi Tamaru and David Reid (Tokyo: Kōdansha International, 1996), Table 1, 185–86.

122. F. Calvin Parker, *The Southern Baptist Mission in Japan, 1889–1989* (Lanham, Maryland: University Press of America, 1991): 127.

ety while in the United States, to open branches in Japan and its colonies.[123] Its pacifist teachings resonated with the Japanese society of the late 1920s, so much so that its popularity is said to have aroused the jealousy of Kanzo Uchimura, a prominent Christian leader who taught similar doctrines on war (for Uchimura, see Appendix 5.1 in Chapter 5).[124] In November 1929, 4,000 Christians filled the largest hall in Tokyo to celebrate the seventieth anniversary of Protestantism in Japan.[125] In the early months of 1940, most Christian missionaries were still able to carry out their assignments without hindrance from the authorities and more missionaries were being sent to Japan from their mission boards abroad.[126]

Elsewhere in the world, the very same church leadership (under Heber J. Grant, 1918–45) did not close a mission in anticipation of a future war or just because the going got tough. In Germany, proselytizing work by American Mormon missionaries continued on in the 1930s despite the constant harassment they were receiving from Nazi officials. Mormon leaders, missionaries, and members were frequently interrogated by police for their beliefs. In 1932, two Mormon missionaries in Hindenburg were attacked by a member of the Nazi Party; one of them was hit by a leather belt over the head and received bad lacerations. In 1934, the German government banned the distribution of certain Mormon publications, presumably because of references they contained to Zion and Israel, and ordered all copies to be burned. In 1938, Mormons in Germany were living under constant fear of *Gestapo* agents spying on church activities. Even so, the First Presidency did not order American missionaries to be evacuated from Germany until 24 August 1939, a week before the Nazi invasion of Poland, when war was a virtual certainty.[127]

7.5. Political and Religious Developments in Interwar Japan

Before evaluating the decision to withdraw the church from Japan, we review below major political developments, how the emerging totalitarian regime progressively tightened its grip on the freedoms of thought and expression, and the impact these developments had on the free exercise of religion, especially by foreign missionaries.

---

123. Masami Inagaki, *Heieki wo Kyohishita Nihonjin* (Tokyo: Iwanami Shoten, 1972), 19–20; Tsurumi, *Wartime Japan*, 47.
124. The society's membership was probably several hundred although it was printing as many as 100,000 copies of its monthly periodical in the mid-1930s. Inagaki, *Heieki*, 56–58.
125. Parker, *Baptist Mission*, 128.
126. Ibid., 128, 158.
127. Scharffs, *Mormonism in Germany*, 80–116.

7.5.1. Political and International Background

Japan's prewar government rested on a delicate balance of power between civilians and career military officers. The prime minister's cabinet included the ministers of the army and the navy, but the prime minister had no authority to appoint them. Those appointments came from the emperor. This meant that the military had virtual veto power on all major state decisions, which in principle required unanimity. The system worked reasonably well during the Meiji period when the real political power was exercised by the *genrō* from the former Satsuma and Choshu domains. As one *genrō* after another passed away, the balance of power became increasingly precarious. The involvement of the military in the political process had an especially negative effect on the country's intellectual and religious climate. Japanese intellectual historians Osamu Kuno and Shunsuke Tsurumi argue that the Ministries of the Army and the Navy, along with the Ministry of Education, were the only organs of the government that subscribed to the exoteric cult of the national myth taught through compulsory education and military training, namely, that the emperor was coeval with heaven.[128] This was a position that most reasonable people could not accept literally but an increasing number of them found it difficult to challenge openly.

Following the conclusion of World War I, Japan emerged as one of the Five Great Powers, with a permanent seat on the Council of the League of Nations (which was established in 1920 by the Paris Peace Conference). Japan lived up to its increased responsibility on the world stage by taking a moderate course in diplomatic and military affairs. The civilian leadership was clearly in the driver's seat. In December 1921, Japan signed the Four-Power Treaty with Britain, France, and the United States, in which it agreed not to seek further territorial expansion and to terminate the Anglo–Japanese Alliance of 1902. Further, in February 1922, Japan agreed to the Five-Power Treaty, which limited the construction of aircraft carriers, battlecruisers, and battleships. This was followed in April 1930 by the London Naval Treaty, which further regulated naval shipbuilding.

On the domestic front, as the culmination of Taisho Democracy, the year 1924 saw the passage in the Diet of the Universal Manhood Suffrage Law, which granted suffrage to all males over the age of twenty-five. Although universal suffrage was not achieved, the law more than quadrupled the electorate, from roughly three million to thirteen million.[129] In commerce and culture, the late Taisho and early Showa years witnessed an improved relationship with the United States. The United States remained Japan's most important trading partner, accounting for

---

128. Kuno and Tsurumi, *Gendai Nihon*, 133, 160.

129. The tax qualifications for voting rights at the outset of parliamentary government meant an electorate of about half a million males. Tax qualifications for the vote had been lowered in 1900 (from fifteen yen to ten) and again in 1919 (to three yen), but rural landowners were disproportionately advantaged relative to unpropertied urban workers. Jansen, *Modern Japan*, 508.

32 percent of its exports and 30 percent of its imports during 1925–34. A number of American companies came to Japan to form joint ventures with Japanese counterparts, including Westinghouse (1924); Carrier (1930); and Associated Oil (1931). Some companies, such as Ford (1925), General Motors (1927), and Victor (1927), built production facilities in Japan.[130] Along with American companies came American-style scientific management practices from the 1920s to the 1930s.[131] Things American, including Tarzan and King Kong movies, started to flood the Japanese market. As baseball became a popular pastime for Japanese, Major League all-star teams that included Lou Gehrig (in 1931) and Babe Ruth (in 1934) came to play against Japanese All Stars.[132]

The military did not welcome these developments wholeheartedly, especially as adverse economic developments in the late 1920s led to a series of cuts in the military budget. The American historian Walter Lafeber, commenting on the lasting legacy of the 1924 Exclusion Act, argued that "American racism [had] led Japan back to the Asian mainland."[133] In part to assert its autonomy and to protect what it perceived to be Japan's national interests from Russian intrusion,[134] a faction within the military began to take unilateral actions on the Asian mainland. In September 1931, the Imperial Army's elite Kwantung Army stationed in Asia staged a bombing of a railway line owned by the Japanese-controlled South Manchurian Railway in order to create a pretext for invading northeast China, known as Manchuria. Then, on 1 March 1932, Japan established the independent state of Manchukuo as a puppet government, and installed Puyi (Xuantong), the last Qing emperor, as the head of state; Japan gave diplomatic recognition to Manchukuo on 15 September 1932.

Japan's adventures on the Asian mainland not only set off an escalation of diplomatic conflict with the Western powers but also dragged the country into a military quagmire that would last for fourteen years. To be sure, the Japanese government was divided about the Manchurian Incident, but the military was determined to dictate its terms. On 15 May 1932, Prime Minister Tsuyoshi Inukai was killed by several navy officers, which according to Walter Lafeber "removed the last important semblance of civilian government in Japan until

---

130. For the Japanese economy of the Meiji and Taisho periods, see Nakamura, *Meiji-Taishō-ki no Keizai*.

131. Taichiro Mitani, *Shinban Taishō Demokurashī Ron: Yoshino Sakuzō no Jidai* (Tokyo: Tōkyō Daigaku Shuppankai, 1995), 70.

132. On 6 November 1934, Joseph C. Grew, United States ambassador to Japan, said of Babe Ruth's visit to Japan: "Of course all Japan has gone wild over him. He is a great deal more effective Ambassador than I could ever be." Joseph C. Grew, *Ten Years in Japan* (New York: Simon and Schuster, 1944), 144.

133. Walter Lafeber, *The Clash: U.S.–Japanese Relations throughout History* (New York: W. W. Norton & Company, 1997), 146.

134. The Japanese presence in Manchuria had been won from Russia in the Treaty of Portsmouth of 1905.

after World War II." On 24 February 1933, following the release of a report by a commission led by A. G. R. Lytton that refused to recognize Manchukuo and its Japanese-imposed head, Japan walked out of the League of Nations (the withdrawal became formally effective in March 1935).

Military authority grew steadily over terrorized civilian politicians and the Foreign Ministry.[135] On 26 February 1936, a group of civilian extremists conspired with young army officers to stage a rebellion ostensibly to restore the emperor's full powers under the rubric of "Showa Restoration."[136] Although the attempt failed to achieve its objectives,[137] the incident had the effect of increasing the influence of the military on the civilian government by introducing a stipulation that only active-duty (as opposed to retired or reserve) officers be allowed to serve as the ministers of the army and the navy, thus giving the military power to cause the government to stand or fall at will.

In November 1936, Japan signed the Anti-Comintern Pact with Nazi Germany,[138] agreeing to assist each other in defending against the spread of communism. This dealt a blow to the Foreign Ministry's hope of maintaining working relationships with the Americans and the British.[139] At the end of that year, Japan let the Washington and London naval treaties expire. In July 1937, Japanese and Chinese forces clashed at the Marco Polo Bridge south of Peking. Japan soon captured a significant portion of China, including the city of Nanking, but the Chinese put up fierce resistance and refused to discuss peace terms; for Japan, to conquer the whole territory of China in any case would have been far beyond the resources at its disposal.

In September 1940 Japan signed a tripartite pact with Nazi Germany and Fascist Italy, which obliged the signatory nations to assist each other if any member was attacked by the Soviet Union or the United States. At this development, United States ambassador Joseph C. Grew, who had believed up to this point that war was avoidable, remarked: "I saw the constructive work of eight years swept away as if by a typhoon, earthquake, and tidal wave combined."[140] From 1940, the United States tried to restrain Japanese expansion through economic sanctions, as Japanese troops advanced into Southeast Asia. In the summer of 1941, the Americans put an embargo on oil and gasoline shipments to Japan and froze Japanese assets. With last-ditch diplomatic efforts failing, on 8 December 1941, Japan attacked the United States naval base at Pearl Harbor in Hawaii.

---

135. Lafeber, *Clash*, 172–73, 180–81.

136. Jansen, *Modern Japan*, 597–99.

137. Thirteen officers and four civilians were sentenced to death.

138. The Comintern refers to the (Third) Communist International founded in 1919 by Vladimir Lenin.

139. Lafeber, *Clash*, 182.

140. As quoted in Lafeber, *Clash*, 194. Grew closed the diary for September by saying: "My heart is heavy. . . . This is not the Japan which I have known in times past." Grew, *Ten Years in Japan*, 339.

Shunsuke Tsurumi, using the framework proposed by the political scientist Masao Maruyama, described the national political system of prewar Japan as consisting of three types of participants: (1) the emperor (authority), (2) the officials (power), and (3) disaffected segments of society, especially in the military, which he called the outlaws (violence). He then argued that, as the Meiji order began to fail, and Japan was thrust into economic and political turmoil following the world panic of 1929 and Japan's invasion of China in 1931, the "growing discontent of the people was expressed by the outlaws, who forced the officials to follow a literal interpretation" of the national myth. The exoteric national cult "overwhelmed" the esoteric cult, and "the Meiji architects collapsed."[141] War became inevitable when the balance between the two permanently broke down in favor of the former.[142]

This occurred sometime after 1931 when Japan's fifteen-year war with China began and patriotic fervor was aroused. State suppression of the freedom of expression intensified (see Section 7.5.2 immediately below), so the literal interpretation of the political ideology of the Meiji state became prevalent even among the national bureaucracy. In 1935, Tatsukichi Minobe, the Tokyo Imperial University professor who had advanced the organ theory of the emperor's role, became the target of a national campaign to discredit him. He was summoned by the public prosecutor (who was his former student) and was asked whether a Japanese subject, under existing law, might criticize an imperial rescript. The day after the trial Minobe's three books on the constitution were banned. Minobe did not retract his theory but resigned from his seat in the House of Peers later in the year.[143]

7.5.2. The Freedoms of Thought, Expression, and Religion under Totalitarianism

The culmination of Taisho Democracy in 1924 came with a price: the Peace Preservation Law of 1925.[144] Initially, the law was aimed at suppressing the activities of anarchism, communism, socialism, and other ideologies incompatible with private ownership and other elements of the national structure. In the 1920s, Marxist analysis became popular in the study of political economy and social problems among Japanese scholars. The authorities thus launched a campaign to eradicate the influence of Marxist thought. In April 1928, about 1,500

---

141. Tsurumi, *Wartime Japan*, 27–30.

142. That the esoteric cult continued to prevail among the elites is illustrated by the following remarks made by Joseph Grew in 1942 upon his return to the United States: "I have lived for ten years in Japan. I have had many friends in Japan, some of whom I admired, respected, and loved. They are not the people who brought on this war. . . . Even during our imprisonment in Tokyo many of those friends used to contrive to send us . . . in spite of the usual obstruction of the police . . . a piece of meat, which was the most precious gift they could confer. . . . They were personally loyal to me to the end." Grew, *Ten Years in Japan*, 535.

143. Ibid., 28–30.

144. Ikimatsu, *Taishōki no Shisō*, 34–35.

members of the Communist Party and their sympathizers were arrested by police and imprisoned. From 1932, left-leaning writers became the target of suppression, and about 400 of them were arrested. More prominent among them was Takiji Kobayashi, a writer of Marxist "proletarian" literature, who was tortured to death at the age of twenty-nine. Many of those imprisoned, under torture or other forms of coercion, recanted their beliefs, a process known as *tenkō* (lit. conversion).[145] In 1933 and 1934, about 90 percent of those who were arrested for harboring anti-state ideologies allegedly experienced a process of *tenkō*.[146]

Tenkō, of course, evinced a spectrum of sincerity. At the most superficial level, those arrested for anti-state ideologies might have signed a statement renouncing their belief just to get out of jail while maintaining their inner convictions; at the other extreme, some may well have seen their patriotic fervor and devotion to the emperor kindled as they were forced to read nationalistic literature while in prison. As *tenkō* became routine from 1933, the authorities recognized the possibility that the previously open ideological conflict had simply become internalized—the possibility that many in society were quietly harboring anti-state ideologies. Thus, from 1935, the authorities launched concerted efforts to place those who had confessed *tenkō* under constant surveillance, including by visiting them in their homes and organizing mutual-support groups. From 1937, as the war with China escalated, it was no longer sufficient to renounce one's belief in anti-state ideologies. *Tenkō* persons were required to actively participate in supporting the war. Many of them voluntarily moved to the Asian continent, in part to get away from constant police surveillance.[147]

The scope of the Peace Preservation Law expanded to religious activities, including those of Buddhist and Shinto sects. Among the Christian denominations, the activities of the Watchtower Bible and Tract Society (*Tōdaisha*), with its pacifist and millennialist beliefs, met with state suppression, even before the revision of the law. In May and June 1933, Watchtower members were arrested in Japan, Korea, and Taiwan, allegedly for defaming the throne; their publications were banned and any remaining copies were destroyed (the raid was inspired by a similar action taken in April by Nazi Germany). This was the first instance of state suppression of a religious group under the Peace Preservation Law. In 1939,

---

145. Tsurumi defined *tenkō* as "a conversion which occurs under the pressure of state power." The thought police had a manual on how to bring about *tenkō*. It was not by imprisonment and torture alone. The policeman would bring the young prisoner, buy him a bowl of chicken and eggs on rice (called "parent-child" bowl), and say nothing about ideology but only "your mother is worried about you." He should not mention the father, as this might encourage the prisoner's defiance of authority. Tsurumi, *Wartime Japan*, 12–13.

146. As a result, communism was virtually eradicated in Japan. Kazutoshi Hamasaki, "Nihon ni okeru Senjika no Bungakushatachi," *Nagasaki Daigaku Kyōyōbu Kiyō* 38 (September 1997), 67–68, 70–71; Akita Ito, *Tenkō to Tennōsei* (Tokyo: Keisō Shobō, 1995), 1, 53, 133–34.

147. Ibid., 245–301.

three members refused to serve in the military, and were sentenced in mid-June to two to three-year prison terms. Immediately, in the early morning of 21 June, the police raided the society's headquarters, arrested twenty-six men and women, and confiscated publications and other properties. This was followed by similar actions in other cities in Japan, Korea, Manchuria, and Taiwan. More than 130 people were arrested; many of them were sentenced to prison terms of two to ten years. Through torture and other means, all but a handful died or were forced to renounce their faith while in prison.[148]

In addition, two churches with British ties were subjected to state harassment. First, in the case of *Nihon Seikō Kai* (the Church of England/Anglican–Episcopal Church), the trigger was the public statement made in 1937 by the archbishop of Canterbury denouncing Japanese military adventures in China. When this became known, Anglicans in Japan were subjected to surveillance by the special higher police (*tokubetsu kōtō keisatsu*, known as *tokkō*) and also became a target of suspicion from the public.[149] Second, in July 1940, the leaders of the Salvation Army were arrested on charges of espionage, and required to sever their ties with their headquarters. Under government instruction, the organization was required to change its name from *Kyūsei Gun* (*gun* means army) to *Kyūsei Dan* (*dan* means group).[150]

In order to control religious activities, in March 1939, the government enacted the Religious Organization Law (*Shūkyō Dantai Hō*), which would take effect in April 1940. The law required a religious group to apply for government approval as a religious organization (*shūkyō dantai*), which would accord it legal protection from confiscation of property, tax exemption, and the freedom to set its own qualifications for priesthood. If a group did not qualify as a religious organization, it was to be known as a religious association (*shūkyō kessha*) and to come under the authority of local officials. Despite the role it would later play in the suppression of the free exercise of religious beliefs, Christians in general welcomed the Religious Organization Law, as it explicitly recognized Christianity, along with Buddhism and Sect Shinto, as one of Japan's three main religions.

A few months before the law took effect, in January 1940, the Ministry of Education issued a set of ministerial regulations governing the implementation of the Religious Organization Law, which included the stipulation that a religious

---

148. After the war, a few of them were about to restore their activities when Akashi learned that the Watchtower in the United States had flown the American national flag and adulated the state at religious meetings during the war while those in Japan were being imprisoned, tortured, and killed for refusing to do the same. When he criticized the American church leadership, he was discharged from the ministry and removed from the official history of the Watchtower. Inagaki, *Heieki*, 48–52, 102, 116–22; Tsurumi, *Wartime Japan*, 47–50.

149. Mitsuru Oe, "Seikōkai," *Senjika no Kirisutokyō: Shūkyō Dantai Hō wo megutte*, ed. Kirisutokyō Shi Gakkai (Tokyo: Kyōbunkan, 2015), 120.

150. Nobuo Kaino, "Nihon Kirisuto Kyōdan," *Senjika no Kirisutokyō*, 34–35.

body must have at least fifty congregations and 5,000 members to qualify as a religious organization. To apply for state recognition, a religious body must file detailed articles of incorporation with the ministry, including an outline of beliefs, which the government must approve. Any change required government approval, and the ministry could dissolve a religious organization if it was deemed injurious to public order and morals. At this time, the ministry instructed Christian groups that no more funds could be received from abroad after April 1941.[151]

While seven denominations belonging to the National Christian Council qualified as religious organizations, the Japanese government exerted pressure on all denominations to consolidate into two groups, a united Protestant group, to be known as the United Church of Christ in Japan (*Nihon Kirisuto Kyōdan*) and a group to be formed from the Roman Catholic Church but without ties to the papacy, to be known as *Nihon Tenshu Kōkyō Kyōdan*. For the Protestants, this meant giving up religious beliefs and practices unique to each denomination, which many considered anathema. In any case, for all religious groups, the statement of beliefs needed to be approved by the government, which meant that it needed to conform to the prescriptions of State Shinto.[152] The government officials, in approving the articles of faith for the United Church, urged the leaders to remove belief in the resurrection of Christ as a childish and outlandish superstition while asking them to place Christ below the emperor.[153] During the war-time years, Christian worship services included certain patriotic rites, such as a reverential bow in the direction of the imperial palace, not unlike the singing of the American national anthem in contemporary Mormon services.

To facilitate the consolidation of otherwise reluctant denominations, Protestant leaders came up with the idea of a "bloc system (*busei*)," in which similar denominations formed separate blocs within the church (a large denomination constituted its own bloc). More than thirty denominations were thus grouped into eleven blocs (e.g., Methodists were Bloc Two, Congregationalists Bloc Three, and Baptists Bloc Four). Thus, the United Church of Christ in Japan was established at a convention of thirty-four Protestant denominations held on 24–25 June 1941. The conception of the United Church as a federation of denominations that allowed some autonomy in creed and mode of worship was soon shattered, however, as the government pressured the Protestants to abolish the bloc system.[154]

---

151. Parker, *Baptist Mission*, 161.

152. The Catholic Church was required to replace foreign priests with local priests and to revise their theology to remove the doctrine of the resurrection and to make it consistent with the imperial philosophy. Miyoshi, "Katorikku Kyōkai (Nihon Tenshu Kōkyō Kyōdan)," *Senjika no Kirisutokyō*, 63–67.

153. This was more than they could take. They succeeded in postponing a decision by the officials indefinitely. Kaino, "Nihon Kirisuto Kyōdan," 40–42.

154. Kaino, "Nihon Kirisuto Kyōdan," 35.

The transition for the Catholics was easier, and not just because they could maintain their identity largely intact. For one thing, the Catholic Church had already permitted its members to engage in Shinto worship as an expression of patriotism. In May 1936, the papacy issued a guideline stating that State Shinto ceremonies only had a civic function, so Catholics were free to participate. In February 1937, Dennis Joseph Dougherty, archbishop of Philadelphia, paid homage to the Meiji and Yasukuni Shrines during his visit to Japan.[155] For another, while the Japanese Catholic organization formally severed its ties with the papacy in order to be recognized as *Nihon Tenshu Kōkyō Kyōdan* in May 1941, Japan soon established a diplomatic relationship with the Holy See in June 1942, allowing the Japanese church to maintain secret communications with the papacy through the Holy See's diplomatic mission in Tokyo. The Vatican was a supporter of Japan's military adventures on the Asian mainland, having given diplomatic recognition to Manchukuo in 1934. Likely, it considered Japan to be an effective force against the spread of communism and the advancement of the Soviet Union in Asia, which it believed was the greater of two evils.[156]

For the other denominations, the difficulty of complying with the new restrictions is illustrated by the experience of *Seikō Kai*. As the Church of England was neither Catholic nor Protestant, the leadership became divided about joining the United Church of Christ in August 1940 when they were pressured by the Ministry of Education to do so. Eventually, in November 1942, the church was split into two groups. One participated in the United Church in November 1943 following the dissolution of the church and allocation of assets, while the other remained as an unrecognized religious association. The group that joined the United Church included eighty-nine congregations, about a third of the total.[157] The authorities dealt harshly with those who refused to participate in the United Church, acting on insider tips from the break-away group. Two leaders were interrogated by the military police in late 1944 and imprisoned in 1945. The Seventh-day Adventists also became the target of state suppression for refusing to participate in the United Church. In 1943, forty-two ministers and chief lay leaders were arrested and jailed; six of them were still in prison when the war ended.[158]

In addition, the authorities attempted to suppress denominations with beliefs in the second coming of Jesus Christ even when they joined the United Church. Those suppressed included the Holiness churches and the Plymouth Brethren. In June 1942, for example, more than 100 ministers of Holiness churches were arrested on charges of violating the Peace Preservation Law. The Holiness movement, which had originated within the Methodist Church in the late nineteenth century, came to Japan in 1901. In 1936, the movement split

---

155. Miyoshi, "Katorikku Kyōkai," 79–82.
156. Ibid., 74–75, 77–78.
157. Oe, "Seikōkai," 136–40.
158. Parker, *Baptist Mission*, 170.

into two groups, *Kiyome Kyōkai* and *Nihon Sei Kyōkai*. In 1940, the former group joined the United Church of Christ as part of Bloc Nine, while the latter joined as part of Bloc Six. At this time, *Kiyome Kyōkai* lost a group, known as *Tōyō Senkyōkai Kiyome Kyōkai*, which refused to join the United Church. These three groups, called the three Holiness churches, were all targeted for state suppression. Of the fourteen ministers who served prison terms, seven died either in prison or shortly after their release. In April 1943, the government withdrew recognition of the Holiness churches and banned them even from forming an association.[159]

The Plymouth Brethren, also a millennialist church, had come to Japan in 1881 but had only two to three hundred members in a little over a dozen cities in 1941. Like the LDS Church, their religious practice is distinguished from other Christian denominations by their reliance on lay clergy to carry out the work of ministry. On 26 September 1941, the police arrested eight leading figures in Kobe, Osaka, and Tokyo on charges of violating the Peace Preservation Law (which was revised in March 1941 to include stipulations on the denial of the national structure and the defamation of Shinto shrines and the imperial family, ostensibly targeted at Christian bodies); this was followed by the arrest of six persons, including four arrested on the previous occasion, on 26 March 1942. It is possible that these actions—the first state suppression of religious activity under the revised Peace Preservation Law—were inspired by a similar action taken against the Plymouth Brethren by Nazi Germany. Four men were sentenced to prison terms of three to four years, while the rest were given suspended prison sentences of varying lengths.[160]

In the meantime, the state suppression of the Holiness churches shook up the Protestant leaders. Up to this time, official control of Christianity had been largely exercised by the Ministry of Education or the military police. Now the Home Ministry's special higher police were suppressing churches on charges of violating the Peace Preservation Law, which was revised in 1941 to allow a broad and discretionary interpretation of what would be considered subversive. "Denial" (as of perpetual imperial rule) was not a physical action, but an activity of the mind. The suppression of millennialistic denominations meant that the government was intent on controlling the thoughts of individuals. This event, taking place in June 1942, led the Protestant leaders to overcome their initial resistance to abolishing the bloc system. At the first convention of the United Church of Christ held in November 1942, the bloc system was formally abolished.[161]

---

159. Sanae Kaminaka, "Hōrinesu," in *Senjika no Kirisutokyō*, 147–48, 166–71.
160. Kasahara, "Kojin Kirisutosha," 77–93.
161. Kaino, "Nihon Kirisuto Kyōdan," 36–37.

7.6. The Withdrawal Decision in Light of Subsequent History

To place the withdrawal decision in historical perspective, a counterfactual question might be posed: what would have happened if the Mormon missionaries had not been pulled out of Japan in 1924? A related question is: when would it have ultimately become necessary to pull them out? To be sure, events could have turned either way from 1924 onward, and war may not have been inevitable. For the sake of argument, however, let us take the view that the Pacific War was destined to commence in 1941, with all the attendant events and developments leading to it.

7.6.1. What Would Have Happened to Mormon Missionaries?

In the light of what we know about subsequent Japanese history, what might have happened to the Mormon missionaries if they had remained in Japan? It would be instructive to consider the experience of Southern Baptist missionary Max Garrott, who was one of just over 100 Protestant missionaries and several hundred Catholic missionaries still remaining in Japan when the Japanese naval forces attacked Pearl Harbor in December 1941. Garrott remained in Japan even after his wife and daughter had sailed home in March, feeling "more strongly than in 1934 that He wants me here." By government decree missionaries were prohibited from teaching the Bible in the schools, preaching in the churches, and doing organized evangelistic work. Their Japanese coworkers were routinely interrogated by police after seeing the missionaries.[162]

On 9 December 1941, the day after Pearl Harbor, Garrot was interned "for his own protection" at a Catholic school and orphanage in Tokyo, some 700 miles away from his home in Fukuoka. He thus became one of the 342 enemy aliens (almost all draft-age men) who were incarcerated in thirty-four detention centers across the country. At this stage, the detainees were well-treated (unless they were suspected of espionage), with opportunities to see their families, recreational activities, and access to kitchen facilities to supplement their meals.[163] In the case of Garrot, kind officials transported his piano from his home in Fukuoka for his use, along with a picture of his wife. After some six months, during which he gained back the 10 pounds he had lost after his wife's departure, in June 1942, Garrott was put aboard an exchange ship for repatriation. Between Japan and the United States, two exchanges of prisoners took place. The first ship, SS *Asama*

---

162. Parker, *Baptist Mission*, 163–65.
163. Mayumi Komiya, "Taiheiyō Sensōka no Tekikokujin Yokuryū: Nihon Kokunai ni Zaijūshita Eibeikei Gaikokujin no Yokuryū nit suite," *Ochanomizu Shigaku* 43 (1999): 4–5, 11–12. At the time of Pearl Harbor, there were an estimated 2,100 enemy aliens living in Japan. Of this total, 342 were incarcerated at detention centers, 105 were in prison for espionage charges, and 258 were diplomats who were kept in their own diplomatic compounds. Of the thirty-seven incarcerated in Tokyo, sixteen were missionaries.

Maru carrying American prisoners in Japan, including members of the American diplomatic mission, left Yokohama on 17 June 1942, while the second ship, SS *Teia Maru*, left on 14 September 1943.[164]

The *Asama Maru* took Garrot to the Portuguese port of Louvenco Marques in Mozambique, East Africa, where the exchange of prisoners took place. Switching to the SS *Gripsholm*, he reached the port of New York on 25 August 1942.[165] Upon returning home, in the summer of 1943, Garrott spoke at a Baptist student conference on the responsibility of American Christians to love the Japanese people: "Jesus told us to love our enemy. And who is our enemy? Japan! Therefore we must love the Japanese." A young Baptist, by the name of Luther Copeland, was in the audience and took this admonition as a call from God to serve as a missionary to Japan to "express to the Japanese that great, indiscriminate love of God by which he embraces all persons as his dear children."[166] True to his conviction, Copeland served an honorable mission to Japan following the end of World War II.

While the Mormon missionaries would have been unharmed, and the worst possible thing would likely have been to be placed on an exchange ship in 1942, the typical approach employed by the Mormon missionaries—personal contacting—would have been ill-suited to produce any results in the increasingly totalitarian environment of the late 1930s. After the outbreak of the China War in 1937, foreign missionaries were increasingly placed under police surveillance and received notices from their embassies and consulates, warning them to leave Japan at once.[167] Some foreign missionaries from other denominations had better reasons to stay in Japan, including their teaching obligations in their schools. Critically, they were missionaries by vocation.[168] In contrast, Mormon missionaries were for the most part young men who came for a fixed length of time and in part as representatives of their families and congregations at home. Their parents and church leaders, feeling responsible for their physical safety, would have wanted their early return. In all likelihood, the Mormon missionaries would have come home in 1937 or 1938.

In any case, the LDS Church would not have survived the Religious Organization Law of 1939 and its implementation during 1940–41. Given its

---

164. Seventy-six enemy aliens left on the first ship, while an additional seventy-three left on the second ship. In addition, a prisoner exchange with Britain took place in July 1942, when sixty enemy aliens were allowed to leave. Komiya, "Tekikokujin Yokuryū," 16, 24.

165. Parker, *Baptist Mission*, 166–67.

166. Luther E. Copeland, *World Mission World Survival: The Challenge and Urgency of Global Missions Today* (Nashville, Tennessee: Broadman Press, 1985), 13.

167. Parker, *Baptist Mission*, 158–60.

168. Except for those who were elderly or sick, no Catholic missionary left Japan. As additional enemy aliens, including women, were incarcerated as the war progressed, Catholic workers constituted more than a quarter of those who remained in detention centers at the close of the war. Komiya, "Tekikokujin Yokuryū," 36.

distinct beliefs, the church could not have joined, or been allowed to join, the United Church of Christ as a Protestant denomination. Because it did not meet the qualifications to be a religious organization on its own (i.e., fifty congregations and 5,000 members), the church would have had to be registered as a religious association and, as such, been subjected to the same kind of harassment as the Seventh-day Adventists, the Watchtower Society, and most of the Anglican–Episcopalians. Its beliefs in the second coming of Jesus Christ, his millennial reign, and the universal resurrection of mankind, let alone modern revelation and the divine origin of the Book of Mormon, would have been scrutinized. Likely, Mormons would have received the same treatment as the Holiness churches or the Plymouth Brethren.

What about the local members who remained? Official records of the special police (*tokkō*) do not contain any reference to religious activity until 1936; no individual names appear in the records before 1937.[169] State suppression and harassment of Christian activity intensified only in July 1937, when the Ministry of Education requested all religious organizations to cooperate with the war efforts following the escalation of the military conflict with China. Even so, in 1939, Hilton Robertson of the Honolulu-based Japanese Mission could freely visit the Japanese members without harassment (see Section 8.5.6 in Chapter 8). Robertson's return to Osaka was openly featured in a positive light by the *Osaka Mainichi* on 27 April. In any case, the LDS Church had no presence in Japan to arouse any suspicion. These counterfactual considerations lead us to a startling conclusion: the ultimate beneficiaries of the church's decision to leave Japan early were the few members who remained faithful. The decision allowed them to maintain their belief without state harassment.

7.6.2. Disentangling Myth from Reality

If the poor harvest was the principal reason for closing the mission, who or what was primarily responsible? The First Presidency clearly took the position that the Japanese were to blame: "[with] over twenty years of hard labor . . . the Lord would justify us if we saw fit to close that mission."[170] This statement justifies as "hard labor" sending into a country half the population of the entire United States no more than twenty missionaries at any time during the mission's tenure, most of whom never attained more than limited language ability. Hilton Robertson, on the other hand, thought differently: "Some of the finest people I have ever met . . . are Japanese. They are not entirely to blame for the failure of the mission as I am sure we have not handled the situation exactly as it should have been due to the many handicaps of the elders."[171]

---

169. Kasahara, "Kojin Kirisutosha," 42.

170. First Presidency of the Church of Jesus Christ of Latter-day Saints, letter to Hilton A. Robertson, 22 February 1924, LDS Church Archives.

171. Robertson, Autobiography, 114.

Too much has been made of such temporary factors as the Great Kanto Earthquake and the passage of the Johnson–Reed Act, especially the supposed rise in nationalism and anti-American sentiment. In 1948, for example, on the occasion of Edward Clissold's call to Japan as mission president, an editorial in the Mormon periodical *Improvement Era* attributed the withdrawal of missionaries in 1924 to "intense nationalism, fanned by ambitious militarists, [which] discouraged every foreign contact and stifled every breath of personal freedom and privilege." It then asserted that "the Church [had] left as the course of events seemed to confirm the Japanese in their belief that the emperor was divine and the Japanese were destined to rule the world."[172] The events described above may accurately describe what happened during the late 1930s, but certainly not before 1924. Also, the issue of closing the mission was already being considered long before the earthquake or the Johnson–Reed Act. History has been rewritten in popular Mormon discourse in order to justify the closing of the mission.[173]

Why did such a myth emerge in the first place? There are two reasons. First, those who witnessed the closing of the mission naturally associated it with what they were observing on the ground at the time. We cannot hold them accountable for their failure to distinguish temporary from structural contributors. Second, most who wrote about the closing of the mission were seeing the event from the vantage point of the postwar era. To them, World War II and the events in Japan that had led up to it were a fait accompli. Combined, these two elements created the narrative that the war of 1941–45 was directly related to what the missionaries saw and experienced during 1923–24. Mormon belief in prophetic power added another dimension to this narrative: President Heber J. Grant, foreseeing the war, withdrew the missionaries—some seventeen years early. Robertson remarked at the April 1947 general conference: "I feel that the Lord knew what was going to transpire and he called the missionaries home and ordered the mission closed temporarily."[174]

Why has the myth persisted for so long? When a half-true story is repeated over and over again, it begins to command respectability. As noted by Reid Neilson and others, there is a definitive culprit: an entry written by prewar Japan missionary Ernest B. Woodward for the official record of the postwar Japanese

---

172. Editorial, *Improvement Era* 51 (1948): 206.

173. This statement applies to popular discourse, not to scholarly writings. Most scholars have recognized that a confluence of factors contributed to the closing of the mission. Neilson, *Mormon Missionary Activities*, 122, 133–39, in particular, emphasized the critical role played by the "poor evangelistic results" while downplaying the impact of international relations or the 1923 earthquake. On the other hand, Nichols, "Japan Mission," 92–96, emphasized the role played by the deterioration in "Oriental–American" relations, relying on the account by Ernest Woodward (see below).

174. He then continued: "Later on we find that the other denominations throughout the world who were proselyting in Japan were forced to close their missions and return to America at great loss and sacrifice." As quoted in Britsch, "Closing," 189.

Mission.¹⁷⁵ The entry is dated 26 July 1949 and describes Woodward's experience following the passage of the "Immigration Restriction Law." Woodward, then a middle-aged man, recalled:

> The talk of "War" with the United States was heard on every hand. . . . As time went on the bitterness became more intense and the attendance at meetings smaller. In our tracting we met with opposition and insult on every hand. We all became discouraged and it reflected in our work.

He then concluded by recalling the greeting the returning missionaries received from Heber J. Grant upon arrival in Salt Lake City: "Thank God you are home because I know what is in store for the people of that land."¹⁷⁶ This memory of a missionary, written a quarter century later, has served as a definitive narrative of why the mission was closed. A review of subsequent Japanese history, however, suggests that the timing of the closure was premature by a dozen or so years, if the decision was based solely on domestic factors.

7.7. Conclusion

The Taisho period (1912–26) saw the liberalizing forces of industrialization and modernization unleashed to counter the suffocating grip of State Shinto. Nationalistic undercurrents remained alive in the public consciousness, but there was a tendency toward intellectual tolerance and pluralism. The LDS Church was a beneficiary of this new climate of intellectual openness and religious tolerance. The productivity of Mormon missionary work was significantly higher during the Taisho period and, from 1915 through 1922, surpassed the productivity observed in the early twenty-first century. The church could have capitalized on this with a more proactive engagement—for example, by addressing the exaggerated dichotomy between Christian belief and patriotism, as the Protestants had done through their successful rebranding efforts, or by increasing the size of the missionary workforce considerably. The Mormons had no strategy, however. Instead, their leaders, fixated on the total number of converts (with little consideration of what inputs were being used to produce that number), concluded that the work was unsuccessful. The result was the closure of the mission during a period of comparative success when confronted with a setback in Tokyo.

Much has been made of the Great Kanto Earthquake and the rising tide of anti-American sentiment in Mormon historical narratives to explain the closing of the mission. But these were temporary factors. Some narratives have even gone so far as to rewrite history by ascribing the withdrawal decision to the church leaders' prophetic insight concerning what would befall the Japan–United States relationship seventeen years later. In reality, the key factor was the lack of convert

---

175. Neilson, *Mormon Missionary Activities*, 142; also Nichols, "Japan Mission," 95–96.
176. Ernest B. Woodward, "Facts Concerning the Japan Mission from 1 January 1924 to the close of the Mission in August 1924," LDS Church Archives, 26 July 1949.

baptisms, and the decision was driven by fundamental considerations. Temporary factors were important only insofar as they determined—possibly hastened—the decision's timing. The personal disposition of a mission president was an important cause of the setback in Tokyo. When the membership and the missionary force were small, individuals mattered greatly. Young as they were, some mission leaders and missionaries did not possess the quality of character or leadership required to make the work successful.

If Japanese history was destined to take the course it took, the Japan Mission would have had to close sooner or later. The duality of prewar Japan meant that there were always two opposing intellectual forces operating in the minds of the public, whose counterpart in the political realm was the precarious balance of power between civilian and military leaders. While liberalism (with emphasis on civil liberties) was in ascendancy during the Taisho period, the 1930s saw a revival of nationalism with totalitarian tendencies. The uneasy balance between the two persisted for some time, but any room for religious tolerance and freedom was virtually gone by 1939.

The contrasting approaches the LDS Church took toward Japan and Germany was noted, but the parallels between the two countries are just as noteworthy. As in Japan, Germany too saw a rise of nationalism with totalitarian tendencies in the 1930s. The National Socialist (Nazi) Party, after coming to power in January 1933, sought to control religious activity, including by banning many Christian denominations. Although the Mormons managed to maintain church activity and tried to promote a cordial relationship with the Nazi authorities, for example, by appealing to the Twelfth Article of Faith,[177] they nonetheless received harassment and physical violence at the local level. Religious harassment and persecution, however, was more vicious and became intense earlier in Germany than in Japan. Whereas Nazi Germany tightened a grip on Catholic and Protestant churches quickly after assuming power, formal control of religious activity in Japan did not take place until the end of the 1930s. Even so, Mormon membership increased by 8 percent from 1930 to 1938 in Germany.[178] It is thus possible that, even in Japan, a Mormon mission would have produced the number of converts commensurate with the number of missionaries through the early years of the 1930s (especially as the Japan–United States relationship flourished in cultural and economic affairs). The Japan Mission could have hung on for another ten to fifteen years, albeit under an insidiously encroaching shadow of hostility.

---

177. The Twelfth Article of Faith states: "We believe in being subject to kings, presidents, rulers, and magistrates, in obeying, honoring, and sustaining the law."

178. Steve Carter, "The Rise of the Nazi Dictatorship and Its Relationship with the Mormon Church in Germany, 1933–1939," *International Journal of Mormon Studies* 3 (2010): 56–89. Scharffs, *Mormonism in Germany*, Table 1, gives an increase in membership of 16 percent from 11,596 in 1930 to 13,480 in 1940.

Chapter 8

Mormonism's Transpacific Interlude: Retreat and Regrouping, 1924–44

8.1. Introduction

This chapter discusses the major events and developments from 1924 through 1944, regarding the work of the Church of Jesus Christ of Latter-day Saints among the people of Japanese ethnicity in Japan, the continental United States, and the Hawaiian Islands. The LDS Japan Mission that had operated in Japan for twenty-three years closed in 1924, leaving several dozen Japanese Mormons outside the formal church structure.[1] This chapter, after summarizing how sixty or so Japanese Mormons initially maintained contact with each other, reviews the attempts by the Utah church authorities to restore formal church activity, albeit on a limited scale. The chapter then shifts attention to the other side of the Pacific, where in the 1920s and 1930s an increasing number of Japanese were becoming converted to Mormonism, as if the work that had been suspended in Japan continued on in another location. Regarding the mainland United States and Hawaii, the chapter first discusses the origin and pattern of Japanese immigration before describing how the LDS Church approached the people of Japanese ancestry.

The church took contrasting approaches in the continental United States and the Hawaiian Islands. In Hawaii, it recognized the Japanese population as a distinct entity and, in the 1930s, established a separate Sunday school program and then a separate mission. On the mainland, the church never made a special attempt to target the Japanese population. In both locations, however, the outcome was similar. It was largely the American-born, second generation Japanese (Nisei) that Mormonism attracted. Whether systematically or spontaneously, the Nisei converts in the interior West and Hawaii served as a bridge between the prewar Japan Mission and the postwar Japanese Mission as many of them would carry the Mormon message to their homeland in subsequent years. Japan came under the jurisdiction of the Honolulu-based Japanese Mission when it was established in 1937. The inaugural mission president made a tour of Japan to visit

---

1. Nominally, there were at most 146 Mormons in Japan at the mission's closing. During the mission's existence, at least thirteen members died, eleven members were excommunicated, and four emigrated to the United States. Undoubtedly many more were unaccounted for, including those who left Japan for its overseas territories or other parts of Asia. For some of these vital statistics, see Annex 8 towards the end of the volume.

the members in 1939, which would be the church's last official contact with the members in the prewar period.

8.2. Resuscitating the Dimming Light

8.2.1. Fujiya Nara and the Shuro, 1925–29

When the last of the American missionaries left Japan in August 1924, Mormonism's priesthood authority became dormant even though some Japanese men held offices in the priesthood. In the terminology of Mormon theology, the priesthood remained but the keys to exercise that priesthood were removed. According to Hilton A. Robertson, the last mission president, "the native priesthood leaders were explicitly prohibited from functioning in that priesthood" and "specifically not allowed to hold meetings of any type."[2] In January 1925, Tokyo member Reiko Mochizuki wrote: "Having lost the church, we have not been able to meet together. When this happened, we began to feel the sense of emptiness that our organization does not exist, at such times as when we see a group of Salvation Army people preaching on the street."[3] There emerged a desire to maintain fellowship among the few members who continued to identify themselves as Mormons. It was Fujiya Nara who took the first step, when in 1925 he began to publish a newsletter entitled *Shuro* (the Palm) for distribution to between sixty-five and seventy-five members whose addresses were known.[4] In 1958, Nara called this decision his "*dokudan* (personal and unauthorized judgment)."[5]

Nara was uniquely qualified for this task. He was an elder in the priesthood and, because of his work with the National Railway, familiar with the members throughout the country (see Annex 4 for Nara's brief biography). The *Shuro* was handwritten, with each issue consisting of personal essays, thoughts on religious themes, poems, and news concerning members. In 1958, Nara recalled having published the periodical for "about four years."[6] It was issued ten times in 1925 and four times in 1926. After 1926, only the winter 1928 issue has survived, but there is a mention of the fall 1929 issue. Presumably publication ceased around that time.[7] Nara later explained this by saying: "*tsuini chikara tsukite* (my strength

---

2. Hilton A. Robertson, as quoted in J. Christopher Conkling, "Members Without a Church: Japanese Mormons in Japan From 1924 to 1948," *Brigham Young University Studies* 16 (1975): 192.
3. *Shuro* 1 (January 1925): 6. Author's translation of the Japanese original.
4. Seiji Katanuma, "The Church in Japan," *Brigham Young University Studies* 14 (1973): 21. The number of subscriptions was estimated to be sixty-five at the inception. *Hattatsu* 1 (1935): 16.
5. Fujiya Nara, "Nihon Dendōbu no Kaiko," *Seito no Michi* 2 (June 1958): 24.
6. Ibid.
7. The Brigham Young University library has thirteen issues between January 1925 and Winter 1928. Conkling, "Members Without a Church," 191n.

was finally exhausted)," which was understandable given that the periodical was entirely dependent upon him with contributions from a few members and friends. In Tokyo, Nara was holding meetings on most Sundays, with such members as Kentaro Mochizuki, Koshi Nakagawa, Genkichi Shiraishi, and Tomigoro Takagi.[8]

Evidently, the state of the few members in Japan was on the minds of former missionaries who returned home. A letter written by Alma O. Taylor to Hilton A. Robertson in 1936 intimates that, on 15 July 1925, Taylor, Robertson, and "some of the other ex-presidents" wrote a letter to the First Presidency recommending that certain actions be taken.[9] We do not know the content of that correspondence, but this, along with the knowledge that Japanese members were communicating with each other, may have been a factor in the decision to authorize Taylor to contact Nara on behalf of Utah headquarters, inquiring about the general conditions of the church and the whereabouts of the members. The May 1926 issue of the *Shuro* printed an excerpt from this letter, stating that an identical copy had been received by members in Osaka and Sapporo.[10] Nara replied to Taylor on 10 June 1926, giving answers to the questions Taylor had posed, including (1) what members were doing in Kofu, Osaka, Sapporo, and Tokyo; (2) if they had organized themselves in any way; and (3) what they would like to do.[11] Nara also provided Taylor with the names of fifty-eight members, including six whose whereabouts he did not know.[12]

8.2.2. Franklin S. Harris and the Mutual Improvement Association, 1926–27

The church's first official action in Japan after August 1924 was to appoint Franklin Stewart Harris (1884–1960), then president of Brigham Young University, as a representative of the church. Harris, an agronomist with a PhD from Cornell University, was about to depart for Japan to participate in the Third Pan-Pacific Science Congress to be held at the Imperial Diet building in Tokyo, from 1 to 11 November 1926; there were excursions and additional meetings planned before and after the formal meetings, so the congress covered more than a month altogether.[13] On 23 August 1926, Harris met with the First Presidency,

---

8. Nara, "Nihon Dendōbu no Kaiko," 24.
9. Alma O. Taylor, letter to Hilton A. Robertson, 27 February 1936. LDS Church Archives.
10. *Shuro* 2 (May 1926): 14–16.
11. According to *Hattatsu* 1 (1935): 16, Taylor contacted three members in February 1926: Katsura in Osaka, Kumagai in Sapporo, and Nara in Tokyo.
12. Fujiya Nara, letter to Alma O. Taylor, 10 June 1926. "Alma O. Taylor Papers, 1904–1935," LDS Church Archives.
13. The congress was held every three years, with the first one in Hawaii and the second in Australia. Harris's invitation to the third congress came because of his expertise in the agriculture of arid land. There were thirty-five scientists from the United States. On 2 November, he was elected chairman of the agricultural section and presented a paper entitled "Soil and Alkali as a Scientific Problem in Pacific Region." Franklin S. Harris,

was instructed to "visit the members of the Church in Japan," and was provided with "copies of correspondence with the members there." They then set him apart for this assignment, with Anthony W. Ivins conducting the ceremony. Leaving Provo on 24 August, he first travelled to Hawaii where on 10 September he "spent most of the forenoon with E. L. Christensen discussing Japan." He arrived in Yokohama on 20 September and checked in at the Imperial Hotel in Tokyo.[14]

Immediately, on 21 September, Harris went to see Fujiya Nara at his office at the "Traffic Bureau, Department of Railways." Later, Nara and three other church members came to see him at the hotel. On 23 September, accompanied by Nara, Harris took an overnight train for Osaka. Upon arriving the next morning, the two located Tsuruichi Katsura, who was at his "factory." After Nara left for Tokyo, in the evening, "a member of the Church" came to see Harris at the hotel and they "had a meeting in which [he] organized an MIA."[15] He left Osaka on 25 September, and made a tour of Korea and China until 12 October. He returned to Japan and, from 18 October, he made a tour of northern Japan with other participants of the Pan-Pacific Congress. When he arrived in Sapporo in the evening of 19 October, "members of the LDS Church were also at the station to meet [him]." On 20 October, "in the evening [he] met with the members of the LDS Church (at 9 p.m.) and organized them into a Mutual Improvement Association for all of Hokkaido. . . . [Their] meeting lasted till twelve." On 23 October, after a tour of Hokkaido, he arrived at Sapporo "about 9:30 p.m. A number of members of the Church were there to greet [him]. Some of them went on the train with [him] till after midnight in order to visit."

He arrived back in Tokyo on 25 October. On Saturday, 30 October, he "called on Brother Nara and arranged about a meeting for Sunday." On Sunday, 31 October, in the afternoon and evening, he "met with Members of the Church in Tokyo and vicinity and organized them as a Mutual Improvement Association. . . . After the meeting in the evening some of the men took [him] for a Japanese supper at a Japanese restaurant. Then they came with [him] to the hotel." After the conclusion of the Pan-Pacific Congress on 11 November, he travelled through Kyoto to depart from Japan and completed the rest of his trip around the world. On 13 November, as his ship was about to sail away from the port of Kobe, a "number of members of the Church from Osaka were at the boat to see [him] off." After making a tour of Asia and Europe, he returned to Salt Lake City on 20 August 1927.[16]

"An International Science Congress: How the World Can Be Made a Paradise for Its Inhabitants," *Improvement Era* 30 (1927): 348–51.

14. Franklin Stewart Harris, "Journal, 1908–1954," LDS Church Archives.

15. The Mutual Improvement Association (MIA) was a Mormon "auxiliary" program that provided young men and women with wholesome recreational, educational, and other cultural activities designed to build faith.

16. Harris, Journal.

On 1 November 1926, Harris, summarizing what he had accomplished up to that point, prepared a letter to Alma O. Taylor, written on an Imperial Hotel letter head:

> I have now completed the work of organizing the Japanese Saints into three Mutual Improvement Associations which the First Presidency authorized me to organize. I am sending them a complete list of the officers and addresses with some suggestions. . . . I am advising you of these facts since you will probably be asked to assist in some of the work. The members here have showed me the letters which you have written them; these they prize very highly. We have a number of very fine groups here, and they are well worth our giving them considerable attention. The officers of the Tokyo association have been given general supervision of the work throughout Japan. Brother Fujiya Nara is the president. He is a wonderfully fine and faithful man of about 30 who is respected by all of the members in Japan. I have developed a real affection for him, as I have for the Japanese Saints generally. . . . I hope that you will be able to devote a little time to the people here. They appreciate it so much.[17]

As foretold by Harris, in early 1927, Taylor was asked by the First Presidency to "co-operate with the General Officers of the Mutual Improvement Associations of the Church" in assisting Nara in Japan. In a letter addressed to Nara, Taylor counseled him to "[a]void vain and personal ambition," "[be] in every way worthy of the respect and confidence given you by the members and by us," and "[be] cheerful and happy so that the saints too will laugh and be glad," explaining that "[true] religion does not make men and women long-faced, solemn and pious." Taylor requested that Nara write to him preferably in English, but if not, then in Japanese character, but never in Romanized Japanese.[18] The *Shuro* became the official periodical of the Japan Mutual Improvement Association.

8.2.3. The Ministry of Fujiya Nara, 1927–33

Based on the achievements of the Japan Mutual Improvement Association, the church authorized ecclesiastical work to resume on a limited scale. On 2 December 1927, Fujiya Nara was appointed as presiding elder for Japan.[19] On 31 March 1928, Taylor informed the First Presidency: "I have received acknowledgement from Elder Fujiya Nara of Tokyo, Japan, accepting his call to be the presiding elder in Japan. He accepts with a humble spirit."[20] On 2 April, the First Presidency responded: "We are pleased to note from your letter . . . that Elder Fujiya Nara has accepted in the proper spirit his call to be the presiding elder in

---

17. Franklin Stewart Harris, letter to Alma O. Taylor, 1 November 1926. "Alma Owen Taylor Papers, 1904–1936," LDS Church Archives.

18. Alma O. Taylor, letter to Fujiya Nara, 25 January 1927. "Alma Owen Taylor Papers, 1904–1936," LDS Church Archives.

19. *Hattatsu* 1(1935).

20. Alma O. Taylor, letter to the First Presidency, 31 March 1928, LDS Church Archives.

Japan; also that the translation of the Presidency's letter of appointment, as published in the "Palm," indicates that the letter has been correctly understood."[21]

Though we do not know the exact content of Nara's appointment letter, it appears that it authorized Nara to "organize branches wherever there were enough members to justify" and allowed "the priesthood . . . to function as far as an Elder could do so."[22] In the terminology of Mormon theology, this means that some of the keys of the priesthood were evidently restored in Japan (though Nara was not formally set apart). In the event, whatever was expected of him was not delivered. Informing the First Presidency in 1935, Taylor noted that under Nara, sacrament meetings had not been started, the performing of other priesthood functions had not been "inaugurated nor authorized by him, contrary to the specific authorization given him," and "no constructive work was done" since his appointment.[23] Taylor criticized Nara scathingly in a letter addressed to Hilton Robertson on 27 February 1936:

> [Right] after this extension of power and assignment of responsibility [as presiding elder], Elder Nara ceased to be as ardent as before, and, finally, he moved to Manchuria and everything flattened out so far as church activity is concerned. . . . It has never been quite clear what happened to him, making him drop his responsibility so suddenly. But that is quite common with Japanese.[24]

In Nara's defense, it must be stated that he had never been a church leader. In fact, no native Japanese had held a leadership position in the Japan Mission (except in auxiliary organizations or at most to conduct meetings). He was therefore unfamiliar with the procedure and protocol of church administration, so it is not clear how much of the instructions he had been given he clearly understood, especially when they were provided in English and only by letter. That "the translation of the Presidency's letter of appointment" was accurate is no guarantee that "the letter has been correctly understood." The thought of taking charge of church affairs in all of Japan may have overwhelmed him; he may have felt unequal to the task. Contrary to Taylor's sharp criticism, it is this author's experience that "[d]ropping [one's] responsibility so suddenly" is not common with Japanese. But it is certainly common for Japanese to say "yes" when what is really meant is "no." Nara was not the kind of spiritual leader Taylor had expected him to be but was a leader nonetheless. In addition to the substantial efforts he made to publish the *Shuro*, keep track of members scattered across Japan, and hold meetings for the members after the mission was closed, Nara also organized a campaign to raise funds from church members and, in February 1930, presented

---

21. First Presidency, letter to Alma O. Taylor, 2 April 1928, LDS Church Archives.
22. Alma O. Taylor, letter to the First Presidency, 14 March 1936. "Alma Owen Taylor Papers, 1904–1936," LDS Church Archives.
23. Alma O. Taylor, letter to the First Presidency, 3 April 1935. "Alma Owen Taylor Papers, 1904–1936," LDS Church Archives.
24. Alma O. Taylor, letter to Hilton A. Robertson, 27 February 1936. LDS Church Archives.

gifts to Heber J. Grant and Alma O. Taylor in anticipation of the centennial of the founding of the LDS Church on 6 April.[25] Such commitment and effort belies Taylor's description.

In December 1933, Nara was assigned by the National Railway to work in Fengtian (present-day Shenyang), Manchuria.[26] In March 1932, Japan had established a puppet government in northeast China, which it called Manchukuo, following the invasion and occupation of Manchuria by the Imperial Army in 1931.[27] The railroads in most of Manchuria were nationalized in March 1933, except for the train lines already operated by the Japanese-controlled South Manchurian Railway Company. A large number of Japanese relocated to Manchuria in the 1930s, by assignment from their employers or in pursuit of new opportunities.[28] The timing of Nara's job relocation coincided with the nationalization and then development of the railroads in Manchukuo. Taylor, thousands of miles away and no doubt unfamiliar with the facts, suggested that Nara left Japan for Manchuria voluntarily, having abandoned his church assignment: "Nothing came of this assignment. Elder Nara dried up and blew away to Manchuria before any priesthood activity got going."[29]

8.3. The Ministry of Takeo Fujiwara, 1934–36

8.3.1. Fujiwara's Call as Presiding Elder

Less than a year after Nara left for Manchuria, Takeo Fujiwara of Sapporo returned home on 27 September 1934, after studying at Brigham Young University (BYU). Before he left Utah, he had been called by the First Presidency of the LDS Church to serve as presiding elder and a special missionary for Japan; he served in this capacity for about a year until illness struck him in August 1935. Fujiwara, bap-

---

25. Photocopy of the prospectus for centennial donation, signed by ten church members, including (in order of appearance): Genkichi Shiraishi, Torao Yamaide, Kentaro Mochizuki, Magoji Kitagawa, Koshi Nakagawa, Shimako Ishida, Fujiya Nara (all of Tokyo), Tsuruichi Katsura (Osaka), Suketomo Nonogaki (Kofu), and Tamano Kumagai (Sapporo), February 1930, in author's possession.
26. Nara, "Nihon Dendōbu no Kaiko," 14.
27. In 1933, the League of Nations declared that Manchuria remained part of China, causing Japan to withdraw from membership.
28. Of these, nearly 220,000 were railroad workers. In addition, as many as 270,000 people were recruited by the government to colonize the land mainly as agricultural workers between 1932 and 1945. During the first year after the end of the war in August 1945, an estimated 80,000 people perished for various reasons; another 10,000 were trapped and unable to return to Japan. Chihō Jinji Chōsa Kai, *Kokutetsu Shi* (Takamatsu: Chihō Jinji Chōsa Kai, 1998), 160; Shinzo Araragi, *Manshū Imin no Rekishi Shakaigaku* (Kyoto: Kōrosha, 1994).
29. Taylor, letter to the First Presidency, 14 March 1936.

tized on 10 May 1924, was one of the last Mormon converts of the Japan Mission era (see Annex 4 towards the end of the volume for a brief biography). Having gone to Utah to study at BYU at the invitation of Franklin D. Harris, he completed his undergraduate and graduate studies in June 1933 and June 1934, respectively.[30]

His Utah experience strengthened his faith in Mormonism. He stated towards the end of his seven-year stay: "The reason I came here is that I might learn the Gospel, and after I finish school . . . I shall go back to Japan and explain that Gospel to my people."[31] He was the first Japanese Mormon to receive sacred rites at the Salt Lake Temple. Following the completion of his studies, on 7 July 1934, Fujiwara was set apart by church president Heber J. Grant to be a missionary to and presiding elder over the church in Japan, with Alma O. Taylor and Hilton A. Robertson assisting.[32] He left promptly and visited, under assignment, the Hawaiian Mission, where all of the church literature in the Japanese language was stored. He stayed in Hawaii from 27 July to 18 September 1934.[33]

On 14 August 1934, Fujiwara wrote to Taylor from Honolulu:

> As I have reported last week on the Church literary books and have inquired the matters which were not clear to me, I have investigated and tracked all the Church literary books in Japanese here in the Hawaiian Mission home. . . . There are about 2000 copies of the Book of Mormon which are in good shape.[34]

With permission, he destroyed some that were damaged beyond any possible use. On the advice of Hawaiian mission president Castle H. Murphy, Fujiwara took a quantity of the literature with him to Japan and stored it in the home of Yoshijiro Watanabe following his arrival in late September. Taylor instructed Fujiwara upon arrival in Japan:

> The official name of the Church in Japan is Japan Mission. . . . [T]he Japan Mission has not been reopened for aggressive proselyting and missionary work among non-members. Your assignment is to the present members of the Church. Naturally the activities of the members will be attractive to their friends, and in that way you and they can spread the Gospel to others. Later there will no doubt be definite steps renewed towards aggressive proselyting.[35]

Fujiwara was paid a monthly allowance of $35 by the church.

---

30. Gene Priday, University Registrar, Brigham Young University, letter to author, 31 October 1995. His master's thesis, entitled "The Political and Military Policies of the Tokugawa Shogunate," was presented on 10 May 1934, his twenty-eighth birthday.

31. Takeo Fujiwara, "Relationship between Shinto and Mormonism," *Improvement Era* 36 (1933): 654–55, 675–76.

32. Taylor, letter to the First Presidency, 3 April 1935. According to the May 1925 issue of the *Hattatsu*, Fujiwara was set apart on 6 July 1934.

33. "Historical Records for the Hawaiian Mission," University Archives, Brigham Young University–Hawaii (hereafter cited as BYU–Hawaii Archives).

34. Takeo Fujiwara, letter to Alma O. Taylor, 14 August 1934, LDS Church Archives.

35. Alma O. Taylor, letter to the First Presidency, 14 April 1935, LDS Church Archives.

8.3.2. Ecclesiastical Work of Takeo Fujiwara

Fujiwara's labors in Japan were frustrating, to say the least. He did not get hold of the membership records until February of the following year.[36] During the long absence of official church contact, practicing members, few to begin with, had weakened in faith and diminished in number. It is also possible that some at least looked with suspicion at Fujiwara, who had just returned from abroad and was as young as he was in a gerontocratic society. His frustration was compounded by his difficulty in finding gainful employment as a school teacher.[37] But when in February 1935 he found a teaching position at Sapporo's First Secondary School, considered to be the best school of secondary education in Hokkaido, he declined the offer, thinking that distance from Tokyo would prevent him from serving effectively as presiding elder for all of Japan.[38] For this decision, he was criticized by his parents, brothers, and the school's principal, and also indirectly by Taylor.[39]

Takeo Fujiwara with Alma O. Taylor, circa 1934. Courtesy Yoshiaki Fujiwara.

From the beginning, Yoshijiro Watanabe and his daughter Tazuko were Fujiwara's most steadfast supporters (see Annex 4 towards the end of the volume for Watanabe's brief biography). One or both of them frequently accompanied Fujiwara when he went out of Tokyo on church business. Yoshijiro, an elder, was called as president of the Tokyo Branch, and Tazuko was appointed as secretary to the Japan Mission. Upon visiting Osaka and Kofu, Fujiwara learned that

---

36. His official report for the period 1 January–30 April 1935 states that, on 29 January, he sent a telegraph to Nara in Manchuria, asking him to send the church records; and, on 10 February, he visited the wife of Fujiya Nara to obtain the records. This was in response to a reply from Nara, dated 30 January, suggesting that Fujiwara obtain the records from his wife who remained in Tokyo. *Hattatsu* 1 (1935): 14.

37. In June 1934, he had been given a teaching credential by the Ministry of Education to teach English in secondary and normal schools.

38. Takeo Fujiwara, "The Official Report from the Japan Mission of the Church of Jesus Christ of Latter-Day Saints, 1 January–30 April 1935," 25 February 1935, LDS Church Archives.

39. Takeo Fujiwara, letter to Tamano Kumagai, 30 March 1935. Photocopy in author's possession. Finding that Fujiwara had declined a teaching job, Taylor replied: "your church appointment does not require you to devote all your time to its duties, and you are free to get yourself established in the line of work you wish to follow, even if such opportunity should come to you from some locality other than Tokyo or where a group of saints are located." Alma O. Taylor, letter to Takeo Fujiwara, 10 September 1935.

no permission had been given to Osaka members to hold meetings, other than MIA meetings, and that Kofu members knew nothing about the visit of Franklin Harris and the organization of the MIA in Japan.[40] In Tokyo, when a welcome party for Fujiwara was held on 2 December 1934, only two friends (Mr. Ono and Mr. Nagata) came out of the thirty-three invitees. On 16 December, however, Reiko Mochizuki and her two children came to church; Reiko was appointed clerk of the Tokyo Branch.[41] When Fujiwara visited Fude Tai, a sister of Tsune Nachie, he found her to have been "faithful to God, Christ and the Church" and "study[ing] often the Book of Mormon with her son and his wife."[42]

Outside Tokyo, Fujiwara organized branches in Kofu (Muraji Yoneyama, a priest, as president), Osaka (Tsuruichi Katsura, an elder, as president), and Sapporo (Takeo Yoshino, a priest, as president). By early August 1935, Fujiwara had been successful in locating about sixty church members, though he had not seen them all, including Morisaburo Sato and Ei Nagao (nee Nachie) who were on the Asian continent.[43] Taylor estimates that Fujiwara contacted about thirty of them personally, of whom about twenty "manifested some interest in the effort to revive the LDS Church in Japan," but only seventeen "ever appeared at the meetings called by the Mission or Branch Presidents."[44] In addition, on 19 May 1935, Fujiwara baptized two of Reiko Mochizuki's children, Terutake Ishikawa and Kyoko Mochizuki, bringing the total number of prewar baptisms to 176.[45]

On 10 May 1935, Fujiwara published the first (and what would become the only) issue of a periodical entitled *Hattatsu* (Progress), with the editorial help of Reiko Mochizuki. The publication was thirty-five pages long, consisting of the Articles of Faith, a greeting from Fujiwara, translations of the official documents indicating the appointment of Elder Fujiwara and the release of Elder Nara, translations of the instructions from Taylor to Nara and Fujiwara, letters from Nara, Heber J. Grant, and Franklin Harris, a statement of gratitude to Nara, a summary of church developments in Japan from the closing of the mission through the end of 1934, letters from former mission presidents Hilton Robertson, Joseph H. Stimpson, and Elbert D. Thomas to Fujiwara, and English letters written by Fujiwara and Tomigoro Takagi for consumption by former Japan missionaries in the United States. The cost of publication was about ¥50 (or $17), entirely paid out of his monthly allowance.[46] The second issue of the *Hattatsu*, planned for

---

40. Takeo Fujiwara, "The Official Records of the Church in Japan, 7 July–31 December 1934," LDS Church Archives.
41. Fujiwara, "The Official Records, 7 July–31 December 1934."
42. Fujiwara, "Official Report," 9 February 1935.
43. Takeo Fujiwara, "The Official Report from the Japan Mission of the Church of Jesus Christ of Latter-Day Saints," 5 August 1935, LDS Church Archives.
44. Alma O. Taylor, letter to the First Presidency, 14 March 1936. "Alma Owen Taylor Papers, 1904–1936," LDS Church Archives.
45. Fujiwara, "Official Report," 6 August 1935, p. 14.
46. Taylor, letter to the First Presidency, 14 March 1936.

September, was never issued on account of Fujiwara's illness (see Section 8.3.3 immediately below).

Alma O. Taylor in Utah acted as the intermediary between Fujiwara and the First Presidency, whose approval was required for priesthood ordinations. In April 1935, Taylor conveyed to the First Presidency Fujiwara's request for a church building or meeting hall, and asked if the church in Utah might support such a facility, noting "the $1,000 building Fund already held in trust by the Church in Utah for the Japanese saints in Utah, as per letter of the First Presidency to Elder Nara dated Dec 2, 1927." Taylor further conveyed Fujiwara's request for permission to ordain Susumu Hisada of Osaka to the priesthood and to the office of priest, along with his endorsement; and to advance Morizo Yoneyama of Kofu to the office of priest, with a recommendation that action be delayed until Taylor makes "inquiry into the potentially undesirable situation in Kofu."[47] Immediately, Taylor conveyed to Fujiwara the decision of the meeting he held with the First Presidency on 2 April 1935,[48] in which all three members were present:

> To them I presented an outline of your letters and reports and your requests—particularly the matter of providing funds for you to have a meeting church or hall and to maintain the same. They promised to give this matter and some of the other matters due consideration. . . . I am glad you now have the records from Bro. Nara. . . . Your appointment of Branch Presidents and Clerks is approved.[49]

The "potentially undesirable situation in Kofu" alluded to must be related to the apparent religious apathy of a member of the Yoneyama family, which Fujiwara described:

> Bro. [Muraji] Yoneyama did not say that he lost his faith to [sic] Jesus Christ and the Church, but he said that he stood against the attitude of the Church in the withdrawing of the Japan Mission so suddenly without much knowledge of the Saints, especially withdrawal of the conference in Kofu. He thinks the Church Mission left Kofu without caring any Saint there, without any instruction or any guidance. He believed that he did his atmost best and whole hearted devotion for the sake of the church in Kofu with all his family. . . . But when the foundation of the Kofu Conference was about founded, the Mission activities were ceased suddenly without telling any reason of closing of their activities. . . . His whole-hearted devotion to the Church was nothing. And he could not bear when he learned that the Church or the Mission had never looked after the Saints in Kofu. Bro. Yoneyama blames the

---

47. Taylor, letter to the First Presidency, 3 April 1935.
48. Approval for the priesthood ordinations was never formally given. Taylor explained to Fujiwara: "The First Presidency have [sic] no doubt forgotten the matter of your request for authorization to ordain Hisada to the office of priest and Yoneyama to the office of priest. They are very busy men. So, I will take the responsibility of authorizing you to make those two ordainments [sic] according to your own judgment with the advice of your associates and the consent of the members of the branch." Alma O. Taylor, letter to Takeo Fujiwara, 10 September 1935. LDS Church Archives.
49. Alma O. Taylor, letter addressed to Takeo Fujiwara, 14 April 1935. LDS Church Archives.

Church for this insincerity, negligence and impatience in doing the Mission activities among the Japanese people.[50]

In short, Yoneyama, despite his devotion to the church,[51] felt betrayed by the church twice, by the sudden closing of the Kofu Branch in January 1922 and of the Japan Mission itself more than two years later. On 5 August 1935, Fujiwara further explained the situation to Taylor.

> [Yoneyama] is rather frank, honest and faithful. That's perhaps a reason why he blamed the sudden action of the Church in the withdrawing of the missionary activities from Japan, especially from Kofu before the closing of the Mission. Since then the Saints in Kofu were left alone without any instructions and some of them said they did not know why it was withdrawn and when the Japan Mission was closed. . . . If we investigate the Saints in Japan, we will find no Saints who can be said to be really faithful and real members of the true Church of Christ.[52]

These and other correspondences reveal both Fujiwara's lack of experience as a church leader and Taylor's unreasonably high expectations for Japanese members who had been cut off from the church for over ten years, with some of them feeling that they had been betrayed by their church.

8.3.3. Fujiwara's Untimely Death and Its Aftermath

Fujiwara's ministry did not last very long. In August 1935, Fujiwara felt so ill that he decided to leave Tokyo for his native village of Garugawa, near Sapporo, in order to rest. In September 1935, Yoshijiro Watanabe, acting presiding elder, Tazuko Watanabe, secretary of the Japan Mission, and Reiko Mochizuki, editor of the *Hattatsu*, wrote a notice to the members, stating that Fujiwara was taken ill and ordered by a physician to rest for a month. This notice was accompanied by a statement, dated 4 September, by Fujiwara that, while he was recovering from illness, he had appointed Watanabe, "chief elder" of the Tokyo Branch, as acting presiding elder.[53] In a letter dated 5 September 1935, Fujiwara asked Taylor to "excuse [him] from official duty and responsibility of Presiding Elder during [his] illness" and informed him of the appointment of "Brother Watanabe (an elder), president of the Tokyo Branch, as Acting Presiding elder who should take care of only office work there."[54]

As Taylor explained to the First Presidency in March 1936, Fujiwara had lived while in Utah for seven years "so nearly on nothing" that his immune sys-

---

50. Fujiwara, "Official Report," 28 April 1935.
51. Yoneyama was the only prewar member whose children were baptized at the age of eight.
52. Takeo Fujiwara, letter to Alma O. Taylor, 5 August 1935. LDS Church Archives.
53. Photocopy of the notice written by Yoshijiro Watanabe, Tazuko Watanabe, and Reiko Mochizuki, September 1935, in author's possession.
54. Takeo Fujiwara, letter to Alma O. Taylor, 5 September 1935. "Japan Mission Miscellaneous documents," LDS Church Archives.

tem was weakened considerably by the time he returned home.⁵⁵ He easily succumbed to tuberculosis, which spread quickly through his circulatory system. Becoming worse, he was hospitalized in Sapporo's Mizushima Hospital in mid-September, never to recover. Takeo passed away at nine o'clock on 27 January 1936. His funeral was held and interment took place at his birthplace on 30 January. The letter Taylor received from Fujiwara's father, postmarked 5 February 1936, noted that "the inability to be working for the Mission was troubling him." His son's dying message was one of apology for having to "quit" without having done anything worthwhile for the church. He had wanted Taylor and the church authorities to be informed of his death immediately. "He hoped the Church in Japan would be continued and the members held together."⁵⁶

The question then was what to do next. Taylor received a letter (in Japanese) from Watanabe and another one (in English) from Tamano Kumagai and others representing the Sapporo members. Watanabe's letter stated that he had consulted with the few members attending the funeral and then went to Osaka to consult with the few members there. Watanabe desired instructions from the church headquarters, concluding with a plea not to "abandon the work in Japan."⁵⁷ The letter from the Sapporo members, likewise asking for instructions, read in part:

> After [Fujiwara's] death what step we shall take, it is a question and I and other saints in Sapporo are asking you to consult with the authorities of the Church and report us, according to his last words. Shall we have another leader to take the place of him or shall we be left without any leader? According to Brother Fujiwara's word, Bro Watanabe is the fittest man and we also all believe so.⁵⁸

Taylor conveyed his low opinion of Watanabe to the First Presidency, and no action was taken.⁵⁹

8.4. Mormonism and the Japanese Population of the American West

8.4.1. Japanese Immigration to the Continental United States

The first Japanese to travel abroad were students, not laborers. Even before the fall of the Tokugawa shogunate in 1868, wealthy domains unfriendly to

---

55. His poverty was not only due to his own lack of funds but undoubtedly also to the fact that his time in Utah coincided with the depression years when many in Utah struggled financially.
56. Alma O. Taylor, letter to the First Presidency, 14 March 1936; Tamano Kumagai, letter to Alma O. Taylor, not dated, LDS Church Archives. Author's interviews with Yuko and Yoshiaki Fujiwara, Sapporo, 3 March 1998 and with Ryoko Murakami, Sapporo, 2 March 1998.
57. Taylor, letter to the First Presidency, 14 March 1936.
58. Tamano Kumagai, Takeo Yoshino, and Kenji Ono, letter to Alma O. Taylor on behalf of Sapporo members, not dated (circa February 1936), LDS Church Archives.
59. Taylor, letter to the First Presidency, 14 March 1936.

the shogun, such as Satsuma and Choshu, had clandestinely sent their students abroad; likewise, some private citizens discreetly left Japan. In 1866, the shogunate felt the need to issue a proclamation requiring those wishing to go abroad for education or business to apply for passports. Subsequent years saw only a moderate rise in the number of Japanese traveling abroad to study. The historian Minoru Ishizuki estimates that 152 Japanese travelled abroad to study before the fall of the Tokugawa regime, with about 32 percent of them going to Britain and about 22 percent to the United States.[60]

The Meiji government, after assuming power in 1868, initially ordered all Japanese students abroad to return home but, recognizing the need for foreign-trained personnel, established in February 1971 a set of selection or approval criteria for those wishing to study abroad.[61] During the first seven years of Meiji, an estimated 550 students went abroad; of this total, 209 went to the United States and 168 to Britain; most likely, these numbers are a gross underestimation of the actual numbers.[62] From around 1880, an increasing number of government-sponsored students began to study in Germany,[63] reflecting the government policy of adopting German institutions, in education, military, and politics, as the model most suitable to Japan.[64] Even so, the United States remained the most popular destination for private students.

The Chinese Exclusion Act of 1882, by halting Chinese labor immigration to the United States,[65] created demand for Japanese laborers in agriculture, in the mines, and on the railroads. Seeing a profitable opportunity, enterprising businessmen employed student-laborers as labor contractors and immigrant leaders.[66] This was the real beginning of Japanese immigration to the United States. The United States Census of 1890 reported only 2,039 Japanese residents, of whom 1,147 were in California and many were student-laborers. The Japanese population expanded from 1891 to 1907, with many of the new arrivals recruited through the labor contracting system: from 1891 to 1900, 27,440 Japanese were admitted to the United States; and from 1901 to 1907, an additional 42,457

---

60. Minoru Ishizuki, *Kindai Nihon no Kaigai Ryūgaku Shi* (Kyoto: Mineruva Shobō, 1972), 28–59, 72–74, 103.

61. Minoru Watanabe, *Kindai Nihon Kaigai Ryūgakusei Shi*, vol. 1 (Tokyo: Kōdansha, 1977), 218–20.

62. Ishizuki, *Kaigai Ryūgaku Shi*, 153–56.

63. For the Meiji period as a whole, about 80 percent of the 683 students sent abroad by the Ministry of Education went to Germany. Watanabe, *Kaigai Ryūgakusei Shi*, 34–36.

64. Ishizuki, *Kaigai Ryūgaku Shi*, 245–46.

65. The Chinese Exclusion Act suspended the entry of Chinese workers for ten years. This was renewed indefinitely in 1902. Stephan Thernstrom, ed., *Harvard Encyclopedia of American Ethnic Groups* (Cambridge, Massachusetts: Harvard University Press, 1980), 490, 492.

66. Yuji Ichioka, *The Issei: The World of the First Generation Japanese Immigrants, 1885–1924* (New York, The Free Press, 1988), 28; William K. Hosokawa, *Nisei: The Quiet Americans* (New York, William Morrow and Company, 1969), 41.

persons were admitted. In 1900, the annexation of Hawaii opened the way for Japanese immigrants in the territory to move to the mainland. From 1901 to 1907, more than 38,000 Japanese laborers entered the mainland from Hawaii.[67]

Early immigrants settled predominantly in California and gradually moved north on the West Coast.[68] Most of them were single men who wanted to make "a quick buck" before returning home; many of the few women were prostitutes. It was only as the population became settled that the proportion of women started to rise. In 1900, there were only 410 married women in the total Japanese population of 24,326. The number increased to 5,581 in 1910 (for the population of 72,157) and further to 22,193 in 1920 (for 111,010).[69]

In 1908, with anti-Japanese sentiment rising, especially on the West Coast, Japanese immigration to the mainland United States virtually ceased. First, the migration of Japanese from Hawaii to the mainland was terminated by President Theodore Roosevelt's executive order of 14 March 1907, prohibiting any alien from entering the United States via its insular possessions, the Canal Zone, or another foreign country if his or her passport had been issued for another destination.[70] Second, the so-called Gentlemen's Agreement of 1907, which came into force in the summer of 1908, stipulated that the Japanese government would not issue passports to laborers for the continental United States, in exchange for ending the segregation of Japanese pupils in San Francisco's public schools. Around this time, there were about 70,000 Japanese residing in the continental United States.

The federal regulation of immigration tightened progressively for all nationalities, but especially for the Japanese who, under the generally accepted interpretation of naturalization laws, were considered ineligible for citizenship.[71] The Quota Act of 1921 (also called the Johnson Act) limited the annual number of entrants of each admissible nationality to 3 percent of the foreign-born population of that nationality as recorded in the census of 1910. The Immigration Act of 1924 (also called the Johnson–Reed Act) reduced the admissible annual total to 165,000 and the annual quota for each nation was set at 2 percent of the foreign-born population of that nationality recorded by the 1890 census. Furthermore, the act barred from entry all aliens ineligible for citizenship, mean-

---

67. Ichioka, *Issei*, 8, 51, 57.

68. Japanese laborers in significant numbers began to arrive in the state of Washington after the mid-1880s with the discovery of silver mines in Coeur d'Alene in Idaho; the pace picked up in 1887 when passenger sea service was launched between Vancouver and Yokohama. Kojiro Takeuchi, *Beikoku Seihokubu Nihon Imin Shi* (Seattle: Daihoku Nippōsha, 1929), 639.

69. Hosokawa, *Nisei*, 96.

70. Ichioka, *Issei*, 69.

71. The United States Supreme Court definitively ruled in 1922 that naturalization was limited to "free white persons and to aliens of African nativity and to persons of African descent." Hosokawa, *Nisei*, 89–91; and Yukiko Kimura, *Issei: Japanese Immigrants in Hawaii* (Honolulu: University of Hawaii Press, 1988), 40.

ing that the immigration of Japanese to the United States, as negligible as it was since 1908, ceased entirely from this time.[72]

8.4.2. Japanese in the Interior West

General pattern of migration. Japanese immigrants moved from the West Coast to the interior West as economic opportunities opened up in the mines, the railroads, and farming. Labor agents played a major role in this relocation process. For example, a labor agent by the name of Tadashichi Tanaka had a contract to supply Japanese workers to the Oregon Short Line.[73] In 1898, Gen Nishiyama, an independent contractor based in Salt Lake City, began furnishing Japanese laborers to the Union Pacific Coal Company in southern Wyoming; in 1899, Nishiyama sent the first group of Japanese workers to coal mines in Rock Springs, Wyoming.[74] In 1900, the E. D. Hashimoto Company of Salt Lake City secured an independent contract with the Denver and Rio Grande Railroad.[75] The Oriental Trading Co. (Tōyō Bōeki Kaisha) of Seattle supplied 15,000 Japanese laborers between 1898 and 1908.[76] Economic incentives often determined the pattern of migration between sectors. In May 1906, for example, a Japanese contractor recruiting agricultural workers for the sugar beet industry "stole" about 200 laborers from the Northern Pacific Railroad by offering higher wages.[77]

By far the largest contractor was Japanese American Industrial Company (Nichibei Kangyōsha). In 1903, the company contracted with the LDS Church-owned Utah Sugar Company (later renamed Utah–Idaho Sugar Company) to furnish laborers to thin, hoe, and harvest sugar beets in Utah and later in Idaho. In 1904, Gen Nishiyama joined the company to supply section hands to the Southern Pacific line east of Sparks, Nevada and the Union Pacific line west of Green River, Wyoming, as well as the Western Pacific Railroad and the Nevada Northern Railway. Railroad contracting complemented sugar beet contracting as it enabled the company to ship laborers to Utah on the Southern Pacific line at no cost. In 1906, the company had more than 3,000 laborers under contract.

By the end of the first decade of the twentieth century, a significant number of Japanese workers were found throughout the interior West. Data for 1909 show, for example, that some 10,000 Japanese were employed as section hands by railroad

---

72. Thernstrom, *American Ethnic Groups*, 492–93.

73. Hosokawa, *Nisei*, 74.

74. In 1907, almost 400 Japanese were working at these mines. Kenkichi Morino, "Hokubei no Tankō Rōdō," *Amerika* 11 (1907): 8–9.

75. Ichioka, *Issei*, 59–60.

76. Hosokawa, *Nisei*, 74.

77. Yuzo Murayama, "Contractors, Collusion, and Competition: Japanese Immigrant Railroad Laborers in the Pacific Northwest, 1898–1911," *Explorations in Economic History* 21 (1984): 302.

companies in the Western states; some 2,000 men were miners in Colorado, Utah, and Wyoming; more than 38,000 were employed in agriculture as field hands during the height of the harvest season. The Japanese workers progressed from one type of work to another. As they accumulated means or as their contracts expired, many remained in the interior to open barber shops, laundries, and restaurants, to farm, mine coal and copper ores, butcher cattle in slaughterhouses, or find employment in lumber camps and steel mills. Many would eventually marry and start families, while some returned to the West Coast or even back to Japan.[78] As a result, the number of first generation Japanese (Issei) who worked for the railroads declined steadily: 10,000 in 1909, 4,553 in 1913, and 4,300 in 1920.

Japanese in Idaho and Utah. The first generation of Japanese immigrants came to Idaho in the 1880s to work on the railroads and farms. When the Oregon Short Line began construction in 1882, recruiters were sent to California and Hawaii. Within two years 1,000 Japanese men were working on the line and, by 1892, the number increased to about 3,500. Japanese labor camps sprang up along the line through southern Idaho, with shop headquarters in Nampa and Pocatello. Many railroad workers took leaves of absence to work for the Utah–Idaho Sugar Company and other firms in the sugar beet fields. In 1907, all the 4,000 acres of sugar beets in Blackfoot, Idaho Falls, Moore, and Sugar City were worked exclusively by Japanese laborers. By 1910 about 1,000 Japanese in southern Idaho were employed in building railroads, constructing irrigation ditches, thinning and topping sugar beets, working as domestic labor, and in boarding houses, shops, and restaurants.[79]

The migration of Japanese workers to Utah began somewhat later. In 1890, the population of persons of Japanese ancestry in Utah consisted only of four men (see Table 8.1). A number started coming to Utah in 1898 to work on rail section gangs,[80] making Utah's Japanese population eleven females and 406 males in 1900.[81] Some Japanese businesses appeared in Ogden and Salt Lake City around this time. It was this small Japanese community in Salt Lake City that gave a reception for the four departing Mormon missionaries to Japan in the Twenty-First Ward meetinghouse on 19 June 1901.[82]

---

78. Ichioka, *Issei*, 72, 149; Hosokawa, *Nisei*, 68–69; Murayama, "Contractors, Collusion, and Competition," 305.

79. Leonard J. Arrington, *History of Idaho*, vol. 2 (Moscow: University of Idaho Press and Boise: Idaho State Historical Society, 1994), 280–82.

80. From the early 1900s to 1942, all of the railroad stops for the Union Pacific Railroad on its routes from Los Angeles to Salt Lake City were maintained mostly by Japanese. Jeanne Matsumiya Konishi, "The Tintic Mountains," in *Japanese Americans in Utah*, ed. Ted Nagata (Salt Lake City: JA Centennial Committee, 1996), 62–64.

81. Elmer R. Smith, "The 'Japanese' in Utah," *Utah Humanities Review* 2 (1948): 134.

82. Japan Mission, "Historical Records and Minutes," 19 June 1901, LDS Church Archives.

Table 8.1. Characteristics of Japanese Population in Utah, 1890–1940

	Population			Share of Nisei (in percent)			Memorandum: Total in the continental US
	Males	Females	Total	Males	Females	Total	
1890	4	0	4	0	0	0	2,039
1900	406	11	417	0	0	0	24,326
1910	2,021	89	2,110	1.5	0	1.4	72,157
1920	2,174	762	2,936	14.2	35.3	19.7	110,010
1930	2,056	1,213	3,269	39.5	59.9	47.1	138,834
1940	1,263	947	2,210	57.5	69.2	62.5	126,947

Census records, as reported in Smith, "Japanese," 134, 136; Daniels, Taylor, and Kitano, *Japanese Americans*, xv; author's estimates.

It was during the 1900s that Japanese immigrants came in substantial numbers to work at copper mines in Bingham Canyon and sugar beet fields in Box Elder County (where a refinery was opened in Garland in 1903). The Japanese farmers settled primarily in Box Elder, Weber, and Salt Lake Counties. The E.D. Hashimoto Company, a labor agency in Salt Lake City, founded the Clearfield Canning Company to help Japanese farmers raising sugar beets. The 1909 report of the Bureau of Immigration, Labor, and Statistics counted 1,025 Japanese farm workers in Utah. Yet, for the first fifteen years of the 1900s, the section gangs were the main source of employment. The 1910 census listed 2,110 railroad workers, while the 1920 census reported 2,936. During the agricultural depression of the 1920s (see Section 7.4.2 in Chapter 7), the industrious Japanese shifted from the cultivation of sugar beets to growing fruits and vegetables.[83]

In the meantime, some Japanese workers came to Ogden and Salt Lake City to establish restaurants, stores, and other businesses to serve the persons of Japanese ancestry. Small areas in Ogden and Salt Lake City began to be designated as Japanese centers where one could find noodle houses and small stores specializing in Japanese food and laundries.[84] In Ogden, J Town was formed from the early 1900s; it was a rectangle bounded by Keisel Avenue on the east, Wall Avenue on the west, Twenty-Fourth Street on the north, and Twenty-Fifth Street on the south.[85] In Salt Lake, *Nihonjin Machi*, founded in 1907, was bounded by South

---

83. Helen Z. Papanikolas and Alice Kasai, "Japanese Life in Utah" in *The Peoples of Utah*, ed. Helen Z. Papanikolas (Salt Lake City: Utah State Historical Society, 1976), 336–40.
84. Smith, "Japanese," 134.
85. Shinji Ichida, et al., "J-Town Ogden," in Nagata, *Japanese Americans*, 36–39.

Temple, State, Third South and Seventh West Streets.⁸⁶ By 1913, there were more than one hundred residents of Japanese ancestry in Salt Lake. At one time, Salt Lake had two Japanese-language newspapers: the *Rokki Jihō* (established in 1907) and the *Utah Nippō* (established in 1914), with a circulation of about 1,000 each by the 1920s.⁸⁷ In 1927, the daily *Utah Nippō* acquired the thrice-weekly *Rokki Jihō* to become the sole Japanese-language newspaper in the region.⁸⁸

Once established, Japanese immigrant families organized Japanese associations (*Nihonjinkai*) in various parts of Idaho and Utah. From the late 1910s to the mid-1920s, as their Nisei children reached school age, many of these associations started Japanese language schools. The schools were typically held in rented halls where the children came to learn the Japanese language and to socialize with each other on their way home from attending public schools or on weekends. The first Japanese school in Utah was opened in Salt Lake City in 1919 in rented space at the Millcreek Ward meetinghouse of the LDS Church (3900 South and 500 East). A vacant building on the Tadehara farm (just east of the present Murray Parkway Golf Course) became the site of the Japanese school known as Jordan Gakuen.⁸⁹ During the 1930s, the population of Japanese in Utah declined as a consequence of economic recession, which caused those less established to return to the Pacific Coast or even to Japan. In 1940, Idaho had 1,191 Japanese and Utah 2,210.⁹⁰

---

86. Haruko Terasawa Moriyasu, "Salt Lake's Nihonjin Machi," in Nagata, *Japanese Americans*, 29–31.

87. Leonard J. Arrington, "Utah's Ambiguous Reception: The Relocated Japanese Americans," in *Japanese Americans: From Relocation to Redress*, revised edition, ed. R. Daniels, S. C. Taylor, H. H. L. Kitano (University of Washington Press, Seattle and London, 1991), 93.

88. The *Utah Nippō* was first published in November 1914 as a daily Japanese-language newspaper by Uneo Terasawa, who had migrated to Utah in 1909. Following the death of Uneo, his wife Kuniko continued the publication. The *Utah Nippō* was closed immediately following the bombing of Pearl Harbor, but permission to resume publication was granted on 25 February 1942 on the condition that only translations of news appearing in the American English newspapers would be used in the Japanese sections of the paper. Each edition of the newspaper was examined by FBI censors for compliance. The English section, which became a permanent addition starting with the 31 August 1942 edition, contained editorials and a variety of items about community activities and happenings important to Nisei in Utah, Idaho, eastern Nevada, western Wyoming, and the internment camps. At its peak, its circulation reached 10,000 because all Japanese-language newspapers had ceased publication on the West Coast. The *Utah Nippō* ended its seventy-seven-year existence in April 1991. Natsuko Masuta, "Terasawa Kuniko," *Sankei Shinbun*, 28 October 2001, 12; 29 October 2001, 13; 30 October 2001, 14; 31 October 2001, 13; 1 November 2001, 18.

89. Smith, "Japanese," 141–42; Moriyasu, "Salt Lake's Nihonjin Machi," 29–31; Papanikolas and Kasai, "Japanese Life" 350; Shake Ushio, "Early Farming," in Nagata, *Japanese Americans*, 79–81.

90. Smith, "Japanese," 132–35.

Jordan Japanese School, Murray, Utah, where Takeo Fujiwara was a teacher. Courtesy Yoshiaki Fujiwara.

8.4.3. The Modality of Conversion to Mormonism

It can be presumed that few of the early Japanese immigrants to the United States converted to Mormonism. Several reasons can be offered. First, most of them were laborers who developed limited English proficiency. Second, many initially settled on the West Coast, where the concentration of Japanese allowed tight communities to be formed and the immigrants to deal almost exclusively with each other. Third, the Mormons did not actively proselytize among the Japanese population, even within their own communities in Idaho and Utah. For one thing, the Mormon concept of "mission" was some place far away. For another, targeting a particular racial group to proselytize among was alien to the Mormon concept of universal brotherhood. Whatever the reason, the conversion of Issei to Mormonism was a rare and sporadic event. In Utah, it was not until after the end of World War II that, in September 1952, the LDS Church organized the Salt Lake Valley Regional Mission with the explicit purpose of proselytizing among the minority groups, including the Japanese.[91]

This does not mean that no Issei joined the LDS Church.[92] In addition to Tomizo Katsunuma, who was baptized in Logan, Utah, in 1895 while attending the

---

91. The first Japanese Sunday school, presided over by Gerald Okabe, was established by Walter R. Bills, president of the North Valley District of the Regional Mission. Most of the fifteen missionaries assigned to this unit had served on previous missions in Hawaii among the Japanese people or in Japan since the re-opening of the mission in 1948. The first Japanese branch in the mainland, the Daiichi Branch, was organized on 10 April 1962 in the Fourteenth Ward meetinghouse. Tomi Sato, "Dai Ichi Ward," in Nagata, *Japanese Americans*, 95.

92. At least three Issei members came to the United States after having been converted to Mormonism in Japan, a young woman and a married couple in their early thirties.

Agricultural College of Utah (see Section 2.1 in Chapter 2), at least one more Issei was converted to Mormonism. Shuichi Sasaki was born in Fukushima Prefecture in 1883, traveled to Tokyo in 1902 to study literature at Tokyo Senmon Gakkō (present-day Waseda University), and arrived in the United States in 1905. After attending school in Oregon for a year, he came to Idaho where he went to school during the winter and worked on sugar beet farms during the summer. It was during this time in Idaho that, in 1908, he reportedly converted to Mormonism in Rexburg.[93] In 1909, following his father's death, he returned to Japan, married, and returned to Idaho after eighteen months. The couple would eventually have seven children. In 1916, Sasaki moved to Salt Lake City where he struggled to support a large family (at one time, he was working for a tire repair shop). He lived in Salt Lake for nearly twenty years before moving to southern California.[94]

Sasaki thought of his true vocation in life as a writer, poet, and journalist. He wrote for the *Utah Nippō* (serving at one time as its chief editor) while in Salt Lake City and authored several books in Japanese under the name Sasabune (lit. bamboo-grass boat), including *Amerika Seikatsu* ("Life in America") and *Yokuryūjo Seikatsu Ki* ("Life in Camp"). The former is a 496-page collection of his biographical essays and poems mostly on American themes, while the latter is a 559-page memoir of his experience following the outbreak of hostilities with Japan, including his arrest in Los Angeles, his six-month incarceration at Missoula, Montana, and his travels to join his family at the Santa Anita Assembly Center in California (the family would eventually spend the remainder of the war at the Granada Relocation Center in Amache, Colorado).[95] Both Katsunuma and Sasaki were relatively educated men, indicating the level of intelligence and English proficiency that was required for Issei to accept the Mormon faith against

---

Chiyo Shioki (nee Koji) was baptized in Sapporo on 7 January 1909, attended church for some time in Tokyo, and moved to Portland, Oregon when she was barely twenty years old. She left Yokohama on 10 April 1912. Her family owned a store catering to Japanese clients. In all likelihood, she was a picture bride. Tomigoro Takagi, "Nihon Dendōbu no Kaiko," *Seito no Michi* 2 (August 1958): 25; Ivins, Journal, 6 September 1911; 2, 9 and 10 April 1912. Tomosuke and Suma Kawano, a married couple from Kofu, left on 21 August 1917 for Oakland, California. "Record of Members Collection." Both were new converts, having been baptized on 26 March 1917 and 14 August 1917, respectively. Tomosuke was thirty-one years old, while his wife was thirty years old. LDS Church Archives.

93. This information comes from Eric Walz, letters to author, 30 October and 24 November 1998. The archived historical records of the three Rexburg wards that existed in 1908 do not record his baptism.

94. Greg Robinson, "The Great Unknown and the Unknown Great: Pioneering Nisei Writer and Physician, Yasuo Sasaki, Fought for Reproductive Freedom," *Nichi Bei Weekly*, 18 October 2012. Sasabune Sasaki, *Yokuryūjo Seikatsu Ki* (Los Angeles: Rafu Shoten, 1950), 519–20.

95. In addition, an essay of his was included in a compendium of literary works authored by Japanese writers living in the United States. Sasabune Sasaki, "Bafun Tetsugaku," in *Amerika Bungaku Shū*, ed. Isshin Yamasaki (Tokyo: Keigansha, 1937), 303–20.

all odds. Curiously, both were from Fukushima Prefecture, and it turns out that Sasaki was a close friend of Katsunuma's nephew, the son of Shutaro Katogi. Sasaki was well acquainted with Tomizo Katsunuma's background, including how he had attended the Agricultural College of Utah and was a prominent figure among the Japanese population of Hawaii.[96] Sasaki may well have known that Katsunuma had affiliated with the LDS Church.

In contrast to the approach the LDS Church took, other Christian denominations actively targeted the Japanese population. Methodists were particularly aggressive, claiming their first three converts of Japanese ancestry as early as 1877—Kanichi Miyama, Etsu Miyata, and T. Saito—eleven years before Japan made it legal for its nationals to leave the country as emigrants. With an increasing number of Japanese adopting Methodism, Japanese Methodist churches were founded in Oakland in 1889, Sacramento in 1891, and Fresno in 1893. Other denominations followed suit from the 1890s to the 1900s, including the Baptists, Congregationalists, Episcopalians, Presbyterians, and Catholics.[97]

In Utah, as early as 1900 a Mrs. Carver organized the Presbyterian Japanese YMCA in Ogden. Eventually, there was a thriving congregation, which was strengthened by the arrival in 1908 of a Japanese-speaking minister, Rev. Yoshinaga Maruyama, from Doshisha University. The Japanese Church of Christ of Salt Lake City, established in October 1918, played a significant role in local Japanese American communities in northern Utah and south-eastern Idaho. Organized through the cooperative efforts of the Japanese Congregational and Presbyterian churches on the West Coast, Rev. H. Toyotomi arrived to become its first minister.[98] During the 1920s, Rev. Kengo Tajima travelled throughout Nevada and Utah to spread Christianity among Japanese miners. In Idaho, the historian Leonard Arrington observed that, by 1920, many Japanese had adopted the dominant religion of the region and affiliated with Christian denominations.[99] In nearly every community of sufficient size, Japanese Christians met in congregations based on ethnicity and presided over by Japanese-speaking ministers.[100]

To understand how conversion to Mormonism occurred among the Japanese population of the interior West, and especially of Utah, it is useful to consider the deconstruction of the Japanese migration process offered by the historian Eric Walz, who described the process in three phases: (1) frontier, (2) settlement, and (3) family. In the frontier phase, predominantly single men worked as gang labor in the mines or on the railroads; in the settlement phase, frontier period immigrants moved out of gang labor jobs into enterprises that offered better opportunities, including as cooks, employees of the mining and railroad companies,

---

96. Sasabune (Shuichi) Sasaki, *Amerika Seikatsu* (Los Angeles: Taishūsha, 1937), 24, 28.
97. Hosokawa, *Nisei*, 126–28.
98. Eric Walz, *Nikkei in the Interior West: Japanese Immigration and Community Building 1882–1945* (Tucson, Arizona: University of Arizona Press, 2012), 133, 137–38.
99. Arrington, *History of Idaho*, 280–82.
100. Walz, *Nikkei*, 145.

and tenant farmers; and, in the family phase, settlement period immigrants called siblings, wives, or children to join them in America to operate barber shops, family farms, hotels, restaurants, and such. The transition from one phase to another could be overlapping and differed from individual to individual, family to family, and community to community.[101]

Within this framework, the systematic conversion of the Japanese population to Mormonism can be understood to have occurred during the last, family phase. First, the LDS Church had no organized proselytizing activity targeted at the Japanese population. This meant that the Japanese population needed to experience sufficient socialization and cultural assimilation before it could be reached by Mormonism. Second, the interior West met this condition earlier than the West Coast. Any existing settlements in the interior were too small to sustain themselves, making it necessary for immigrants to develop face-to-face relationships with the host community. As a result, the Japanese communities in the interior West never developed the same level of cohesiveness or the sense of isolation from the host community that existed on the West Coast. Japanese businesses did develop in some locations, such as Ogden and Salt Lake City, but they still needed to rely on the larger community for patronage; in rural areas Japanese farms were seldom located contiguous to one another.[102] Third, while these conditions promoted social interactions between the Mormons and the Japanese population, systematic conversion to Mormonism needed to wait until Nisei were at least of school age, as it was predominantly the American-born Nisei that Mormonism was able to reach.

Systematic conversion of Nisei began in the 1920s. The Mormon faith was attractive to young Nisei with a desire to participate in the social lives of their non-Japanese classmates and neighbors. The Primary Association, an organization involving children ages three through twelve and meeting one week-day each week, offered non-Mormon Nisei children an opportunity to become exposed to Mormonism. After school, some Nisei students would follow their Mormon schoolmates to Primary and by the 1920s significant numbers of them were attending the Primary program. These typically did not lead to baptisms.[103] Children could not be baptized until they were eight years old and, as a general rule, required parental permission. Thus, Nisei children needed to be of post-primary age before they had the judgement, let alone the support of their families, to join the LDS Church. Shigeki Ushio, baptized in 1922 at the age of eight, may well have been among the first Nisei to join the church. Yukus Inouye, baptized in Union, Utah, in 1928, was another early Nisei convert. Other early Japanese converts from this period included Mike Masaru Masaoka (see Appendix 8.1), Minoru Matsumori, Tom Matsumori, and Jim Ushio.[104] George (or Joji) Matsumoto, whose father

---

101. Ibid., 61, 89.
102. Ibid., 91, 98.
103. Ibid., 146–47; Eric Walz, letter to author, 10 July 1998.
104. Author's interview with Yukus and Betty Inouye, Tokyo, 24 May; 12 June, 20 July; and 29 October 1998. Inouye stated that he had joined the LDS Church, with

owned a store between West Temple and Second Street and Second South in Salt Lake City, was another early Nisei convert. Interestingly in his case, he was baptized on 17 September 1922 in Osaka after returning to Japan in 1921.[105]

8.5. Mormon Missionary Work among the Japanese of Hawaii

8.5.1. Evangelization of Japanese Immigrants in Hawaii

Following the arrival of some 150 *gan-nen-mono* in 1868 (see Section 2.3.2 in Chapter 2), no further group of Japanese immigrants arrived in Hawaii until the launch of Japanese government–sponsored emigration in 1885. The first group of government-sponsored contract laborers, numbering 945 people, arrived aboard the *City of Tokio* on 20 January 1885. From 1885 to 1894, nearly 30,000 laborers emigrated from Japan to the Hawaiian Islands under government auspices as contract laborers. In addition, there were merchants, ministers and priests, newspaper correspondents, physicians, students, and teachers who were not under contract when they came to Hawaii.[106] In 1898, Hawaii became a territory of the United States and in 1900 Congress passed the Organic Act, making the laws and constitution of the United States applicable to Hawaii, thereby nullifying contract labor immigration. From 1900 to 1907, known as the period of free immigration, more than 68,300 Japanese came to Hawaii. As a result, the population of Japanese swelled from 12,610 in 1890 to 157,905 in 1940 (see Table 8.2), despite the fact that a number of the emancipated plantation laborers left for the West Coast.[107]

In Hawaii, the spiritual needs of Japanese immigrants were met by what was for them a new religion (Christianity) that welcomed them, as well as by an old and familiar one (Buddhism) that followed them. The first proselytization attempt was made by the local Protestant community. As early as 1885, the Congregational Board of Missions started Bible classes for the Japanese immigrants by securing Japanese-speaking preachers from Japan or the mainland United States. The first one to assist a local preacher (C. M. Hyde) was Kenjiro Aoki, a theology student from Doshisha University in Kyoto. Following Aoki's departure in 1887, the congregational board invited Kanichi Miyama from

---

strong parental encouragement, because most of his friends were Mormons. Also Yukus Inouye, letter to author, 3 November 1998.

105. Hilton A. Robertson, Autobiography, 2 November 1921 and 15 May 1922.

106. From March 1894, these individuals were required to pay $50 as proof that they could support themselves without becoming public charges while waiting for jobs. Kimura, *Issei*, 11.

107. The rush of more than 35,000 Japanese plantation workers to the West Coast after Hawaii's annexation to the United States intensified the anti-Japanese agitation already present there. Kimura, *Issei*, 13–14, 142.

Table 8.2. People of Japanese Ancestry in Hawaii, 1890–1940

	Number of Japanese	Share in total population	Memorandum: Total in the continental US
1890	12,610	14	2,039
1900	61,111	40	24,326
1910	79,675	42	72,157
1920	109,274	43	110,010
1930	139,631	38	138,834
1940	157,905	37	126,947

Thernstrom, *American Ethnic Groups*, 562, Tables 1 and 2; author's estimates.

California; subsequently, additional Protestant ministers arrived from Japan. It was in July 1888 that the first Japanese Christian church, under the name of the Japanese Mission Society, was started at the Miyama residence on Nuuanu Street. As various denominations arrived over the subsequent years, forty-two Japanese Christian churches existed in 1940 representing seven different denominations.

There was a lag of several years before Buddhism reached the Japanese immigrant community in Hawaii. The first *Jōdo Shinshū* monk, Soryu Kagahi, arrived in 1889, but did not stay very long. It was some eight years later that the Nishi Honganji Temple of the *Jōdo Shinshū* school established the first permanent Buddhist mission in Hawaii. In 1897, Keijun Miyamoto surveyed local conditions. The Nishi Honganji Temple, according to this survey, set up preaching stations in Hilo and Honolulu.[108] Buddhism over time became the dominant religion of Hawaii's Japanese population, and Buddhist priests commanded considerable respect in the community.

In the 1920s, as the Japanese presence in Hawaii became permanent, Hawaii's *Haole* establishment that controlled the plantation economy became alarmed that the generation born with the rights of American citizenship could use constitutional means to eventually control the political life of the territory. Thus began the Americanization movement, with the goal of eliminating Japanese tendencies and promoting American values. Key features of the Americanization movement involved the education and Christianization of the Nisei. In June 1920, Christian leaders began an "Americanize and Christianize the Plantations" movement, which strove to establish a Sunday school on every plantation.[109]

---

108. Soen Yamashita, *Nippon Hawai Kōryū Shi* (Tokyo: Daitō Shuppansha, 1943), 370–72; Kimura, *Issei*, 157–60, 169.
109. Gary Y. Okihiro, *Cane Fires: The Anti-Japanese Movement in Hawaii, 1865–1945* (Philadelphia: Temple University Press, 1991), 129–30, 132, 138, 151.

8.5.2. Establishing the Japanese Mission in Hawaii

The Americanization movement of the 1920s coincided with the beginning of Mormon missionary work among Hawaii's Japanese population. The first recorded instance of Mormon proselytizing took place in 1919. The LDS Hawaiian Mission diary for 12 October 1919 records: "proselyting work had begun among the Japanese of Kauai." This was notably followed by the efforts of Elizabeth Hyde and Jane Jenkins in 1922 at Laie. Hyde and Jenkins, teachers at Laie's LDS church school, converted Haruichi Matsumoto, Ochie Matsumoto, Otokichi Matsumoto, and Hisashi Ogawa to Mormonism. When David O. McKay and Hugh Cannon visited Laie on their way from Japan in early 1921 (see Section 3.7.1 in Chapter 7), they found among the student body several nationalities, including Japanese.[110]

Even so, the work of the LDS Hawaiian Mission focused almost exclusively on the native Hawaiian population. The Japanese, cliquish as they were, remained outside the reach of normal Mormon missionary activity. In 1933, when Kichitaro Ikegami, a non-Mormon who was attending church in Salt Lake City, brought his family to Honolulu, he suggested the possibility of holding a Sunday school in the Japanese language for the benefit of his family and friends. In early 1934, Edward L. Clissold, president of the Oahu District Council and Ikegami's immediate superior at work, discussed the matter with mission president Castle H. Murphy.[111] It was then decided in a 6 April meeting of key individuals, which included Tomizo Katsunuma and Tsune Nachie, that a Japanese Sunday school would be held from 6 May at the Kalihi chapel. Nachie, who had been converted in Japan and emigrated to Hawaii, and Elwood L. Christensen, who had earlier served as a missionary in Japan, were appointed as teachers. Twenty-eight Japanese members and friends attended the first session.[112]

By this time, a fair amount of Mormon literature was available in the Japanese language. The first shipment of the Book of Mormon to Hawaii was

---

110. Sharlene B. C. L. Furuto, "Japanese Saints in Hawaii and Japan: Values and Implications for Baptism," *Proceedings of the Eleventh Annual Conference of the Mormon Pacific Historical Society* (Laie, Hawaii: Brigham Young University–Hawaii, 1990), 2; Lanier R. Britsch, *Moramona: The Mormons in Hawaii* (Laie, Hawaii: The Institute for Polynesian Studies, Brigham Young University, Hawaii, 1989), 143; Francis M. Gibbons, *David O. McKay: Apostle to the World, Prophet of God* (Deseret Book Company, Salt Lake City, 1986), 110–11.

111. Clissold had moved in August 1926 from Salt Lake City to Honolulu as sales manager for the State Savings and Loan, a Utah institution, and invited Kichitaro Ikegami, the institution's part-time employee in Utah to Hawaii in 1927 or 1928 in order to head the Japanese department. David Takeshi Ikegami, interview with author, Kobe, 30 June 1996; Edward L. Clissold Oral History, interviews by R. Lanier Britsch, 1976, James Moyle Oral History Program, LDS Church Archives.

112. John A. Widtsoe, "The Japanese Mission in Action," *Improvement Era* 42 (1939): 88–89, 125; Edward L. Clissold, "Missionary Work among the Japanese in the Hawaiian Islands." Central Pacific (Japanese) Mission, "Mission President's Reports, 1937–1949," BYU–Hawaii Archives.

LDS Kalihi chapel in Honolulu, where the first meeting of the Japanese Sunday school was held in May 1934. Courtesy BYU–Hawaii Archives.

made in April 1924 before the closing of the mission in Japan, for the explicit purpose of aiding the proselytizing efforts.[113] When the Japan Mission closed in the summer of that year, most of the 5,000 copies from the second printing of the book were sent to Hawaii, along with any remaining copies of the Japanese-language tracts.[114] According to a report filed with Alma O. Taylor by Takeo Fujiwara in August 1934, there were about 2,100 copies of the Japanese Book of Mormon, 1,000 copies of James E. Talmage's *Articles of Faith*, 350 copies of the Sunday school song book, and a limited number of copies of various tracts.[115] It was from this stock that Fujiwara sent copies of relevant publications back to Japan (see Section 8.3.1).[116]

Takeo Fujiwara, on his way to Japan as presiding elder, attended one of the early meetings of the Japanese group in 1934 and described the group as having been "organized only two or three months ago with only 6 members." Fujiwara further stated:

---

113. Hilton A. Robertson, Autobiography, 17 April 1924.

114. Elwood L. Christensen Oral History, interview by R. Lanier Britsch, 1978, James Moyle Oral History Program, LDS Church Archives, 15; Alma O. Taylor, letter to the First Presidency, 3 April 1935. LDS Church Archives.

115. Takeo Fujiwara, "Report on the Church Literary Books in Japanese at the Hawaiian Mission," not dated (believed to be written in the first week of August 1934), LDS Church Archives.

116. Takeo Fujiwara, letter to Alma O. Taylor, not dated (believed to be written in early August 1934; Alma O. Taylor, letter to the First Presidency, 3 April 1935. LDS Church Archives.

> We, Pres. Murphy, Mr. Christensen . . . Sister Nachie and myself, are planning to do more work among the Japanese people here. . . . I have been tracting with other Elders who are unable to talk Hawaiian and Japanese. I have helped them at many Japanese houses where I have had good conversations on our religion.[117]

In June 1935, the presence of this group received the attention of visiting Mormon authorities, Heber J. Grant and J. Reuben Clark of the First Presidency, who came to organize the church's first stake outside North America. The two men arrived in Honolulu on 20 June 1935 and organized the Oahu Stake on 30 June 1935, with Ralph E. Woolley as president, Edward L. Clissold as first counselor, and Arthur K. Parker as second counselor. During their sojourn in Honolulu, a group of Japanese members gave a party in their honor at a Japanese teahouse, and requested that Grant confirm the nine adults and children, including Kichitaro Ikegami, who had just been baptized into the LDS Church.[118] Grant is said to have replied: "That's more than I confirmed during all the time I was in Japan. I'll be glad to do it."[119]

Christensen later recalled a conversation he had exchanged with Clark at the Japanese teahouse:

> While we were finishing our dinner, President Clark came. . . . He asked me about the suggestion made by President Wooley and President Clissold and others that a Japanese mission be established. . . . I was the only one [in Hawaii] who had been on a mission to Japan. He said, "You know, it's against the principles of the gospel to have segregation." . . . I said, "I agree 100 percent that it's not the right way. But, President Clark, it's the only way we'll ever get the Japanese started. And I think it would be a wonderful thing to get them started, even if we have to do it in a way that's not the best way. . . . [A]s they become members of the Church, . . . I think the time will come when the mission to the Japanese, which is wrong in concept, would no longer be necessary."[120]

Clark then foresaw the far-reaching implication of a decision the church was about to make:

> [It] would seem not improbable that Hawaii is the most favorable place for the Church to make its next effort to preach the Gospel to the Japanese people; and it would further appear that a strong colony of Japanese Saints in Hawaii could operate from there into their homeland in a way that might bring many Japanese to a knowledge . . . of the restored Gospel.[121]

In 1936, consistent with these considerations, a decision was made to create a mission for the Japanese, to be known as the Japanese Mission. In November,

---

117. Fujiwara, letter to Taylor, not dated.
118. Hawaiian Mission, "Historical Records"; J. Reuben Clark, Jr., "The Outpost in Mid-Pacific," *Improvement Era* 38 (1935): 530–35.
119. Clissold Oral History, 7; Christensen Oral History, 18–19.
120. Christensen Oral History, 19–20.
121. Clark, "Outpost," 533.

Hilton A. Robertson, the last person to preside over the mission in Japan, was called as mission president.

8.5.3. From the Japanese to the Central Pacific Mission

Hilton and Hazel Robertson arrived in Honolulu on 24 February 1937 and found a small group of seventeen Japanese members.[122] Mormon apostle John A. Widtsoe characterized this as a *reopening* of the Japanese Mission.[123] Apparently, former presidents of the Japan Mission had conceived of missionary work among Hawaii's Japanese population as a way of restarting the work suspended in Japan. In a letter addressed to Robertson in Honolulu, in February 1937, Alma O. Taylor referred to "the communication you and I and some of the other ex-presidents directed to the First Presidency under date of July 15th, 1925," and stated that "your present appointment is rather in line with what was then recommended." In the same letter, Taylor updated Robertson on what had happened in Japan since the closing of the mission, including the Franklin Harris visit and the ministries of Nara and Fujiwara.[124]

Robertson remained in Honolulu until 1 September 1940, when he was replaced by Jay C. Jensen of Salt Lake City, who had served a mission to Japan from 1908 to 1913.[125] Jensen was released in December 1942, as he fell ill with a malignant tumor.[126] Edward L. Clissold, first counsellor in the Oahu Stake presidency, took over the reins of the mission on 7 December initially as acting president.[127] It was during his tenure that, on 13 May 1944, the name of the mission was changed from Japanese to Central Pacific Mission. Previous authors have explained the name change as necessary to remove the stigma attached to the name Japanese, once the war with Japan had started.[128] Since the name change took place in 1944, more than two years after the start of the war, this explanation is not entirely

---

122. Japanese Mission, *Nipponjin Dendobu Tayori*, April 1939, 9; Widtsoe, "Japanese Mission," 88–89, 125.
123. Widtsoe, "Japanese Mission," 88–89, 125. Widtsoe's dates for Fujiwara's death and the establishment of the Japanese Mission in Hawaii are incorrect.
124. Alma O. Taylor, letter to Hilton A. Robertson, 27 February 1937. LDS Church Archives.
125. The new president arrived in Honolulu on 21 August 1940. Central Pacific Mission, "Historical Records," BYU–Hawaii Archives.
126. He was flown to the mainland on 13 December but died on 31 January 1943. Central Pacific Mission, "Historical Records."
127. He was formally set apart as president of the Japanese Mission in Hawaii by David O. McKay on 13 April 1944.
128. Russell T. Clement and Sheng-Luen Tsai, "East Wind to Hawaii: Contributions and History of Chinese and Japanese Mormons in Hawaii," *Proceedings of the Second Annual Conference of the Mormon Pacific Historical Society* (Laie, Hawaii, Brigham Young University–Hawaii, 1981), 11–19; James R. Moss, et al., *The International Church* (Provo, Utah: Brigham Young University Press, 1982).

The Japanese Mission in Hawaii, circa 1937 or 1938. Sitting immediately to the left of Hilton Robertson (center) are Tsune Nachie and Tomizo Katsunuma. Courtesy BYU–Hawaii Archives.

convincing. Clissold, notifying the missionaries of the name change through a letter dated 15 May 1944, explained that the Utah authorities had felt that "this Mission, like all other Missions of the Church . . . should bear the name of its geographical area rather than of a racial group."[129] It is also possible that the First Presidency wanted the scope of the mission to go beyond the Japanese population. On 11 September 1944, official word was received from the First Presidency that the Chinese of Oahu were part of the Central Pacific Mission.[130]

In May 1944, Clissold was called into active duty outside the islands as a reserve naval officer.[131] Before he left Hawaii, on 8 May, he met with President Castle H. Murphy of the Hawaiian Mission and President Ralph E. Woolley of the Oahu Stake to agree that the Hawaiian Mission president "should take over the supervision of the Temple, the Temple Bureau and all of the work of the Hawaiian and Japanese Missions on the outside islands." At a missionary meeting held that evening, Murphy officially turned over to Clissold "all local missionary brethren as they are to labor on Oahu island henceforth."[132] On 13 May 1944, a wire was received by Clissold from the First Presidency informing him that Murphy was to take charge of affairs of the Japanese Mission (now to be

---

129. Edward L. Clissold, letter to the missionaries of the Central Pacific Mission, 15 May 1944, LDS Church Archives.

130. Central Pacific Mission, "Historical Records."

131. Up to this time, Clissold's duty was confined to day time work within Hawaii, allowing him to serve the church. He was released as president of the Japanese Mission on 14 May 1944. Central Pacific Mission, "Historical Records."

132. Hawaiian Mission, "Historical Records."

called the Central Pacific Mission) in view of his impending departure.[133] Thus, Murphy assumed the duty as president, concurrently, of the Hawaiian Mission, the Central Pacific Mission, and the Hawaiian Temple, as stated formally in a letter from the First Presidency received on 9 June 1944.[134] The Central Pacific and Hawaiian Missions, however, continued as separate entities. Following the conclusion of the war, in 1946, Melvyn A. Weenig was called to preside over the Central Pacific Mission until 1950 when it was formally merged with the Hawaiian Mission.

8.5.4. Achievements of the Japanese/Central Pacific Mission

In October 1937, the first three missionaries, Preston D. Evans, Roy W. Spear, and Melvyn A. Weenig, arrived in the mission. With the arrival of additional missionaries, work spread to the Big Island of Hawaii in 1938 (the Hilo Branch opened on 19 October), Maui and Kauai in 1939 (January and February, respectively), and Kauai in September 1940.[135] In early February 1938, Chiye Terazawa, born in Sugar City, Idaho, and a member of the Pasadena Ward in California, became the first Nisei to serve a mission at her own expense.[136] As of April 1939, there were four conferences: Hilo, Honolulu (including branches in Beretania, Kakaako, Kalihi, Lanakila, and Honolulu), Kauai, and Maui.[137]

The mission saw its first baptisms on 18 August 1938, when thirteen people were baptized at the Kalihi chapel: Elaine Sumiko Imanaka, George Izumi, Florence Kametani, Yasuyuki Ernest Koroki, Betty Masako Mori, Lawrence Asao Nakano, Sayeko Nakano, Winifred Wakako Nakano, Sonokichi Okagi, Tsukiyo Okagi, James Morio Okawa, Wallace Natsuo Okimoto, and Melvyn Shigeru Prestige. Some of these people were baptized by Tomizo Katsunuma. The second group of converts was baptized on 1 April 1939, also at the Kalihi chapel, including: Herbert Kenkichi Fujimoto, Chiyoko Higa, Masako Ishizaki, Robert Makoto Takeuchi, and Thomas Tsutomu Takeuchi.[138] In reviewing the work for the year 1939, Robertson noted that it was most effective "among the younger people from ages ranging from fifteen to twenty-five."[139]

At least during the first years, the productivity of the Japanese Mission of Hawaii differed little from that of the Japan Mission in Japan: somewhat less

---

133. Ibid.

134. *Hui Lau Lima News*, 24 November 1957, T11. Murphy had arrived in Honolulu on 17 March 1944 to take charge of the Hawaiian Mission. Hawaiian Mission, "Historical Records."

135. Central Pacific Mission, "Historical Records."

136. Her sister Toshi served as a missionary in the postwar Japanese Mission in Japan from 1952 to 1954. Chiye and Toshi Terazawa Mission Papers, 1838–39, 1952–54, LDS Church Archives; Widtsoe, "Japanese Mission," 88.

137. Japanese Mission, *Nipponjin Dendobu Tayori*, April 1939, 11, 16.

138. Japanese Mission, *Nipponjin Dendobu Tayori*, April 1939, 12.

139. Mission President's Report for 1939, Central Pacific Mission, "Historical Records."

The Oahu District Council of the Central Pacific Mission, 1944. Among the standing are mission president Castle H. Murphy (center) and Adney Y. Komatsu (left); among the sitting are Kichitaro Ikegami (third from left) and Koichi Takeuchi (third from right). Courtesy BYU–Hawaii Archives.

than one baptism per year per missionary from 1937 to 1941 (Table 8.3). With the outbreak of war in December 1941, however, productivity soared even as the number of missionaries declined. During 1942, for example, 156 people joined the LDS Church when the number of missionaries (at the end of the year) was only eighteen.[140] By the end of the war, membership in the Central Pacific Mission was approaching 500. It was from among these young converts of Japanese ancestry that a large number of postwar missionaries to Japan, including several mission presidents, would be called.

The outbreak of the Pacific War in December 1941 directly affected the Japanese Mission. On 8 May 1942, word was received from the First Presidency, notifying the mission that all missionaries were to return home "at or about the time their two years [were] completed." On the next day, all lady missionaries were told to transfer to the Northern California Mission "as soon as possible."[141] Moreover, no missionary from the mainland was sent to Hawaii in 1944 and 1945 (the last two mainland missionaries, Morris S. Bushman and John Floyd,

---

140. Among the Nisei baptized in Hawaii during 1942 was Chieko Nishimura, a then fifteen-year old girl who would become the first non-Caucasian to serve on any general board of the LDS Church in 1961. In 1990 she was called as first counselor in the church's Relief Society General Presidency. Chieko N. Okazaki, *Aloha* (Salt Lake City: Deseret Book, 1995), 43–45. She married Edward Y. Okazaki, who would serve as the first president of the Japan–Okinawa Mission when it was organized in September 1968. See Section 11.1 in Chapter 11.

141. On 14 March 1943, however, the term was extended by six months "if agreeable at home." Mission President's Report for 1939, Central Pacific Mission, "Historical Records."

Table 8.3. Japanese/Central Pacific Mission in Hawaii, 1937–44

	1937	1938	1939	1940	1941	1942	1943	1944	1945
Number of Missionaries (end-year)	5	19	32	54	55	18	13	7	4
Number of baptisms	4	13	26	37	48	156	72	48	34
Number of members (end-year)[1]	17	30	60	101	150	302	375	437	484

[1] From 1939 on, the eight members baptized by Robertson in Japan were included in this figure for "statistical purposes."

"Historical Records for the Central Pacific Mission." Missionary Annual Reports, as quoted in Conkling, "Members without a Church," 210.

were released on 24 July 1944). With a declining missionary force, it was no longer possible to maintain all the areas where meetings had been held. Members in the areas from which missionaries had been pulled out were encouraged to attend meetings of the Hawaiian Mission, where feasible. To keep the mission afloat, mission president Castle H. Murphy called local missionaries in 1944 and 1945. A total of thirty-one local members, including married couples, responded to the call. Of this total, twelve served as full-time missionaries and nineteen as part-time missionaries for various lengths of time.[142]

8.5.5. Cultural Assimilation of Japanese and the End of an Era

A separate mission for the ethnic Japanese was known to be a temporary expedience. No purpose would be served from having a separate mission if the Japanese population became culturally integrated with the rest of Hawaiian society. Moreover, even though the target audience of the Central Pacific Misson missionaries was the people of Japanese ancestry, it was mainly the Hawaii-born, English-speaking Nisei who were attracted to Mormonism. As a result, difficulties quickly arose from having overlapping jurisdictions with the Hawaiian Mission. As early as January 1942, Clissold suggested to David O. McKay that the Japanese and Hawaiian Missions be combined under one president. Given the desire of the Japanese members to be considered "wholly Americans," Clissold argued, the policy of racial segregation had "served its maximum usefulness." Clissold was sensitive to the feeling of Japanese members:

---

142. "Mission President's Personal Report for 1945," Central Pacific Mission, "Historical Records."

> [We] believe from the standpoint of the Japanese saints it is particularly desirable at this time that the Japanese president not be released and the Japanese mission taken over by the Hawaiian mission president but that the Hawaiian mission president be released and his duties be taken over by the Japanese president. Thus it would not appear that we are in any way lessening our efforts to bring the gospel to the Japanese people in the Territory of Hawaii.[143]

Nothing, however, was done, even though the downsizing of both the Japanese and Hawaiian Missions would have been a sufficient reason to combine the resources of the two. Speaking of the difficulty caused by the existence of two overlapping missions in the same location, Clissold recalled in an interview held in 1976:

> When I got back from the war in [19]46 and we began talking of a mission in Japan and the necessity of opening the work there, I wrote to President McKay about [the difficulty]. I realized that we had a problem in Hawaii in these two missions.... There was confusion, particularly I think out in the country districts, where the Saints were in the minority.... It quite often happened that the Hawaiian missionaries would go out the back door as the [Central Pacific] missionaries came in the front of the same house [of a member family]. And it wasn't fair to the Saints.[144]

Though the possibility of consolidating the missions was clearly on the minds of the church authorities in Salt Lake City,[145] the Central Pacific Mission was retained. In February 1946, Melvyn A. Weenig was installed as president to succeed Castle H. Murphy, who remained as president of the Hawaiian Mission.[146]

The difficulty intensified, undoubtedly owing to the fact that Murphy had previously been in charge of both missions. Weenig wrote to Murphy in November 1946:

> I want you to know that as far as I am concerned, I am trying hard to be in harmony with the action of the First Presidency in establishing a Central Pacific Mission in the Territory of Hawaii. Their letters to me in calling me to this position and the blessings pronounced upon my head clearly state that this Mission, the Central Pacific Mission, is to labor with the Japanese people. However, in several parts of the Mission, and in instructing your missionaries to baptize in your Mission, Japanese people, I am convinced that you are not in agreement with this action of the First

---

143. Edward L. Clissold, letter to David O. McKay, 26 January 1942. A copy in the possession of author.

144. Clissold Oral History, 9.

145. Report to the First Presidency and the Twelve was filed by Spencer W. Kimball and Matthew Cowley on 12 August 1946. The report, citing the conflicts and duplication of efforts between the Central Pacific and the Hawaiian Missions, concluded: "Because of the mixture of the races the problem continues to arise and be most vexing, as to whom each of the two groups of missionaries shall proselyte, who shall baptize the converts, and to which mission they shall belong.... We are persuaded that consideration should be given to the re-establishment of a mission in Japan." As quoted in Clement and Tsai, "East Wind to Hawaii," 11–19.

146. Weenig was to take over as soon as "the affairs of the mission are turned over to you by Brother Murphy." First Presidency, letter to Melvin A. Weenig, 7 February 1946, LDS Church Archives.

Presidency. In view of this fact, I would like, President Murphy, to have you address a letter to the First Presidency and tell them how you feel in regard to this separation—where and when you feel this separation should and should not take place—and get their opinion on the matter.

In this accusatory letter, albeit written in the restraining spirit of brotherhood, Weenig cited examples of people of Japanese ancestry who had been or were being baptized into the Hawaiian Mission and expressed his opinion that "even though the Mission [was] not geographically divided, it definitely [was] racially divided." He then inquired about the validity of the Hawaiian Mission missionaries' intimation that Murphy had received a letter from Utah to the effect that "as soon as I should take a trip to Japan, the Central Pacific Mission shall again be dissolved into the Hawaiian Mission." Finally, he summarized the crux of the matter:

> [Since] both the Hawaiian and CPM [Central Pacific Mission] elders are laboring in the same Territory for the same Church, confusion arises between them as to who is responsible for which people and exactly where their duties should begin.[147]

8.5.6. Hilton Robertson's Visit to Japan, 1939

One of the achievements of Hilton Robertson as president of the Honolulu-based Japanese Mission was a month-long tour of Japan he made in 1939 to minister to the spiritual needs of any remaining members there. Robertson left Honolulu on 4 April aboard the *Tatsuta Maru* amid a large group of well-wishers that included Tomizo Katsunuma, and he arrived in Yokohama on 13 April. His stay lasted nearly a month, during which he visited Tokyo (twice), Osaka, and Sapporo, ordaining men to the priesthood, baptizing the children and sibling of Japanese members, and administering the sacrament to those who assembled on Sundays. Robertson left Japan on 11 May, arriving back in Honolulu on 19 May 1939.[148]

The first person Robertson tried to locate was Nami Suzuki, whose family lived on the mission home property for some time following the Great Kanto Earthquake of September 1923 in which they had lost their home. Knowing that she was in Yokohama, he went out in search of her while his ship was still docked at the pier. He records what transpired then:

> I enquired of a policeman as to the address I had of Sister Suzuki and was informed that I should take a rikashaw [sic] which I did. Not having a complete address I enquired at different intervals along the way, and was just asking a man on the street when a young lady came out of a bath house on the opposite side of the street and started in the opposite direction to which we were headed, when she saw we were enquiring she came across the street and ask [sic] who we were enquiring about and

---

147. Melvin A. Weenig, letter to Castle H. Murphy, 15 November 1946, LDS Church Archives.

148. Robertson, Journal, 4 and 13 April; 11 and 19 May 1939.

of course we told her, Suzuki, Nami. Well she said "that is my mother & if you will follow me I will take you to our home."¹⁴⁹

After checking in at the Daiichi Hotel in Tokyo, on 14 April, the next person he located was Yoshijiro Watanabe, who had assisted Takeo Fujiwara in his ministry as presiding elder and served as acting presiding elder when Fujiwara fell ill. Robertson describes his encounter with Watanabe: "He was surely surprised to see me and I was more so to see him with long hair and a beard. He said he was trying to follow the custom of the Savior."¹⁵⁰ Robertson found that one of the rooms in Watanabe's house was full of church books and tracts, which Fujiwara had shipped from Hawaii. He quickly arranged for them to be repacked and shipped back to Honolulu. On Sunday, 16 April, Robertson held sacrament meeting with Yoshijiro and his daughter Tazuko in their home, and learned that 109 yen was kept in a postal savings account for the church.¹⁵¹ After meeting members Shojiro Kimura, Reiko Mochizuki and family, and Tomigoro Takagi, who was "in charge of the Foreign Affairs Association," Robertson left on the evening of 20 April for Osaka "on the sleeper."¹⁵²

Hilton A. Robertson of the Japanese Mission in Honolulu leaves on a tour of Japan, 4 April 1939. Courtesy Carolyn McDonald/Bill McIntyre.

When Robertson arrived in Osaka on 21 April, Tazuko Watanabe was there to help him. During their stay in Osaka, which lasted until 29 April, Robertson met a number of members and friends, including Taki Arai, Susumu Hisada, Tsuruichi Katsura, Ichitaro Ohashi, and Muneharu Teranishi. He found Susumu Hori in Kobe, successfully engaged in manufacturing "steel supports or ties for railroad rails." When Robertson entered Hisada's home, "he threw his arms around me in joy and appreciation and it was mutual for I love him very dearly, as do I brother Katsura and others in Osaka. He hasn't changed in looks, action, nor [sic] faith. He is still looking forward to the time when the elder [sic] will re-

---

149. Ibid., 13 April 1939.
150. Ibid., 14 April 1939.
151. Ibid., 16 April 1939.
152. Ibid., 17, 18, 20 April 1939.

turn." Comparing these members with "the hundreds and thousands of Japanese" he had seen, Robertson remarked on 23 April: "The cleanliness of their thoughts and living has had a decided effect upon their entire physical makeup. There was a look of contentment and satisfaction written upon each face."[153]

While in Osaka, Robertson performed two significant actions. First, on 25 April 1939, he took the families of Katsura and Teranishi "to the river on the outskirts of the city and there after prayer and song" baptized Katsura's daughter (14-year-old Kazuko) and four of Teranishi's children (16-year-old Nagayo, 13-year-old Akiko, 12-year-old Haruko, 9-year-old Michio). They were all confirmed by Katsura. Second, on 28 April, Robertson ordained Ichitaro Ohashi to the office of elder in the Melchizedek Priesthood. This action was taken in view of the fact that Hisaichi Hamada had passed away. Robertson, in consultation with Katsura, thought that it would be good to have two elders in Osaka. Robertson left for Sapporo on 29 April after exhorting Katsura, Ohashi, and others to "contact each other often and regularly, and to keep in touch with [him] in Hawaii."[154]

After arriving in Sapporo on 1 May 1939, Robertson first went to locate Tamano Kumagai "at the Hokkaido Times office." There was a gathering of members and friends on the following day, which included Kumagai and family, Kenji Ono, and Takeo Fujiwara's father. On 3 May, Robertson baptized and confirmed Yoshino Kumagai, Tamano's sister. On the way back to Kumagai's house, Robertson visited Professor Tsuchinai of Hokkaido Imperial University (formerly Sapporo Agricultural College), who was a friend of Tomizo Katsunuma in Hawaii. On the next day, he left for Tokyo and arrived there on 5 May.[155]

From 5 May to the day he left Japan, Robertson sought to see additional members in Tokyo. On 7 May, he had a "very splendid" meeting with Shojiro Kimura, Reiko Mochizuki with her son and daughter, Masagiku Saigo, Nami Suzuki, Yoshijiro and Tazuko Watanabe, and "Sister Ishida" and her two sons.[156] On 9 May, he went to see Nami Suzuki at her house and spoke for "a couple of hours." In this meeting, "Suzuki felt she had not done the right thing . . . in not having taught [her children] the Gospel but she expressed a strong desire to have those who would accept baptism." Accordingly, on 10 May 1939, the day before Robertson was to leave Japan for Hawaii, he baptized two of Nami's children: 23-year-old Tsuneko and 14-year-old Naruko. They were both confirmed by Yoshijiro Watanabe.[157] These were the 183th and 184th baptisms and the last ones to be performed in pre–World War II Japan.

Robertson's diary indicates that he delivered three consistent messages to the few members he met in Japan. The first was the assurance that missionary work would resume in Japan. On 20 April, for instance, he told Yoshijiro Watanabe

---
153. Ibid., 22, 23, 24 April 1939.
154. Ibid., 25, 26, 28 April 1939.
155. Ibid., 29 April; and 1, 2, 3 May 1939.
156. Her maiden name, hence her identity, is not known, at least to this author.
157. Robertson, Journal, 10 May 1939.

that "in the Lord's own due time the missionaries would again be brought back to labor in Japan." The second message was related. As missionaries would return, "it was the duty of the saints now living in Japan to remain faithful and true until that time, be united and interested." On 7 May, he pleaded with those assembled "to remain faithful" and told them that "if they did they need not fear, God would protect and guide them and their families." The third message was the progress of work in Hawaii among the Japanese people. The Osaka saints, Robertson recorded, were "astounded" by this news and "astonished at the progress we are making."[158]

8.6. Conclusion

This chapter has reviewed the major events and developments from 1924 through 1944, covering Japan, the continental United States (Utah in particular), and Hawaii. When the Utah church authorities closed the Japan Mission, there were four faithful Japanese elders: Hisaichi Hamada and Tsuruichi Katsura of Osaka (both ordained on 27 November 1921), Fujiya Nara of Tokyo (14 January 1923), and Yoshijiro Watanabe (18 October 1922). Watanabe, converted in Tokyo, was attending church in Osaka but he would later relocate back to Tokyo. Following the mission's closing, the church did not allow these and other men to exercise their priesthood, for example, by holding meetings or performing ordinances. Japanese Mormons were suddenly left without any support to sustain their faith, other than the light they already possessed within themselves. Initially, it was the self-motivated, self-initiated efforts of Nara that held the remaining members together.

In all fairness, it must be acknowledged that the LDS Church did not possess the luxury of resources to maintain extensive contact with its members so far away from Utah. The subsequent appointment of Nara and Takeo Fujiwara as presiding elders, from late 1927 to early 1936, was a workable idea designed to sustain a minimum level of church activity in Japan, but little came out of it. Nara was too inexperienced and ill-prepared to take on the assignment of watching over the church members scattered across hundreds of miles. Fujiwara was a case of zeal without knowledge; young and inexperienced as he was, he cannot be blamed for any of his failings. He did the best he knew how before succumbing to a fatal attack of tuberculosis. Here, it becomes clear that among the many failures of the prewar Japan Mission was a failure to train and develop local leadership. One wonders how things might have evolved differently if Nara had been appointed to serve alongside American mission leaders before they departed, or at the very least called as presiding elder (and formally set apart by the departing mission president) upon the closing of the mission, when he was still motivated and full of energy.

---

158. Ibid., 20 April; 7 May 1939.

It is unfortunate in this context that Alma O. Taylor was playing the intermediary between the Japanese members and the First Presidency. His service in Japan (1901–10) had ended too many years earlier to know the prevailing conditions in Japan, especially outside Tokyo. The Japan he knew was Meiji Japan, not the Japan of the Taisho period. One wonders, for example, if Osaka's Tsuruichi Katsura could have succeeded Fujiwara, given his experience, maturity, and the fact that he was a person of some means. He had his own business and was married to a Mormon woman. Osaka had a core group of members who supported each other, as would be revealed during Hilton Robertson's visit in 1939. Some of them, if not Katsura himself, could have communicated occasionally with the church headquarters in English. The outcome might have been different if Taylor had consulted with Robertson before giving his critical piece of advice on the succession question.

From a church-wide perspective, the work among the ethnic Japanese of the United States could be considered a continuation of the work suspended in Japan. Following the end of World War II, a number of the American and Hawaiian converts of Japanese ancestry would return to the land of their forefathers as servicemen and civilian employees of the American occupation forces and as missionaries in the postwar Japanese Mission to be established in 1948. In Hawaii, where an ethnically-defined mission was created in 1937 to proselytize exclusively among the Japanese population, what was left of the Japanese-language literature produced by the prewar Japan Mission was sent to aid the work. To think that what appeared to be a failed experiment in prewar Japan was in fact a preparation for successful work among the Japanese population across the Pacific, however, would be too simplistic an interpretation of history. The ethnic Japanese who converted to Mormonism outside Japan were mostly the Nisei who did not need the aid of Japanese-language literature. Their conversion occurred as part of their socialization and assimilation with the host society, and the number was small in absolute terms.

It is ironic that the Issei were beginning to migrate to Utah and its surrounding region just about the time the first four Mormon elders left Salt Lake City for Japan. Unlike other Christian denominations, the Mormons did not appear to give serious consideration to systematically targeting their evangelical work on ethnic minorities in their midst. While most of the early Japanese in the interior West were contractual laborers in the mines and on the railroads, the Mormons could have benefited from developing relationships with the more educated among them. A few of these individuals, such as Tomizo Katsunuma and Shuichi Sasaki, did join the church. With more proactive engagement, many more Japanese could have been converted to Mormonism, and their knowledge and contacts in Japan exploited to the benefit of the Japan Mission. But church activity in three locations operated largely independent of each other, with no coordination to speak of. The human eye did not see a transpacific scheme of divine origin.

Appendix 8.1. Mike Masaoka and the Japanese Americans During World War II

The story of Mike Masaru Masaoka (1915–91), a Nisei converted to Mormonism in Salt Lake City, along with his close association with Elbert D. Thomas (1883–1953), a Utah Democratic senator and a former Mormon missionary from the prewar Japan Mission,[159] would make a fitting appendix to this discussion of Mormonism's transpacific interlude. Towards the end of World War II, it was Senator Thomas, in consultation with Masaoka and others, and acting as chairman of the Senate Military Affairs Committee, who advised that President Harry Truman order the United States armed forces not to destroy the ancient cultural assets of Japan. The head abbots of six leading Buddhist temples in Nara,[160] in recognition of the contribution of Masaoka (as the only surviving member of the four men who in their view helped save Japan's cultural assets),[161] presented him with a letter of gratitude, which read in part:

---

159. Thomas was a member of the United States Senate from 1933 to 1951, when he was appointed as United States high commissioner for the Trust Territory of the Pacific Islands.

160. They were the Hōryūji, Kōfukuji, Saidaiji, Tōdaiji, Tōshōdaiji, and Yakushiji.

161. According to Tamotsu Murayama, a Seattle-born Japanese journalist and an honorary citizen of Salt Lake City, who was personally acquainted with Masaoka through their activities with the Japanese American Citizens League, Thomas called a meeting with former ambassador Joseph C. Grew, Harvard art historian Langdon Warner, and Mike Masaoka. He then conveyed the consensus view of the meeting to Truman. Masaoka kept quiet about his role for over twenty years. Unfortunately, Murayama does not make clear the context of the meeting, so one cannot be sure when it was held or whether it concerned atomic or conventional bombs (both Kyoto and Nara were subjected to conventional bombing, albeit on a far more limited scale than comparable cities). According to the Japanese historian Morio Yoshida, declassified United States government documents show that, in early May 1945, Kyoto was the highest priority target for atomic bombing. Yoshida further shows, based on official and personal records, that, in late July, Henry L. Stimson, United States secretary of war, successfully persuaded Truman and top military leaders to remove Kyoto from the list of targets for the first two atomic bombs. It is possible that the purpose of the meeting Thomas called was to influence the outcome of (or even to strengthen Stimson's position in) the ongoing military decision making process from May to July 1945. One should not think that Thomas and his associates single-handedly saved Kyoto from atomic bombing. Nara would have been spared in any case given the lack of strategic importance. Tamotsu Murayama, *Shūsen no Koro: Omoide no Hitobito* (Tokyo: Jiji Tsūshinsha, 1968), 297–303; Morio Yoshida, *Nihon no Koto wa Naze Kūshū wo Manukareta Ka* (Tokyo: Asahi Shinbunsha, 2002), 96, 108–9, 135–37, 167–68, 200. Stimson's own account of the role he played in removing Kyoto from "the list of suggested targets" is found in Henry L. Stimson, "The Decision to Use the Atomic Bomb," *Harper's Magazine* 194 (February 1947): 105. For a recent scholarly treatment of the topic, see Jason M. Kelly, "Why Did Henry Stimpson Spare Kyoto from the Bomb?: Confusion in Postwar Historiography," *Journal of American-East Asian Relations* 19 (2012): 183–203.

This is to acknowledge with a profound sense of gratitude your significant contribution to the preservation of the religious and cultural heritage of Japan. We feel deeply indebted to you for the sacrificial efforts which you made during World War II to preserve the innumerable cultural assets, of worldwide importance, in Nara and Kyoto, from bombardment.[162]

Mike Masaoka was born in Fresno, California, on 15 October 1915 and moved at the age of three to Salt Lake City, where he converted to Mormonism. While at Salt Lake City's West High School, he developed into an accomplished debater.[163] As such, Masaoka became well acquainted with Elbert D. Thomas, who as professor of political science at the University of Utah served as a judge at state high school speech and debate contests.[164] Following his graduation from high school in 1932, and before entering the University of Utah with a full scholarship in 1933, Masaoka helped as a volunteer worker with Thomas's campaign to run on the Democratic ticket for the seat occupied by Republican senator Reed Smoot. As the campaign progressed, Masaoka held "minor leadership positions," including speaking on the candidate's behalf before small groups.[165] Thomas was swept into office in the Franklin Roosevelt landslide.

Americans of Japanese ancestry faced increasing racial prejudice and discrimination in the early decades of the twentieth century. In order to promote their rights as American citizens, they formed associations of one type or another. One such, the American Loyalty League of Fresno, founded in 1923, grew by 1930 to become a national organization known as the Japanese American Citizens League (JACL). While still in high school, Mike was one of the Utah residents who were recruited by Tamotsu Murayama, a JACL representative. Later, in 1941, Mike was asked by JACL president Saburo Kido to become "national secretary and field executive" as Kido considered Masaoka to be "cocky, aggressive, [and] extrovert"—qualities that most Japanese Americans lacked. At the encouragement of Senator Thomas, Masaoka accepted the offer. In August 1941, he resigned from a position at the University of Utah and headed for San Francisco.[166]

Utah was no exception to the prevailing culture of racial prejudice and discrimination against men and women of Japanese ancestry. Even the Hotel Utah, a Mormon enterprise, refused to accept Japanese guests. In larger Utah towns, Japanese were barred from better restaurants and had to sit in the balconies of theaters.[167] The situation intensified following the outbreak of war in December 1941. Utah State Agricultural College president, Elmer G. Peterson, announced

---

162. Mike Masaoka, with Bill Hosokawa, *They Call Me Moses Masaoka: An American Saga* (New York, William Morrow and Company, 1987), 7–8.
163. Masaoka wrote a manual for the LDS Church, *Outline of Debate*. More than 5,000 copies were distributed.
164. Masaoka, *Moses Masaoka*, 34.
165. Ibid., 37.
166. Hosokawa, *Nisei*, 203–5; Masaoka, *Moses Masaoka*, 59.
167. Walz, *Nikkei*, 96.

that "it would be in their best interest not to admit [Japanese students]." In October 1943, Tom Wilson of Pleasant View, Jim Rooney of Idaho, Roy Barton of Pleasant Grove, and Reed Frandsen and Harvey Park of Orem were arrested for firing a shotgun and a .30 calibre rifle at buildings in a farm labor camp in Provo where many Japanese worked.[168] Utah governor Herbert B. Maw, a liberal Democrat, an LDS Church official, and a humanitarian, was also a politician anxious to be reelected.[169] He advised the University of Utah not to admit Japanese students;[170] he also publicly expressed opposition to Japanese evacuees settling in the Wasatch front. In fact, all but two county representatives were opposed to receiving them.[171]

Even so, the Church of Jesus Christ of Latter-day Saints was a moderating influence. The general authorities of the church taught and practiced tolerance towards people of Japanese ancestry. Mike Masaoka later recalled the acts of individual kindness offered to his family by James Wolfe, a justice of the Utah Supreme Court, and C. Clarence Neslan, his bishop. Both of these men took personal interest in Mike's welfare following the loss of his father.[172] From 1942 through 1946, even as over five thousand evacuees arrived, the situation in Utah was not as hysterical as in neighboring states.[173] This was among the reasons why the national headquarters of the JACL and the Buddhist Mission relocated to Utah. Salt Lake mayor Ab Jenkins waited at the state border to welcome the caravans from San Francisco and escorted them into the capital.[174] In a town in the Upper Snake River Valley, where a number of Nisei and Issei farmers joined the large number already there, a member of the local stake presidency took the lead in organizing a group opposed to the sale of real estate to Japanese. In response, the LDS Church, on 4 December 1945, issued a statement in the church-owned *Deseret News* decrying "these foolish prejudices."[175]

On 27 March 1942, the army activated a program of compulsory evacuation and began building fifteen "assembly centers." Between March and June 1942, all citizens and aliens of Japanese descent were transferred. Then, the War Relocation Authority transferred 110,000 residents of the assembly centers to ten newly constructed "relocation centers" in far-removed places in seven states during the summer and fall of 1942, including the Central Utah Relocation Center

---

168. Alice Kasai, "Wartime Years: Discrimination against Japanese-Americans during WWII," in Nagata, *Japanese Americans*, 138–41.
169. Arrington, "Ambiguous Reception," 93.
170. Leonard J. Arrington, *The Price of Prejudice: The Japanese-American Relocation Center in Utah during World War II* (Logan, Utah: Faculty Association, Utah State University, 1962), 15–18.
171. Arrington, *Price of Prejudice*, 7.
172. Masaoka, *Moses Masaoka*, 28–29, 32.
173. Arrington, *Price of Prejudice*, 36–38.
174. Papanikolas and Kasai, "Japanese Life," 358.
175. Arrington, *Price of Prejudice*, 41.

in Topaz, Millard County. The population of Topaz at its peak reached over eight thousand people, making it the fifth most populous city in Utah.[176] During the fall of 1942, about a thousand evacuees from Topaz were permitted to work in Utah. When they returned to camp in January 1943, approximately 85 percent indicated that they had a "good" reception (as opposed 3 percent "poor" and 12 percent "fair").[177] A number of the evacuees joined the LDS Church during their residency at Topaz, and were given special relocation assistance by the Church Newcomers Committee in early 1945.[178]

In the meantime, the question of how to improve the conditions of American citizens of Japanese ancestry and their parents in the relocation centers was constantly on the minds of JACL officials. In the early summer of 1942, Masaoka was sent on a mission to "find and cultivate influential friends, consult and cooperate with the federal government to get the most equitable terms possible for the evacuees."[179] It was in part based on his efforts that, in January 1943, the secretary of war announced plans for formation of an all-volunteer Nisei fighting unit, to give them the chance to prove their loyalty to the United States and to elevate their status. The 442nd Regimental Combat Team, an all-volunteer Nisei unit, saw its first combat duty in June 1944 and subsequently fought as shock troops in eight major campaigns in Italy and France. Although the unit never numbered more than 3,000 men at any time (altogether about 14,000 men served), it won 18,143 individual decorations, including 9,486 Purple Hearts while losing 680 soldiers.[180]

Following the end of World War II, Mike Masaoka became a lobbyist in Washington. In 1949, he was described as "Washington's most successful lobbyist" by Readers' Digest magazine. In 1952, he was instrumental in helping with the passage of the McCarran–Walter Act, which allowed Asians to become American citizens. At his funeral held on 2 July 1991 in Chevy Chase, Maryland, the eulogy offered by his brother-in-law and member of congress Norman Y. Mineta called him "one of the greatest Americans of the twentieth century."[181]

---

176. Ibid., 8–10.
177. Arrington, "Ambiguous Reception," 96–97.
178. Arrington, *Price of Prejudice*, 41.
179. Hosokawa, *Nisei*, 379.
180. Masaoka, *Moses Masaoka*, 23.
181. *Nichi Bei Times*, 4 July 1991, 1–2.

Chapter 9

The Eagle and the Scattered Flock: Early Mormon Activities in Occupied Japan, 1945–48

9.1. Introduction

This chapter reviews some of the events and personalities of major significance in the history of the Church of Jesus Christ of Latter-day Saints in Japan from the beginning of Allied occupation in September 1945 to the time the Japanese Mission was established in March 1948, a mostly undocumented period of about thirty months when there was no organized church structure. The purpose here is not only to uncover and preserve important events as accurately as possible and restore some forgotten individuals to their rightful place in history, but also to place the early Mormon activities in the broader context of that singular period in Japan's history when changes in the structure of society were being initiated by an occupying foreign power, of which the church was a part.

When war broke out in the Pacific in December 1941, the LDS Church had long been gone from Japan. The Japan Mission, established in 1901, was closed in 1924 when the church authorities determined that the fruits (amounting to 174 baptisms by a total of eighty-eight missionaries over twenty-three years) did not justify the continued stationing of a few missionaries (see Section 7.4. in Chapter 7).[1] Although they allowed the few remaining practicing members, perhaps never exceeding forty, to hold meetings on a limited scale from September 1926 to January 1936, there was no effective local leadership to take advantage of this provision to keep the church really alive (see Section 8.2.3 and 8.3 in Chapter 8). From 1936 on, the members entirely lost contact with church authorities, except for a one month-long visit made in 1939 by Hilton A. Robertson, president of the Honolulu-based Japanese Mission, which was established in February 1937 to proselytize among the Japanese population of Hawaii. From early April to early May of 1939, Robertson visited the members in Tokyo, Osaka, and Sapporo, baptizing and confirming eight individuals and performing

---

1. On the basis of year-end figures, the average number of missionaries in Japan during 1901–1924 was thirteen. The number never exceeded twenty at any given time. Andrew Jensen, comp., "History of the Japan Mission," 1934, LDS Church Archives.

an ordination to the office of elder. These were the last baptisms and priesthood ordination of the prewar era (see Section 8.5.6 in Chapter 8).

Hostilities ended in most of Japan on 15 August 1945, as the Japanese government had a day earlier notified the Allied Powers of its decision to surrender by accepting the terms of the Potsdam Declaration of 26 July. By this time, Japan had paid a dear price in terms of human and material loss, even within the mainland. A total of sixty-six Japanese cities had been devastated by over 30,000 air raids from the long-range B-29 bombers stationed initially on the Asian continent and subsequently in the Mariana Islands. Over 250,000 civilians were killed by conventional bombing, while an almost equal number in Hiroshima and Nagasaki were killed by atomic bombs, which virtually destroyed their cities on 6 and 9 August, respectively.[2] In Okinawa (the modern Japanese name for the Ryukyu Islands) where the only ground battles were fought, almost 200,000 lives (of which about half were civilian) were lost by the time most of the islands were conquered by the advancing American troops in June. In terms of material loss, the country had lost 42 percent of its national wealth during the war, and manufacturing production had fallen to less than 10 percent of the 1935–37 average.[3]

Towards the end of August, American troops, commanded by General Douglas MacArthur of the United States Armed Forces in the Pacific (AFPAC), began to land in various parts of mainland Japan. When MacArthur landed at the Atsugi airfield near Yokohama on 30 August, he came in his capacity not only as commander-in-chief of the AFPAC but also as the newly appointed Supreme Commander for the Allied Powers (SCAP), charged with the assignment to execute the terms of the Potsdam Declaration. Following the signing of the surrender documents on the battleship *Missouri* on 2 September, he located his General Headquarters (GHQ/AFPAC) in the Daiichi Life building and dozens of other commandeered office buildings in downtown Tokyo.

To execute this complex military and civil undertaking, MacArthur added to his general staff sections (named G-1 through G-4, corresponding to personnel, intelligence, operations, and supply/logistics) special staff sections in various branches of civil affairs, such as the Economic and Scientific Section (ESS) on 15 September, and the Civil Information and Education Section (CIE) on 22 September. The reorganization of the GHQ was completed on 2 October as the GHQ/SCAP, which had both military and civil functions to perform.[4] With the

---

2. Alvin D. Coox, "The Pacific War," *The Cambridge History of Japan*, vol. 6, ed. Peter Duus (Cambridge and New York: Cambridge University Press, 1988), 369, 373–75. The exact numbers are not known.

3. Japanese government data, as quoted in Shinji Takagi, "From Recipient to Donor: Japan's Official Aid Flows, 1945 to 1990 and Beyond," *Princeton Essays in International Finance*, no. 196 (Princeton, New Jersey: International Finance Section, Department of Economics, Princeton University, 1995).

4. Edwin M. Martin, *The Allied Occupation of Japan* (New York: American Institute of Pacific Relations, 1948), 9–13; Justin Williams, Sr., *Japan's Political Revolution under*

agenda for post-surrender reforms already in place, the GHQ/SCAP immediately launched on a major program of reform, designed to restore and strengthen democracy and human rights in Japan.

Possibly the most lasting accomplishment of the occupation in changing the basis of Japanese society was the new Constitution of Japan, which was promulgated on 3 November 1946. The new constitution denounced war as a means of settling international disputes and guaranteed basic human rights. Even prior to the drafting of the new constitution, the GHQ/SCAP had already begun to implement a series of democratic reforms through "Potsdam directives," which superseded all existing Japanese statutes. Significantly, as early as 4 October 1945, the GHQ/SCAP issued a memorandum to the Japanese government, directing that all "restrictions on political, civil and religious liberties and discrimination on grounds of race, nationality, creed or political opinion" should be removed; and that the "operation of all provisions of all laws, decrees, orders, ordinances and regulations which . . . [establish] or maintain restrictions on freedom of thought, of religion, of assembly and of speech" should be abrogated and immediately suspended.[5]

Likewise, in a memorandum dated 15 December 1945, the SCAP directed the Japanese government to terminate any public support for State Shinto while stipulating that no one would "be discriminated against because of his failure to profess and believe in or participate in any practice, rite, ceremony, or observance of State Shinto or of any other religion."[6] Pursuant to these directives, on 28 December, the Japanese government issued a Religious Corporation Ordinance, declaring that the restrictive Religious Organization Law of 1939 and the associated statutes had lost force, and that a religious organization could now be incorporated simply upon notification to the authorities and filing of registration with a local court.[7] Equally important was the SCAP memorandum of 22 October 1945 on educational reform, which directed the Japanese government to discontinue "dissemination of militaristic and ultra-nationalistic ideology" and to encourage inculcation of "concepts and establishment of practices in harmony with representative government, international peace, the dignity of the individual, and such fundamental human rights as the freedom of assembly, speech, and

---

MacArthur: A Participant's Account (Athens, Georgia: University of Georgia Press, 1979), 5; and Eiji Takemae, *GHQ* (Tokyo: Iwanami Shoten, 1983), 45–46.

5. Japanese Government, Foreign Office, Division of Special Records, comp., *Documents Concerning the Allied Occupation and Control of Japan*, vol. 2 (Tokyo: Japanese Government, Foreign Office, 1949).

6. Japanese Government, *Documents*.

7. Japanese Government, *Kanpō*, no. 5689, 28 December 1945. According to the Religious Organization Law of 1939, the incorporation of a religious group required government approval and the government retained the authority to restrict or prohibit the practice or preaching of a religious group if it was deemed prejudicial to peace and order or antagonistic to the performance of duties as Japanese subjects. See Section 7.5 in Chapter 7.

religion." With these and other reforms, the religious soil and climate of Japan surely began to change.

9.2. Chaplain Nelson and the First Postwar Baptisms

With the defeat of Japan, on 15 August, MacArthur made a major reorganization of the AFPAC and placed the Sixth and Eighth Armies on occupation duty in western and eastern Japan, respectively. The SCAP's directives were to be transmitted to the regional and prefectural military government (or civil affairs) teams through the separate headquarters of the Sixth Army (in Kyoto) and the Eighth Army (in Yokohama).[8] With the staging of troops throughout the country, it is estimated that, by the end of December 1945, the number of American servicemen in occupied Japan reached a peak of about 430,000.[9] Crudely judging from the share of Utah (about 0.4 percent) in the total population of the United States at the time, the number of Mormon soldiers in the occupation forces might have been slightly less than two thousand, of which perhaps several hundred were religiously active. In fact, the first postwar conference of Mormon military personnel held in Tokyo on 7 April 1946 had the attendance of about five hundred from all of Japan and the Philippines, attesting the accuracy of such estimates as rough ballpark figures.[10]

At one time during the war, it is estimated that over 100,000 Mormon men were serving in the United States armed forces in either Europe or the Pacific.[11] Obviously, meeting the spiritual needs of these men was of great concern to the Mormon authorities. In part to address this issue more effectively, a special committee was organized in late 1942, with Hugh B. Brown as coordinator. Beginning in July 1943, assistant coordinators were called to assist Brown, each with a specific geographical area to work with. The assistant coordinators gave counsel, ordained men in the priesthood, directed baptismal services, located meeting places, and set apart group leaders who were to organize groups in their various theaters of war, conduct meetings, administer the sacrament and, under certain circumstances, baptize converts.[12] In this program, initially called the MIA group leader program (where MIA stood for the Mutual Improvement Association, a Mormon auxiliary program), qualified men set apart as group leaders had in their possession a certificate stating that authorization, and were expected to organize

---

8. Robert E. Ward and Frank Joseph Shulman, eds., *The Allied Occupation of Japan, 1945–1952* (Chicago: American Library Association, 1974), 297.
9. Takemae, *GHQ*, 22–27, 45.
10. "Mormon Meeting Held in Tokyo," *Stars and Stripes*, 10 April 1946.
11. Joseph F. Boone, *The Roles of the Church of Jesus Christ of Latter-day Saints in Relation to the United States Military, 1900–1975* (PhD diss., Brigham Young University, 1975), 434.
12. Boone, *Roles of the Church*, 658–59.

Mormon soldiers into a group whenever such action had not been taken, and to select two counselors to aid them in their work.[13]

Another channel of church influence was through Mormon chaplains. During World War II, the LDS Church was represented by a total of forty-five chaplains, of whom about twenty served in the Pacific, including John W. Boud, Theodore E. Curtis, Roy M. Darley, Warren Richard Nelson, and Vadal W. Peterson. At the war's end in August 1945, the number of Mormon chaplains on active duty had reached a peak of forty. In November 1945, there were still thirty-nine chaplains on duty but, by 1 July 1946, the number had dwindled to ten, all of whom were in the army.[14] It should be noted that the first duty of a Mormon chaplain was to serve as a Protestant chaplain, and only after that assignment was completed and only if time allowed did he work with members of his own faith. In that case, he organized men into MIA groups, organized conferences for members of the church, and conducted Mormon programs and services, including blessing of children, baptisms and confirmations, and priesthood ordinations. The Mormon chaplain also played a vital role in the MIA group leader program as he had the authority to seek out and set apart group leaders.[15]

Thus, by the end of 1945, there must have been a number of Mormon servicemen's groups meeting together in various parts of the country, presided over by group leaders possibly with their counselors. Some groups were short-lived. As the number of troops began to decline in 1946, soldiers were pulled out of some areas altogether. Even within more permanent military installations, Mormon servicemen came and went, creating and then dissolving MIA groups. Some groups were active in proselytizing activities, generally among their fellow servicemen, but sometimes even among the local population. Undoubtedly, the missionary zeal reflected the response to the call of their ecclesiastical leaders, which was voiced from the pulpits of general conference and other religious meetings during the war years. For example, at the April 1945 conference, Mormon apostle Ezra Taft Benson stated that while "our number of full-time missionaries has been reduced, we have . . . almost one hundred thousand of our young men in the service of their country, hundreds and thousands of whom are doing effective missionary work."[16]

Back in those days, the Mormon authorities were quite tolerant of members serving in informal capacities, so that the majority of Mormon servicemen engaged in missionary activities in occupied Japan did so without a formal call

---

13. C. W. Nielsen, "Chaplain Corps of the US Navy, and the Church of Jesus Christ of Latter-day Saints," May 1952, LDS Church Archives; and Thomas E. Bauman, "personal history," not dated.

14. Richard Thomas Maher, "For God and Country: Mormon Chaplains during World War II" (MA thesis, Brigham Young University, 1975), 55–56. Boone, *Roles of the Church*, 548, 551, however, gives the total number of Mormon chaplains during World War II as forty-six.

15. Maher, "God and Country," 94, 98, 101; and Boone, *Roles of the Church*, 568.

16. As quoted in Boone, *Roles of the Church*, 501.

from the church. As late as 1954, the First Presidency expressed the view that it would be inadvisable to set servicemen apart as part-time missionaries, meaning that they could act as proselytizing missionaries without formal authorization. Official instructions given to group leaders during World War II discussed how to interview prospective members, how to baptize and ordain them, and how to prepare their membership records, indicating that some servicemen were indeed joining the church as a result of these efforts.[17] Japan was not an exception. Some of the early fruits of the church in occupied Japan came out of these self-motivated efforts of American servicemen in uniform.

As far as can be ascertained at the present, the first person baptized in Japan after the end of World War II was Eugene Johnson of Deposit, New York, who was stationed in the military city of Kokura (now part of the city of Kitakyushu) on the island of Kyushu. He was befriended by his Mormon barrack mate Clair L. Roberts and expressed a desire for baptism. At the request of the group leader, Mormon chaplain Warren Richard Nelson, serving at the time with the 25th Division (then headquartered in Nagoya), came and interviewed Johnson and approved his baptism. The baptism took place in the afternoon of Sunday, 27 January 1946 in an abandoned public bathhouse, which Roberts had located. According to the printed program of the baptismal service, the ordinance was performed by Kirk R. Christensen, with Roberts doing the confirmation. In all likelihood, this was the first baptism performed in Japan since the baptisms of Naruko and Tsuneko Suzuki on 10 May 1939, which were performed by Hilton Robertson, president of the Honolulu-based Japanese Mission during his one-month tour.[18]

In general, language and some physical separation confined the scope of Mormon servicemen's self-motivated missionary activities to their fellow American associates. Occasionally, some local Japanese attended Mormon military meetings, when their language ability permitted. Such were Tatsui and Chiyo Sato, a married couple in their forties, and Mamoru Iga, a thirty-year old man soon to be engaged to his Japanese American girlfriend.[19] As a result of Mormon soldiers' efforts, in the summer of 1946 they became the first native Japanese to be baptized into the LDS Church in the postwar period. The baptisms of Tatsui and Chiyo Sato (on 7 July) and Mamoru Iga (on 13 August) all took place in a swimming pool on the campus of Kansei Gakuin University, a Methodist school located upon a hill in Nishinomiya, a midpoint between Kobe and Osaka.[20] Also

---

17. Boone, *Roles of the Church*, 496.

18. Clair L. Roberts, letter to author, including a photocopy of the minutes of the baptismal service for Eugene Johnson, 12 March 1997. The program lists seven people in attendance at the baptism: Reo S. Archibald, Kirk R. Christensen, Harvey H. Field, Ray J. Green, Eugene Johnson, Clair L. Roberts, and Daniel F. Wood. Judging from the leading role played by Harvey H. Field in the program, he might have been the group leader.

19. Roberts, letter to author. Also, Mamoru Iga, letter to author, 15 June 1997.

20. Iga was a recent graduate of Kansei Gakuin University in English literature. It is likely that he had secured the use of the swimming pool on both occasions.

Chaplain Warren Richard Nelson presides over a baptismal service for Tatsui and Chiyo Sato in Nishinomiya, 7 July 1946. Courtesy C. Elliott Richards.

baptized along with Iga was a Japanese American woman working for the United States military in Kobe, by the name of Ikuko Rose Matsuda. Matsuda, a native of Salt Lake City, had been trapped in Japan when she was visiting her relatives at the break of the war. Iga was baptized by Joseph Barrett Richards and confirmed by John H. Moore; Rose was baptized by Shigeru Mori and confirmed by Clair L. Roberts, who had been transferred from Kokura to Kobe in April.

The Satos had been taught by Mormon soldiers in the town of Narumi just outside of Nagoya, about a hundred miles east of Osaka. In June, some three months after all Mormon soldiers had left the area, Chaplain Nelson returned to Narumi to interview the couple and invited them to be baptized in Osaka (see Section 9.3 below for a more detailed account). Mamoru Iga (1916–98), born on the island of Shikoku and a recent graduate of Kansei Gakuin University, had been introduced to the church by his would-be fiancée, Marye Matsuura of Rexburg, Idaho. Marye was raised as a Mormon, came to Japan at the age of twelve to receive education, and returned to the United States. When the war broke out, she was back in Japan teaching English while staying with her grandparents, and was trapped. Marye began to attend the Mormon services in Kobe as soon as she heard of the presence of Mormon servicemen.[21]

---

21. Mamoru accompanied Marye when she returned to the United States. He attended graduate school at Brigham Young University (MA in 1951), obtained a PhD from the University of Utah in 1955, and after a distinguished academic career, retired as a professor of sociology at California State University, Northridge.

Baptisms of Mamoru Iga and Ikuko Rose Matsuda in Nishinomiya, 13 August 1946. Courtesy Clair L. Roberts.

By now, it may be apparent that the thread that connects all these early postwar baptisms was Warren Richard Nelson, the Mormon chaplain who tirelessly travelled across western Japan (presumably the territory covered by the 25th Division) from the town of Narumi in central Honshu to the city of Kokura on the island of Kyushu. It was he who interviewed the candidates for baptism and then presided over at least two of the baptismal services. He showed no hesitation in inviting native Japanese to be baptized. This was in sharp contrast to the apparent attitude of Vadal W. Peterson, another Mormon chaplain stationed in Yokohama,[22] who either did not see a need or was reluctant to allow native Japanese to be baptized. We know that, in the Tokyo area, at least two individuals, Motoko Nara (the wife of prewar convert Fujiya Nara) and Miyoshi Sato (who was introduced to the church by American servicemen and became a regular participant in Mormon meetings) were made to wait until after the opening of the mission to be baptized. Technically, there should not have been a rule against baptizing a native Japanese person, if the chaplain or some other military leader concerned had only been willing. To have an insight into the more positive inclination of Chaplain Nelson towards native baptisms, it helps to know something about his experience in war-time Utah.

Warren Richard Nelson (1912–56) was born on 24 May 1912 at Bear River City, Utah. He attended the University of Idaho–Southern Branch in Pocatello during 1933–34 and the Utah State Agricultural College in Logan during 1935–37, graduating with a bachelor of science degree. After teaching vocational

---

22. "Mormon Meeting Held in Tokyo," *Stars and Stripes*.

agriculture in high school and working for the United States Department of Agriculture as a county farm supervisor for some years, he served a full-time mission for the LDS Church in Brazil for three years. Upon coming home in the fall of 1942, Nelson was asked by the head of the department of education at the Utah State Agricultural College to help set up a vocational agriculture department in Topaz, near Abraham, where a federally-operated relocation center had just been constructed for citizens and aliens of Japanese ancestry who were being evacuated from the Pacific Coast.

In the atmosphere of war-time hysteria and racial prejudice that followed the Japanese attack on Pearl Harbor on 7 December 1941, President Franklin D. Roosevelt had signed Executive Order 9066 on 19 February 1942, giving blanket power to the army to deal with the "enemy alien" problem. At that time, more than 112,000 persons of Japanese ancestry were living on the Pacific Coast, including 40,000 first generation immigrant (Issei) Japanese who were being excluded from becoming American citizens by law. Following about a month of voluntary evacuation from the coastal area, on 27 March 1942, a program of compulsory evacuation was instituted, allowing each person to take with him only what he could carry in his hands.

From March to June 1942, all citizens and aliens of Japanese ancestry were transferred to hastily-built barracks at fifteen assembly centers. Then, during the summer and fall of 1942, the 110,000 residents of the assembly centers were moved to ten newly-constructed "relocation centers," including the Central Utah Relocation Center in Millard County. The Central Utah Relocation Center, which came to be known as Topaz after the nearby mountain, was located sixteen miles northwest of Delta, surrounded on all four sides by mountains, had a climate range of 106 degrees in summer to 30 degrees below zero in winter, and was characterized by the wind that kept up "a seldom interrupted whirl of dust" and the "nonabsorbent soil which, after a rain, is a gummy muck, ideal as a breeding ground for mosquitoes." Built between July 1942 and January 1943, the center was made up of "row after row of low, black barracks of frame and tar paper construction." Still under construction, the Topaz relocation center began to receive evacuees on 11 September 1942, and accommodated over 8,000 persons during the fall of 1942.[23]

About thirty-six Latter-day Saints lived as workers at the Topaz facility, with only one car among them when the facility opened.[24] They received permission to hold church meetings right at the facility, and the Topaz Branch was organized. Richard Nelson was called to be the president, and he served in that capacity from October 1942 to June 1943. His wife Maurine writes of her experience at Topaz:

> I learned a great deal from my association with the Japanese people. They are very industrious, very clean, polite and respectful. They appreciate culture.... The people

---

23. Leonard J. Arrington, *The Price of Prejudice: The Japanese–American Relocation Center in Utah during World War II* (Logan, Utah: Faculty Association, Utah State University, 1962).
24. Maurine Larsen Nelson, "My Marriage," not dated.

were not bitter about being uprooted from their homes. I wonder how we would have acted under similar circumstances.[25]

Richard must have developed similar feelings towards the Japanese Americans and their alien parents of Topaz. This, along with his innate disposition, may explain the apparent zeal and willingness with which Chaplain Nelson invited the native Japanese to be taught and baptized into the LDS Church before the opening of the mission. His love for the Japanese people was such that he later named one of his daughters Chiyo, after the name of one of Maurine's closest coworkers at Topaz.[26]

In November 1943, Nelson was enlisted with the army and was set apart as a group leader by Mormon naval chaplain John Boud. After serving in the army for more than a year, in February 1945, he received a commission as a chaplain and was assigned to the 27th Infantry Regiment of the 25th Division. In that capacity, he served in the Philippines, Japan, and Korea, spending eight and a half months in combat, four months as assistant division chaplain, and four and a half months as acting division chaplain. The apparent freedom with which he travelled for his church can be explained by the position he held during those months.[27]

9.3. The Conversion of Tatsui Sato

The story of Tatsui Sato and his wife Chiyo deserves a section of its own because of the important role Sato would later play in the development of the LDS Church in postwar Japan as the official translator of the Japanese Mission.[28] Much has already been written on the subject in various places; however, there is unfortunately much error and contradiction in published and unpublished accounts, calling for a more definitive account of what happened. What follows is based principally on newly acquired primary sources (mostly contemporary letters), supplemented by other available documents.[29]

---

25. Nelson, "My Marriage."

26. Coincidentally, it was also the name of the wife of the first native Japanese convert in the postwar period, whose baptismal service Nelson would conduct in Japan.

27. Warren Richard Nelson, "Personal and Family Data," 1955. See also "Reservist Chaplain First To Be Set Apart for Duties," *Deseret News*, Church Section, 29 November 1950. Even after his initial discharge, Nelson's relationship with Japan would continue. In November 1950, the outbreak of the Korean War called him again into active duty as an army chaplain, this time to serve in California, Japan, and Korea. For additional information on Chaplain Nelson, see "Five Chaplains Return From Ft. Lewis Duty," *Deseret News*, Church Section, 1 August 1953 and "Funeral Held for Chaplain," *Deseret News*, Church Section, 21 July 1956.

28. Sato's biographical information comes from several published accounts, as checked against his letter to Harold B. Lee, circa 1946, LDS Church Archives. Whenever there was a discrepancy, the information in the letter was presumed to be correct.

29. It appears that most of the factual errors were first committed by Harrison T. Price, "A Cup of Tea," *Improvement Era* 65 (1962): 160–61, 184, 186, and were subsequently

Tatsui Sato was born on 16 October 1899 in the town of Narumi (now part of the city of Nagoya). In his early years, he was influenced by Christianity and, at the age of eighteen, baptized in the Methodist Church. After completing his secondary education, he moved to the northern city of Sendai to pursue higher education at Second Higher School and Tohoku Imperial University (also in Sendai), from which he graduated with a bachelor's degree in chemistry in March 1925. For some reason (possibly related to health), it took him four years to complete a three-year course of study in chemistry. He was the last of the fifteen chemistry students in the entering class of 1921 to graduate.[30]

The prewar system of higher education in Japan was a double track system, where those wishing to acquire higher education upon graduation from secondary schools (with a 5-year course) had the choice of either going to what was called *senmon gakkō* (literally "speciality school") to study in a specified field for three years, or enrolling in *kōtōgakkō* (literally "higher school") to study general or liberal arts subjects for two to three years, followed by three years of specialized training at *daigaku* (or university). In terms of social status and prestige, there was a differentiation between *senmon gakkō* and comparable institutions (designed to produce technicians) and the *kōtōgakkō–daigaku* sequence (intended to produce leaders).[31] Of the higher schools, the government-sponsored schools numbered one to eight were considered to be the very best; of the universities, likewise, the seven government-sponsored institutions, called imperial universities, were in a class by themselves. In other words, the Second Higher School/Tohoku Imperial University sequence was among the very best courses of education available in Japan. Given the program of generally six years of instruction, those completing the higher school/university sequence were receiving an equivalent of today's master's degree, which did not exist in prewar Japan.

Upon graduation from Tohoku Imperial University, Tatsui was immediately employed as an assistant researcher there. In 1937, after several years of secondary and normal school teaching and some more research work at the university, Tatsui moved to the city of Kawasaki just outside Tokyo, to take up a position as research supervisor at Nippon Metal Industrial Company, which produced stainless steel exhaust pipes for aircraft. Tatsui, by now married to Chiyo, lived in Yokohama until

---

picked up by unsuspecting authors. See, for example, Terry G. Nelson, "A History of the Church of Jesus Christ of Latter-day Saints in Japan from 1948 to 1980" (MA thesis, Brigham Young University, 1986); and Spencer J. Palmer, *The Church Encounters Asia* (Salt Lake City: Deseret Book Company, 1970). New errors were committed by George M. McCune, "A Tribute to Brother Tatsui Sato," June 1996, possibly because the author relied too much on the dimming memories of Tatsui Sato himself.

30. Tōhoku Teikoku Daigaku, *Tōhoku Teikoku Daigaku Ichiran* (Sendai: Tōhoku Teikoku Daigaku, 1924 and 1925).

31. In 1903, *senmon gakkō* were allowed to call themselves *daigaku* (university), but the government did not regard them as such until the University Ordinance (*Daigaku Rei*) of 1918 legalized the establishment of private universities.

1944, when he resigned from the company not only on account of illness but also because he thought "from the standpoint of an expert of special alloy steels" that Japan could never win the war.[32] Tatsui returned to the town of Narumi where food was more plentiful, thus joining the millions of other Japanese who similarly moved out of large cities to their ancestral homes in rural areas in the immediate postwar period. With no jobs available, Tatsui began to sell locally produced products in the black market. Given his proficiency in English, he soon began to help the local kimono merchants to sell kimono to newly arrived American servicemen.[33] Kimono and silk in general were popular souvenir items for American soldiers, and the local kimono store in Narumi became a popular spot for them to hang around, Narumi being conveniently located on a major road connecting Nagoya and Camp Okazaki in Uto (just outside the city of Okazaki).

Many American soldiers had come to Nagoya and its surrounding areas, because the headquarters of the 25th Division were initially placed there. The first group of soldiers from the division entered the port of Nagoya on 25 September 1945, but bad weather prevented the sweeping of mines in the port, so the rest of the troops did not begin to land until 26 October, when about 600 soldiers landed in one day, followed by an additional 10,000 soldiers on the next day. Some of these soldiers stayed in Nagoya, others went to Gifu to the north, and the rest to Camp Okazaki, a replacement depot for soldiers returning home.[34] In a major reorganization of the occupation structure, however, the Kyoto-based Sixth Army was relieved of occupation duty and moved out of Japan to Korea on 31 December 1945. As a result, in February 1946, the 25th Division moved its headquarters to Osaka, as the previously Osaka-based First Corps moved its headquarters to Kyoto. Soon, in March 1946, Camp Okazaki was closed, diminishing the number of soldiers visiting the town of Narumi.[35]

It was in the evening of Thursday, 15 November 1945, that Tatsui met the first group of Mormon soldiers stationed at Camp Okazaki, which included Mel Arnold, Raymond E. Hanks, and possibly Norton Nixon.[36] They may have become engaged in a religious conversation of some sort, but no explicit mention was made of the LDS Church.[37] Nevertheless, Hanks was sufficiently impressed to tell his good Mormon friend Reed Davis about Tatsui when he returned to the base that evening. A week later, on 22 November, when Arnold and Hanks decided to go back to see Tatsui, they invited Davis to go along. According to Sato's own account upon which most of the subsequent writers have based their stories, when he saw them outside the shop, they appeared to be waiting for

---

32. Sato, letter to Lee.
33. McCune, "Tribute."
34. C. Elliott Richards, letter to author, 7 December 1995.
35. Jun Eto, *Nihon Hondo Shinchū* (Tokyo: Kōdansha, 1982), 278–79.
36. Norton D. Nixon, letters to author, 10 December 1995 and 17 January 1996.
37. Reed Davis, telephone interview with author, 19 January 1996. Also, Reed Davis, letter to author, 4 January 1996.

transportation back to the base. In reality, unbeknown to Sato, the soldiers were there with the express purpose of seeing him.[38]

As an educated person, Sato had read about the Mormons. He somehow remembered a passage he had read as a child, which in glowing terms described the Salt Lake Temple illuminated against a snowy night sky.[39] When he heard Hanks mention the name Mormons, "the memory of thirty years ago, that ever so beautiful part of the memory vividly came back to [his] mind." "Particularly, when I heard that they did not drink either tea or coffee for a religious reason, I felt a greater desire to listen to their message."[40] The first of the series of religious discussions began in the morning of 28 November in the humble Sato home, initially with Arnold, Davis, and Hanks. Discussions lasted for a few months, with a number of additional participants, such as Nixon, Chaplain Nelson, and C. Elliott Richards. The soldier-missionaries commuted from Camp Okazaki to Narumi by military vehicle, GI truck, or local train. At least once, they walked back to the base when the discussion went beyond the departure time of the last scheduled train.[41]

Along with the relocation of the 25th Division headquarters from Nagoya to Osaka in February 1946, some Mormon military personnel (including Hanks and Chaplain Nelson) were transferred to Osaka. Partly owing to the deteriorating physical conditions of the Camp Okazaki facilities, the camp itself was closed in March. Besides, as a natural part of post-war troop reduction and discharges, the number of American soldiers necessarily began to decline from the beginning of 1946. Davis left for Osaka on 26 February 1946. C. Elliott Richards, one of the very last ones to remain and visit the Satos, left for Camp Zama outside Yokohama on 4 March 1946.[42] By 15 March, all Mormon soldiers were gone. Concerning this state of affairs, Tatsui wrote to Reed Davis in March 1946:

> After your leaving, all LDS members soon left for their destinations one by one and Mr. Swett was the last one who left Uto . . . on the 14th of March. I am attending every day to the Sensor [sic] Office in Nagoya. . . . Now that all LDS members have gone, no meeting is held on Sunday, but I am reading the Book and pamphlets which were given to me.[43]

At this time, Tatsui was using his English language skills to censor personal letters and possibly other materials written by Japanese nationals, as the Mormon

---

38. Davis, telephone interview.
39. This passage is found on pages 17–21 of a best-selling travelogue by Sojinkan Sugimura entitled *Hankyū Shūyū* (Tokyo: Yūrakusha, 1909). Sugimura, who arrived in Salt Lake City on 6 April 1908 and left on the next day, ate dinner at a Japanese restaurant, learned about the Mormon practice of polygamy, and saw the Mormon Temple. While rain changed to snow at night, the scene is not exactly how Sato remembered it.
40. Tatsui Sato, "Watashi no Kaishū," *Seito no Michi* 2 (December 1958): 13–15. The author's translation of the Japanese original.
41. C. Elliott Richards, letter to author, 7 November 1995.
42. Japanese Mission, "Proselyting Area Histories, 1945–1952." LDS Church Archives.
43. Tatsui Sato, letter to Reed Davis, March 1946.

soldiers had arranged a position for him at the Civil Censorship Detachment in Nagoya in January. While the GHQ/SCAP proclaimed the freedoms of the press and expression as the essential components of democracy, it immediately established a strict military censorship, exercised by the Civil Censorship Division of the Civil Intelligence Section (CIS). Much of the actual work was done through the military channels under the supervision of the G-2's Public Safety Division. The purpose was to gather information to determine if the Japanese public was complying with the occupation policies. Through local civil censorship detachments, the GHQ/SCAP censored communications, publications, and radio programs, tapped private telephone conversations, and inspected private letters. With the passage of time and the progress of the Cold War, the emphasis increasingly shifted toward the surveillance of communist activities. The civil censorship operations were massive indeed. As of June 1947, over 5.9 million domestic letters, 2,400 telephone calls, and 2.2 million domestic telegraphs had been subjected to censorship, not to mention the numerous publications, radio programs, plays, and other communication media of more public nature.[44] No wonder, through the intermediation of Mormon soldiers, Tatsui's English language skills were immediately put to work.

Some of the departed soldiers continued to write to Tatsui and his family, who in turn wrote back to them. C. Elliott Richards was one of those who kept in touch with the Sato family. By early May, the Satos had developed a desire to be affiliated with the LDS Church.[45] Perhaps sensing these developments, Chaplain Nelson decided to visit them towards the end of June. He was on an assignment in Gifu, a city that lies between Kyoto and Nagoya. He took advantage of that proximity to visit the Satos on 27 June 1946, and invited them to be baptized in Osaka following a conference scheduled for early July.[46]

In the meantime, unaware of these developments, Richards remained concerned about the Sato family in his barrack in Zama. On 29 June 1946, Richards wrote to Ray Hanks, who had already returned home:

> I have been receiving some mighty fine letters from the Sato's.... Ray, I wish that before I leave here, I could see the Sato's baptized in the Church. And it is our prayer that the Lord will open up the way for them to be received in the waters of baptism and receive the laying on of hands for the gift of the Holy Ghost. I know that . . . other teachers will come to complete the work that you started. They are humble people, and have a mission to perform here among their own people.

---

44. Shiro Haga, *Nihon Kanri no Kikō to Seisaku* (Tokyo: Yūhikaku, 1951), 157; Takemae, *GHQ*, 102–6; and Kazuo Kawai, *Japan's American Interlude* (Chicago: University of Chicago Press, 1960), 213–14.
45. Tatsui Sato, letter to Reed Davis, 12 May 1946.
46. Japanese Mission, "Proselyting Area Histories."

The Eagle and the Scattered Flock

His excitement over these letters was so great that he could not hide it from his newly found friend, Boyd K. Packer,[47] whom he had earlier met at a conference of Mormon servicemen. He later explained to Hanks:

> Five weeks ago I met Boyd Packer, who has become my closest friend. . . . [O]ne night while we were studying I had him read two of the Sato's [sic] letters, [which] so impressed him that we went up into the woods behind my quarters and knelt down in prayer, praying that the way would be opened for them to be received into the waters of baptism. . . . As we were leaving Boyd felt impressed to say that it would come about and that we would see it! At the time there was absolutely no outward indication of such a possibility.[48]

What seemed impossible came true, as Richards continued to explain to Hanks:

> Shortly after, Boyd was transferred to Osaka, and when he arrived there and contacted Chaplain Nelson he found that W. Richard had just returned from seeing the Sato's in Narumi . . . and he felt so strongly that this was the time for them to be baptized that he had made arrangements for them to go to Osaka that weekend in order to take care of the ordinance. I phoned Boyd the 30th, and you can imagine the thrill I received when he told me the marvelous news. I was being casualized the 3rd, so there was nothing stopping me from going down—not even a request disapproved by the Colonel. He finally saw it my way, and I took off Thursday on TDY. If the baptism had been set for any other time, I don't see how I could have made it (might have been on the ship that left yesterday). . . . Conference was being held Sunday, and naturally the Sato's were the highlight. . . . We all fasted morning and noon, so right after the first session we piled into our caravan of jeeps and trucks and rode out to the chosen spot—an open air swimming pool. Chaplain Nelson conducted the Service. . . . As we sang "Oh It Is Wonderful," I couldn't keep the tears from coming. . . . [I]t wasn't Boyd and I down there in the water, it was you, Reed, Mel, Hap, Ross, Koch, Swett, Morley, and all the others who helped to bring a knowledge of the Gospel to them. . . . I shall never forget the 7th of July as long as I live.[49]

This is how Tatsui and Chiyo Sato became the first native Japanese Mormons in the post–World War II period, by being baptized by C. Elliott Richards and Boyd K. Packer, respectively, in the Kansei Gakuin University swimming pool in Nishinomiya on 7 July 1946.[50]

---

47. Boyd K. Packer would serve as a member of the Quorum of the Twelve Apostles of the LDS Church, from 1970 to 2015.

48. C. Elliott Richards, letter to Ray Hanks, 29 June 1946; emphasis in original. Also, letter to Ray Hanks, 9 July 1946 and 10 July 1946.

49. Ibid.

50. McCune, "Tribute," erroneously states that these were the first baptisms after the 1925 [sic] closing of the Japan Mission and that they took place on the Kansai University campus in Sannomiya, Kobe [sic]. The mistaken idea that the Satos were baptized at Kansai University is also repeated in many other places, including Palmer, *Church Encounters Asia*, and is likely based on Price, "A Cup of Tea," which confused Kansai University (located in Osaka, and not Sannomiya) with Kansei Gakuin University, a Methodist institution located in Nishinomiya. The characters for *Kansai* and *Kansei* are identical in Japanese,

The story of Tatsui Sato does not end here. At this time, there was no church presence in Nagoya, let alone Narumi. This meant that Tatsui and Chiyo were being baptized into a church that could not nurture them in the faith. The very fact that the baptisms were performed in Nishinomiya, just outside of Osaka, was reflective of this fact. Things began to change later that year, however, as the Fifth Air Force moved into Japan, with headquarters in Nagoya.[51] With the arrival of some Mormon airmen and officers, Sunday school was started at the Sato home on Christmas Day, with Wadsworth Shigeru Uyetake as president, and Thomas E. Bauman and E. Carling Whetten attending.[52]

Thomas Bauman, an epidemiologist with the Fifth Air Force, describes the conditions existing in the fall of 1946 in his personal history:[53]

> It seems that I arrived on the scene in Narumi and met Brother Sato about the time I was needed. Brothers Richards and Davis had both been transferred home. The group was dwindling. There were no group leaders at that time, but the Sunday services continued. . . . I had access to a jeep when I needed it and would help with the transportation of Brother Sato and his neighbors on Sunday. Quite often I visited in their home during the week. . . . Considering everything, this was really a happy time of my army life. I looked forward to visits with Brother Sato and his neighbors.

Bauman then explains how he was prompted to help with the spiritual development of the Sato family:

> It was about this time that I was surprised to receive a promotion to the rank of Captain. The colonel had arranged for another doctor to work on epidemiology also. Our work overlapped quite a bit and I was getting a little bored with my office work. For some time I had been thinking about asking for a transfer, but I kept hesitating because of my activities with Brother Sato. I felt that perhaps I was really needed there to give support to the little branch. One day after I had been pondering this problem for some time. . . . I decided to make my problem of whether or not to ask for a transfer a matter of prayer. . . . Instead of going to lunch that day, I went to my room and knelt at the side of my bed and prayed for guidance in trying to make a decision. After I had finished my prayer, I got into my jeep and was driving back to

---

and this confusion is not uncommon even among native Japanese who are unfamiliar with the higher education scene. If the verbal statements of some participants and the records of the Central Pacific Mission are not sufficient to establish this error, one can resort to the well-established fact that Kansai University had no swimming pool in 1946, so that the swimming team was practicing in a facility located in Takarazuka in Hyogo Prefecture. Kansai Daigaku, *Kansai Daigaku Hyakunen Shi* (Osaka: Kansai Daigaku, 1987), 1051. Also see Ray Hulet, mission recorder of the Central Pacific Mission, letters to Russell Horiuchi, 5 December 1947 and to Edward L. Clissold, president of the Japanese Mission, 19 February 1948, LDS Church Archives; and Boyd K. Packer, letter to author, 8 September 1995.

51. With the renaming of AFPAC as the Far East Command on 1 January 1947, the Fifth Air Force came under MacArthur's command, and MacArthur was renamed Commander-in-Chief, Far East, or CINCFE. Eto, *Hondo Shinchū*, 47.

52. Japanese Mission, "Proselyting Area Histories."

53. Thomas E. Bauman, "Personal History," not dated.

Thomas E. Bauman (left) and E. Carling Whetten (right) bring gifts, with Yasuo Sato, around Christmas 1946. Courtesy Thomas E. Bauman.

my office. While turning the corner at one of the busy intersections, I suddenly and unexpectedly felt something that is impossible for me to adequately describe. . . . I knew at that moment that I was to stay.

In a letter addressed to Bauman, dated 7 March 1949, Sato called him "truly a God-sent distinguished Mormon missionary to my family" and that his assignment in Nagoya was a "definite plan of the Lord to save my family."[54] Six months later, on 5 July 1947, Sato's son Yasuo was baptized by Wadsworth Shigeru Uyetake at the Ohama beach, about twenty miles southeast of Narumi, thus becoming the fourth and the last native Japanese to be baptized into the LDS Church in the postwar era before the opening of the Japanese Mission.[55]

9.4. Edward L. Clissold and the Tokyo Saints

Concurrent with these developments in western Japan, Mormon military meetings were being held throughout occupied Japan wherever and whenever there were an appointed group leader and any number of Mormon servicemen.

---

54. Tatsui Sato, letter to Thomas Bauman, 7 March 1949.
55. Tatsui Sato, letter to Reed Davis, 20 August 1947.

As late as the summer of 1947, a *Church News* report of the centennial conference held on 19–20 July makes references to Mormon military groups in Beppu, Fukuoka, Kobe, Kumamoto, Kyoto, Nagoya, Sapporo, Sasebo, Sendai, Tokyo, and Yokohama.[56] Undoubtedly, there had been many more groups in late 1945 and early 1946, when there was a greater presence of Mormon servicemen in Japan. Of these, the Tokyo group was by far the most important, not only because it had the greater semblance of permanency (with the attendance of perhaps several dozens, meeting at the SCAP-commandeered Meiji Life building in downtown Tokyo), but also because it was proximate to many of the dozen or so Japanese Mormons from the prewar period who still identified themselves as Mormons. The first bridge between the military church and the Japanese members was made in late 1945 by Edward L. Clissold, a naval officer with the Civil Information and Education (CIE) section of the GHQ/SCAP.

Edward Lavaun Clissold (1898–1985) was born on 11 April 1898 in Salt Lake City, and attended East High School and the University of Utah.[57] During World War I (1918–19), he served aboard the USS *Arkansas* in the North Sea. After marrying Irene Picknell in September 1920, he served a full-time mission for the LDS Church in the Hawaiian Islands from 1921 to 1924. After a brief visit home, he returned to Hawaii in 1925 as assistant manager of the Honolulu branch of the American Building and Loan Association (later renamed American Savings and Loan Association), a Utah institution. In 1926, he became manager of the Honolulu branch of the State Building and Loan Association (later renamed State Savings and Loan Association), also a Utah institution. It was because of his banking business that he became interested in acquiring some skills in the Japanese language; he hired a private tutor and attended classes at the University of Hawaii. An overwhelming majority of his clients were Japanese and he saw a further opportunity among the culturally exclusive Japanese population.

Clissold became a person of some prominence in Hawaii, having successful business and church careers. In church service, he was a counselor in the inaugural presidency of the Oahu Stake (1935–44), twice president of the Hawaiian Temple (1936–38, 1942–44), and president of the Hawaii-based Japanese Mission (1942–44), whose name was changed to the Central Pacific Mission in May 1944, in order to comply with the established church policy that the mission should "bear the name of its geographical area rather than of a racial group."[58] As a church leader, he was closely associated with the members of Japanese ancestry, having been instrumental in the organization of the Japanese Sunday school in

---

56. "Centennial Conference is Held in Tokyo," *Deseret News*, Church Section, 23 August 1947.

57. Basic biographical information on Clissold comes from Honolulu Star-Bulletin, *Men and Women of Hawaii* (Honolulu: Star-Bulletin, 1954 and 1966); and miscellaneous documents in the possession of Richard L. Clissold.

58. Edward L. Clissold, letter to missionaries of the Central Pacific Mission, 15 May 1944.

The Eagle and the Scattered Flock 309

May 1934 and the establishment of the Japanese Mission in February 1937 (see Sections 8.5.2 and 8.5.3 in Chapter 8).

His assignment with the GHQ/SCAP was a result of his position as a reserve naval officer and his (limited) command of the Japanese language. In 1936, he joined the navy reserves as a lieutenant junior grade, and attained the rank of full lieutenant in 1937. He was recalled to active duty on 7 December 1941 and served in communications censorship in Hawaii for two years; he then accepted an assignment as a member of the civil affairs corps in preparation for Japan's surrender. From 9 June to 22 July 1944, he attended the School of Allied Military Government, located on the campus of the University of Virginia at Charlottesville, and was promoted to the rank of lieutenant commander. From 30 July 1944 to 27 January 1945, he attended the Far Eastern Civil Affairs Training School (CATS) located at the University of Chicago. Clissold was thus among the 2,500 or so officers who received training for service with military government units at the military government schools located at seven major universities (including Virginia and Chicago) and the Civil Affairs Holding and Staging Area (CASA) at Monterey, California. These officers were being trained to help govern the Japanese nationals in conquered areas, as the troops advanced further to conquer additional areas in Japan.[59]

It turned out that most of these officers were never needed in Japan, as the surrender of Japan came much more quickly than had been anticipated, and without land battles on the mainland.[60] Moreover, unlike in Germany, a system of military government was never established in Japan; instead, a system of indirect rule was adopted as a more practical alternative. The Japanese government remained intact with most of its functions. General policies and directives would be issued by the Allied Powers (or the United States), but they would be implemented by the organs of the Japanese government. For this reason, many of the officers trained in civil affairs were never called to go to Japan, and those who did (numbering about a thousand) were incorporated into the GHQ/SCAP or the Eighth (and briefly Sixth) Army. Many of them left Japan after a brief stay.[61]

Clissold was disappointed to learn that he was assigned to the CIE, a section charged with the democratization and demilitarization of the spiritual fabrics of Japanese society, including education, religion, and culture in general. He had hoped that he would be given a prefectural assignment as a military governor. In fact, he protested and spoke to the chief of staff, but was told that he had "[his] assignment and had better get to it," which ended his "vain dream of a prefectural assignment and because of the press of the work [he] turned to [his] duties in the CIE section with all the energy [he] had."[62] It would turn out, however, that

---

59. Williams, *Political Revolution*.
60. Takemae, *GHQ*, 17–20.
61. Ward and Shulman, *Allied Occupation*, 100; and Takemae, *GHQ*, 74.
62. Edward L. Clissold, "Personal Experiences in the Life of Edward L. Clissold," not dated. During the month of October, Clissold made a trip to Kyoto. Japanese Mission,

his affiliation with the CIE (charged with religious affairs) was helpful when he returned to Japan in 1948 as the founding president of the Japanese Mission.

With his vast church experience, Clissold naturally began to think not only of the need to organize a group of Mormon servicemen, but also of the conditions of the Japanese members. He writes in his own words:

> While in Japan I gave much thought to the status of the Japanese saints. . . . I also knew that there had been very little contact by the church authorities with the saints. So I took upon myself to call a meeting and had notices placed in the Japanese newspaper and the occupation "Stars and Stripes." A large group turned out to the meeting, mostly servicemen, but among them a handful of Japanese members. After the meeting I talked with these people and learned that they had been carrying on without leadership to the best of their ability and were waiting patiently for the reestablishment of the mission in Japan. Soon after returning to Salt Lake City . . . I called on President McKay and told him of my meeting with the saints in Japan. I apologized for presuming to act in the leadership capacity without authority. He told me I had done the right thing and he was delighted that the contact had been made. He said that steps must be taken immediately to restore some organization contacts to these people.[63]

The "handful of Japanese members" must be an exaggeration, or else "the meeting" must be referring not to any single meeting but to a series of meetings, both formal and informal. We know that Genkichi Shiraishi, a fifty-five-year old prewar convert (baptized in Asahikawa in 1909) with some command of English, saw a notice addressed to the members of the church on the streets of Tokyo and attended a meeting of servicemen held at the Meiji Life building in the very early part of the occupation, possibly in early October.[64] Moreover, the notice which Clissold placed in the advertisement section of the *Mainichi Shinbun*, one of the three major dailies in Tokyo at the time, on 30 October 1945, caught the attention of Tazuko Watanabe, another prewar convert. It was not difficult. Because of the shortage of paper, the newspapers in those days were only two pages long (or just one piece of paper) and, given the eagerness of the people to gather critical information, they must have read the papers from top to bottom. The poorly translated notice, occupying a tiny fraction of the bottom column of the second (and last) page, said:

> Urgent Notice—would immediately desire to get in touch with members of the Church of Recent-day Saints of Jesus Christ (Mormonism). Lieutenant Commander Edward Clissold, Room 548, Daiichi Hotel.[65]

Although "Latter-day" was translated as "Recent-day" and the word order was mixed up, the notice was sufficient to do the intended job.

"Historical Records and Minutes," 15 March 1949, LDS Church Archives.
63. Clissold, "Personal Experiences."
64. Nara, Fujiya, "1945 nen niokeru Kaigō Hōkoku," January 1946.
65. The author's translation of the Japanese original.

Tazuko Watanabe decided to act upon it. Tazuko was the daughter of Yoshijiro Watanabe who, as the fifth Japanese man to be ordained an elder in the LDS Church (in October 1922), briefly served as president of the Tokyo Branch under Takeo Fujiwara's tenure as presiding elder from late 1934 to January 1936. On her part, Tazuko was appointed as secretary of the provisional Japan Mission under Fujiwara's leadership, assisted him in his travels, and nursed him when he fell ill (see Section 8.3 in Chapter 8). On 5 November 1945, Tazuko decided to see Fujiya Nara, another prewar convert with some command of English, and told him about the notice she had seen. It is not clear if they had kept in touch with each other over the years because Nara was in Manchuria during much of that time. Regardless, Tazuko knew that Nara worked at the National Railway, and she must have located him through that knowledge.

Immediately, on 5 November, Tazuko and Nara went to see Clissold who was staying at the Daiichi Hotel, the living quarters for officers of the occupation forces. They together discussed the conditions of the members in Japan and their desire that a mission be opened in Japan. In this meeting, Clissold promised that he would introduce them to Russell N. Horiuchi (a Nisei servicemen converted to the Mormon faith in Hawaii).[66] To act on that promise, on 6 November, Clissold took Nara to the GHQ/SCAP to see Horiuchi. Thus, contact with the Japanese members was established two months after the occupation of mainland Japan began. In the meantime, along with many other officers trained in civil affairs whose services were no longer needed, Clissold was released from active duty on 7 December 1945.[67]

9.5. Russell N. Horiuchi and the Nara Sunday Group

With Clissold's departure in December 1945, the torch was passed on to a Nisei serviceman by the name of Russell Horiuchi. With his ability to speak both English and Japanese, he was an effective bridge between the military church and the Japanese members while the LDS Church was not yet formally established in Japan. Horiuchi would remain in Japan until April 1948, a month after the return of Clissold as the founding president of the Japanese Mission. He was thus an effective bridge not only in terms of language, but also in terms of time, covering the period from the departure of Clissold as a military officer to his arrival as a duly appointed religious leader.

---

66. Nara, "1945 nen niokeru Kaigō Hōkoku."
67. Clissold was released early because he had accumulated sufficient points by that time, as his two and a half year service in Hawaii was counted as an overseas assignment. Clissold, "Personal Experiences."

Russell Nozomi Horiuchi (1923–2011) was born on 25 January 1923 in Lahaina, Maui, Hawaii, to Mitsutaka Horiuchi and Kikuyo Koyama.[68] After graduating from high school, he moved to Honolulu to attend a vocational school. It was there that, on 14 February 1943 at the age of twenty, he was baptized by Kenneth L. Aubrey of the Honolulu-based Japanese Mission. In 1944, he was drafted and sent to Minnesota to receive training in military intelligence. In September 1945, he was stationed in Japan and attached to the Banking and Finance Division of the GHQ/SCAP's Economic and Scientific Section (ESS), one of the principal organs of post-surrender reform, charged with such matters as banking, public finance, trade, labor, investment, utilities, anti-trust, foreign exchange, and science and technology.

After the departure of Clissold, Horiuchi informally took charge of the affairs of the LDS Church with respect to the Japanese members. Several meetings of key individuals took place from December 1945 to January 1946. The first meeting was held at the Marunouchi Hotel on 21 December. In attendance were Nara and his wife Motoko (not yet a member), Shiraishi, Kentaro Mochizuki, and Tazuko Watanabe, with Preston D. Evans and Horiuchi from the American side. Nara recorded the minutes of additional meetings on 26 December, 11 January, 18 January, and 2 February, all taking place at Nara's office. The last and perhaps the most significant meeting was held, also at Nara's office, on 9 February 1946, in which it was announced that (1) the Mormon military leadership in Tokyo had appointed Nara as presiding elder for the Japanese members, with Shiraishi and Mochizuki as his assistants, (2) a suitable rental building would be located to hold meetings, and (3) the Japanese members were invited to attend the sacrament meetings of Mormon servicemen. During the military sacrament meeting held at the Meiji Life building on 10 February 1946, the officers of the Japanese group were sustained.[69]

This was the second time Nara voluntarily assumed a leadership role among the Japanese Mormons. Earlier, when the Japan Mission was closed in 1924, he took upon himself the task of holding the Japanese members together for some time by publishing newsletters called "*Shuro* (Palm)." In view of this and his other efforts, on 2 December 1927, Nara was appointed by letter to be presiding elder by the First Presidency. Perhaps with little visible success, however, he was discouraged and virtually abandoned his assignment as presiding elder as early as the fall of 1929, and left for Manchuria in January 1934 (see Section 8.2 in Chapter 8). In 1958, he recalled the sentiment he felt during his years in Manchuria:

---

68. Basic biographical information on Horiuchi comes from Russell N. Horiuchi, personal interview with author, Orem, Utah, 20 March 1996. Upon returning to the United States, he pursued graduate studies at the University of California, Berkeley, and the University of Washington before becoming a professor of geography at Brigham Young University.

69. Nara, "1945 nen niokeru Kaigō Hōkoku"; Fujiya Nara, "1946 nen niokeru Kaigō Hōkoku," January 1947.

Fujiya Nara's Sunday group in Tokyo, most likely in front of the Shirozaki residence in Gotanda, circa 1946. Standing in the middle of the back row are Fujiya and Motoko Nara. The man in civilian clothes standing on the right is Mike Kiyoshi Tsukayama. Courtesy Aiko Horiuchi.

> Although I was given an honorable mission with the keys of authority as a holder of the Melchizedek priesthood, I could not fully perform it. This was indeed regrettable, and for this I only ask God for forgiveness.[70]

Perhaps, it was in part to make up for those unfulfilled years that Nara assumed an active role in the work of starting up the church in Japan after the conclusion of World War II.

Whatever the motive, it was Nara who took the lead in arranging regular Sunday meetings for the Japanese members of the Tokyo area. The first meeting was held at 2 o'clock on 14 April 1946 in the living room of the Russell Horiuchi residence, with ten people (including three American servicemen) in attendance. The meeting was conducted by Nara, and the invocation was given by Shiraishi. The program was a simple one, consisting of three hymns and two talks (by Nara and Shiraishi), and the benediction was offered by Kenneth L. Aubrey, a former missionary who had baptized Horiuchi in Honolulu. In the second meeting held on 21 April, the sacrament was administered by Nara and Shiraishi. On 19 May, however, it was announced that the sacrament would not be administered in these meetings. Following the pattern established in the first meeting, these Sunday meetings consisted only of hymn singing, talks, scripture recitation,

---

70. Fujiya Nara, "Nihon Dendōbu no Kaiko," *Seito no Michi* 2 (July 1958): 27–29. The author's translation of the Japanese original.

and sometimes a lesson on a religious theme. It was not exactly a contemporary Mormon Sunday school class, but more like a Protestant service.

Starting on 16 June 1946, the meeting place was moved to Toyo Eiwa Women's High School in Roppongi, where Aubrey's troop was stationed. It was during this period (in July) that Nara wrote a letter to Japanese members, informing them of the Sunday meeting being held in Roppongi, and stating that they were invited to the American servicemen's sacrament meetings held on the seventh floor of the Meiji Life building in Marunouchi at 2 o'clock in the afternoon.[71] Initially, some of the Japanese members attended the servicemen's sacrament meetings on first Sundays. After a while it appears that they ceased to meet with American servicemen. It is not clear whether they were discouraged by the language barrier and voluntarily stopped attending, or they were explicitly discouraged by new military church leaders who later arrived at the scene.

American Mormons of Japanese ancestry continued to attend and assist with the Japanese Sunday meetings. Included in Nara's minutes were such surnames as Akagi, Akita, Arima, Ikeda, Komatsu, Shino, Sonoda, Takahashi, and Tsukayama. Of these individuals, Mike Kiyoshi Tsukayama went so far as to remain in Japan as a civilian employee of the occupation forces after his discharge from military service, so that he could continue to help the Japanese members. From 12 January 1947, with the assistance of some of the same Nisei members, an afternoon Sunday school for children was started at the Nara residence in Shimo-Kitazawa, with the average attendance of twenty to thirty pupils.[72] This was apparently a response to the increased number of children attending the morning meeting. During the month of December 1946, for example, between seven and nine children were attending the meeting, necessitating a special program for them.

Concerning these activities of the Japanese group, a *Church News* report of the centennial conference held on 19–20 July 1947 says:

> One of the outstanding groups is the Tokyo Japanese branch. Mike Tsukayama, an intelligent young fellow of 23 years of age, from Hawaii, and three Nisei friends and coworkers, [Allan Ebesu], Russell Horiuchi, and Sister Alma [Sonoda] conduct Sunday church services in the morning with an average of 7 members and about 19 investigators present. . . . Mike also has a Sunday School class every Sunday afternoon with an average attendance of 30 children in the age group of from 2 to 12.

The reference to the "Japanese branch," which technically did not exist, may be indicative of the way American servicemen perceived the group of Japanese members and investigators.[73]

---

71. Fijiya Nara, letter to Japanese members, July 1946.
72. Fujiya Nara, "1947 nenchu niokeru Shūkai Hōkoku," July 1947.
73. "Centennial Conference," *Deseret News*, Church Section.

On 28 July 1947, the morning session was moved to the large residence of a man by the name of Shirozaki in Gotanda.[74] The use of the Shirozaki residence for Mormon meetings was apparently arranged by a Toyo Eiwa teacher by the name of Ko Sakai.[75] These Sunday meetings, namely, the "Sunday meeting" in Gotanda in the morning and the "Sunday school" in Shimo-Kitazawa in the afternoon, continued until the arrival of Edward L. Clissold in March 1948. Records show that attendance was small but steady throughout the period, with morning attendance ranging between fifteen and thirty, and afternoon attendance relatively constant in the neighborhood of twenty children and three adults. In addition to Fujiya Nara and Genkichi Shiraishi, Tazuko Watanabe was a frequent native member participant. Kentaro Mochizuki, Koshi Nakagawa, Nami Suzuki, and a few others attended every once in a while. Motoko Nara, Aiko Mori, and Miyoshi Sato were frequent non-member participants. Towards the end of the period, some non-Nisei American members were also attending the morning meetings, most notably Spencer Savage, an air force officer.[76]

9.6. Reestablishing the Church in Japan

Mention was already made of Clissold's meeting with David O. McKay in Salt Lake City shortly after his discharge from military service in December 1945, in which McKay indicated the need to take some steps to make "organization contacts" with the Japanese members. At about the same time, Preston E. Evans and Russell Horiuchi met with the key Japanese members to discuss the possibility of establishing a branch of the LDS Church in Tokyo. In a letter dated 15 December 1945, Evans wrote to Clissold:

> I have been talking to Russell and we feel that we may be able to start a small meeting here in the Japanese tongue. . . . We would like to know if it is possible to have someone designated to take care of the work here and if it could receive the sanction of the mission there in Hawaii.[77]

It is interesting to note that the idea expressed here was not to establish a separate mission in Japan but to create a unit of the already established Central Pacific Mission (CPM) in Hawaii, undoubtedly reflecting the understanding that Japan was part of the territory covered by the CPM. Clissold forwarded the letter to the First Presidency, who in turn forwarded it to Melvin A. Weenig of Ogden who had just been called to preside over the CPM. In the cover letter dated 23

---

74. Fujiya Nara, "1946 nenchu niokeru Shūkai Hōkoku," January 1947.
75. Horiuchi, interview.
76. Horiuchi, interview.
77. Preston D. Evans, letter to Edward Clissold, 15 December 1945.

January 1946, the First Presidency wrote to Weenig that they would "discuss this matter further" with him when he was set apart for his mission.[78]

As things turned out, nothing really was done to reestablish "organization contact" with the Japanese members. Perhaps, the church authorities were too preoccupied with the more critical situation in Europe, where there was an established church structure with thousands of religiously active members in desperate conditions. In fact, just around this time, Ezra Taft Benson was called as president of the European Mission to give spiritual guidance and to initiate the provision of welfare supplies to the members in Europe, particularly in Germany.[79] The first ship carrying food from the United States arrived in Hamburg on 11 October 1946, and the shipment of supplies lasted for almost three years until the summer of 1949.[80] In contrast to Germany, the situation in mainland Japan was not as critical. Given the fact that there were at most three dozen religiously active members in Japan, perhaps it was felt best to concentrate the efforts in Germany and to leave those few Japanese members to the care of American servicemen, at least for the time being. About the two intervening years of no apparent action (from 1945 to 1947), Clissold writes that "the problem was considered by the brethren" and he was advised by the First Presidency of "the progress being made."[81]

Attempts were made to ship welfare supplies to Japan, beginning on 29 October 1945. It is said that, by 25 March 1946, 356 parcels of clothing, bedding, and food had been mailed to Japan.[82] In all likelihood, these supplies were not necessarily meant for the Japanese members per se. For one thing, it was not until early September of 1946 that the GHQ/SCAP allowed the resumption of international mail service between Japan and foreign countries, subject to the condition that gift "parcels to Japan will be limited to eleven pounds in weight and contents will be restricted to relief items such as non-perishable foods, clothing, soap, and mailable medicines."[83] It is thus almost certain that these parcels were sent to Mormon servicemen, who in turn distributed them to Japanese people, including some church members. In a meeting held on 9 February

---

78. Weenig was officially appointed on 7 February 1946. First Presidency, letters to Melvyn A. Weenig, 23 January and 7 February 1946, LDS Church Archives.

79. Gilbert W. Scharffs, *History of the Church of Jesus Christ of Latter-day Saints in Germany between 1840 and 1968* (PhD diss. Brigham Young University, 1969), 149–66; and Boone, *Roles of the Church*, 364–66.

80. Scharffs, *Church in Germany*, 161, 165; and Boone, *Roles of the Church*, 365–66.

81. Clissold, "Personal Experiences."

82. Boone, *Roles of the Church*, 364–65.

83. A press release issued on 12 September announced that international "postal service became effective September 10" on a limited scale "between Japan and all other countries except Germany," and that "the service will be restricted to postal cards to and from Japan; one-way gift parcel post to Japan." Japanese Government, *Documents*.

1946, Nara and other Japanese members received gifts from Russell Horiuchi.[84] Perhaps, the gifts represented some of the parcels sent from Utah.

After the resumption of international mail service to Japan in September 1946, welfare packages began to arrive at some of the members' homes with known addresses. In the summer of 1946, the CPM began to prepare welfare packages for the members in Japan.[85] In a letter addressed to the General Welfare Committee dated 25 March 1947, Nara acknowledged the receipt of packages, stating that he would distribute the goods to other members of the church.[86] Tomigoro Takagi, another prewar convert, received his first welfare package from Hawaii on 24 November 1947, containing candies, canned rice, medicine, socks, and sugar, and underwear. By January 1948, he said, he had received four additional packages from Hawaii and Utah. As a journalist, Takagi had first worked for the *Yomiuri Shinbun*, then for the *Utah Nippo*, a Japanese language newspaper published in Salt Lake City, from 1920 to 1922, and spent his war years in China as the chief editor of the *Tōa Shinpō*, a Japanese-language newspaper founded in 1939 in Peking. He had only returned from China at the end of April 1946 (see Annex 4 towards the end of this volume for a more detailed biography).[87]

Obviously, the possibility of initiating formal missionary work in Japan was in the minds of those at the CPM, who were charged with the responsibility for Japan. That Japan was under the jurisdiction of the CPM is beyond dispute. For one thing, it was with this understanding that Hilton Robertson, Honolulu-based president of the then Japanese Mission, visited the church members in Japan in 1939. For another, the membership records of Tatsui and Chiyo Sato, Mamoru Iga, and Ikuko Rose Matsuda were kept in the CPM headquarters until the opening of the Japanese Mission in Japan in 1948.[88] In keeping with this understanding, in early 1946, CPM president Weenig requested Wadsworth Shigeru Uyetake, a former member of his mission now serving in the occupation forces in Japan, to inform him of the prospect for missionary work there.[89] Again, in reporting the memorial service for Shigeru Mori (an American soldier who was killed in a plane accident on 10 December 1946 while on duty near Kobe, Japan) held in Honolulu on 16 February 1947, the CPM newsletter explained that "Brother Mori was acting, at the time of his death, as a Group Leader within

---

84. Fujiya Nara, "1946 nen niokeru Kaigō Hōkoku."
85. Melvyn A. Weenig, letter to the First Presidency, 1 August 1946, LDS Church Archives.
86. Fujiya Nara, letter to the General Church Welfare Committee, 25 March 1947.
87. Tomigoro Takagi, "Hikari wo Futatabi Uketa Koro," *Seito no Michi* 5 (1961): 23–26; 62–65; 126–27.
88. For the baptisms of Tatsui, Chiyo and Yasuo Sato, see Hulet, letters to Horiuchi and Clissold, 5 December 1947 and 19 February 1948, respectively. For the baptisms of Iga Mamoru and Ikuko Rose Matsuda, see Ray Hulet, letter to Edward L. Clissold, 20 February 1948, LDS Church Archives.
89. The text of the letter written by Uyetake was reprinted in "Japanese Convert Writes from the Land of His Forefathers," *Deseret News*, Church Section, 10 August 1946.

the area covered by that mission."⁹⁰ In 1946, Weenig proclaimed that he had "great aspirations to fulfill the destiny of the Central Pacific Mission here in the islands and prepare ourselves to establish a mission in Japan."⁹¹

Hence, the initial assignment of reestablishing the LDS Church in Japan naturally fell upon Melvyn Weenig, as president of the CPM. In a letter addressed to Edward Clissold dated 23 April 1947, the First Presidency stated that for "sometime past the General Authorities have considered the advisability of having members of the Church in Japan visited officially by the President of the Japanese Mission" and that a unanimous decision was made in the meeting of the First Presidency and the Council of the Twelve held in the Salt Lake Temple on 17 April 1947, that "President Weenig should go to Japan to set things in order, and that he should be accompanied by Brother Clissold."⁹² This is how things stood in the summer of 1947, when William Paul Merrill, Tokyo area group leader, expressed his hope that Weenig and Clissold would be able to come to Japan to "reestablish this mission."⁹³

In a letter addressed to the First Presidency dated 3 July 1947, Weenig stated that he had made an application with the War Department in Washington, D.C. on 27 May, for entry permits for him and Clissold and was told that the application was forwarded to the State Department, and expressed hope that they would be able to attend a conference in Japan scheduled for 19–20 July.⁹⁴ In presenting the case, it appears that the LDS Church appealed to the visit of Hilton Robertson in 1939, giving rise to the folklore in some circles that somehow Robertson's visit cleared the way for the LDS Church to return to Japan when it did.⁹⁵ In reality, that was not the case. In any event, it took the church almost nine months to obtain clearance.⁹⁶ Naturally, Weenig and Clissold could

---

90. Central Pacific Mission, "News of Happenings in the Mission Fields," 16 February 1947.

91. Melvin A. Weenig, "Report of Mission President," 1946, as quoted in Murray L. Nichols, "History of the Japan Mission of the L.D.S. Church 1901–1924" (MS thesis, Brigham Young University, 1957), 102.

92. First Presidency, letter to Edward L. Clissold, 23 April 1947, LDS Church Archives.

93. "Centennial Conference," *Deseret News*, Church Section.

94. Melvyn A. Weenig, letter to the First Presidency, 3 July 1947, LDS Church Archives.

95. Muriel Jenkins Heal, "We Will Go: The Robertson Response," *Ensign* 12 (1982): 32–35, claims that "it was this trip in 1939 that made it possible for the Church to enter Japan after World War II."

96. In contrast, the Foreign Mission of the Southern Baptist Convention received an invitation in early 1946 from the GHQ to "send one mature, level-headed former missionary to Japan," who had not been away from Japan for more than eight years. The first Southern Baptist missionary, Edwin Dozier, arrived in Kobe on 30 October 1946. By June 1947, some eighty Protestant missionaries from the United States and Canada had returned to Japan. In the fall of 1947, missionaries' wives and children ages twelve months or above were permitted to enter Japan. F. Calvin Parker, *The Southern Baptist Mission in Japan, 1889–1989* (Lanham, Maryland: University Press of America, 1991), 174, 177.

not attend the conference on 19–20 July (at which Paul Merrill expressed the hope that they would arrive soon).

On 22 October 1947, the First Presidency explained the situation to Weenig by quoting from the letter they had received from officials in Washington:

> The only possibility of entrance would appear to be as a 'representative missionary' temporarily to be supported from United States Army sources on a reimbursable basis. Since your church has not carried on mission work in Japan for over twenty years, it would have to be treated as a special case in order to receive favorable consideration, since the requirement of having 'carried on missionary activities prior to the war' has been interpreted to mean the years immediately preceding the war. Under this policy, only one person could be admitted from your church as a representative missionary in any case.

The First Presidency then quoted from a statement on Department of Army policy:

> Organizations which carried on missionary activities in Japan prior to the War but which have no missionaries in Japan to give assurances may send a representative who will be temporarily supported from U.S. Army sources on a reimbursement basis until such time as they can become self-sufficient. Until these representatives have resided for one year in Japan the provisions relating to missionaries regularly admitted do not apply.

It was under these circumstances that the First Presidency informed Weenig of their decision to establish a separate mission in Japan and to appoint Clissold as president, given the fact that he had recently been in Japan as a military officer and "had an opportunity to become acquainted with both civic and military rules and regulations governing the present-day situation."[97] In view of many years of absence from his business affairs, Clissold accepted the call with the understanding that he be released as soon as the mission was established and running smoothly.[98] On 22 October 1947, the day when the First Presidency wrote the letter to Weenig of its decision, Clissold was set apart by George Albert Smith as president of the new Japanese Mission.

With clearance from the American authorities, Clissold arrived in Yokohama harbor on Saturday, 6 March 1948 aboard the *President Cleveland*. He was then forty-nine years old, going to turn fifty in about a month. On the first weekend, he stayed in Yokohama at the home of William Paul Merrill. From there, in the morning of Sunday, 7 March, he attended the Japanese Sunday meeting, which was still being held at the Shirozaki residence in Gotanda, and went to the Tokyo military group meeting in the afternoon. In the morning meeting, he was welcomed by forty-three people in attendance. On Monday, he reported to the SCAP's CIE section, which was then headed by Lt. Col. Donald R. Nugent, with

---

97. First Presidency, letter to Edward L. Clissold, 22 October 1947, LDS Church Archives.
98. Clissold, "Personal Experiences."

All-mission missionary conference at Nikko, 9–13 August 1951. Courtesy Robert A. Swenson.

the chief of the religious division being Lt. Comdr. William Bunce.[99] Clissold was assigned a room in the Daiichi Hotel, which "oddly enough was across the hall from the room [he] occupied as an officer two and a half years before," and was given certain instructions.

> The written instructions given me stated that as a representative of the church I could live in the hotel for six weeks but after that would be required to find my own housing accommodations or leave Japan. It [sic] further stated that I was to report to the CIE Section for whatever direction or help I needed in my work.

Then, Clissold was hit by a profound realization that "my original assignment to the CIE section was not by chance. As I went to this office and entered the door a number of officers with whom I had served before rose to greet me and I was assured that I would receive every possible assistance from them."[100] With Clissold's arrival in March 1948, a Mormon mission was finally established in Japan, after well over two years of American occupation, and twenty-four years of official absence.

---

99. Ward and Shulman, *Allied Occupation*, 841. As of February 1948, the staff of the CIE was made up of about five hundred sixty people (including over three hundred Japanese employees), of whom fourteen were military officers. Takemae, *GHQ*, 128.

100. Clissold, "Personal Experiences." The probationary period given by the CIE was sixty days, and not six weeks.

9.7. Conclusion

This chapter has reviewed some of the events and personalities of major significance in the history of the Church of Jesus Christ of Latter-day Saints in Japan during the first thirty months of the post-World War II era from September 1945 to March 1948. During this period, no organizational church existed in Japan, so it was with the self-motivated, and often unauthorized, initiatives of American Mormon servicemen that the work of the LDS Church was carried out. The church owes much to the work of Warren Richard Nelson, Edward L. Clissold, Russell N. Horiuchi, and other men and women in military uniform for initiating missionary work, reestablishing contact with the prewar members, and keeping the church alive until the mission was reopened in March 1948. To be sure, the environment of apparent institutional laxity, within which self-appointed church workers liberally exercised their initiatives in the Mormon cause, reflected the extraordinary climate of the period, when administrative control from Utah was necessarily limited. At the same time, it may also have reflected the less "correlated" administrative style of church president George Albert Smith (1945–51), which placed greater value on local initiative and stewardship than may be the case today.[101]

With the establishment of the Japanese Mission in March 1948, the LDS Church entered a period of institution building for the first time in Japan. In the coming years, the church was incorporated and registered as a religious organization, real properties were purchased for the first time, and organizational structure began to be perfected. Work spread from Tokyo to a dozen or so places throughout the country. Within three years, the cumulative number of missionaries in the post-war Japanese Mission had exceeded the cumulative number in the pre-war Japan Mission. When all the eighty or so missionaries of the mission gathered together at a special conference held in the mountain resort of Nikko on 9–13 August 1951, the sight was something to behold for Hilton Robertson, the last president of the prewar Japan Mission and the first president of the Honolulu-based Japanese Mission, who came in his capacity as president of the Chinese Mission in San Francisco.[102] The sight was even more moving to another guest, who was none other than Chaplain Warren Richard Nelson of the United States Army, who had returned to Japan to serve in the Korean War. A hero of the past had come back to admonish the eighty or so successors of what was once his one-man show.

---

101. I owe this insight to Armand Mauss.
102. Following the outbreak of the Korean War, the Chinese Mission in Hong Kong was moved to Chinatown, San Francisco in May 1951. Robertson would return to Japan again in October 1953 as the third president of the postwar Japanese Mission.

Chapter 10

Riding on the Eagle's Wings: The Japanese Mission under American Occupation, 1948–52

10.1. Introduction

This chapter reviews major ecclesiastical developments in the Japanese Mission of the Church of Jesus Christ of Latter-day Saints from its establishment in March 1948 to the time the San Francisco Peace Treaty took effect in April 1952, a period of approximately four years during which Japan remained occupied by the Allied forces. With the fabrics of the old militaristic and totalitarian regime shattered, the people were generally open to new ideas and new ways of doing things, especially during an early part of the period; the LDS Church and its missionaries also enjoyed a special status as representatives of an occupying power. Our purpose is to trace the LDS Japanese Mission's early beginnings in occupied Japan within the broader historical context of that period, and to present historical analyses of why things happened the way they did when they did.

By the time the LDS Church returned to Japan, the post-surrender transformation of Japan's economic, political, and social foundation had substantially been achieved. In religious matters, the important reforms had included the directives issued in October and December 1945 by General Douglas MacArthur, the Supreme Commander for the Allied Powers (SCAP), requiring that no one should "be discriminated against because of his failure to profess and believe in or participate in any practice, rite, ceremony, or observance of" any religion, and establishing "such fundamental human rights as the freedom of assembly, speech, and religion."[1] The Religious Corporation Ordinance was issued in December 1945, stipulating that a religious organization could now be incorporated simply upon notification to the authorities and filing of registration with a local court.[2] As a culmination of these and other developments, the new Constitution of Japan was promulgated on 3 November 1946, upholding the principles of

---

1. Japanese Government, Foreign Office, Division of Special Records, comp., *Documents Concerning the Allied Occupation and Control of Japan*, vol. 2 (Tokyo: Japanese Government, Foreign Office, 1949).
2. Japanese Government, *Kanpō*, no. 5689, 28 December 1945.

democracy, the dignity of the individual, and all basic human rights (see also Section 9.1 in Chapter 9).

For one reason or another, the LDS Church as an organization did not immediately respond to this changed religious climate in Japan. The Japan Mission, closed in 1924 for lack of success, remained closed. No official contact was attempted with the few dozen Japanese converts from the prewar era who still identified themselves as Mormons. So it was with the self-motivated, and often unauthorized, initiatives of American Mormon servicemen that the work of the church was carried out. During the first three years of the post-World War II era, the church relied on such individuals as Warren Richard Nelson (an army chaplain), Edward L. Clissold (a naval officer), and Russell N. Horiuchi (a staffer at the SCAP's General Headquarters [GHQ]) to initiate missionary work, reestablish contact with the prewar members, and keep the church alive. As noted in the previous chapter, the conversion of Tatsui Sato and his family in Narumi (just outside of Nagoya) and the initiation of Sunday meetings for the Japanese members in Tokyo by prewar convert Fujiya Nara were among the achievements of these men and women in military uniform (see Chapter 9).

It was in the spring of 1947 that the Mormon authorities in Utah took the first concrete step to reestablish the church in Japan by appointing Melvyn Weenig, president of the Honolulu-based Central Pacific Mission (CPM) to visit Japan, accompanied by Edward L. Clissold.[3] Entry restrictions were placed by the occupation authorities, however, because the LDS Church had not "carried on missionary work" during "the years immediately preceding the war," allowing only one "representative missionary" to enter Japan, and requiring nearly ten months to grant clearance. Under these circumstances, it was decided to create a separate mission in Japan and to appoint Clissold as president, given his previous experience in occupied Japan as a naval officer. Clissold was set apart by George Albert Smith on 22 October 1947.

10.2. The Japanese Mission Begins Work

10.2.1. Successive Mission Presidents

The formal ministry of the LDS Church in Japan in the postwar period began in the spring of 1948, when Clissold finally obtained clearance to enter Japan. In anticipation of his departure for Japan, on 13 January 1948, Clissold had written a letter from Honolulu to the members of the church in Japan. The letter, typed in Japanese, read in part:

> Our Church of Jesus Christ of Latter-day Saints will reopen a mission in Japan. I have been appointed as Japanese Mission president and will be in charge of setting

---

3. The Japanese Mission changed its name to Central Pacific Mission in May 1944.

up the mission and organizing branches. I am scheduled to leave in mid-February, when entry permit will be granted by the authorities. At present, it is planned that the headquarters will be established in either Tokyo or Yokohama. As soon as suitable facilities are found after my arrival, a notice will be placed in newspapers, informing you of the location.[4]

The letter reached the Japanese members with known addresses in early February. Clissold's departure was delayed however, and he arrived in Yokohama on Saturday, 6 March 1948. On the following day, Sunday, 7 March, guided by Tokyo military group leader William Paul Merrill, he attended Fujiya Nara's Japanese Sunday meeting in Gotanda, and was welcomed by a group of over forty people in attendance.

Edward L. Clissold, the first president of the postwar Japanese Mission, 1948–49. Courtesy BYU–Hawaii Archives.

Edward Lavaun Clissold, born on 11 April 1898 in Salt Lake City, was ideally suited for his assignment. A successful banker in Hawaii, he also had vast experience in LDS church leadership, having been at different times a counselor in the inaugural presidency of the Oahu Stake (1935–44), twice president of the Hawaiian Temple (1936–38, 1942–44),[5] and president of the Hawaii-based Japanese Mission (1942–44). Given his (limited) Japanese language skill, he was closely associated with the members of Japanese ancestry in Hawaii. Of equal importance and relevance to his assignment was his previous experience in occupied Japan as a naval officer attached to the GHQ/SCAP's Civil Information and Education Section (CIE), charged with responsibility for religious matters. Clissold's term in office as mission president lasted only until August 1949. In view of many years of absence from his business affairs, he had accepted the call with the understanding that he would be released as soon as the mission was established and running smoothly.[6]

---

4. As quoted in Tomigoro Takagi, "Hikari wo Futatabi Uketa Koro," *Seito no Michi* 5 (1961): 23–26; 62–65; and 126–27. Tomigoro received the letter on 3 February 1948. The author's translation of the Japanese original.

5. He would serve in this capacity again from 1963 to 1965.

6. Edward L. Clissold, "Personal Experiences in the Life of Edward L. Clissold," not dated. Following his return to Hawaii, Clissold succeeded E. Wesley Smith of the Hawaiian Mission and Weenig of the Central Pacific Mission to become the first president of the combined Hawaii Mission. For his activities, see Edward L. Clissold Oral History, interviewed by R. Lanier Britsch, 1976, James Moyle Oral History Program, LDS Church Archives.

The first full-term president of the Japanese Mission was Vinal G. Mauss, who succeeded Clissold in August 1949 and served for four years in office until October 1953, about eighteen months beyond the end of the occupation in April 1952. Mauss, born in Murray, Utah, on 16 October 1900, had served as a Mormon missionary in the prewar Japan Mission from 1922 until 1924, when his term was cut short by the decision to close the mission. In 1931, he moved to California and worked as a broker in real estate and insurance. He was a prominent Mormon in the Oakland area and was serving as bishop at the time of his call as mission president. He was set apart by George Albert Smith on 2 August 1949, and arrived in Yokohama on 20 August, accompanied by wife Ethel Louise and three children.

10.2.2. Finding a building for the Mission Home

When the mission was established in March 1948, the first order of business was to find a mission home in the bombed out city of Tokyo, not least because Clissold's legal presence in Japan beyond the probationary period of sixty days was contingent upon finding accommodation.[7] After "several days of continuous driving all over Tokyo in search of a house for rent or sale, all to no avail," he begins in his lengthy report of his experience, "I went for rest and relaxation to visit my former acquaintance."[8] His friend was not there, but his family was able to introduce Clissold to a Mr. Kawasoe, the business advisor of Prince Takamatsu. Through this contact, on Saturday, 20 March, Clissold was driven to see "the skeleton of a once palatial residence in a very good neighborhood opposite a park" in the Azabu district. He was immediately impressed with the site, which he learned on 22 March was for sale for ¥2,000,000 (or $10,000 at the prevailing, though overvalued, exchange rate). On 27 March, Clissold arranged for an inspection by architects and engineers from Kajima Construction Company (one of the largest construction companies in Japan) as well as church members with the Army Engineers, who "all pronounced the skeleton in good condition and the house very well constructed, as evidenced by the little damage done by three direct bomb hits."

Because of foreign exchange controls, the church did not have the means of raising the yen funds needed to purchase the property. Upon learning that the building belonged to a businessman by the name of Hachiro Shimizu,[9] Clissold decided to see the man. He writes:

---

7. Clissold, "Personal Experiences." See also "Pres. Clissold Takes Hold of New Field upon Arrival in Japan," *Deseret News*, Church Section, 24 April 1948.

8. Unless noted, all quotations of Clissold concerning the acquisition the Mission home are from Edward L. Clissold, "Acquiring a Mission Home in Japan," 5 December 1948, LDS Church Archives.

9. Hachiro Shimizu was president of Taiyō Engyō, Ltd., a company that took over the management of Mitsui's salt manufacturing operations in Niigata Prefecture in December 1947. Jinji Kōshinsho, *Zennihon Shinshi Roku* (Tokyo: Jinji Kōshinsho, 1950). According to Clissold's report, he also had a foreign automobile dealership. No doubt, he was a

I liked Mr. Shimizu right away and was sure we could do business with him. In fact, after much praying over this matter I felt we would eventually get the property no matter what the obstacles.

After exploring different options to get around the problem posed by the exchange controls, Shimizu agreed to "deed the property to the church free of encumbrances and that the church would give him a letter agreeing to pay him $10,000 or the then equivalent in yen when the law permitted." It turned out that no mention of foreign monetary value could be made in a commercial transaction, so the only feasible solution was to make "an agreement in which the sale price of the property would be mutually determined at a future date." Undaunted, Shimizu said that "he had decided to let us have the property and that the word of the Church through me was security enough for him."

On 19 April, in accordance with the requirement of the Religious Corporation Ordinance of 28 December 1945, Clissold filed a notification of incorporation for the "Japanese Mission of the Church of Jesus Christ of Latter-day Saints" in its English form with the Ministry of Education. On 20 April, with the certificate of incorporation issued,[10] Clissold and Shimizu signed the papers deeding the property to the church, in exchange for a "deposit slip showing $10,000 credited to a special account in the National City Bank of New York and my word that the money would be held there by the Church subject to his order." Clissold summarized his feeling at the conclusion of the six-week search for a mission home:

> We left his office with all the signed papers and I marvelled at the trust and kindness of the man. Mr. Yamamoto, a lawyer, remarked he had never seen anything like this piece of business in all his experience!

On 24 April, a contract was signed with Kajima Construction Company to refurbish the building for ¥2,700,000. Work began on 1 May and lasted until Thanksgiving Day, 25 November 1948.[11] In keeping with Japanese custom, on 19 May, an inauguration ceremony was held in which Kajima's vice president and the former owner Shimizu spoke, followed by a prayer offered in Japanese by Clissold. To give weight to the occasion, the LDS Church was represented by Chojiro Kuriyama, a prewar convert who was serving in the House of Representatives.[12] In the meantime, on 11 August 1948, the mission gave

---

well-to-do man for his day. According to government records, Shimizu had purchased the property only in October 1947 from Shinzo Mihashi, a prominent businessman affiliated with Mitsui. Tokyo Legal Affairs Bureau, Ministry of Justice.

10. The application to register the mission property was made on 21 April 1948. Tokyo Legal Affairs Bureau, Ministry of Justice.

11. Edward L. Clissold, "Mission Head Reports Japanese Mission Baptisms," *Deseret News*, Church Section, 15 December 1948.

12. Chojiro Kuriyama (1896–1971), a journalist educated at the University of Utah and Harvard, held executive positions at the *Mainichi Shinbun*, was elected to the House of Representatives from the Tokyo second district on a Japan Liberal Party ticket in April 1946, and served in the house until March 1953. He held several important appointments,

Mission home in Tokyo under extensive renovation, summer 1948. Courtesy LDS Church Archives.

Shimizu a check for ¥2,915,000, "paying him in full for the mission home property," indicating that Shimizu made an exchange gain of ¥915,000 by waiting for four months. As to the restoration work on the building, the final figure came out to be ¥6,220,000, and Kajima was paid in full on 23 December 1948. Clissold summed up his experience in acquiring the mission home in these words:

> Through [the CIE's] help and the channels which I understood through military government training I was able to purchase land, obtain materials, and labor, and establish the mission ready to receive my wife and five missionaries who arrived five [*sic*] months later.[13]

10.3. The Arrival of Missionaries

10.3.1. The First Missionaries

Concurrent with the progress of restoration work on the mission building, Clissold was busy getting ready to receive missionaries from North America and Hawaii. At the time of Clissold's call, two missionaries had already been called to assist him and were temporarily assigned to the CPM under Weenig's supervision. In making that assignment, the First Presidency wrote to Weenig that

---

including as chairman of the Foreign Affairs Committee and parliamentary vice minister of education. See Annex 4 towards the end of this volume for a more detailed biography.

13. Clissold, "Personal Experiences."

"Brother Clissold feels that after he has been in Japan for a while he will be able to make necessary arrangements for these two Elders and others to join him" and requested that Weenig "go over your list of missionaries, and be in a position to make recommendations to appoint some of them to Japan as soon as the mission headquarters has been established and conditions warrant their going."[14] In order to secure the clearance of the occupation authorities to allow missionaries to enter Japan, what Clissold needed was evidence of logistical support.

The help came from Shigenori Yajima, whom Clissold met on 19 March 1948 through their mutual acquaintance by the name of Nagai. Yajima, born in 1909, had served in the Japanese Imperial Army in Shanghai and Manchuria during World War II. After the conclusion of the war, in November 1945, he established a school to teach English conversation, called Clover Beikaiwa Gakuin (Clover American Conversation Institute). In time, the school grew in enrollment and American soldiers began to teach as volunteers.[15] By securing the address of a relative of Yajima's by the name of Tomokazu Iwata in Saitama Prefecture,[16] on 25 March, Clissold filed an application with the occupation authorities for clearance for four missionaries (Paul C. Andrus, Wayne McDaniel, Harrison Theodore Price, and Raymond Price) to enter Japan. He continued to file applications for more missionaries, including wife Irene, daughter Carol, and Kooji Okauchi on 11 May, Kenji Akagi, Kojin Goya, Jeaune Iwaasa, Kimiaki Sakata, and Kiyoshi Yoshii on 25 August, Bessie Yukiko Okimoto and Tomiko Shirota on 30 August, and Paul S. Carter, Daniel E. Nelson, and Murray L. Nichols on 29 October.[17]

While the entry of foreigners into Japan was in principle strictly controlled by the occupation authorities and "the provisions relating to missionaries regularly admitted" did not apply to the LDS Church for one year (because of its failure to carry out missionary work during the years immediately preceding the war), it appears that clearance for additional missionaries was liberally granted. This may have been a special favor extended to Clissold from his former colleagues at the CIE. Alternatively, it may well have simply reflected the more general relaxation of the entry restrictions after the summer of 1947.[18] To some extent, the ease with which

---

14. First Presidency, letter to Melvyn A. Weenig, 22 October 1947, LDS Church Archives.

15. Later, Mormon missionaries helped with the teaching. Both Yajima and his wife joined the LDS Church (6 May 1949 and 6 November 1948, respectively) and participated in its activities for some time. Shigenori Yajima, letter to author, 31 December 1995; and Shigenori Yajima, interview with author, Tokyo, 19 September 1996.

16. Tomokazu Iwata operated a large rubber factory in Saitama Prefecture. Yajima, interview. In the application, the name was erroneously spelled as Tomoichi, instead of Tomokazu.

17. In all subsequent applications, the address of the newly acquired mission home in Azabu was used. From late 1951, the mission was no longer required to file an affidavit for logistical support with the occupation authorities. Vinal G. Mauss, letter to Ernest A. Nelson, 3 January 1952, LDS Church Archives.

18. On 15 August 1947, as many as four hundred trade representatives from various countries were invited to enter Japan and to reside indefinitely, provided that the purpose

the LDS Church obtained clearance for additional missionaries may also have reflected the Christian orientation of the occupation. While the CIE was opposed to General MacArthur's idea of Christianizing Japan on the ground of separation of church and state, it may have been hospitable to the idea of bringing more Christian missionaries to indoctrinate Japanese thinking along Western Christian lines.[19]

Whatever the reason, missionaries began to arrive in Japan at a steady pace. The first group of five missionaries (Andrus, McDaniel, Okauchi, and the two Price brothers) arrived on 26 June 1948. Of the five missionaries, McDaniel and Ted Price had been working in the CPM since early December of 1947, while waiting for permits to enter Japan. Likewise, Andrus had been laboring in the CPM since February, and Okauchi and Ray Price since May. Until the mission home was completed, Andrus and Ray Price lived with the Merrills in Yokohama, while McDaniel, Okauchi, and Ted Price lived with the family of an air force officer, Spencer R. Savage, in western Tokyo.[20] Following the arrival (by plane) of wife Irene on 4 September, the second group of seven missionaries (Akagi, Goya, Iwaasa, Okimoto, Sakata, Shirota, and Yoshii) arrived on 21 October. They were all Nisei missionaries, and all but one came from Hawaii. Iwaasa, a Canadian, was scheduled to arrive with the first group, but immigration complications had prevented him from arriving in Honolulu in time.[21] They were followed by the arrival, on 28 December, of three missionaries (Carter, Nelson, and Nichols).

Mormon serviceman Ross Allen in front of Clover American Conversation Institute, used as the Ogikubo Branch of the LDS Church, circa 1948. Courtesy Einar Erickson.

10.3.2. The Changing Religious Climate in Japan

Japan's society went through a tremendous transformation during the occupation period, and with it the country's religious climate too changed. The initial phase of the occupation focused on reforming the social fabrics of society,

---

of the visit was deemed contributory to the goals of the occupation.

19. Eiji Takemae, *GHQ* (Tokyo, Iwanami Shoten, 1983).

20. Harrison Theodore Price, letter to author, 29 December 1995.

21. He labored in the CPM until the departure of the second group. Jeaune Iwaasa, letter to author, 16 January 1996.

Mission president Edward Clissold (left) with first five Mormon missionaries in postwar Japan. Courtesy Wade Fillmore.

including educational and religious institutions; the defeat of their country, and especially the collapse of the national myth, also created a spiritual vacuum. From around 1948, however, the broad aim of the occupation gradually shifted to economic rehabilitation. As economic prosperity slowly returned, the public's initial religious openness began to wane. Mormon missionaries arrived in Japan during this transition period, which explains why their experience and the mission's proselytizing success varied over time.

During the occupation period, a total of 108 missionaries from North America and Hawaii (including two locally called American missionaries, two mission presidents, and their wives) served in Japan. In addition, two native Japanese elders, Toshiro Murakami and Yotaro Yoshino, were called to serve full-time missions, with financial support from American members of the armed services in Japan. Both were from Takasaki, though living in Tokyo at the time of their calls, and were set apart on 30 December 1951.[22] From a force of only seventeen at the end of 1948, the number of missionaries quickly increased, reaching a peak of eighty-four in March 1951; it then declined as the Korean War progressed and an increasing number of mission-age Mormon men were drafted (see Figure 10.1). The church saw 527 baptisms (excluding American servicemen) during the occupation period, of which 332 (or 63 percent) were females.

---

22. See also "First Japanese Elders Called from Local Units," *Deseret News*, Church Section, 16 January 1952.

Figure 10.1. Number of Mormon Missionaries in Occupied Japan, June 1948–April 1952

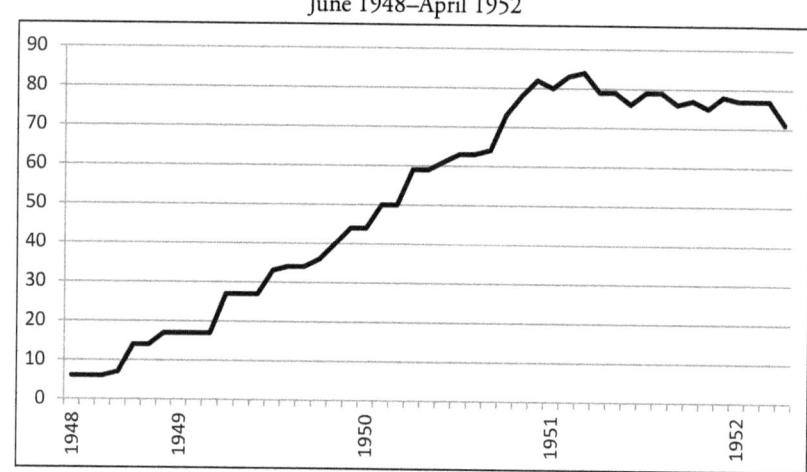

Author's estimates based on official records.

Initially, these missionaries found a particularly receptive soil in Japan, as the void created by the outcome of the war had undoubtedly led to much soul searching and an openness to things American. In fact, during the Clissold era, hundreds of Japanese people were flocking to the LDS Church. In April 1949, for example, over eleven hundred people were said to be attending various Mormon meetings in Tokyo alone.[23] Mormon apostle Matthew Cowley assessed the situation, as it stood in the summer of 1949, in the following words:

> In Japan we have one of the greatest opportunities for missionary service I have ever heard of or read of in the history of this Church. While I was there . . . [twenty-one hundred people] were coming to the missionaries; the missionaries were not seeking them out as we do in other missions of the Church.[24]

Not all the missionaries who served during the occupation period experienced the same fertile soil. After the arrival of Vinal Mauss as mission president, the situation began to change. In March 1950, a newly arrived missionary wrote in his diary:

> The Japanese Mission is quite a bit different than I was led to believe. . . . I was told back in the U.S. that the people were seeking out the L.D.S. missionaries and the people were ready for the Gospel. . . . [T]hey don't come looking for the Elders nor do they seem to be ready for the Gospel. . . . [T]hey aren't particularly interested in the Gospel.[25]

---

23. According to Clissold's report, as quoted by David O. McKay at the April 1949 general conference. *Conference Report*, April 1949.
24. *Conference Report*, September/October 1949.
25. Dennis H. Atkin, Journal, 11 March 1950.

To appreciate this sudden change in religious climate, one must understand the profound economic and political changes that were taking place in Japanese society at that time, largely attributable to a shift (or the "reverse course") in American occupation policy.²⁶ With the escalation of the Cold War in 1947, the emphasis of American policy shifted from demilitarization and democratization to economic recovery and independence, as a way of ensuring that Japan would become a prosperous ally of the United States. With the increasing chance of communist victory in China, the reorientation became even more pronounced in early 1949.²⁷ The outbreak of the Korean War in June 1950, moreover, increased the urgency to conclude a peace treaty with Japan.

In December 1948, in order to place the Japanese economy firmly on a rehabilitation path, the United States government demanded that a major stabilization program be adopted to arrest the mounting inflation that was running at the annual rate of over 100 percent, and it dispatched Detroit banker Joseph Dodge as special advisor to the GHQ/SCAP.²⁸ The Dodge plan, consisting of an austerity budget, a unification of multiple exchange rates, rationalization of administered prices, and gradual relaxation of economic controls, was implemented from April 1949. While the Dodge plan initially caused deflationary pressure, with price stability ensured and the market mechanism largely in place, the Japanese economy began to recover, and the pace of recovery became strong and steady after the outbreak of the Korean War. This marked improvement in economic conditions was accompanied by an increased prospect of regaining political sovereignty. As a way of excluding the Soviet Union from the peace treaty process, President Harry S. Truman and Secretary of State Dean G. Acheson appointed John Foster Dulles to conduct bilateral negotiations with potential signatory nations, and the agreed Treaty of Peace with Japan was signed by Japan and forty-eight countries in San Francisco on 8 September 1951, to become effective on 28 April 1952.

No doubt, the apparently increasing religious apathy of the people in the early 1950s was related to these economic and political developments. Mauss noted this negative correlation between temporal improvements and religious inclination in his annual report of 1951:

> With the expected peace treaty coming into effect it is generally felt there will naturally be considerable adjusting and a period of levelling off which may bring some difficulties. The past year has been a prosperous year for Japan as a whole and we have noticed it in the attitude of the people. There has developed the spirit of indifference which always seems to come when there is an abundance of material things.²⁹

---

26. Justin Williams, Sr., *Japan's Political Revolution under MacArthur: A Participant's Account* (Athens, Georgia: University of Georgia Press, 1979), 208–15.

27. Shiro Haga, *Mihon Kanri no Kikō to Seisaku* (Tokyo, Yūhikaku, 1951), 46.

28. Shinji Takagi, *Conquering the Fear of Freedom: Japanese Exchange Rate Policy since 1945* (Oxford: Oxford University Press, 2015), chapter 1.

29. "Report of Mission President," in "Mission Annual Reports, 1951," as quoted in Murray L. Nichols, "History of the Japan Mission of the L.D.S. Church 1901–1924"

Thus, the occupation period was by no means uniform in terms of religious climate. In fact, it was a period of declining religious interest, ending with a level of apathy not too much distinguishable from that observed in the succeeding years of relative economic prosperity. As a result, average annualized productivity declined from 3.7 (converts per missionary per year) in 1949 to 2.4 in 1951 and further to 1.7 in 1952.[30]

10.4. Clissold Completes His Mission

10.4.1. Achievements in Mormon Ministry

During Clissold's term as mission president, the work of the Japanese Mission spread from Tokyo (where some organizational structure was put in place) to other areas. The size of the missionary force, however, limited the geographical expansion to eight additional areas, six of which were places where members (including American military members) were known to reside: Kofu, Narumi, Osaka, Sapporo, Sendai, and Takasaki. He visited additional areas to explore, but it was Vinal Mauss, his successor, who actually launched missionary work in these and other places (see Section 10.5 below). Clissold also reached out to locate prewar members and held a reunion of some fifteen such members in April 1949.

Initially, Clissold's activities were confined to the Tokyo area. On 28 March 1948, in order to accommodate a greater number of participants, he moved the Japanese Sunday meeting from a private home in Gotanda to Yajima's Clover Institute in Ogikubo, where a formal Sunday school structure was instituted on 22 August, with Fujiya Nara as superintendent and Genkichi Shiraishi and Koshi Nakagawa as his assistants. On 6 April, he baptized Nara's wife Motoko and Miyoshi Sato, an investigator who had been active with the Nara Sunday group.[31] In the absence of missionaries, Clissold reached out to American servicemen for assistance, including nineteen-year old Einar Erickson of Ruth, Nevada, who often acted as his companion.[32] Active in missionary work among Americans and Japanese alike, Erickson was instrumental in the baptisms of eleven men, including Yutaka Shimotoku (baptized on 14 May 1949), and the conversion of several others. The mission's quarterly report entry for 18 May 1949, noting his departure from Japan, called him "a one-man mission force."

(MS thesis, Brigham Young University, 1957), 107.

30. The denominator is the average number of missionaries for a particular year, calculated from end-of-month figures.

31. Clissold, "Japanese Mission Baptisms."

32. Einar C. Erickson was born on 7 August 1928 in Ruth, Nevada and spent twenty-seven months in Japan from February 1947 to May 1949. He was stationed at the Tachikawa air base in western Tokyo. Einar C. Erickson, letter to author, 9 August 2014.

After the first group of missionaries arrived in June, Clissold began to make a systematic effort to locate the old prewar members. In a letter dated 20 July 1948, Clissold wrote to the Japanese members:

> As soon as the mission home is completed, I would immediately like to visit the members outside Tokyo. . . . (By the end of the year) the missionaries will begin to labor in the different areas where you members live. So please be patient for a little while. We intend to make up for our absence since the closing of the mission.[33]

Then he requested help in updating the church membership records. As a result of these and other efforts, both in Tokyo and later in other areas, about fifty (out of 184) prewar members had been found by April 1949.[34]

In the summer of 1948, the work began to spread beyond the Tokyo area. During his tenure, Clissold visited all the places where known members resided, including Narumi (1 August 1948), Takasaki (27 October), Osaka (19–21 November), Sapporo (9–10 March 1949), and Kofu (26 April). Among these places, Sapporo, Kofu, and Osaka had been the only viable centers of missionary activities in the prewar Japan Mission. Missionary work went on in Sapporo from October 1905 until the closing of the mission, Kofu from February 1907 until January 1922, and Osaka from September 1911 until the closing of the mission (see Section 5.6 in Chapter 5). On these visits, Clissold met such old-timers as Susumu Hisada, Tsuruichi Katsura, and Ichitaro Ohashi in Osaka, Tamano Kumagai, Kenji Ono, and Masaichiro Soman in Sapporo, and Muraji Yoneyama and his son Morizo in Kofu. In Narumi, Clissold met Tatsui Sato and called him to be the official translator for the mission. In Takasaki, a hundred miles north of Tokyo, there was a prewar member by the name of Morisaburo Sato, who had returned from spending the war-time years in China.[35]

American servicemen were a part of the LDS missionary scene during the occupation period. Einar Erickson (far left) poses with missionaries, fellow servicemen, and Japanese investigators. Courtesy Einar Erickson.

---

33. Takagi, "Hikari wo Futatabi Uketa Koro." The author's translation of the Japanese original.
34. McKay, *Conference Report*, April 1949. With deaths, emigration, and excommunications, the number on church records still living in Japan may have been 120–140.
35. Takagi, "Hikari wo Futatabi Uketa Koro."

Reunion of prewar converts at Tokyo mission home, 8 April 1949. Front row (right to left): Saigo, Takagi (non-member), Tada, Nara, Matsumoto, Suzuki, Kodama, Ishida; back row (right to left): Nara, Kuriyama, Matsuki, Takagi, Clissold, Shiraishi, Mochizuki, Watanabe, Nagao. Courtesy Toshiko Yanagida.

Clissold was frequently on the road, for both business and pleasure, visiting such places as Karuizawa, Nara, Sendai, and Shizuoka, and returned on a few occasions to the Narumi–Nagoya, Osaka–Kobe–Kyoto, and Takasaki–Tomioka areas. Towards the end of his tenure, in early June 1949, he visited the rice producing region of Niigata to investigate an offer of land to the LDS Church (see Section 10.5 below for details). In early August, shortly before his release, he visited Komatsu on the Sea of Japan coast to explore the prospect for missionary work. He gave a number of talks at educational or vocational institutions. On 5 October 1948, he spent some time with Prince Takamatsu at his mansion in Takanawa, discussing religious matters.

He accompanied Apostle Matthew Cowley, president of the Pacific Mission of the LDS Church,[36] on a tour of Japan during June and July 1949. By this time, Clissold had already been informed by the First Presidency that he would soon be succeeded by Vinal G. Mauss. Thus, this tour of Japan was the opportunity to report his mission to his superior and help him become familiar with the conditions in Japan. Cowley and his wife arrived in Japan on 11 June 1949 by plane from Honolulu. Immediately, Cowley left with Clissold by train to Nagoya where, on the following day, he ordained Tatsui Sato an elder and set him apart as

---

36. The Pacific Mission structure of the LDS Church (as an umbrella organization over individual missions) was discontinued in November 1949. It was decided that the various missions of the Pacific would be visited by any one of the general authorities on assignment.

Matthew Cowley (left), wife Elva, and Edward Clissold in front of Tatsui Sato home in Narumi, 23 June 1949. Courtesy Ryoko Murakami.

the interpreter and translator for the people of Japan "for the rest of your life."[37] While in Japan, Cowley travelled extensively, visiting such places as Hiroshima, Kamakura, Karuizawa, Kashikojima (in Mie Prefecture), Kobe, Kyoto, Nara, Okayama, Osaka, Takasaki, and Tenno. From 2 to 16 July, Cowley was in Hong Kong to install a new mission president.

10.4.2. The Dedication of the Mission Home

While Clissold thus visited several areas of Japan, met with most of the prewar members who still identified themselves as Mormons, and dispatched what few missionaries he had to several locations (see Section 10.5 below for details), his most lasting accomplishment was the acquisition and refurbishing of the mission home. It was thus fitting that the closing part of his mission was highlighted by a special conference, which featured a dedicatory prayer for that building. On Sunday, 17 July 1949, a general session was held at one o'clock in the auditorium of Junshin Girls' High School in Hiroo, just several blocks from the mission home. Those in attendance at the conference included Tsuruichi Katsura from Osaka, Tamano Kumagai from Sapporo, Morisaburo Sato from Takasaki, and Tatsui Sato from Nagoya (Narumi). Following the general session, a group of members and missionaries moved to the mission home to attend a dedicatory service, which was held at five o'clock.[38]

---

37. As remembered by Ted Price who was present at the scene. Harrison Theodore Price, letter to author, 27 November 1995.
38. Takagi, "Hikari wo Futatabi Uketa Koro."

In the dedicatory service, Clissold spoke and Cowley, after making a few remarks, offered a solemn prayer, dedicating the new mission home to divine purposes. Ted Price, quoting from his journal entry on 17 July 1949, reported to the Church Historian in Utah:

> In this inspired and inspiring prayer Elder Cowley gave thanks for the countless blessings in the Lord's work here to date, and went on to prophesy.... "THERE WILL SOME DAY BE MANY CHURCH BUILDINGS—AND EVEN TEMPLES BUILT IN THIS LAND." I was sitting on the first row in this gathering and clearly heard these words. As was my practice I wrote these important things in my journal that same evening while they were still fresh in my mind.[39]

In October 1980, Cowley's prophecy was partially fulfilled in the dedication of the Tokyo Temple on that very spot.[40] Clissold was released on 31 August 1949 and left for Hawaii on 5 September.

10.5. Geographical Expansion under Clissold and Mauss

The sequence in which new areas outside Tokyo were opened for missionary work might appear perplexing to an outside observer, particularly regarding the early openings of such seemingly insignificant places as Shibata and Tenno (opened prior to Niigata), Komatsu (opened prior to Kanazawa), and Hirao (opened prior to Hiroshima). To understand these puzzling facts, one must recognize that decisions were sometimes made in response to the whims of circumstances (see Appendix 10.1 below for a summary of how each area was opened to Mormon missionary work). As these and other places would turn out to be too small to sustain missionary activities, some of them would subsequently be closed down, with the few remaining members left behind (see Section 11.2.2 in Chapter 11). With the benefit of hindsight, the limited number of missionaries may well have been better deployed with more proactive planning.

10.5.1. Reaching the Members Outside the Tokyo Area

The choice of the first five areas opened outside Tokyo was logical, as members were known to be residing there. The very first was Narumi (pop. 22,000 in 1950), just outside of Nagoya, where Tatsui Sato and his family lived.[41] The

---

39. Harrison Theodore Price, letter to the Office of the Church Historian, 31 December 1956, LDS Church Archives; emphasis in original.

40. Clissold may have had a premonition that a temple would be built on the precise spot. Einar Erickson was present when Clissold made that statement. Erickson, letter to author. Cowley's prophecy fully came true with the dedication of the Fukuoka Temple in June 2000 as a second temple in Japan.

41. The population figures in this section are approximate for 1950, obtained from official government statistics, accessed 24 November 2015, http:// www.e-stat.go.jp.

priority given to Narumi is evident by the fact that Kojin Goya, a member of the second group of missionaries, was sent there with Ted Price on 22 October 1948, only a day after the group had landed in Japan, indicating that Clissold sent the two missionaries as soon as the arrival of additional missionaries had increased the missionary force from five to twelve. Immediately after the arrival of the third group on 28 December 1948, sets of missionaries were sent to Osaka (pop. 2 million) and Takasaki (pop. 93,000) in early January 1949.[42] With the arrival of the fourth group on 29 April 1949,[43] missionaries were sent to Sapporo (pop. 300,000) on 30 April and to Kofu (pop. 120,000) on 9 May. It is thus clear that these five cities with known members received the first allotments of missionaries. In each of these cases, Clissold had first visited the area to meet with the members, and subsequently sent the missionaries.

The first area without known members to be opened was Sendai (pop. 350,000), to which Kenji Akagi and Lynn Oldham were sent on 24 July 1949.[44] The decision to open Sendai was no doubt related to the fact that missionary work had been performed there in the prewar mission. In fact, Akagi and Oldham spent 24 July "attempting to locate old members." In the prewar period, missionaries were stationed in Sendai from July 1905 to October 1907, and again from July 1922 to the mission's closing in July 1924, and two baptisms were recorded (see Section 5.6 in Chapter 5).[45] Although Clissold was not successful in locating the members during his visit, he must have decided to open Sendai just in case the church could possibly capitalize on its early presence. It was not a bad decision in any case, because Sendai is a principal city in the Tohoku region and opening the city for missionary work would have been only a question of time. The presence of American military members in the city may also have facilitated the decision.

10.5.2. The Opening of Rural Districts

The early opening of the next three places, namely, the city of Shibata (along with the adjoining farmland of Tenno) in the rice producing region of Niigata Prefecture in July 1949, the city of Komatsu on the Sea of Japan coast in August

---

42. In a two-day conference held on 6–7 January 1949, the following assignments were made: (1) Kojin Goya and Ted Price to Narumi (Nagoya); (2) Murray Nichols and Kiyoshi Yoshii to Osaka; (3) Kooji Okauchi and Ray Price to Takasaki; (4) Kenji Akagi and Paul Carter to Denenchofu in Tokyo; (5) Daniel Nelson and Kimiaki Sakata to Takanawa in Tokyo, (6) Bessie Okimoto and Tomiko Shirota to the mission office and the Azabu vicinity; (7) Jeaune Iwaasa and Wayne McDaniel to Ogikubo in Tokyo; and (8) Paul Andrus as Tokyo District president or, effectively, assistant to the mission president.

43. Their arrival was delayed by three months because of a shipping strike. H. Lynn Oldham, telephone interview with author, 13 January 1996.

44. Tenno was opened on the same day. See Section 10.5.2 immediately below.

45. Shizuo Kikuchi and Hiroo Yamauchi, both males, were baptized, respectively, on 16 April and 30 June 1924, shortly before the mission was closed.

Mormon missionaries Oldham, Akagi, and Pusey (left to right) speak to a street crowd in Sendai, circa 1950. Courtesy H. Lynn Oldham.

1949, and the town of Hirao (along with the adjoining town of Yanai) on the Inland Sea coast of Yamaguchi Prefecture on the southern tip of Honshu in February 1950, may require some explanation.

First, the opening of Shibata (pop. 35,000), along with the adjoining farmland of Tenno in the village of Nakaura (pop. 9,000), was related to the offer of land to the LDS Church, made by a wealthy landholder named Noriatsu Ichishima in early 1949, in connection with the agricultural land reform of 1946–49 (see Appendix 10.2 below for details). Faced with the prospect of losing a substantial fraction of his land, and responding to the suggestion of his associate by the name of Seigo Mogi who had once lived among the industrious Mormon farmers of Mexico, Ichishima came up with the idea of donating the land (or its use) to the LDS Church. Clissold seriously considered using the land to build an agricultural school for the church, and even invited Cowley to inspect the place. Concerning the opening of Shibata and Tenno, Cowley spoke at a session of general conference on 30 September 1949:

> President Clissold and I went . . . to the city of Shibata. The mayor of the city heard that we were coming . . . and he asked us to come with him. We followed him upstairs over a bank building to a large chamber, and there assembled were one hundred and six of the leading businessmen and civic leaders of the city. . . . After he introduced us, he asked us to speak to those people as we saw fit.

District meeting held at Ichishima home in Tenno, 25 March 1951. Courtesy Gideon Stanford Jarvis.

The mayor requested that missionaries be sent and, on 9 August, Frances Parker and Katherine Takeuchi arrived in Shibata. The mayor turned over to them a large assembly room in another bank building for their use "until we have a chapel in the city." Cowley continues:

> Just outside the city of Shibata there is a man named Mr. Ichishima, who was the second largest landowner in Japan prior to the war. When we visited him, he had with him his banker, his lawyer, and two or three others, and after they had held a meeting together for an hour or so, they joined President Clissold and me, and Mr. Ichishima made a formal offer of his seventeen hundred acres, which surrounded his home, to the Church.... [He] said: "Well, send missionaries immediately, not next month, not next year, but immediately." And so the following week two missionaries were sent to Mr. Ichishima's home, and he turned part of his home over to them as a residence.... On his land is a private chapel which belongs to the estate, a Buddhist chapel, and they have boarded off the figure of the Buddha and are using it as a chapel for our Church. Mr. Ichishima is the organist for the services.[46]

The first missionaries to the area, Samuel Kalama and Wayne McDaniel, arrived at the Ichishima home on 24 July 1949 (the same day as the opening of Sendai) and held their first Sunday school on 31 July, with two hundred twenty people in attendance. After the arrival of the two lady missionaries in Shibata about a week later, the elders continued to live at the Ichishima home in Tenno. The Ichishima land deal never materialized, but church meetings continued on the Ichishima property until around early 1952, when the Tenno operation was

---

46. *Conference Report*, September/October 1949. This talk was reprinted as Matthew Cowley, "The Language of Sincerity," *Improvement Era* 52 (1949): 715, 762.

consolidated into Shibata. Still later in 1957, Shibata, too, would be closed (see Section 11.2.2 in Chapter 11).

Second, the opening of Komatsu (pop. 63,000) was made in apparent response to the request of a widowed woman by the name of Yukiko Nojima for missionaries. Nojima was introduced to the LDS Church through a relative by the name of Shigeo Masukawa who was a recent convert in Tokyo. The first missionaries, William Akau and Gerald Okabe, were sent to Komatsu on 18 August, and began to live at the Nojima home. Work would gradually shift to the neighboring principal city of Kanazawa (pop. 250,000), and the Komatsu Branch would be terminated in 1957 (see Section 11.2.2 in Chapter 11).

Finally, the opening of the small town of Hirao (pop. 6,000) was made in response to the request of a Hawaiian Mormon by the name of Koichi Takeuchi, who was a close acquaintance of Clissold.[47] Takeuchi was born in Hirao in 1889, emigrated to Hawaii in 1904 at the age of fifteen, worked on a sugar plantation on the island of Hawaii, and became successful in the construction business in Honolulu. Ever since joining the LDS Church in 1936, Takeuchi's desire was to see the church established in his home town, and he offered assistance to the church for that end.

To initiate the work, mission president Vinal Mauss sent Bessie Okimoto and Sarah Pule to Hirao on 27 February 1950. Upon arrival, they were met by Takeuchi himself, who had returned from Hawaii to give personal assistance. Not even a week later, Kojin Goya and William Oppie were sent to Hirao to assist the lady missionaries who had called Mauss for elders' assistance. As the town turned out to be too small to support four missionaries, the elders decided to locate themselves in the neighboring principal city of Hiroshima (pop. 300,000) on 6 March, and to commute to Hirao on Sundays or as circumstances necessitated.[48] Later, meetings began to be held concurrently in the slightly more populous adjoining town of Yanai (pop. 20,000) and, in 1954, the smaller Hirao operation was absorbed (see Section 11.2.2 in Chapter 11).

10.6. Organizational Developments under Mauss

10.6.1. Organization of Tokyo branches and the Mission Presidency

On 6 November 1949, as an initial step toward perfecting the organizational structure of the LDS Church in Japan, Mauss announced the upgrading of three meeting places in Tokyo (Aoyama, Ogikubo, and Yukigaya) to branch status. At the same time, in order to better reach the northern portion of Tokyo, it was decided to

---

47. The major economic activities of Hirao were farming, fishing, and salt making. In 1955, Hirao absorbed the smaller adjoining communities to increase its population to sixteen thousand. Hirao-chō, *Hirao-chō Shi* (Hirao, Yamaguchi: Hirao-chō, 1978).

48. William H. Oppie, interview with author, Kobe, 18 December 1995.

In April 1952, a full mission presidency was organized for the first time in Japan. From left to right: Peter Nelson Hansen (first counselor), Vinal G. Mauss, and Dwayne N. Andersen (second counselor). Courtesy Bill McIntyre.

create a unit in Ikebukuro out of the Aoyama Branch. Three older Japanese elders were called as branch presidents: Fujiya Nara for Yukigaya, Genkichi Shiraishi for Ogikubo, and Tomigoro Takagi for Ikebukuro, which came into existence at the beginning of 1950.[49] In March 1950, the Yukigaya Branch was moved to Meguro, becoming the Meguro Branch. On 7 October 1951, the four Tokyo branches (Aoyama, Ikebukuro, Meguro, and Ogikubo) were consolidated to form the Tokyo First Branch (from Ikebukuro and Ogikubo)—to be presided over by Takagi—and the Tokyo Second Branch (from Aoyama and Meguro)—to be presided over by Nara—in order to "get as perfect an organization as possible."[50]

On 13 April 1952, a full mission presidency was organized for the first time in the history of the LDS Church in Japan, with Peter Nelson Hansen as first counselor and Dwayne N. Andersen as second counselor. They were both older missionaries who had "answered the call of the Church to return to the mission field" to make up for the declining missionary force associated with the Korean War.[51]

---

49. Genkichi Shiraishi (born 1890) had been ordained an elder on 6 November 1948, while Tomigoro Takagi (born 1894) was ordained an elder on 8 November 1949. Japanese Mission, "list of ordained elders," not dated, LDS Church Archives.

50. Atkin, Journal, 8 October 1951. According to Japanese Mission, "Historical Records and Minutes" (10 September 1951), the reason given for this change was the "decreasing number of missionaries being called." It is not clear how much of this (given retroactively by the mission historian sometime during 1952) should be taken at face value because these branches were staffed mostly by Japanese members.

51. Japanese Mission, "Historical Records and Minutes."

10.6.2. Experimental Division Structure, 1950–52

During the occupation portion of the Mauss presidency, there were necessarily frequent changes in the geographical setup of the LDS Church in Japan. Of particular interest was an experimental structure, tried for sixteen months from 30 September 1950 to 7 February 1952, in which Mauss divided the mission into "divisions," each headed by a supervising elder. A division was made up of several districts, which in turn were made up of one or more branches. This seemingly duplicative and superfluous structure was designed, in the words of its originator, "to facilitate the work and give more help to the various districts and branches." Initially, four of the first five missionaries were given the assignment to supervise the divisions, with Ray Price over the Hokkaido Division, Wayne McDaniel over the Northern Division, Paul Andrus (released as the Tokyo District president) over the Central Division, and Ted Price over the Southern Division.[52]

It may be that the division structure was intended to be a vehicle for opening new areas for missionary work, whereby an older (in terms of age) and seasoned (in terms of experience) missionary could travel freely in a relatively large portion of the mission in search of a new area and, if found, easily incorporate it into one of the existing districts. Supervising elders did travel widely within their divisions. Most notably, it was under this division structure that supervising elder Ted Price opened Fukuoka for missionary work in November 1950. Others had similar intentions. In a report filed sometime in 1951, Andrus stated that the "city of Shizuoka with a population of 225,000 could be opened up with good success just as soon as missionaries are available" and that "the larger cities on the Chiba [sic] Peninsula have not yet been investigated but looks [sic] very well."[53] In early February 1951, shortly before his release, McDaniel visited such places as Fukushima, Kitakata, Koriyama, Morioka, Sakata, and Yokote, all in the Tohoku region.[54] Of these cities, Morioka was opened in October 1951.[55]

---

52. This organizational structure was announced at a special leadership meeting held in Tokyo on 30 September, and was communicated to the missionaries in a letter of 2 October. Initially, the Hokkaido Division consisted of the Asahikawa, Muroran, Otaru, and Sapporo Districts. The Northern Division consisted of the Gunma, Miyagi, and Niigata Districts. The Central Division consisted of the Kanagawa, Nagano, Tokyo, and Yamanashi Districts. Finally, the Southern Division consisted of the Aichi, Hiroshima, Ishikawa, and Osaka Districts. Japanese Mission, "Proselyting Area Histories, 1945–1952," LDS Church Archives.

53. Japanese Mission, "Proselyting Area Histories."

54. Atkin, Journal, 28 January–9 February 1951. Atkin was McDaniel's companion.

55. By then, Lynn Oldham was supervising elder for the Northern Division (which had incorporated the Hokkaido Division). The first missionaries, Gene Millward and Herbert Sproat (previously Oldham's companion), arrived in Morioka on 26 October 1951, accompanied by Oldham, Amy Igarashi, and Zona Walker, who were on their way to Hokkaido to help put the new Sunday school plan into effect. The decision to open Morioka may have been influenced by the fact that proselytizing work was performed there during the prewar mission, from 1907 to 1911 (see Section 5.6 in Chapter 5).

For this system to function well, it required a constant inflow of additional missionaries to support the opening of new areas, as well as the availability of older and seasoned missionaries who could be entrusted with a relatively large geographical responsibility. Perhaps contrary to the initial expectations of Mauss, it became increasingly clear that these conditions would not be met. First, with the breakout of hostilities on the Korean Peninsula in June 1950, and the associated drafting of a greater number of young Mormon men into military service, a sizable increase in the missionary force could no longer be expected. In fact, the number of missionaries peaked in March 1951 and declined subsequently through the end of the Korean War, even though the term of three years was applied to male missionaries called to Japan.[56] Second, with the release of the earlier groups of missionaries, who were almost all World War II veterans in their mid to late twenties, the average age of the remaining cohorts of missionaries began to decline. To supervise a division may have been a task beyond the ability of most of the remaining younger missionaries. For these and possibly other reasons, the division structure was terminated in February 1952, when two of the three supervising elders (Marvin Follett and Lynn Oldham) were released to return home.[57]

Whatever the original intent may have been, no additional area was opened for missionary work during this period, except for Fukuoka (pop. 400,000) in November 1950 and briefly Morioka (pop. 120,000) in October 1951, though there was a geographical enlargement to cover Mormon servicemen in Guam, Korea, Okinawa, and the Philippines.[58] In addition to the lack of missionaries, the general lack of geographical expansion in the early 1950s may also have reflected the seemingly rising religious apathy of the Japanese people, as earlier noted. In fact, average attendance at *all* meetings (presumably with double counting) throughout Japan declined from 2,046 in 1951 to 1,414 in 1952. Attendance at a typical meeting in a branch ranged from a few to forty.[59] Thus, this short-lived

---

Gene C. Millward, Journal, 24 October–17 December 1951. Morioka was closed on 30 November 1952.

56. The regular term of full-time missionaries from North America was two and a half years for foreign missions and two years for domestic missions. The length for those called to Japan was reduced back to two and a half years in 1959.

57. Earlier, on 19 June 1951, the four divisions were reduced to three, and many of the districts were combined to form larger districts, "in the face of a decreasing number of workers being called due to the present world conditions." Japanese Mission, "Quarterly Historical Reports," LDS Church Archives.

58. On 23 June 1951, Guam, Korea, Okinawa, and the Philippines were added to the mission, in view of the increasing number of Mormon servicemen in the area following the outbreak of the Korean War. Mauss made his first tour of Guam, Okinawa, and the Philippines from October to November and of Korea in late December, all in 1951. "Japanese Mission Head Reports Tour of Islands," *Deseret News*, Church Section, 2 January 1952 and "Pres. Mauss Reports Visits to Servicemen," *Deseret News*, Church Section, 16 January 1952.

59. Based on unidentified branch attendance statistics, in author's possession.

attempt at the division structure provides important insights into the aspirations, constraints, and realities under which the LDS Church was operating in Japan during the very last part of the occupation era.

10.7. Conclusion

This chapter has reviewed major ecclesiastical developments in the Japanese Mission of the Church of Jesus Christ of Latter-day Saints from its establishment in March 1948 to the end of American occupation in April 1952. During this period, the LDS Church was a beneficiary of the American military presence. The initial opening itself and the setting up of the mission home were supported by the military resources made available on a reimbursement basis. The missionaries received temporary accommodations at military member homes and installations, rode on military trains, used the military medical facilities for treatment, and otherwise enjoyed the status accorded by being the citizens of the occupying powers.

While the LDS Church received an extraordinary level of public attention at the very beginning of the Japanese Mission, religious apathy increased as the standard of living rose and political independence approached, and the church began to suffer from declining attendance and dwindling interest in its message. Even so, over five hundred individuals joined the LDS Church during the occupation period, three times the total prewar figure (see also Section 12.3 in Chapter 12). Japanese society's cultural affinity towards things American remained strong, even beyond the occupation period. The LDS Church may well have been able to capitalize on that favorable socio-cultural (if not religious) climate, had it increased the size of the missionary force during the rest of the 1950s, which it did not (see Section 11.2.1. in Chapter 11).

Ironically, American military presence in Japan became permanent at the conclusion of the occupation era. When Japan regained sovereignty under the terms of the San Francisco Peace Treaty in April 1952, the new Japan–United States Security Treaty (succeeded subsequently by the Treaty of Mutual Cooperation and Security of 1960) took effect, allowing the United States continued access to military installations in Japan. With the permanence of United States military presence, the presence of American Mormon servicemen also became permanent in the few places where the military bases were maintained, giving rise to the emergence of a parallel church structure within Japan, with little or no interaction with the local church. This parallel structure presents a sharp contrast to the close relationship that existed between American and Japanese Mormons during the occupation period.

American servicemen and missionaries of the occupation era made an important contribution to the establishment of the LDS Church in Japan. Throughout this early period, the church structure remained fluid, and there were frequent organizational changes. Even after the end of the occupation period, there would still be additional changes, including the closing of a few areas and the opening of some others. Yet, the geographical scope of the LDS Church in Japan would remain essentially unchanged until the latter half of the 1960s, with the exception of the geographical expansion of missionary work to Okinawa and Korea in 1956 (see Sections 11.2.2 and 11.3.2 in Chapter 11).[60] After all is said and done, the groundwork for Mormon ministry during the first twenty years of postwar Japan was laid by those men and women who had come riding on the Eagle's wings.

APPENDIX 10.1. SELECTED AREA BEGINNINGS BY DISTRICT

This appendix presents a brief summary of how areas were opened for Mormon missionary work during the occupation period.[61] The areas are organized by district, as constituted at the beginning of 1953, when the organizational structure of the LDS Church in Japan became relatively stable. In addition to the areas covered here, missionary work was conducted briefly in Morioka (pop. 120,000; from 26 October 1951 to 30 November 1952) and the Togura district (near Lake Towada) of Akita Prefecture (from 12 May to 2 August 1952).

HOKKAIDO DISTRICT

(1) SAPPORO (POP. 300,000). Sapporo was the fourth area to receive Mormon missionaries outside the Tokyo area. On 9 and 10 March 1949, mission president Edward Clissold was in Sapporo and visited with prewar Mormon converts Tamano Kumagai, Kenji Ono, and Masaichiro Soman. According to the arrangement made, Paul Andrus and Jeaune Iwaasa arrived in Sapporo on 30 April and were met at the station by Kumagai, who took them to a first-class Japanese inn called Yamagataya. Later, Kumagai called her boss at the newspaper office about the "big news" of the Mormon missionaries' arrival.[62] On 1 May, Andrus was featured in the *Hokkaido Shinbun* as an American servicemen who had returned to Japan as a Mormon missionary. On 15 May, the missionaries held a meeting on a nearby American military base. On 16 May, they visited the family of the late Takeo Fujiwara, the second and last Mormon presiding elder for Japan during the time when the mission was closed (see Section 8.3 in Chapter 8). The first Sunday school was held at Sapporo Keizai High School (on Fourteenth Street South) on 12 June, with fifty-two people present.

---

60. Outside of Okinawa and Korea, the only major area to be opened after the occupation period but before the 1960s was Okayama (pop. 200,000) in 1955. See Section 11.2.2 in Chapter 11.

61. Unless noted otherwise, information in Appendix 10.1 comes from Japanese Mission, "Proselyting Area Histories, 1945–1952;" "Historical Records and Minutes;" and "Missionary District Journal, November 1948–December 1949," LDS Church Archives. The population figures are approximate for 1950, obtained from official government statistics, accessed 24 November 2015, http:// www.e-stat.go.jp.

62. Paul C. Andrus, letter to author, 10 January 1996.

(2) OTARU (POP. 180,000). On 3 April 1950, preparation was made to open work in Otaru by Sapporo missionaries Dennis Atkin and Jeaune Iwaasa. On 11 April, all Sapporo missionaries and two members went to Otaru to hold a cottage meeting with over fifty investigators.[63]

(3) MURORAN (POP. 110,000). On 10 July 1950, Dennis Atkin and Jeaune Iwaasa visited Muroran, with a Mr. Itoi, to check into the possibility of opening the area for missionary work.[64] On 19 August 1950, Hideo Kanetsuna and Ray Price arrived in Muroran at 5:30 p.m. and found temporary lodging at the home of Norimitsu Kuribayashi at 135 Tokiwa-cho. On 21 August, they found living quarters in Bokai, a suburb of Muroran. Price returned to Sapporo and sent Keith Munk to be Kanetsuna's companion.

(4) ASAHIKAWA (POP. 120,000). Asahikawa was opened for missionary work by Daniel Nelson and Milton Shaum on 31 October 1950. During the first week, they lived at the Hokuetsu Hotel. They then secured a room in the home of Kotaro Bando at 6 jo-dori 2-chome.

NORTHERN DISTRICT

(1) NIIGATA (INCLUDING NIITSU, SANJO, SHIBATA, AND TENNO). Mormon missionary work in Niigata Prefecture began not in the principal city of Niigata, but in the smaller communities about fifteen miles southeast of the city, namely, the agri-based city of Shibata (pop. 35,000) and the adjoining farmland of Tenno (or Tenno-Shinden) in the village of Nakaura (pop. 9,000). The place name Tenno (or Tenno-Shinden) was essentially identical with the farm and the house that belonged to the wealthy landlord Noriatsu Ichishima, and so was the name of the train station.[65] As stated in the text (and further elaborated in Appendix 10.2 below), the decision to send missionaries to the sparsely populated rural district of Niigata Prefecture was directly related to the prospective offer of land made in the early summer of 1949 by the Ichishima family, in connection with the GHQ/SCAP-directed program of agricultural land reform.

To investigate the land, on 9 June 1949, mission president Edward Clissold arrived at Tenno-Shinden, accompanied by church members Fujiya Nara, Morisaburo Sato, and Tomigoro Takagi. Another visit was made on 30 June by Clissold, accompanied by Mormon apostle Matthew Cowley. On the basis of

---

63. Atkin, Journal.
64. Ibid.
65. After the divestiture of Ichishima's agricultural landholdings, on 1 September 1950, the name of the station was changed from Tenno-Shinden to Tsukioka. Keishikai, "Ichishima-ke no Kankei Shiryō" (Shibata, Niigata: Keishikai, 1991).

the arrangement made, on 24 July 1949, the first missionaries, Samuel Kalama and Wayne McDaniel, arrived at Tenno-Shinden, accompanied by Mr. Doi, Ichishima's agent. The first Sunday school was held at the Ichishima home on 31 July, with two hundred twenty people in attendance, about 25 percent of whom were adults.

On 3 August 1949, Clissold came to visit the place again. On 9 August, Frances Parker and Katherine Takeuchi arrived at Tenno-Shinden station, accompanied by Mrs. Mogi, the wife of Ichishima's associate. They were to live in the city of Shibata, just a few miles east of Tenno. The first Mutual Improvement Association (MIA) meeting was held in Shibata on 18 August.[66] From this time on, church meetings were held both at the Ichishima home in Tenno and in Shibata. On 27 August, Clissold arrived at Tenno-Shinden, accompanied by incoming mission president Vinal Mauss. Clearly, the purpose of the visit was to introduce the new mission president to Ichishima and the general conditions surrounding the prospective offer of land to the church.

The church authorities tried hard to negotiate to acquire the land. As late as 22 August 1951, Vinal Mauss visited the Ichishima estate, accompanied by Hilton A. Robertson of the Chinese Mission (then in San Francisco) in order to clear up "the mess concerning the property."[67] Robertson had been "sent by the First Presidency to assist in the final disposition of the property under Tenno, Niigata Prefecture which had been offered to the Church by Mr. Ichishima."[68] Ichishima was away, most likely on purpose, but the talk with his agent "was fruitless, disgusting to say the least."[69] LDS church records only state that the offer of land "had been withdrawn" and that Robertson and "President Mauss made several trips to Niigata and tried to see Mr. Ichishima but were denied an interview, nor did Mr. Ichishima offer any explanation for why the offer had been withdrawn." The elders moved out of the Ichishima home on 20 August 1951, but church meetings continued to be held there until around early 1952.[70]

Concurrently, work was extended to adjoining communities, such as Niitsu (pop. 37,000), Sanjo (pop. 47,000), Suibara (pop. 13,000), and the city of Niigata (pop. 220,000). This work was intermittent, initially performed by the missionaries living in Tenno–Shibata. Niitsu was opened for missionary work on 24 February 1950 by Ralph Sperry and Samuel Kalama, assisted by a Mr. Doi, a "prominent resident" of Shibata. On 3 March, they were finally established in

---

66. The Mutual Improvement Association was a Mormon "auxiliary" program offering young men and women wholesome recreational, educational, and other cultural activities.

67. Gideon Stanford Jarvis, Journal, 22 and 23 August 1951.

68. Japanese Mission, "Historical Records and Minutes," 5 September 1951.

69. Jarvis, Journal, 22 and 23 August 1951.

70. "Proselyting Area Histories" under "Tenno" sates that a special sacrament meeting was held on 14 October 1951 and that MIA meetings were being held in Tenno on Wednesdays in November. As the section on Tenno ends with an entry on 23 November, it is not possible at this time to identify exactly when the Tenno operation was terminated.

a private home after eight days of searching. Sanjo was opened in early 1951. The city of Niigata was officially opened by Robert Boyack and Darrell Hadley on 30 June 1951 when they moved into a home within the city, although it was closed on 22 May 1952. After Shibata and Sanjo were closed in the fall of 1957, the Niigata Branch (by then reopened again) became the only branch in Niigata Prefecture (see Section 11.2.2 in Chapter 11).

(2) Sendai (pop. 350,000). Sendai was the sixth place to be opened for Mormon missionary work outside the Tokyo area in the postwar era. On 11 and 12 March 1949, mission president Edward Clissold visited Sendai and met with members in the armed forces. On 24 July, the first missionaries, Kenji Akagi and Lynn Oldham, arrived and spent the day attempting to locate old members. They stayed with "Brother and Sister Versluis," who were with the occupation forces. The first Sunday school was held sometime in September.[71] The first convert, Masao Watabe, was baptized on 6 November 1949. A large Japanese house would be purchased on 16 December 1952, as the second church-owned meetinghouse in Japan (see Section 11.4.1 in Chapter 11).

(3) Yamagata (pop. 100,000). Work in Yamagata began on 19 September 1950, with missionaries Dennis Atkin and Kooji Okauchi commuting from Sendai. At that time, it took about three hours to get there from Sendai by train.[72] On 12 October 1950, Max Christensen and Howard Theodore Gorringe were stationed in Yamagata on a permanent basis.

Central District

(1) Tokyo (pop. 5.4 million, in twenty-three special wards). On 22 August 1948, the Ogikubo Sunday School (meeting at Clover American Conversation Institute) was fully organized, with Fujiya Nara as superintendent, Genkichi Shiraishi as first assistant, Koshi Nakagawa as second assistant, and Motoko Nara as secretary. The first classes were held in Denenchofu on 31 October 1948 and in Takanawa on 28 November 1948. On 29 May 1949, Nara was sustained as superintendent of the Denenchofu Sunday School; Shiraishi took over Nara's position at the Ogikubo Sunday School.

On 6 November 1949, mission president Vinal Mauss announced the upgrading of the Aoyama (changed from Takanawa in June 1949), Ogikubo, and Yukigaya (changed from Denenchofu) Sunday Schools to branches, each to be headed by a native Japanese elder. At this time, it was decided to create a unit out of the Aoyama Branch in the northern Ikebukuro section of Tokyo, so the

---

71. Oldham, telephone interview.
72. Atkin, Journal.

Ikebukuro Branch came into existence in January 1950. In March 1950, the Yukigaya Branch was moved to Meguro, thus becoming the Meguro Branch. Apparently, the Aoyama Branch remained in central Tokyo, which the mission staff (including Tatsui Sato) continued to attend.

In September 1951, it was decided to consolidate the four Tokyo branches (Aoyama, Ikebukuro, Meguro, and Ogikubo) to form the Tokyo First Branch (from Ikebukuro and Ogikubo) and the Tokyo Second Branch (from Aoyama and Meguro). This was implemented in early October. A large Japanese house would be purchased in the Namikibashi section of Shibuya on 10 April 1953 in order to accommodate these two branches, which began to meet in the same building. This was the third church-owned meetinghouse in Japan (see Section 11.4.1 in Chapter 11).

(2) YOKOHAMA (POP. 950,000). Yokohama, a port city located thirty miles south of Tokyo, is part of Tokyo's metropolitan area. It was in Yokohama that mission president Edward Clissold landed on 6 March 1948 and spent the first few days at the home of William Paul Merrill, an American civilian employee of the occupation forces. After the arrival of the first group of missionaries on 26 June 1948, two of them, Paul Andrus and Ray Price, labored in Yokohama while living at the Merrill home, pending the completion of the mission home. The work in Yokohama continued for some time with missionaries resident in Tokyo but was terminated in July 1949 when Kenji Akagi was transferred to Sendai. On 28 November 1949, Marvin Follett and Wayne Herlin were permanently assigned to Yokohama.

(3) TAKASAKI (POP. 93,000). On 27 October 1948, mission president Edward Clissold and wife Irene went to Takasaki and met Morisaburo Sato, a prewar convert.[73] During this visit, Clissold also met with some of the dignitaries of the city, including the mayor and members of the city council. A man by the name of Nakahara invited the missionaries to live at his house if and when some were assigned. On 5 January 1949, Kooji Okauchi and Ray Price spent the day at Takasaki, making plans for opening the area. On 10 January, they arrived in Takasaki to live temporarily with Mr. Nakahara.

Morisaburo Sato had spent his war-time years in China, being engaged in trading business and, later, petroleum sales. He had returned to Takasaki after the war.[74] At the priesthood session of the general conference held on 4 April 1949, David O. McKay, a counselor in the LDS Church's First Presidency, quoted from the report of Clissold:

---

73. Morisaburo Sato later became a custodian of the Takasaki building. Toshiko Yanagida, telephone interview with author, 11 January 1996.

74. Tomigoro Takagi, "Nihon Dendōbu no Kaiko," *Seito no Michi* 2 (1958): 29–31.

One of the faithful members of the former mission and a man of considerable influence in Takasaki, a city ninety miles north of Tokyo, has been of great assistance to the missionaries assigned to that district. He helps them with a large Sunday School and several weekly meetings, including an MIA gathering of over four hundred young people.[75]

The first person to be baptized into the LDS Church from Takasaki (on 2 April 1949), Toshio Murakami, became the first Japanese full-time Mormon missionary, along with Yotaro Yoshino (also from Takasaki) who was baptized on 28 May. Murakami and Yoshino were both ordained elders and set apart for full-time missions on 30 December 1951.[76] Following Clissold's visit on 5 May 1949, Howard Theodore Goringe and Kooji Okauchi opened a Sunday school in the adjoining city of Tomioka on 15 May 1949 while living in Takasaki.

On 29 October 1951, the LDS Church purchased a large Japanese-style house in Takasaki. Besides the mission home, this was the first church-owned property in Japan and the only one during the occupation period. The registration of the property was made in the name of the Corporation of the Presiding Bishop of the Church of Jesus Christ of Latter-day Saints, 47 East South Temple Street, Salt Lake City, Utah, U.S.A.[77] In 1958, Takasaki absorbed Maebashi to become the Gunma Branch (see Section 11.2.2 in Chapter 11).

(4) KOFU (POP. 120,000). Kofu was the fifth place to be opened for Mormon missionary work outside the Tokyo area in the postwar era. In the early afternoon of 26 April 1949, mission president Edward Clissold arrived in Kofu, accompanied by Shigenori Yajima. They tried to locate some of the old members, but the addresses proved useless. The mission records state what transpired next:

> Having exhausted every possible resource, President Clissold offered a silent prayer as he walked along the crowded street asking the Lord to direct him to someone who knew something about the people he was seeking. A few moments later he was in the Military Government Office and felt impressed to ask the corps of translators for any information they might have. As the Military Government Office had closed, all the interpreters had left for the day with the exception of one. He remembered seeing a Book of Mormon in someone's house and although the incident occurred over twenty-five years ago, he finally associated the book with the name of Yoneyama, which was the name of one of the members whom President Clissold was seeking. In the course of a few minutes he had Brother Yoneyama on the phone. . . . [He] and his father arrived at the station one-half hour before the train left and gave President

---

75. *Conference Report*, April 1949.
76. Soon after returning home, Murakami became disenchanted with the church. Ryoko Murakami, letter to author, 9 November 1997; telephone interview with author, 17 November 1997. Yoshino later went to the United States to study at Brigham Young University, Columbia Business School, and Stanford Business School. He briefly returned to Japan in 1962 and served as counselor to Dwayne Andersen in the mission presidency.
77. Takasaki branch office, Maebashi Legal Affairs Bureau, Ministry of Justice.

Clissold some valuable information about Kofu and the saints who were still living in the area.

In consequence, Hideo Kanetsuna and Ray Price were sent to Kofu. On 6 May 1949, they spent the day in Kofu and returned to Tokyo at night. On 9 May, they left for Kofu to open the area for missionary work. The first Sunday school was held on 29 May.

(5) MAEBASHI (POP. 97,000). On 22 April 1950, Ray Price and William Sproat, who had been living in Takasaki but laboring in Maebashi, physically relocated to Maebashi. Maebashi was consolidated back into Takasaki in 1958 (see Section 11.2.2 in Chapter 11).

(6) MATSUMOTO (POP. 86,000). The Nagano District was opened for missionary work on 22 June 1950 by Kenji Akagi and Dallas Peterson, who began their work in Higashi Minowa, twenty miles south of Matsumoto in the Japan Alps. On 2 July 1950, Akagi and Peterson visited the city of Matsumoto, a "very nice city, quite clean, with about 85 thousand people living there." They moved from Higashi Minowa to Matsumoto on 1 September 1950.

South Central District

(1) NARUMI (POP. 22,000). On 1 August 1948, mission president Edward Clissold came to Narumi, just outside the city limit of Nagoya, and was greeted by a large number of Sunday school children meeting at the Tatsui Sato home. On 29 August, Paul Andrus and Ray Price came, accompanied by prewar member Tomigoro Takagi.[78] On 22 October, Kojin Goya and Ted Price came to open Narumi for missionary work and, on 8 November, began to hold regular meetings. On 22 November, Clissold made a surprise visit to Narumi. Narumi was closed in March 1956 and consolidated with Nagoya (see Section 11.2.2 in Chapter 11).

(2) NAGOYA (POP. 1 MILLION). The history of the LDS Church in Nagoya is intertwined with that in Narumi. When mission president Edward Clissold and his missionaries came to Narumi on different occasions in 1948, they first arrived in Nagoya and stayed with an American military family stationed there, by the name of Major Bock and wife Comfort. It appears that work in Nagoya officially began with the calling of Lynn Oldham and Kimiaki Sakata on 29 April 1949, which allowed the other two missionaries (Daniel Nelson and Ted Price) to labor in Nagoya while leaving them in Narumi. A separate branch was opened in

---

78. Tatsui Sato, letter to Reed Davis, 25 September 1948.

Nagoya in 1950 and, in March 1956, absorbed the Narumi Branch (see Section 11.2.2 in Chapter 11).

(3) Osaka (pop. 2 million). On 19 November 1948, mission president Edward Clissold arrived in Osaka in the evening. Prewar convert Tsuruichi Katsura was to meet him at the station, but they missed each other as they were at different ends of the station. Clissold stayed at the Naniwa Hotel that night. On 20 November, he met Katsura, and later Susumu Hisada and Ichitaro Ohashi, at the Katsura home.

On 7 January 1949, Murray Nichols and Kiyoshi Yoshii were assigned to labor in the Osaka and Kyoto areas. In the evening of 12 January, they arrived at Sannomiya station in Kobe, where they were to stay at the house of American member William Paul Merrill, who had just moved from Yokohama in early December. The first trip to Osaka was made on 14 January. They looked for living quarters and meeting places in Kobe, Osaka, and Ashiya (a midpoint between the two cities), finally settling in the Ishibashi (Toyonaka) area, north of the city of Osaka. On Sunday, 30 January, they held meetings in Kyoto at the house of an American Mormon woman by the name of Kundrick in the morning and at the Katsura home in Osaka at night.

The first public meeting was held on Sunday, 13 February at the "Japan Democratic Hall" in Osaka, with about thirty in attendance. On 20 February, the meeting was held at the same place, but they used an "upstairs room, the auditorium being in use, only few present." It is not certain what building the "Democratic Hall" referred to, as American soldiers had different names for buildings than Japanese did.[79] Tomigoro Takagi quotes a story told him by Ei Nagao (a prewar Mormon convert) to the effect that she had attended Sunday school sessions held at "Osaka Kōkaido," but that the meeting place (evidently referring to what the American missionaries called the "auditorium") was inappropriate for church meetings as it was too large.[80] Most likely, the building was "Chūō Kōkaidō" located in Nakanoshima, the heart of Osaka.

Later, Katsura and other members located a more suitable meeting place at Yodogawa High School (renamed Yodogawa Girls' High School in 1953) in Juso, close to a commuter train junction linking Kobe, Kyoto, and Takarazuka. Through the generosity of Toshio Hirata, the principal of the school, the LDS Church was given use of the school facilities free of charge, including utilities. The first Sunday school in Juso was held on 8 May 1949, with about a hundred forty in attendance, including Mamoru Iga, Katsura, and Nagao. In the summer of 1950, another branch was opened in Abeno in southern Osaka.

---

79. Neither Mamoru Iga nor Murray Nichols had a recollection of where the building was located, when the author contacted them. Mamoru Iga, letter to author, 15 June 1997 and Murray L. Nichols, letter to author, 18 January 1996.

80. Takagi, "Nihon Dendōbu no Kaiko," 31.

(4) KOBE (POP. 760,000). Kobe, a port city twenty miles west of Osaka, is located on the western end of the Hanshin (Osaka–Kobe) metropolitan area. As American member William Paul Merril had moved to Kobe from Yokohama at the beginning of December 1948, in January 1949, the first missionaries to the Osaka area, Murray Nichols and Kiyoshi Yoshii, initially stayed in Kobe at the Merrill home until living quarters could be found closer to Osaka. They arrived at Sannomiya station on 12 January and stayed in Kobe until late February. It was not until October 1957 that the first permanent branch of the LDS Church, the Sannomiya Branch, was established in the city of Kobe (see Section 11.2.2 in Chapter 11).

(5) KYOTO (POP. 1 MILLION). Kyoto is the ancient capital of Japan located some forty miles northeast of Osaka. Mission president Edward Clissold visited Kyoto in conjunction with his trip to Osaka in November 1948 and attended a servicemen's meeting on 21 November. Kyoto was included in the geographical assignment of the first missionaries sent to Osaka, Murray Nichols and Kiyoshi Yoshii. It is possible that Kyoto was included because an American Mormon woman by the name of Kundrick was living there. The missionaries held a meeting at her home on Sunday, 30 January. It was not until February 1950 that Yoshii came to live in Kyoto, along with Hal Furguson, as permanent missionaries. They lived at the home of Uzuru Hotta for about two months. Kyoto's first Mormon convert, Tomio Katayama, was baptized on 11 June 1950.[81]

(6) KOMATSU (POP. 63,000). Mission president Edward Clissold first visited Komatsu on 12 August 1949 shortly before he was released to go home. On Thursday, 18 August 1949, William Akau and Gerald Okabe arrived in Komatsu. Shigeo Masukawa, a recent Mormon convert in Tokyo, was to meet the missionaries at the station but failed to do so because of misunderstanding. After a short search, they located the home of Yukiko Nojima, where Clissold had earlier made an arrangement for them to stay.[82] On the following day, the "assistant mayor . . . suggested to call the airport commanding officer. . . . The army officer arrived and it was learned that he was a Mormon also from Utah, by the name of Lt. Law. He offered the missionaries every possible aid."

The Mormon missionaries arranged English classes to be taught at Rojo Junior High School. The first Sunday school was held at Zenrinkan at 10 a.m. on 28 August, with thirty-nine people present. "Brother Masukawa first gave a short introductory talk and Elder Okabe conducted the meeting from then on." The first convert, Kan Watanabe, was baptized on 22 April 1950. For a time, the

---

81. Tomio Katayama, interview with author, Kobe, 31 December 1995.

82. Yukiko Nojima soon joined the LDS Church and became an exemplary member but died of cancer. Atkin called her "a wonderful lady whose only and greatest concern is the welfare of the missionaries." Atkin, Journal, 11 October 1952.

Komatsu missionaries also labored in the neighboring town of Daishoji (pop. 14,000). In September 1957, the Komatsu Branch was closed and the members requested to attend the Kanazawa Branch, more than an hour away by public transportation (see Section 11.2.2 in Chapter 11). Work in Komatsu would resume only in May 1970.

(7) KANAZAWA (POP. 250,000). Kanazawa is the principal city of the Hokuriku region, lying twenty miles northeast of Komatsu. On 1 June 1950, William Akau and Murray Nichols first began missionary work there, while living in Komatsu. They commuted daily but, on 24 July 1950, moved permanently from Komatsu to Kanazawa.

Southern District

(1) HIRAO (POP. 6,000)–YANAI (POP. 20,000). In the late afternoon of 27 February 1950, Bessie Okimoto and Sarah Pule, both of Hawaii, arrived in Yanai in Yamaguchi Prefecture and were met by Koichi Takeuchi and taken to their living quarters in Hirao. On 6 March 1950, mission president Vinal Mauss called Kojin Goya, the mission recorder at the time, into his office and asked him to go to assist the lady missionaries in Hirao as a result of a telephone conversation with them. It was a "sudden decision." On Friday morning, Goya caught a train to Nagoya, picked up William Oppie, and continued on to Yanai, arriving there on the following day, and took a taxi to Hirao. Meetings began in Yanai from 1950. In February 1954, the Hirao Branch would be consolidated into the Yanai Branch (see Section 11.2.2 in Chapter 11).

(2) HIROSHIMA (POP. 300,000). On 16 March 1950, after spending several days in Hirao, the missionaries decided to establish headquarters in Hiroshima. In Hiroshima, on 19 March, Kojin Goya ran into an acquaintance from Tokyo by the name of Yarita. To Goya, it was "in answer to the prayer and desire . . . we elaborated on the problems of housing. . . . Yarita-san consented to help us and so we made arrangements to meet him on Monday at the Hiroshima station." Monday, they "arrived in Hiroshima from Hirao where we are temporarily quartered. This day we spent the whole day looking for homes in and around Hiroshima." They found a temporary place and returned to Hirao to get their belongings. After a few days, a woman came to the house who claimed to have had a dream about two angels and insisted that the missionaries come and live with her family for a nominal rent.[83] The woman, Miyoko Kamotani (born 30 August 1913) and daughter Michiko (born 28 February 1937) were both baptized into the LDS Church on 1 October 1950.

---

83. Oppie, interview.

An interesting incident took place while Goya and William Oppie were in Hiroshima. On 22 May, apparently in response to a request of the mission president, they left by train to Nagasaki Prefecture to locate Susumu Hori, a prewar convert from the Osaka area. They travelled by way of Shimonoseki and Moji, arrived in Kikitsu, and took a bus to what appears to be the town of Tarami (fifteen miles east of the city of Nagasaki) to locate Hori. "He was filled with tears and joy." In June 1951, Hori became a ground keeper for the mission home.[84]

(3) Fukuoka (pop. 400,000). Fukuoka is the principal city on the island of Kyushu. Ted Price, supervising elder of the Southern Division, arrived in Fukuoka on 14 November 1950 to make arrangements for the opening of the area for missionary work. Pursuant to the arrangement made, on 24 November, Murray Nichols and Robert Swenson arrived and began to live in the house of Sumiko Fukuda, the widowed younger sister of Masako Fukuda, then a Japan Socialist Party member of the Diet.[85] The first Sunday meeting was held on 26 November at Sumiyoshi Women's Hall. The first baptisms, Kyoko An and Yuki Sato (both women), took place on 13 April 1952.

Robert Swenson had earlier been in Nagoya, as a member of the Fifth Air Force band from January 1947 to May 1949. It was while there that he met and married his wife (in September 1948). As immigration restrictions prevented him from taking his wife to the United States when he returned home in May 1949, he sought an early discharge from the air force in November 1949 by availing himself of the special provisions applicable to those entering the ministry, and returned to Japan as a Mormon missionary. During his mission in Japan, he lived in Nagoya with his wife for about six months, during which time he baptized her (in June 1950). In April 1952, he was released and allowed to return home, this time with his wife.[86]

Appendix 10.2. The Ichishima Land Deal

The Ichishima family made a fortune in the seventeenth century from selling medicine and marine products, and they began to accumulate land holdings in the eighteenth century by reclaiming the vast wetlands of Niigata and by taking advantage of the favors received from the ruling families in exchange for its generous donations. In the latter part of the nineteenth century, the family was also involved in banking and politics,[87] establishing their residence in Tenno in the village of Nakaura.

---

84. Oppie, interview; Oldham, telephone interview; and Yanagida, telephone interview.
85. Nihon Tosho Sentā, *Nihon Josei Jinmei Jiten* (Tokyo: Nihon Tosho Sentā, 1993).
86. Robert A. Swenson, telephone interviews with author, 25, 28 and 30 January 1996.
87. Noriatsu's grandfather was the founding president of the Fourth National Bank in Niigata in 1874, and his father was the first member of the Imperial Diet's House of

As an heir to the family wealth, Noriatsu Ichishima (1893–1959), upon graduation from Keio University in Tokyo, launched a major program to reclaim a nearby lagoon (called Fukushima-gata), the title to which he had fully obtained in 1911. His ventures were so successful that, by 1924, a government survey identified Noriatsu's agricultural landholdings, huge by any standard to begin with, as the largest in the prefecture of Niigata and the third largest in Japan, with 1,350 hectares (approximately 3,300 acres) of agricultural land that was being cultivated by 2,488 tenant households. In the following year, his income was reported as ¥297,900, the highest in Niigata. His residential property was 28,000 square meters (approximately 300,000 square feet) in size, and included thirteen buildings with a total floor space of 2,000 square meters (22,000 square feet). At the end of World War II, his wealth remained undiminished. As of 3 March 1946, the government assessed his assets at ¥15,420,000, the third highest in Niigata, which compared favorably with the asset value of ¥26,000,000 claimed by the fifteenth wealthiest person in Japan at that time.[88]

During the course of post-surrender reforms, the seemingly feudalistic system of tenant farming caught the attention of the occupation authorities. To be sure, the wide-spread practice of tenant farming was not a vestige of feudalism, as there had been a major land reform in the 1870s, clearly defining property rights and giving land to the cultivating farmers. Concentration of landholding actually proceeded subsequent to the land reform of the 1870s, owing to the bursts of declining agricultural prices in the 1880s and 1920s, which forced many of the farmers to sell their land.[89] Be that as it may, by the end of the war the concentration of agricultural land ownership had reached the point where only about 30 percent of all the farmers owned enough land for their sustenance. In terms of acreage, almost half of all agricultural land was cultivated by tenants, with about two thousand individuals holding one hundred acres or more each.[90] The Japanese themselves had earlier attempted to tackle the problem of tenant farming on several occasions, but no major reform was possible given the resistance of the politically powerful landlords. They needed the support of the occupation authorities to implement any substantive change, but the GHQ/SCAP went far beyond what the Japanese had thought reasonable.

With the passage of the Agricultural Land Adjustment Law (and the associated Owner-Farmer Establishment Special Measures Law) in October 1946, absentee landlordism was wholly prohibited. A landlord could keep up to one hectare (or approximately two and a half acres) in the community in which he

---

Peers appointed from Niigata in 1890. Keishikai, "Ichishima-ke no Kankei Shiryō" and "Echigo no Kyodai Jinushi: Ichishima-ke," not dated.

88. Keishikai, "Ichishima-ke no Kankei Shiryō" and "Echigo no Kyodai Jinushi."

89. Toshihiko Kawagoe, "Nōchi Kaikaku," in *Sengo Nihon no Keizai Kaikaku: Shijō to Seifu*, ed. Yutaka Kosai and Juro Teranishi (Tokyo: Tōkyō Daigaku Shuppankai, 1993).

90. Kazuo Kawai, *Japan's American Interlude* (Chicago: University of Chicago Press, 1960): 171–73.

lived. An actual cultivator was allowed to own as much as three hectares (approximately seven and a half acres) for his own use. Except in the extreme north, all land in excess of these limits, as well as absentee-owned land, was to be bought up by the government, which in turn was to sell it on easy terms to former tenants.[91] As it turned out, with the rampant inflation and the time it took to complete the transfer of land, the predetermined land prices became worthless when the payment was actually made by the government to the landlords; thus the program amounted to a virtual confiscation of land.[92] Much of the actual work was done by locally elected land commissions, each consisting of five tenant farmers, two owner-cultivators, and three landlords.[93] Most of the transfers had been made by late 1949, with the registration of titles remaining to be completed.

The questions that naturally arise, then, are what Ichishima was trying to accomplish by donating land (or use thereof) to the LDS Church and why he chose not to do so after all. Although the full answers to these questions are lost to history, a few remarks may be offered. First, in 1949, there was a small probability that the conservative cabinet of Shigeru Yoshida, which came into power in January 1949, would scale down, if not completely rescind, the scope of land reform. The minister of agriculture was an outspoken critic of agricultural land reform and was seeking to obstruct its completion. In fact, it was the action of the minister of agriculture, supported by the minister of finance, that halted the land registration work in October 1949, to which Douglas MacArthur issued a sharp warning. A contemporary American observer, writing in the early part of 1950, noted the "lingering uncertainties" and remarked that "conservative elements, in many cases genuinely believing that the reform is not in Japan's best interest, have not surrendered, and can be expected to continue their efforts to bring it down, overtly if feasible and otherwise by indirection."[94] Possibly, offering the LDS Church use of his land was conceived as a convenient means of effectively holding onto his land until the dust settled.

Second, in any case, Ichishima must have been resigned to the fact that he would have to yield the major portion of his agricultural land that was being cultivated by tenant farmers. In fact, most of the transfer transactions had already been completed at that time, although the registration was being halted. Thus, the land in question was strictly the land that was not being cultivated by tenants, namely, the newly reclaimed areas around the lagoon and possibly the lagoon itself. This conjecture is consistent with the statement of Apostle Matthew

---

91. Kawai, *American Interlude*, 171–73.

92. In some cases, an acre of land was sold at a price "equivalent to the black-market price for one carton of cigarettes and was then sold to the former tenants at a correspondingly low price payable in instalments spread over a thirty-year period at 3.2 percent interest." Kawai, *American Interlude*, 173; also Kawagoe, "Nōchi Kaikaku," 167–68.

93. Kawai, *American Interlude*, 171–73.

94. Robert A. Fearey, *The Occupation of Japan: Second Phase, 1948–50* (New York: Macmillan, 1950), 95.

Cowley that Ichishima was offering the church "1,700 acres, which surrounded his home." Concerning this land, the determination of eventual ownership would be made by the local land commission, over which Ichishima must have yielded some influence. By offering the LDS Church use (if not the ownership) of his land, he may have been trying to establish that the land was being used for public good, so as to sway the decision of the land commission in his favor.

Third, if he was genuinely interested in making an outright donation of the land, it may have been because he had no heir at that time. Then, the decision not to give the land after all may be related to the fact that he later adopted a son (named Noriaki), who was born in 1949. Voluntarily or involuntarily, sometime in the 1950s, Noriatsu sold the lagoon to the government, permanently moved to Tokyo, and died there in 1959.[95] Ironically, his adopted son decided not to succeed the Ichishima family, so the family ceased as a legal entity on 8 May 1968.[96] On the government-owned lagoon, now fully reclaimed, currently stands a wild-bird observation station. The residential compound, with all the buildings, is now a designated cultural treasure of the prefecture of Niigata and is maintained by the non-profit foundation *Keishikai*. It is a popular spot for tourists who come to savor the life style of a giant landholder of prewar Japan.

---

95. Futazo Nakamura, office chief, Keishikai, interview with author, Tenno, Toyouracho, Niigata, 10 March 1998.

96. Keishikai, "Ichishima-ke no Kankei Shiryō" and "Echigo no Kyodai Jinushi."

Chapter 11

Enlarging the Borders: Modern Ecclesiastical Developments, 1952–68

11.1. Introduction

This chapter reviews major ecclesiastical developments in the Church of Jesus Christ of Latter-day Saints in Japan from the end of the occupation in April 1952 through the end of August 1968. This period saw the LDS Church experience real, sustained growth in Japan for the first time. The missionary force tripled, while the membership increased more than ten-fold. The church purchased properties and began to build meetinghouses throughout the country, and called local members to assume greater leadership roles. Five men successively presided over the church as mission president: Vinal G. Mauss of Oakland, California (August 1949–October 1953), Hilton A. Robertson of Provo, Utah (October 1953–November 1955), Paul C. Andrus of Kaneohe, Hawaii (December 1955–July 1962), Dwayne N. Andersen of Folsom, California (July 1962–August 1965), and Adney Y. Komatsu of Honolulu (August 1965–July 1968).

These men all came with previous experience in Japan. Mauss and Robertson had been Mormon missionaries in the prewar Japan Mission (Robertson was the last mission president and subsequently the first president of the Honolulu-based Japanese Mission). Andrus, at thirty-one years of age when he arrived, was one of the first five missionaries of the postwar Japanese Mission. Andersen, a former missionary in the Hawaiian Islands, had fought in the Battle of Okinawa during the final days of the war and, from 1951 to 1953, served his second mission in Japan; he served as a counselor to Mauss for seventeen of his twenty-two months in the field.[1] Finally, Komatsu, born in Honolulu as a son of Japanese immigrants from Hiroshima, had been a member of the American occupation forces in Japan.

By the end of the occupation, the work of the LDS Church in Japan was firmly defined, if not established, with every indication that it was there to stay: there was a newly renovated mission home; seventy or so full-time missionaries were serving in the field; and more than 500 Japanese Mormons lived across

---

1. When the number of missionaries declined as a result of the Korean War, his ward was assigned by the First Presidency to provide a missionary. Andersen responded to the assignment though he was by then married with a young child.

Japan in more than twenty locations. For the church, the next phase in Japan would be a period of institutional consolidation followed by expansion. In July 1955, the Northern Far East Mission was created to take over the work previously performed by the Japanese Mission, with a geographical focus that expanded to Okinawa and the Republic of Korea (hereafter cited simply as Korea).

It should be noted at the outset that this chapter does not discuss developments related to military and civilian members associated with the American armed forces,[2] except when they had a bearing on the local church. Mormon military districts in Japan, with more than a thousand members, remained roughly the same in number as Japanese member districts during this period,[3] requiring mission presidents to devote to them a considerable amount of their administrative time. Ecclesiastical decisions with respect to military units, however, were almost entirely demand-driven: the church organized (or discontinued) a unit as warranted by the number of members in a particular location, which in turn was determined by the American military authorities. In none of these decisions was the geographical location of these units (i.e., Japan) consequential. They functioned as if they were extraterritorial entities of the American church, to which full-time missionaries were not assigned. The Mormon missionaries were even instructed to keep their distance from the American servicemen.[4]

The rest of the chapter reviews the evolution of the full-time missionary force, the organization, termination, and consolidation of member branches and districts, the opening of work in Okinawa and Korea that followed the establishment of the Northern Far East Mission, the systematic purchases by the church of properties throughout Japan, and the development of local leadership. On 16 July 1968, Walter R. Bills arrived to begin preparatory work to divide the mission.[5] This took place on 1 September, when the Japan Mission (headquartered in

---

2. At the end of the occupation, about 260,000 American military personnel were stationed in Japan (excluding Okinawa). The number would fall to 46,000 in 1960. Takenori Inoki, *Keizai Seichō no Kajitsu 1955–1972* (Tokyo: Chūō Kōron Shinsha, 2000), 108.

3. The Mormon military church structure in postwar Japan initially stabilized with five districts and approximately 1,000 members: Northern Honshu–Hokkaido (four groups with 90 members in October 1956), Central Honshu (seven branches, 500 members), Southern Honshu (two groups, 50 members), Southern Honshu–Kyushu (six groups, 175 members), and Okinawa (three branches and one group, 200 members). *Church News*, 27 October 1956. By the end of 1961, the five districts had been consolidated into three districts reflecting the parallel consolidation of American military installations into fewer locations. *Success Messenger* 6 (March 1962): 6–7. As of July 1965, there were 2,146 members in fourteen branches organized into three districts. Dwayne N. Andersen, "Dwayne N. Andersen's Experience with the Japanese People," not dated, 15.

4. On 15 November 1955, Robertson instructed the missionaries to stay "away from the servicemen's meetings. There is no need for missionaries to hang around the servicemen as we have no responsibilities with them. Our duties are with the Japanese people." Japanese Mission, "Quarterly Historical Reports," LDS Church Archives.

5. Authority was formally transferred to Bills on 19 July 1968. "Quarterly Historical Reports."

Tokyo, with Bills as president) and the Japan–Okinawa Mission (headquartered in Kobe, with Edward Y. Okazaki as president) came into existence, marking the end of the period covered by this volume.

11.2. The Evolving Scope of Missionary Work

11.2.1. The Missionary Force

At the beginning of the post-occupation era,[6] in May 1952, there were seventy full-time Mormon missionaries serving in Japan, including the mission president and his wife (eight were women and two were native Japanese men). In addition, the post-occupation era saw an estimated 1,032 full-time missionaries arrive through the end of August 1968, including mission presidents and their wives but excluding those on a temporary assignment. Women (numbering 162) constituted about 16 percent of the missionary force, while Japanese men (forty) and women (forty-nine) accounted for about 9 percent. As noted below, fifty-one of these missionaries (not including a native Korean elder) spent at least part of their missions in Korea. Combined, they gave an estimated 2,137 man-years of service within Japan, which is equivalent to the work of 1,165 missionaries spending twenty-two months each in the field.

During the early years of the post-occupation era, the number of full-time missionaries serving in Japan (including Okinawa) saw a moderate, gradual increase, from about seventy to ninety based on end-month figures (Figure 11.1). It was only after late 1960 or early 1961 that the number began to rise noticeably. The number initially peaked at 188 in October 1963 before declining. It began to increase again in mid-1965 to reach a new peak of 251 in October 1967. When the mission was split at the beginning of September 1968, there were 221 missionaries. Of these, 116 missionaries were assigned to the Japan Mission covering northeast Japan and 105 to the Japan–Okinawa Mission covering southwest Japan.[7]

Following the establishment of the Northern Far East Mission in July 1955, preparation was made to initiate missionary work in Korea. The first set of missionaries, Richard L. Detton of Honolulu and Don Gayle Powell of Rexburg, Idaho, left for Korea in April 1956 after receiving clearance from the Korean government, followed by Gail E. Carr of Lynwood, California, and Larry D. Orme of Ashton, Idaho, in August 1956. At the time they left for Korea, these men had been serving in Japan for 16–26 months. In contrast, except for two instances,[8]

---

6. The occupation formally ended on 28 April 1952.

7. These numbers include the mission president and his wife for the Japan Mission but not for the Japan–Okinawa Mission.

8. These involved Robert T. Stout of Boise, Idaho, who stayed in Japan from April to December 1957; and James R. Bradshaw of Beaver, Utah, who remained in Japan from November 1958 to March 1959.

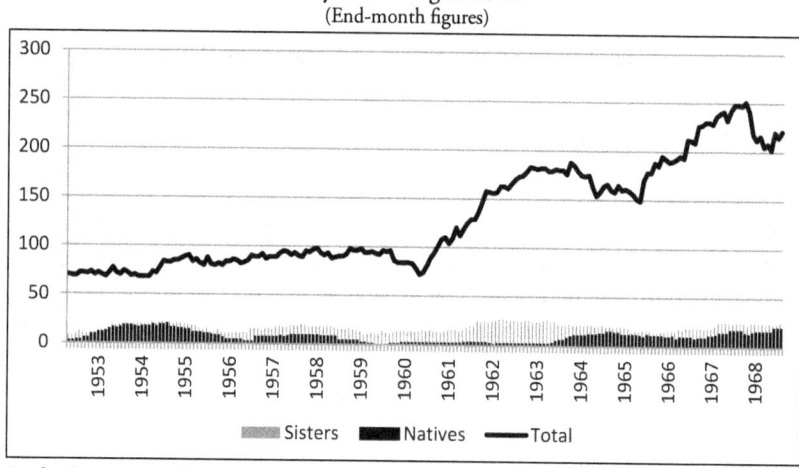

Figure 11.1. Number of Full-time Mormon Missionaries in Japan, May 1952–August 1968 (End-month figures)

Author's estimates based on various church records.

all the missionaries who arrived in Japan after Paul C. Andrus took office as mission president in December 1955 appear to have received the assignment to serve in Korea immediately upon arrival in the mission (if not before);[9] they only stayed in Tokyo long enough to obtain clearance from Korean authorities. All in all, fifty-two full-time elders, including native Young Bum Lee, served in Korea between April 1956 and July 1962, when the Korea Mission was separated out of the Northern Far East Mission. During the period under review, no lady missionary was sent to Korea, in view of "most austere" living conditions, about which Andrus said he would not be surprised "if they [were] the worst in the world."[10] Except for six men who served in Japan for four months or more, the

---

9. Visa applications were often made ahead of their arrival in Tokyo, indicating that assignments to serve in Korea were made before their arrival. Not all missionaries on whose behalf visa applications had been filed actually served in Korea, possibly indicating that assignments were withdrawn upon their arrival in the mission. Northern Far East Mission, "Released Missionary Files," LDS Church Archives.

10. "Quarterly Historical Reports," 29 January 1957. Writing in June 2003, Ronald K. Nielsen of Rexburg, Idaho, recalled the manner in which the call to serve in Korea had been extended to him in February 1962 upon arriving in Tokyo: "President Andrus interviewed each of us one by one . . . I remember only one thing from his interview. He asked me, 'Elder Nielsen, are you willing to give your life for the Church?' Trying to say the right thing I meekly stammered, 'I don't know, I guess so.' 'Good, you will be assigned to labor in the Korea District.'" Accessed 26 October 2014, Northern Far East Mission Alumni Site (mission.net/northern-far-east/index.php). Andrus recalls that missionaries first had to live off of what they could get on the black market. Paul C. Andrus Oral History, interviews by R. Lanier Britsch, 1974, James Moyle Oral History Program, LDS Church Archives, 20.

Table 11.1. Full-Time Mormon Missionaries Who Arrived and Completed Their Missions, May 1952–August 1968

	Total	Number of those released early				Average length of service (in months)
		Health reasons	Misconduct	Personal reasons	Reassigned to the United States	
Foreign elders (arrived before December 1956)	583 (96)	14 (8)	9 (2)	10 (0)	5 (0)	29.7 (34.0)
Foreign sisters	97	2	0	0	1	23.9
Japanese elders	31	3	0	0	0	22.4
Japanese sisters	38	1	0	2	0	17.5

Excludes those who served in Korea, mission presidents, and their wives. Missionary term was shortened from thirty-six to thirty months in September 1959, allowing any currently serving missionary to take advantage of the new policy. The first missionaries to do so had arrived in February 1957. Author's estimates based on various church records.

men assigned to Korea are not included in the number of full-time missionaries in Figure 11.1 or in our subsequent narratives on Japan.

In principle, the prescribed term of Mormon missionary service was eighteen months for Japanese sisters and two years for non-native sisters and Japanese elders. For non-native elders, the term was initially three years but was shortened to thirty months in September 1959.[11] The new policy for non-native elders also applied to those who were already serving in the field at the time. Franklin S. Black of Laramie, Wyoming and Peter Kent Maughan of Wellsville, Utah, became the first missionaries to be released under the new policy, on 24 September 1959, after having served in Japan for thirty-one months each. The shortening of the term of service in part explains why there was a significant decline in the number of missionaries from September 1959 to May 1960, when Andrus complained that the mission was "experiencing a critical shortage of missionaries" (see Figure 11.1).[12] It should not be thought, however, that the average term of elders actually declined by six months because more than 10 percent of the non-native elders had returned home early for health and other reasons during the early part of the post-occupation era (Table 11.1).

Part of the reason why so many elders went home early may have been the generally poorer hygienic conditions in early postwar Japan. Sisters were less susceptible because their time in Japan was shorter and also typically spent in larger cities,

---

11. A letter dated 9 September 1959 from the First Presidency informing the mission of this change was received on 15 September 1959. "Quarterly Historical Reports."
12. "Quarterly Historical Reports," 12 May 1960.

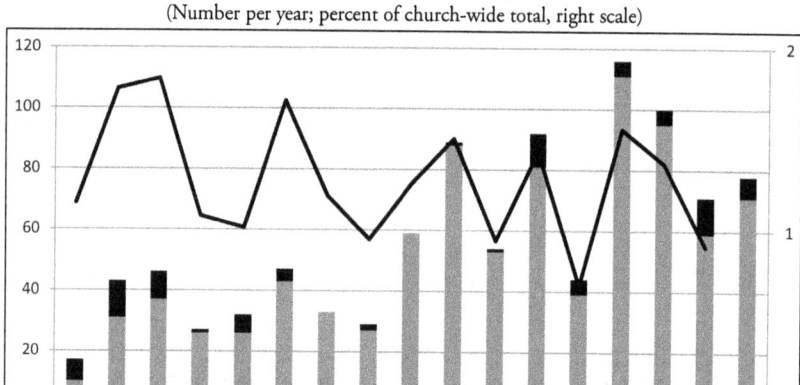

Figure 11.2. The Arrival of Mormon Missionaries in the Japanese and Northern Far East Missions, 1952–68
(Number per year; percent of church-wide total, right scale)

The numerator includes only those who were set apart for missionary service in North America. Author's estimates based on various church records; *1974 Church Almanac* (Salt Lake City: Deseret News).

especially Tokyo and Osaka, where streets were paved, refuse removal systems were more developed, and perhaps modern amenities were more readily available (the average tenure for sisters was almost exactly twenty-four months over the entire period, see Table 11.1). Also, the term for elders, set at thirty-six months in principle, was quite flexibly applied in practice in either direction. While some served shorter than three years, others served much longer. For example, Don C. Lundberg of Newhall, California, served for forty-four months, from November 1953 to July 1957, while three others remained in the field for forty-two months.[13] During the 1960s, the share of elders who went home early for health reasons dramatically declined (to about 1 percent) presumably as living conditions in Japan improved. Just about every elder stayed in Japan for almost exactly thirty months by that time, unless they were sent home early for various reasons. This also reflects the stricture with which the tenure policy was applied in these later years.

A look at the number of annual arrivals indicates that the LDS Church allocated to Japan on average about 1.2 percent of those set apart as missionaries in North America (see Figure 11.2). From 1952 to 1968, the number of missions increased from forty-three to eighty-three. As a result, Japan's share was somewhat higher during the earlier period, even though the absolute number

---

13. They are Norman D. Shumway of Stockton, California, Ira R. Telford of Washington, D.C., and Theodore Franklin Welch of Los Angeles, who all served during 1954–58.

sent to Japan rose in the 1960s. The same data indicate that the decline in the missionary force observed in the late 1950s reflected not only the shortening of the term of service but also the decline in the number of missionaries allocated to Japan. The share of local Japanese missionaries in new arrivals saw its peak during 1952–54 (twenty-eight Japanese vs. seventy-eight foreign arrivals). In order to compensate for the Korean War–associated decline in the number of missionaries, the mission leaders made concerted efforts to recruit Japanese missionaries with financial support from American military members. The first called were Toshiro Murakami and Yotaro Yoshino, who were both set apart on 29 December 1951; both were from Takasaki but were living in Tokyo at the time of their call. They were followed by Hide Kishigami of Otaru, the first Japanese sister ever to serve a mission, who was set apart on 22 July 1952. Church records state that the first self-supporting local missionary was Nobuko Tanaka of Gunma, who served from June 1963 to December 1964.

11.2.2. Early Closing and Opening of Branches

By the end of the occupation, Mormon missionary work had commenced in as many as twenty locations throughout Japan, namely (going roughly from northeast to southwest): Asahikawa,[14] Sapporo, Otaru, Muroran, Sendai, Yamagata, Niigata (including Niitsu, Sanjo, Shibata, and Tenno),[15] the neighboring cities of Maebashi and Takasaki, Tokyo (Tokyo First and Second Branches), Yokohama, Kofu, Matsumoto, Kanazawa, Komatsu, Nagoya (with the adjacent town of Narumi), Kyoto, Osaka (Abeno and Juso Branches), Hiroshima, the neighboring towns of Hirao and Yanai, and Fukuoka. The district structure, still in a state of flux at the time, began to stabilize in early 1953, with branches and proselytizing areas organized into five districts: Hokkaido, Northern, Central, South Central, and Southern (see Figure 11.3).

Over the subsequent years, some of these branches would be closed, consolidated, or reorganized, while new ones would be opened. These decisions should be understood against the background of a relatively stable number of full-time missionaries in the field through the early 1960s. Paul Andrus repeatedly requested more missionaries from Salt Lake, but to no avail.[16] Under these circumstances, new areas could only be opened if some of the existing ones were closed. Pressure on

---

14. Early postwar records spell the name of this city as Asahigawa. The alternative spelling used here has become increasingly established, with the city hall, the main railroad station, and the airport spelling the name as Asahikawa. The mormon.org website currently spells the city as Asahikawa. The city was always spelled Asahikawa in the prewar Japan Mission.

15. The branch in the city of Niigata itself was closed on 22 May 1952, with the members incorporated into the Tenno-Shibata Branch and the missionaries transferred to the Sanjo Branch. A reversal of this would occur in 1956 when the work in Niigata Prefecture was consolidated in the Niigata Branch, which had been reopened on 31 July 1955.

16. Author's interview with Paul C. Andrus, 1 February 1997, Kaneohe, Hawaii.

First Japanese missionaries: (from left to right) Matsumoto, Aki, Kishigami, Murakami, and Yoshino. Courtesy Hide Matsubara.

missionaries intensified when Okinawa and Korea were opened to missionary work in early 1956 (see Section 11.3 for details). This too needed to be accommodated within the existing resources. As the first of a series of such actions, on 21 February 1954, work in Hirao was consolidated into Yanai, the larger of the two locations.

The first area to be opened permanently during the post-occupation era was Okayama, but this required the closing of Fukuoka, a larger city. Why this happened is not clearly explained in the historical records of the LDS Church. In May 1955, Hilton Robertson pulled the missionaries out of Fukuoka without giving a reason to the few members who resided there. In part, lack of success could have been a factor, but it also appears that the church lost use of a meeting place as well as a housing arrangement for the missionaries, possibly as a result of a personal issue between a missionary and the landlord.[17] On 9 May 1955, Thomas T. Takeuchi of Wakaiki, Hawaii, president of the Southern District, came to Fukuoka to close the branch. On 26 June, a small group of members was organized, with Mitsuru Kawasaki as group leader and Toshiro Yoshizawa as assistant. This allowed the few members who lived in Fukuoka to continue meeting for church worship without the support of full-time missionaries.

In the meantime, on 9 May 1955, the Fukuoka missionaries Harold D. Slade of Kaysville, Utah, and Richard Toyn of Ogden, Utah, transferred all branch belongings and materials to the Hiroshima Branch.[18] On the next day,

---

17. Author's telephone conversation with Thomas Tsutomu Takeuchi, 22 February 1996.
18. "Quarterly Historical Reports."

Figure 11.3. Latter-day Saint Districts with Proselytizing Areas in Japan, 1953

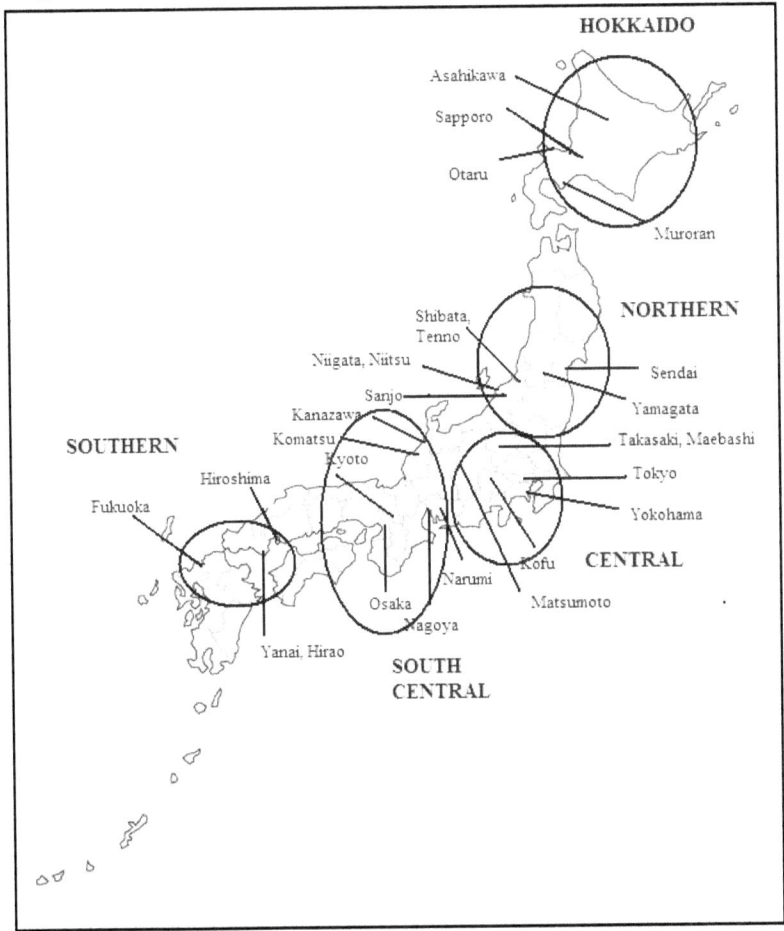

Takeuchi and Toyn left Hiroshima for Okayama in search of new proselytizing possibilities. On 1 June, Toyn and Howard Moffitt of Duchesne, Utah, were sent to Okayama, with instructions from Robertson to proselytize for four months and to close it down if there were no prospects. On 10 June, with a boarding arrangement having been secured, they moved to Okayama. The first two baptisms there would take place in December 1956.[19]

When Paul Andrus arrived in Japan as mission president in early December 1955, he wondered why missionary work had been terminated in Fukuoka, the principal city on the island of Kyushu and the place where Andrus had spent

---

19. *Seito no Michi* 1 (September 1957): 15–17.

most of his days as an American serviceman.[20] Immediately, Andrus decided to reopen the city for missionary work, informing the members of his intention on 10–11 December. On 28 December, less than twenty days after Andrus's arrival in Japan, two missionaries resumed proselytizing work in Fukuoka and reopened the branch. Effectively, the reopening of Fukuoka was the first official task Andrus performed as mission president.

Over the coming months, Andrus systematically closed down branches in smaller cities and towns, and transferred the missionaries to larger population centers. In this, he was being guided by counsel received from Delbert L. Stapley of the Council of the Twelve Apostles in Honolulu. In setting Andrus apart as mission president, Stapley instructed him "to organize the work . . . so that stakes could be organized as soon as possible." In Andrus's mind, it was obvious that the first stakes should be organized in the great population centers of Tokyo and Osaka. "Accordingly I systematically went about organizing four more branches in Tokyo which with the Yokohama Branch would naturally grow into a stake. I likewise organized four [sic] branches in the Osaka–Kobe area which with the Kyoto Branch would naturally grow into a stake."[21] Even when the number of missionaries began to increase in the early 1960s, Andrus opened no new areas, but allocated the extra missionaries to the two metropolitan areas.

Within a year from his arrival, Andrus increased the number of branches within the Tokyo and Osaka metropolitan areas. From August to November 1956, he disbanded the Tokyo First and Tokyo Second Branches to create five new branches: Tokyo West (August 26), Tokyo North (October 28), Tokyo East (November 4), Tokyo Central (November 11), and Tokyo South (November 18). The mission records characterized "the organization of these five branches in Tokyo" as "a real milestone on the road to our goal of organizing a stake."[22] About a year later, in the Osaka area, branches were established in the city of Kobe (known as Sannomiya Branch) on 1 October 1957 and in the city of Nishinomiya, which lies between Kobe and Osaka, on 4 December 1957. The name of the branch in Kobe came from the name of the central station, which is located in the city's Sannomiya district (the name would remain even after the branch found property several miles east of the city center).[23]

---

20. Robertson left for home on 28 November 1955 while Andrus arrived in Japan on 9 December, disallowing any formal transfer of business between the departing and succeeding presidents. Robertson was apparently ill and flew back to the United States, while the Andrus's traveled to Japan by boat. Andrus Oral History, 13.

21. Paul C. Andrus, "Summary Report by Paul C. Andrus of His Term of Service as President of the Northern Far East Mission from December 9, 1955 to July 19, 1962," 10 September 1975.

22. Northern Far East Mission, Quarterly Historical Report, 18 November 1956.

23. Sannomiya Branch was renamed as Kobe Branch following the establishment of the Japan–Okinawa Mission in 1968 in line with the LDS Church's new naming policy.

In contrast, missionary work in smaller cities was terminated. On 9 December 1956, the Narumi Branch, one of the first branches established by Edward Clissold, was merged with the Nagoya Branch. From August to September 1957, lack of success prompted the closing of the Shibata and Sanjo Branches (August 18, both merged with the Niigata Branch), the Komatsu Branch (September 1, merged with the Kanazawa Branch), and the Kyoto Branch (September 8). The closing of a branch in Kyoto may appear odd in view of the size of the city, its large student population, and the fact that the city is located in the larger Osaka metropolitan area,[24] but it is also a stronghold of Japanese Buddhism. The closing of Kyoto in any case allowed resources to be freed up to create branches in two cities closer to Osaka, namely Kobe and Nishinomiya, as noted above.[25] Earlier on 22 August 1956, Andrus visited the Matsumoto Branch to discuss the possibility of closing the branch with the members, but he decided against it during the course of the meeting. Similar resource considerations would have closed down the branch in Yanai (which had absorbed Hirao in February 1954), a small rural city in Yamaguchi Prefecture, but the circumstances surrounding its opening and Hawaiian member Koichi Takeuchi's contribution toward the purchase of land in the city made closure difficult.[26]

Members, missionaries, and investigators protested the closing of branches. In Sanjo, for example, Sunday meetings had seen only two missionaries and two or three additional people in attendance, but in May 1956 when Andrus "went up there to close the branch they had ten or twelve members show up all opposed to closing it." Andrus promised to keep the branch open if they would "really get with it and cooperate and work hard to make the branch successful." After a period of time, it "fell right back into the same situation," and the branch was closed about a year later.[27] The Niigata Branch appears to have made outreach efforts to maintain contact with the Sanjo and Shibata members. An article in the January 1964 issue of the *Seito no Michi* reported that, from December 1963, sacrament meeting had begun to be held at 7 P.M. in Shibata on every third Sunday, concluding with a hope that this would continue until a branch was reestablished again.

---

24. Kyoto was the capital of Japan from the late eighth century to the middle of the nineteenth century. Though it is a large city, the prevalence of strong traditional values may have diminished the receptiveness of the people to a foreign religion to a greater extent than in other large cities.

25. The Kyoto Branch would reopen in October 1961.

26. Author's interview with Andrus. Koichi Takeuchi of Hawaii made a down payment of $500 towards the land purchase on 29 September 1955. Paul C. Andrus, letter to Koichi Takeuchi, 1 December 1956. Northern Far East Mission, "Presidents' Correspondence, 1956–1966," LDS Church Archives.

27. Andrus Oral History, 34. Andrus's visit may have been prompted by a letter he received from Sanjo, dated 17 May 1956 and signed by twenty-one members and investigators. Northern Far East Mission, "Presidents' Correspondence." Also, "Quarterly Historical Reports," 21 May 1956.

Within the larger Tokyo metropolitan area, on 11 August 1957, the Tokyo East Branch was closed because its location had proven to be too far from the other units to function effectively. This allowed resources to be concentrated on the Tokyo–Yokohama [Keihin] corridor west of Tokyo Bay.[28] In the summer of 1958, Andrus considered opening a second branch in Yokohama, to be known as Yokohama South Branch, but the plan did not materialize.[29] About sixty miles north of Tokyo, the Maebashi Branch was closed on 30 April 1958 and merged with the Takasaki Branch to form the Gunma Branch (to be located in Takasaki).[30]

Along with the reorganization of branches, the districts were consolidated. Effective 1 July 1958, the Southern and South Central Districts were merged to become the West Central District (Abeno, Fukuoka, Hiroshima, Kanazawa, Nagoya, Nishinomiya, Okamachi,[31] Okayama, Sannomiya, and Yanai); the Northern and Central Districts were merged to become the East Central District (Gunma, Kofu, Matsumoto, Niigata, Sendai, Tokyo Central, Tokyo North, Tokyo South, Tokyo West, Yamagata, and Yokohama). In the meantime, the Hokkaido District in the far north remained intact, with four branches (Asahikawa, Muroran, Otaru, and Sapporo) and, following the opening of work in Okinawa, a new district was created with branches in Futenma (29 April 1956) and Naha (17 March 1957). This four-district structure would last for nearly ten years. The number of units also remained stable, except that the reopening of branches in Kyoto (1 October 1961) and Tokyo East (1 July 1962) raised the number from twenty-seven to twenty-nine.[32]

---

28. The Tokyo East Branch would reopen in July 1962.

29. It apears that the plan was abandoned when the request to purchase a meetinghouse site was not approved by the First Presidency. The "Quarterly Historical Report" entry for 4 July 1958 states that Andrus signed an option to purchase a meetinghouse site in Yamatecho within sixty days, which if "authorized by the First Presidency . . . will be known as Yokohama South Branch." There is no record to show that the requested approval was granted.

30. It was initially planned to hold sacrament meetings once a month each in Maebashi and in Tomioka.

31. The name was changed from Juso in late 1956 on account of a relocation. The first Sunday meeting was held at the newly acquired meetinghouse on 2 December 1956. List of attendees prepared by Haruko Sakamoto, 3 December 1956, in author's possession.

32. For a brief period of time, from December 1963 to January 1965, there was a dependent branch in Sasebo on the island of Kyushu. *Seito no Michi* 8 (1964): 157. It was on account of "a great deal of interest in the Church" the LDS servicemen had aroused that, on 16 December 1963, Alan M. Uyehara of Honolulu and Masahisa Watabe of Yokohama were sent to start missionary work there. "Quarterly Historical Reports," 16 December 1963. Nobuyasu Yano, a convert from Tokyo who had moved to Nagasaki, attended the branch. The branch closed on 24 January 1965, and the few members there began to meet in the servicemen's branch. Author's interview with Nobuyasu Yano, Fukuoka, 5 January 1996.

11.2.3. Opening of Additional Areas after 1966

It was only in 1966 that an increase in the missionary force (see Figure 11.1) began to allow additional areas to be opened for missionary work. From 10 January 1966 to 21 March 1966, President Komatsu sent Masayoshi Isomura of Nagoya and George M. McCune of Nephi, Utah, on a tour of the island of Kyushu to explore proselytizing possibilities. Upon their return to Tokyo, they recommended that Kitakyushu, Kumamoto, and Nagasaki be opened immediately for missionary work. On 1 November 1966, three sets of missionaries were assigned to these cities: Rowland S. Blake of St. Paul, Minnesota and Dennis J. Meurer of Santa Barbara, California, to Kitakyushu; Rondy Bentley of Nampa, Idaho, and Kenneth L. Christopherson of Salt Lake City to Kumamoto; and David P. Fillmore of Ontario, Oregon, and Allen F. Hill of Salt Lake City to Nagasaki. This was followed by the opening of two other cities, with the assignment on 23 November 1966 of Dwight M. Kakazu of Honolulu and Ben S. Markham of Spanish Fork, Utah, to Fukushima, north of Tokyo; and the assignment on 30 May 1967 of Robert S. DaBell of Rexburg, Idaho, and Richard S. Meng of Teton City, Idaho, to Takamatsu, the first city on the island of Shikoku.

From late 1967, based on the fruits of labor in the new areas and perhaps also in the context of preparing for a division of the mission, Komatsu organized additional branches outside the Tokyo and Osaka metropolitan areas. On 17 December 1967, the Nagoya North Branch was created out of the Nagoya Branch. On 1 January 1968, new branches were established in the new proselytizing areas of Fukushima, Kitakyushu, Kumamoto, Nagasaki, and Takamatsu. With the establishment of three additional branches in Kyushu, in a conference held on 27–28 January 1968, the Fukuoka Branch was removed from the West Central District to form a four-branch Kyushu District, with Osamu Ishikawa as president. The geographical expansion of the mission, however, remained modest. It was only after the division of the mission, and the doubling of the missionary force (to a combined total of 370 in 1970), that the LDS Church began to penetrate every corner of Japan.

11.3. The Opening of Work in Okinawa and Korea

11.3.1. The Northern Far East Mission

On 27 July 1955, the Northern Far East Mission was organized by Joseph Fielding Smith of the Council of the Twelve Apostles during a missionary conference held in Karuizawa, a mountain resort north of Tokyo. Smith proposed on that occasion that the Japanese Mission be divided into two entities.[33] The

---

33. At the conference, a vote was taken by those assembled to approve the division of the mission. Wherever Smith held conference from that time on, the same procedure

Northern Far East Mission, headquartered in Tokyo, would be responsible for work in mainland Japan, Okinawa, and Korea. The Southern Far East Mission would be responsible for work in Hong Kong, which had been suspended in May 1951 but would soon resume;[34] work was also expected to commence in Taiwan (in 1956) and the Philippines (in 1961). In anticipation of the commencement of Mormon missionary work in these and other areas in the region, Smith traveled after the conference to dedicate the land of Korea (2 August),[35] Okinawa (14 August), the Philippines (21 August), and Guam (25 August) for the preaching of the gospel.[36] During the middle of the tour, on 15 August, Smith installed Herald Grant Heaton as president of the Southern Far East Mission.

Since 23 June 1951, the geographical responsibility of the Japanese Mission had covered Guam, Korea, Okinawa, and the Philippines where American members of the armed forces resided.[37] Though no missionaries had been assigned to these areas, missionary-minded American servicemen had converted a number of their associates to Mormonism and they would continue to do so. Also, it appears that the Japanese Mission assumed geographical responsibility for China in May 1951 when the Chinese Mission headquartered in Hong Kong was relocated to San Francisco. The mission's quarterly historical report records that Vinal Mauss traveled to Hong Kong in March 1953 to visit with the members. When Hilton Robertson was set apart on 10 September 1953 by David O. McKay to preside over the Japanese Mission, he was formally charged to serve concurrently as president of the Chinese Mission, over which he had previously presided from July 1949 to January 1953 both in Hong Kong and in San Francisco.[38]

Thus, the creation of the Northern Far East Mission meant a splitting of Robertson's responsibility, which had previously extended to the whole area to be covered by the two missions. More important, it meant an expansion of

---

was repeated. The decision to divide the Japanese Mission had been made by the First Presidency and the Council of the Twelve Apostles in early April and announced to the public on 5 May. Dong Sull Choi, *A History of the Church of Jesus Christ of Latter-day Saints in Korea, 1950–1985* (PhD Diss., Brigham Young University, 1990), 125.

34. Hong Kong had already been dedicated for the preaching of the gospel on 14 July 1949 by Matthew Cowley.

35. The dedication of Korea was not a planned event. Before his trip to the Far East, Smith had requested Captain Vernon J. Tipton of the United States Army to survey living conditions in Korea to determine if Korea could sustain missionaries. Captain Tipton's conclusion was negative, seeing Korea too hazardous for missionaries. While in Korea, however, Smith was impressed to move ahead to dedicated the land and to begin missionary work. Choi, *History*, 128.

36. Joseph Fielding Smith, "Report from the Far East Missions," *Improvement Era* 58 (1955): 917–18.

37. The "Quarterly Historical Report" entry on 23 June 1951 notes: "Effective this date . . . [the] servicemen in those areas will now operate under the direction of the mission." Also see *Church News*, 2 January 1952, 10.

38. Muriel Jenkins Heal, "We Will Go: The Robertson Response," *Ensign* 12 (1982): 32–35.

Mormon missionary work beyond the borders of mainland Japan to Okinawa and to Korea, where converts had already been made but no missionaries had yet been sent. Even so, no concrete steps were taken while Robertson remained in office. Perhaps, knowing that he would be released soon, he thought it was more appropriate for the process to be initiated by his successor. Indeed, it was Paul Andrus who initiated the work, according to the instruction he had received when he was set apart by Delbert L. Stapley: "the Brethren would like [him] to push ahead with the work in Korea and Okinawa."[39] Andrus visited Okinawa and Korea immediately after arriving in Japan to put in motion the work of preparing to send missionaries.

11.3.2. Work in Okinawa

Okinawa, the modern Japanese name for the geographical area covered by the Ryukyu Islands, remained under American occupation even after Japan regained its sovereignty in April 1952. Article 3 of the San Francisco Peace Treaty allowed the United States to administer the Nansei Islands south of 29 degrees north latitude, including the Ryukyu Islands, for an indefinite period.[40] Given their proximity to communist China, these islands, especially the main island of Okinawa, became the American military's bastion in the Pacific. The islands were administered by the United States military government (renamed, in December 1950, as the United States Civil Administration of the Ryukyu Islands or USCAR) headed by a military governor (known from June 1957 as the high commissioner). That Japan retained residual sovereignty over Okinawa was not disputed,[41] with the implicit understanding that it would be returned to Japan someday. This became a real possibility on 19 March 1962, when President John F. Kennedy issued a proclamation recognizing "the Ryukyus to be part of the Japanese homeland." In accordance with an agreement reached between the Japanese and United States governments on 21 November 1969, Okinawa was returned to Japanese sovereignty on 15 May 1972 after twenty-seven years of American rule.

From late 1950, the American military authorities granted partial autonomy to the local population as normalcy gradually returned. In April 1952, the Government of the Ryukyu Islands (GRI) was established, with independent judicial, legislative, and executive branches, the last of which was headed by a

---

39. Andrus, "Summary Report by Paul C. Andrus."
40. The United States voluntarily returned the Amami Islands to Japan on 25 December 1953.
41. Japan's residual sovereignty over Okinawa (as well as the Bonin Islands) was reaffirmed in a joint statement issued on 21 June 1957 by Prime Minister Nobuhiko Kishi and President Dwight D. Eisenhower; on 19 June 1961, President John F. Kennedy agreed in a meeting with Prime Minister Hayato Ikeda, to allow the Japanese national flag to be hoisted at public buildings in Okinawa. Inoki, *Keizai Seichō no Kajitsu*, 107, 138.

chief executive.⁴² While the people were given the right to elect local and national officials, who in turn could pass local and national laws, the outcomes of an election or a legislative process could be vetoed by the USCAR.⁴³ Okinawa residents traveling to mainland Japan, as well as mainland residents traveling to Okinawa, were subjected to inspection at ports of disembarkation and embarkation. They were required to present travel documents (in lieu of passports), along with clearance from the American military authorities, at ports of entry (Japanese border officials would stamp the travel documents of Okinawans arriving in Japan with a seal indicating "returned home"). A special military currency (formally known as supplementary type-B yen or simply B-yen) circulated as legal tender until September 1958, when it was replaced by the United States dollar.⁴⁴

One of the fiercest battles of the Pacific War was fought on Okinawan soil between the Japanese and American forces, especially on the main island. The Battle of Okinawa, which lasted from 26 March to 20 June 1945, reportedly claimed nearly 300,000 lives on both sides, including 100,000 civilians. The economic and social infrastructure remained in a shambles. With the confiscation of much productive land for American military use, it is not difficult to imagine the intensity of anti-American sentiment that existed in Okinawa when the LDS Church was about to launch its missionary work there. A contemporary American observer, in explaining in 1958 why "most Okinawans dislike[d] Americans," blamed the personal behavior of American troops and the way their commanders administered the civilian affairs of Okinawa.⁴⁵ The observer continued:

---

42. The chief executive of the Ryukyu government was appointed by the high commissioner from 1952 to 1965, elected by the legislature from 1965 to 1968, and popularly elected from 1968 to 1972.

43. In practice, all draft bills were "pre-adjusted" with the USCAR before being submitted to the legislature, and a bill passed by the legislature was cleared again by USCAR officials before being sent to the chief executive for signature. This was done to avoid the publicity of a veto. Rafael Steinberg, "Our Unhappy Asia Bastion," *Washington Post*, 3 May 1964, E2.

44. Shinji Takagi, Mototsugu Shintani, and Tetsuro Okamoto, 2004, "Measuring the Economic Impact of Monetary Union: The Case of Okinawa," *Review of Economics and Statistics* 84 (2004): 858–67.

45. An American journalist described Okinawa as "a dumping ground for Army misfits and rejects from more comfortable posts." He reported that, from April to September 1949, American soldiers committed twenty-nine murders, eighteen rapes, sixteen robberies, and thirty-three assaults. Frank Gibney, "Okinawa: Forgotten Island," *Time*, 28 November 1949, 24. According to another American journalist, American servicemen "tend[ed] to consider every woman they [saw] a prostitute and treat[ed] them accordingly," and in search of excitement, they "plung[ed] easily into drunkenness, hoodlumism, and gang street-fighting." In the summer of 1956, almost 800 men were involved in a Navy vs. Marines free-for-all which spread quickly from town to town; 30 percent of the patients in the military hospital were there because of injuries sustained in street fights. Barton M. Biggs, "The Outraged Okinawans," *Harper's Magazine* 217 (December 1958): 58–59.

When a Communist was elected mayor of Naha, the Armed Forces High Commissioner changed the election laws, deposing the new mayor and disqualified him permanently from office. With so many anti-American grievances already ripe for exploitation, it is not surprising that the Communists should have little trouble in igniting others. Today about one-third of the towns on Okinawa have Communist mayors and the party is growing.[46]

Things did not change much in the 1960s. Another American journalist, writing in 1964, observed:

> Ruled by an American general who makes plain his feeling that he knows better than they do what is good for them, unprotected by any constitution and unable to carry on normal commerce and travel with Japan, which all of them consider their homeland, the people of Okinawa today are convinced that the United States has let them down.[47]

Some in the military, however, went out of their way to solicit the goodwill of the Okinawans through charitable activities.[48] It was through such activities of Mormon men and women that three Okinawans had joined the LDS Church before the arrival of the first Mormon missionaries. On 25 December 1955, Ayako Nakamura, Nobu Nakamura, and Kuniko Tamanaha were baptized in the East China Sea near Futenma, where Camp Zukeran was located. Nobu Nakamura, a prominent civic leader, was the head of the Okinawa Prefectural Federation of Associations of Women; she was initially introduced to the LDS Church by Ralph W. Bird of Ogden, Utah, who had earlier served as a missionary in the Japanese Mission from November 1950 to December 1953.[49] Futenma was the administrative center of the village of Ginowan (now part of the city of Ginowan). The collateral damage the village had suffered during the final days of the Battle of Okinawa was severe, with about 3,700 of the total population of 14,000 (as of March 1945) having been killed. Following the American occupation of Okinawa, about 40 percent of the land, including a large plot to be used to build an airfield, was confiscated.[50]

The first Mormon missionaries called to Okinawa were Clarence Leroy B. Anderson of Thornton, Idaho, and Sam K. Shimabukuro of Honolulu, who had been serving in Japan since February and September 1954, respectively. For Shimabukuro, this meant bringing the gospel to the land from which his parents had come. Three weeks after receiving their call, on 11 April, Anderson and

---

46. Ibid., 56–60.
47. Steinberg, "Unhappy Asia Bastion."
48. Biggs, "Outraged Okinawans," 57.
49. Bird, stationed elsewhere in the Pacific, was on a temporary military assignment in Okinawa when he met Nakamura. As Andrus remembers the story, she was praying for religious guidance when Bird introduced himself in Japanese. Andrus Oral History, 19.
50. The airfield was built immediately after the Americans arrived in the spring of 1945, to be used as a base from which to attack Japan's mainland. In 1953, the runway was lengthened from 7,900 feet to 8,800 feet. Ginowan Kyōiku Iinkai, *Ginowan-shi Shi* (Ginowan, Okinawa: Ginowan Kyōiku Iinkai, 1994), 390–94, 403–4.

Shimabukuro departed from the port of Yokohama aboard the *Hakusan Maru* and six days later (17 April) sailed into Naha's Tomari port. The two missionaries were immediately taken by LDS servicemen to the home of Nobu Nakamura in Futenma, some fifteen miles north of Naha. Late in 1955, a small plot of land had been purchased there to build a meetinghouse. The missionaries were to live with the Nakamuras until 8 November 1956, when a Quonset donated by the United States Army was completed as their living quarters.[51] Thus, the work in Okinawa began, not in Naha, but in a small town in central Okinawa. On 29 April 1956, the first Mormon meeting conducted in Japanese was held at Nodake Junior High School, which had served as the headquarters of the 96th Division of the United States Army during the final days of war.[52] On 2 September 1956, Anderson was sustained and set apart as the first president of the Okinawa District. It was not until 17 March 1957 that a branch was organized in Naha, when four elders and two sisters arrived, and the first meeting was held at a community hall.[53]

11.3.3. The Work Spreads to Korea

A similar situation existed in Korea, where American servicemen had been the instrument of carrying out Mormon missionary work, including among the local population. The bloody conflict on the divided Korean Peninsula, triggered when North Korean forces crossed the 38th parallel in June 1950, had barely ended at this time, after claiming half a million civilian and military lives in South Korea alone.[54] The center of Mormon missionary activity was in the southern port city of Pusan, which had become "a haven for the homeless, a place for those who had lost their families, and a gathering place for those who had become separated from their families in their haste to flee from the advancing Communist armies."[55] Mormon soldiers began to hold English and religious classes in the evenings, which attracted young Korean men and women. The work, which began in early 1952 under personal initiatives, became an organized effort in early 1953 under the leadership of Leon Ballard and Howard W. Bradshaw of the LDS Pusan group. In March 1953, the work was strengthened with the arrival in the Pusan area of Mormon chaplain Spencer D. Madsen. Missionary efforts by these and other servicemen saw their first fruits on 3 August 1952, when four local individuals were baptized into the LDS Church at Songdo near Pusan.

Those baptized on this occasion included two children of Ho Jik Kim. Kim was born under Japanese colonial rule in what is now part of North Korea, edu-

---

51. "Quarterly Historical Reports."
52. Gibney, "Okinawa," 24.
53. "Quarterly Historical Reports"; Sam K. Shimabukuro, letter to author, 28 November 1995.
54. An armistice agreement, which formally ended hostilities, was signed on 27 July 1953.
55. Choi, *History*, 111.

cated in the Japanese educational system, and graduated from Tohoku Imperial University in Sendai, Japan. Kim had joined the LDS Church during the previous year (July 1951) at the age of forty-six while attending a doctoral program at Cornell University in New York. Following his return to Korea in September 1951, he assumed a number of influential positions in Korean society, including vice minister of education in President Syngman Rhee's cabinet and Korea's chief representative to the United Nations Educational, Scientific and Cultural Organization (UNESCO).[56] At this time, Kim was president of the National Fisheries College in Pusan. About a year later, in May 1953, Kim was ordained an elder by Chaplain Madsen; in August 1955, he was called and set apart by Apostle Joseph Fielding Smith to serve as president of the Korea District of the newly organized Northern Far East Mission.

Paul Andrus, in preparing to launch missionary work in Korea, naturally requested Dr. Kim's personal involvement. In March 1956, Andrus informed Kim of his desire to send missionaries to Korea "in the next two or three weeks if possible" in a letter hand-carried by Colonel Robert H. Slover, chairman of the LDS Far East Military Coordinating Committee. After stating that he had selected the "two best missionaries," he asked if they could stay at Kim's house until suitable quarters could be found and requested his assistance in facilitating the issuance of entry visas.[57] In reply, Kim informed Andrus that suitable quarters for the missionaries had been secured and that he had sent letters of guarantee to be filed with Korea's diplomatic mission in Tokyo.[58] In the absence of support guaranteed by an established organization in Korea, where the LDS Church was not yet incorporated, Dr. Kim gave his personal guarantee, which Korean officials accepted. As vice-chairman of the Seoul Board of Education (to which he was appointed in 1956), moreover, Kim subsequently argued successfully for the LDS Church's incorporation in Korea.

As noted in the previous section, the first Mormon missionaries assigned to labor in Korea were Richard Lee Detton and Don Gayle Powell, who had been serving in Japan since February and March 1954, respectively. Andrus, explaining how the system should work when they arrived, stated that (1) Powell would be the supervising elder in the Korea District (over missionary work); (2) Groves would be the president of the Korea Servicemen's District; and (3) Kim would remain as the president of the Korea District (over members and general church affairs). Andrus further stressed that the three men would be responsible for "separate spheres of action" and noted that "in the future the servicemen's

---

56. Choi, *History*, chapter 4.

57. Paul C. Andrus, letter to Ho Jik Kim, 19 March 1956. Northern Far East Mission, "Presidents' Correspondence," LDS Church Archives.

58. Japan and Korea did not have a formal diplomatic relation at this time. The Korean mission in Tokyo provided consular services in Japan. Paul C. Andrus, letter to Ho Jik Kim, 31 March 1956. "Presidents' Correspondence."

organizations and the Korean organizations [would] become completely separate and apart from each other."[59]

In the early morning of 20 April 1956, Detton and Powell took a Northwest Airlines flight out of Haneda airport for Seoul. At this time there were about sixty-six Korean members.[60] The first all-Korea conference was held on 3 June 1956 at Seoul Senior High School, attended by thirty members. By summer six more missionaries had arrived. The early missionaries to Korea suffered hardships, not the least of which was the poor hygienic conditions. In the summer of 1958, five of the ten missionaries in Korea contracted hepatitis. Immediately Andrus flew in from Tokyo to assess the situation. The missionaries, asked to express their feelings concerning whether or not to close the Korea District, each reportedly stated that they were "prepared to give their lives if necessary so that the work could continue in Korea."[61] Language was another challenge. No literature was available in the Korean language. Though most spoke Japanese, use of the former colonial language was unacceptable to the Koreans (though Andrus evidently conversed with Kim in Japanese).

In the Korea District of the Northern Far East Mission, missionary work was conducted only in Seoul and Pusan. The number of missionaries slowly picked up throughout the 1950s; the number peaked at twenty-three in May 1961. Initially, the supervising elder concurrently served as counselor to the district president. After the untimely death of Dr. Kim at the age of fifty-four in August 1959, it became established practice to have one of the Korea elders serve as a counselor in the mission presidency. This would continue until the creation of a separate mission in Korea. On 8 July 1962, Andrus proposed in a conference held in Seoul that the Northern Far East Mission be divided and that the Korean Mission be organized, with Gail E. Carr as president. At this time, there were nineteen missionaries serving in Korea, with more than 1,100 baptisms having been recorded since the formal opening of missionary work in April 1956.

11.4. Securing Places of Worship

11.4.1. Early Property Purchases

At the end of the occupation, the LDS Church owned only one building, besides the mission home in Tokyo; it was in Takasaki and had been purchased in October 1951 (see Table 11.2). Each time a new area was opened, the first order of business was to find a place to meet on Sundays and for other activi-

---

59. Andrus then concluded: "I suggest, therefore, that Elder Powell serve as one of your counselors in the District Presidency. It is not necessary that Brother Gardener be released as your counselor, but I suggest that when he goes home that he is not to be replaced by a serviceman." Paul C. Andrus, letter to Ho Jik Kim, 26 April 1956. "Presidents' Correspondence."

60. Choi, *History*, 130.

61. Ibid., 131.

Table 11.2. Property Purchases by the LDS Church in Japan, 1948–65

	Municipality	Date of purchase[1]	Remarks
1	Tokyo—Hiroo (Azabu)	21 April 1948	Mission home. Registered The Japanese Mission of the Church of Jesus Christ of Latter-day Saints (English).
2	Takasaki	29 October 1951	Gunma Branch. Registered The Corporation of the Presiding Bishop of the Church of Jesus Christ of Latter-day Saints (English).
3	Sendai	16 December 1952	Registered The Foreign Land Corporation of the Church of Jesus Christ of Latter-day Saints (English).
4	Tokyo—Shibuya (Namikibashi)	10 April 1953	Tokyo Central Branch. Registered The Japanese Mission of the Church of Jesus Christ of Latter-day Saints (English). Sold 11 February 1963.
5	Sapporo—Kita-2 jo	15 July 1953	Registered The Japanese Mission of the Church of Jesus Christ of Latter-day Saints (English). Building burned 30 March 1965.
6	Hiroshima	14 October 1953	Registered The Japanese Mission of the Church of Jesus Christ of Latter-day Saints (English).
7	Yokohama	22 June 1954	
8	Kofu	10 October 1954[2]	
9	Otaru	28 December 1954	
10	Ginowan	9 December 1955[3]	Land. Futenma Branch. Registered Al G. Youngberg, Henry H. Griffith, Lew W. M. Cramer of the Church of Jesus Christ of Latter-day Saints (English).[4]
11	Nagoya	24 March 1956	
12	Muroran	17 November 1956	Sold 14 January 1988.
13	Toyonaka	10 December 1956	Okamachi Branch.
14	Yanai	12 December 1956	Land.

	Municipality	Date of purchase[1]	Remarks
15	Asahikawa	30 April 1957	Land. Sold 4 April 1990.
16	Tokyo—Senzoku	27 December 1957	Tokyo South Branch.
17	Tokyo—Nakano	15 August 1958[5]	Land. Tokyo North Branch.
18	Kobe	26 December 1958	Sannomiya Branch.
19	Tokyo—Musashino	13 July 1959	Land. Tokyo West Branch.
20	Osaka	7 December 1959	Abeno Branch.
21	Tokyo—Aoyama (Omotesando)	18 June 1960	Tokyo West and then Tokyo Central Branch. Sold 12 November 1973
22	Nishinomiya	26 November 1960	
23	Fukuoka—Yakuin	23 January 1961	Building burned 5 March 1963.
24	Naha	16 May 1962	Land. Registered Paul C. Andrus.[6]
25	Tokyo—Koiwa	10 December 1962	Tokyo East Branch.
26	Yamagata	29 May 1963	
27	Kanazawa	4 July 1963	
28	Fukuoka—Josui	29 February 1964	
29	Kyoto	8 July 1964	
30	Sapporo—Minami 20-jo (Moiwa)	10 February 1965	Land.
31	Matsumoto	9 March 1965	Land. Part of property sold on 13 August 1984.

[1] Date of registration, if the date of purchase is not recorded; [2] Additional piece purchased on 16 December 1954; [3] Additional purchases of adjoining land were made on 17 December 1956 and 17 August 1959; [4] Registration changed to the Corporation of the President of the Church of Jesus Christ of Latter-day Saints, May 1956. Additional purchases of adjoining land were made under the Corporation of the President of the Church of Jesus Christ of Latter-day Saints on 17 December 1956 and 17 August 1959. The Futenma property was purchased in seven transactions made on three separate days over four years. Registration changed to *Matsujitsu Seito Iesu Kirisuto Kyōkai*, March 1979; [5] The Tokyo North property was purchased in three separate transactions (covering two local jurisdictions) made on two separate days over two years; [6] Registration changed to *Matsujitsu Seito Iesu Kirisuto Kyōkai*, December 1975.

Land registration records held at the respective legal affairs bureaus of the Ministry of Justice: Takasaki, Sendai, Shibuya (Tokyo), Sapporo, Hiroshima, Yokohama, Kofu, Otaru, Ginowan, Showa (Nagoya), Muroran, Toyonaka, Yanai, Asahikawa-Higashi, Omori (Tokyo), Shinjuku and Nakano (both Tokyo), Kobe, Musashino (Tokyo), Higashi-Osaka, Nishinomiya, Fukuoka, Edogawa (Tokyo), Yamagata, Naha, and Matsumoto.

ties on weekdays. Initially, they would find a community meeting hall of some sort, which could be identified at short notice and used for a nominal fee. Then, they would typically find a school building as a more permanent location. For example, from May 1949 to December 1956, the Juso Branch met at Yodogawa Girls' High School, whose principal allowed the church to use the facilities free of charge. From time to time, meetings needed to move from one school building to another. In 1959, the church periodical carried announcements that the Tokyo North Branch had just moved to the fourth floor of a sewing school (Musashino Dressmaking School) near Ikebukuro station (though weekday meetings were being held at different locations) and the Abeno Branch to a kindergarten in Osaka's Higashi Sumiyoshi ward.[62]

The Nishinomiya Branch building, purchased in 1960, was a typical old-vintage Japanese house, with a large garden. Courtesy Kyoko Tanaka.

As membership grew, the LDS Church began to purchase buildings in various locations, including Sendai (December 1952), Tokyo (April 1953), Sapporo (July 1953), and Hiroshima (October 1953). These and others to follow were typically large, vintage Japanese-style houses of two-story construction. The first floor had a kitchen and several rooms, which were separated from each other by sliding doors. When the sliding doors were removed, two or three rooms could be made into a large meeting room that could accommodate sixty or even up to a hundred people. The rooms upstairs could be used as the living quarters for missionaries. A few were nonresidential buildings, such as a warehouse or a medical clinic no longer in use.

These early properties were registered under the Corporation of the Presiding Bishop, the Foreign Land Corporation, or the Japanese Mission (English title). It appears that Mauss rather accidentally discovered that the church was required to register under the new Religious Corporation Law of April 1951 in order to enjoy tax-exempt status for property transactions. The church's Japanese Mission, though not the church itself, had been registered as a religious corporation under the SCAP-directed Religious Corporation Ordinance of December 1945, which formally abolished the Religious Organization Law of 1939 (that took effect in April 1940). Unlike its war-time predecessor, which had given the govern-

---

62. *Seito no Michi* 3 (March 1959): 27; (April 1959): 26.

ment power to control religious activity, the Religious Corporation Ordinance liberally permitted free exercise of religion, allowing any religious organization to be registered as a tax-exempt juridical entity simply upon notification. The new Religious Corporation Law, though more elaborate and comprehensive, was meant to preserve essentially the same liberal orientation of the Religious Corporation Ordinance, which was expiring at the end of the occupation. Article 1 describes the purpose of the law as giving religious organizations legal power to own and manage assets, so as to facilitate the achievement of their purposes.

Under the new law, the LDS Church was required to follow a certain procedure (including designating three or more responsible officers and formally notifying the members of the intention to incorporate) to file an application as a religious corporation before 3 October 1952.[63] This point was reiterated when Mauss sought advice from a law firm on transferring the title of the Takasaki property to the Foreign Lands Corporation according to the instructions he had received from the Office of the Presiding Bishop in August 1952. The law firm advised that such a transfer would involve a registration tax, and the transfer was not made.[64] The letter received in September 1952 from the law firm of McIvor, Kauffman & Yamamoto noted the requirements of the law and offered assistance in "preparation of various documents required for the above application if you so desire" (the public notice of the incorporation of the church had already appeared in the monthly *LDS Messenger*, dated 10 August 1952). The government records show that the religious corporation was registered only on 11 February 1954.[65] With the LDS Church formally incorporated, the titles for these properties were transferred to the tax-exempt *Matsujitsu Seito Iesu Kirisuto Kyōkai* (the name for the Japanese corporation of the Church of Jesus Christ of Latter-day Saints) in early 1954.[66]

The situation was different in Okinawa, where Japanese law did not apply. When a group of American servicemen purchased a small plot of land in Futemna in December 1955, the title was initially registered to "Al G. Youngberg, Henry H. Griffith, and Lew W. M. Cramer of the Church of Jesus Christ of Latter-day Saints (English)."[67] The land, upon which a Quonset would be placed in the fall of 1956 to accommodate the newly arrived missionaries, proved to be too small to

---

63. Otherwise, the church would be deemed to have been dissolved on that day.

64. Office of the Presiding Bishopric, letter to Vinal G. Mauss, 13 August 1952; McIvor, Kauffman & Yamamoto, letter to Vinal G. Mauss, 9 September 1952, LDS Church Archives.

65. The "Quarterly Historical Report" entry for 11 March 1954 states: "The Church's registration was completed today with the Japanese government—in process for several months." The date must be an error.

66. Registration was changed to *Matsujitsu Seito Iesu Kirisuto Kyōkai* in February 1954 for Hiroshima, in March 1954 for Sapporo, in March 1955 for the two Tokyo properties, and in February 1954 for Takasaki and Sendai.

67. The title was changed to the Corporation of the President of the Church of Jesus Christ of Latter-day Saints in May 1956.

build an adequate meeting facility. The church thus decided to purchase adjoining plots of land. As told by Sam Shimabukuro, given strong anti-American feeling in Okinawa, resistance was expected from the landlords to selling the land to what was perceived as an American institution. The first landlord they visited was absent, so was the second. The last landlord lived quite far away from Futenma. When the missionaries arrived at the house, a man in his seventies appeared at the door and upon hearing the purpose of their visit told them that he had lived in Utah some fifty years earlier and learned to appreciate the honesty of the Mormon people. Not only did he agree to sell his property to the LDS Church, but also he offered to persuade the other two landlords to sell their properties as well. Additional purchases of adjoining land were made under the Corporation of the President of the Church of Jesus Christ of Latter-day Saints in six transactions on 17 December 1956 and 17 August 1959. Likewise, in May 1962, the purchase of the Naha property was initially made in the name of Paul C. Andrus.[68] The titles to these properties were transferred to the LDS Church's Japanese religious corporation in the 1970s following the return of Okinawa to Japanese administration in May 1972.

To defray the costs of property acquisition, branches frequently organized fundraising activities of various types. The most common were bazaars that sold food and miscellaneous donated items. A notable fundraising event of this period was the formation, under the directorship of Ronald D. Pexton of Salt Lake City, of a combined Maebashi–Takasaki Branch choir (named the "Gunma LDS Chorus") that made a tour of eight cities in August 1952. From March to July 1953, another group of Mormon musicians made a tour of the mission, helping each branch where a concert was held to raise building funds by selling the tickets. The group, called the "Melody Men," consisted of five musically talented missionaries—Wendell W. Jensen of Salt Lake City, David H. Moikeha of Lanakila, Hawaii, Russell W. Oakey of Boise, Idaho, and Richard R. Olsen of Preston, Idaho, in addition to Ronald Pexton. The program consisted of selections of vocal (solo and quartet) and instrumental (piano and violin) music in the classical and popular traditions. The tour began in Asahikawa on 1 March 1953 and traveled southward, holding more than sixty concerts.

Curiously, these and earlier large-scale fundraising events all took place when Vinal Mauss was the mission president.[69] The personal disposition of his successors may be a factor explaining why such activities ceased under their presiden-

---

68. As Andrus recalls, George Lowe, a civilian employee, worked with the American authorities on these transactions. Author's interview with Andrus.

69. Earlier large-scale fundraising events included a "Fashion Show" in November 1950 and a major music and dance production called "Hawaii Calls" in June 1951; both of these events were held in Tokyo and yielded net profits of $2,000 and $4,500, respectively. The Hawaiian show was conceived and carried out by the mission's Hawaiian contingent, including Samuel Kalama, Dorothy A. Koolau, and Philomena Andrade who wrote the script. The show, featuring volunteer singers and dancers recruited from the public, was performed on two evenings in front of a sell-out crowd at the 2,500-capacity

Members and missionaries pose in the back garden of the Sannomiya Branch building, circa 1962. Courtesy Ryoko Konishi.

cies. It may also well be the case that Robertson was too old or too old-fashioned to devote his energy to a complex managerial task, while to Andrus the shortage of missionaries did not justify engaging in such unconventional activities.[70] Regardless, as their incomes rose, the Japanese people were beginning to enjoy greater opportunities for recreation and to demand higher standards for artistic performance. Novelty was no longer sufficient to justify charging the admission fee for an amateur performance, however good it might be. Andrus continued to challenge the members to raise funds through various activities as well as by donating ¥100 a month to the building fund.[71]

11.4.2. Acceleration of Property Purchases under Andrus

Andrus accelerated the acquisition of real estate by purchasing more than twenty existing buildings or building sites, starting with Nagoya and Toyonaka (Okamachi) in 1956. When a large Japanese-style house was found in the city of Toyonaka, a northern suburb of Osaka, near Okamachi station on the Hankyu

---

Kyōritsu Hall. Philomena Clawson, letters to author, 11 February 1996 and 12 March 1996, along with supporting documents.

70. This was an explicit decision on Andrus's part. Andrus, later explaining why he did not sponsor "missionary quartets or basketball teams or any of the things that were being done in other missions at that time," questioned the wisdom of taking "missionaries away and develop[ing] a traveling musical show" when "we could get more investigators... just by going out and holding a street meeting." Andrus Oral History, 45–46.

71. Paul C. Andrus, president's message, *Seito no Michi* 2 (December 1958): 8.

commuter line, the branch that had been meeting in Juso in northern Osaka (fifth station south on the same train line) was relocated; the name was accordingly changed from Juso Branch to Okamachi Branch. These were all registered under the LDS Church's Japanese religious corporation.

The biggest real estate purchase of the period was made in June 1960 when the church acquired a 2,600 square meters (or about 28,000 square feet) lot with a large house in the fashionable Aoyama district of Tokyo for about ¥245 million (or approximately $680,000).[72] The purchase of this rather expensive property was prompted by the emerging need to find a replacement for the Tokyo Central Branch building whose physical condition was deteriorating. The plans to demolish the old building and construct a new one on the existing Namikibashi property had been abandoned when a satellite ticket office of the Japan [Horse] Racing Association (JRA) was built next door. Because purchasing the new Aoyama property would involve a large sum of money, it was a major decision requiring a consultation between the First Presidency and Gordon B. Hinckley,[73] who, as Assistant to the Twelve, was a frequent visitor to the mission at the time.

The transaction was finalized over a three-week period between 27 May (when Hinckley met with Motoyuki Ibata) and 18 June 1960 (when the payment was made in full). The decision to buy the property was facilitated by the prospect of being able to sell the Namikibashi property for a considerable sum of money.[74] On 29 May 1960, Hinckley talked on the telephone with Henry D. Moyle of the First Presidency regarding the purchase. On the next day, 30 May 1960, a telegram arrived from Salt Lake approving the purchase, and the contract was signed on 3 June. On 25 June, Don Peter Lassig of Salt Lake City and John W. Wanlass of Ogden, Utah, moved into the property.[75]

The property faced the busy Omotesando Avenue, which led to the front gate of the Meiji Shrine, a memorial to Emperor Meiji. The building that stood on the plot was a large stately house with a beautiful Japanese garden. It was later discovered that the stone lanterns found on the property (numbering eleven) were sixteenth-century Tokugawa vassals' gifts to the memory of shogun Tokugawa Iemitsu, whose funeral was held at the Kan-ei-ji Temple, and that they were in

---

72. The equivalent value in 2014 would be about ¥1.3 billion based on the consumer price index (www.e-stat.go.jp). This amounts to $13.2 million at the exchange rate of 100 yen to a dollar.

73. Gordon B. Hinckley (1910–2008) would serve as a member of the Quorum of the Twelve Apostles from October 1961 and become the LDS Church's fifteenth president in 1995.

74. The Namikibashi property had been purchased at ¥7.2 million ($20,000) in 1953. It would be sold for ¥198 million ($550,000) in 1963. Author's interview with Kazuo Imai, 9 and 27 January 1996. See also Andrus Oral History, 30–32. Where there are discrepancies between the two accounts, the Imai account was deemed more accurate. He was a church accountant serving as president of the Tokyo Central Branch at the time.

75. "Quarterly Historical Reports."

In 1960, the LDS Church acquired this 28,000 square foot property on the fashionable Omotesando Avenue (left), a boulevard leading up to the front gate of the Meiji Shrine. The large house thereon (right) was used as a meetinghouse first for the Tokyo West Branch and then for the Tokyo Central Branch. Courtesy Masao Watabe.

fact misplaced temple treasures.[76] The LDS Church contacted the temple and, on 15 June 1964, returned the artifacts in a ceremony that was widely covered in the press.[77] Mormon leaders had a grand plan to take advantage of the location as a showcase for the church. In July 1962, the church announced that permission had been granted by the First Presidency to construct on this property a building that would accommodate more than 1,200 people as the East Central District Center.[78] The plan never materialized. The house would be used by the church as a meetinghouse for thirteen years (initially for the Tokyo West Branch, followed by the Tokyo Central Branch from 1963, and the Tokyo Ward of the Tokyo Stake from 1970).

Andrus later learned that he and Hinckley had been "criticized for wasting the Church's money and paying such a high price for such a small piece of land." The LDS Church, after abandoning the plan to build a large district center, instead sold the property in November 1973 for ¥6.4 billion (approximately $24 million at the prevailing exchange rate of ¥265 per United States dollar; about 25 times the purchase price),[79] and used the proceeds to pay for the cost of constructing church buildings throughout the country, including the costs associated with the construction of the Tokyo Temple. Andrus received a letter from Hinckley, dated 16 August 1973, which stated that the Omotesando property purchase

---

76. The Kan-ei-ji Temple was one of the two Tokugawa family temples, along with the Zōjōji Temple. During the Edo period, the temple was given a large, 250-acre plot of land that included most of what is now Ueno Park, but lost most of its buildings during the civil war (Boshin War) in 1868. Subsequently, much of the land was confiscated by the newly established Meiji government.

77. The event was not only broadcast on air by public Nihon Hōsō Kyōkai (NHK) news but also covered by the *Asahi* and *Mainichi Shinbun*, two of the largest national dailies. *Seito no Michi* 8 (1964): 398–401.

78. *Church News*, 7 July 1962, 4; also *Seito no Michi* 6 (1962): 550.

79. The equivalent value in 2014 would be about ¥16 billion based on the consumer price index (www.e-stat.go.jp). This amounts to $160 million at the exchange rate of 100 yen to a dollar.

The Muroran Branch building, completed in late 1959, was the first Mormon meetinghouse constructed in all of Asia. Courtesy Kyoko Sato.

"certainly is the most profitable real estate deal the Church has ever made," thus vindicating the original purchase. On this spot now stands the landmark Oak Omotesando building that provides upscale retail space to *Emporio Armani* and *Coach* on the ground floor.[80]

Most buildings acquired were in need of a renovation to make them suitable as a meetinghouse. In particular, the renovation work on the Tokyo East Branch property (acquired in December 1962) and the Yamagata Branch property (May 1963) was extensive as they had been originally built, not as residential homes, but as a warehouse and a medical clinic, respectively.[81] Another major renovation took place in Muroran. The 40-plus year-old Muroran Branch property (purchased in November 1956) had deteriorated so much that it was decided to replace the whole upper structure.[82] Most considered this to be a new building when the work was completed in late 1959. On 31 March 1960, Gordon B. Hinckley, accompanied by Paul C. Andrus, made a tour of the "new building." The Muroran meetinghouse became the first "chapel-like" building ever constructed by the LDS Church in all of Asia. No thought was given, however, to formally dedicating the building to church use.[83]

Far south in the mission, on the island of Okinawa, another attempt was made to build a chapel in the 1950s. According to the 25 February 1956 issue

---

80. Andrus Oral History, 30–32.
81. *Seito no Michi* 7 (1963): 686.
82. *Seito no Michi* 3 (September 1959): 22–23.
83. Author's interview with Andrus.

of the *Church News*, ground was broken on 4 February in Futenma for "the first Mormon chapel to be constructed on this tiny Pacific island in a solemn ceremony" presided over by Paul C. Andrus.[84] In the event, the plan to build on this site a "$25,000 chapel . . . by late summer" to be used by "all LDS groups on the island" did not materialize and the Quonset continued to serve as a meetinghouse.[85] Speaking in 1997, Andrus explained this incident as a case of young servicemen "carried away" by the zeal to build a chapel all on their own. While the First Presidency may have considered the "general concept" of building a chapel in Futenma approvingly, there was no explicit approval of the plan by the LDS Church. In addition, the land itself was too small to accommodate an adequate meeting facility at the time.[86] Talks of building a meetinghouse in Futenma lingered on for some time until 1960, when the plan was formally scrapped in favor of first constructing a building in Naha.[87]

All in all, properties had been acquired for all but two of the original branches by the end of the Northern Far East Mission.[88] Real estate transactions were handled by the Far East Construction Office following its establishment in July 1962. Eight of the twenty-seven branches with their own properties, including Futenma, owned only land; these land purchases were made with the future prospect of building a church-designed meetinghouse in mind. In these branches, the LDS Church continued to hold Sunday and other meetings in rented facilities. In Asahikawa, for example, the church-owned land was leased to a car dealer while missionaries lived and held meetings in a rented house.[89] In the Tokyo North Branch, a 30,000 square-foot plot of land that stands across the boundaries of Tokyo's Shinjuku and Nakano wards was purchased in August 1958, reportedly for ¥20 million ($55,555),[90] while the branch continued to meet in a rented school building in Ikebukuro, as noted previously.[91]

---

84. *Church News*, 25 February 1956, 7.
85. Author's interview with Keisei Nagamine, 24 March 1998.
86. Author's interview with Andrus.
87. "This afternoon, Brother Hinckley and President Andrus met with the Okinawa Building Committee and reviewed the proposed building at the Futenma Branch. After an extensive review and a discussion of the present status of this project, Brother Hinckley suggested that the present plans be abandoned, that a smaller building be erected on the present Futenma property, and that a suitable site be obtained in Naha for a large Church building. The Committee unanimously agreed to this suggestion." "Quarterly Historical Reports," 12 June 1960.
88. The two branches without their own buildings or land were the Niigata and Okayama Branches. Obviously, none of the newly established branches (Fukushima, Kitakyushu, Kumamoto, Nagasaki, and Takamatsu) owned properties.
89. Dick Nanto, e-mail to author, 19 November 1996; telephone interview with Takuzo Yasuda, 21 February 1997; Tsugumi Yamada, letter to author, 15 January 1997.
90. The equivalent value in 2014 would be about ¥114 million based on the consumer price index (www.e-stat.go.jp). This amounts to $1.14 million at the exchange rate of 100 yen to a dollar.
91. *Seito no Michi* 3 (May 1959): 32–33.

11.5. Developing Local Leadership

11.5.1. Branch Leadership

Most Japanese members were young, in their teens and early twenties, at the time of their conversion to Mormonism. The LDS Church therefore needed to wait for about ten years, until the late 1950s, before the first cohort of converts became mature enough to assume leadership roles, especially as branch presidents. To be sure, a few had earlier served as branch presidents, but these were older men, including prewar converts Fujiya Nara and Tomigoro Takagi.[92] While they were not particularly experienced in church administration, at least they had the wisdom and judgment that came with age. Given the limited supply of such men, the church could not rely on them to carry on its work indefinitely.

It was toward the end of 1957, in the context of an overhaul of the organizational structure in Tokyo, that five Japanese men were called as branch presidents: Kohei Tanaka (Tokyo West, 1 December), Masaji Otsuka (Tokyo North, 8 December), Kazuo Imai (Tokyo Central, 15 December), Shozo Suzuki (Yokohama, 15 December), and Kan Watanabe (Tokyo South, 29 December). They were probably all in their late twenties and had been in the church for five to eight years;[93] three of them had previously served full-time proselytizing missions. Outside the Tokyo area, branch president positions were filled by local men on a regular basis from 1961, beginning with the Nagoya Branch (Tokichi Yanagida, 26 February 1961). On 19 March 1961, Andrus reorganized six branches during a conference of the West Central District, with six local men as presidents: Hiroshi Aki (Nishinomiya), Tadao Hayashi (Yanai), Tamahiko Shudo (Abeno), Tokuichi Tsukuda (Hiroshima), Kenjiro Uenoyama (Okamachi), and Yoichi Yamamura (Sannomiya). These were followed by the appointment on 26 March 1961 of Toshio Yanagisawa as the president of the Sapporo Branch.[94] In some of the smaller units, proselytizing missionaries would continue to serve as branch presidents when these men were released and no suitable local men could be found.[95]

---

92. When Vinal Mauss created three branches in Tokyo in November 1949, he called three local men to preside in each: Fujiya Nara (Yukigaya Branch, 20 November), Genkichi Shiraishi (Ogikubo), and Tomigoro Takagi (Ikebukuro, 27 November). These members were all prewar converts who had been baptized in 1915, 1909, and 1915, respectively, and were fifty-one, fifty-nine, and fifty-five years of age (see Section 10.6.1 in Chapter 6). On 3 May 1953, Masao Watabe was set part as president of the Sendai Branch at the age of thirty-eight.

93. As the most recent convert, Shozo Suzuki had been baptized in August 1952.

94. In March 1963, prewar convert Suketomo Nonogaki (then seventy-five years old) was called to preside over the Kofu Branch. He had been baptized as Suketomo Suda in Kofu in 1907.

95. In July 1965, Dwayne Andersen observed that, of the twenty-nine branches, eighteen were headed by local Japanese men; of the eleven missionary leaders, more than

11.5.2. District and Priesthood Leadership

Mormon district leadership requires greater experience and maturity in the church, preferably including experience as a branch president. Thus, the first Japanese man to serve as district president was not called until 1960.[96] During the East Central District conference held in Tokyo on 2 October 1960, Kazuo Imai was sustained as president, with Masaji Otsuka as his first counselor and Shozo Suzuki as his second. When the announcement was made, a reporter for the mission periodical *Seito no Michi* recorded, an audible sigh of surprise and disbelief was expressed among those assembled.[97] Outside the Tokyo area, local men assumed district leadership roles over the subsequent years. On 18–19 November 1961, Shozo Suzuki was sustained as president of the West Central District.[98] This was followed in the Okinawa District on 18 November 1962 when Kensei Nagamine was sustained as president.

At the end of 1960, the number of Japanese men ordained to the Melchizedek priesthood was approaching one hundred, prompting Paul Andrus to organize them into an elders quorum. Thus, on 23 October 1960, the first quorum of elders was organized, with Kan Watanabe as president. This covered all elders in Japan (including Okinawa), but not those in Korea or American servicemen. In two years, the number of elders in the mission exceeded 150. In November 1962, Dwayne Andersen divided the first quorum into two quorums, with the first quorum (with Hideji Hotta as president) responsible for elders in Tokyo and north of Tokyo and the second quorum (with Kan Watanabe as president) for those south of Tokyo; where feasible, a group leader was called in each branch. Then, the fifth quorum was created out of the first quorum on 27 March 1964, with Kenichi Sagara as president, to cover northern and eastern Japan outside of Tokyo.[99] This was followed by the sixth quorum on 6 December 1964 and the seventh quorum (for local elders in the Hokkaido District) on 28 May 1966, with Yasuhioro Matsushita as president.

---

half were local Japanese missionaries. Andersen, "Dwayne N. Andersen's Experience with the Japanese People," 15. Towards the end of the Northern Far East Mission, in early 1968, eight of the thirty-five branches were headed by missionaries: Fukushima, Kitakyushu, Kumamoto, Matsumoto, Nagasaki, Niigata, Okayama, and Takamatsu. Three of these had only been created in late 1967. *Seito no Michi* 12 (1968).

96. As part of the December 1957 branch reorganization in Tokyo and Yokohama, however, a district council had been partially organized, with Fujiya Nara, Zenjiro Noguchi, Tatsui Sato, and Tomigoro Takagi.

97. *Seito no Michi* 4 (1960): 322.

98. The district conference was held simultaneously in Osaka and Fukuoka. Suzuki was formally set apart on 20 November 1961. *Seito no Michi* 6 (February 1962).

99. The third quorum of elders, organized on 22 October 1962 was for all servicemen in Japan. On 10 March 1963, the fourth quorum of elders was organized to split the geographical area of the third quorum.

11.5.3. Mission Leadership

The first Japanese person to serve as a counselor in the mission presidency was Yotaro Yoshino, who was set apart as first counselor to Andersen on 5 October 1962 (the second counselor was Masaru T. Shimizu, a proselytizing missionary from Butler, Utah). Yoshino was one of the first two local missionaries to serve a full-time Mormon mission; following his mission he studied at Brigham Young University (BS in business, 1957), and subsequently obtained an MBA from Columbia Business School in 1959 and a PhD from Stanford Business School in 1962.[100] At the time of his call, he was engaged in a research project in Japan on the business practices of Japanese corporations. On 15 June 1963, Yoshino was released to allow him to return to the United States to pursue his professional career, which would eventually include a faculty position at Harvard Business School. At that time, he was replaced by Goro Yamada in the mission presidency. Yamada too had served a full-time Mormon mission and acquired proficiency in English, a qualification essential to serve as a counselor to Dwayne Andersen whose proficiency in Japanese was limited.

On 4 August 1963, Kan Watanabe, another speaker of English, was set apart as second counselor in the mission presidency. Watanabe, who was living in Osaka while working for the Swiss chemical company CIBA, was given the responsibility of coordinating the work of the West Central District. Born in Komatsu on 23 March 1941, he was baptized into the LDS Church in the Tedori River in Ishikawa Prefecture on 22 April 1950. Upon graduation from high school, he enlisted in the newly established National Police Reserve (present-day Self-Defense Forces),[101] moved to Tokyo towards the end of his two-year service in 1952, and worked briefly as assistant to church translator Tatsui Sato before serving a full-time Mormon mission from 1953 to 1955. Upon completing his mission, he was called to be the first president of the Tokyo South Branch in 1957 and, following his move to Osaka in 1960, became the first president of the first quorum of elders (and continued as president of the second quorum in 1962 when the first quorum was split). In 1967, Watanabe would become the area manager for the church's Translation Services Department, and in March 1970 called as the first native Japanese mission president—to preside over the newly organized Japan West Mission.[102]

---

100. *Success Messenger* 6 (October 1962): 13–15.

101. Although Japan's military was disbanded at the end of World War II, Douglas MacArthur, Supreme Commander for the Allied Powers, ordered the establishment of a special police unit (with greater firepower) when occupation forces were dispatched to Korea in 1950 at the outbreak of the Korean War.

102. *Seito no Michi* 2 (February 1959): 13–15. Kan Watanabe, interview with author, Tokyo, 18 April 1997. See also Kan Watanabe, "Japanese Baseball Fan Reaches Home," in *No More Strangers*, vol. 2, ed. Hartman and Connie Rector (Salt Lake City: Bookcraft, 1973), 99–102.

Adney and Judy Komatsu (in the center) pose, with young Japanese mission leaders. Kenji Tanaka (left in back row), Kan Watanabe (third from left in back row), Goro Yamada (left in front row) are among the people seen. To the right of Judy Komatsu is Toshiko Yanagida. Courtesy Toshiko Yanagida.

In the meantime, a Japanese woman assumed the leadership of adult women in the mission for the first time. On 21 June 1964, Toshiko Yanagida was set apart as president of the Northern Far East Mission Relief Society, a position that had previously been filled by the wife of an incumbent mission president. Yanagida, baptized into the LDS Church in Tokyo on 18 August 1949, was a daughter of Tomigoro Takagi, a prewar convert. She would serve in this capacity until the division of the mission in 1968.

Goro Yamada emigrated to Canada in late 1966,[103] prompting Adney Komatsu to reorganize the mission presidency. On 30 October 1966, as Yamada was released as first counselor, Kan Watanabe took his place and Kenji Tanaka was called to take Watanabe's place as second counselor. Tanaka was then serving as president of the East Central District, a position he had held since 13 June 1965.[104] Previously, Tanaka had served as president of the Yokohama Branch since October 1960, when Shozo Suzuki was called to be a counselor in the East Central District presidency. Tanaka was born of Christian parents on 25 May 1926 in Hiroshima, moved to Tokyo at the age of six months, and had been baptized into the LDS Church in Maebashi on 19 April 1953. As a student of the Bible, he readily accepted Mormonism when it was presented to him, receiving a spiritual confirmation at the peak of the snow-covered Mt. Akagi. After teaching chemistry, dairy farming, mathematics, and mechanical engineering at the Nasu farm of Jiyū Gakuen, a noted Christian academy in Tochigi Prefecture, he moved

---

103. *Seito no Michi* 10 (December 1966).
104. Hitoshi Kashikura was called to take his place as president of the East Central District.

to the Tokyo area in 1957. At the time of his call, he was the Yokohama plant manager of a large agricultural machinery manufacturing firm, Netsu-ponpu Kōgyō K. K. In March 1970, he would become the first stake president in all of Asia and would be called to preside over the Japan Nagoya Mission in 1976.[105]

11.6. Conclusion

The period of 1952–68 saw the LDS Church in Japan grow in numbers, geographical scope, and physical assets. Over the course of this period, the missionary force tripled, membership increased by more than ten-fold, and the church purchased properties for use as meetinghouses in all but a handful of existing branches. Most Mormon converts were in their late teens and early twenties, but as some of them matured and gained experience in the church, they progressively assumed leadership roles at the branch, district, and mission levels. Following the creation of the Northern Far East Mission out of the Japanese Mission, in early 1956, missionary work spread to Okinawa, then under American control, and to Korea. Concentration of resources in the Tokyo and Osaka metropolitan areas to create stakes meant that the branch and district structure remained stable at twenty-seven to twenty-nine branches under four districts. It was only in 1966 that a significant pickup in the number of missionaries allowed new areas to be opened, which ultimately led to the breakup of the mission into the Japan and the Japan–Okinawa Missions in September 1968.

Long-time Japanese members fondly remember the time in the history of their church when Kan Watanabe and Kenji Tanaka served as counselors to Nisei mission president Adney Komatsu in the Northern Far East Mission presidency. Because Komatsu devoted relatively more energy to supervising full-time missionaries and the administrative affairs of American military members, Watanabe and Tanaka effectively served as the public face of the LDS Church in all of Japan. Members looked to them for spiritual guidance and leadership, considering them as exemplary disciples of Jesus Christ, a role model to emulate. The LDS Church in Japan has since grown numerically and in maturity, but in some sense has never surpassed the pinnacle of local leadership exemplified by the Komatsu presidency. Admittedly, this is not a fair assessment of the depth of local leadership that exists today, with seasoned men and women filling positions of leadership in literally hundreds of units. Even so, the concluding days of the Northern Far East Mission, when three men with Japanese faces presided over the church in all of Japan and spoke directly to the people in their native language, have not been repeated.

---

105. Kenji Tanaka, interview with author, Tokyo, 19 September 1996.

Chapter 12

Leafs, Steeples, and Testimonies: Building the Foundation for Future Growth, 1948–68

12.1. Introduction

This concluding chapter presents a historical analysis of the experience of the Church of Jesus Christ of Latter-day Saints in Japan from 1948 to 1968, focusing on events and activities that had a lasting impact on its future growth. By 1955, the Japanese economy had recovered from the devastation of World War II and begun to grow rapidly.[1] From 1952 to 1970, real annual growth averaged 9.5 percent; average growth was 10.7 percent during the 1960s (see the bar chart in Figure 12.1). In April 1964, Japan was invited to join the Paris-based Organization for Economic Cooperation and Development (OECD), thus becoming the first non-Western nation to achieve developed country status. The size of the Japanese economy, about 5 percent of the gross domestic product (GDP) of the United States in 1952, grew to reach 20 percent by 1970; in the process, it overtook France in 1966, the United Kingdom in 1967, and West Germany in 1968 to become the world's second largest economy (see the line chart in Figure 12.1).

Along with the size of the economy, Japan's per capita income also rose: from $202 per year (about a tenth of the level in the United States) in 1952 to nearly $2,000 (40 percent) in 1970 (see Figure 12.2). It was this economic prosperity that allowed the LDS Church in Japan to construct meetinghouses from the early 1960s and an increasing number of Japanese Mormons to participate in mission-organized excursions to the Hawaii Temple from the mid-1960s. The LDS Church also benefited from its early property purchases (see Section 11.4 in Chapter 11). Although the rise in urban land prices (averaging 20 percent per year) exceeded the growth of nominal income throughout the period, the rise was spectacular from 1959 to 1961, especially in large metropolitan areas where

---

1. Per capita real income and consumption, which had fallen to 63.5 and 57.1 percent, respectively, of the prewar (1934–36) level in 1946, both recovered to regain that level in 1953. Takenori Inoki, *Keizai Seichō no Kajitsu 1955–1972* (Tokyo: Chūō Kōron Shinsha, 2000), 30–31.

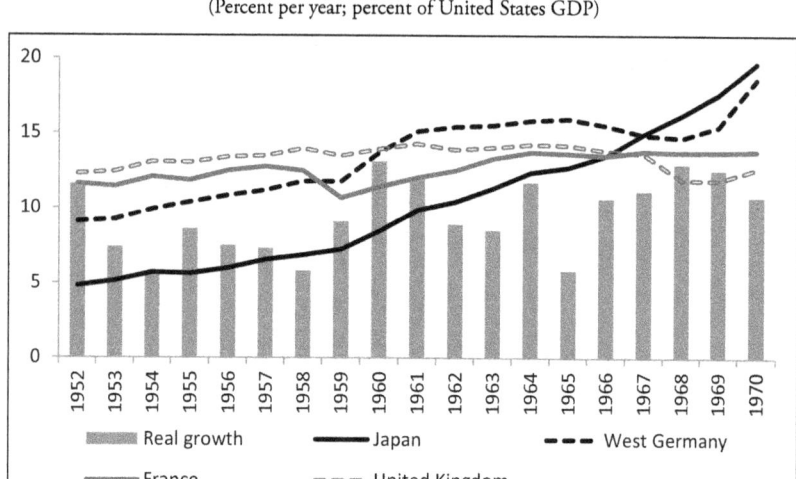

Figure 12.1. Japan's Real Gross Domestic Product (GDP) Growth and Nominal GDP in Major Industrial Countries, 1952–70
(Percent per year; percent of United States GDP)

International Monetary Fund, *International Financial Statistics*, various issues.

the increase was more than 300 percent.[2] Because most of the properties were held in prime locations, the increase in the value of the church's land holdings was likely even greater. The church, having purchased most of the properties well before the property boom, could build meetinghouses relatively inexpensively on existing land and made large capital gains (of more than $23 million) by selling a property in central Tokyo in 1973, the proceeds from which were used to obtain additional land throughout the country.

The rest of this chapter reviews the LDS Church's program of institution building through publications, construction, systematic missionary teaching methods, and opportunities for temple worship from 1948 to 1968, when a single mission was in charge of all of Japan. In particular, it discusses the translation and publication in 1957 of the standard works, especially the Book of Mormon and the Doctrine and Covenants; the missionary teaching plans of 1957 and 1961, which led to a sharp pickup in convert baptisms; the labor missionary program under which the church began to build meetinghouses across the country; the church's translation and publication program; and the mission-organized excursions to the Hawaii Temple in 1965 and 1967, designed to build the faith and testimonies of Japanese Mormons. The chapter then attempts to place the postwar growth of the LDS Church against the background of major demographic and social changes taking place during Japan's high growth period.

---

2. Japanese Government, Bureau of Statistics, *Nihon no Chōki Tōkei Keiretsu*, Table 15–18, accessed 24 November 2015, http:// www.stat.go.jp.

Figure 12.2. Per Capita Gross Domestic Product
in Japan and the United States, 1952–70
(In United States dollars)

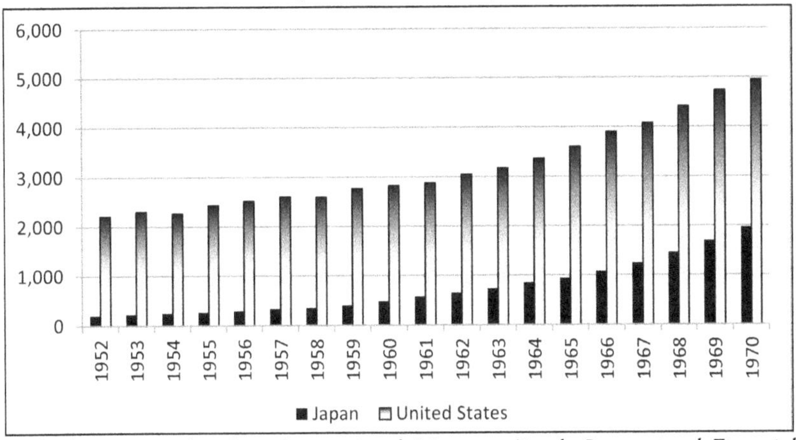

■ Japan   □ United States

Author's estimates based on International Monetary Fund, *International Financial Statistics*, various issues; United Nations, *Department of Economic and Social Affairs, World Population Prospects: The 2012 Revision*, DVD edition, 2013.

12.2. The Translation of LDS Scriptures

12.2.1. Early Translation Work

President Vinal G. Mauss of the Japanese Mission initiated a formal program of translation and publication. The most important task, of course, was to translate the three books of Mormon scripture (which, together with the Bible, constitute the "standard works" in Mormon terminology). On 22 August 1949 (before the departure of Edward L. Clissold), he organized an eight-member translation committee, consisting of Mauss himself as chairman, Paul C. Andrus as vice-chairman, Mitsue Fujiwara, Kotoe Kodama, Fujiya Nara, Tatsui Sato, Genkichi Shiraishi, and Tomigoro Takagi as members. By this time, Tatsui Sato had already been set apart as the official mission translator, and he was spending half of each month in Tokyo working on translation. In January 1950, Sato moved to Tokyo with his family and began to live in a detachment of the mission home. Over the coming years, Sato, assisted by others, was to translate the Book of Mormon, the Doctrine and Covenants, and the Pearl of Great Price, as well as to publish tracts in Japanese from time to time.

The committee's very first task was to revise the translation of the sacrament prayers and the Articles of Faith, which were part of the Doctrine and Covenants and the Pearl of Great Price, respectively. The new translation of the sacrament

Church translator Tatsui Sato (standing on the left), with Fujiya Nara (sitting on the left), Zenjiro Noguchi (standing on the right), and Tomigoto Takagi (sitting on the right). They were the first members of the first district council created in Japan. Circa. 1958. Courtesy Toshiko Yanagida.

prayers, along with that of the Articles of Faith, was published in the April 1953 issue of the *LDS Messenger*. This means that it took nearly four years to translate, review, and authorize the publication of a set of relatively short passages of less than 100 words each.[3] A controversial element of the newly translated sacrament prayers is the way the Chinese characters for *the Son* (literally "honorable child") were to be pronounced in Japanese. Instructions written in phonetic letters appeared in the May 1953 issue of the *LDS Messenger* in an apparent attempt to dispel the confusion, noting that they should be pronounced as *onko*, and not *miko*, which is the standard, established pronunciation among Protestant churches in Japan. While the alternative pronunciation follows the reading used in the 1909 translation of the Book of Mormon, it does not appear that this was widely in use in the prewar church. Though the reading may have been in some use among the Catholics,[4] following the publication in 1978 of the joint Protestant–Catholic translation of the Bible, which accepted *miko* as the pronunciation, the Latter-day Saints remain the only major group of Christians who refer to Christ as *onko*. Why Tatsui Sato, with his Protestant background, decided to retain this unusual reading remains a mystery.

---

3. The delay resulted from the time it had taken the First Presidency to approve the translation. Because there was no language expertise in Salt Lake City, what procedure the headquarters followed to approve the translation, and why it took so long, is not clear.

4. This reading was adopted in the 1910 Catholic translation of the New Testament by Belgian missionary Émile Reguet.

Mormon publications began to come out in rapid succession. Around Christmas time, in December 1949, the first issue of the monthly newsletter, the *LDS Messenger*, was published. Though poorly edited, the newsletter contained much useful information, including conference announcements, doctrinal expositions, excerpts from the sermons and writings of general authorities, Sunday school lessons, and various reports (such as missionary arrivals and new branch presidents). Most issues from mid-1951 to early 1954 contained translations of the *Life of Christ* (a Sunday school textbook by Kenneth S. Bennion) and James E. Talmage's *Articles of Faith*. When the work of translation was completed, these were published in book form as *Kirisuto no Shōgai* (1956) and *Shinkō Kajō no Kenkyū* (1959), respectively. This was not the first time Talmage's *Articles of Faith* was translated into Japanese. Before the modern translation was complete, the LDS Church published a reprint of its prewar translation *Shinshō Kōgi* (1915) in October 1951. Also, during 1951, reprints of two other prewar publications were published: *Morumon Kei* (1909), Alma O. Taylor's classical translation of the Book of Mormon, in June; and *Batsujitsu Seito Iesu Kirisuto Kyōkai Ryakushi* (1907), a translation of Edward H. Anderson's *Brief History of the Church*, in October.[5]

The Book of Mormon was already available in the 1909 classical Japanese translation, so the decision to translate the book again may appear to be related to a need to change the style from classical (written) to contemporary (colloquial) Japanese (see Section 6.2 in Chapter 6). This was not the case. The purpose was to retain the classical style but to make it more easily understandable to contemporary readers. Sato felt that (1) the 1909 translation often used expressions not in contemporary use; (2) it employed too many Chinese characters, which contemporary readers would find difficult; and (3) a number of typographical errors and missing fonts were found. In 1957, Sato stated:

> [A] new translation was not attempted because the original translation of the Book of Mormon was imperfect. I have read the original translation a number of times as I began to make a new translation. The translation is superb, and I became convinced that it had the hands of a prominent scholar of English literature.[6]

Little did he know that a man of Choko Ikuta's ability perfected Alma O. Taylor's draft translation in classical style (see Section 6.3 in Chapter 6 for details).

The idea of rendering the translation in contemporary style based on the grammar of spoken language was suggested by Tomigoro Takagi, when Sato was already working on the Second Book of Nephi. Concurrently, similar efforts were being made in Japan's small Protestant community, with the Japan Bible Society preparing a colloquial style translation of the entire Old and New Testaments. When the society's translation was eventually published (in 1954 for the New

---

5. An appendix on polygamy (written by Alma O. Taylor) originally found in the 1907 edition of *Brief History* was deleted from the 1951 reprint.

6. Tatsui Sato, "Shinyaku Morumonkei no Shuppan ni saishite," *Seito no Michi* 1 (July 1957): 8.

Testament and in 1955 for the Old Testament), the reaction of Japanese intellectuals was generally critical, considering the colloquial style lacking the dignity and grace the Bible commanded. Aware of these developments, Sato consulted with Apostle Joseph Fielding Smith during his tour of Japan in 1955. The outcome was to use a mixed style—classical style for prayers and the words of the deity (except for passages from the Book of Isaiah) and contemporary style for most of the narratives, which Sato called "a type of strange writing." On the other hand, no Japanese translation of the Doctrine and Covenants or the Pearl of Great Price had been published.[7] For these, because most of the accounts are the words of the deity, the entire volumes, including any narratives, were rendered in classical style.

It then becomes legitimate to ask if the retranslation of the Book of Mormon was necessary at all. If the purpose was to make it easier for contemporary readers to understand, the retranslation should have been made entirely in colloquial style. If the purpose was to correct typographical errors and missing fonts, and to rephrase certain expressions no longer in use (if such was necessary at all), the work would not have required several years to complete. Nor was there a need to replace the literary masterpiece that the 1909 translation was with a piece that was not. There is no question that the Doctrine and Covenants and the Pearl of Great Price needed to be made available in Japanese. But why in the classical style, which an increasing number of young people were finding difficult to understand as the national school curriculum, starting from the 1920s, progressively did away with it? One must conclude that the mission leadership, perhaps without consultation with outside experts, too easily bought into the need to retranslate the Book of Mormon and Sato's idea of how best to present the standard works in Japanese. In any event, the Sato translation would remain in official use until 1995, when the LDS Church published a fully colloquial translation of all three standard works.

12.2.2. The Publication of Standard Works

When Paul C. Andrus returned to Japan as president of the Northern Far East Mission in December 1955, the work of translating the three standard works was still in progress.[8] At this time, Andrus recalled the years it had taken to receive approval from the First Presidency to publish the newly retranslated sacrament prayers.[9] Accordingly, on 25 April 1956, Andrus wrote to the First Presidency, requesting permission to form a committee composed of himself,

---

7. The Doctrine and Covenants was translated into Japanese but was never published in prewar Japan (see Section 5.7.5 in Chapter 5).

8. The mission's "Quarterly Historical Report" notes that the completed translation of the Doctrine and Covenants and the Pearl of Great Price was sent to the First Presidency on 15 December 1953. This may have been the first draft.

9. Paul C. Andrus Oral History, interviews by R. Lanier Britsch, 1974, James Moyle Oral History Program, LDS Church Archives, 22–23.

his two counselors (Ben Oniki of Detroit, Michigan and Don C. Lundberg of Newhall, California), Tatsui Sato, and Tomigoro Takagi "to do the final reading of the translations and to be empowered to make the final recommendations for publication." In response, on 9 May, the First Presidency authorized the committee to be formed but did not empower it to make final recommendations, stating that when the work was completed they would be "pleased to receive a recommendation concerning methods of checking interpretation of doctrine and related items."[10] When it was suggested in May that Tatsui Sato should be sent to Salt Lake City to complete the translation, Andrus expressed privately his opposition to "an incompetent committee, meeting at irregular and infrequent intervals,"[11] implying that the translation should be completed in Japan where his own committee could meet regularly and frequently. None of his committee members, however, had real language expertise.

With First Presidency approval, on 4 June 1956, the special translation committee in Tokyo began its work. Working four to five hours a day five to six days a week, it examined the manuscripts for the three standard works until 13 August 1956: the review of the Book of Mormon was completed on 7 July, and the committee agreed to request First Presidency approval to publish it; the review of the Doctrine and Covenants was completed on 2 August; and the review of the Pearl of Great Price was completed on 13 August. Permission to print 10,000 copies of the new translation of the Book of Mormon arrived from the First Presidency on 27 October 1956, and proofreading of the Book of Mormon began before the end of the year. The first five copies were delivered from Sanseidō Printing Company on 31 May 1957,[12] and the rest were received by 3 June except for 2,000 copies which would be leather-bound with the Doctrine and Covenants and the Pearl of Great Price. In the last two weeks of December 1957, 3,000 copies of the translations of the Doctrine and Covenants and the Pearl of Great Price were delivered to the mission office (with an additional 2,000 copies to be leather-bound with the Book of Mormon).

In a series of articles published in the Northern Far East Mission monthly *Seito no Michi* from August 1957 to February 1958, Sato explains how the new translation differed from the old one.[13] Though the new translation follows the same sentence structure of the old translation, it (1) uses more current expressions; (2) employs fewer Chinese characters (about 41,000 characters eliminated); and (3) uses modern phonetic rules (e.g., *kyō* for *kefu*; *zō* for *za*). Some corrections and

---

10. Northern Far East Mission, "Presidents' Correspondences, 1956–1966," LDS Church Archives. The letter was received on 16 May 1956.

11. Paul C. Andrus, letter to Hilton A. Robertson, 29 May 1956. "Presidents' Correspondence."

12. Paul C. Andrus, "Kanzen no Mama no Fukuinsho—Shinyaku Morumonkei wo Shuppansu," *Seito no Michi* 1 (June 1957): 1–2.

13. Sato, "Shinyaku Morumonkei," 7–9; Tatsui Sato, "Shinyaku Morumonkei nitsuite," *Seito no Michi* 1 (August 1957): 4–5; (September 1957): 7–8; (October 1957): 5–6; (November 1957): 5–6; (December 1957): 10–11; 2 (January 1958): 13–14; (February 1958): 13–14.

replacements were made. For example, *tenshu* was changed to *shu* for the Lord, in conformity with established Protestant terminology; *shinrei* to *baputesuma* for baptism, again in conformity with established Protestant terminology; *tenpu* to *onchichi* or *ten no onchichi* for Father; and *seihan* to *shinken* for priesthood. He concluded by saying that language changes with time and that the new translation would need to yield to a "more perfect" translation several decades later.

12.3. Assessing the Quality of the 1957 Translation

12.3.1. The Book of Mormon

Though about 90 percent of the Sato translation of the Book of Mormon was rendered in contemporary style, a number of Japanese Mormons and investigators of the Mormon faith increasingly found the translation to be difficult to read, if not to understand. Part of the reason is that 10 percent of the text, corresponding to prayers and the words spoken by the deity, was rendered in classical style. Even where the contemporary style was used, the translation retained the syntax and vocabulary of the original translation and, as noted below, the verb conjugation of classical grammar. In addition, the 1957 translation had recurring linguistic problems, which made reading it difficult. For example, Jiro Numano, after asking ten native Japanese to participate in a "cloze test" in which every tenth word was deleted from a text, found that they missed 25 percent of the missing words, about a third of which were due to common, recurring problems.[14]

For example, textual analysis shows that punctuation marks are fewer, and sentences are longer, compared to what Numano considers standard translated texts in Japanese:[15] there are on average thirty-one words per sentence in the Book of Mormon compared to nineteen words in the New Testament; likewise, there are twelve words between punctuation marks compared to seven words in the New Testament. Another major issue is the manner in which Sato translated an English sentence containing a subordinate clause, in which there are two subjects in direct sequence, such as: "Mr. A said that Mr. B was wrong." Sato consistently uses the Japanese subject-marker participle *"wa"* for both subjects, causing serious difficulties when a complex structure is involved. An experienced writer of Japanese would have used an alternative subject-marker particle *"ga"* for the subordinate clause (Mr. B in this example) or altogether eliminated the subject of the main clause (Mr. A in this example) when the context makes it clear.

---

14. Jiro Numano, "The Japanese Translation of the Book of Mormon: A Study in the Theory and Practice of Translation" (MA thesis, Brigham Young University, 1976).

15. As a reference Numano selected, in addition to the colloquial translation of the New Testament, translations published in the *Chūō Kōron*, a national magazine addressed to Japanese intellectuals.

Numano further notes a number of "odd" or "peculiar" expressions throughout the translation, such as "*sukuwareru koto ga dekiru*" for "to be able to be saved" in Alma 24:16; frequent use of passive forms of intransitive verbs, such as "*jōju sareta*" for "to be fulfilled" in 2 Nephi 5:20, when the active form should have been used in standard Japanese; retention in countless verses of classical verbs in a colloquial sentence, such as "*shinzuru*" for "to believe" when the colloquial "*shinjiru*" should have been used (see Appendix 6.1 in Chapter 6); and frequent occurrence of vulgar words, such as "*kū*" (to eat) for "*taberu*," as well as outright non-idiomatic expressions, such as "*uwasa ga okonawareru*" (2 Nephi 25:12: "they shall have . . . rumors"), "*shinkō wo suru*" (Helaman 6:4: "faith"), "*takai minotake ga atta*" (Ether 14:10: "was . . . of great stature"), "*kami no meirei wo iya to iu*" (Mosiah 17:20: "deny the commandments of God"), and "*nintai de aijō ni tomi*" (Mosiah 3:19: "patient, full of love"). The last two expressions are grammatically incorrect. Whatever the justification, the mixed style of the Sato translation should have been avoided.

Even a cursory reading of Sato's translation clearly shows that it closely follows the 1909 translation. Thus, it retains the literary characteristics of the 1909 translation, as described in Chapter 6: that is to say, excessively interpretive and explanatory. As in the 1909 translation, for example, the new translation adds words where they do not exist in the original: "the moon shall not cause her light to shine" (2 Nephi 23:10) is translated as "*tsuki wa nobottemo terasanai*" (the moon shall rise but not shine); "justice cannot be denied" (Jacob 6:10) as "*seigi no yōkyū wo kobamu koto wa dekinai*" (the demand of justice cannot be denied); "[many wounds] were severe" (Alma 49:24) as "*itami no hananadashii mono ga sukunaku nakatta*" (there were not a few that were severely painful); and "another people receiving the land for their inheritance" (Ether 13:21) as "*takoku kara kite kono chi wo sono uketsugi no chi to suru takoku no tami*" (another people from another country receiving this land for their inheritance). Likewise, it deletes words from the original: "bowels of mercy" (Alma 34:15) is rendered simply as "*awaremi*" (mercy) and "the hand of the Lord" (Ether 1:1) as "*shu*" (the Lord). These and many like them are colloquial renditions of the equivalent expressions in the 1909 translation.[16]

The Sato translation also follows the 1909 translation in using a word interpretatively when an alternative Japanese word could better convey the meaning of the original: "fountain" (1 Nephi 2:9) is translated as "*umi*" (sea); "flocks" (Alma 17) as "*hitsuji*" (sheep); "touch not the evil gifts" (Moroni 10:30) as "*warui tamamono . . . ni kakawatte ha naranai*" (do not be involved with the evil gifts). Many of these are colloquial renditions of the equivalent expressions in the 1909 translation, but Sato at least in two instances replaced a more literally

---

16. As an exception the Sato translation deleted "blood" from the atoning blood of Jesus Christ in translating Helaman 5:9 whereas the 1909 translated had explicitly translated the word.

translated word with an alternative one: "at Jerusalem" (Alma 7:10) is translated as "*erusaremu no atari de*" (near Jerusalem) and "esteemed as the potter's clay" (2 Nephi 27:27) as "*mueki to omowaren*" (esteemed as useless). To be explanatory, Sato often follows the 1909 translation in replacing pronouns in the original English text (such as "this," "it," "he," or "these things") with what in his view they explicitly refer to. Commentary-like expressions are a feature of the 1909 translation that Sato inherited. Sato's own expressions include: "*korera wa mizukara no nashitaru okonai no mukui wo uku*" (they receive the rewards of their own works) for "their works do follow them" (3 Nephi 27:12) and "*jinrui no shison ga daraku shitaru kekka*" (as a result of the progenitor(s) of the human race falling) for "because of the fall" (Ether 3:2).

A new feature of the Sato translation is the use of Mormon doctrines to translate certain words. For example, "soul" is almost always translated as "body and spirit" (e.g., 2 Nephi 4:15, Alma 5:7, 3 Nephi 20:28, Mosiah 19:7), whereas this rendition appears only in a few instances in the 1909 translation (e.g., Helaman 3:30, Mosiah 2:21). Likewise, "one God" is translated as "one Godhead" (Alma 11:44, 3 Nephi 11:27), whereas this rendition appears only once in the 1909 translation (e.g., 2 Nephi 31:21). Sato, in rendering "God" as "Godhead," however, introduces an error in Mosiah 15:4, where the Father and the Son are referred to as "one God," clarifying the dual role of Christ as father and son. The Mormon concept of "death" as "separation," is used to translate "die as to things pertaining unto righteousness" (Alma 12:16) as "*tadashii koto kara tachikirareta arisama ni naru*" (become cut off from righteous things) and "their lost and fallen state" (Mosiah 16:4) as "*darakushite kami no onmae kara oidasareteiru kyōgai*" (their state of being fallen and cut off from the presence of God).

Many of the questionable translations of the 1909 translation remain because the Sato translation was substantially a revision of the earlier translation. Of the nine outright cases of mistranslation identified in Chapter 6, only three were corrected by Sato (i.e., Mosiah 15:3, Helaman 14:9, and Ether 2:15). Sato introduced new errors, in addition to the one noted above (Mosiah 15:4). He translated "be perfected in Christ" (Moroni 10:32) as "*kirisuto niyori mattaku naru*" (be made perfect by Christ), whereas the 1909 translation had "*kirisuto nioite mattakare*" (be perfect in Christ). Many of the other errors are innocuous, but two are more serious and are to be noted. First, Sato translated "ye can turn the right hand of the Lord unto the left" (3 Nephi 29:9) as "*shu no migite wo sono hidarite ni kaerukoto ga dekiru*" (you can change the right hand of the Lord into his left hand), whereas the 1909 translation had it as "*tenshu no migi no te wo sono hidari ni utsushi ubeshi*" (you can shift the right hand of the Lord to his left). Second, the entire verse of 2 Nephi 2:10 is rendered convoluted, incoherent, and likely incorrect by translating "the ends of the law" and "the ends of the atonement" as "*okite no mokuteki*" (the purposes of the law) and "*migawari no shokuzai no mokuteki*" (the purposes of the atonement). This verse can be better translated by considering "the ends" as the "consequence" or "outcome" (the 1909 translation had it as "the demands," which also made it a coherent translation). These two cases of mistranslation have not been corrected in the 1995 translation of the Book of Mormon currently in use.

12.3.2. The Doctrine and Covenants

Sato's translation of the Doctrine and Covenants is free from the linguistic weaknesses associated with the colloquialism of his Book of Mormon translation. After all, Sato had been educated in classical Japanese and knew far better how to write in that style. Even so, the 1957 translation of the Doctrine and Covenants has the same interpretive tendency of the Book of Mormon translation. For example, "the unbelieving and rebellious" (D&C 1:8) is translated as "*fukuin wo shinzezu oshie ni somuku mono tachi*" (those who do not believe in the gospel and rebel against the teachings); "the Lord is nigh" (DC 1:12) as "*shu no kuru wa chikakereba nari*" (the coming of the Lord is near); "from on high" (D&C 38:32) as "*ten yori*" (from heaven); "without faith no man pleaseth God" (D&C 63:11) as "*shinkō nakereba nanibito mo kami no mimune ni kanawazu*" (without faith no man conforms with the will of God); "the messenger of salvation" (D&C 93:8) as "*sukui no shimei wo motsu mono*" (the one who has the mission of salvation); "all the elements" (D&C 122:7) as "*fū-u-ka-seki*" (winds, rains, fire, and stones), a literary expression in Japanese.

Aside from these idiosyncrasies, the Sato translation of the Doctrine and Covenants is a competent one. Cases of outright mistranslation are few. For example, it renders "I will require this at their hands" (D&C 10:23) as "*ware wa karera ni kono koto wo nasu wo motomemu*" (I will require them to do this thing), which is nonsensical as the Lord is here holding the wicked accountable for their actions, not causing them to commit evil. Another example is D&C 88:40 where "mercy hath compassion on mercy and claimeth her own" is rendered "*awaremi wa awaremi wo kaerimite mizukara no awaremi wo shuchō shi*" (mercy has regard to mercy and claims its own mercy). Here, the English expression "its own," while vague, can be translated in the light of Alma 42:23–24, where what mercy claims as its own is stated as "the penitent" or "the truly penitent."[17] Likewise, "power of godliness" is consistently mistranslated as "kami no chikara" (power of God) in Japanese (D*C 84:20; also JS-H 1:19 in the Pearl of Great Price). Godliness is a human quality of being godly, not an attribute of the deity. This problem is not unique to the Japanese translation.[18] Perhaps the most serious er-

---

17. For convenience, "its own" could be translated as "*mizukara no ryōiki*" (its own domain). The 1995 translation renders it as "*mizukara no kenri*" (its own rights), which does not seem right.

18. When the word godliness appears in the New Testament, it is nearly in every instance the King James translation of the Greek word *eusebeia*, a compound noun formed from *eu* ("well") and *sebomai* ("to be devout"). The King James translation follows Tyndale, who had translated *eusebeia* in old English as "godly lyvynge" (2 Tim. 3:5) or

ror of the 1957 translation of the Doctrine and Covenants occurs in Section 9:8, where "you must study it out in your mind; then you must ask me if it be right" was translated as "*nanji kokoro no naka ni yoku omoi hakari sono nochi negau koto moshi tadashikaraba nanji negawazaru bekarazu*" (you must study it out in your mind, and if it is right, you must ask me). This mistranslation caused confusion on numerous occasions when the principle of prayer was taught in Mormon classrooms for many years.

Perhaps the most important contribution that the 1957 translation of the Doctrine and Covenants made was to establish (if not create anew) a number of uniquely Mormon doctrinal words in Japanese. Some of the more important of these included: president (of the church) as "*daikanchō*"; celestial, terrestrial, and telestial as "*hi no sakae no*," "*tsuki no sakae no*," and "*hoshi no sakae no*"; quorum as "*teiinkai*"; priesthood as "*shinken*"; patriarch (as an office in the Mormon priesthood) as "*shukufukushi*"; dispensation (as a period of time when priesthood authority is available to man) as "*shinken no jidai*"; exaltation as "*saikō no sakae*"; and high council as "*kōtō hyōgiin kai*."

In translating "telestial," which is strictly a Mormon word, Sato followed the practice established in the prewar period to apply the meaning of the word given in the scripture, that is, the glory of the stars, and used their counterparts "the glory of the sun" and "the glory of the moon" for celestial and terrestrial, rather than using the established Japanese words for them. While most of these words

---

"godlynes" (2 Pet. 3:11). Tyndale in turn may have been inspired by Martin Luther's German translation of the Greek word as "*gottseligen Wesen*" (literally, God-blessed nature). With an origin in Greek philosophy, *eusebeia* denotes "that piety which, characterized by a God-ward attitude, does that which is well-pleasing to Him" (William Edwy Vine, *Vine's Concise Dictionary of the Bible* [Nashville: Thomas Nelson, 1997]). In the *Vulgata* (Latin Bible), it is translated as *pietas* (piety), as is also the case with more recent biblical translations in a number of contemporary languages, including Chinese (*jingqian*), French (*piété*), Japanese (*shinjin*), Russian (*blagochestie*) and Spanish (*piedad*). Even some English translations use piety in place of godliness (e.g., Wycliffe and Darby). New Testament writers used godliness in the sense of inward character (vs. outward behavior) and of a duty to God (vs. duties to men). For example, in 1 Timothy 2:2 Paul contrasted "godliness" against "honesty" (*semnotes* in Greek, meaning "propriety of conduct"); in 2 Peter 3:11 Peter likewise paired "godliness" with "conversation" (meaning "conduct" in Middle English) (Matthew Henry, *Commentary on the Bible*, edited by L. F. Church [Grand Rapids: Zondervan, 1961]; Robert Jamieson, A. R. Fausset, and David Brown, *Commentary Critical and Explanatory on the Whole Bible*, 1871, in the public domain, accessed 24 November 2015, http://biblestudy.churches.net/CCEL/INDEX.HTM). In one place being godly is implied to be a prerequisite for becoming the "partakers of the divine nature" (2 Pet 1:3–4). In Mormon scriptural usage, the "god" in the expression is so striking that the power of godliness is often rendered as the "power of God" (JS–H 1:19) or the "power of divinity" (D&C 84:20) in several foreign language editions of the LDS scriptures, including the 1957 and 1995 Japanese translations as well as in French, German, Italian, Mongolian, Portuguese, Russian, and Spanish.

were used in the prewar literature (see Section 5.5.5 in Chapter 5), none appeared firmly established. The publication of the Japanese-language Doctrine and Covenants established their use by giving them legitimacy. In Mormon parlance, however, *shinken no jidai* (dispensation) and *kōtō hyōgiin kai* (high council) were shortened over time to *shinken jidai* and *kōtō hyōgi kai*, respectively; *saikō no sakae* (exaltation) never took root but was replaced by *shōei*.

Overall, Tatsui Sato made a better translation of the Doctrine and Covenants (though an increasing number of Japanese would find its classical language difficult to read and comprehend) than of the Book of Mormon. This was largely due to Sato's inability to use colloquial Japanese as skillfully as he did classical Japanese. With his prewar education, this was understandable. Sato was also a novice in translation; he had only started his new career when he was forty-nine years old. He did develop translation skills with practice. For example, his 1965 translation of David O. McKay's message entitled "The Realm of Women" was rendered in beautiful colloquial Japanese (though the translation itself was not fully accurate).[19] His masterpiece, in terms of accuracy, beauty, and dignity, proved to be the translation of the Mormon temple ceremonies in 1965, which was done with heavy classical flavor utilizing the seven-and-five syllable meter of Japanese poetry to facilitate ready memorization. It is unfortunate that his translation of the Book of Mormon came early in his career as a translator.

12.4. Revamping the Approach to Missionary Work

An estimated 9,570 converts were baptized into the LDS Church in Japan (including Okinawa but excluding the American military units) between the establishment of the Japanese Mission in March 1948 and the split of the Northern Far East Mission at the end of August 1968. Missionary productivity, however, was not uniform across time. Productivity quickly declined from the initial peak in 1949 to reach a low point during the term of Hilton A. Robertson (see Figure 12.3). If we divide the total number of converts by the average number of full-time missionaries for each year, productivity in 1955 was 0.7 converts per year per missionary, a figure comparable to what we observe in early twenty-first century Japan.[20] Then, productivity picked up all of a sudden in 1957, when 92.4 missionaries claimed an estimated 482 converts for a productivity per missionary of

---

19. *Seito no Michi* 9 (October 1965): 476–89. For the original, see *Improvement Era* 68 (August 1965): 676–77.

20. Part of the reason for the low productivity under the presidency of Hilton Robertson may have been the high standards he expected (if not required) investigators to meet before baptism: (1) read the Book of Mormon and James E. Talmage's *Articles of Faith*; (2) pay a full tithe; (3) keep the Word of Wisdom; and (4) attend Sunday meetings. It often took months for an investigator to satisfy such standards. Norman D. Shumway, *Times and Seasons of Norman D. Shumway: An Autobiography* (self published, 2009), 69.

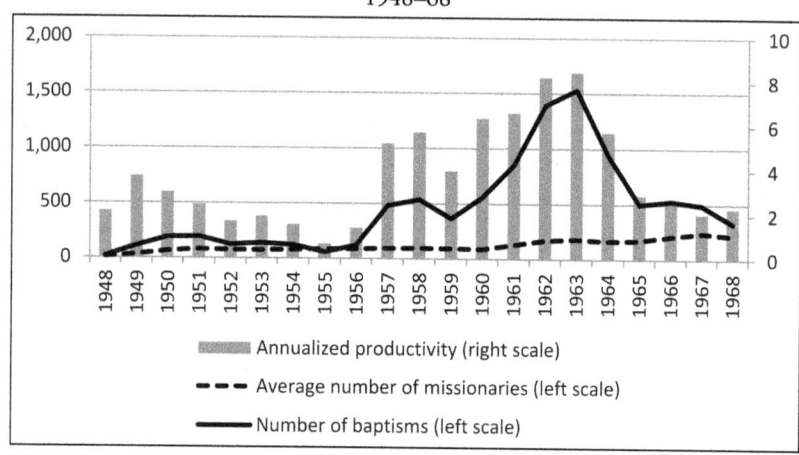

Figure 12.3. Productivity of Full-time Mormon Missionaries in Japan, 1948–68

Through August for 1968; productivity is annualized for comparability. Author's estimates based on various church records.

5.2. The figure remained elevated through 1964—the peak was in 1963 when 181 missionaries baptized an estimated record 1,532 converts—before declining.[21]

What could possibly explain the sudden surge in Mormon missionary productivity in 1957? On the demand side, it is tempting to attribute part of this to a more hospitable religious climate that emerged after the end of World War II. The religious climate certainly explains the sudden burst of interest in the Mormon message that the missionaries encountered when they first arrived in Japan in 1948, but the public's interest quickly waned as prosperity gradually returned (see Section 10.3.2 in Chapter 10). The change in the religious climate cannot explain the sudden pickup in convert baptisms in 1957. Another potential demand factor is the transformation of Japanese society, from rural to urban—from agrarian to industrial—which attended Japan's rapid economic growth during much of this period. Such socio-economic factors may explain the higher productivity of urban versus rural areas or the age and gender composition

---

21. In arriving at this figure, we included the mission president, his wife, and mission home staff in the denominator, but excluded part-time missionaries—district missionaries—who served locally in their own units. For example, of the 1,322 baptisms recorded during 1961 in all of the Northern Far East Mission, including Korea, 1,160 were by full-time missionaries, ninety-two by part-time missionaries, thirty-six by LDS servicemen, and thirty-four were children of records. *Missionary Messenger* 6 (January 1962): 1–2. During 1962, full-time missionaries claimed 1,523 baptisms as compared to eighty by part-time missionaries. *Success Messenger* 7 (February 1963): inside cover. The net effect of the offsetting influences is likely to have over-estimated the true productivity by a small margin.

of Mormon converts (see Section 12.6 below for further discussion), but not the timing of the surge in baptisms.

The higher missionary productivity experienced in Japan from the late 1950s to the early 1960s was a church-wide phenomenon. In fact, the Northern Far East Mission lagged behind many other missions of the LDS Church in terms of both missionary productivity and total converts. During the year 1961, for example, the Northern Far East Mission (including the Korea District whose productivity was higher than the rest of the mission) was the eighteenth out of the sixty-seven existing missions in terms of converts per missionary (8.14). The church average at the time was 8.28 converts per missionary, with the most productive mission being the Samoan Mission (47.67). The Northwestern States Mission was the highest baptizing mission, with 4,901 converts for the year, compared to 1,196 for the Northern Far East Mission.[22] The explanation for the sudden surge in missionary productivity in Japan must therefore be sought in a factor common across the entire church: a spontaneous revamping of the approach to missionary work.

The spontaneous change was in fact triggered by the book *Teaching the Gospel with Prayer and Testimony* self-published in 1956 by Willard Allen Aston, who was around that time serving in the presidency of the Great Lakes Mission.[23] The book is based on Aston's observation of what contributes to missionary success. After highlighting the importance of attitude, desire, and other character traits, the book emphasizes the need to use simple words, not to dwell on what other churches teach, to refrain from argument over points of doctrine, and to frame questions in such a way as to prompt answers in the affirmative—in short, the importance of what the author calls "direct-to-the-point teaching."[24] It further encourages the missionary to be direct in asking his investigators if they are interested in the teachings; if not, the missionary is encouraged to move on to find another person, so that "months" would not be wasted.[25] The missionary is to meet with the investigator frequently in order to keep his interest and to minimize any outside interference.[26] Some sample lessons are offered, among others, on the godhead, the apostasy, the restoration, the plan of salvation, and the first principles. Aston argues that by focusing on teaching simple lessons "no later than the fourth week some investigators will be ready for baptism."[27]

---

22. *Success Messenger* 6 (February 1962): 10–11. The same data show that total converts in the LDS Church rose steadily from 1957 to 1961: 20,075, 22,972, 23,026, 36,723, and 76,827.

23. Willard A. Aston, *Teaching the Gospel with Prayer and Testimony* (self-published, 1956). His biographical information comes from Wade Fillmore, e-mail to Bob and Marcia Sorenson, copied to author, 5 December 2014.

24. Aston, *Teaching*, 98.

25. Ibid., 83.

26. Ibid., 88–89.

27. Ibid., 185.

This book fell into Paul C. Andrus' hands in late 1956. Andrus recalls:

> One of the missionaries, Elder Lyman Godfrey [of Clarkston, Utah] had some of his friends send him a copy of *Teaching the Gospel with Prayer and Testimony* by Willard Aston. Elder Godfrey . . . said, "Here's a book that makes a lot of sense. I would like to have you take a look at it." . . . One of the basic principles of that book is that you teach the gospel, bear testimony, and invite the people to be baptized, naturally. . . . At the end of 1956 I called together our leading elders and talked about this.[28]

The ideas advocated by the book would revolutionize the way Mormon missionary work was conducted in Japan, where each missionary had thus far been left to devise his own way of teaching the Mormon message.[29] Andrus ordered enough copies for every missionary and, in the words of mission office elder Norman D. Shumway of Stockton, California, "its suggestions and methods began to reverberate through the mission. Within just a few weeks, we had incorporated many of its ideas into an emerging new system."[30] In March 1957, all district leaders met in Tokyo and drafted an outline of a new teaching plan. James J. Jones, Jr. of Honolulu, serving as second counselor in the mission presidency, was assigned to prepare sample lessons, while Shumway was asked to write up the plan and a mission handbook.

The new package, already in sporadic use, was formally presented to all Mormon missionaries in Japan in a special mission-wide conference held at the Lakeside Hotel in Nikko on 25–28 June 1957. At the first session of the conference, James Jones presented the plan and, in the afternoon of 26 June, explained how it was to be used in cottage meetings. Commenting in his quarterly report for 30 September 1957, Andrus noted: "The results of that conference have shown up sharply in the third quarter of the year."[31] Indeed, the number of monthly baptisms picked up, rising from the average of 4.7 in 1955 to 40.2 in 1957 (see Figure 12.4). Andrus, speaking some ten years later, attributed this success directly to the introduction of the new six-lesson teaching plan designed specifically for the Japanese.[32]

In 1961, the spontaneous use of the Aston plan in various missions was formally sanctioned by the LDS Church. Commencing on 26 June 1961, a seminar for all mission presidents was held in Salt Lake City, where a new "uniform system" for teaching was introduced for use throughout the world.[33] This system, called "A Systematic Program for Teaching the Gospel," was based substantially on the Aston plan and would be registered with the United States Copyright Office under Willard Allen Aston, Gordon Bitner Hinckley, and The Church of

---

28. Andrus Oral History, 25.
29. Shumway, *Times and Seasons*, 69.
30. Ibid., 81.
31. Northern Far East Mission, "Mission President's Quarterly Summary" 30 September 1957.
32. Andrus Oral History, 25–27.
33. "Mission President's Quarterly Summary," 30 June 1957.

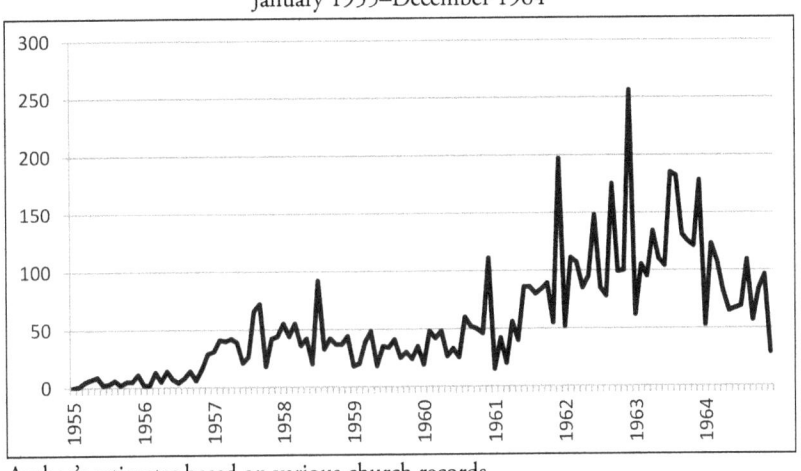

Figure 12.4. Monthly Mormon Baptisms in Japan, January 1955–December 1964

Author's estimates based on various church records.

Jesus Christ of Latter-day Saints.[34] The draft of the plan, which Andrus brought back to Japan in mid-July, was immediately translated by Ronald N. Inouye of American Fork, Utah, and Katsuhiro Kajiyama of Hiroshima into Japanese, with revisions by Paul Andrus and Tatsui Sato. When the final English version was received in September, Andrus and Sato revised the Japanese translation to reflect any changes. All missionaries in Japan were in possession of the English and Japanese versions of the uniform plan by the end of September 1961.[35] The momentum created by the Aston plan in 1957 was maintained, with average monthly baptisms increasing to exceed a hundred in 1963 and 1964.

12.5. The Building Program

12.5.1. The Labor Missionary Program

In 1958 and 1959, as the pace of missionary work picked up and the number of Mormon converts increased, President Paul C. Andrus of the Northern Far East Mission repeatedly noted in his presidential messages and quarterly reports to Salt Lake City that the lack of adequate meeting facilities was the single most critical issue facing the mission. In March 1958, for example, he wrote:

---

34. Fillmore, e-mail to Sorenson.
35. "Mission President's Quarterly Summary," 30 September 1961.

Our greatest single need is for ten or twelve full-scale meeting houses. With such facilities strategically located, the converts baptized each year would soon number in the thousands in Japan alone, even with no increase in missionaries. . . . Our crying need at present is for a few strategically located full-scale meeting houses. It is sincerely hoped that the Church will take the necessary action to provide the needed facilities in order to properly take advantage of these magnificent opportunities.[36]

In June 1958, he warned his leaders in Salt Lake City that if they did not "take the necessary action right away, the tremendous opportunity that exist[ed] in Japan today [would] subside and it [would] be many times more difficult for the church to become strongly established in Japan."[37] In his view, a suitable meetinghouse meant a building capable of accommodating between 200 and 250 people, with thirty to fifty seats upon the stand, ten to twelve classrooms, and a cultural hall adjacent to the chapel capable of holding an additional 300 people.[38]

In his 1959 New Year's message, Andrus challenged the Japanese Mormons to raise funds to construct meetinghouses (with a target of ¥7 million for the year), adding that no adequate physical facility existed in Japan.[39] The sense of urgency had another reason. From around 1956, conservative elements in Japanese society, alarmed by the rise of many dubious religious organizations, were seeking to tighten the criteria a religious group must meet to qualify as a religious corporation under the 1951 Religious Corporation Law.[40] In January 1959, Andrus was under the impression that legislation was just about to be introduced in the Diet to require each branch of the church, not the church as a whole, to own suitable assets for religious purposes.[41] In retrospect, such a possibility was slim. A proposal to that effect was offered by the education minister's advisory panel, but vehement opposition from the Buddhist and Shinto establishments to any idea of tightening the provisions of the law as equivalent to a reinstatement of the war-time Religious Organization Law virtually killed any chance that the Diet would consider, much less pass, such legislation.[42] In connection with this legislative agenda, the government conducted a survey of religious corporation assets

---

36. Northern Far East Mission, "Quarterly Historical Reports," LDS Church Archives, 31 March 1958.
37. "Quarterly Historical Reports," 30 June 1958.
38. December 1958 message.
39. *Seito no Michi* 3 (January 1959): 6–7.
40. Zen Nippon Bukkyōkai, *Zenbutsu Tsūshin*, 25 January 1957, 8.
41. *Seito no Michi* 3 (January 1959): 6–7.
42. The Religious Corporation Council issued a report on 22 April 1958. Noting that the 180,000 or so religious corporations registered under the 1951 Religious Corporation Law included not a few inappropriate ones, it recommended that explicit criteria be established to qualify an entity as a religious corporation; in particular, a facility inside a residential home should not qualify as a place of worship. For a complete text, see *Zenbutsu Tsūshin*, 25 November 1959, 4.

from the fall of 1958.[43] It is possible that the LDS Church too was subjected to this survey, hence Andrus's sense of urgency.

Andrus's plea to Salt Lake notwithstanding, the LDS Church was slow to move. It was only in June 1960 that Wendell B. Mendenhall, chairman of the Church Building Committee, accompanied by J. Howard Dunn, came to the mission to survey the situation and to consult with a local architect. In October 1960, Harold W. Burton, the LDS Church's supervising architect, came to inspect future building sites throughout Japan and to consult with local architects. It was only toward the very end of Andrus's term as mission president, however, that he was finally informed of the church's decision to introduce a labor missionary program in Japan.

The labor missionary program was conceived in 1955 as an economical way of building meetinghouses throughout the world; the program had initially focused on the South Pacific, including New Zealand and Australia, but spread by this time to Europe, Mexico, and the rest of Latin America.[44] Under this program buildings were constructed by local men who were called by the mission president to serve as full-time labor missionaries for a period of time (two years in principle). These men were supervised by experienced and capable building supervisors (typically from Canada and the United States) called by the First Presidency. The housing, meals, and other necessities of full-time labor missionaries had to be provided by the members of the mission, particularly by those in the branches where the missionaries were working; supervisors were provided with housing and a modest stipend from the church.[45]

In the president's message of May 1962, Andrus noted that, through the efforts of Gordon B. Hinckley, the Church Building Committee had approved the construction of several buildings in Japan. From 27 February to 3 March 1962, Mendenhall, accompanied by Joseph Wilson, head of the church-wide labor missionary program, had visited the potential building sites and, with Gordon B. Hinckley, formulated a building construction plan for Japan. On the basis of this survey, it was decided that buildings would first be constructed in Tokyo and its surrounding area, followed by some in Osaka and its surrounding area.

---

43. *Zenbutsu Tsūshin*, 25 September 1958, 3; 25 October 1958, 4.

44. Far East Construction Office, *Far East Construction News* 2, 28 February 1963.

45. H. Dyke Walton, *They Built With Faith* (Bountiful, Utah: Horizon Publishers, 1979), 15. The system ultimately proved to be unsatisfactory as the church could not dismiss missionaries even when they were inefficient or unproductive as building supervisors. The church thus phased out the program from 1965 to 1966 by starting to pay salaries to building supervisors. When this happened, a number of supervisors requested to be released because it was the idea of being called on a mission that had led them to quit their jobs in service of their church. The whole building missionary program would also be phased out from the late 1960s, beginning in the United States and Canada, as it became cheaper to pay cash than to donate labor. Horace A. Christiansen, interview by Bruce Blumell, 1973, LDS Church Archives, 5–6, 9.

Work was anticipated to commence as early as the summer of 1962, starting with the Tokyo North and Tokyo West Branch meetinghouses (the construction of a larger building on the Omotesando property to serve as the East Central District Center would start in the spring of 1963).[46]

The details of how the building program would work were explained to the members, both by Andrus and Dwayne N. Andersen, who succeeded Andrus in July 1962 and would actually oversee the work. In a nutshell, the members were required to pay 20 percent of the cost of land (up to $50,000)[47] and 20 percent of the cost of construction.[48] As the cost of constructing a typical building (excluding the cost of the land) was about ¥70 million, this meant that the local unit needed to come up with about ¥15 million when a typical salaried worker in Japan at the time made about ¥500,000 a year.[49] The labor missionary program was meant to cut the required financial contributions of members by counting the value of labor provided by locally called labor missionaries, as well as the value of labor donated by local members, as a credit towards the required local contributions. The monetary value of providing for the necessities of labor missionaries, including food, lodging, and other miscellaneous expenses (such as laundry), was also counted toward the local share.

As the work commenced, Andersen supplied additional details to the membership. In Japan, he said, the share of labor in the cost of a building was set at 30 percent. So if all of this labor was contributed by the members, the 10 percent in excess of the 20 percent could be applied to the cost of land. In practice, not all the required labor could be provided by local members because some work, including electrical and plumbing, could only be performed by skilled technicians. Thus, the mission president encouraged the members to seek a donation of skilled labor and usable materials from their friends outside the church, which would be counted toward their credit. Clearly, the labor missionary program did not entirely eliminate the need for cash contributions. Andrus instructed

---

46. *Seito no Michi* 6 (1962): 263–65. The 7 July 1962 issue of the *Church News* reported that the construction of a meetinghouse on the Omotesando property to serve as the district center had been approved by the First Presidency. It was stated that the building would have the maximum capacity of 525 people in the chapel, with the additional accommodation of 676 people, twenty-four rooms and a Japanese garden in the center. See also *Seito no Michi* 6 (1962): 550. For unknown reasons, the plan never materialized and the property itself was sold in 1973.

47. That is to say, the member contribution would be limited to a maximum ceiling of $10,000.

48. Prior to the start of the labor missionary program, the LDS Church policy applicable to Japan was for local members to pay 10 percent of the cost of land and construction. On this basis, Andrus had challenged each branch to raise ¥6–9 million ($17–25,000), given the high price of land in Japan. Paul C. Andrus, "Gisei wo Motomeru Sakebi," *Seito no Michi* 2 (December 1958): 8–9.

49. Tōyō Keizai Shinpōsha, *Shōwa Kokuzei Sōran*, vol. 1 (Tokyo: Tōyō Keizai Shinpōsha, 1991), Table 14-28.

the members throughout the mission to organize a building committee in each branch and each member to pay ¥100 a month to support the program.[50] In addition, the branches throughout Japan frequently hosted bazaars and other similar functions as fundraising activities.

Preparation began in July 1962, when the area supervisor Melvin D. Hales of Maywood, Idaho, and the area treasurer Samuel K. Kalama of Honolulu arrived in Tokyo to set up the Far East Construction Office, only ten days before Andrus's departure from the mission.[51] This was followed by the arrival of two building supervisors: Melvin R. (Bud) Hales of La Puente, California, the son of Melvin D., on 24 August to work on the Tokyo West Branch; and Clarence Katwyk of Salt Lake City on 8 October to work on the Tokyo North Branch.[52] Both the area supervisor and the building supervisors were men of considerable prior experience in the construction business. In particular, Melvin D. Hales not only had been a building contractor by profession but also had previously served as a labor missionary in Hawaii. During the remaining years of the Northern Far East Mission, Hales would be succeeded by Rex Alton Cheney of San Gabriel, California (from late September 1963) and then by Marvin S. Harding of Salt Lake City (from July 1966) as the area supervisor responsible for the church building program in Japan (including Okinawa) and Korea.

12.5.2. Early Construction Activity

Actual construction work began on 30 September 1962, with a groundbreaking ceremony in the Tokyo North Branch; the second meetinghouse to be constructed was the Tokyo West Branch in the city of Musashino, with groundbreaking taking place on 6 January 1963 (see Table 12.1). To initiate the work, three full-time proselytizing missionaries were given short-term assignments as labor missionaries: Nonaina H. Makahi of Honolulu (effective 10 October 1962), Merle B. Hult of Martinez, California (27 October), and Marden L. Wolsey of Wellington, Alberta (17 December); four more proselytizing missionaries would serve as labor missionaries between February and November 1963: Kenneth K. Higa of Lanai City, Hawaii, James L. Shirk of St. Louis, Missouri, James W. Smith of Lompoc, California, and Rodney P. Zaugg of Sterling, Alberta.[53] Some of these elders rendered valuable service in facilitating communication between those building supervisors with little knowledge of Japanese and the local build-

---

50. It was decided to locate the office in a detached building on the Omotesando property. *Seito no Michi* 7 (1963): 275–77; *Success Messenger* 7 (May 1963): 7–9.

51. *Seito no Michi* 6 (1962): 550.

52. See Annex 11 towards the end of this volume for a complete list of early American labor missionaries who came as supervisors.

53. In addition, Paul K. Laimana of Kailua, Hawaii worked on a building site as a volunteer from his discharge in September 1962 to January 1963.

Table 12.1. LDS Church Constructed Buildings in Japan, 1948–67
(In order of dedication)

	Unit	Groundbreaking	Date of dedication	Dedicated by
1	Mission Home[1]	19 May 1948	17 July 1949	Matthew Cowley
2	Muroran[1]	N.A. (work began 20 September 1959)	Not dedicated.[2]	N.A.
3	Tokyo North	30 September 1962	26 April 1964[3]	Gordon B. Hinckley
4	Tokyo West	6 January 1963	26 April 1964[4]	Gordon B. Hinckley
5	Gunma	5 January 1964	16 October 1966[5]	Marion D. Hanks
6	Naha	23 June 1964	16 October 1966	Gordon B. Hinckley
7	Abeno	14 June 1964	23 October 1966[6]	Marion D. Hanks
8	Yokohama	19 April 1964	22 April 1967[7]	Gordon B. Hinckley
9	Tokyo South	7 June 1964	23 April 1967	Gordon B. Hinckley
10	Sapporo (Minami 20-jo)	18 May 1965	24 April 1967[8]	Hugh B. Brown
11	Tokyo East[1]	N.A. (work began in January 1967)	11 May 1967	Marion D. Hanks
12	Asahikawa	10 June 1968	17 April 1969[9]	Ezra Taft Benson
13	Okamachi	16 December 1967	21 April 1969[10]	Ezra Taft Benson

[1] Renovation of existing facilities.
[2] Open house held on 12 December 1959.
[3] Service held at 10 A.M.; the dedicatory prayer is reprinted in *Seito no Michi* 8 (1964): 324–25.
[4] Service held at 3 P.M.
[5] Service held at 11 A.M.
[6] The dedicatory prayer is reprinted in *Seito no Michi* 10 (1966): 8–9.
[7] The dedicatory prayer is reprinted in *Seito no Michi* 11 (1967): 14.
[8] The dedicatory prayer is reprinted in *Seito no Michi* 11 (1967): 30.
[9] The dedicatory prayer is reprinted in *Seito no Michi* 13 (1969): 308–9.
[10] The dedicatory prayer is reprinted in *Seito no Michi* 13 (1969): 498–99.

Seito no Michi, various issues; Northern Far East Mission, "Quarterly Historical Reports," respective dates

ing missionaries (some supervisors were former proselytizing missionaries with proficiency in Japanese).

Mission leaders began to call local men to serve as labor missionaries in the early fall of 1962. On 6 November, the first set of local building missionaries were set apart: Zenjiro Ishikawa (from Tokyo West), Hironori Koizumi (Yokohama), Shunichi Kudo (Tokyo North), Retsui Matsushima (Tokyo West), Masahiro Ohashi (Tokyo North), and Charles Tabata (Tokyo South). In addition, prewar convert Fujiya Nara and wife Motoko were set apart to serve as the "house parents" to take care of the meals and other basic needs of locally called labor missionaries. The first set of missionaries, all assigned to work on the Tokyo North and West Branch sites, lived on the Omotesando property, where a warehouse had been converted into a dormitory.[54] It was the Naras' responsibility to take care of their basic needs. In August 1963, they were succeeded in this assignment by Masanobu and Fumie Nitta, recent converts from the Yokohama Branch.[55]

The construction of the two meetinghouses in Tokyo was followed by that of additional buildings: Gunma (ground breaking in January 1964), Yokohama (April 1964), Naha (June 1964), Abeno (June 1964), Tokyo South (June 1964), and Sapporo (May 1965). In addition to Katwyk, Walter R. Chedister, Alden White, Jean D. (J.D.) Larson, and Evan Larson served successively as supervisors for these buildings. Concurrently, the first-phase renovation of a storehouse purchased for the Tokyo East Branch proceeded from February 1963 under the supervision of H. Theodore (Ted) Gorringe; from August 1963 to August 1965, a three-story addition to the Tokyo mission home was constructed under the supervision of Le Roy Johnson.[56] The construction of two more buildings, in Asahikawa and Okamachi, would start before the end of the Northern Far East Mission though they would not be completed.

The Naha building would have been constructed sooner had no difficulty been encountered in obtaining a building permit. In fact, Theodore Willis, who had been assigned to work on the Naha property as building supervisor, arrived in Tokyo on 14 July 1963 (he was the fourth building supervisor to arrive). As it had become evident that the building permit was not forthcoming anytime soon, he was reassigned to the Salt Lake building office in September. The problem was that the property adjoined the remains of the Sōgenji Temple, which had served as the royal tomb for the Shō Dynasty who ruled the Kingdom of the Ryukyus for generations. Destroyed during the last days of the Battle of Okinawa, the temple ground was made into a park with the original stone gate designated as a cultural treasure. It was only through the intervention of American military authorities that the building permit was ultimately granted.[57] After a long delay, a ground breaking ceremony took place on 23 June 1964.

While this incident is often told as a story of divine intervention in the face of political opposition to free exercise of religion, the context and the counterfactual must be understood in order to place it in proper historical perspective. First, it is not clear whether appeal to the authority of a foreign occupying power was used as a means of arm-twisting or as an occasion to persuade the local authorities that the proposed meetinghouse could be made consistent with the dignity

---

54. The garage was converted into an office for the Far East Building Committee. "Quarterly Historical Reports," 21 July 1962.

55. Masanobu and Fumie Nitta, from Tsurumi, Kanagawa, had only recently been baptized into the LDS Church in April 1963. *Far East Construction News* 2, 31 August 1963.

56. Ibid.

57. On 18 May 1964, Dwayne Anderson received a call informing him of the city's decision to grant the LDS Church permission to build on the property.

and historical value of the neighborhood.[58] Second, would the LDS Church have suffered irreparable damage if it had been required to find an alternative plot of land elsewhere in the city? Given the strong anti-American sentiment existing in Okinawa, precisely on account of the capricious and high-handed manner with which the United States Civil Administration of the Ryukyu Islands (USCAR) ruled Okinawa, one must ask if sufficient sensitivity was exercised towards the feelings of the very people whom the church was trying to serve.

LDS church records are sporadic when they come to the accounting of local members who served as labor missionaries. A perusal of the mission's official history, the newsletters of the Far East Construction Office, and the monthly *Seito no Michi* allows about a hundred names (often only their surnames) to be identified, including four older members who served as "dorm parents" in Tokyo.[59] Perhaps there were many more, especially if we include those who served on shorter assignments. For the most part, they were young men in their late teens and early twenties who gave up two of their early years to their church. They were required to lead a disciplined daily routine, which included scripture study time designed to build faith and testimony.

A story is told of the lonesome mother of one such missionary, Toyoharu Tanabe of Okamachi, who came up to Tokyo to take home her eldest son from the building site at the Tokyo North Branch. "Project supervisor Katwyk . . . proceeded with explaining the program to this mother and the boy's uncle." After a tour of the project she is said to have told Katwyk, "If this is what my son is doing, your church can keep him." They left the project site in Tokyo for their home in Osaka just as they came—without the boy.[60] Another story is told of early labor missionary Zenjiro Ishikawa, who fell upside down from the roof to a cement floor of the Tokyo North construction site but walked out unharmed after resting for two hours. Recalling this experience when he was released, Ishikawa saw in this divine protection.[61]

The December 1963 issue of the *Far East Construction News* reports the amount of labor inputs into the construction of the first two buildings, which were nearly complete at the time (Table 12.2). The Tokyo West Branch building was completed in record time, from January to November 1963, whereas the Tokyo North Branch building took considerably longer, from October 1962 to January 1964, despite the fact that it received much larger labor inputs. Taking the average of the two, one might suppose that the construction of a meetinghouse on average took 16,000 hours of labor missionary time, which is translated

---

58. Kensei Nagamine, who was president of the Okinawa District at the time, thinks that American members used the USCAR to pressure the municipal authorities to change the local ordinance. Kensei Nagamine, interview with author, 24 March 1998.

59. See Annex 12 towards the end of this volume for a partial list of locally called labor missionaries, including proselytizing missionaries on temporary assignments.

60. *Far East Construction News* 2, 31 July 1963, 1–2.

61. *Seito no Michi* 8 (1964): 661–62.

Table 12.2. Labor Inputs in the First Two Mormon Building Projects in Japan, December 1963

	% completed	Missionaries total hours accrued	Members total hours accrued
Tokyo North	98	19,067.0	8,326.7
Tokyo West	100	13,359.0[1]	5,318.0[1]

[1] Through October.

Far East Construction Office of the Church of Jesus Christ of Latter-day Saints, *Far East Construction News* 2, 1 December 1963.

into 400 40-hour weeks or 7.7 man-years. Then, constructing eleven buildings (including the renovation of the mission home but excluding the refurbishing of the Tokyo East Branch building) would have required about fifty-seven full-time labor missionaries if we further assume that they served on average for eighteen months. In addition, members provided labor inputs equivalent to more than 40 percent of what the missionaries did. Many of these came from American members of the United States Armed Services, especially in areas where American military installations were located in close proximity of the building sites, such as Tokyo and Naha.[62]

Normally construction took about a year-and-a-half, and the building was immediately ready for use by members. The dedication of the building, however, could not be performed until after the 20 percent local contribution had been paid in full; and it could only be done by a visiting general authority. For this reason, it was not unusual for a building to be dedicated two or three years after completion. The Tokyo North Branch building was the first building to be dedicated (as it was also the first building to be started). The Tokyo West Branch building was the second one to be dedicated, on the same day. On 26 April 1964, Gordon B. Hinckley, after dedicating the Tokyo North Branch building in a ceremony that started at 10 am, traveled west to dedicate the Tokyo West Branch building in a meeting that started at 3 pm. About 500 people were in attendance at each of these dedicatory services.

Outside Tokyo, on 16 October 1966, the Naha Branch building and the Gunma Branch building were dedicated by Gordon B. Hinckley and Marion D. Hanks, respectively. A week later, 23 October 1966, Hanks traveled to Osaka to dedicate the Abeno Branch building. In April 1967, buildings were dedicated in Yokohama (22 April, by Gordon B. Hinckley), Tokyo South (23 April, by Gordon

---

62. The breakdown of labor inputs in the Tokyo North and West Branch sites, as of the end of February 1963, was as follows: labor missionaries, excluding building supervisors, 75.9 percent; American military members, 9.4 percent; local members, 13.3 percent, and full-time proselytizing missionaries, 1.4 percent. *Seito no Michi* 7 (1963): 217.

The Tokyo North Branch meetinghouse was one of the first two Mormon buildings to be completed under the labor missionary program in Japan. Courtesy Kenji Tanaka.

B. Hinckley), and Sapporo (24 April, by Hugh B. Brown) during a tour of Japan by Hugh B. Brown and Gordon B. Hinckley. It was during this tour that Brown famously remarked at the Abeno chapel that a Japanese man would someday be called to the Council of the Twelve Apostles.[63] On 11 May 1967 Hanks dedicated the Tokyo East Branch building, but this was not a new, church-designed building but the refurbishing of a storehouse the church had purchased earlier. This was the last building to be dedicated in the Northern Far East Mission, though construction work would continue in Asahikawa and Okamachi.

12.6. Building the Testimonies of Japanese Mormons

12.6.1. Translation and Publication Program

In 1957, the mission office purchased a new printing machine, which enabled an upgrading of the publication program. In June 1957, the monthly *Seito no Michi* (literally, the Way of the Saints) replaced the *LDS Messenger*. Whereas the *Messenger* had been in four-page tabloid format during most of its existence (several issues were mimeographed copies), the *Seito no Michi* had the format of

---

63. Brown remarked in part: "Some of you who are listening to me tonight will live to see the day when there will be a Japanese man in the Council of the Twelve Apostles of the Church." Hugh B. Brown, "Prophecies Regarding Japan," *Brigham Young University Studies* 10 (1970): 159–60. The footnote ascribing the talk to the Abeno chapel dedication in April 1967 is incorrect. The meetinghouse had already been dedicated by Marion Hanks six months previously.

Okamachi members and labor missionaries at the construction site, circa 1968.

a magazine. Initially 20–30 pages long, the length would eventually exceed 50 pages. A typical issue included the translation of a message from LDS Church president David O. McKay (from a previous issue of the *Improvement Era*), a message from the mission president (or a member of the mission presidency on a few occasions), doctrinal expositions (including those by local members), translations of the sermons and writings of general authorities, and reports of district conferences and events in local branches. Translations of the "Your Question" section of the *Improvement Era* by Joseph Fielding Smith frequently appeared. Increasingly towards the end of the period, the monthly periodical was used to disseminate lessons to be used for family home evenings and in auxiliary programs, such as the Sunday School and Relief Society organizations.

The *Seito no Michi* served as the principal means of augmenting the doctrinal and historical knowledge of Japanese Mormons, to whom little information was available in their native language beyond the church curriculum material. From June 1959 to April 1963, Tatsui Sato wrote a total of thirty-seven articles entitled "*Morumon no Kyōgi* (doctrines of Mormonism)," covering such topics as the resurrection, the second coming, the scattering and gathering of Israel, the millennium, baptism for the dead, and the like. These doctrinal expositions are among the best that have ever been written in Japanese, in translation or otherwise, in terms of the comprehensiveness of coverage and the clarity of exposition. In addition, translations of excerpts appeared from three classic Mormon publications from 1960 to 1964: Joseph Fielding Smith's *Essentials in Church History*,[64] Lucy Mack

---

64. *Essentials in Church History* appeared in forty-seven issues from January 1960 to December 1964, covering through Chapter 28 of Part 4: The Nauvoo Period or the first

Smith's *History of Joseph Smith by His Mother*,[65] and *Lectures on Faith* attributed to Joseph Smith.[66] None of these were ever published in book form. Besides James E. Talmage's *Articles of Faith*, his *Jesus the Christ* (published as *Kirisuto Iesu* in 1962) was the only translation of non-curriculum material published as a book.

Except for those noted above, the mission's translation resources were devoted to supporting the Sunday school and other curricula of the LDS Church. Even so, some of these paperbacks had enduring value beyond their immediate use as manuals and textbooks, and the titles remained on a "publications" page of the *Seito no Michi* for a long time as items for sale. They include, among other books, *Kodai no Shito* (1953, *Ancient Apostles*, by David O. McKay), *Bannin no Yoki Otozure* (1953, *Good Tidings to All People*, by Carl F. Eyring), *Kansei eno Michi* (1957, *The Way to Perfection*, by Joseph Fielding Smith), *Kaifukusareta Kami no Kyōkai* (1957, *The Divine Church Restored*, by Roy A. Welker), *Morumon Kei no Shin-kenkyū* (1959, *An Approach to the Book of Mormon*, by Hugh W. Nibley), *Kodai Amerika no Seikatsu* (1959, *Life in Ancient America*, by Leland H. Monson), *Shion-san no Sukuite-tachi* (1959, *Saviors on Mount Zion*, by Archibald F. Bennett), *Kushiki Miwaza* (1963 and 1964, *A Marvelous Work and a Wonder*, by LeGrand Richards), *Kami no Ōkoku* (1964, *Kingdom of God*, by Oscar W. McConkie), and *Kami to Hito* (1965, *God and Man*, by Oscar W. McConkie). Richards' *A Marvelous Work and a Wonder* was translated as a two-volume Sunday school text, not by a team of mission office translators headed by Tatsui Sato, but by a group of six volunteer translators appointed by the mission Sunday school organization.[67]

As might be expected from the prevailing lack of professionalism in the LDS Church at that time, the quality of translation and writing was generally poor. This is not surprising, given that few members, if any, had the experience and qualification as writer or translator. For the purposes at hand, Mormon translators of this period need not be held to the higher standards required of canonical translation. As long as the translated material conveyed basic information accurately, how well it read was of secondary importance. Nor were the recipients of the material sufficiently qualified or experienced to judge the translation's quality. This broad characterization has not fundamentally changed in Japan, where the educational system places little emphasis on the importance of writing in favor of memorization of facts. An important exception was the modern translation of LDS hymns by Toshiko Yanagida and her father Tomigoro Takagi, who had earlier assisted in

---

237 pages of the 1950 edition. The February 1962 piece was virtually a duplication of the previous month's issue and is not counted. This shows the poor manner in which the magazine was edited.

65. *History of Joseph Smith* appeared in twenty-four issues from October 1962 to September 1964, covering through Chapter 38, which describes the arrival of Lucy Smith in Kirtland, or the first 208 pages of the 1958 edition.

66. *Lectures on Faith* appeared in five issues from October 1962 to March 1963, covering Lecture One, Lecture Two (verses 1–48 only), and Lecture Three (verses 1–20 only).

67. *Seito no Michi* 8 (1964): 104–5.

the prewar translation of LDS hymns (see Section 5.7.4 in Chapter 5). The new hymnal, completed towards the end of 1960, was published in 1961. Many of the hymns, accurately and beautifully rendered in Japanese and skillfully committed to accompanying music, are still in use in Mormon worship services today.[68]

The fledging translation and publication program in Japan became a casualty of the LDS Church's correlation movement in 1968.[69] Up to this point, the mission office had maintained a team of translators and an editorial committee to oversee the production of local publications. On 24 October 1967, Victor L. Brown, second counselor in the church's Presiding Bishopric visited Japan with J. Thomas Fyans, director of the church's Translation and Distribution Department, to explain to local leaders how the work of translation and publication would be organized in Japan, going forward. On 5 January 1968, Kan Watanabe was appointed as the oriental area manager of the Translation and Distribution Center in Tokyo, which was to oversee the work of translators in the Japanese, Chinese, and Korean languages. Six individuals were hired as Japanese translators, including: Japanese language coordinator Yasuhiro Matsushita (previously a high school English teacher), Masako Koguro, Sachiko Masuda, Jiro Numano, Masao Watabe (a former mission office translator), and Shuichi Yaginuma (Tatsui Sato had by this time emigrated to the United States).[70] Kiyoshi Sakai served as executive assistant to Kan Watanabe.

Although it was announced at the time of the Victor Brown visit that the program would become fully operational from 1 September 1968, in March 1968, the locally produced *Seito no Michi* was replaced by the translation of a "unified" magazine produced in Salt Lake City, with a few local pages. The establishment of the translation services department in Tokyo meant that the translation and publication work, which up to that time had been done by the mission office, would begin to be performed by the church on a scale sufficient to support its full, worldwide curriculum. Though this action was taken as part of the church correlation program, designed to eliminate duplication and to standardize the operation of the church throughout the world, it was also a foreshadowing of the impending breakup of the Northern Far East Mission into the Japan and Japan–Okinawa Missions.

---

68. Toshikio Yanagida, "Atarashii Sanbika ni Omou," *Seito no Michi* 5 (1961): 378–80.

69. As the scale and complexity of church administration grew with an expanding worldwide membership, the church initiated the process of consolidating and coordinating the activities of various units and programs in the church in the early 1960s. The "correlation" movement, which lasted through the end of the decade, led to centralizing the production of magazines, manuals, and textbooks under the supervision of general authorities. James B. Allen and Glen M. Leonard, *The Story of the Latter-day Saints* (Salt Lake City: Deseret Book, 1976), 595–622; Armand L. Mauss, *The Angel and the Beehive: The Mormon Struggle with Assimilation* (Urbana, Illinois: University of Illinois Press, 1994), especially 163–67.

70. *Seito no Michi* 12 (1968): 38, 64–65.

12.6.2. Trips to the Hawaii Temple, 1965 and 1967

The Hawaii Temple Trip of 1965. Most of the new Mormon converts who responded to the new teaching plan from the late 1950s were young people. Dwayne Andersen characterized the LDS Church in Japan when he first arrived as mission president in 1962 as "a high school or college social club," observing that "the rate of those becoming inactive was about equal to the number of baptisms." The LDS Church had attracted mainly high school and college students. Once they graduated or had family, they would stop coming to church. As a result, there was "no real growth."[71] Though an extreme example, the active membership in the Futenma (Okinawa) Branch dwindled to one at some point in the early 1960s.[72] To better meet the spiritual needs of adult members, Andersen set out to train the local priesthood and Relief Society leadership and to give greater attention to "the family as the center of the church."[73]

It was as a culmination of these efforts that, from 22 to 31 July 1965, 141 adults and twenty-six children made a trip to the Hawaii Temple in Laie, Hawaii.[74] In the evening of Thursday, 22 July, the Mormon travelers all met at the Tokyo Central Branch and proceeded by bus to Tokyo's Haneda airport. Chaperoned by mission president Dwayne Andersen and his wife, most of the group took a chartered Japan Airlines Douglas DC-8 aircraft, while fourteen of them, including mission presidency counselor Goro Yamada, flew ahead on a regularly scheduled commercial flight.[75] Japan's foreign exchange controls, progressively eased in the early 1960s, had just been fully liberalized in April 1964 to allow Japanese residents to travel abroad without formality.[76] Because it was

---

71. Dwayne N. Andersen, "The First Japanese Temple Excursion: Hawaii Temple, 1965," April 1982, 3; Dwayne N. Andersen and Peggy H. Andersen, "History of the Northern Far East Mission (Japan and Okinawa), July 1962–August 1965," not dated, 1–2; Dwayne N. Andersen, president's message, *Seito No Michi* 9 (1965): 437. The average sacrament meeting attendance in 1963 was 23 percent for the mission (Hokkaido 28 percent; Okinawa 14 percent), considerably higher than the activity rate of around 15 percent in the early twenty-first century. *Success Messenger* 8 (February 1964): 7.

72. It was only at the suggestion of Gordon B. Hinckley that the branch was kept open. Nagamine, interview with author.

73. Andersen, "The First Japanese Temple Excursion," 3.

74. Dwayne N. Andersen, "The First Japanese Temple Excursion"; Yoshihiko Kikuchi, "Shu yo Ware wa Nani wo Nasubeki ka," *Seito no Michi* 9 (1965): 62–63; Masao Watabe, "Hawai Shinden Hōmon Ki," *Seito no Michi* 9 (1965): 449–57. Where there is a discrepancy, Watabe (1965), written at the time by the official mission recorder, is taken to be more accurate.

75. The fourteen people could not be accommodated on the chartered plane because the seating capacity proved to be smaller than agreed in the initial charter contract. They were flown by the airline free of charge in its regularly scheduled flight. Andersen, "The First Japanese Temple Excursion," 8; Dwayne N. Andersen, letter to Sister Davis, 29 July 1965.

76. Article 22 of the Constitution of Japan guarantees Japanese nationals' freedom to emigrate, which is generally understood to include freedom to travel abroad. The government

Japanese Mormons at Haneda airport on their way to Hawaii, 22 July 1965. Courtesy Kenji Tanaka.

rare in those days to see a large group, especially with children, travel abroad, the event was widely covered in the media, including newspapers and television.

The event, involving mostly branch, district, and mission leaders, had been carefully planned and prepared on both sides of the Pacific, with Paul Andrus acting as chairman of the welcoming committee in Hawaii. The temple ceremonies had been translated into Japanese by Tatsui Sato, who received a special assignment from the First Presidency to relocate to Hawaii in early 1965 to perform the task. On their part, the Japanese Mormons had submitted for processing 1,000 or so family group sheets to the Genealogical Society of Utah in Salt Lake City. One of the requirements for participation was to secure the names and other particulars of ten ancestors on direct lines.[77]

The Mormon pilgrims crossed the international dateline to arrive in Honolulu on the same day. They were met at the airport, not only by Andrus, but also by Edward Clissold, now president of the Hawaii Temple and Gordon B. Hinckley. Masao Watabe, a participant, recorded what he saw:

> After we passed through the customs officers, the first thing that came into my sight was the large, dear stature of former mission president Andrus, chairman of the wel-

---

regulation of that freedom therefore took the form of restrictions on the ability of Japanese residents to obtain foreign exchange. As the exchange controls were fully lifted in April 1964 for the making of payments and transfers for current international transactions, about 300,000 Japanese residents traveled abroad in 1964 and 1965 alone. Inoki, *Keizai Seichō no Kajitsu*, 144. See also Shinji Takagi, *Conquering the Fear of Freedom: Japanese Exchange Rate Policy since 1945* (Oxford: Oxford University Press, 2015), chapter 2.

77. Dwayne Andersen, president's message, *Seito no Michi* 9 (1965): 318.

coming committee. As I spontaneously ran over to him to shake hands, he embraced me into that big chest and wept openly.[78]

The group was then taken by bus to the Church College of Hawaii (present-day Brigham Young University–Hawaii) in Laie where they took accommodation in its dormitories.

The Japanese Mormons not only participated in temple ceremonies but also attended Oahu Stake leadership meetings or accompanied Oahu Stake leaders on their church assignments in order to deepen their understanding of how a stake should function. Members also participated in family home evenings hosted by Oahu Stake members, and some of them received patriarchal blessings, special personal blessings faithful Mormons receive from patriarchs ordained for that purpose. On 30 July 1965, the commercial flight that took off five hours after the chartered flight back to Japan carried Tatsui Sato, who had completed his translation assignment in Hawaii, and Adney Komatsu who had just been called to preside over the Northern Far East Mission.

How the Project Was Conceived. The idea for organizing a trip to the United States came from Kenjiro Yamanaka, who had joined the LDS Church in June 1963 at the age of sixty through the instrumentality of an American serviceman. His initial proposal was to take a group of Japanese Mormons to Salt Lake City, but Anderson thought in view of cost considerations that Hawaii would be a more logical destination; moreover, he thought, the temple should be made the focus of the trip as a means of developing local leaders.[79] A decision was thus made to organize a trip to the Hawaii Temple; initially this was to take place every summer.[80]

At that time, the Mormon mission leaders estimated the cost of airfare per person to be ¥170,000 (or $472.22). Because most members would participate as a couple, this meant the total costs of ¥340,000 for a typical household. It was decided that members would be required to pay half the cost, while the church would raise funds to cover the balance. According to Ministry of Labor statistics, an average Japanese salaried worker earned about ¥600,000 per year in 1965. By contemporary standards, making a temple trip was comparable to buying a

---

78. Watabe, "Hawai Shinden Hōmon Ki," 449–57. The author's translation of the Japanese original.

79. Earlier in 1961, missionary Wade W. Fillmore of Spanish Fork, Utah, had written a letter to the First Presidency proposing the idea of organizing temple trips for Japanese members with financial support from American members. The response he received was not supportive of the idea. Wade W. Fillmore, "Shinden Projekuto," *Seito no Michi* 7 (1963): 672–73; Andersen, letter to Sister Davis. Fillmore's idea predated the decision of the LDS Church to establish a General Temple Patron Assistance Fund in 1992, designed to assist members in developing areas whose financial conditions put a visit to the temple outside their reach.

80. Fillmore, "Shinden Projekuto," 672–73.

luxury vehicle for a young school teacher.[81] Without the subsidy from the church, the trip would have been difficult for many members. As it turned out, the cost of airfare was nearly cut in half by chartering a plane, so the church's financial contribution in the end was modest.[82]

In order to raise funds for this purpose, in October 1963, the mission temple project committee launched a fundraising project named "Project Temple." The project essentially involved the resale of 4,000 pearls purchased through Yamanaka and the sale of 3,000 LP records of hymns and Japanese folk songs featuring local Mormon singers. The LP album titled "*Nihon no Seito wa Utau* (Japanese Saints Sing)" was recorded on 21 October 1963 at the reputable Teichiku Records studio. The first and second quorums of elders were put in charge of selling the record albums and pearl tiepins.[83] The prices were set at ¥1,200 (or $3.33) for the record and ¥1,300 ($3.61) for the tiepin;[84] for each sale, ¥150 (¢42) and ¥100 (¢28), respectively, could be retained by the unit in which the sale was made toward the branch building fund.[85]

Some old-time members were skeptical of such a money-making scheme especially when they realized that Yamanaka was a pearl merchant. An "insider" in the mission office reported this to the tax office as an activity falling outside the purview of a tax-exempt religious corporation. Andersen calls him a "prominent member" in his written summary of the temple trip; he has privately identified the person as Tatsui Sato.[86] That Sato was opposed to the project was public knowledge. Not only was he planning to stay out of the trip but he initially turned down Andersen's offer of a free trip to Hawaii plus wages to translate the temple ceremony into Japanese. Opposition from "some of the older members in the Tokyo area" was such that it was only in May 1965 that "the bills were paid off and we could start putting money into the temple fund."[87] In the event, about ¥3.2 million—some $60 per adult participant—was raised (of which ¥1.4 million was used to pay for the expenses incurred in Hawaii).

---

81. Tōyō Keizai Shinpōsha, *Shōwa Kokusei Sōran* (Tokyo: Tōyō Keizai Shinpōsha, 1991), Table 14-28. The most affordable *Subaru* cost ¥430,000 at that time when few owned private automobiles in Japan.

82. According to Andersen, each couple paid $500 plus food, housing, passport fees, and transportation to and from Tokyo, and the mission fund paid the balance. Andersen, "The First Japanese Temple Excursion," 9. The cost of chartering the DC-8 was ¥13,856,400 ($38,490). "Quarterly Historical Reports," 2 March 1965.

83. *Seito no Michi* 7 (1963): 786.

84. It was explained that the retail price of a tiepin of similar construction was ¥2,000–2,500.

85. *Seito no Michi* 7 (1963): 668–79.

86. Andersen, "Japanese Temple Excursion," 9; Dwayne N. Andersen, letter to author, 6 February 1997. Evidently Sato's feelings were hurt because he was kept out of the planning for the trip by Andersen who considered him "too traditional and stubborn."

87. Andersen, "Japanese Temple Excursion," 6.

Assessing the First Temple Project. Andersen repeatedly and publicly called Kenjiro Yamanaka "a wonderful member who made devoted efforts to make this temple excursion plan a reality."[88] It is true that Yamanaka had an acquaintance in the sales department of Japan Airlines and literally gave hundreds of hours of his time to the project. But the fact that he was in the pearl business legitimately created the perception of conflicts of interest, justifying the suspicion some prominent local Mormons felt about the motive for his involvement. Also at issue was his depth of conversion and activity in the church. Not only did he not participate in the trip himself, but he remained a marginal member during the rest of his life. The tale that Yamanaka was somehow a prominent person, as perpetuated by unsuspecting history tellers, is not supported by evidence.[89] More likely, he was a regular person in his sixties who had developed normal business contacts throughout his working life.[90] Andersen's view of him only indicates the rarity of older Japanese businessmen in the LDS Church, where even the top local leaders were barely in their thirties.

One wonders, with the benefit of hindsight, if the sale of LP records and pearl tiepins was the right approach to helping defray the costs of the temple trip. Aside from the propriety of the church engaging in a commercial activity,[91] most of the merchandise was sold to members, especially those who would be participating in the trip. The total declared profit of ¥3.2 million was modest, but the net contribution was even smaller, too small to be justified by thousands of hours of work expended over eighteen months. More fundamentally, the scheme had an element of unfairness in the allocation of available spots. As priority was given to branch, district, and mission officers, some members who wanted to participate could not be accommodated even though they were requested to help fund the project.[92] In any case, the fundraising project amounted to almost noth-

---

88. Dwayne Andersen, president's message, *Seito no Michi* 9 (1965): 317–18.

89. The following characterization of Yamanaka is typical of this literature: "His experience in government, business and education enabled him to help the Church out of many binds. . . . He had made many influential friends in all walks of life in Japan." No objective facts, other than what Andersen said, are offered to support such a glorified view of what appears to this author to be an ordinary individual. Terry G. Nelson, "History of the Church of Jesus Christ of Latter-day Saints in Japan from 1948 to 1980" (MA thesis, Brigham Young University, 1986), 59–60.

90. From 1947 to 1951, he was a member of the city council in Musashino, where he unsuccessfully ran for mayor in 1955. Subsequently he appeared to have a series of odd jobs. The 1965 alumni directory of Waseda University, where he had graduated as an English major, lists his whereabouts "unknown." Waseda Daigaku Kōyūkai, *Kaiin Meibo*, 1965 edition (Tokyo: Waseda Daigaku Kōyūkai, 1966).

91. After the matter was settled with the tax office, the mission emphasized that records and tiepins were given free of charge to those who made the donations. The rhetoric did not change the substance of the commercial transaction involved.

92. In fairness, it should be noted that the mission's idea was to organize a trip every summer so that everyone worthy and able could eventually be accommodated. Fillmore,

ing. The LDS Church's greater contribution to the project was in successfully negotiating with Japan Airlines a contract to charter a plane on reasonable terms.

Planning Additional Temple Trips. The second trip to the Hawaii Temple was made from 5 to 14 June 1967, with 125 adults and seventeen children. For twenty-five of the 125 adults, including Kan Watanabe and Kenji Tanaka, this was the second trip to the Hawaii Temple.[93] It was announced early in the year that ten spots remained unfilled, which implies that everyone who wanted to participate in a trip to the temple had been accommodated by the first two excursions.[94] Arriving in the morning of 5 June aboard a chartered Japan Airlines Douglas DC-8 aircraft, they were welcomed at the airport by Andersen, Andrus, and temple president Harry B. Brooks, and they were taken by bus to Laie. As with the first temple trip in 1965, the program included, in addition to participation in temple sessions, attendance at local congregations, a homestay at local members' homes on Saturday, and a sightseeing tour of the island.

During the existence of the Northern Far East Mission, another temple excursion was planned, though the trip would take place in the summer of 1969 after the mission's split. In February of 1968, it was announced that an estimated cost would be about ¥150,000 per person, including ¥100,500 in airfare; the fifth quorum of elders was put in charge of planning and logistics.[95] For this, as well as for the previous trip, there was no fundraising activity. As per capita income continued to rise, the financial sacrifice required of members to make the trip was becoming smaller. Most of the leaders of Japan's first three stakes—Tokyo (organized in 1970), Osaka (1972), and Yokohama (1974)—came from among the participants in these Hawaii Temple trips.

12.7. Understanding the Postwar Growth of the LDS Church in Japan

Although the earlier analysis of the surge in missionary productivity from the late 1950s to the early 1960s (see Section 12.4 above) was based on "supply-side considerations" (how the message was presented), fuller understanding of what took place must also consider the "demand side" (the public's receptivity to Mormonism). The importance of demand-side considerations is obvious because the level of productivity was not sustained for very long even though the church's approach remained virtually the same thereafter. The establishment of religious freedom was a constant factor, so it cannot be used to explain the ups and downs in missionary productivity. True, Mormon missionaries encountered an increasing number of people educated in the postwar educational system in which State

---

"Shinden Projekuto," 672–73.
  93. *Seito no Michi* 11 (April 1967): 26.
  94. *Seito no Michi* 11 (February 1967): 5–6.
  95. *Seito no Michi* 12 (February 1968): 36.

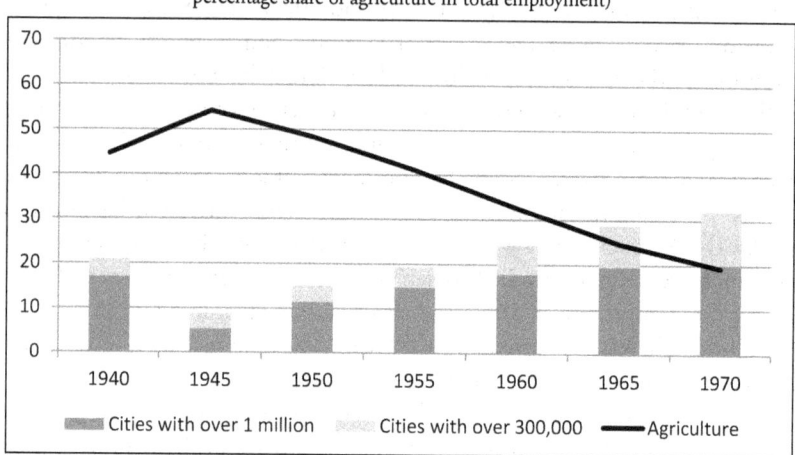

Figure 12.5. Urbanization and Industrialization in Japan, 1940–1970
(Percentage shares of population in cities with over 300,000 and one million people; percentage share of agriculture in total employment)

For labor statistics, 1945 should read as 1947. Author's estimates based on Japanese government census data, as reported in Yano Kōta Kinen Kai, *Sūji de Miru Nihon no Hyakunen*, second edition (Tokyo: Kokuzeisha, 1981), Tables 2-12 and 2-17.

Shinto played no formal role, but the secular humanism of postwar education worked against the Mormon message. To understand the Mormon experience in postwar Japan requires understanding the demographic and social changes associated with Japan's rapid economic growth.

Japan at the beginning of the postwar period was more agrarian than it had been during the previous two decades. City families sent their children to their ancestral homes in rural areas during the final days of the Pacific War as the major cities were subjected to aerial bombing. As factories were destroyed and military production was terminated, hundreds of thousands of people left the places of their employment in the cities for their ancestral homes in search of food and shelter. Rural population swelled further as military personnel and civilians living abroad were repatriated in the early postwar years.[96] As a result, the share of Japan's total population living in cities with more than 300,000 people declined from 20.9 percent in 1940 to a mere 8.8 percent in 1945 (see Figure 12.5). Likewise, the employment share of agriculture rose from 44.6 to 54.2 percent. In this light, it was reasonable that the church, when initiating missionary work in the late 1940s, often started in small agricultural communities. Action, activity, and people were more concentrated there during the early postwar years.

---

96. It is estimated that about three million military personnel and an equal number of civilians were stationed abroad, predominantly in China, Indonesia, Korea, and Manchuria, at the conclusion of World War II. Tokyo Shinbun, "Shūsen no Hi wo Kangaeru," 8 August 2010.

Many of the newcomers to agriculture added little to production, meaning that their marginal product of labor was virtually zero. Essentially, agriculture provided them with disguised unemployment or underemployment at best. The rapid industrialization that followed was initially made possible by transferring the surplus workers in agriculture into the manufacturing sector, whose major centers of activity were located along the 650-mile Pacific seaboard stretching in a southwesterly direction from Tokyo to Osaka, and then to Kitakyushu.[97] From the early 1960s, agricultural productivity rose, releasing additional workers without sacrificing output, as mechanization and use of chemical fertilizers and pesticides progressed. In Japan, paddy (wet) fields are used to cultivate rice, the main crop, such that seedlings are planted under water during the monsoon season. In this type of agriculture, little labor is required during the growing season. Mechanization of planting and harvesting therefore allowed labor inputs to be reduced considerably.[98]

Migration of labor from rural communities to urban areas accelerated in 1960. The employment share of agriculture declined from 32.6 percent in 1960 to 24.7 percent in 1965; the decline was equivalent to 20 percent (or about 3 million people) of the total agricultural labor force.[99] The population share of the largest metropolitan areas increased steadily throughout this period, from 14.8 percent in 1955 to 19.6 percent in 1965 (see Figure 12.5). In actual number, from 1955 to 1970, the three largest metropolitan areas of Tokyo, Osaka, and Nagoya saw an increase in population of as many as 15 million people. Almost all of the migrants were recent junior or senior high school graduates, who came to big cities either to obtain work in the manufacturing or service sector or to attend college or vocational school.

More than anything, it was these demographic factors that the LDS Church benefited from, especially as it increasingly concentrated its resources on the major population centers of Tokyo and Osaka. In fact, the overwhelming majority of the converts came from these two areas, which accounted for an estimated 26.9 and 18.8 percent, respectively, of the total (Tokyo's share was understandably larger during the first few years because few other areas were open for missionary work). On an annual basis, the combined share of the two population centers never fell below 40 percent from 1958 to 1967; the combined share of Tokyo and Osaka exceeded 50 percent during 1963–66 when the annual number of converts as well as missionary productivity saw their peaks (see Figure 12.6).

---

97. Kitakyushu (literally, North Kyushu) refers both to the northern part of the island of Kyushu and to the city of Kitakyushu, which was formed by the amalgamation of Kokura, Moji, Tobata, Yahata, and Wakamatsu in 1963.

98. Yield per 100 m^2 increased from 357 kg in 1951 to 497 kg in 1968, while yield per 10 hours of labor increased from 17.8 kg to 37.4 kg over the same period. Inoki, *Keizai Seichō no Kajitsu*, 169, 173.

99. Inoki, *Keizai Seichō no Kajitsu*, 162. Yasukichi Yasuba and Takenori Inoki, eds., *Kōdo Seichō* (Tokyo: Iwanami Shoten, 1989), 17, 182.

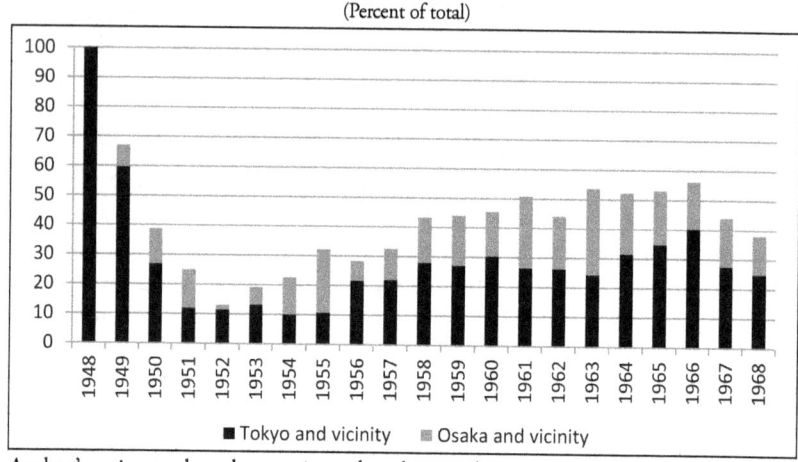

Figure 12.6. Mormon Converts in Largest Metropolitan Areas in Japan, 1948–68 (Percent of total)

Author's estimates based on various church records.

Part of this reflects the larger number of missionaries assigned to these areas, where there were multiple branches. At the same time, there is evidence to believe that missionary productivity was higher in larger cities.[100] One is tempted to conclude that the larger baptismal shares of Tokyo and Osaka reflected both the larger number of missionaries and their generally higher missionary productivity.

As an important feature of labor and other population migration during Japan's high growth period, mobility was considerably higher among men than among women. For example, Tokyo Prefecture received net inflows of men and women in 1959, which translated to 2.65 and 2.14 percent, respectively, of the total population (see Table 12.3). On the opposite side, in 1961, Kagoshima Prefecture saw net outflows of men and women equivalent to -2.65 and -1.82 percent, respectively, of the total population. A similar migratory pattern was observed within prefectures. For example, more men than women were migrating to the city of Sapporo from rural communities in the rest of Hokkaido Prefecture. In other words, Mormon missionaries working in large cities faced comparatively more men than women on the streets where a lot of contacting took place.

These demographic developments show up in the gender composition of Mormon convert baptisms (see Figure 12.7).[101] Initially, the LDS Church at-

---

100. For example, the share of total converts per branch in Tokyo and Osaka was in the order of 4–6 percent, which was comparable to the shares of Sapporo (5.1 percent) and Nagoya (4.2 percent). On the other hand, these figures were smaller in less populous cities, such as Yanai (1.2 percent), Muroran (1.8), Kanazawa and Komatsu (2.2 percent, combined), and Otaru (2.4 percent).

101. For the period as a whole, women constituted about 55 percent of total baptisms.

Table 12.3. Net Migration in Selected Urban and Rural Prefectures in Japan, 1959–61
(Percent of total population)

Prefecture	Gender	1959	1960	1961
Urban (positive numbers indicates net in-migration):				
Tokyo	Men	2.65	2.41	2.05
Tokyo	Women	2.14	1.96	1.76
Aichi (Nagoya)	Men	1.29	1.91	2.16
Aichi (Nagoya)	Women	1.06	1.39	1.34
Osaka	Men	2.62	3.32	3.38
Osaka	Women	2.04	2.29	2.62
Rural (negative numbers indicates net out-migration):				
Akita	Men	-1.37	-1.84	-2.14
Akita	Women	-0.98	-1.22	-1.46
Miyazaki	Men	-1.14	-1.59	-2.18
Miyazaki	Women	-1.05	-1.30	-1.30
Kagoshima	Men	-1.82	-2.45	-2.65
Kagoshima	Women	-1.62	-1.84	-1.82

Nihon Tōkei Kyōkai, *Nihon Chōki Tōkei Sōran*, vol. 1 (Tokyo: Nihon Tōkei Kyōkai, 1987), Table 2-41.

tracted men as well as women (the share of men was 52.3 percent in 1949) but, as prosperity gradually returned, the share of men declined precipitously to 24.6 percent in 1952—perhaps because men were working longer hours or had more after-work commitments. The share then picked up again from 1958 and eventually exceeded 50 percent in 1964 and 1965. Dwayne Andersen later explained the increase in male baptisms from 1962 to 1963 as resulting from his instruction that the elders should "turn all the female contacts over to the sister missionaries" and "concentrate on male converts."[102] Demographic factors were also at play. Whatever the impact of Andersen's instruction, elders now had enough male contacts to occupy themselves with.

Most converts to Mormonism were young and joined the church predominantly in large cities. This had social and spiritual aspects. First, the LDS Church offered opportunities to socialize and cheap forms of entertainment when per capita income in Japan was still low. Especially for those who came from rural areas, the church was a place to make friends and to find support in times of

---

102. Dwayne N. Andersen, "Dwayne N. Andersen's Experience with the Japanese People," not dated, 11.

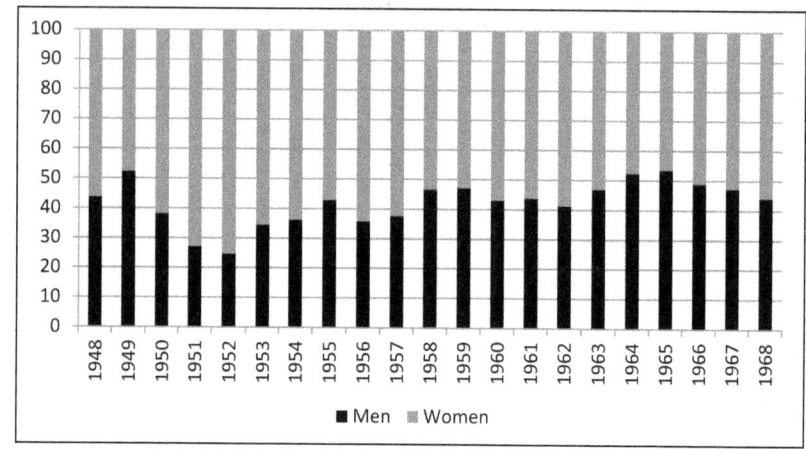

Figure 12.7. Gender Composition of Mormon Converts in Japan, 1948–68

Author's estimates based on various church records.

need. No wonder, then, Andersen found the church in Japan when he arrived in the summer of 1962 resembling a high school or college social club. This aspect of the conversion process in the 1960s is consistent with the findings of the recent literature on the sociology of religion, which emphasizes the importance of networks in large-scale conversion.[103]

Second, it was not religious freedom per se but the freedom from Edo Buddhism that raised the receptiveness of the Japanese soil to the Mormon message. The vestiges of Edo Buddhism, along with traditional social ties, remained stronger in rural communities than in urban areas. Irrespective of their religious belief, families were tied to local temples as parishioners; each home had a family altar known as *butsudan*, which was handed down from generation to generation, typically through the eldest son. Migrants to the cities were often freed from these familial or social obligations of Edo Buddhism, allowing them to believe and practice what they pleased. This was driven, not so much by religious freedom, but by Japan's rapid economic transformation. In the terminology of the economics of religion, freedom from religious tradition reduced the opportunity cost of conversion to Mormonism while increasing competition in the religious marketplace.[104]

The LDS Church, while a beneficiary of these societal changes, was a minor player among the new religious groups that rose to the occasion. Among the most

---

103. Rodney Stark and Roger Finke use the benefit of networks to explain the early, large-scale success of Mormonism. Rodney Stark and Roger Finke, *Acts of Faith: Explaining the Human Side of Religion* (Berkeley and Los Angeles: University of California Press, 2000), 127–35.

104. It has been observed that a society tends to become more religious overall as it is religiously deregulated. Stark and Finke, *Acts of Faith*, 218–58.

prominent of such "new religions" (*shinkō shūkyō*) were lay groups that affiliated themselves with the *Nichiren Shōshū* sect of Buddhism, such as *Reiyūkai*, *Risshō Kōseikai*, and *Sōka Gakkai*.[105] As common features, they all created a community for those young people who had migrated to urban areas, where they had no friends or family; they offered a promise of temporal salvation from sickness, poverty, and alienation. A large body of sociological literature has emerged to explain how Sōka Gakkai,[106] the most successful of these so-called new religions, could so effectively recruit converts.[107] Not unlike the LDS Church, it is organized in geographically defined units; a cottage meeting known as *zadankai* is held once a month in a member home to gather together members living in a given area and to share their life experiences; someone is assigned to new initiates to provide social and collective support; the relationship between the introducer and the introduced is especially close and important; most significantly, an object of worship known as *gohonzon* is given, which could be placed in a family altar, allowing the convert to sever ties with the religion of his or her ancestors.[108] Sōka Gakkai developed into a major force in Japanese society, with membership increasing phenomenally from 70,000 households in 1953 to 1.7 million in 1960, and further to 5.9 million in 1965.[109]

---

105. Byron Earhart uses the term "new religions" for religious movements that appeared after the late Tokugawa period and became a powerful force after World War II. H. Byron Earhart, *Japanese Religion: Unity and Diversity*, fourth edition (Belmont, California: Wadsworth/Thomson, 2004), 187–89. New religions are not unique to Japan. For the sociology of new religious movements (NRMs) in American society, see E. Burke Rochford, Jr., "The Sociology of New Religious Movements," in *Religion and the Social Order, vol. 13: American Sociology of Religion: Histories*, ed. Anthony J. Blasi (Boston: Brill Academic Publishers, 2007), 253–90.

106. Sōka Gakkai, organized in 1930 as an educational organization, developed into a religious organization as the founder developed faith in *Nichiren Shōshū*.

107. See, for example, Hiromi Shimada, *Sōka Gakkai* (Tokyo: Shinchōsha, 2004); Kazushi Tamano, *Sōka Gakkai no Kenkyū* (Tokyo: Kōdansha, 2008). English-language references include: Noah S. Brannen, *Sōka Gakkai: Japan's Militant Buddhists* (Richmond, Virginia: John Knox Press, 1968); James Allen Dator, *Sōka Gakkai, Builders of the Third Civilization: American and Japanese Members* (Seattle and London: University of Washington Press, 1969); Hideo Hashimoto and William McPherson, "Rise and Decline of Sokagakkai: Japan and the United States," *Review of Religious Research* 17 (1976): 82–92; and Daniel A. Metraux, *The Soka Gakkai Revolution* (Lanham, Maryland: University Press of America, 1994). Its spread to the United States is discussed by John Kie-chang Oh, "The Nichiren Shoshu of America," *Review of Religious Research* 14 (1973): 169–77; and Lorne L. Dawson, "The Cultural Significance of New Religious Movements: The Case of Soka Gakkai," *Sociology of Religion* 62 (2001): 337–64.

108. Tamano, *Sōka Gakkai no Kenkyū*, 13–14, 18, 157.

109. Hashimoto and Mcpherson, "Rise and Decline of Sokkagakkai," Table 1; see also Shimada, *Sōka Gakkai*, 54.

The LDS Church, with its Christian message, probably did not directly compete with these and other religious groups based on traditional beliefs. What it found was a niche in a society being swept by societal changes associated with rapid industrialization. Compared to those who were attracted to traditional "new religions," a greater number of the Mormon converts were somewhat more educated, and came from somewhat higher strata of society. Even so, the LDS Church benefited from the same social changes that were promoting the growth of "new religions" in Japan.

Long-time Japanese Mormons look back at the 1960s as the golden age for the church, when young people in large numbers came to church to socialize in weekday activities and Sunday meetings never ended. True, many of them did not stay active very long as the cost of religious participation rose with increasing economic and social commitments, but there were always new waves of converts to fill their place. In this, they see a parallel between their church and their country, for which the 1960s were also the golden age. People were poorer and less sophisticated, but they were young and full of hope for the future.

12.8. Conclusion

In 1968, the LDS Church in Japan claimed approximately 10,000 members, of whom about 2,000 were actively engaged in thirty-five branches organized into five districts. It had the Book of Mormon, the Doctrine and Covenants, and the Pearl of Great Price translated into the Japanese language (though they were rendered in a style readers were increasingly finding difficult to understand); a number of manuals and textbooks were available in Japanese (though the translation and writing were not of high quality). The church had a stately mission home in a diplomatic section of Tokyo, nine modern meetinghouses across the country, and two buildings under construction. There were about 250 relatively young but experienced members, who had been endowed in the temple of God and were ready to take on greater leadership roles in the kingdom.

It was upon this foundation that, on 1 September 1968, the LDS Church divided the Northern Far East Mission into the Japan Mission (based in Tokyo), with Walter R. Bills as president and the Japan–Okinawa Mission (based in Kobe), with Edward Y. Okazaki as president. As the church saw the great potential for future growth, it began to devote greater resources to Japan. On 10 November 1967, the church filed an application to host a pavilion at a world fair (Expo '70) to be held in Osaka in 1970; in 1969, a Japanese version of the church's motion picture, "Man's Search for Happiness," was filmed with a well-known Japanese lead actor and actress.[110] Also, in 1969, the church's language mission program was

---

110. *Church News*, 4 October 1969, 4. About 10 percent of the 65 million visitors to the fair attended the Mormon Pavilion between the opening day on 15 March and the

expanded to include instruction in the Japanese language;[111] in early February, the first group of Japan-bound missionaries entered the Language Training Mission located at the Church College of Hawaii. Coinciding with the opening of Expo '70 on 15 March 1970, the Tokyo Stake was organized as the church's first stake in Asia, with Kenji Tanaka called to be its president; at that time, it was announced that two more missions would be created, with Kan Watanabe as president of the Japan West Mission and Russell N. Horiuchi as president of the Japan East Mission.[112]

Mormon Pavilion at Expo '70 in Osaka, March–September 1970. Courtesy Keiichi Mizuno.

Although missionary work was temporarily boosted by self-referrals made at Expo '70, the momentum of the early 1960s had largely dissipated by the end of the decade. Japan was maturing as an advanced industrial economy, meaning that no large-scale labor migration was to be expected; urbanization had essentially run its course, and the period of high growth was over. Many of those young people who had earlier flooded commuter train stations in big cities were now married with children; with the demands of work and other responsibilities, they no longer had time for religion. As the LDS Church doubled and then quadrupled the number of missionaries in the early 1970s, it opened new areas for proselytizing efforts to reach virtually every corner of the populated segments of the country. But this inevitably meant going into less urban, more tradition-bound areas where productivity was not expected to be high. One can only wonder what the outcome might have been if the LDS Church had increased the number of missionaries when the productivity was at its peak—from the late 1950s to the mid-1960s.

---

closing day on 13 September 1970. Bernard P. Brockbank, "The Mormon Pavilion at Expo '70," *Improvement Era* 73 (1970): 120–22.

111. Effective 8 February 1969, the term for all missionaries, including lady missionaries, was standardized at two years regardless of the mission. *Church News*, 18 January 1969, 3.

112. The establishment of the Tokyo Stake and two new missions was timed to coincide with the opening of Expo '70 in order to accommodate the travel schedule of Apostle Ezra Taft Benson. Work began in the new missions when Horiuchi arrived in Sapporo on 16 March and Watanabe in Fukuoka on 18 March. At this time, the name of the Japan–Okinawa Mission was changed to Japan Central Mission.

The early postwar period was a time when Asia suddenly caught the attention of the American church. Japan was at the forefront of this eastward trek of American Mormonism. During this period, through exposure to and experience with the people of Asia, American Mormons substantially overcame much of the prejudice they may have previously entertained. The sermon delivered by Joseph Fielding Smith at the fall 1955 general conference following his return from the Far East is instructive in this respect:

> Now I want to say to you mothers, particularly, fathers, too, who have sons in the mission field in any of these Eastern countries. . . . If your sons are called to go to the Far East to labor among the Japanese people, the Korean people . . . do not feel disappointed. Do not feel sorry and wish that they had been appointed to some European country or somewhere within the borders of the United States or the South Pacific. These people in these lands who have joined the Church are just as good as we are. Those people in those Far East countries are human beings, with like feelings and passions. They can love and they can hate just as you and I may love and hate. When they receive the gospel of Jesus Christ, they are just as good as we are.[113]

While spoken in part to counter lingering anti-Asian sentiments from the war and to encourage American Mormons to embrace their church's expansion into countries where American soldiers had died during a war started by Japanese aggression, these remarks may sound ludicrous if not offensive from the vantage point of the early twenty-first century. They show not only how much the world has changed in a remarkably short period of time but also how far Mormonism has traveled in its cautious but determined *Trek East*.

---

113. Joseph Fielding Smith, "Report from the Far East Missions," *Improvement Era* 58 (1955): 917–18.

Annexes

1. The Iwakura Mission in Salt Lake City
2. George Jarvis: Was He the First Mormon Missionary to Japan?
3. The Rise and Fall of Walter Murray Gibson
4. Notable Japanese Mormons from the Prewar Period
5. Mormon Mission Presidents, 1901–68
6. Selected Major Newspapers in Japan that Published Articles, Editorials, and Letters on Mormonism Between August and September 1901
7. Mormon Missionaries in the Japan Mission, 1901–24
8. Converts and Children of Record Baptized in Prewar Japan, 1902–39
9. Mormon Converts Baptized in Occupied Japan, 1946–52
10. Mormon Missionaries in the Japanese and Northern Far East Missions, 1948–68
11. Early American Labor Missionaries in Japan, 1962–69
12. Partial List of Locally Called Labor Missionaries in the Northern Far East Mission, 1962–68

Annex 1

The Iwakura Mission in Salt Lake City

In 1871, acting upon advice received from Guido Verbeck (Verbeek), a Dutch Reformed missionary, educator, and government advisor, the new Meiji government dispatched a high-level delegation to foreign powers in order to conduct exploratory renegotiations of the Ansei treaties (which gave their nationals extraterritorial privileges in Japan) and to observe their advanced institutions that might be helpful for Japan's modernization. The delegation was headed by Prince Tomomi Iwakura, junior prime minister and ambassador extraordinary, and included four senior government officials as vice ambassadors extraordinary, namely, Takayoshi Kido (state councilor), Toshimichi Okubo (minister of finance),[1] Hirobumi Ito (vice minister of public works), and Masuka Yamaguchi (vice minister for foreign affairs). In addition, a number of clerks, junior officials, servants, and students on their way to study abroad accompanied the delegation, making the full complement when they left Japan on 23 December over one hundred people.[2] This came to be known as the Iwakura Mission (or Embassy) in Japanese history.

The journey lasted nearly twenty-one months, beginning with a visit to the United States. The delegates traveled from the port of San Francisco, where they arrived on 15 January 1872, to Washington D.C. by train passing through Chicago and Pittsburgh. After spending nearly seven months in the United States, they left Boston on 6 August for Britain where they would spend the next four months, visiting such industrial cities as Birmingham, Glasgow, and Manchester, in addition to London. The delegates' visit to continental Europe began in mid-December with a stop in France and continued with brief stays in Belgium and Holland. The visit to Germany included an audience with German chancellor Otto von Bismarck, whose remarks are said to have influenced the thinking of Meiji politicians on constitu-

---

1. Kido and Okubo represented the former Choshu and Satsuma domains, which played leading roles in the overthrow of the Tokugawa shogunate. Although a government reshuffling on 11 August 1871 had relegated Okubo to a subordinate position, his influence remained strong in the State Council (later the Central Board). Masakazu Iwata, *Okubo Toshimichi: The Bismarck of Japan* (Los Angeles: University of California Press, 1964), 142–43.

2. According to the lunar calendar then in use, the date of departure was 12 November of the fourth year of Meiji. Historical records give the number of delegates proper variously as forty-six, forty-eight, forty-nine, and fifty-one. The rest were servants and students. Takashi Miyanaga, *Amerika no Iwakura Shisetsudan* (Tokyo: Chikuma Shobō, 1992), 6; Nagao Nishikawa and Hideharu Matsumiya, eds., *Beiō Kairan Jikki wo Yomu* (Kyoto: Hōritsu Bunkasha, 1995), 1. An English-language summary of the Iwakura Mission is provided by Ian Nish, "Introduction," in *Japan Rising: The Iwakura Embassy to the USA and Europe 1871–1873*, comp. Kunitake Kume (Cambridge and New York: Cambridge University Press, 2009), xi–xxix. For a detailed, contemporary account, see Charles Lanman, *The Japanese in America* (New York: University Publishing Company, 1872).

The Iwakura Mission upon arrival in San Francisco, January 1872. From left to right: Kido, Yamaguchi, Iwakura, Ito, and Okubo. Courtesy National Diet Library

tional, military, and other matters. Following visits to additional countries by various members of the mission, the main party arrived back at Yokohama on 13 September 1873.[3] All in all, twelve countries were visited by various members of the mission.

The Iwakura Mission's encounter with the Mormons took place at the beginning of the trip, in February 1872. On the early morning of 4 February, the Japanese delegates arrived in Ogden, where they were welcomed by a delegation from Salt Lake City, which included George Q. Cannon, a Mormon apostle and the managing editor of the *Deseret News*. While at breakfast, they were informed that the railroad tracks to the east had become unpassable on account of snow and hurriedly made arrangements to travel down by the Utah Central Railroad to Salt Lake City. With the main party accommodated at Townsend House, the mission was to remain in Salt Lake until the snow cleared on 22 February. While in Salt Lake, they were entertained by citizens of the city, met the governor, the mayor, members of the municipal and territorial legislatures in a formal reception, attended a Mormon service, and had an audience with seventy-one-year-old Brigham Young.

Concerning this meeting with Brigham Young, the 7 February issue of the *Deseret News* reported:

> The Embassy, having expressed a great desire to see President Young, took the earliest opportunity of visiting him at his mansion, he being the first of our citizens to whom they paid their respects. . . . The interview was an exceedingly agreeable one, the members of the Embassy evincing great interest in learning that all the improvements in the territory had been accomplished within 25 years.

---

3. Japan had formally adopted the solar calendar on 1 January 1873 or 3 December of the fifth year of Meiji, which became 1 January of the sixth year of Meiji.

Annex 1. The Iwakura Mission in Salt Lake City 445

The Salt Lake Tribune of the same day reported a different story, stating that Prince Iwakura, upon learning that Brigham Young was under house arrest (on a charge of polygamy), had declined the invitation for a meeting from Young's emissary by remarking: "We came to see the President of this great nation; we do not know how he would like for us to call on a man who had broken the laws of his country and was under arrest."[4] This story was picked up by a number of newspapers across the United States.[5] Galen M. Updike convincingly argues that such a conversation between Iwakura and Young's emissary never took place.[6] Regardless, that the Iwakura Mission met Brigham Young is an indisputable fact attested by official records, but it is not certain if Iwakura himself was at the meeting. He was quite ill at the time.

A debate of some interest took place among the members of the mission concerning the future of Christianity in Japan. One evening in Salt Lake City, Hirobumi Ito and Masuka Yamaguchi, the two more progressive members of the mission, came to the room of Takayuki Sasaki, a "commissioner" assigned to the ambassadors, to discuss the subject of lifting the centuries-long ban on Christianity (see Sections 4.2.2 and 4.4.1 in Chapter 4). Sasaki expressed his view to his superiors that it would be impossible to retain the ban indefinitely but preconditions must be met in terms of legal and social institutions before freedom of religion could be established. The next morning Sasaki reported this to Prince Iwakura, who remarked that he had earlier engaged in a heated discussion on the subject with Ito, but he himself had no immediate intention to lift the ban.[7] In the meantime, Jonathan Goble, a Baptist missionary who traveled with the Iwakura Mission to San Francisco, was writing letters to the editors of newspapers in major cities, calling on American churchmen to promote the cause of Christianity when the Japanese envoys visited their cities.[8]

The Iwakura Mission's visit to Salt Lake was reported widely in the Japanese press, from the end of February through March 1872, including in the *Yokohama Mainichi Shinbun*, Japan's first daily established in 1870,[9] and the mission's periodic report for public consumption called *Taishi Shinpō*.[10] The Salt Lake visit and the Mormon practice of plural marriage were covered on the front page of the very first issue of the *Tokyo Nichinichi Shinbun*, Tokyo's first daily, on 29 March 1872.[11]

---

4. *The Salt Lake Daily Tribune and Utah Mining Gazette*, 7 February 1972.
5. See also Lanman, *Japanese in America*, 23–24.
6. Galen M. Updike, "The Iwakura Mission: The Mormons' First Encounter with Japan," unpublished, Brigham Young University, 1974, 18–22.
7. Miyanaga, *Amerika no Iwakura Shisetsudan*, 90–91.
8. See, for example, Jonathan Goble, letter to editor, *New York Times*, 20 February 1872, 8.
9. The issue is reprinted in Yutaka Kitane, eds, *Nihon Shoki Shinbun Zenshū*, vol. 35 (Tokyo: Perikansha, 1992), 181–82. The paper later moved to Tokyo and changed its name to *Mainichi Shinbun*.
10. Nishikawa and Matsumiya, *Beiō Kairan Jikki*, 434–35. The issue is reprinted in Kitane, *Nihon Shoki Shinbun Zenshū*, vol. 35, 267–68 and vol. 36, 294. This public relations effort lasted until March 1873.
11. The lunar date was 21 February of the fifth year of Meiji.

Annex 2

George Jarvis:
Was He the First Mormon Missionary to Japan?

It has been claimed that the first Mormon missionary to Japan was George Jarvis (1823–1913). Jarvis was born in Harlow, Essex, England on 25 March 1823. He became a sailor at the age of seventeen and made several trips to far corners of the earth, including Ceylon, China, North America, and South Africa. He then joined the British Navy on an expedition to the West Indies, where he became ill and was blinded in one eye. Following his marriage to Ann Prior in 1846, he worked as a ship-keeper for the British Navy in Woolwich, where he and his wife were converted to the Mormon faith by Franklin D. Richards (future apostle) and Lorenzo Snow (future apostle and church president). They were baptized on Christmas Day 1848. George continued to work as a seaman, occasionally going on short voyages, in order to save enough money to emigrate to Utah. George, Ann, and five children boarded the ship *George Washington* at Liverpool on 28 March 1857 and arrived in Boston on 20 April. The couple, joined by seven additional children, would eventually settle in St. George, Utah.[1]

That George Jarvis might have been the first missionary to reach Japan became widely known with the publication of an article in the 4 December 1954 issue of the *Church News*, which noted that G. Stanford Jarvis, then serving in Japan, was the third generation of missionaries. His father Erastus had served in Japan some fifty years before, while his grandfather George "had been there in 1850, with authority to preach Mormonism to the Japanese people but circumstances prevented." The article goes on to say: "When Queen Victoria sent her royal freighter to the Orient in the spring of 1850 for a cargo of spices, George Jarvis was one of the sailors she interviewed personally for the voyage. As mission officials learned of George Jarvis's assignment . . . they set him apart to do missionary work in China and Japan."[2]

George's experience during his last voyage to the Orient was told to his family when he gave his missionary son Erastus a departing blessing on 20 June 1902, wherein he stated:

> When I undertook one last voyage to China in order to obtain funds to bring my family to Utah, Elder Purdy, President of the Poplar Branch of the London Conference, called me into his office. He ordained me an elder and then set me apart

---

1. The family group record and biographical information of George Jarvis were provided to the author by G. Stanford Jarvis, his grandson. See also Zora Smith Jarvis, comp., "Sketches from the Lives of Brigham Jarvis, Sr. and Mary Forsythe Jarvis" (St. George, Utah, 1967).

2. "Father and Son Fill Missions to Japan Fifty Years Apart," *Church News*, 4 December 1954, 7, 10.

for a mission to preach the Gospel during this voyage to all the English-speaking people I should meet in China and Japan. . . . The ship's schedule was overdue when the cargo of spices arrived. Cholera broke out on board, and as the captain took it, I became acting captain of the ship. At Yokohama, after giving orders, I went ashore with a heavy heart. . . . We left Yokohama at three-thirty P.M.[3]

He concluded by stating that after much prayer and fasting he had received a spiritual assurance that he "shall live to witness one of [his] descendants carry the Gospel to Japan." George then used his influence as the patriarch of the St. George Stake to have his son's mission assignment changed from the Southern States to the Japan Mission in 1902.

There are internal inconsistencies in the memory of George Jarvis. First, Yokohama did not exist as a port until 1 July 1859, when the Ansei treaties with the Five Powers took effect. Second, no British ship was allowed to come into a Japanese port until the Anglo–Japanese Friendship Treaty of 1854 opened Hakodate and Nagasaki in 1855 for provisioning (but not for commerce).[4] Third, there was no outbreak of cholera in Japan between 1822 and 1858.[5] It is a logical impossibility that George Jarvis landed at the port of Yokohama in 1850. Given the fact that he left Liverpool for Boston in March 1857 and that this was his last voyage to the Orient, the only possible window of time for his presumed visit to Japan was the warm summer months of 1856 or even possibly 1855 (the spread of the disease tends to rise with warmer climate). The port was likely Nagasaki, which George confused with Yokohama in his old age. While there was no outbreak of cholera in Japan, there was one in China during 1855–56. It is entirely reasonable that the captain of the ship contracted the disease during his stay in China (if so, this was confined to the ship). One cannot rule out the possibility that George Jarvis did not reach Japan.

---

3. Typed copy of the blessing given by George Jarvis to his son Erastus. Provided to author by G. Stanford Jarvis of Magna, Utah. Copy in possession of author.

4. This followed the Treaty of Kanagawa signed in March 1854 with the United States, which opened the ports of Hakodate and Shimoda to American ships for provisioning. Until 1855, when the treaty came into force, only Dutch ships (or ships chartered by the Dutch East India Company) were allowed to come into Deshima in Nagasaki harbor upon inspection by Japanese and resident Dutch officials, including presentation of proof that they had sailed from Batavia (present-day Jakarta). Kazuo Katagiri, *Hirakareta Sakoku* (Tokyo: Kōdansha, 1997), 39–72.

5. The nineteenth century saw five cholera pandemics: (1) 1817–23; (2) 1826–37; (3) 1840–60; (4) 1863–79; and (5) 1881–96. As part of these pandemics, there were outbreaks of cholera in Japan in 1822 (when the disease was transmitted through Nagasaki or Tsushima), 1858–60 (when the disease was transmitted through Nagasaki by the American ship *Mississippi* from China), 1862, 1879, 1882, 1886, 1890, and 1895. More than 10,000 people died in each of these years. Shoji Tatsukawa, *Byōki no Shakai Shi* (Tokyo: Nihon Hōsō Shuppan Kyōkai, 1971), 173–83; Hideo Fukumi, "Nihon no Korera Ryūkō Shi (I)," *Kagaku* 47 (1977): 458–59.

Annex 3

The Rise and Fall of Walter Murray Gibson

Walter Murray Gibson was born at sea in 1817 (or 1822) of English parents en route to the United States.[1] He spent his childhood in New York and New Jersey before his family settled in the backwoods of South Carolina. He taught school, married, had three children, was widowed, became a merchant, traveled in Central America, and ran into trouble with the Dutch authorities in the East Indies (he was tried, imprisoned, escaped, and returned to the United States). Witnessing the plight of the Mormons suffering persecution, he conceived the idea of relocating the entire Mormon population from their mountain and desert homes to New Guinea or some other island in the Pacific or Indian Ocean. Failing to persuade United States president James Buchanan to finance his venture, he decided to talk directly to LDS Church president Brigham Young.

When Gibson arrived in Salt Lake City in the fall of 1859, he was warmly welcomed by the Mormons mostly out of curiosity and became a popular speaker in the valley. Brigham Young was not so gullible. Gibson was told to investigate the doctrines of the church and, if convinced of their truthfulness, to be baptized. Then, it was promised, he would be ordained an elder and sent to the South Pacific to preach the gospel. Gibson took Young's advice and was baptized into the LDS Church on 15 January 1860. After six months of church service in the eastern United States, he was set apart to go to the Pacific, "fully authorized to negotiate with all the nations of this world who would obey the gospel of Christ."[2] Gibson left Salt Lake City "for Japan" on 21 November 1860.

After spending several months in San Francisco, Gibson arrived in Honolulu in July 1861. Initially, he was told that the LDS Church had virtually ceased to function in Hawaii with the departure of Utah missionaries in 1858.[3] In time, however, he discovered that, although membership had dwindled and some branches had ceased to function, the church was still functioning under local leadership. He seized the first opportunity to take control of the church by attending a semi-annual conference held in Wailuku, Maui on 6 October. Upon presenting his credentials in the form of letters of appointment and recommen-

---

1. Unless otherwise noted, the information on Gibson in this annex comes from Frank W. McGhie, "The Life and Intrigues of Walter Murray Gibson" (MS thesis, Brigham Young University, 1958); Esther Leonore Ferreira Sousa, "Walter Murray Gibson's Rise to Power in Hawaii" (MA thesis, University of Hawaii, 1942), supplemented by Britsch, *Unto the Islands of the Sea*, chapter 7; Ralph S. Kuykendall, *The Hawaiian Kingdom, Vol. II: 1854–1874 Twenty Critical Years* (Honolulu: University of Hawaii Press, 1953), 102–3.

2. *Deseret News*, 18 November 1860, as quoted in McGhie, "Walter Murray Gibson," 70.

3. In the light of generally fruitless labors, the Utah elders were called home because of the Utah War.

dation from Brigham Young, he assumed the presidency of the Hawaiian Mission and obtained control of the church in Hawaii.

By November 1861, Gibson was in Lanai, an island previously chosen to be the gathering place for the Hawaiian Mormons. Following the departure of the Utah elders in 1858, the Hawaiian Latter-day Saints had struggled on the poor soil of Lanai, but some still remained when Gibson arrived. Gibson began a major initiative to expand the colony by purchasing or leasing additional land. To finance the operation of this scheme, he began to sell priesthood offices and membership certificates for money, and to receive contributions in both money and kind from the members. The newly acquired land was registered under his own name.

Although cultivation was hard, from 1861 to 1864, great achievements were made under Gibson's direction in raising the temporal and cultural welfare of the people of Lanai. Success was particularly remarkable in the raising of cattle and sheep on the greener hillside of the island, and in the building of schools, meetinghouses, and better homes for the people. Against these great temporal achievements, Gibson's failure in the spiritual realm was obvious to the more discerning members of the colony. In addition to simoniac practices, he introduced pagan and superstitious elements, and established a hierarchical command structure in which he was on the top. Mormon writers have generally interpreted his motive as that of establishing a temporal kingdom for his own personal gains.[4]

In early 1862, responding to the letters of complaint written by the more experienced and thus suspecting members in Lanai, Brigham Young decided to send a committee of seasoned leaders to investigate the situation. The committee, which included apostles Ezra T. Benson and Lorenzo Snow, left Salt Lake City on 2 March 1864, arrived in Honolulu on 27 March, and came to Lanai on 2 April. In a special conference held on 6 April, Joseph F. Smith, a member of the visiting committee and a former Hawaiian missionary fluent in the Hawaiian language, gave a stirring admonition to the members, counseling them to leave Lanai for their homes. On 8 April, Gibson was excommunicated from the LDS Church in a council meeting held in Lahaina, Maui. After this incident, Gibson remained on Lanai and became the dominant owner and lessee of the island of Lanai.

The second round of Gibson's rise and fall began in 1872, when he moved to Honolulu to try his hand in Hawaiian politics. By this time, he had mastered the Hawaiian language and had become a naturalized citizen of Hawaii (in 1866). In May 1873, he began to publish a newspaper called the *Nuhou* to influence the

---

4. Although such an interpretation is probably correct and his journal entries do attest that his motives were dishonest and impure, it is only one aspect of the picture. In October 1862, an editorial in the *Polynesian* published in Honolulu praised Gibson as a philanthropist and social reformer among the natives of the kingdom, stating that he had shown what a "calm, clear-headed, energetic and devoted man" could do for the social improvement of the Hawaiians. Britsch, *Moramona*, 54–55; Sousa, "Walter Murray Gibson," 59.

public opinions of the natives.[5] His platform was "Hawaii is for the Hawaiians," placing him as the champion of the Hawaiian people and the friend of the "downtrodden natives."[6] After taking up residence in Lahaina, Maui, he was elected to the Legislative Assembly in 1878. As King Kalakaua's right-hand man and principal advisor, Gibson was appointed to various positions in the government, including the premier and minister of foreign affairs (May 1882–July 1887). It was during his tenure as foreign minister that the immigration convention with Japan was signed.

With Gibson's characteristic propensity towards dominance, pomposity, and power, problems were to be expected with the administration of King Kalakaua. In fact, there was much corruption and waste of public funds. He also made personal enemies. As early as 1882, some of his political enemies published a scathing criticism of Gibson called *The Shepherd Saint of Lanai*, exposing his past career as a Mormon leader.[7] Following the failed and disastrous naval expedition to Samoa, made in 1886–87 in a vain attempt to establish Hawaiian primacy in an eventual confederation of Polynesian states, ill will towards Gibson intensified even more. The final straw was the revelation, in June 1887, of bribery on the part of the king and the premier associated with Chinese opium trade. This resulted in a popular uprising against the king and his cabinet, especially Gibson.

The historian Ralph S. Kuykendall states that Gibson was "one of the leading figures in the public life of the kingdom" and summarizes his person in the following words: "He was without doubt a remarkable character, possessed of an ingratiating personality, a brilliant mind, and much adroitness in his dealings with others. He had many excellent ideas, but his own personal aggrandizement seems to have been his ultimate objective."[8] His relationship with the Mormons was brief. Despite the dishonorable way in which he was discharged from the LDS Church, however, Gibson is said to have shown no malice towards the Latter-day Saints. He later spoke warmly of his respect for the church and donated $50 to the Laie chapel building fund in 1882.[9] One may interpret this to mean that whatever may have been his intention with the Mormons his motive was never priestly—that of becoming a spiritual leader. Following the rebellion of 1887, Gibson was dismissed, jailed and, in peril of his life, allowed to leave Hawaii. After six months of exile, he died in San Francisco in January 1888.

---

5. The publication of the *Nuhou* lasted until April 1874. He then purchased the influential *Pacific Commercial Advertiser*. Sousa, "Walter Murray Gibson," 184; McGhie "Life and Intrigues," 110.

6. McGhie "Life and Intrigues," 103, 108 and 110; and Sousa, "Walter Murray Gibson," 104.

7. *The Shepherd Saint of Lanai, Priest of Melchisedec, President of the Isles of the Sea, Rich "Primacy" Revelations* (Honolulu: Thos. G. Thrum, 1882). The book was a compilation of letters and other documents that had previously been published in the *Saturday Press*. The negative impact of this was limited, as it was written in English. McGhie, "Life and Intrigues," 112.

8. Kuykendall, *Hawaiian Kingdom*, 102.

9. Britsch, *Moramona*, 58; McGhie, "Walter Murray Gibson," 96.

Annex 4

Notable Japanese Mormons from the Prewar Period

1. Takeo Fujiwara (1906–36)

Takeo Fujiwara, baptized in Sapporo on 10 May 1924, was one of the very last converts in the prewar Japan Mission. He responded to an invitation from President Franklin S. Harris of Brigham Young University to study at his institution, spent seven years in Utah, and returned to Japan in 1934 as presiding elder and a special missionary. He lived on a limited budget while studying in Utah. Years of poor diet had weakened his immune system by the time he came home. He soon succumbed to tuberculosis, which entered his blood causing the disease to spread quickly.[1] At the tender age of twenty-nine, Fujiwara died as a single man at Sapporo's Muzushima Hospital. His ministry as presiding elder lasted less than eighteen months (see Section 8.3 in Chapter 8). On 23 February 1979, some forty-three years after this untimely death, his nephew, Yoshiaki Fujiwara, with wife Yuko and daughter Ayumu, joined the LDS Church, without prior knowledge of Uncle Takeo's Mormon connection.[2] Yoshiaki has since served as a bishop and Ayumu as a full-time proselytizing missionary for the church.

Takeo Fujiwara was born on 10 May 1906 in Garugawa, Teine-cho, Sapporo-gun,[3] which was, in the 1930s, about 30 minutes by train from the center of Sapporo. At 1 m 54 cm (or 5' 1"), according to his passport, he was a man of short stature.[4] Upon graduation from Sapporo First Secondary School (five-year curriculum) in March 1925, he worked for Hokkaido's district court system. He was in the prosecutors' department in the Sapporo District Court from May to February 1926, when he was appointed as clerk by the Ministry of Justice to work for the Kushiro District Court, the position he held until September 1927. It was while in Kushiro that he took a leave of absence to meet and interpret for Harris during his visit to Sapporo in 1926.

Upon graduation from Brigham Young University High School in June 1929, Takeo enrolled at BYU as a freshman. Four years later, in June 1933, he

---

1. This is according to his younger brother, who was a physician. Author's interview with Akitake Yamada, telephone, 27 March 1998.

2. Takeo's father, Masatsugu Fujiwara, had twelve sons. Yoshiaki is a son of Masajiro, the eldest son of Masatsugu and an elder brother of Takeo. Author's interview with Yuko and Yoshiaki Fujiwara, Sapporo, 3 March 1998.

3. The biographical information in his *Improvement Era* article (that he was born in 1907) is incorrect. Fujiwara, "Shinto and Mormonism," 654. Conkling gives the year of Takeo's birth as 1905. This is also incorrect. J. Christopher Conkling, "Members without a Church: Japanese Mormons in Japan from 1924 to 1948," *Brigham Young University Studies* (1975): 200.

4. Photocopy of the cover page of Fujiwara's passport, in author's possession.

received a bachelor of arts degree, with a major in English and a minor in French.[5] With a tuition waiver granted by the university,[6] he moved on to pursue graduate studies, obtaining a master of arts degree in June 1934, whereupon he was given a credential by the Japanese Ministry of Education to teach English in secondary and normal schools.[7] His master's degree was in history, with a thesis entitled, "The Political and Military Policies of the Tokugawa Shogunate." Takeo Fujiwara is the first Japanese Latter-day Saint to receive ordinances in the Salt Lake Temple. He was "known around Utah and Idaho as a Japanese lecturer and entertainer, and [had] given many lectures and entertainments at high schools and various places."[8]

Takeo Fujiwara, a graduate of Brigham Young University, 1933. Courtesy Yoshiaki Fujiwara.

2. Tsuruichi Katsura (1891–1982)

Tsuruichi Katsura, born on 6 February 1891 and baptized in Osaka on 25 December 1913, was one of only seven Japanese men who received the Melchizedek priesthood in the prewar Japan Mission (the ordination took place on 27 November 1921). He was a man of some means, self-employed as the operator of a small factory. This explains why Katsura frequently invited the missionaries for dinner at his house.[9] Within four years of joining the LDS Church, Katsura was already playing a leading role in Osaka. In May 1917, mission president Joseph H. Stimpson recorded in his journal: "Bro. Katsura and I took up the time in Preaching Meeting." In late 1921, missionary Hilton A. Robertson recorded: "In the Evening Brothers Katsura and Ohashi came to the church to arrange speakers for Sunday night"; "Brother Katsura took charge of the Sunday School which was well attended."[10]

---

5. Gene F. Priday, University Registrar, Brigham Young University, letter to author, 31 October 1995.

6. Takeo Fujiwara, "The Political and Military Policies of the Tokugawa Shogunate" (MA thesis, Brigham Young University, 1934), ii.

7. Photocopy of Fujiwara's resume, circa 1934, in author's possession.

8. Fujiwara, "Shinto and Mormonism," 655.

9. For example, Robertson recorded: "In the afternoon Brother Katsura invited us to his home for dinner. We had a very splendid time and enjoyed being with them." Robertson, Autobiography, 3 January 1922.

10. Robertson, Autobiography, 3 and 6 November 1921.

Annex 4. Notable Japanese Mormons from the Prewar Period

Following the closing of the mission, in 1926, Katsura was appointed by BYU president Franklin S. Harris to be president of the Mutual Improvement Association (MIA) in Osaka. When a semi-formal church structure was restored in 1934 under presiding elder Takeo Fujiwara, Katsura was made president of the Osaka Branch. When Robertson visited Osaka in 1939 as president of the Honolulu-based Japanese Mission, Katsura was the first to receive him and gathered the few faithful who remained (see Section 8.5.3 in Chapter 8). Following the resumption of missionary work in 1948, Katsura was again the first to receive a visit from mission president Edward Clissold in Osaka (see Section 10.4 and Appendix 10.1 in Chapter 10). He died a faithful Mormon on 8 April 1982 at the age of ninety-one.[11]

Tsuruichi Katsura, with wife Tsuru, at the entrance of their house in Osaka. Courtesy Carolyn McDonald/Bill McIntyre.

In the 1920s, Robertson described the respect Katsura commanded from the local members:

> All present [in a testimony meeting] . . . expressed joy in the fact that our faithful member, brother Katsura, had brought happiness into their lives through his efforts in being instrumental in teaching them and other [sic] the gospel.[12]

Robertson then summarized his character:

> No fine [sic] meaning man walks Japanese soil than Brother Katsura. He has stood with us night after night in the church and on the [street] corners preaching the gospel reminding me . . . of that wonderful character Samuel, the Lamanite. . . . He is not only good but he is humorous & kind.[13]

3. Tamano Kumagai (1892–1978)

Tamano Kumagai, baptized on 19 December 1908, was a female member in Sapporo who remained faithful to the LDS Church throughout her life of eighty-six years. She was present at each critical event affecting the church in Sapporo (as well as in Japan). For example, she was at Yokohama harbor on 6

---

11. Kanji Moriya, email to author, 9 October 2015; Kohei Kawano, letter to author, 21 November 2015. Kawano was a family friend and former employee of Katsura.
12. Robertson, Autobiography, 5 March 1922.
13. Robertson, Autobiography, 14 December 1923.

August 1924 to see some of the last set of missionaries depart from Japan.[14] She was there in 1926 when BYU president Franklin Harris came to organize an MIA in Sapporo. Following the end of World War II, it was Kumagai who first saw mission president Edward Clissold and assisted the first missionary Paul Andrus in the reopening of Sapporo (see Section 10.4 and Appendix 10.1 in Chapter 10). She participated in the Northern Far East Mission's second Hawaii Temple trip in 1967 (an injury had prevented her participation in the first) and attended the October 1970 general conference in Salt Lake City. She died on 2 June 1978.

Born on 2 January 1892, Kumagai graduated from a secondary school for women that was affiliated with *Jōdō Shinshū* Buddhism. She married church member Mitsuo Sakuma on 13 February 1914,[15] but the marriage did not last very long. Evidently, Lewis H. Moore, the last missionary to serve in prewar Japan, proposed marriage to her, but mission president Hilton A. Robertson disapproved. After discussing this matter with Kumagai during his visit to Sapporo in 1939 (see Section 8.5.3 in Chapter 8), Robertson recorded: "Had [Kumagai] gone to America with [Moore], his parents, society and the public generally would not have accepted her and she would not have been able to enter the country with him. Her happiness in the future would have been entire [sic] crashed." He told her "how happy and satisfied I had felt at my decision."[16] In 1928, she seriously considered attending Brigham Young University to study, but the plan never materialized.[17] As a pioneer female journalist in Hokkaido, she spent most of her ensuing years working for the *Hokkai Taimusu* (later renamed *Hokkaido Shinbun*).[18]

Kumagai's youthful faith is demonstrated by a letter she wrote to the editor of the *Juvenile Instructor* in January 1918:

> It is just ten years since I received baptism. . . . It must be nice in Utah where most of the people belong to the Church. There are many churches in Japan. Recently the Church of England built a nice church only a block away from ours and we were afraid we would lose some of our children, but we haven't yet. I am very thankful that God has seen fit to establish His Church in Japan, for in it some Japanese have found satisfaction. . . . I think the reason there are no more who join is because this is

---

14. Of this event, Robertson recorded: "I sure felt sorry for Sister Kumagai." Robertson, Journal, 6 August 1924.

15. Mitsuo Sakuma was born on 18 January 1883 and baptized on 23 December 1907.

16. Robertson, Journal, 1 May 1939.

17. In February 1928, she applied for a passport at the Hokkaido prefectural office, wherein she stated her occupation as a newspaper reporter and her intention to attend Brigham Young University to study home economics. Photocopy of the passport request submitted by Tamano Kumagai, 20 February 1928, in author's possession. Takeo Fujiwara wrote to Kumagai on his way to Utah describing his experiences on the ship and with the immigration and customs procedures in San Francisco. This seems to intimate that Kumagai's planned departure was imminent. Takeo Fujiwara, letter to Tamano Kumagai, 27 October 1927. Photocopy in author's possession.

18. Mitsuo Kurami, "Nihon no Dendō Shoki no Kaishūsha Kumagai Tamano Shimai Jūnana Sai no Nikki ni miru Shinkō no Ibuki," *Seito no Michi* 27 (June 1985), local pages, 1–2.

Annex 4. Notable Japanese Mormons from the Prewar Period

the higher law and perhaps harder to obey. The Word of Wisdom sounds very strange to many people as tea drinking is a universal custom in Japan. But we are not discouraged at the scarcity of numbers, and are perhaps the more thankful to think we are among the chosen few.[19]

Takeo Fujiwara was a compatriot of Kumagai from Sapporo. Perhaps feeling that their friendship was sufficiently strong, Fujiwara in his capacity as a friend and presiding elder chastised Kumagai for refusing to serve in the church just because she had no one to help her. Noting that meetings were beginning to be held in Kofu, Osaka, and Tokyo but not in Sapporo, he wrote to her: "I earnestly desire you to have a faith with works."[20] On 6 August 1935, Fujiwara reported to Taylor: "Sister Tamano Kumagai, the supposed, most faithful saint, would never communicate us for the sake of the Church work in Sapporo. She says she has faith, but it is without work."[21]

Tamano Kumagai, a member in Sapporo. Courtesy Carolyn McDonald/Bill McIntyre.

Even so, she had faith strong enough to have her sister baptized into the LDS Church in 1939 during Robertson's brief visit to Sapporo as president of the Honolulu-based Japanese Mission.[22] On this occasion, she handed him a letter for his wife that stated: "My sister was baptized today and we are all very happy."[23] Hokkaido scholar Seiji Katanuma reports, based on an interview with Kumagai, that she held Sunday school at her house when the church was closed, but fewer and fewer men started coming as some were called to work at factories or into the battlefield and that policemen often came when they were singing hymns, the music of an enemy.[24] This experience must refer to the actual war-time years when any suspicious activity was under surveillance by the thought police. As imperfect and discouraged as she may have been, her faith was sustained during this period.

---

19. Tamano Kumagai, "Letter from a Japanese Convert," *Juvenile Instructor* 53 (1918): 180.

20. Takeo Fujiwara, letter to Tamano Kumagai, 30 March 1935. Photocopy in author's possession. The author's translation of the Japanese original.

21. Takeo Fujiwara, "The Official Report from the Japan Mission of the Church of Jesus Christ of Latter-day Saints," 5 August 1935, 9, LDS Church Archives.

22. Yoshino Kumagai was baptized in Sapporo on 3 May 1939.

23. Tamano Kumagai, letter to Hazel Robertson, 3 May 1939.

24. Seiji Katanuma, "The Church in Japan," *Brigham Young University Studies* 14 (1973): 21.

4. Chojiro Kuriyama (1896–1971)

Chojiro Kuriyama, born on 7 September 1896 and baptized in Tokyo on 25 August 1919, would become perhaps the most prominent member of the LDS Church in postwar Japanese society. In April 1946, he was elected to the National Diet in the lower House of Representatives on a Japan Liberal Party ticket. During his parliamentary tenure, which lasted until March 1953, he served as parliamentary vice-minister of education from October 1948 to February 1949 and as chairman of the Foreign Affairs Committee in 1952.[25] He gave a speech in the United States Senate in August 1950 as a representative of the Japanese parliamentary delegation. In the postwar acquisition of property for the LDS Church, Kuriyama did what he could to assist mission president Edward Clissold and spoke at a ground-breaking ceremony for the construction of the mission home. Other than this, it does not appear that he took his religion seriously during much of his life. He died on 8 July 1971.

Shortly after his baptism, in May 1920, Kuriyama left Japan to further his education in the United States.[26] He first attended the University of Utah before moving on to Harvard. While in Salt Lake City, he was a contemporary of Japanese member Tomigoro Takagi, who was working for the *Utah Nippō* as chief editor.[27] They met but neither of them attended Mormon services regularly. He returned to Japan in 1924 and attended church for some time.[28] Hilton Robertson recorded of him:

> I talked to Brother Kuriyama, who has recently returned from Salt Lake City, and others [*sic*] part of the U.S.A. where he has been attending school, during the past four years. I talked to him for about three hours. I ask[ed] him what he thought of our people and he said he was somewhat disappointed in them. He felt that many of our people, especially the young people of the church, were not standing true to the faith and that our people were narrow and what not. I inquired as to his living and to whether he attended regularly to his church duties but he informed he had not. He said, however, that he hadn't ever questioned the authenticity of the Church. . . . I am sorry to hear him express himself as he does, for I realize, too well after talking to him, the reason for his feelings. I am sure if he had been living as he should he would have seen different people in Utah, while not perfect by a long ways, yet leading the world as a whole.

Robertson commented a few days later: "We have had him to church more since he came home than he attended while he was in Salt Lake City."[29]

---

25. Takayoshi Miyagawa, ed., *Rekidai Kokkai Giin Keireki Yōran* (Tokyo, Seiji Kōhō Sentā, 1990).

26. Jenson, "History of the Japan Mission," 15 May 1920.

27. Takagi, "Nihon Dendōbu no Kaiko," October 1958, 24.

28. Hilton Robertson recorded: "At our night meeting Brother Kuriyama, just recently returned from Salt Lake City and Brother Hicken were the speakers." Robertson, Autobiography, 2 March 1924.

29. Robertson, Autobiography, 26 February 1924; 2 and 4 March 1924.

Becoming a journalist, Kuriyama was stationed in New York City as the chief correspondent for the *Osaka Mainichi* and *Tokyo Nichinichi*, which were under the same management.[30] At this time, Elbert D. Thomas, a former Japan missionary, was a member of the United States Senate. Thomas thought that he could use Kuriyama's position to influence the deteriorating course of events in Japan. In March 1935, he sent a telegram asking Kuriyama to use his influence as the New York correspondent for an influential newspaper to change the sentiment of the Japanese government and people towards withdrawal from the League of Nations.[31] A letter from Thomas to the First Presidency, dated 5 August 1950, states: "Brother Kuriyama told me that he not only got this telegram to his paper, and it was widely circulated, but he also got it into government circles. The results, of course, were nil."[32]

5. Ei Nachie (1892–1982)

Ei Nachie, born on 1 October 1892 and baptized in Tokyo on 26 March 1908 at the age of fifteen, was an adopted daughter of Tsune Nachie (see below). She lived in the mission home while her mother served as a maid and cook. Her name appears frequently in the journals of H. Grant Ivins and Joseph H. Stimpson when they were mission presidents, indicating that she was attending church regularly throughout the 1910s. In December 1920, she married Yoshio Nagao, a non-member, and lived in Manchuria during part of the interwar years.[33] When Hilton Robertson visited Japan in 1939 as president of the Honolulu-based Japanese Mission (see Section 8.5.3 in Chapter 8), she was in Tokyo but too sick to see him.[34] It is possible that this illness had brought her back to Japan. Robertson learned that "Ei san" had received her mother's belongings, which he had earlier sent to her following Tsune's death in Hawaii (see the account of Tsune Nachie immediately below).

Following the end of World War II, she was in Osaka (where her husband was from) and attended the first Mormon meeting held in that city by postwar missionaries. Ei subsequently moved to Yokohama and remained a faithful Mormon until her death on 11 May 1982. She lived long enough to see her

---

30. *Hattatsu* 1 (1935): 11.
31. Elbert D. Thomas, telegram to Chojiro Kuriyama, 25 March 1935, LDS Church Archives.
32. Elbert D. Thomas, letter to the First Presidency, 5 August 1950, LDS Church Archives.
33. Takeo Fujiwara, "The Official Report from the Japan Mission of the Church of Jesus Christ of Latter-day Saints, 1 January–30 April 1935," LDS Church Archives. Her husband, a 1916 graduate of Keio University, left for Manchuria in August 1921, though it is not known when he returned to Japan. Kenichi Takenaka, ed., *Jinmei Jiten: Manshū ni Watatta Ichiman Nin* (Tokyo: Kōseisha, 2012), 1006.
34. Robertson, Journal, 19 April 1939.

husband join the LDS Church in 1980 and to have their marriage solemnized in the newly dedicated Tokyo Temple on 19 March 1982.[35] Alma O. Taylor said of her when he was about to leave Japan on 9 January 1910:

> I said a special farewell to my young Sister in the gospel Ei Nachie, who has lived at headquarters with her mother for several years. During the past year I have been paying her way at school and have taken great pains to have her grow up as the Lord would have her do. As a token of my interest in her and my love for her and as a reminder of the instructions given to her I gave her a small pearl ring. . . . I have loved this little girl as a sister and regret more the farewell to her than I did the farewell to my own blood sisters when I left America. In fact this is the first time in my life that I have had a sister in the same home with me.[36]

6. Tsune Nachie (1856–1938)

Tsune Nachie was baptized in Tokyo on 26 September 1905 while working as a maid and cook at the mission home. Nachie was perhaps the greatest fruit of Mormonism in prewar Japan and one reason why the Japan Mission was not a failure. She was born in what is now Yamanashi Prefecture on 9 May 1856 (or 6 April in the third year of Ansei).[37] She left her husband because of abuse and moved to Tokyo where she made a living as a cook in foreign homes. She was a self-educated woman. Having become a member of the Church of England (Anglican–Episcopal Church), she was familiar with the Bible. Her interest in Mormonism arose from her misgiving about infant baptism. She was forty-nine years of age when she joined the church.[38]

She became a towering spiritual figure in the church during its formative years and, as a Sunday school teacher, a mentor to young converts and investigators. In 1958, member Tomigoro Takagi said of her:

> Although we had no literature to help us gain a deep understanding of the doctrines and did not have the means of obtaining deep knowledge, the testimony that the Church of Jesus Christ of Latter-day Saints was the only true church restored through the Prophet Joseph Smith became stronger every day. Particularly, the solemn and intense testimony of Sister Tsune Nachie was wonderful enough to shake up the souls of us young people. Now, I cannot help but feel and be thankful that we were coming to church, being led by her faith. Later, when Sister Nachie left for Hawaii to be engaged in the work of baptisms for the dead, I fell into a sense of sadness, not knowing where to rest my heart.[39]

---

35. *Seito no Michi* (June 1982): local pages, 68; Toshiko Yanagida, "Takagi Tomigoro ni tsuite," interview by Jiro Numano, *Morumon Fōramu* 6 (Spring 1991): 45.

36. Taylor, Journal.

37. Her church membership record shows the date of birth as 12 May. This is probably an error because 6 April appears to be the correct lunar date.

38. Anonymous, "The Life of Sister Tsune Nachiye." Photocopy in author's possession.

39. The author's translation of the Japanese original. Takagi, "Nihon Dendōbu no Kaiko," September 1958, 25.

Annex 4. Notable Japanese Mormons from the Prewar Period

Tsune Nachie (front row, far left) and her daughter Ei (to her right) pose for a picture on the occasion of David O. McKay's visit to Tokyo, circa December 1920. Courtesy LDS Church Archives.

Her desire to do work for her ancestors grew strong as she matured in the LDS Church. On 10 May 1923, she left Yokohama for Hawaii at the age of sixty-six.[40] When she arrived at Honolulu, Hawaii Temple president William M. Waddoups took her to Laie. She lived in the missionary living quarters as if a member of the Waddoups family. At least initially, Nachie may have had a desire to return to Japan. She wrote to Japanese member Fujiya Nara in July 1925 that she would be willing to return to Japan "if everyone worked hard" (by implication, if the church was restored in Japan).[41] Nachie returned to Japan from 22 July to 25 September 1928. She met with several members in Tokyo, teaching them the Mormon doctrine of baptism for the dead.[42] That was her last visit to Japan.

She was actively engaged in missionary work among the Japanese population of Hawaii, not only in Oahu but also in the island of Hawaii and Maui. Russell Clement and Sheng-Luen Tsai quote Hawaiian mission president Castle H. Murphy as saying:

> Sister Nachie lived with us, in a small apartment connected with our Mission Home in Honolulu. She went out each morning with her little bundle of Church books and a few pamphlets tied together in a handkerchief and diligently visited among her people.[43]

---

40. Orlando Fowler was there to see her off. Richins, "Orlando Fowler," 29. He had helped Nachie prepare genealogical records.

41. *Shuro* 1 (September 1925): 10–12.

42. *Hattatsu* 1 (1935): 17.

43. Russell T. Clement and Sheng-Luen Tsai, "East Wind to Hawaii: Contributions and History of Chinese and Japanese Mormons in Hawaii," in *Proceedings of the Second Annual Conference of the Mormon Pacific Historical Society* (Laie, Hawaii: Brigham Young University–Hawaii, 1981), 11–19.

For a time she worked at the "information bureau at the Temple."[44] She did not differentiate between Mormons and non-Mormons in her charitable service. She gave her time freely whenever there was a need and walked miles if necessary to aid the sick.[45] Nachie died on 3 December 1938 at the "Japanese" (presumably Kuakini) Hospital in Honolulu after an illness of only a few days. She was buried in Laie, in a cemetery overlooking the Mormon Temple.[46]

Those who knew her spoke of her direct personality, valiance in the practice of her religion, and deep knowledge of Mormon doctrines. In 1978, Hawaii member and former Japan missionary E. L. Christensen said of her: "She was very unlike the average Japanese woman, who is very shy. She was not shy about the gospel. She would tell the men when they were wrong. . . . She knew the gospel from A to Z."[47] Hawaii church leader Edward Clissold, recalling in 1976, called her "a saint, if ever there was one, a wonderful woman."[48] On 26 October 1922, Japan missionary Hilton Robertson said of her: "There never was a more faithful soul in the church than Sister Nachie. She has certainly been a friend to the Elders." According to Murphy, when the aged Nachie died in December 1938, Robertson seeing the coincidence of her death with the timing of the establishment of the Japanese Mission, stated that the Lord had kept her until he had twenty-five missionaries to replace her.[49]

7. Fujiya Nara (1898–1992)

Fujiya Nara, baptized in Tokyo on 13 June 1915, was one of the seven Japanese men who were ordained to the Melchizedek priesthood in the prewar mission (the ordination took place on 14 January 1923); Nara was the sixth Japanese convert to be so ordained.[50] On 6 April 1924, Nara married Motoko, who was not yet a member, in a Mormon ceremony officiated by mission presi-

---

44. Takeo Fujiwara reported from Hawaii: "Grandma Nachie told me that she sold some copies of the Book of Mormon and the Sunday School song books when she was working at the information bureau in the Temple." Takeo Fujiwara, letter to Alma O. Taylor, 14 August 1934, LDS Church Archives.
45. Tatsui Sato, "Nachie Tsune Shimai no Ato wo Tazunete," *Seito no Michi* 9 (1965): 508–10.
46. Central Pacific Mission, "Historical Records," BYU–Hawaii Archives.
47. Christensen, Oral History, 18.
48. Edward L. Clissold Oral History, interviews by R. Lanier Britsch, 1976, James Moyle Oral History Program, LDS Church Archives, 7.
49. As quoted in Conkling, "Members without a Church," 211.
50. Yukiko Konno, "Fujiya Nara: Twice a Pioneer," *Ensign* 23 (1993): 31–33, is a summary statement of the widely-held Japanese church folklore which, in its desire to elevate him, commits several factual errors concerning his place in history, stating to the effect that he was the first (and only) Japanese member to be ordained an elder and to be married in a Mormon ceremony during the prewar period, and that he was the one who read Clissold's notice in the *Mainichi* newspaper, all of which are untrue.

Annex 4. Notable Japanese Mormons from the Prewar Period

Fujiya Nara was married to wife Motoko in a ceremony officiated by Mormon mission president Hilton A. Robertson, 6 April 1924. Courtesy Carolyn McDonald/Bill McIntyre.

dent Hilton A. Robertson. The wedding date—an anniversary of the founding of the LDS Church in 1830—should indicate the depth of his commitment to the church. Nara became a key figure to lead the church when the mission closed in 1924 (see Section 8.2 in Chapter 8). Following the end of World War II, he helped the church re-establish itself in Japan (see Section 9.4 in Chapter 9). When the mission was reopened, he served as one of the first Japanese branch presidents in Tokyo (see Section 10.6 in Chapter 10); in September 1973, he was ordained as a stake patriarch. Thus, Nara's church service spanned over fifty years encompassing the prewar and the postwar periods.

Fujiya Nara was born in Akita Prefecture on 10 May 1898. In 1911, at the age of twelve or thirteen, he became acquainted with the LDS Church in Sapporo where his father's work had taken the family (his father was a government worker in charge of imperial forests). In 1913, he moved to Tokyo to attend a railroad school (a vocational school to train railroad workers) and began attending church regularly. It was during this time that he was baptized. Upon graduation, he was assigned to work for the National Railway in Kofu, which was one of the four areas of Japan where a branch of the LDS Church existed. In April 1920, he returned to Tokyo to attend college. By the time the mission closed in 1924, he was back with the National Railway, this time at the headquarters in Tokyo. He travelled frequently for work, including to Kofu, Osaka, and Sapporo, thus allowing him to get to know most of the active church members throughout Japan. As mis-

Nami Suzuki (left), with postwar mission president Hilton A. Robertson, circa 1954. Courtesy Carolyn McDonald/Bill McIntyre.

sion clerk, he was also familiar with church records and had access to the addresses of the members.[51] He had some command of the English language.

Nara was thus uniquely qualified to assume a leadership role, initially on a voluntary basis, when the mission closed in 1924. In January 1925, he started the publication of a newsletter called "*Shuro* (Palm)" to be distributed among the members; in the fall of 1926, Nara was appointed by President Franklin S. Harris of Brigham Young University to oversee the formally organized Mutual Improvement Association in Japan; in December 1927, he was appointed by letter from the First Presidency to be presiding elder, with authorization to restore limited church activity. With little visible success, however, he perhaps became discouraged. He virtually abandoned his assignment as early as the fall of 1929 and, in December 1933, left for Manchuria, where Japan, having just established a puppet government, began to develop its economy, including by managing or building the railroad infrastructure.[52] He returned to Tokyo in 1944 about a year before the end of the war.[53]

8. Nami Suzuki (1881–1974)

Nami Suzuki (nee Hakii) was a maid in the mission home when she was baptized on 20 December 1903 as the fifth person and first woman to join the LDS Church in Japan. Later in life she claimed that she had been at the site when Heber J. Grant dedicated the land of Japan for the preaching of the gospel on 1 September 1901, a story that has been perpetuated by unsuspecting Mormons.[54] This cannot be true because she did not meet the missionaries until they arrived in Tokyo; also Alma Taylor's journal makes it clear that the dedication was attended only by the four elders. Rather, her recollection must be referring to a

---

51. Fujiya Nara, "Nihon Dendōbu no Kaiko," *Seito no Michi* 2 (May 1958): 31–32 and (June 1958): 24–25; Fujiya Nara, interview by Shinichi Yano, *Morumon Fōramu* 4 (Spring 1990): 26–36.

52. Nara thus became one of the more than 200,000 railway workers assigned to work in Manchuria. Chihō Jinji Chōsa Kai, *Kokutetsu Shi* (Takamatsu: Chihō Jinji Chōsa Kai, 1998), 160.

53. Nara, Interview by Yano, 28; Nara, "Nihon Dendōbu no Kaiko," June 1958, 25.

54. *Seito no Michi* 9 (May 1965): 217.

special devotional held on the same spot in Yokohama on the second anniversary of the event. Uneducated as she was, and with no command of English, she had no clue as to what was taking place. Married to a non-Mormon, she lost a home in the Great Kanto Earthquake in September 1923, so her family lived in a small house located on the property of the mission home near Shinjuku station. Hilton A. Robertson made time to see them during his brief Japan visit in 1939 as president of the Honolulu-based Japanese Mission; he had gotten to know them when they lived on the same property for some months (see Section 8.5.3 in Chapter 8). She died a faithful Mormon on 26 May 1974.

Tomigoro Takagi (center), with Kazuo Imai (standing right) and another postwar convert, circa 1951. Courtesy Toshiko Yanagida.

9. Tomigoro Takagi (1894–1973)

Tomigoro Takagi, baptized in Tokyo on 1 June 1915, was a journalist who worked in Japan, the United States, and China at various times. He was one of the few dozen people who participated in Mormon activities both in the prewar and in the postwar period. He helped with the translation of Latter-day Saint hymns on two occasions, for the 1915 hymnbook and for the 1961 hymnbook (see Section 5.7.4 in Chapter 5). Following the reopening of missionary work in Japan after the end of World War II, Takagi helped the missionaries with locating prewar members, served as one of the first local branch presidents in Tokyo, and brought his daughter Toshiko Yanagida into the church. In June 1964, Toshiko would become the first Japanese woman to serve as president of the mission Relief Society.

Born in a fishing village on Hokkaido on 27 March 1894, Tomigoro Takagi began attending Mormon services in Tokyo during the fall of 1909. His brother (Nikichi Takahashi, 1892–1923), having been baptized in Sapporo, had urged him to do so. He studied politics at Waseda University from February 1913 to July 1914. He was a reporter for the *Yomiuri Shinbun* from February 1915 to May 1919. His job often took him away from church on Sundays. In June 1920, he went to Salt Lake City to work for the *Utah Nippō*, a Japanese-language newspaper, as chief editor, and remained there until March 1922. Between May 1922 and November 1933, he went to China and Manchuria six times as a reporter for the *Chūgai Shōgyō Shinpō* (present-day *Nihon Keizai Shinbun*).[55] He learned of the closing of the mission while in Peking. From December 1941 to September 1945, he was the chief editor of the *Tōa Shinpō*, a Japanese-language newspaper founded in 1939 in Peking. He returned to Japan in April 1946.[56]

Takagi was never a zealous church member. He was hardly seen at church when he was in Salt Lake City. He remained aloof from the church during the administration of Takeo Fujiwara as presiding elder, though they were in contact. When the subject of who, if anybody, should become presiding elder following Fujiwara's death arose, former mission president Alma O. Taylor wrote to the First Presidency:

> There is also in Tokyo at this time Tomigoro Takagi (42 years old). . . . He came to America and resided in Salt Lake City for some years. So far as I know he was not very active in any church activity or church attendance while here. . . . He is fairly well educated, has a position with a "Foreign Relations Association" and he has a fairly good physical personality. The kind that perhaps isn't so proud of his religion unless it is set in an imposing structure, not in a cottage.[57]

This is too harsh and unfair a characterization of him, especially given the fact that Taylor did not know Takagi personally. More likely, he simply practiced his religion on his own terms, at his own pace.

10. Yoshijiro Watanabe (1873–circa 1940)

Yoshijiro Watanabe, baptized in Tokyo on 1 June 1915, was one of the seven Japanese men who were ordained to the Melchizedek priesthood in the prewar Japan Mission (the ordination took place on 18 October 1922). In October 1922, he moved to the city of Nara and began to attend church in Osaka, where Hilton A. Robertson described him as "one of the most faithful saints in Japan."[58] Following the closing of the mission in 1924, he was appointed by BYU president Franklin S. Harris as counselor to Tsuruichi Katsura in the Osaka MIA.

Watanabe subsequently returned to Tokyo, where during the time Takeo Fujiwara was presiding elder he served as president of the Tokyo Branch. When Fujiwara fell ill, Watanabe assumed the role of acting presiding elder. When nearly everyone had dropped out of church activity, Watanabe, along with his

---

55. A history of the Nihon Keizai Shinbun Company records two of these trips, one in September 1931 to Manchuria (as chief political correspondent) and the other in July 1933 to northern China and northern Korea (as chief foreign correspondent). Nihon Keizai Shinbunsha Hyaku-sanjū-nen-shi Henshū Iinkai, ed., *Nihon Keizai Shinbunsha Hyaku-sanjū-nen Shi* (Tokyo: Nihon Keizai Shinbun, 2006), 689.

56. Yanagida, "Takagi Tomigoro ni tsuite," 38–48; Tomigoro Takagi, "Nihon Dendōbu no Kaiko," *Seito no Michi* 2 (August 1958): 25–26; (September 1958): 23–25; and (October 1958): 24–26.

57. Alma O. Taylor, letter to the First Presidency, 14 March 1936, "Alma Owen Taylor Papers, 1904–1936," LDS Church Archives.

58. Robertson, Autobiography, 26 October 1922.

Annex 4. Notable Japanese Mormons from the Prewar Period

Yoshijiro Watanabe (left) with an unidentified man. Courtesy Carolyn McDonald/Bill McIntyre.

daughter Tazuko (as secretary to Fujiwara), remained a confidant and loyal friend to Fujiwara. When Robertson visited Japan briefly in 1939 as president of the Honolulu-based Japanese Mission, he located Watanabe and found his residence being used as storage space for church publications. He quickly arranged for them to be shipped to Hawaii.

Born on 1 February 1873, Yoshijiro Watanabe became a Methodist and, after apprenticing under a master by the name of Tessai Kano, became an ivory carver and assumed the artist name Dassai. Alma O. Taylor, in his journal entry for 4 March 1907, recorded:

> Had a talk with Mr. Yoshijiro Watanabe, a man I met while labouring in Nakanegishi, Tokyo, three years ago and with whom I had many talks on the gospel. . . . He is about to leave for London, England. . . . He confessed that he has never been able to discharge from his mind the testimony I bore to him and that he has reflected upon our teachings and compared them to the teachings of the Methodist Episcopal Church to which he belongs and felt that the Church of Jesus Christ of Latter-day Saints is the true church and that he was connected with a church having no authority.[59]

Robertson considered Watanabe "an exceptionally good ivory carver," and thought of his trip to England as having been made to exhibit his carving.[60] Watanabe did go to London, but it was in March 1907 that Taylor mentioned his immediate departure, whereas the Japan–British Exhibition was held in London

---

59. Taylor, Journal, 4 March 1907.
60. Robertson, Autobiography, 26 October 1922.

from May to October 1910. It is more likely that Watanabe went to London to do carpentry work on the traditional Japanese-style buildings being constructed on the exhibition site as he was also skilled in wood carving. This, however, remains the author's speculation.

Watanabe is the main character of a 1949 essay entitled, "Kijin Dassai (Dassai the Eccentric)," by the famed novelist Naoya Shiga (1883–1971).[61] Shiga had met Watanabe for the first time in Nara about twenty-three or twenty-four years before, that is, in 1925 or 1926. As the essay tells the story, Watanabe was the son of a steeplejack and became an ivory carver, but failing to make a living, turned to wood carving. His wife left him when their daughter was about three years old. He became a disciple of Tessai Kano and was given the name Dassai (datsu means void—void of human character). When Tessai moved to Nara, Shiga continues, Dassai went with him.[62] He was fond of public speaking in support of political candidates. Shiga, noting that Watanabe had become a Mormon, saw Watanabe walking with a tall Westerner in Nara,[63] where his daughter was working as a nurse. Dassai liked Japanese chess but was not very good. Subsequently Watanabe moved to Tokyo "when he was around sixty years old" in search of work. Shiga describes Watanabe as dull, dumb, lazy, and uncreative, calling him "good for nothing but somehow likeable." Shiga concludes by stating that he had written about Watanabe with affection.

By all accounts, Watanabe was an uneducated and unsophisticated man. Taylor, who knew him only as an investigator, conveyed a poor opinion of him to the First Presidency when they were considering steps to take following the death of Takeo Fujiwara, describing him as "an ignorant man, both in speech and in general knowledge."[64] On the other hand, Robertson, who attended church with Watanabe in Osaka, had a better estimate of him:

> He has plenty of good common sense and with it a fairly good knowledge of the Gospel. I commended him for his faithfulness and integrity and counselled to remain true and steadfast and to study each day some principal [sic] of the Gospel. He told me Elder McKay stood with him and Brother Stimpson at the front gate of the Emperor's Palace at one time and President McKay remarked to him, that the

---

61. Naoya Shiga, "Kijin Dassai," in *Shiga Naoya Zenshū*, vol. 4 (Tokyo: Iwanami Shoten, 1973), 369–82, 731.

62. This was presumably in October 1922. A farewell party for Watanabe was held in Tokyo on 17 October 1922. Richins, "Orlando Fowler." Osaka missionary Robertson met Watanabe for the first time on 26 October 1922. Robertson, Autobiography, 26 October 1922.

63. On 14 June 1923, Robertson recorded: "We took our lunch and spent the day in Nara. While there visited Brother Watanabe for about two hours." Likewise, on 29 December 1923: "In the afternoon Elder Jensen and I went to Nara to see Bro. Watanabe." One of these occasions may have been the one witnessed by Shiga. Robertson, Autobiography, 176.

64. Alma O. Taylor, letter to the First Presidency, 14 March 1936, "Alma Owen Taylor Papers, 1904–1936," LDS Church Archives.

Emperor was now and would continue for sometime to govern the people of that great nation but the time would come if he remain faithful . . . that he would rule over nations of people. At first he smiled as he thought Brother McKay was just jesting with him, but today he realizes what was meant at that time and believes it.[65]

Following the end of World War II, in the fall of 1945, the American naval officer Edward Clissold placed a notice in the *Mainichi Shinbun* expressing his desire to meet Japanese members. Tazuko Watanabe and Fujiya Nara responded to the notice, but Yoshijiro was not there. He must have died sometime before 1945. Shiga says that Watanabe died at sixty-five or sixty-six years old. If so, he must have died shortly after Robertson's visit in 1939.

---

65. Robertson, Journal, 20 April 1939. The same event was described by David O. McKay at the October 1948 general conference: "I am reminded of an incident that happened in front of the Japanese emperor's palace in Tokyo. Three or four of us Mormon missionaries were there, and with us a Japanese convert, a carver of ivory, wearing the cloak of the ordinary working man. As we stood there, I noticed the obeisance this Japanese, though a member of the Church, paid the grounds and particularly the palace. I turned to him and said: 'Do you know, Brother Watanabe, that you have something which is of more value than all the wealth you are looking at, and something which the emperor cannot have unless he follows the same road that you have followed?' The man looked up in surprise to think that he, a humble carver, would have something which was of more value than the emperor's palace or all his possessions. And through the interpreter, Brother Stimpson, he said: 'What is it?' 'Why,' I said, 'it is the priesthood of the Almighty. You are an elder in the Church of Jesus Christ, and that is of more worth to you than all the wealth you are now looking at.'" *Conference Report*, October 1948, 173–74; reprinted in David O. McKay, *Gospel Ideals: Selections from the Discourses of David O. McKay* (Salt Lake City: Deseret Book Company, 1953), 513.

Annex 5

Mormon Mission Presidents, 1901–68

	Name	Hometown	Term in office[1]
	Japan Mission, Tokyo		
1	Heber Jeddy Grant (1854–1945)	Salt Lake City, Utah	August 1901 – September 1903
2	Horace Samuel Ensign (1871–1944)	Salt Lake City, Utah	September 1903 – July 1905
3	Alma Owen Taylor (1882–1947)	Salt Lake City, Utah	July 1905 – January 1910
4	Elbert Duncan Thomas (1883–1953)	Salt Lake City, Utah	January 1910 – October 1912
5	Heber Grant Ivins (1889–1974)	St. George, Utah	October 1912 – July 1915
6	Joseph Henry Stimpson (1885–1964)	Riverdale, Utah	July 1915 – February 1921
7	Lloyd Oscar Ivie (1890–1967)	Salina, Utah	February 1921 – January 1924
8	Hilton Alexander Robertson (1891–1983)	Springville, Utah	January 1924 – August 1924
	Japanese Mission (Central Pacific Mission), Honolulu		
1	Hilton Alexander Robertson (1891–1983)	Springville, Utah	February 1937 – September 1940
2	Jay Clair Jensen (1888–1943)	Salt Lake City, Utah	September 1940 – December 1942
3	Edward LaVaun Clissold (1898–1985)	Honolulu, Hawaii	December 1942[2] – May 1944
4	Castle Hadlock Murphy (1886–1985)	Ogden, Utah	June 1944 – February 1946
5	Melvyn Alma Weenig (1915–2000)	Ogden, Utah	February 1946 – March 1950
	Japanese Mission (Northern Far East Mission), Tokyo		
1	Edward LaVaun Clissold (1898–1985)	Honolulu, Hawaii	March 1948 – August 1949
2	Vinal Grant Mauss (1900–92)	Oakland, California	August 1949 – October 1953
3	Hilton Alexander Robertson (1891–1983)	Provo, Utah	October 1953 – November 1955
4	Paul Charles Andrus (1924–)	Kaneohe, Hawaii	December 1955 – July 1962
5	Dwayne Nelson Andersen (1921–2012)	Folsom, California	July 1962 – August 1968
6	Adney Yoshio Komatsu (1923–2011)	Honolulu, Hawaii	August 1968 – July 1968

[1] From arrival (or predecessor's departure) to departure
[2] Served initially as acting president. Formally set apart in April 1944.

Annex 6

Selected Major Newspapers in Japan that Published Articles, Editorials, and Letters on Mormonism Between August and September 1901

A6.1. By Date

13 August
Japan Advertiser (Yokohama, English)

14 August
Jiji Shinpō (Tokyo)

15 August
Japan Herald (Yokohama, English)
Yamato Shinbun (Tokyo)

16 August
Chūkyō Shinpō (Nagoya)
Japan Herald (Yokohama, English)
Japan Mail (Yokohama, English)
Jiji Shinpō (Tokyo)
Kobe Yūshin Nippō (Kobe)
Niigata Shinbun (Niigata)
Shizuoka Minyū Shinbun (Shizuoka)
Tōhoku Nippō (Niigata)
Yamato Shinbun (Tokyo)

17 August
Hinode Shinbun (Kyoto)
Hokkoku Shinbun (Kanazawa)
Japan Herald (Yokohama, English)
Japan Mail (Yokohama, English)
Kahoku Shinpō (Sendai)
Niroku Shinpō (Tokyo)
Osaka Asahi (Osaka)
Yamato Shinbun (Tokyo)

18 August
Hinode Shinbun (Kyoto)
Kahoku Shinpō (Sendai)
Kyōgaku Hōchi (Kyoto)
Niroku Shinpō (Tokyo)
Yamato Shinbun (Tokyo)

19 August
Hōchi Shinbun (Tokyo)
Japan Herald (Yokohama, English)
Kyōgaku Hōchi (Kyoto)
Niroku Shinpō (Tokyo)
Osaka Asahi (Osaka)
Yamato Shinbun (Tokyo)
Yomiuri Shinbun (Tokyo)

20 August
Chūgoku (Hiroshima)

Hinode Shinbun (Kyoto)
Hōchi Shinbun (Tokyo)
Japan Mail (Yokohama, English)
Japan Times (Tokyo, English)
Jiji Shinpō (Tokyo)
Kahoku Shinpō (Sendai)
Kyōgaku Hōchi (Kyoto)
Niroku Shinpō (Tokyo)
Osaka Asahi (Osaka)
Osaka Mainichi (Osaka)
Yamato Shinbun (Tokyo)

21 August
Chūkyō Shinpō (Nagoya)
Japan Mail (Yokohama, English)
Kyōgaku Hōchi (Kyoto)
Mainichi Shinbun (Tokyo)
Moji Shinpō (Moji)
Niroku Shinpō (Tokyo)
Osaka Asahi (Osaka)
Osaka Mainichi (Osaka)
Shizuoka Minyū Shinbun (Shizuoka)
Yamato Shinbun (Tokyo)
Yorozu Chōhō (Tokyo)

22 August
Kyūshū Shinbun (Kumamoto)
Kyūshū Nippō (Fukuoka)
Moji Shinpō (Moji)
Niroku Shinpō (Tokyo)
Yamato Shinbun (Tokyo)
Yorozu Chōhō (Tokyo)

23 August
Chūō Shinbun (Tokyo)
Japan Herald (Yokohama, English)
Japan Mail (Yokohama, English)
Kyōgaku Hōchi (Kyoto)
Niroku Shinpō (Tokyo)
Osaka Mainichi (Osaka)
Shinano Mainichi Shinbun (Nagano)
Yonezawa Shinbun (Yonezawa)

24 August
Hinode Shinbun (Kyoto)
Japan Herald (Yokohama, English)
Kyōchū Nippō (Kofu)

Kyōgaku Hōchi (Kyoto)
Osaka Asahi (Osaka)
Osaka Mainichi (Osaka)
Tokyo Asahi Shinbun (Tokyo)
Yamato Shinbun (Tokyo)
Yonezawa Shinbun (Yonezawa)

25 August
Chūkyō Shinpō (Nagoya)
Dokuritsu Shinbun (Tokyo)
Hokkoku Shinbun (Kanazawa)
Jiji Shinpō (Tokyo)
Kyōgaku Hōchi (Kyoto)
Shinano Mainichi Shinbun (Nagano)
Yamanashi Nichinichi Shinbun (Kofu)
Yamato Shinbun (Tokyo)

26 August
Japan Mail (Yokohama, English)
Kobe Yūshin Nippō (Kobe)
Kyōgaku Hōchi (Kyoto)
Yamato Shinbun (Tokyo)

27 August
Chūkyō Shinpō (Nagoya)
Japan Herald (Yokohama, English)
Japan Mail (Yokohama, English)
Kyōchū Nippō (Kofu)
Kyūshū Nichinichi Shinbun (Kumamoto)
Kyūshū Nippō (Fukuoka)
Niroku Shinpō (Tokyo)
Osaka Asahi (Osaka)
Yamanashi Nichinichi Shinbun (Kofu)
Yamato Shinbun (Tokyo)

28 August
Kobe Yūshin Nippō (Kobe)
Kyōchū Nippō (Kofu)
Miyako Shinbun (Tokyo)
Tokyo Nichinichi Shinbun (Tokyo)

29 August
Hinode Shinbun (Kyoto)
Japan Herald (Yokohama, English)
Kyūshū Nippō (Fukuoka)
Ryūkyū Shinpō (Naha)
Yonezawa Shinbun (Yonezawa)

30 August
Kyōgaku Hōchi (Kyoto)

31 August
Japan Herald (Yokohama, English)
Kobe Yūshin Nippō (Kobe)
Shizuoka Minyū Shinbun (Shizuoka)

1 September
Ryūkyū Shinpō (Naha)

2 September
Japan Herald (Yokohama, English)
Yamato Shinbun (Tokyo)

3 September
Japan Mail (Yokohama, English)

4 September
Japan Herald (Yokohama, English)
Japan Mail (Yokohama, English)
Kyōgaku Hōchi (Kyoto)

5 September
Mainichi Shinbun (Tokyo)

6 September
Japan Mail (Yokohama, English)
Kyōgaku Hōchi (Kyoto)

7 September
Japan Mail (Yokohama, English)
Mainichi Shinbun (Tokyo)

8 September
Mainichi Shinbun (Tokyo)

9 September
Osaka Asahi Shinbun (Osaka)
Ryūkyū Shinpō (Naha)

10 September
Japan Herald (Yokohama, English)
Kyōchū Nippō (Kofu)
Kyōgaku Hōchi (Kyoto)

13 September
Japan Mail (Yokohama, English)
Kyōgaku Hōchi (Kyoto)

14 September
Jiji Shinpō (Tokyo)

Kyōgaku Hōchi (Kyoto)

15 September
Kyōgaku Hōchi (Kyoto)

18 September
Kyōgaku Hōchi (Kyoto)

19 September
Kyōgaku Hōchi (Kyoto)

20 September
Kyōgaku Hōchi (Kyoto)

21 September
Osaka Asahi Shinbun (Osaka)
Tokyo Nichinichi Shinbun (Tokyo)

23 September
Kyōgaku Hōchi (Kyoto)
Yamato Shinbun (Tokyo)

24 September
Kyōgaku Hōchi (Kyoto)

A6.2. By City and Date

1. Fukuoka
Kyūshū Nippō
22 August, p.1, Mormon missionaries refused lodging at boarding house; p.7, "Mormonism is a Polygamist Religion"
27 August, p.1, "Mormon Invasion"
29 August, p.1, "Mormonism in Germany"

2. Hiroshima
Chūgoku
20 August, p.3, "Our Constitution and Mormon Proselytizing Work"

3. Kanazawa
Hokkoku Shinbun
17 August, p.4, Arrival of Mormon missionaries
25 August, p.5, Authorities on Mormons

4. Kobe
Kobe Yūshin Nippō
16 August, p.1, "Mormons Arrive"
26 August, p.1, Mormons and authorities
28 August, p.1, Authorities on Mormons
31 August, p.1, Emigration of European Mormons to Utah

5. Kofu
Kyōchū Nippō
24 August, p.1, "Mormonism (1)"
27 August, p.1, "Mormonism (2)"; p.1, "Mormonism and the Home Ministry"
28 August, p.1, "Mormonism (3)"
10 September, p.2, Mormon missionaries visit Kanagawa prefectural government

Yamanashi Nichinichi Shinbun
25 August, p.2, "A Japanese Mormon"
27 August, p.2, "Mormons and the Home Ministry"

6. Kumamoto
Kyūshū Nichinichi Shinbun
27 August, p.1, "The Authorities and Mormonism"
Kyūshū Shinbun
22 August, p.5, "On Mormon Proselytizing Work"

7. Kyoto
Hinode Shinbun
17 August, p.2, Arrival of Mormon missionaries
18 August, p.2, Interview with Grant
20 August, p.2, "The Imperial Constitution and Mormonism"
24 August, p.2, "Mormonism"
29 August, p.1, Authorities on Mormons
Kyōgaku Hōchi
18 August, p.1, Arrival of Mormon missionaries
19 August, p.1, Basic beliefs of Mormonism; p.1, "A Mormon Elder Shakes Hands with Marquis Ito"
20 August, p.2, Heber J. Grant and his business career
21 August, p.1, Mormon missionaries refused at boarding house
23 August, p.1, Mormon missionaries support themselves; p.2, Woodruff's Manifesto; p.3, History of Mormonism
24 August, p.1, Negative comments quoted from *Japan Mail* and *Japan Times*; p.2, Doctrines of Mormonism
25 August, p.1, "The Authorities and Mormonism"
26 August, p.3, "Mormon Polygamy"
30 August, p.1, "Mormon Proselytizing Work"

Annex 6. Selected Major Newspapers in Japan   475

4 September, p.1, "Mormons Begin Their Proselytizing Work"
6 September, p.1, Mormons housed in Bluff boarding house
10 September, p.1, "Mormonism Preparing for Proselytizing Work"
p.1, "Mormon Missionaries Visit the Kanagawa Police Department Head"; p.1, "An Update on Mormonism"
13 September, p.3, "The Mormon Bible"
14 September, p.1, Arrival of Mormons as greatest event of recent times
15 September, p.2, "The Origin of the Name Mormonism"; p.2, Spaulding origin of the Book of Mormon
18 September, p.2, Mormons first go to Niigata; p.4, Persecution of Mormons
19 September, p.1, Mormons go to look around Tokyo
20 September, p.3, Origin of Mormon polygamy
23 September, p.1, Mormons request license to preach
24 September, p.2, Mormons called back to appear before Kanagawa prefectural government
p.3, Truths of Buddhism must be explained before Mormons win poor

8. Moji (now part of Kitakyushu)
Moji Shinpō
21 August, p.2, "On Mormon Proselytizing Work"
22 August, p.2, Mormon missionaries refused at boarding house

9. Nagano
Shinano Mainichi Shinbun
23 August, p.1, Mormon priests said to visit Marquis Ito
25 August, p.2, Mormonism should be banned

10. Nagoya
Chūkyō Shinpō
16 August, p.2, Mormon missionaries soon to arrive
21 August, p.5, Mormon missionaries refused lodging at boarding house
25 August, p.1, Authorities on Mormons
27 August, p.1, "A Proclamation to the Antagonists of Mormonism"

11. Naha (Okinawa)
Ryūkyū Shinpō
29 August, p.1, "Mormon Missionaries Arrive"
1 September, p.1, Mormon missionaries refused lodging at boarding house
9 September, p.1, "The Authorities and Mormonism"

12. Niigata
Niigata Shinbun
16 August, p.1, "Mormon Priests Arrive"
Tōhoku Nippō
16 August, Appendix, "Mormon Priests Arrive"

13. Osaka
Osaka Asahi
17 August, p.2, "A Mormon Elder Shakes Hands with Marquis Ito"
19 August, p.2, "An Update on Mormonism"
20 August, p.1, "Mormon Missionaries Arrive"
21 August, p.1, Mormon missionaries refused lodging at boarding house
24 August, p.5, "The Authorities and Mormonism"
27 August, p.1, Statement of Japanese Christian leader on Mormonism quoted from Christian magazine
9 September, p.1, "Mormons Preparing to Preach"
21 September, p.2, "Mormons File Application"
Osaka Mainichi
20 August, p.3, Mormon proselytizing work
21 August, p.1, "What in the World Should Prevent Them?"; p.5, "Mormonism (1)"
23 August, p.5, "Mormonism (2)"
24 August, p.3, "Mormonism (3)"

14. Sendai
Kahoku Shinpō
17 August, p.2, Arrival of Mormon missionaries, in English
18 August, p.3, "An Interview with a Mormon Missionary (1)"
20 August, p.3, "An Interview with a Mormon Missionary (2)"

15. Shizuoka
Shizuoka Minyū Shinbun
16 August, p.2, Arrival of Mormon missionaries
21 August, p.1, "State vs. Religion (Mormonism)"
31 August, p.5, "Education and Religion"

16. Tokyo
Chūō Shinbun
23 August, p.2, "Mormonism Must Be Banned"
Dokuritsu Shinbun
25 August, p.1, "How About Studying Mormonism?"
Hōchi Shinbun
19 August, p.3, Mormon missionaries refused lodging at boarding house
20 August, p.1, Letter to editor, in English
Japan Times (English)
20 August, p.2, "The Mormons in Japan"
Jiji Shinpō
14 August, p.7, Arrival of Mormon missionaries
16 August, p.4, "An Interview with Mormon Missionaries"
20 August, p.2, Editorial on arrival of Mormon missionaries
25 August, p.2, Editorial on refusal of Mormon missionaries at boarding house
14 September, p.2, Editorial on attitude of Japanese women towards men and Mormonism
Mainichi Shinbun
21 August, p.1, "Foreign Mormonism, Domestic Mormonism"
5 September, p.1, "Mormonism Evaluated (1)"
7 September, p.1, "Mormonism Evaluated (2)"
8 September, p.1, "Mormonism Evaluated (3)"
Miyako Shinbun
28 August, p.1, Authorities on Mormons; p.2, "Disappointment of Mormon Missionaries"
Niroku Shinpō
17 August, p.2, "A Visit with a Mormon Missionary (1)"
18 August, p.2, "A Visit with a Mormon Missionary (2)"

19 August, p.1, Portrait of Heber J. Grant; p.1, "To the Great and Progressive Nation of Japan (1)" by Grant, in English with Japanese translation; p.2, "A Visit with a Mormon Missionary (3)"; p.2, Mormon missionaries refused at boarding house; p.3, Cartoon of Mormon missionaries as Buddhist saints
20 August, p.1, Portrait of Joseph Smith; p.1, "To the Great and Progressive Nation of Japan (2)" by Grant, in English with Japanese translation
21 August, p.2, "A Visit with a Mormon Missionary (4)"
22 August, p.2, "Mormons"
23 August, p.2, "A Visit with a Mormon Missionary (5)"
27 August, p.1, Reprint of Grant's letter to editor of *Japan Daily Mail*, dated 22 August, with Japanese translation

Tokyo Asahi Shinbun
24 August, p.1, "Mormonism and the Home Ministry"

Tokyo Nichinichi Shinbun
28 August, p.3, "On Mormon Proselytizing Work"
21 September, p.4, "Mormons Request License to Preach"

Yamato Shinbun
15 August, p.1, "Mormonism Arrives"
16 August, p.1, "Let Our Nobility Be All Mormons (1)"
17 August, p.1, "Let Our Nobility Be All Mormons (2)"; p.1, Mormon polygamy explained
18 August, p.1, "Mormonism (1)"
19 August, p.1, "Mormonism (2)"
20 August, p.1, "Mormonism (3)"
21 August, p.1, "Mormonism (4)"
22 August, p.1, "Mormonism (5)"
24 August, p.1, "Mormonism (6)"
25 August, p.1, "Mormonism (7)"; p.1, "Mormonism and the Home Ministry"
26 August, p.1, "Mormonism (8)"
27 August, p.1, "Mormonism (9)"
2 September, p.1, "Mormons Begin Proselytizing"
23 September, p.1, "Mormon Missionaries Called to Appear"

Yomiuri Shinbun
19 August, p.3, Mormon missionaries refused lodging at boarding house

Yorozu Chōhō
21 August, p.1, Quotation from *Jiji Shinpo* and *Japan Times*
22 August, p.1, Quotation from *Osaka Asahi* and *Mainichi*

17. Yokohama
Japan Advertiser (English)
13 August, Arrival of Mormon missionaries

Japan Herald (English)
15 August, "Latter-Day Saints in Japan"
16 August, "Mormonism"; "The Earnestness of Mormon Missionaries"; Mormons refused lodging at boarding house
17 August, Criticism of *Japan Mail* editorial
19 August, Grant's letter, dated 18 August
23 August, Reprint of Grant's letter to *Japan Mail*
24 August, "The Mormon Mission"; Mormons in Japanese press
27 August, Response to *Japan Mail* article on Staniland
29 August, "The Mail and Its Protégé"
31 August, "Mormon Missions"
2 September, "The Mormons in Japan"
4 September, "The Mail as a Controversialist"
10 September, Mormon missionary work in different lands

Japan Mail (English)
16 August, Mormons refused lodging at boarding house
17 August, "The Mormon Mission"
20 August, Discussion of *Niroku* cartoon of Mormon missionaries on 19 August
21 August, "The Mormons and the *Jiji Shimpo*"
23 August, "Mormon Creed"; Grant's letter to editor, dated 22 August
26 August, "The Home Department and the Mormons"
27 August, "Mr. Staniland and the Mormons"
3 September, Grant's letter to editor, dated 30 August
4 September, "The Mormon Controversy"
6 September, "The Mormon Question"
7 September, "Mr. Grant's Explanation"; "Mormons and Polygamy"; Grant's letter to editor, dated 5 September
13 September, "Mormonism"

18. Yonezawa (Yamagata)
Yonezawa Shinbun
23 August, p.2, Mormon proselytizing work
24 August, p.2, "Mormonism and Marquis Ito"
29 August, p.1, "Mormonism and the Authorities"

Annex 7

Mormon Missionaries in the Japan Mission, 1901–24

(By date of arrival; by name)

	Name (*second time)	Hometown	Date of Arrival	Date of Departure
1	Horace S. Ensign	Salt Lake City, Utah	12 August 1901	8 July 1905
2	Heber J. Grant	Salt Lake City, Utah	12 August 1901	8 September 1903
3	Louis A. Kelsch	Salt Lake City, Utah	12 August 1901	9 August 1902
4	Alma O. Taylor	Salt Lake City, Utah	12 August 1901	30 March 1910
5	Frederick A. Caine	Salt Lake City, Utah	17 July 1902	30 March 1910
6	Mary W. Ensign	Salt Lake City, Utah	17 July 1902	8 July 1905
7	Joseph F. Featherstone	American Fork, Utah	17 July 1902	21 December 1904
8	Marie S. Featherstone	American Fork, Utah	17 July 1902	13 July 1904
9	Augusta W. Grant	Salt Lake City, Utah	17 July 1902	8 September 1903
10	Mary Grant	Salt Lake City, Utah	17 July 1902	8 September 1903
11	Sanford W. Hedges	Salt Lake City, Utah	17 July 1902	1 May 1906
12	Erastus L. Jarvis	St. George, Utah	17 July 1902	21 December 1904
13	John W. Stoker	Lehi, Utah	17 July 1902	3 June 1908
14	John L. Chadwick	North Ogden, Utah	1 June 1905	16 September 1908
15	William R. Fairbourn	Crescent, Utah	1 June 1905	18 January 1911
16	Justus B. Seely	Ephraim, Utah	1 June 1905	28 April 1909
17	James Anderson	Richfield, Utah	29 June 1905	25 February 1910
18	Daniel P. Woodland	Downey, Idaho	29 June 1905	16 September 1908
19	John H. Roskelley	Smithfield, Utah	23 August 1906	19 April 1911
20	Joseph P. Cutler	Salt Lake City, Utah	14 December 1906	19 April 1911
21	Joseph H. Stimpson	Riverdale, Utah	14 December 1906	6 July 1912
22	Moroni S. Marriott	Ogden, Utah	26 July 1907	9 August 1911
23	Elliot C. Taylor	Coalville, Utah	26 July 1907	21 July 1910
24	Warren E. Harris	Emmett, Idaho	28 September 1907	25 February 1910
25	Charles W. Hubbard	Bench, Idaho	28 September 1907	26 July 1909
26	Edna H. Thomas	Salt Lake City, Utah	12 October 1907	24 October 1912
27	Elbert D. Thomas	Salt Lake City, Utah	12 October 1907	24 October 1912
28	William S. Ellis	Pleasant View, Utah	23 November 1908	19 April 1913
29	Jay C. Jensen	Heber City, Utah	23 November 1908	11 January 1913
30	Melvin F. Barton	Kaysville, Utah	28 June 1909	21 July 1910
31	Robert H. Barton	Kaysville, Utah	28 June 1909	22 March 1913
32	Walter W. Steed, Jr.	Syracuse, Utah	28 June 1909	26 July 1909
33	Thomas L. Chipman	American Fork, Utah	15 July 1910	21 January 1914
34	James Scowcroft	Ogden, Utah	15 July 1910	31 August 1914
35	Ezra L. Anderson	Salem, Idaho	23 November 1910	5 June 1912
36	Heber Grant Ivins	Salt Lake City, Utah	23 November 1910	24 July 1915
37	James A. Miller	Murray, Utah	23 November 1910	14 January 1914
38	Henry R. Emmett	Dee, Oregon	19 February 1911	31 December 1912
39	Lloyd O. Ivie	Salina, Utah	19 February 1911	23 October 1915
40	Leonard E. Harrington	American Fork, Utah	10 November 1911	21 January 1914
41	Alvin B. Hintze	Murray, Utah	10 November 1911	31 August 1914
42	James Leo Hatch	Panguitch, Utah	9 May 1912	31 August 1914

	Name (*second time)	Hometown	Date of Arrival	Date of Departure
43	Esther Spackman	Lewiston, Utah	9 May 1912	10 June 1916
44	Edwin J. Allen, Jr	Salt Lake City, Utah	13 November 1912	14 October 1916
45	Arthur F. Crowther	Provo, Utah	13 November 1912	27 January 1917
46	Arthur Cutler	Salt Lake City, Utah	13 November 1912	28 May 1915
47	Edwin A. Bennion	Logan, Utah	19 June 1913	14 January 1914
48	Amacy W. Clark	Rexburg, Idaho	19 June 1913	25 March 1916
49	Blair H. Stringham	Provo, Utah	19 June 1913	26 January 1914
50	John V. Adams	Logan, Utah	23 December 1913	3 November 1917
51	George A. Turner	Largo, Utah	23 December 1913	11 August 1917
52	Charles R. Amott	Salt Lake City, Utah	7 March 1914	21 March 1918
53	Harold Kingsford	Franklin, Idaho	7 March 1914	21 March 1918
54	Joseph H. Stimpson*	Riverdale, Utah	11 March 1915	18 February 1921
55	Mary E. Stimpson	Riverdale, Utah	11 March 1915	18 February 1921
56	Lagayette Cox Lee	Hinckley, Utah	25 November 1915	13 December 1919
57	Pearl M. Lee	Hinckley, Utah	25 November 1915	13 December 1919
58	Varsall L. Cowley	Venice, Utah	18 March 1916	5 March 1920
59	Valentine W. Palmer	Logan, Utah	18 March 1916	5 March 1920
60	Joseph R. Stoddard	Richmond, Utah	18 March 1916	8 November 1919
61	Lillian L. Broadbent	Ogden, Utah	14 November 1916	11 August 1917
62	Albert R. Olpin	Pleasant Grove, Utah	14 November 1916	30 October 1920
63	Bryan L. Wright	Ogden, Utah	14 November 1916	30 October 1920
64	Myrl L. Bodily	Fairview, Idaho	8 April 1917	3 May 1921
65	Owen McGary	Shelley, Idaho	8 April 1917	3 May 1921
66	Joseph S. Pyne	Provo, Utah	21 December 1917	23 November 1921
67	Louring A. Whittaker	Circleville, Utah	21 December 1917	23 November 1921
68	Irwin T. Hicken	Heber City, Utah	20 May 1920	28 March 1924
69	Deloss W. Holley	Slaterville, Utah	20 May 1920	21 January 1924
70	A. Howard Jensen	Brigham, Utah	20 May 1920	28 March 1924
71	Lloyd O. Ivie*	Salina, Utah	11 February 1921	22 January 1924
72	Nora B. Ivie	Kaysville, Utah	11 February 1921	22 January 1924
73	William E. Davies	Ogden, Utah	22 March 1921	24 July 1924
74	Orlando Fowler	Henefer, Utah	22 March 1921	17 May 1923 (died)
75	Aldo Stephens	Ogden, Utah	22 March 1921	31 May 1923
76	Earnest B. Woodward	Wellsville, Utah	22 March 1921	7 August 1924
77	Hazel M. Robertson	Springville, Utah	6 June 1921	7 August 1924
78	Hilton A. Robertson	Springville, Utah	6 June 1921	7 August 1924
79	F. Wallace Browning	Ogden, Utah	11 July 1922	24 July 1924
80	Louese M. Browning	Ogden, Utah	11 July 1922	24 July 1924
81	Arva B. Christensen	Brigham, Utah	11 July 1922	7 August 1924
82	Elwood L. Christensen	Brigham, Utah	11 July 1922	7 August 1924
83	Sylvia P. Glover	Brigham, Utah	11 July 1922	8 July 1924
84	William L. Glover	Brigham, Utah	11 July 1922	8 July 1924
85	Rulon Esplin	Orderville, Utah	7 December 1922	7 August 1924
86	Vinal Mauss	Murray, Utah	7 December 1922	7 August 1924
87	Milton B. Taylor	Harrisville, Utah	7 December 1922	24 July 1924
88	Lewis H. Moore	Vernal, Utah	26 June 1923	7 August 1924

Andrew Jenson, "History of the Japan Mission," LDS Church Archives.

Annex 8

Converts and Children of Record Baptized in Prewar Japan, 1902–39

	Name	Gender	Date of baptism	Place	Remarks[1]
1	Hajime Nakazawa	Male	8 March 1902	Tokyo	Excommunicated
2	Saburo Kikuchi	Male	10 March 1902	Tokyo	
3	Yoshiro Oyama	Male	8 October 1902	Tokyo	Excommunicated
4	Kenzo Kato	Male	11 October 1903	Tokyo	Excommunicated
5	Nami Hakii	Female	20 December 1903	Tokyo	Married M. Suzuki
6	Rin Kamiyama	Female	8 May 1904	Tokyo	
7	Tsuta Kato	Female	8 May 1904	Tokyo	
8	Tsune Nachie	Female	26 September 1905	Tokyo	Emigrated to US
9	Aritatsu Kawanaka	Male	3 August 1906	Sapporo	
10	Yasubeiye Chiba	Male	29 August 1906	Tokyo	Married I. Daikoku
11	Fude Tai	Female	1 November 1907	Tokyo	
12	Hachiro Mori	Male	25 November 1907	Tokyo	Excommunicated
13	Mitsuo Sakuma	Male	23 December 1907	Sapporo	Married T. Kumagai[2]
14	Toshichi Sato	Male	15 January 1908	Sapporo	
15	Yoshiei Osaki	Male	7 February 1908	Sapporo	
16	Ei Nachie	Female	26 March 1908	Tokyo	Married Y. Nagao
17	Eisaburo Kuga	Male	30 May 1908	Tokyo	Excommunicated
18	Hana Yoneyama	Female	29 July 1908	Kofu	
19	Muraji Yoneyama	Male	29 July 1908	Kofu	Alternative reading: Ren
20	Itsu Watanabe	Female	11 August 1908	Sapporo	
21	Joji Shirai	Male	1 September 1908	Kofu	
22	Nikichi Takahashi	Male	5 September 1908	Sapporo	Died
23	Kino Nakachi	Female	28 September 1908	Sapporo	Died
24	Sai Ishikawa	Female	19 December 1908	Sapporo	
25	Tamano Kumagai	Female	19 December 1908	Sapporo	Married M. Sakuma[2]
26	Chiyo Tanifuji	Female	19 December 1908	Sapporo	Married I. Ishigaki; died
27	Yasue Iso	Female	25 December 1908	Kofu	Married I. Nakajima
28	Chiyo Koji	Female	7 January 1909	Sapporo	Married Shioki; emigrated to US
29	Sue Ogawa	Female	7 January 1909	Sapporo	Married R. Takahashi
30	Tokujiro Taue	Male	5 April 1909	Tokyo	
31	Genkichi Shiraishi	Male	29 September 1909	Asahikawa	
32	Suketomo Suda	Male	3 November 1909	Kofu	Married Nonogaki[3]
33	Katsuzo Horikawa	Male	22 November 1909	Kofu	
34	Ioe Shioiri	Female	23 November 1909	Kofu	Married G. Usami
35	Kuma Nabeshima	Female	27 November 1909	Tokyo	Married F. Midorikawa
36	Katsuzo Nasa	Male	20 December 1909	Tokyo	Excommunicated
37	Shosuke Matsuki	Male	1 January 1910	Sapporo	
38	Hana Kato	Female	5 January 1910	Sapporo	Died 1929
39	Yuki Kato	Female	5 January 1910	Sapporo	
40	Masagiku Saigo	Female	8 January 1910	Tokyo	
41	Takeshiro Sakuraba	Male	24 February 1910	Tokyo	Married A. Takahashi[3]
42	Morizo Yoneyama	Male	18 March 1910	Kofu	Child of record

	Name	Gender	Date of baptism	Place	Remarks[1]
43	Shunichi Yamakawa	Male	14 May 1910	Kofu	Died
44	Morisaburo Sato	Male	11 June 1910	Tokyo	Excommunicated 1952
45	Tamigoro Oyama	Male	18 June 1910	Kofu	Excommunicated
46	Cho Ogura	Female	10 September 1910	Tokyo	Married K. Arai
47	Masaichiro Soman	Male	1 January 1911	Sapporo	
48	Fujio Sato	Male	10 July 1911	Tokyo	
49	Tatsusaburo Nanbu	Male	3 August 1911	Morioka	
50	Naoe Hirano	Male	19 August 1911	Sapporo	Excommunicated
51	Ichiro Nakajima	Male	3 November 1911	Kofu	Married Y. Iso
52	Giichi Usami	Male	3 November 1911	Kofu	
53	Koto Fujimoto	Female	17 May 1912	Tokyo	
54	Sakari Komagamine	Male	6 September 1912	Tokyo	
55	Seiji Sawaguchi	Male	11 October 1912	Sapporo	
56	Eitaro Hirata	Male	21 December 1912	Osaka	
57	Otofumi Horikiri	Male	1 February 1913	Tokyo	
58	Tomomitsu Noguchi	Male	16 April 1913	Tokyo	Died
59	Takashi Tsushima	Male	16 April 1913	Tokyo	
60	Tsuneko Yoneyama	Female	12 June 1913	Kofu	Child of record
61	Hisaichi Hamada	Male	15 July 1913	Osaka	
62	Masakichiro Ito	Male	7 August 1913	Sapporo	
63	Sueto Oyama	Male	24 September 1913	Tokyo	
64	Tsune Maeda	Female	23 October 1913	Tokyo	Alternative name: Tsuneko
65	Tsuruichi Katsura	Male	25 December 1913	Osaka	
66	Shigetaka Suzuki	Male	12 July 1914	Osaka	
67	Yoshiaki Nakashima	Male	29 August 1914	Kofu	
68	Tomeko Ishiwara	Female	1 June 1915	Tokyo	Died
69	Tomigoro Takagi	Male	1 June 1915	Tokyo	
70	Yoshijiro Watanabe	Male	1 June 1915	Tokyo	
71	Fujiya Nara	Male	13 June 1915	Tokyo	
72	Hitoshi Sano	Male	27 June 1915	Kofu	
73	Fumiko Ito	Female	30 June 1915	Kofu	
74	Keishi Tan	Male	30 June 1915	Kofu	
75	Taki Arai	Female	22 July 1915	Osaka	
76	Jiro Imai	Male	9 September 1915	Osaka	
77	Hisashi Iwata	Male	27 September 1915	Kofu	
78	Shozo Iwata	Male	27 September 1915	Kofu	
79	Nanshu Sakaita	Male	20 December 1915	Tokyo	
80	Katsuro Kitai	Male	23 March 1916	Osaka	
81	Tsurui Ikegami	Female	18 April 1916	Osaka	
82	Sho Osaragi	Female	18 April 1916	Osaka	
83	Jiro Fujita	Male	24 June 1916	Sapporo	Excommunicated
84	Tsuyoshi Shikama	Male	18 July 1916	Sapporo	Died
85	Keizo Yoneyama	Male	5 August 1916	Kofu	Child of record
86	Eikichi Iwata	Male	30 September 1916	Kofu	
87	Nobuko Iwata	Female	30 September 1916	Kofu	
88	Toyo Takahashi	Female	18 November 1916	Tokyo	Died
89	Eiko Yamamoto	Female	25 November 1916	Kofu	
90	Tadashi Okuda	Male	11 February 1917	Tokyo	Died
91	Mitsuko Ozaki	Female	12 February 1917	Osaka	

Annex 8. Converts and Children of Record Baptized in Pre-war Japan

	Name	Gender	Date of baptism	Place	Remarks[1]
92	Kentaro Yokoi	Male	13 February 1917	Tokyo	Excommunicated
93	Tomosuke Kawano	Male	26 March 1917	Kofu	Emigrated to US
94	Kuranosuke Saito	Male	5 July 1917	Sapporo	
95	Kenzo Seino	Male	30 July 1917	Sapporo	
96	Suma Kawano	Female	14 August 1917	Kofu	Emigrated to US
97	Momozo Takemura	Male	30 August 1917	Osaka	
98	Shuncho Matsumoto	Male	19 September 1917	Tokyo	Alternative spelling: Shincho
99	Go Inouye	Male	21 October 1917	Osaka	
100	Fukujiro Yamazaki	Male	7 November 1917	Tokyo	
101	Katsu Ogura	Female	10 February 1918	Osaka	
102	Toriko Kimura	Female	12 June 1918	Kofu	Died
103	Kenji Yoneyama	Male	12 June 1918	Kofu	Child of record; died 1935
104	Takeo Yoshino	Male	5 July 1918	Sapporo	
105	Ryozo Suzuki	Male	5 August 1918	Tokyo	
106	Tazuko Watanabe	Female	5 August 1918	Tokyo	
107	Sumie Naruse	Female	25 August 1918	Osaka	
108	Chojiro Hashimoto	Male	1 September 1918	Osaka	Died
109	Kumao Matsumoto	Male	1 September 1918	Osaka	
110	Koichi Iwatsu	Male	6 October 1918	Osaka	
111	Kotoe Morimoto	Female	6 May 1919	Tokyo	
112	Tokihei Shimizu	Male	14 May 1919	Kofu	Died
113	Chojiro Kanda	Male	6 July 1919	Osaka	
114	Torao Yamaide	Male	23 August 1919	Kofu	
115	Chojiro Kuriyama	Male	25 August 1919	Tokyo	
116	Eiko Toyokusa	Female	25 August 1919	Kofu	
117	Tsuneyo Toyokusa	Female	25 August 1919	Kofu	
118	Mitsuko Yamaide	Female	25 August 1919	Kofu	
119	Tamotsu Ishikawa	Male	26 August 1919	Kofu	
120	Muneharu Teranishi	Male	31 August 1919	Osaka	
121	Teiichi Ito	Male	2 September 1919	Tokyo	
122	Matsuyo Takusagawa	Female	22 September 1919	Kofu	
123	Masashi Nakayama	Male	1 December 1919	Kofu	
124	Keiji Ueda	Male	4 February 1920	Osaka	
125	Atsushi Shioiri	Male	8 February 1920	Osaka	
126	Setsu Tabata	Female	28 February 1920	Sapporo	
127	Moto Ueno	Female	28 February 1920	Sapporo	
128	Umon Minai	Male	3 May 1920	Kofu	Alternative spelling: Yubun
129	Kentaro Mochizuki	Male	11 May 1920	Tokyo	
130	Reiko Mochizuki	Female	11 May 1920	Tokyo	Alternative name: Rei
131	Sadako Nakayama	Female	18 August 1920	Kofu	
132	Kaneko Takahashi	Female	27 October 1920	Tokyo	
133	Kazuo Fukuda	Male	28 January 1921	Tokyo	
134	Masajiro Goshima	Male	28 January 1921	Tokyo	
135	Junzo Hashimoto	Male	6 February 1921	Osaka	
136	Yukio Haneda	Male	23 March 1921	Tokyo	Married T. Yamada
137	Ichitaro Ohashi	Male	8 June 1921	Osaka	
138	Yoshitoku Tanimura	Male	4 July 1921	Tokyo	
139	Takeshi Yamada	Male	4 July 1921	Tokyo	
140	Kennosuke Nakazawa	Male	14 August 1921	Tokyo	

	Name	Gender	Date of baptism	Place	Remarks[1]
141	Yukie Nakazawa	Female	14 August 1921	Tokyo	
142	Tadashi Yamashita	Male	21 October 1921	Sapporo	Excommunicated
143	Michio Kashima	Male	12 February 1922	Osaka	Married M. Kabata 1935[3]
144	Yosaburo Ueda	Male	19 March 1922	Osaka	
145	Magoji Kitagawa	Male	11 July 1922	Tokyo	
146	Shima Nagai	Female	11 July 1922	Tokyo	
147	Koshi Nakagawa	Male	11 July 1922	Tokyo	
148	Fumi Takezawa	Female	11 July 1922	Tokyo	
149	Ishi Yamada	Female	11 July 1922	Tokyo	
150	Kenji Ono	Male	19 July 1922	Sapporo	
151	Tadasuke Kurashige	Male	23 July 1922	Sapporo	
152	Midori Kikuchi	Female	29 July 1922	Sapporo	
153	Susumu Hori	Male	30 July 1922	Osaka	
154	Tsuru Katsura	Female	30 July 1922	Osaka	
155	Joji Matsumoto	Male	20 August 1922	Osaka	Alternative spelling: George
156	Kinzo Abe	Male	3 September 1922	Sapporo	
157	Shizue Goto	Female	3 September 1922	Tokyo	
158	Hirosuke Okudaira	Male	3 September 1922	Tokyo	
159	Susumu Hisada	Male	10 September 1922	Osaka	
160	Koto Kasu	Male	10 September 1922	Osaka	Died
161	Iwao Matsuo	Male	19 November 1922	Osaka	
162	Tamiko Matsumoto	Female	3 December 1922	Osaka	
163	Kinue Asai	Female	10 June 1923	Osaka	
164	Shizue Mizuki	Female	12 August 1923	Tokyo	
165	Kimi Sudo	Female	14 October 1923	Sapporo	
166	Akira Suzuki	Male	14 October 1923	Sapporo	
167	Saburo Sada	Male	16 December 1923	Sapporo	
168	Shojiro Kimura	Male	19 February 1924	Tokyo	
169	Shizuo Kikuchi	Male	26 April 1924	Sendai	
170	Takeo Fujiwara	Male	10 May 1924	Sapporo	
171	Maki Katsuta	Female	22 June 1924	Sapporo	
172	Hiroo Yamauchi	Male	30 June 1924	Sendai	
173	Chika Kumagai	Female	13 July 1924	Sapporo	Died 1928
174	Yosaku Morita	Male	16 July 1924	Tokyo	
175	Terutake Ishikawa	Male	19 May 1935	Tokyo	
176	Kyoko Mochizuki	Female	19 May 1935	Tokyo	
177	Kazuko Katsura	Female	25 April 1939	Osaka	
178	Akiko Teranishi	Female	25 April 1939	Osaka	
179	Haruko Teranishi	Female	25 April 1939	Osaka	
180	Michio Teranishi	Male	25 April 1939	Osaka	
181	Nagayo Teranishi	Female	25 April 1939	Osaka	
182	Yoshino Kumagai	Female	3 May 1939	Sapporo	
183	Naruko Suzuki	Female	10 May 1939	Tokyo	
184	Tsuneko Suzuki	Female	10 May 1939	Tokyo	

[1] Partial information; year indicated if event took place after August 1924; in Mormon terminology, a child of record in the context of baptism means a member's child who is baptized at the age of eight before the ninth birthday
[2] Divorced afterwards.
[3] Took on wife's surname.
Record of members, LDS Church Archives; various church records.

Annex 9

Mormon Converts Baptized in Occupied Japan, 1946–52[1]

	Name	Gender	Place [2]	Date of Baptism (*before)
1	Chiyo Sato	Female	Narumi	7 July 1946
2	Tatsui Sato	Male	Narumi	7 July 1946
3	Mamoru Iga	Male	Kobe	13 August 1946
4	Ikuko Rose Matsuda	Female	Kobe	13 August 1946
5	Yasuo Sato	Male	Narumi	5 July 1947
6	Motoko Nara	Female	Tokyo	6 April 1948
7	Miyoshi Sato	Female	Tokyo	6 April 1948
8	Toshiro Ishida	Male	Tokyo	6 November 1948
9	Tokusaburo Kanno	Male	Tokyo	6 November 1948
10	Matsuko Matsumoto	Female	Tokyo	6 November 1948
11	Yutaka Mizuko	Male	Tokyo	6 November 1948
12	Kenichi Mochizuki	Male	Tokyo	6 November 1948
13	Micnhiko Morisaki	Female	Tokyo	6 November 1948
14	Toshiko Nakayama	Female	Tokyo	6 November 1948
15	Takako Watanabe	Female	Tokyo	6 November 1948
16	Toshiko Yajima	Female	Tokyo	6 November 1948
17	Umeko Akimoto	Female	Tokyo	29 December 1948
18	Shigeo Masukawa	Male	Tokyo	29 December 1948
19	Takazo Matsushita	Male	Tokyo	29 December 1948
20	Hiroshi Musashino	Male	Tokyo	29 December 1948
21	Hiroko Ogawa	Female	Tokyo	29 December 1948
22	Shotaro Eguchi	Male	Tokyo	8 January 1949
23	Hideko Hata	Female	Tokyo	8 January 1949
24	Nobuo Ishida	Male	Tokyo	8 January 1949
25	Ichigi Kuribayashi	Male	Tokyo	8 January 1949
26	Etsu Mochizuki	Female	Tokyo	8 January 1949
27	Yae Mochizuki	Female	Tokyo	8 January 1949
28	Yasuhiro Ono	Male	Tokyo	8 January 1949
29	Chiyoko Sagara	Female	Tokyo	8 January 1949
30	Yoshiko Ishino	Female	Tokyo	5 February 1949
31	Masako Kimura	Female	Tokyo	5 February 1949
32	Shizuko Mochizuki	Female	Tokyo	5 February 1949
33	Haruko Sato	Female	Tokyo	5 February 1949
34	Osamu Sho	Male	Tokyo	5 February 1949
35	Makoto Suzuki	Male	Tokyo	5 February 1949
36	Fujiko Watanabe	Female	Tokyo	5 February 1949
37	Yaeko Arai	Female	Tokyo	19 February 1949
38	Michiko Masukawa	Female	Tokyo	19 February 1949
39	Nobuko Murakami	Female	Tokyo	19 February 1949
40	Toriko Tateuchi	Female	Tokyo	19 February 1949
41	Keiko Yamaguchi	Female	Tokyo	19 February 1949
42	Kikue Yoshino	Female	Tokyo	19 February 1949

	Name	Gender	Place [2]	Date of Baptism (*before)
43	Midori Ezoi	Female	Tokyo	5 March 1949
44	Misayo Hachiya	Female	Tokyo	5 March 1949
45	Fumio Iketani	Male	Tokyo	21 March 1949
46	Tsuneo Kiuchi	Male	Tokyo	26 March 1949
47	Ukio Nakahigashi	Male	Tokyo	26 March 1949
48	Shokichi Sugahara	Male	Tokyo	26 March 1949
49	Toshio Murakami	Male	Takasaki	2 April 1949
50	Minoru Musashino	Male	Tokyo	23 April 1949
51	Kisa Kuno	Male	Tokyo	6 May 1949
52	Katsue Ueda	Female	Tokyo	6 May 1949
53	Shigenori Yajima	Male	Tokyo	6 May 1949
54	Hideko Hara	Female	Takasaki	14 May 1949
55	Yoshiko Kaneko	Female	Takasaki	14 May 1949
56	Yutaka Shimotoku	Male	Tokyo	14 May 1949
57	Kohei Tanaka	Male	Takasaki	14 May 1949
58	Katsuko Arai	Female	Takasaki	28 May 1949
59	Masaru Suzuki	Male	Takasaki	28 May 1949
60	Yotaro Yoshino	Male	Takasaki	28 May 1949
61	Minoru Ishii	Male	Tokyo	4 June 1949
62	Ichiro Kikuchi	Male	Tokyo	4 June 1949
63	Tomiko Mizuko	Female	Tokyo	4 June 1949
64	Ayako Kishikawa	Female	Tokyo	10 July 1949
65	Shigeru Kishikawa	Male	Tokyo	10 July 1949
66	Mitsue Ota Fujiwara	Female	Tokyo	14 July 1949
67	Mitsuo Ishida	Male	Tokyo	14 July 1949
68	Taeko Ishida	Female	Tokyo	14 July 1949
69	Yasuko Iwata	Female	Tokyo	14 July 1949
70	Noriko Ono	Female	Tokyo	14 July 1949
71	Akira Watanabe	Male	Tokyo	14 July 1949
72	Harue Obayashi	Female	Tokyo	23 July 1949
73	Kazuo Fukuzaki	Male	Tokyo	2 August 1949
74	Minoko Hirose	Female	Nagoya	18 August 1949
75	Sachiko Masuda	Female	Tokyo	18 August 1949
76	Hiroko Matsumoto	Female	Tokyo	18 August 1949
77	Nobuko Negishi	Female	Tokyo	18 August 1949
78	Masaji Otsuka	Male	Takasaki	18 August 1949
79	Tomohiko Sagara	Male	Tokyo	18 August 1949
80	Sumiko Sakagawa	Female	Tokyo	18 August 1949
81	Kimie Sakamoto	Female	Tokyo	18 August 1949
82	Hisae Shimada	Female	Tokyo	18 August 1949
83	Kazuko Shimizu	Female	Nagoya	18 August 1949
84	Yasuko Takahashi	Female	Tokyo	18 August 1949
85	Sachiko Tamon	Female	Nagoya	18 August 1949
86	Kiyoko Tanaka	Female	Tokyo	18 August 1949
87	Teiko Tanaka	Female	Takasaki	18 August 1949
88	Isamu Todoroki	Male	Nagoya	18 August 1949
89	Toshiko Yanagida	Female	Tokyo	18 August 1949
90	Sadao Ishihara	Male	Osaka	21 August 1949

Annex 9. Mormon Converts Baptized in Occupied Japan

	Name	Gender	Place [2]	Date of Baptism (*before)
91	Yoshihito Kiso	Male	Osaka	21 August 1949
92	Haruko Murakami	Female	Osaka	21 August 1949
93	Hatsuko Murakami	Female	Osaka	21 August 1949
94	Kenjiro Murakami	Male	Osaka	21 August 1949
95	Takayashi Yoshioka	Male	Osaka	21 August 1949
96	Yoneo Ishii	Male	Tokyo	28 August 1949
97	Hiroshi Ogasawara	Male	Sapporo	10 September 1949
98	Kazuo Ogasawara	Male	Sapporo	10 September 1949
99	Yoshie Adachi	Male	Nagoya	12 September 1949
100	Kazuo Imai	Male	Tokyo	17 September 1949
101	Reiko Kobayashi	Female	Tokyo	17 September 1949
102	Zenjiro Noguchi	Male	Tokyo	17 September 1949
103	Masao Yamamoto	Male	Osaka	18 September 1949
104	Tokichi Yanagida	Male	Tokyo	30 September 1949
105	Makoto Tanaka	Male	Takasaki	1 October 1949
106	Hiroshi Goto	Male	Tokyo	15 October 1949
107	Hatsue Kobayashi	Female	Tokyo	15 October 1949
108	Emiko Mitomi	Female	Tokyo	15 October 1949
109	Kazutora Shoji	Male	Tokyo	15 October 1949
110	Toshiko Yamashita	Female	Tokyo	15 October 1949
111	Masao Watabe	Male	Sendai	6 November 1949
112	Ichiro Hata	Male	Sapporo	14 November 1949
113	Eiko Arai	Female	Takasaki	28 November 1949
114	Kesaitsu Takei	Male	Kofu	30 November 1949
115	Masayuki Tanaka	Male	Kofu	30 November 1949
116	Takekazu Tanaka	Male	Takasaki	1 December 1949
117	Hiroshi Aki	Male	Osaka	4 December 1949
118	Masataro Yanagisawa	Male	Sendai	18 December 1949
119	Akiko Fukuda	Female	Kofu	20 December 1949
120	Shinichi Kitta	Male	Kofu	20 December 1949
121	Yoshio Moteki	Male	Takasaki	24 December 1949
122	Hiroshi Sato	Male	Takasaki	24 December 1949
123	Tomiko Watanabe	Female	Takasaki	24 December 1949
124	Osamu Iwasawa	Male	Kofu	27 December 1949
125	Emiko Harayama	Female	Takasaki	31 December 1949
126	Kyutaro Kishiwagi	Male	Kofu	31 December 1949
127	Tadaashi Matsumoto	Male	Takasaki	31 December 1949
128	Tamotsu Matsumura	Male	Takasaki	31 December 1949
129	Jun Ochiai	Male	Takasaki	31 December 1949
130	Hideo Tomomatsu	Male	Takasaki	31 December 1949
131	Akira Akao	Male	Tokyo	21 January 1950
132	Hideji Hotta	Male	Tokyo	21 January 1950
133	Katsuko Inagaki	Female	Tokyo	21 January 1950
134	Susumu Ishii	Male	Takasaki	21 January 1950
135	Toshiko Shimizu	Female	Takasaki	21 January 1950
136	Eiichi Hirose	Male	Takasaki	4 February 1950
137	Iwao Ishiuchi	Male	Takasaki	4 February 1950
138	Kenji Otani	Male	Takasaki	4 February 1950

	Name	Gender	Place [2]	Date of Baptism (*before)
139	Teruo Otsuka	Male	Tokyo	4 February 1950
140	Yoshio Shigoka	Male	Takasaki	4 February 1950
141	Shigeru Nakajo	Male	Takasaki	11 February 1950
142	Yoshimitsu Yoshida	Male	Takasaki	11 February 1950
143	Toshio Igarashi	Male	Shibata	12 February 1950
144	Satako Fukuzawa	Female	Takasaki	4 March 1950
145	Tokiko Hara	Female	Takasaki	4 March 1950
146	Toshiko Minegishi	Female	Takasaki	4 March 1950
147	Kimiko Mogi	Female	Takasaki	4 March 1950
148	Hisako Arai	Female	Takasaki	11 March 1950
149	Kiyoko Araki	Female	Tokyo	11 March 1950
150	Fumiko Fujiki	Female	Tokyo	11 March 1950
151	Shiro Imura	Male	Yokohama	11 March 1950
152	Mikio Ito	Male	Takasaki	11 March 1950
153	Nobue Minegishi	Male	Tokyo	11 March 1950
154	Fumie Saito	Female	Tokyo	11 March 1950
155	Masaw [sic] Sakuma [3]	Female	Tokyo	11 March 1950
156	Yaeko Shirai	Female	Shibata	11 March 1950
157	Hisao Uchiyama	Male	Tokyo	11 March 1950
158	Kenzo Arai	Male	Tokyo	17 March 1950
159	Tsuji Tsuchiya	Male	Tokyo	17 March 1950
160	Yasuchika Taki	Male	Nagoya	18 March 1950
161	Haruyuki Sekiya	Male	Takasaki	23 March 1950
162	Yasuhiko Asama	Male	Takasaki	25 March 1950
163	Yukio Sugiyama	Male	Osaka	26 March 1950
164	Emiko Ishikawa	Female	Kofu	27 March 1950
165	Minoru Kawashima	Male	Takasaki	1 April 1950
166	Masaki Omura [4]	Female	Takasaki	8 April 1950
167	Hiroyuki Watanabe	Male	Tokyo	8 April 1950
168	Kiyoko Yamagishi	Female	Takasaki	8 April 1950
169	Sadao Takashima	Male	Tokyo	9 April 1950
170	Shinzo Takashima	Male	Tokyo	9 April 1950
171	Kyoko Koya	Female	Tokyo	14 April 1950
172	Koji Yatabe	Male	Tokyo	14 April 1950
173	Kan Watanabe	Male	Komatsu	22 April 1950
174	Atsuko Amemiya	Female	Kofu	1 May 1950
175	Shigeru Muramatsu	Female	Kofu	1 May 1950
176	Kazuko Yamamoto	Female	Sapporo	1 May 1950
177	Kiyono Aoyama	Female	Takasaki	5 May 1950
178	Matsuko Arimura	Female	Takasaki	6 May 1950
179	Nobuko Hasegawa	Female	Tokyo	6 May 1950
180	Masayoshi Ogihara	Male	Tokyo	6 May 1950
181	Matsue Tsukamoto	Female	Tokyo	6 May 1950
182	Tokiko Ohara Vance	Female	Tokyo	6 May 1950
183	Michiko Kanai	Female	Tokyo	7 May 1950
184	Atsushi Matsumoto	Male	Tokyo	7 May 1950
185	Yoshiko Nobuchi	Female	Tokyo	7 May 1950
186	Tamiko Watanabe	Female	Tokyo	7 May 1950

Annex 9. Mormon Converts Baptized in Occupied Japan

	Name	Gender	Place [2]	Date of Baptism (*before)
187	Yoshiyuki Amano	Male	Tokyo	20 May 1950
188	Masako Fukazawa	Female	Takasaki	20 May 1950
189	Yoko Hamajima	Female	Nagoya	3 June 1950
190	Harumi Hattori	Female	Nagoya	3 June 1950
191	Kazuki Kashiwagi	Male	Nagoya	3 June 1950
192	Yuya Kuroki	Male	Tokyo	3 June 1950
193	Ryuzo Nakayama	Male	Nagoya	3 June 1950
194	Fumie Suzuki Swenson	Female	Nagoya	3 June 1950
195	Kazuo Takagi	Male	Nagoya	3 June 1950
196	Tatsuya Tomita	Male	Nagoya	3 June 1950
197	Akiko Kitai	Female	Tokyo	4 June 1950
198	Norihiro Tsunoda	Male	Tokyo	4 June 1950
199	Michiko Hamano	Female	Osaka	11 June 1950
200	Kimiko Himeno	Female	Kyoto	11 June 1950
201	Isao Ito	Male	Osaka	11 June 1950
202	Fusae Iwamoto	Female	Osaka	11 June 1950
203	Tomio Katayama	Male	Kyoto	11 June 1950
204	Toyonori Shimada	Male	Tokyo	17 June 1950
205	Toshio Fujiyama	Male	Tokyo	28 June 1950
206	Sakiko Suzuki	Female	Tokyo	1 July 1950
207	Michiyo Hatsuya	Female	Sapporo	2 July 1950
208	Naotaro Hosaka	Male	Sapporo	2 July 1950
209	Miiko Kosaka	Female	Sapporo	2 July 1950
210	Keiko Ohashi	Female	Sapporo	2 July 1950
211	Atsushi Fukuda	Male	Sendai	4 July 1950
212	Shozo Nagao	Male	Sendai	4 July 1950
213	Toshiko Shimada	Male	Sendai	4 July 1950
214	Masahisa Watabe	Male	Sendai	4 July 1950
215	Shisako Watanabe	Female	Sendai	4 July 1950
216	Junko Iwasa	Female	Takasaki	15 July 1950
217	Takako Koganezawa	Female	Takasaki	15 July 1950
218	Tsuneya Kuroki	Male	Tokyo	15 July 1950
219	Chomatsu Mizuno	Male	Nagoya	15 July 1950
220	Kinsaku Sekiguchi	Male	Tokyo	15 July 1950
221	Haruo Todoroki	Male	Nagoya	15 July 1950
222	Takashi Miyakawa	Male	Tokyo	*16 July 1950
223	Tsukasa Maki	Female	Kyoto	23 July 1950
224	Michiko Nishimoto	Female	Kyoto	23 July 1950
225	Setsuko Ikeda	Female	Sendai	27 July 1950
226	Yoko Takahashi	Female	Sendai	27 July 1950
227	Teruyoshi Nakamura	Male	Niigata	8 August 1950
228	Toshiko Sakurai	Female	Niigata	8 August 1950
229	Nagao Tanaka	Male	Takasaki	8 August 1950
230	Teruko Hashi	Female	Sendai	9 August 1950
231	Teiko Murakami	Female	Sendai	9 August 1950
232	Seijiro Adachi	Male	Komatsu	12 August 1950
233	Chieko Aoyama	Female	Nagoya	12 August 1950
234	Hideyuki Doba	Male	Komatsu	12 August 1950

	Name	Gender	Place [2]	Date of Baptism (*before)
235	Keiko Fukuda	Female	Komatsu	12 August 1950
236	Emiko Hirose	Female	Nagoya	12 August 1950
237	Nobuko Kameda	Female	Komatsu	12 August 1950
238	Sonoko Motoshima	Female	Nagoya	12 August 1950
239	Emiko Murota	Female	Komatsu	12 August 1950
240	Yasu Nishide	Female	Komatsu	12 August 1950
241	Yukiko Nojima	Female	Komatsu	12 August 1950
242	Hisako Ogura	Female	Nagoya	12 August 1950
243	Suemasa Todoroki	Male	Nagoya	12 August 1950
244	Hajime Wakayama	Male	Nagoya	12 August 1950
245	Shinako Hisada	Female	Osaka	13 August 1950
246	Haruko Sakamoto	Female	Osaka	13 August 1950
247	Imada Yoshida	Male	Takasaki	26 August 1950
248	Kiyoshi Hashimoto	Male	Takasaki	2 September 1950
249	Matsuo Nakajima	Male	Takasaki	2 September 1950
250	Junichi Takada	Male	Tokyo	2 September 1950
251	Wataru Takahashi	Male	Tokyo	2 September 1950
252	Yoshio Katsumata	Male	Takasaki	9 September 1950
253	Miyako Kondo	Female	Takasaki	9 September 1950
254	Nobuko Onda	Female	Takasaki	9 September 1950
255	Michiko Musashino	Female	Yokohama	10 September 1950
256	Takasuke Nagao	Male	Yokohama	10 September 1950
257	Masayoshi Sawayama	Male	Yokohama	10 September 1950
258	Junko Shimada	Female	Yokohama	10 September 1950
259	Atsuko Uda	Female	Tokyo	10 September 1950
260	Kazuko Yamada	Female	Kyoto	10 September 1950
261	Mitsuko Yamashita	Female	Kyoto	10 September 1950
262	Chieko Abe	Female	Sendai	12 September 1950
263	Masako Endo	Female	Tokyo	16 September 1950
264	Tsuneko Kita	Female	Tokyo	16 September 1950
265	Chiyono Yamasawa	Female	Tokyo	16 September 1950
266	Sachiko Kawajo	Female	Osaka	21 September 1950
267	Michie Izuka	Female	Takasaki	23 September 1950
268	Yoshiko Otsuki	Female	Takasaki	23 September 1950
269	Michiko Kamotani	Female	Hiroshima	1 October 1950
270	Miyoko Kamotani	Female	Hiroshima	1 October 1950
271	Masayo Igarashi	Male	Kyoto	8 October 1950
272	Miyoko Nishimoto	Female	Kyoto	8 October 1950
273	Haruko Nishimura	Female	Kyoto	8 October 1950
274	Sadako Takagi	Female	Kyoto	8 October 1950
275	Keiko Kato	Female	Hiroshima	23 October 1950
276	Yuko Hayashi	Female	Nagoya	28 October 1950
277	Mitsuko Kojima	Female	Nagoya	28 October 1950
278	Chizuko Murakami	Female	Nagoya	28 October 1950
279	Sachiko Murase	Female	Nagoya	28 October 1950
280	Sakiko Nakano	Female	Nagoya	28 October 1950
281	Asako Ochiai	Female	Nagoya	28 October 1950
282	Mubeko Ogawa	Female	Nagoya	28 October 1950

Annex 9. Mormon Converts Baptized in Occupied Japan

	Name	Gender	Place [2]	Date of Baptism (*before)
283	Sakae Takei	Female	Nagoya	28 October 1950
284	Kikue Yamane	Female	Hiroshima	3 November 1950
285	Goro Arima	Male	Tokyo	4 November 1950
286	Sachiko Arima	Female	Tokyo	4 November 1950
287	Yaeko Sasaki	Female	Sendai	12 November 1950
288	Tomoko Tanaka	Female	Sendai	12 November 1950
289	Chieko Umetsu	Female	Sendai	12 November 1950
290	Ikuko Yamada	Female	Sapporo	12 November 1950
291	Tomiko Imai	Female	Shibata	18 November 1950
292	Misu Inomata	Male	Shibata	18 November 1950
293	Masa Isobe	Female	Shibata	18 November 1950
294	Tokuichi Kaneta [5]	Male	Takasaki	18 November 1950
295	Katsue Nakajima	Female	Shibata	18 November 1950
296	Kyubei Nakano	Male	Niigata	18 November 1950
297	Yoko Yamakawa	Female	Tokyo	18 November 1950
298	Chieko Kuboki	Female	Kofu	22 November 1950
299	Rintaro Nakashima	Male	Hiroshima	22 November 1950
300	Tomio Yamashita	Male	Kofu	22 November 1950
301	Tamahiko Shudo	Male	Osaka	*2 December 1950 [6]
302	Toshihiro Kaze	Male	Yokohama	2 December 1950
303	Toshiko Okuni	Female	Tokyo	2 December 1950
304	Toshiichi Shimizu	Male	Takasaki	2 December 1950
305	Ritsuko Maekawa	Female	Osaka	10 December 1950
306	Muneyuki Nakagawa	Male	Osaka	10 December 1950
307	Mitsuyo Onishi	Female	Osaka	10 December 1950
308	Teruo Tanaka	Male	Osaka	10 December 1950
309	Shokichi Aizawa	Male	Kofu	16 December 1950
310	Yoshio Inouye [4]	Female	Niigata	16 December 1950
311	Etsuko Kon	Female	Niigata	16 December 1950
312	Hitomi Horino	Female	Sendai	17 December 1950
313	Tomoko Miyazawa	Female	Sendai	17 December 1950
314	Yuriko Nakano	Female	Sendai	17 December 1950
315	Atsuko Yamazaki	Female	Takasaki	25 December 1950
316	Kazuyuki Fukasawa	Male	Kofu	27 December 1950
317	Tomiko Iwata Demello	Female	Yamagata	11 February 1951
318	Yoshiko Seino	Female	Yamagata	11 February 1951
319	Etsuko Kawashima	Female	Shibata	17 February 1951
320	Tsuru Ozawa	Female	Takasaki	24 February 1951
321	Eiko Tanaka	Female	Takasaki	24 February 1951
322	Yoshie Yajima	Female	Takasaki	24 February 1951
323	Eiko Akito	Female	Otaru	25 February 1951
324	Eiko Masegawa [7]	Female	Otaru	25 February 1951
325	Nakubo Shinozuka	Female	Otaru	25 February 1951
326	Sumi Sugiyama	Female	Otaru	25 February 1951
327	Toshiaki Nakata	Male	Asahikawa	28 February 1951
328	Tsuruko Kanehara	Female	Tokyo	3 March 1951
329	Juza Kimura	Male	Tokyo	3 March 1951
330	Matsumi Mizusawa	Female	Takasaki	3 March 1951

	Name	Gender	Place [2]	Date of Baptism (*before)
331	Sumiko Morikawa	Female	Tokyo	3 March 1951
332	Tetsuro Morikawa	Male	Tokyo	3 March 1951
333	Hideo Nakayama	Male	Tokyo	3 March 1951
334	Michiko Okada	Female	Yokohama	5 March 1951
335	Kozaburo Sugimoto	Male	Narumi	6 March 1951
336	Hiroshi Masuko	Male	Shibata	10 March 1951
337	Kazutaka Furui	Male	Sapporo	21 March 1951
338	Shizue Kamakura	Female	Sapporo	21 March 1951
339	Sadako Shingu	Female	Sapporo	21 March 1951
340	Tadahiro Takeda	Male	Sapporo	21 March 1951
341	Mihoko Wada	Female	Sapporo	21 March 1951
342	Kiyoshi Ito	Male	Osaka	24 March 1951
343	Sachiko Kamitani	Female	Kyoto	24 March 1951
344	Tadahiro Kono	Male	Osaka	24 March 1951
345	Yukiko Maki	Female	Kyoto	24 March 1951
346	Masao Matsumoto	Male	Osaka	24 March 1951
347	Fumiko Mizoguchi	Female	Osaka	24 March 1951
348	Takako Nagamoto	Female	Kyoto	24 March 1951
349	Shizuko Nasu	Female	Osaka	24 March 1951
350	Kay Elizabeth Nishida	Female	Kyoto	24 March 1951
351	Koichiro Omura	Male	Osaka	24 March 1951
352	Ikuyo Sakamoto	Female	Osaka	24 March 1951
353	Masako Sugie	Female	Kyoto	24 March 1951
354	Takiko Sugie	Female	Kyoto	24 March 1951
355	Nobuko Takizawa	Female	Osaka	24 March 1951
356	Emiko Teranishi	Female	Osaka	24 March 1951
357	Tsumiko Yamamoto	Female	Kyoto	24 March 1951
358	Eiko Nakamura	Female	Otaru	25 March 1951
359	Kazuko Nakamura	Female	Otaru	25 March 1951
360	Toshiko Nakamura	Female	Otaru	25 March 1951
361	Fumie Kogure	Female	Yanai–Hirao	26 March 1951
362	Yoko Yanagi	Female	Yanai–Hirao	26 March 1951
363	Kinichiro Kameda	Male	Komatsu	31 March 1951
364	Tokiji Murakami	Male	Komatsu	31 March 1951
365	Wakako Murata	Female	Komatsu	31 March 1951
366	Yoshiko Okubo	Female	Kofu	31 March 1951
367	Takako Yamakawa	Female	Komatsu	31 March 1951
368	Yuko Sugimoto [8]	Female	Narumi	3 April 1951
369	Hiroshi Yasuda	Male	Narumi	3 April 1951
370	Miyoko Harikoshi	Female	Takasaki	5 April 1951
371	Sasayoshi Shibusawa	Male	Maebashi	5 April 1951
372	Susumu Yanai	Male	Maebashi	5 April 1951
373	Akira Imai	Male	Takasaki	6 April 1951
374	Akiko Fujii	Female	Tokyo	7 April 1951
375	Risako Fujii	Female	Tokyo	7 April 1951
376	Harumi Kadomoto	Female	Yanai–Hirao	7 April 1951
377	Yoshiko Koizumi	Female	Tokyo	7 April 1951
378	Toshio Shokawa	Male	Yanai–Hirao	7 April 1951

Annex 9. Mormon Converts Baptized in Occupied Japan 491

	Name	Gender	Place [2]	Date of Baptism (*before)
379	Masashi Yanagida	Male	Nagoya	7 April 1951
380	Chizuko Narita	Female	Tokyo	21 April 1951
381	Chieko Sasa	Female	Tokyo	21 April 1951
382	Sonoe Muramatsu	Female	Kofu	29 April 1951
383	Tokuko Tsuchiya	Female	Kofu	29 April 1951
384	Toshiko Tsunoda	Female	Kofu	29 April 1951
385	Shizu Kato	Female	Otaru	5 May 1951
386	Hide Kishigami	Female	Otaru	5 May 1951
387	Mii Kobayashi	Female	Sanjo	5 May 1951
388	Akiko Miya	Female	Tokyo	5 May 1951
389	Fumiko Nakamura	Female	Otaru	5 May 1951
390	Takako Ochi	Female	Otaru	5 May 1951
391	Yoko Sakagami	Female	Otaru	5 May 1951
392	Sumi Ssasaki	Female	Otaru	5 May 1951
393	Kimie Shirakami	Female	Otaru	5 May 1951
394	Nitsuko Takenara	Female	Otaru	5 May 1951
395	Kyoko Wada	Female	Otaru	5 May 1951
396	Kyoto Horiuchi	Female	Muroran	6 May 1951
397	Mitsue Horiuchi	Female	Muroran	6 May 1951
398	Akiko Katakura	Female	Muroran	6 May 1951
399	Toriko Kosaka	Female	Muroran	6 May 1951
400	Yoshiko Miyoshi	Female	Muroran	6 May 1951
401	Shigemasa Nagai	Male	Muroran	6 May 1951
402	Yoko Endo	Female	Shibata	19 May 1951
403	Motoe Hiraga	Female	Kofu	19 May 1951
404	Takao Igarashi	Male	Shibata	19 May 1951
405	Yoshiichi Koiwa	Male	Sanjo	19 May 1951
406	Terumi Maeda	Male	Sanjo	19 May 1951
407	Nobuko Maruyama	Female	Shibata	19 May 1951
408	Shizuko Miyaguchi	Female	Sanjo	19 May 1951
409	Keiko Onta	Female	Shibata	19 May 1951
410	Mitsue Sato	Female	Sanjo	19 May 1951
411	Yayako Seito	Female	Shibata	19 May 1951
412	Hideyo Shirai	Female	Shibata	19 May 1951
413	Noriko Tanabe	Female	Shibata	19 May 1951
414	Asaka Tsuchida	Female	Shibata	19 May 1951
415	Miwako Yoshida	Female	Shibata	19 May 1951
416	Noburo Komine	Male	Maebashi	21 May 1951
417	Tetsuro Omi	Male	Sapporo	26 May 1951
418	Shimeko Sato	Female	Sapporo	26 May 1951
419	Akihito Hiranuma	Male	Osaka	27 May 1951
420	Tomoe Tomotake	Female	Osaka	27 May 1951
421	Yasuko Hageshita	Female	Komatsu	2 June 1951
422	Junko Miyamoto	Female	Kanazawa	2 June 1951
423	Chie Shibata	Female	Komatsu	2 June 1951
424	Mineko Takagi	Female	Komatsu	2 June 1951
425	Setsuko Takane	Female	Muroran	3 June 1951
426	Reiko Ueda	Female	Muroran	3 June 1951

	Name	Gender	Place [2]	Date of Baptism (*before)
427	Sozaburo Kakimoto	Male	Komatsu	6 June 1951
428	Tairoku Hashimoto	Male	Shibata	9 June 1951
429	Yoshikoza Narita [9]	Male	Nagoya	9 June 1951
430	Hidegi Namekawa	Male	Tokyo	16 June 1951
431	Yoshiko Iwabe	Female	Yokohama	17 June 1951
432	Isako Doi	Female	Shibata	23 June 1951
433	Kazuko Numata	Female	Kofu	23 June 1951
434	Aiko Shibayama	Female	Shibata	23 June 1951
435	Setsuko Takeuchi	Female	Shibata	23 June 1951
436	Kazuko Karasawa	Female	Matsumoto	30 June 1951
437	Fukiko Shimizu	Female	Matsumoto	30 June 1951
438	Itoko Shimizu	Female	Matsumoto	30 June 1951
439	Ichiro Hirota	Male	Nagoya	3 July 1951
440	Chwa Jung Yui	Male	Narumi	3 July 1951
441	Sachiko Umeki	Female	Otaru	7 July 1951
442	Ikuko Yanagihara	Female	Otaru	7 July 1951
443	Ichiko Momoi	Female	Sendai	18 July 1951
444	Shinsuke Niino	Male	Sendai	18 July 1951
445	Emiko Honma	Female	Asahikawa	23 July 1951
446	Tamae Minegishi	Female	Takasaki	28 July 1951
447	Yoko Watanuki	Female	Takasaki	28 July 1951
448	Marekuni Kamakura	Male	Matsumoto	30 July 1951
449	Kazue Okuhara Goto	Female	Hiroshima	31 July 1951
450	Kikkuyo Ishibashi Kamotani	Female	Hiroshima	31 July 1951
451	Umeyo Sugime Matsuo	Female	Hiroshima	31 July 1951
452	Eiko Sugimoto	Female	Hiroshima	31 July 1951
453	Kitsuko Fukuda	Female	Yanai–Hirao	4 August 1951
454	Yashiko Ishida	Female	Takasaki	4 August 1951
455	Sachiko Kobayashi	Female	Takasaki	4 August 1951
456	Tamayo Osawa	Female	Takasaki	4 August 1951
457	Mitsu Kaneta	Female	Takasaki	7 August 1951
458	Kiyoko Saito	Female	Takasaki	8 August 1951
459	Yuko Saito	Female	Takasaki	8 August 1951
460	Masako Emuro	Female	Kofu	19 August 1951
461	Kyoko Azegami	Female	Tokyo	23 August 1951
462	Takao Deguchi	Male	Hiroshima	1 September 1951
463	Setsuko Makino	Female	Sapporo	2 September 1951
464	Kazuko Yamakawa	Female	Shibata	4 September 1951
465	Tsutomu Shimomura	Male	Tokyo	7 September 1951
466	Toshie Murooka	Female	Takasaki	12 September 1951
467	Yasuko Okamoto	Female	Yanai–Hirao	15 September 1951
468	Yoshiyuki Tawa	Male	Asahikawa	15 September 1951
469	Yuki Toyokawa	Female	Asahikawa	15 September 1951
470	Etsuko Kato	Female	Muroran	16 September 1951
471	Kuniko Sakai	Female	Muroran	16 September 1951
472	Yoneko Tominari	Female	Muroran	16 September 1951
473	Hikojiro Oshika	Male	Nagoya	19 September 1951
474	Masahiro Sekiya	Male	Takasaki	25 September 1951

Annex 9. Mormon Converts Baptized in Occupied Japan

	Name	Gender	Place [2]	Date of Baptism (*before)
475	Shizuko Yonehara	Female	Hiroshima	2 October 1951
476	Shigeko Takahashi	Female	Tokyo	5 October 1951
477	Miyoko Furazawa	Female	Osaka	7 October 1951
478	Kayo Murakawa	Female	Osaka	7 October 1951
479	Kiyoki Owamoto	Female	Osaka	7 October 1951
480	Keietsu Maezawa	Male	Tokyo	13 October 1951
481	Yoshimi Ota	Female	Sanjo	13 October 1951
482	Aiko Okamoto	Female	Yokohama	18 October 1951
483	Sayoko Arai	Female	Otaru	28 October 1951
484	Koichi Hashizume	Male	Otaru	28 October 1951
485	Osamu Ishida	Male	Otaru	28 October 1951
486	Masako Kato	Female	Otaru	28 October 1951
487	Shigetoshi Kato	Male	Otaru	28 October 1951
488	Kiyono Numazawa	Female	Yamagata	28 October 1951
489	Toshiko Ikeda	Female	Tokyo	31 October 1951
490	Masako Miyajjima	Female	Tokyo	31 October 1951
491	Katsue Kudo	Female	Muroran	3 November 1951
492	Kazuko Maki	Female	Hiroshima	3 November 1951
493	Setsuko Nakano	Female	Muroran	3 November 1951
494	Fumio Yamaguchi	Male	Sapporo	11 November 1951
495	Namiko Yamamoto	Female	Sapporo	11 November 1951
496	Miyoko Sakamoto	Female	Tokyo	24 November 1951
497	Ichiro Okamoto	Male	Tokyo	9 December 1951
498	Susumu Yanai	Male	Maebashi	9 December 1951
499	Hiroaki Hitano	Male	Otaru	24 December 1951
500	Hirofumi Kimura	Male	Asahikawa	24 December 1951
501	Akemi Horino	Female	Sendai	25 December 1951
502	Mitsuro Ogawa	Male	Osaka	25 December 1951
503	Chizuko Sho	Female	Sendai	25 December 1951
504	Sakuno Teranishi	Female	Osaka	25 December 1951
505	Masaji Koike	Male	Osaka	30 December 1951
506	Fusako Miyano	Female	Shibata	30 December 1951
507	Kazuaki Watanabe	Male	Shibata	30 December 1951
508	Teruko Yamamoto	Female	Kofu	4 January 1952
509	Ichiro Kanasashi	Male	Tokyo	12 January 1952
510	Hiroko Sato	Female	Sendai	2 February 1952
511	Masaji Watanabe	Male	Sendai	2 February 1952
512	Teiko Araki	Female	Tokyo	11 February 1952
513	Hiroshi Ishii	Male	Tokyo	11 February 1952
514	Fumiko Matsumoto	Female	Tokyo	11 February 1952
515	Yukiko Matsuda	Female	Sendai	1 March 1952
516	Junko Shio	Female	Sendai	1 March 1952
517	Chieko Somekawa	Female	Sendai	1 March 1952
518	Taeko Takaizumi	Female	Sendai	1 March 1952
519	Toshiko Takizawa	Female	Sanjo	7 March 1952
520	Tomoko Kiryu	Female	Kanazawa	16 March 1952
521	Toshiyo Naniwa [10]	Female	Yamagata	22 March 1952
522	Kaneko Takahashi	Female	Yamagata	29 March 1952

	Name	Gender	Place [2]	Date of Baptism (*before)
523	Nobuo Hazokawa	Male	Otaru	30 March 1952
524	Tsuyoshi Kobayashi	Male	Otaru	30 March 1952
525	Haruhiko Komima	Male	Otaru	30 March 1952
526	Kyoko An	Female	Fukuoka	13 April 1952
527	Yuki Sato	Female	Fukuoka	13 April 1952
528	Hideyuki Hayashi	Male	Sendai	19 April 1952
529	Kazuo Koike	Male	Takasaki	*20 April 1952
530	Hiromi Wakita	Male	Takasaki	*20 April 1952
531	Etsuko Sasanuma	Female	Yamagata	23 April 1952

[1] Excludes military and civilian baptisms associated with American armed forces.
[2] Home unit or place of residence; may not be the place of baptism.
[3] The spelling of the name is uncertain; gender could be male.
[4] Gender could be male.
[5] Name could be Kameta.
[6] Alternative date is 25 December 1951.
[7] Name could be Hasegawa.
[8] Gender could be male if the name is pronounced Yūkō.
[9] Name is more likely to be Yoshikazu.
[10] Name could be Namiwa.

Japanese Mission, "Historical Records and Minutes," LDS Church Archives; various church records.

Annex 10

Mormon Missionaries in the Japanese and Northern Far East Missions, 1948–68

(Alphabetical order; chronological order for the same surname)[1]

Name (* female)	Home country, U.S. state, or Japan town	Month of arrival (+estimate)	Month of departure [2] (+estimate)
Aamodt, Wayne G.	Utah	March 1951	March 1953
Abe, Chieko*	Sendai	January 1953	May 1954
Abo, Tomosue	Hawaii	April 1949	May 1951
Abo, Betty*	Hawaii	February 1953	February 1955
Adachi, Ikuko*	Sapporo	January 1967	July 1968
Adams, Lloyd K.	California	October 1950	October 1953
Adams, John Reed	Idaho	July 1957	February 1960
Adams, Louis Jerold	Arizona	July 1959	December 1961
Adams, Robert Maurice	Idaho	March 1960	Korea D.
Adams, Bruce Kent	Idaho	September 1961	Korea D.
Aimoto, Sudori*	Tokyo	July 1968	Japan M.
Aipoalani, Earl	Hawaii	April 1950	March 1953
Akagi, Kenji	Hawaii	October 1948	September 1951
Akamine, Arleen Teruko*	Hawaii	May 1956	May 1958
Akau, William Ah You	Hawaii	July 1949	May 1952
Aki, Hiroshi	Osaka	September 1952	September 1954
Akita, Eiko*	Otaru	December 1953	June 1955+
Akiyama, Mikiko*	Idaho	August 1965	July 1967
Akuna, Beverly Ah Fee	Hawaii	January 1952	October 1952
Albrecht, William Steve	Utah	August 1966	Japan–Okinawa M.
Alleman, Carol Ann*	Utah	October 1958	September 1960
Allen, Lloyd Edward	Montana	October 1963	March 1966
Allen, Robert William	Utah	August 1966	Japan M.
Allen, Gary S.	Utah	February 1967	Japan M.
Alley, Sharon*	Utah	March 1967	Japan M.
Amemiya, Akiko*	Kofu	April 1965	October 1966
Amemiya, Ikuko*	Tokyo	August 1967	Japan–Okinawa M.
Ames, Walter Lansing	California	September 1965	March 1968
Andersen, Dwayne N.	Utah	October 1951	July 1953
Andersen, Dean Martin	Utah	March 1956	Korea D.
Andersen, Thomas Martin	California	October 1957	April 1960
Andersen, Neils Roger	Idaho	March 1961	September 1963
Andersen, Dwayne N.[3]	California	July 1962	August 1965
Andersen, Peggy*[4]	California	July 1962	August 1965
Andersen, Paul H.	Utah	August 1963	February 1966
Anderson, Clarence LeRoy	Idaho	February 1954	February 1957
Anderson, Jean Lucile*	Idaho	December 1960	December 1962
Anderson, Marc Alfred	Idaho	February 1962	Korea D.
Anderson, Stanley Nelson	Utah	September 1966	Japan M.

Name (* female)	Home country, U.S. state, or Japan town	Month of arrival (+estimate)	Month of departure [2] (+estimate)
Anderson, Bonnie Fae*	Utah	March 1967	Japan M.
Anderson, Sherman Farel	Utah	February 1968	Japan M.
Anderson, Paul L.	California	April 1968	Japan–Okinawa M.
Andrade, Philomena*	Hawaii	April 1949	May 1951
Andrus, Paul Charles[5]	Utah	June 1948	February 1951
Andrus, Paul Charles[3]	Hawaii	December 1955	July 1962
Andrus, Frances Parker*[4]	Hawaii	December 1955	July 1962
Andrus, Antone Marlon	Utah	July 1958	January 1961
Aoyagi, Hideo	Tokyo	March 1967	Japan–Okinawa M.
Aoyagi, Koichi	Yokohama	June 1968	Japan M.
Apana, Wilma K. L. H.*	Hawaii	April 1958	April 1960
Apo, Joy Kalehua*	Hawaii	May 1960	May 1962
Arave, Joseph Brent	Utah	January 1968	Japan–Okinawa M.
Arbon, Richard Donl	Utah	October 1959	May 1962
Arnold, Keith Eugene	California	September 1963	March 1966
Asada, Tsunenori	Sapporo	August 1956	July 1958
Ashby, Claude Stewart	Utah	December 1961	Korea D.
Ashby, Howard Bennet	Utah	October 1962	April 1965
Asher, Grant Edwin	Idaho	October 1963	February 1966
Ashman, Harold Lowell	Utah	July 1957	June 1960
Astin, Delbert Fullmer	Utah	July 1955	July 1958
Astle, Wilford Bevan	Utah	June 1956	June 1959
Atchley, Danny Wayne	Montana	December 1962	June 1965
Atkin, Dennis H.	Utah	February 1950	February 1953
Atkinson, Jerry LeMar	Utah	July 1955	July 1958
Atkinson, John David	West Virginia	June 1965	December 1967
Auld, James Adams Uilakulani	Hawaii	July 1949	March 1951
Austin, John Maxfield	Utah	November 1953	November 1956
Austin, Richard Maxfield	Utah	February 1955	February 1958
Austin, Roger Lee	California	March 1962	September 1964
Averett, Leah Mae*	Utah	July 1959	July 1961
Awa, George Kahakili	Hawaii	May 1954	May 1957
Axelson, Terry Robert	California	February 1968	Japan M.
Bair, John Richard	Utah	November 1962	May 1965
Baird, Maryellen*	Utah	December 1966	Japan M.
Baker, Conway	Utah	February 1953	June 1955
Ball, Jr., Alfred Vernon	Idaho	July 1955	July 1958
Ball, Stephen Lynn	Idaho	June 1968	Japan M.
Bandy, Thomas Joseph	Idaho	July 1961	December 1963
Barcarse, Damaso Alan	Hawaii	November 1959	May 1962
Barney, Lee Alva	California	September 1966	Japan M.
Barrett, Eulene*	Utah	October 1958	October 1960
Barrett, Warren B.	California	December 1966	May 1967
Barrow, Marlin Hobson	Utah	November 1965	May 1968
Bartholomew, Wynn Evan	California	September 1966	Japan M.
Bartholomew, Bruce	Utah	May 1968	Japan M.
Barton, David Reid	Utah	March 1957	October 1959

Annex 10. Mormon Missionaries in the Japanese and Northern Far East Missions

Name (* female)	Home country, U.S. state, or Japan town	Month of arrival (+estimate)	Month of departure [2] (+estimate)
Bassett, James Edmond	California	May 1965	November 1967
Beagley, Steven George	Utah	December 1966	Japan M.
Beaman, Bruce	California	October 1954	November 1957
Beardall, Armel Owen	Utah	March 1963	September 1965
Beckstrand, Paul H.	Utah	June 1960	December 1962
Belcher, Steven Monty	Utah	May 1963	November 1965
Bell, Wallace K.	Hawaii	May 1951	May 1954
Bell, Jeffrey White	Utah	October 1963	March 1966
Bell Jr, Stewart Kanakea	Hawaii	October 1963	April 1966
Bell, Lincoln R.	California	January 1966	July 1968
Bennett, Richard L.	Utah	October 1953	October 1956
Bentley, Rondy	Idaho	January 1965	July 1967
Berger, Terryl Franklin	Idaho	July 1958	December 1960
Berkey, Kent G.	California	June 1967	Japan M.
Beste, Alan Paul	Utah	August 1966	Japan–Okinawa M.
Bills, Walter Larae	Utah	February 1962	August 1964
Bills, Donald Ole	Utah	September 1964	March 1967
Bills, Jon Kenneth	Utah	April 1966	Japan M.
Bills, Bruce R.	Utah	April 1967	Japan–Okinawa M.
Bills, Walter Rudolph[3]	Utah	July 1968	Japan M.
Bills, Elsie Mathea Torgerson*[4]	Utah	July 1968	Japan M.
Bingham, Darold	Idaho	October 1953	October 1956
Bingham, Robert Larry	Washington	July 1958	January 1961
Bingham, Carolyn*	Idaho	May 1961	May 1963
Bingham, Kendell Rex	Idaho	June 1962	December 1964
Bingham, Danny Kay	Arizona	January 1963	July 1965
Bird, Ralph W.	Utah	November 1950	December 1953
Black, Franklin S.	Wyoming	February 1957	September 1959
Black, Peter Humphries	Utah	July 1959	April 1961
Black, Timothy Jaques	Utah	March 1966	Japan M.
Blackmore, Barclay V.	Canada	October 1960	April 1963
Blackwelder, Donald Lee	Florida	March 1962	September 1964
Blake, Rowland Sumsion	Minnesota	July 1964	December 1966
Blakely, Glen B.	Kentucky	November 1965	May 1968
Blalock, Merrill Legrande	Mississippi	July 1962	February 1965
Blau, Delray R.	Arizona	April 1957	November 1959
Bodily, David M.	Idaho	June 1954	July 1957
Booth, Steven William	Utah	February 1966	August 1968
Bowen, Paul G.	Utah	June 1954	June 1957
Bowman, Wallace Neal	Idaho	December 1957	Korea D.
Boyack, Robert Noble	Wyoming	October 1949	September 1952
Boyd III, Norman Kent	Utah	September 1960	March 1963
Boyd, Bill Gerald	Wyoming	October 1960	April 1963
Boyer, Michael Keith	Arizona	August 1962	November 1963
Bradford, William	Utah	November 1953	October 1954
Bradshaw, James R.	Utah	November 1958	Korea D.
Brady, Feurman Neil	Nevada	March 1965	September 1967

Name (* female)	Home country, U.S. state, or Japan town	Month of arrival (+estimate)	Month of departure [2] (+estimate)
Bragg, Donald G.[6]	Utah	November 1960	June 1961
Brigham, Wayne James	Utah	January 1961	July 1963
Broadhead, David Robert	Utah	July 1954	July 1957
Brossand, Robert L.[6]	Utah	August 1964	January 1965
Brown, Carol Rae*	Utah	September 1957+	August 1959
Brown, Lowell Edward	California	October 1957	Korea D.
Brown, Roger Dee	Utah	June 1963	December 1965
Brown, Paul Victor	Utah	July 1963	January 1966
Brown, Roger Alexander	Utah	October 1963	March 1966
Brown, Lamar Delbert	Washington	August 1965	February 1968
Brown, Wayne H.	California	March 1966	August 1968
Brown, Kenneth Bellamy[7]	Florida	July 1967	Japan M.
Bryant, III, John Webster	New Hampshire	September 1965	March 1968
Budden, Brent Ray	Oregon	November 1965	May 1968
Bullock, Karl Hart	Utah	April 1957	November 1959
Bullock, Brian Lee	Canada	March 1964	September 1966
Bunderson, Sue*	Idaho	August 1965	August 1967
Burkholder, Patricia Ellen*	Nevada	March 21, 1963	March 1965
Burnham, Francis	Idaho	August 1953	August 1956
Burton, David Jeff	Utah	October 1961	April 1964
Burton, Fred David	Utah	May 1965	November 1967
Burton, Kent Austin[7]	Utah	July 1967	Japan M.
Butler, David Conwey	Utah	November 1960	Korea D.
Butler, Bart Lerwell	Utah	December 1961	Korea D.
Butler, Michael T.	New Mexico	August 1967	Japan–Okinawa M.
Campbell, Cline G.	Utah	January 1958	Korea D.
Campbell, Bruce Larsen	Utah	February 1961	August 1963
Candall, Alice Ilene*	Idaho	May 1964	May 1966
Canfield, Paul Clifton	Utah	November 1950	November 1953
Carbine, James Wendell	Utah	December 1965	June 1968
Carr, Gail Edwin	California	January 1955	Korea D.
Carter, Paul Smith	Utah	December 1948	September 1951
Carter, Barton Lamar	Utah	September 1960	March 1963
Case, Budd Eugene	California	August 1960	February 1963
Causey, Charles Scott	Texas	June 1965	March 1967
Chadwick, John Dick	Utah	June 1959	Korea D.
Chantrill, Earl Preator	California	September 1962	March 1965
Chapman, Richard Smedley	Utah	March 1963	September 1965
Chappell, Alton Judd	Utah	June 1963	December 1965
Chase, John Dunn	Idaho	October 1957	April 1960
Childs, Tim Kay	Utah	October 1967	Japan–Okinawa M.
Ching, Lester Sin Fook	Hawaii	April 1950	April 1953
Chocco, Franklin Dee	California	July 1964	January 1967
Christensen, Max B.	Idaho	April 1950	March 1953
Christensen, Kay	Oregon	February 1953	March 1955
Christensen, Ned Lewis	Utah	March 1957+	October 1959
Christensen, Paul Elwood	Hawaii	July 1960	January 1963

Annex 10. Mormon Missionaries in the Japanese and Northern Far East Missions

Name (* female)	Home country, U.S. state, or Japan town	Month of arrival (+estimate)	Month of departure [2] (+estimate)
Christensen, Mark W.	Utah	August 1962	March 1965
Christensen, Burke Arthur	Utah	June 1965	September 1965
Christopherson, Kenneth Lee	Utah	November 1964	May 1967
Clark, Jeremiah H.	Utah	December 1950	December 1953
Clark, Scott F.	Idaho	May 1968	Japan M.
Clarke, Fauntella J.*	Utah	December 1949	November 1951
Clater, Charles Ronald	Virginia	September 1966	Japan–Okinawa M.
Clawson, John R.	Utah	April 1949	May 1951
Clawson, James G.[7]	Idaho	July 1967	Japan M.
Clement, Dallas Brent	Idaho	September 1961	Korea D.
Clement, Morgan Don	Idaho	March 1966	August 1968
Cleveland, Donald Ellsworth	California	March 1963	September 1965
Clifford, Alfred Floyd	Arizona	December 1950	December 1953
Clifford, John Robert[7]	Oklahoma	July 1967	Japan–Okinawa M.
Clissold, Edward LaVaun[3]	Hawaii	March 1948	August 1949
Clissold, Irene Picknell*[4]	Hawaii	September 1948	July 1949
Cluff, Ralph Richard	Oregon	October 1960	April 1963
Collings, Howard Earl	Utah	July 1961	December 1963
Conklin, Jon Christopher	California	May 1968	Japan M.
Cook, Marion H.	Idaho	July 1954	July 1957
Cook, Mary Elaine*	Utah	September 1961	September 1963
Cook, Gary Lee	Nevada	July 1966	Japan M.
Cook, Krehl Osmond	Utah	February 1968	Japan M.
Cook, Vaughn D.	Idaho	March 1968	Japan–Okinawa M.
Coon, David Parley	Utah	September 1966	Japan M.
Cooper, Cherril Dean	Utah	February 1950	February 1953
Cosgriff Jr., John Cornelius	California	March 1965	September 1967
Cox, Neal La Vaun	Utah	June 1968	Japan M.
Crabb, Kelly Charles	Utah	February 1966	August 1968
Cragun, Wallace Frank	Utah	March 1959	September 1961
Crane, Boyd L.	Idaho	February 1951	February 1954
Cranney, Spencer Albert	Idaho	October 1963	March 1966
Crapo, Lloyd Bruce	Utah	January 1963	July 1965
Crook, Mary*	Nevada	July 1957	February 1959
Crosby, Richard V.	California	February 1967	Japan–Okinawa M.
Crump, Gary Roy	Utah	July 1957	August 1957
Cuellar, James Emil	California	January 1966	June 1968
Cundiff, Jr., James Alfred	California	September 1965	March 1968
Cutright, Craig P.	Utah	June 1968	Japan M.
DaBell, Robert Steven	Idaho	February 1966	August 1968
Dahl, Richard A.	Utah	April 1953	March 1956
Dalley, Eugene S.	Utah	March 1968	Japan M.
Dalton, Frederick R.	Utah	December 1956	October 1959
Davis, Robert Stevens	Utah	July 1957	December 1959
Davis, Larry H.	Utah	January 1960	July 1960
Davis, Allen E.	Utah	June 1967	Japan–Okinawa M.
Davis, Dale Carroll	Utah	June 1967	Japan M.

Name (* female)	Home country, U.S. state, or Japan town	Month of arrival (+estimate)	Month of departure [2] (+estimate)
Day, Paul Reuben	Utah	September 1965	March 1968
Dearden, John F.	Utah	May 1968	Japan M.
Decelle, II, Robert Eugene	California	January 1965	February 1966
Deeben, Glen Bazil	Utah	November 1965	May 1968
Deets, Albert Floyd	Tokyo	April 1963	October 1965
DeLong, Jr., Richard Peter	Minnesota	August 1966	Japan–Okinawa M.
Denham, Larry Ross[7]	Utah	July 1967	Japan M.
Densley, Vernon L.	Utah	June 1960	December 1962
Deskins, III, Lilburn Sydney	Missouri	November 1965	May 1968
Despain, Frank Johnson	Wyoming	November 1964	May 1967
Despain, Albert W.	Idaho	June 1968	Japan M.
Detton, Richard Lee	Hawaii	February 1954	Korea D.
Dickie, Jr., Edward	Canada	October 1961	April 1964
Dimick, Dennis Lynn	Utah	September 1960	March 1963
Dixon, Stephen Bruce	Colorado	October 1963	April 1966
Doba, Hideyuki	Komatsu	October 1953	September 1955
Doman, Alan James	Colorado	June 1964	December 1966
Durfee, Milo	Utah	April 1953	May 1955
Earl, Dennis Roland	Utah	November 1961	May 1964
Easthope, Clarence Laroy	Utah	June 1968	Japan–Okinawa M.
Edwards, William Foster	Utah	June 1965	December 1967
Egan, Ray Marshall	Utah	March 1962	September 1964
Eggertsen, Lars Elliott	Utah	July 1960	December 1962
Ehlert, Richard Craig	Canada	November 1966	Japan–Okinawa M.
Elder, Kathren Marie*	Washington	November 1965	November 1967
Eliason, Orville LeGrande	Utah	November 1949	November 1952
Ellis, Steven B.	Utah	February 1956	February 1959
Ellis, Klark Barry	Utah	April 1959	Korea D.
Ellis, Elaine*	Utah	May 1961	May 1963
Empey, Thomas Henry	Utah	June 1965	December 1967
Endo, Irene Masako*	Hawaii	October 1955	November 1957
Endo, Fumikata	Matsumoto	August 1956	July 1958
Enniss, Noel H.	Utah	December 1953	November 1956
Ensign, Gary Myron	California	Mach 1962	September 1964
Erickson, Louis Albin	Oregon	November 1964	May 1967
Eskelson, Mark Kekane	Utah	November 1964	May 1967
Eskelson, Gary Kekanelua	Utah	September 1965	March 1968
Eubank, Richard R.	California	May 1964	November 1966
Evans, Frederick P.	Utah	February 1968	Japan M.
Eyre, Ray Dennis	California	July 1965	December 1967
Fairbanks, Richard George	Utah	June 1965	November 1967
Farnsworth, III, Harold Davis	New Jersey	February 1968	Japan–Okinawa M.
Faught, Roy B.	Nevada	November 1961	May 1964
Fenske, Gary Leroy	Utah	June 1965	December 1967
Ferguson, Hal Goerge	Utah	October 1949	September 1952
Fillmore, Wade Wride	Utah	March 1961	October 1963
Fillmore, David Parker	Oregon	July 1964	January 1967

Annex 10. Mormon Missionaries in the Japanese and Northern Far East Missions 501

Name (* female)	Home country, U.S. state, or Japan town	Month of arrival (+estimate)	Month of departure [2] (+estimate)
Fish, Harold Bruce	Utah	May 1963	November 1965
Fletcher, Robert Waldron	Utah	February 1954	February 1957
Fletcher, Karl Samuel	Arizona	May 1956	Korea D.
Follett, Marvin D.	Arizona	April 1949	February 1952
Follett, Scott S.	Utah	June 1968	Japan–Okinawa M.
Forbes, Glora Belle*	California	July 1959	July 1961
Forsythe, Francis G. Kaoao	Hawaii	March 1959	October 1961
Foster, David Louis	Oregon	November 1963	May 1966
Fowers, Craig Emerson	Arizona	September 1964	February 1967
Fox, Lowell Jimmy	Utah	October 1956	October 1959
Fox, Russell Ellis	Wyoming	September 1966	Japan–Okinawa M.
Francis, Arthur Lynn	Utah	April 1967	Japan M.
Francom, Stephen Paul	Utah	September 1961	April 1964
Fraser, Margaret R.*	Canada	November 1961	November 1963
Freeman, Norman A.	Wyoming	February 1961	August 1963
Fry, LeeRoy	Washington	November 1958	Korea D.
Fuchigami, Ronald S.	Hawaii	August 1960	March 1963
Fuchigami, James Hisao	Hawaii	June 1966	Japan–Okinawa M.
Fujii, Shigeo	Sendai	November 1963	November 1965
Fujimoto, Tom Tomotsu	Idaho	November 1962	May 1965
Fujimoto, Kazutoshi	Hawaii	October 1966	Japan–Okinawa M.
Fujimoto, Bryan T.	Idaho	February 1968	Japan–Okinawa M.
Fukuda, Makoto	Sendai	August 1956	July 1958
Fuller, Leon Hunt	Arizona	July 1958	January 1961
Funakoshi, Mizue*	Hiroshima	April 1966	October 1967
Funk, Helen June*	Utah	July 1955	July 1957
Funk, Lewis James	Utah	November 1955	November 1958
Furniss, Robert Charles	California	March 1965	August 1967
Gahan, Geraldine Leihaulani*	Hawaii	December 1965	December 1967
Galbraith, Brian Earl	Idaho	June 1968	Japan M.
Gambles, Harry B.	Idaho	August 1953	August 1956
Gehring, Brent D.	Washington	November 1963	May 1966
Geigle, Ray Albert	Utah	September 1959	March 1962
George, Ronald Glen	Utah	March 1961	September 1963
George, Sterling Gardner	Utah	May 1961	Korea D.
Giles, Kirby L.	Utah	June 1968	Japan M.
Gill, David Raeburn	Utah	February 1961	August 1963
Gillespie, Gilbert Bryan	California	March 1965	September 1967
Ginn Jr., Edmund Chaplin	California	November 1960	June 1963
Gleed, JoAnn*	Idaho	January 1961	January 1963
Gleed, Myrle*	Idaho	May 1964	February 1966
Goaslind, Donald H.	Utah	February 1957	October 1959
Godfrey, Lyman Rulon	Utah	November 1955	November 1958
Goodey, Veldon Claude	Utah	September 1958	April 1961
Goodfellow, Nola Gay*	Utah	October 1961	October 1963
Goodman, Robert Merle	Arizona	June 1956	April 1959
Goodsell, Wayne Lewis	Idaho	June 1965	December 1967

Name (* female)	Home country, U.S. state, or Japan town	Month of arrival (+estimate)	Month of departure [2] (+estimate)
Goodwin, Robert Donald	California	October 1954	September 1957
Gorringe, Howard Ted	Utah	April 1949	June 1951
Goth, Gary Leroy	Canada	June 1964	December 1966
Gougler, George Michael	Utah	May 1964	November 1966
Goya, Kojin	Hawaii	October 1948	May 1951
Graham, Michael Clark	Washington	October 1963	April 1966
Grames, Conan Paul	Utah	April 1966	Japan M.
Grant, Bruce Kent	Nevada	August 1960	Korea D.
Grant, Royce T.	Nevada	March 1961	Korea D.
Grant, Randall E.	Utah	April 1968	Japan–Okinawa M.
Gray, John David	Arizona	June 1965	November 1965
Gray, Johnny Brian	Utah	August 1966	Japan M.
Green, Donald Wilmer	Oregon	September 1954	September 1957
Green, Steven Douglas	Utah	September 1963	March 1966
Green, Thomas Reed	Wyoming	July 1965	December 1967
Griffin, Charles Robert	California	November 1957	May 1960
Griffiths, Rex King	Utah	November 1960	May 1963
Grimmett, William Steven	Idaho	March 1966	Japan–Okinawa M.
Groberg, Delbert Holbrook	Idaho	September 1960	March 1963
Gubler, Greg	Utah	July 1963	January 1966
Gunderson, David R.	Utah	July 1958	January 1961
Gunn, Benjamin Junior	Idaho	February 1955	November 1955
Gurr, Robert Marsh	Utah	March 1967	Japan M.
Gushiken, Hideko*	Futenma	February 1967	August 1968
Gustafson, Wayne Reid	Utah	November 1964	May 1967
Haag, Thomas Ronald	Utah	November 1957	May 1960
Haag Jr., Richard Owen	California	September 1964	March 1967
Hadfield, William Elden	Utah	October 1963	March 1966
Hadley, Darrell LeRoy	Idaho	December 1950	December 1953
Hadley, Raymond B.	Utah	November 1965	May 1968
Hale, Lester Darrel	Wyoming	October 1956	October 1959
Hall, Robert Walter	California	July 1955	July 1958
Halling, Reed Denton[6]	Utah	March 1964	May 1964
Halvorsen, James M.	Washington	January 1967	Japan M.
Hamson, Marcus Lee	Utah	May 1961	November 1963
Hanamaikai, William Masato Kane	California	December 1962	June 1965
Hanamaikai, Robert K. H.	California	August 1968	Japan M.
Hansen, Peter Nelson	Idaho	February 1952	February 1955
Hansen, Jerry V.	Utah	June 1965	December 1967
Hansen, Larry Dean	Utah	January 1966	July 1968
Hanson, Leonard Chester	Canada	October 1961	April 1964
Hanuna, Thomas Tadao	Hawaii	June 1962	December 1964
Haraguchi, Wallace Kazuo	Hawaii	October 1961	April 1964
Harbican, James Lee	California	December 1959	June 1962
Harrell, Jr., Mason Douglas	Nebraska	December 1962	June 1965
Harris, Gene*	Utah	August 1952	August 1954
Harris, Gaylen L.	Utah	July 1958	January 1961

Annex 10. Mormon Missionaries in the Japanese and Northern Far East Missions

Name (* female)	Home country, U.S. state, or Japan town	Month of arrival (+estimate)	Month of departure [2] (+estimate)
Harris, Lamont Dee	Utah	September 1958	April 1961
Harris, Darryl Wayne	Idaho	July 1961	Korea D.
Harris, Alan Reed	Idaho	March 1966	Japan M.
Harvey, Bruce Douglas	Utah	November 1961	May 1964
Hasegawa, George M.	Canada	July 1960	January 1963
Hashimoto, Alma*	Hawaii	December 1955	August 1957
Haslam, Larry O.	Utah	October 1953	August 1956
Hatch, Sheridan G.	Utah	November 1950	December 1953
Hatch, Christopher Randal	Arizona	July 1965	January 1968
Hatch, William James	Maryland	September 1965	March 1968
Hauritz, Lionel David	Australia	April 1964	November 1966
Hawkes, Steven Jay	Utah	March 1968	Japan–Okinawa M.
Hawkins, Farell Ray	Utah	October 1957	Korea D.
Hawkley, Daniel Leland	Idaho	November 1963	May 1966
Hayasaka, Takashi	Sendai	June 1968	Japan–Okinawa M.
Hayashi, Hideo Howard	California	October 1961	April 1964
Hayashi, Keiko*	Sapporo	September 1966	Japan M.
Hayes, Robert E.[6]	California	October 1958	July 1959
Heaton, Wayne G.	Utah	December 1960	June 1963
Heggie, Bruce Garner	Canada	February 1963	August 1965
Heiner, Daniel Glenn	Wyoming	March 1968	Japan M.
Heise, Donald Paul	Utah	April 1954	May 1957
Henderson, Jay Willie	California	March 1962	September 1964
Herlin, Wayne R.	Utah	July 1949	July 1952
Herrick, Michael Vern	Utah	April 1966	Japan–Okinawa M.
Hess, Leanora Ellen*	Utah	July 1961	July 1963
Hicken, Donald Clegg	Utah	August 1962	March 1965
Higa, Lily Yuriko*	Hawaii	November 1956	November 1958
Higa, Rose S.*	Hawaii	April 1958	April 1960
Higa, Kenneth Kosuke[8]	Hawaii	August 1960	March 1963
Higgins, John C.	Nevada	October 1954	December 1956
Higgins, Richard Ames	Utah	January 1967	Japan–Okinawa M.
Hill, Roy P.	Utah	February 1951	February 1954
Hill, Donald Bruce	California	November 1959	Korea D.
Hill, Allen Flake	Utah	July 1965	January 1968
Hills, Ronald Cree	Utah	May 1956	May 1959
Hilton Jr., Kenneth Clyde	Utah	March 1962	September 1964
Hilton, James Harvey	Utah	June 1963	December 1965
Hinchcliff, Guy Howard	Utah	November 1966	Japan M.
Hironaka, Timothy Glenn	Canada	December 1965	June 1968
Hisatake, Thelma*	Hawaii	July 1953	August 1955
Hobbs, Clint Lorenzo	Idaho	June 1967	Japan–Okinawa M.
Hoffmann, Albert William	Utah	July 1959	Korea D.
Hoggan, James C.	Idaho	December 1949	December 1952
Hoggan, Stephen Drummond	Idaho	November 1960	May 1963
Hoki, Murray Mitsuo	Hawaii	October 1954	November 1957
Holbrook, Paul Ward	Utah	October 1958	April 1961

Name (* female)	Home country, U.S. state, or Japan town	Month of arrival (+estimate)	Month of departure [2] (+estimate)
Holbrook, Charles J.	Idaho	March 1966	August 1968
Holdaway, Richard M.	Utah	June 1964	December 1966
Holm, James Briant	Oregon	September 1966	Japan–Okinawa M.
Honda, Yasohachi	Osaka	June 1968	Japan–Okinawa M.
Hoover, Mark William	Utah	January 1955	February 1958
Horikami, Tamaru	Hawaii	May 1954	April 1957
Horman, Gerald De La Haye	Utah	March 1954	February 1957
Horton, Gary J.	Utah	September 1959	March 1962
Howell Jr., James Russell	Utah	September 1961	March 1964
Howell, Jr., Barton John	New York	September 1963	March 1966
Hudson, Robert J.	Idaho	September 1964	March 1967
Hug, Marilyn B.*	Utah	February 1957	February 1959
Hulet, Oscar Kent	Utah	June 1950	June 1953
Hulme, John Edward	California	September 1965	March 1968
Hult, Merle Blythe[8]	California	April 1960	November 1962
Humphries, Len C.	Idaho	December 1950	December 1953
Hunsaker, Weldon Reuel	Utah	July 1961	January 1964
Idehara, Junko*	Nagoya	May 1957	May 1959
Igarashi, Amy Keiko*	Hawaii	April 1950	April 1952+
Igarashi, Toshiro	Shibata	May 1953	March 1955
Ikeda, Joe Noboru	Idaho	November 1958	June 1961
Ikeda, Thomas T.	Idaho	November 1962	May 1965
Ikegami, David T.	Hawaii	September 1952	September 1954
Imai, Kazuo	Tokyo	November 1952	November 1954
Imai, Tomiko*	Shibata	November 1954+	May 1956+
Inokuchi, Carl Hisashi	Hawaii	May 1954	November 1956
Inouye, Ronald Noriyuki	Utah	July 1960	January 1963
Inouye, Dillon Kazuyuki	Utah	June 1964+	November 1966
Inouye, Jay Dee	Utah	April 1968	Japan M.
Isaac, JoAnn R.*	Utah	February 1957	February 1959
Isaacs, Clyde Kanuumealani	Hawaii	October 1950	September 1953 (died)
Ishida, Chieko*	Kanazawa	August 1954	February 1956
Ishii, Ronald S.	California	April 1968	Japan–Okinawa M.
Ishikawa, Osamu[9]	Fukuoka	February 1966	July 1967
Ishizaka, Koichi	Tokyo	December 1966	Japan–Okinawa M.
Isomura, Masayoshi	Nagoya	March 1964	March 1966
Ito, Robert Kiichi	Utah	May 1966	Japan M.
Ito, Masako*	Sapporo	December 1967	Japan–Okinawa M.
Ito, Ami*	Nagoya	January 1968	Japan M.
Ito, Tetsuji	Yokohama	June 1968	Japan–Okinawa M.
Iwaasa, Jeaune	Canada	October 1948	February 1951
Iwaasa, David Brian	Canada	December 1967	Japan–Okinawa M.
Iwamura, Noriyuki	Hawaii	May 1951	May 1954
Jack, Alvin W.	New Mexico	December 1955	November 1958
Jackson, Jr., Udell Thomas	Utah	June 1965	December 1967
Jacobsen, Heber Smith	Utah	November 1965	May 1968
Jacobson, Ross Allan	Utah	March 1966	Japan M.

Annex 10. Mormon Missionaries in the Japanese and Northern Far East Missions

Name (* female)	Home country, U.S. state, or Japan town	Month of arrival (+estimate)	Month of departure [2] (+estimate)
Jaggi, Wayne George	Utah	September 1966	Japan–Okinawa M.
James, Thomas A.	Utah	November 1950	November 1953
James, Morris H.	California	October 1960	Korea D.
Jameson, Roger Marx	Utah	September 1965	March 1968
Jansen, Anthon Howard	Idaho	July 1965	January 1968
Jarvis, Gideon Stanford	Utah	February 1951	February 1954
Jaynes, Lavard Dee	Utah	May 1963	November 1965
Jenkins, Jack R.	Washington	January 1959	Korea D.
Jenkins, Deane Grant	Utah	August 1965	February 1968
Jenkins, Edith Connie*	Idaho	December 1966	Japan–Okinawa M.
Jensen, Wendell W.	Utah	July 1950	July 1953+
Jensen, Douglas Nile	Utah	July 1954	July 1957
Jensen, Terry Kent	Utah	May 1963	November 1965
Jensen, Douglas Evans	Utah	October 1963	April 1966
Jensen, Stewart Allen	Idaho	March 1966	Japan M.
Jeo, Eleanor*	Idaho	August 1960	August 1962
Johnson, Archie C.	Idaho	December 1953	April 1956
Johnson, Robert Allen	California	November 1959	May 1962
Johnson, William David	Illinois	November 1963	May 1966
Johnston, William David	Utah	December 1964	December 1966
Johnson, Geraldine*	Utah	December 1964	December 1966
Johnson, Robert Donald	California	September 1965	March 1968
Johnson, Bradley Wayne	Minnesota	September 1966	Japan–Okinawa M.
Johnson, Norman Kay	Idaho	September 1966	Japan M.
Johnson, II, Blaine H.	Utah	May 1968	Japan–Okinawa M.
Jones, Jr., James Jackson	Hawaii	May 1954	August 1957
Jones, Ralph Clifford	Utah	October 1956	November 1959
Jones, Stanford Garth	Utah	January 1961	July 1963
Jones, Kenneth Oscar	Utah	January 1963	September 1964
Jones, Bruce David	Utah	September 1965	March 1968
Jones, Robert Clive	Nevada	September 1966	Japan M.
Kaanaana, Kahanamau*	Hawaii	May 1951	June 1953
Kagoshima, Tami*	Sanjo	November 1954	May 1956+
Kahananui, Jr., Alfred Kelii	Hawaii	July 1960	January 1963
Kailikea, Wayne Mark	Hawaii	December 1960	June 1963
Kajiyama, Katsuhiro	Hiroshima	September 1959	January 1962
Kakazu, Dwight Manabu	Hawaii	June 1965	December 1967
Kaku, James Isao	Hawaii	July 1963	January 1966
Kalama, Samuel	Hawaii	April 1949	June 1951
Kamekona, Daniel K.	Hawaii	December 1955	November 1958
Kamiya, Tomiyasu	Asahikawa	August 1956	July 1958
Kanahale, George S.	Hawaii	October 1950	May 1954
Kaneko, Mihoko*	Nagoya	June 1954	December 1955
Kaneko, Kenichi David	Utah	August 1960	March 1963
Kanekoa, Curtis Kealoha	Hawaii	February 1961	August 1963
Kaneshiro, Hatsue*	Hawaii	May 1953	May 1955
Kanetsuna, Hideo	Hawaii	April 1949	June 1952
Kapololu, William K.	Hawaii	September 1967	Japan M.

Name (* female)	Home country, U.S. state, or Japan town	Month of arrival (+estimate)	Month of departure [2] (+estimate)
Karaki, Gordon Wataru	Canada	August 1960	May 1962
Karasawa, Kazuko*	Matsumoto	April 1954	November 1955+
Kartchner, Ila Rae*	Arizona	November 1961	November 1963
Kashiwa, Florence*	Hawaii	July 1953	August 1955
Katsuda, Peggy Sumie*	Hawaii	October 1955	November 1957
Kaui, Lorraine Waimaka*	Hawaii	April 1950	April 1952
Kawai, David Yoshio	California	July 1964	January 1967
Kawasaki, Mitsuru	Fukuoka	August 1953	December 1953
Kekaula, Mary*	Hawaii	May 1953	November 1954
Kekauoha, George W.	Hawaii	August 1952	August 1955
Kekoolani, Amy C. K.*	Hawaii	August 1952	August 1954
Kekoolani, Charles Paleiholani	Hawaii	December 1955	November 1956
Kenney, Kenneth B.	Utah	October 1950	September 1953
Kiilau, Charles [10]	Hawaii	June 1966	June 1968
Kiilau, Haruko M.*[10]	Hawaii	June 1966	June 1968
Kikuchi, Yoshihiko	Muroran	May 1961	November 1963
Kilauano, Carolyn Uluwehi*	Hawaii	July 1956	July 1958
Killian, Kenneth Glen	Utah	November 1964	May 1967
Killpack, J. Duane	Utah	May 1963	November 1965
Kimball, Newell Elliott	Utah	May 1956	Korea D.
King, DeRees	Utah	June 1957	December 1959
Kingsbury, Frances Ilene*	Utah	March 1959	April 1961
Kishigami, Hide*	Otaru	July 1952	June 1954
Kiyabu, Richard Hideo	Hawaii	June 1966	Japan M.
Kiyosumi, Yoko*	Matsumoto	July 1965	December 1965
Knowlton, III, Hooper	Utah	June 1965	December 1967
Kobayashi, Marvin Katsuki	California	July 1963	January 1966
Kochi, Nancy*	Hawaii	September 1954	October 1956
Koga, Lincoln Kunito	Hawaii	October 1961	April 1964
Koga, Donald Harumi	Hawaii	February 1965	August 1967
Koga, Gary Msayuki	Hawaii	June 1966	Japan M.
Kogure, Fumie*	Yanai	December 1955	July 1957
Komatsu, Adney Yoshio[3]	Hawaii	July 1965	July 1968
Komatsu, Judy Nobue[4]	Hawaii	July 1965	July 1968
Koolau, Dorothy Anna*	Hawaii	April 1950	April 1952
Korth, Mary Rose*	Idaho	July 1961	July 1963
Krauss, Walter Kenneth	Arizona	May 1957	November 1959
Krueger, Roice N.[7]	Utah	July 1967	Japan–Okinawa M.
Kua, Alexander Palmer	Hawaii	January 1959	August 1961
Kubo, Kyoko*	Nishinomiya	December 1967	Japan M.
Kubota, James	Canada	December 1951	March 1954
Kwak, Richard D. S.	Utah	July 1950	July 1953
Laimana, Paul Kalei	Hawaii	July 1960	September 1962
Lamb, Kenneth Eldon	Utah	June 1965	December 1967
Lambert, Glen Lionel	Utah	November 1961	May 1964
Lamph, Alan Neil	California	August 1960	February 1963
Lang, Janet*	Nevada	February 1966	January 1968

Annex 10. Mormon Missionaries in the Japanese and Northern Far East Missions

Name (* female)	Home country, U.S. state, or Japan town	Month of arrival (+estimate)	Month of departure [2] (+estimate)
Langston, Lynn Connor	Arizona	April 1963	October 1965
Langston, Jay L.	Arizona	February 1967	Japan M.
Larkin, Scott Francis	Utah	June 1965	December 1967
Larsen, Evan Allan	Utah	February 1955	February 1958
Larsen, Wallace Junior	Utah	November 1961	May 1964
Larsen, Steven H.	Utah	August 1963	February 1966
Larsen, Larry James	Wyoming	September 1965	March 1968
Larson, Gordon Thomas	Arizona	September 1961	March 1964
Larson, Kerry B.	Louisiana	August 1964	January 1967
Lassig, Don Peter	Utah	June 1958	January 1961
Law, Delmont C.	Idaho	December 1956	October 1959
Laws, Gordon D.	Texas	March 1968	Japan M.
Lea, Gary Wayne	Canada	January 1967	Japan M.
League, William Donaldson	Hawaii	November 1966	Japan M.
Leasure, John R.	California	May 1961	Korea D.
Leatherman, Richard D.	Utah	April 1966	Japan M.
Leavitt Jr., Donnell Eugene	Utah	July 1965	December 1967
Lee, Young Bum	Korea	September 1956	Korea D.
Lee, Janice*	Utah	February 1961	February 1963
Lee, Ronald Eugene	Washington	July 1962	January 1965
Lee, Terrence Delbert	Utah	January 1963	July 1965
Lee, Michael Robert	Arizona	February 1963	August 1965
Lee, Dennis Maclay	Canada	November 1964	May 1967
Lee, Jr., Barney Lindley	Oregon	March 1966	Japan M.
Lee, John David	Utah	July 1967	Japan M.
Leifson, June*	Hawaii	October 1959	October 1961
Leishman, Garth Waldrum	Idaho	July 1957	January 1960
Lewis, Roger Pierpont	Utah	March 1962	September 1964
Lewis, William Claude	Utah	January 1963	July 1965
Leymaster, Craig E.	Idaho	June 1968	Japan–Okinawa M.
Lindsey, Thelma Lulu*	Hawaii	August 1961	August 1963
Linn, David R.	Utah	July 1965	January 1968
Livingston, Parley J.	Utah	October 1950	September 1953
Livingston, Marcia Ann*	Massachusetts	November 1964	November 1966
Longman, Allen Thatcher	Utah	April 1957	June 1957
Lowry, Steven Douglas	Idaho	May 1961	November 1963
Ludlow, Grent Greg	Utah	August 1968	Japan M.
Lui, Hilton Joseph	Hawaii	August 1961	February 1964
Luke, Carl Eugene	Florida	November 1960	Korea D.
Lundberg, Don C.	California	November 1953	July 1957
Lundberg, John Peter[7]	California	August 1961	October 1963
Lyman, Joseph Hansen	Utah	September 1963	March 1966
Mabey, Thomas T.	Utah	March 1968	Japan–Okinawa M.
MacBeth, Dennis R.	Utah	March 1968	Japan M.
MacKay, Martin	Oregon	October 1967	Japan M.
Mackelprang, Joseph William	Utah	December 1954	November 1957
Mackley, James Reed	Idaho	September 1954	September 1957

Name (* female)	Home country, U.S. state, or Japan town	Month of arrival (+estimate)	Month of departure [2] (+estimate)
Madsen, Veneta*	Utah	September 1961	September 1963
Madsen, Michael Philip	Florida	July 1963	January 1966
Madsen, Edward Keith	Utah	January 1965	June 1967
Maetani, Howard Hidemi	Hawaii	August 1967	Japan–Okinawa M.
Maezawa, Keietsu	Tokyo	August 1956	February 1958
Makahi, Merlin Kaimiola	Hawaii	August 1959	March 1962
Makahi, Nonaina Hoopili[8]	Hawaii	May 1960	December 1962
Malo, David Kalanikoa	California	April 1959	October 1961
Mancini, Armen Nicholas	California	June 1965	December 1967
Mano, Kenneth H.	Utah	November 1958	June 1961
Mano, Ronald Makoto	Utah	November 1961	May 1964
Mano, Richard M.	Utah	October 1967	Japan–Okinawa M.
Marker, Melvin Maddock	Utah	March 1963	September 1965
Markham, Ben Stephen	Utah	March 1965	September 1967
Marlowe, Kent W.	Utah	July 1958	January 1961
Marlowe, Roy Hilding	Utah	July 1961	December 1963
Marsh, Don W.[7]	Utah	July 1967	Japan M.
Martinez, Steven Jon	California	December 1965	June 1968
Marx, Gary Ervin	Utah	November 1960	April 1963
Mather, Stephen S.	Utah	July 1965	December 1967
Matsui, Kazue*	Tokyo	February 1964	August 1965
Matsumori, Douglas	Utah	November 1966	Japan M.
Matsumoto, Masao	Osaka	September 1952	September 1954
Matthews, Thomas P.	Idaho	June 1968	Japan–Okinawa M.
Maughan, Peter Kent	Utah	February 1957	September 1959
Maughan, Arlene*	Utah	July 1961	July 1963
Mauss, Vinal G.[3]	California	August 1949	October 1953
Mauss, Ethel L.*[4]	California	August 1949	October 1953
Mauss, Margueriete L.*	Tokyo	September 1950	September 1952
Maw, George Glayde	Utah	March 1960	Korea D.
McAllister, Jr., Edmond Luther	Arizona	September 1965	March 1968
McArthur, James A.	Utah	August 1963	February 1966
McCann, Gary R.[6]	Utah	March 1961	February 1962
McClellan Jr., Warren Eugene	Washington	January 1960	July 1962
McClellan, Sandra	Illinois	August 1968	Japan–Okinawa M.
McCook, William D.	Arizona	June 1968	Japan M.
McCune, George Moody	Utah	September 1963	March 1966
McDaniel, Wayne Proctor[5]	Utah	June 1948	February 1951
McKay, David Alden	Utah	January 1966	July 1968
McKell, Kent B.	Utah	February 1967	Japan M.
McNaughton, Mary*	Hawaii	October 1959	October 1961
McNeil, Jeffrey E.[7]	Utah	July 1967	Japan M.
Mead, Jr., Hyrum Anderson	Colorado	September 1966	Japan M.
Meng, Richard S.	Idaho	June 1965	December 1967
Mesquita, Ida Kahaumeliala*	Hawaii	June 1960	March 1962
Messinger, Steven S.	Utah	August 1968	Japan M.
Meurer, Dennis James	California	November 1964	May 1967

Annex 10. Mormon Missionaries in the Japanese and Northern Far East Missions

Name (* female)	Home country, U.S. state, or Japan town	Month of arrival (+estimate)	Month of departure [2] (+estimate)
Meyer, Sterling Drake	Utah	September 1966	Japan–Okinawa M.
Meyers, Bruce Kunio	Hawaii	October 1957	April 1960
Meyers, Sylvia Lei*	Hawaii	September 1963	September 1965
Miike, Stanford Sadao	Hawaii	October 1961	April 1964
Mikami, Miako*	Utah	March 1962	May 1964
Mikami, Sumiko*	Utah	March 1962	May 1964
Miles, Lynn W. Child	Arizona	June 1965	December 1967
Miles, Bowen Douglas	Utah	November 1966	Japan M.
Miller, Don LeRoy	Idaho	December 1953	November 1956
Miller, Harold Lewis	Utah	July 1954	May 1957
Miller, Donald Thomas	Idaho	March 1961	September 1963
Miller, Gordon Vernon	Idaho	August 1963	February 1966
Miller, Marilyn*	Utah	August 1965	July 1967
Miller, Terryl G.	Utah	July 1966	Japan–Okinawa M.
Millet, Robert William	Utah	March 1966	Japan M.
Mills, Richardson Pua	Hawaii	September 1959	March 1962
Millward, Gene Cleon	Idaho	June 1950	June 1953
Millward, Jr., Franklin Curtis	California	April 1954	March 1955
Miura, Merrill Sadami	Hawaii	June 1966	Japan M.
Miura, Kaye*	California	September 1967	Japan–Okinawa M.
Miya, Akiko*	Tokyo	April 1954	November 1955
Miyamoto, Given K.	Hawaii	September 1967	Japan M.
Miyara, Takeshi	Naha	December 1966	Japan M.
Miyasaki, Rodney Alan	Idaho	September 1965	March 1968
Mizukawa, John Hideo	Utah	April 1966	Japan–Okinawa M.
Moffat, Craig M.	Utah	June 1967	Japan–Okinawa M.
Moffat, Gregory M.	Idaho	June 1968	Japan M.
Moffitt, Jr., Howard	Utah	July 1954	July 1957
Moikeha, David Hoolanaikamanao	Hawaii	August 1952	August 1955
Moikeha, Mona Amy Hooipoipo*	Hawaii	July 1963	July 1965
Monson, Glenn A.	Utah	August 1968	Japan M.
Moon, Lamont Willis	Utah	October 1961	April 1964
Moore, Clara Louise*	Utah	July 1956	July 1958
Morgan, Jack C.	Utah	December 1953	February 1957
Morgan, Jon Leo	Utah	March 1962	September 1964
Morgan, Richard Scott	Utah	April 1967	Japan M.
Morgan, Michael J.	Utah	June 1968	Japan–Okinawa M.
Mori, Steven Hiroyuki	Utah	October 1962	April 1965
Morikawa, Shirley Hanako*	Hawaii	July 1957	August 1959
Moriyama, Sherwin R.	Canada	October 1967	Japan–Okinawa M.
Morris, Stewart Mann	California	May 1964	November 1966
Morrison, Craig L.[7]	Utah	July 1967	Japan–Okinawa M.
Morse, Colldene Hatch	Utah	September 1958	February 1961
Moss, Thomas Elmer	Idaho	December 1957+	July 1960
Moss, James Edgar	Utah	September 1965	March 1968
Mouritsen, Maren M.*	Utah	Mary 1962	May 1964
Mulnix, Russell James	Illinois	March 1965	September 1967

Name (* female)	Home country, U.S. state, or Japan town	Month of arrival (+estimate)	Month of departure [2] (+estimate)
Munk, Keith M.	Utah	June 1950	June 1953
Murakami, Toshiro	Tokyo	December 1951	June 1953
Murakami, Yukie*	California	September 1957+	September 1959
Murakami, Chihiro*	Fukuoka	November 1963	December 1964
Musick, Richard L.	California	February 1968	Japan M.
Nacey, James Jensen	Utah	January 1963	July 1965
Nagata, Terrel Teruo	Ohio	March 1963	September 1965
Nagata, Byron I.	Utah	September 1966	Japan–Okinawa M.
Nakagawa, Kiyoko*	Tokyo	March 1967	Japan–Okinawa M.
Nakanishi, Sharon Naomi*	Hawaii	September 1967	Japan–Okinawa M.
Nakano, Kyubei	Shibata	April 1953	March 1955
Nakasone, Wayne K.	Hawaii	September 1967	Japan–Okinawa M.
Nakata, Constance*	Hawaii	September 1963	September 1965
Nako, Aldon Katayuki	Hawaii	February 1966	August 1968
Naluai, Robert G. K.	Hawaii	November 1957	May 1960
Naluai, Calvin Blake Kakela	Hawaii	October 1963	April 1966
Nanjo, Hiroko*	Tokyo	February 1962	February 1964
Nanto, Robert Masayuki	Washington	January 1958	July 1960
Nanto, Dick K.	Washington	October 1960	April 1963
Naumu, Alvin Kalaialii	Hawaii	October 1961	April 1964
Naumu, Ronald Nohili	Hawaii	July 1965	January 1968
Nebeker, Gordon Alston	Utah	June 1965	December 1967
Needham, Ruth K.*	Hawaii	April 1949	April 1951
Nelson, Daniel E.	Utah	December 1948	April 1951
Nelson, James Clair	Utah	July 1961	December 1963
Nelson, Brent Alan	Utah	June 1965	December 1967
Nelson, Keith L.	Utah	May 1968	Japan M.
Nelson, Mark R.	Utah	August 1968	Japan–Okinawa M.
Newman, Claude Wayne	Idaho	July 1956	Korea D.
Nicholes, Michael Erin	Utah	September 1961	Korea D.
Nichols, Murray Leo	South Carolina	December 1948	September 1951
Nielsen, Ronald Kalmar	Idaho	February 1962	Korea D.
Nielsen, Floyd Jens	Utah	November 1965	May 1968
Nielson, Jan Lyle	Utah	January 1963	July 1965
Nihipali, Clyde Kauluwahi	Hawaii	January 1966	July 1968
Nii, Kiyoshi	Idaho	April 1950	August 1952
Niiyama, Yasuo	Yanai	May 1963	May 1965
Nilsson, William Bert	Canada	October 1962	April 1965
Nishihara, Katsuko*	Hiroshima	April 1966	October 1967
Nishimoto, Michiko*	Kyoto	August 1953	November 1953
Nishimoto, Kenneth	Hawaii	October 1961	April 1964
Nishimoto, Castle Kei	California	February 1966	August 1968
Nishimoto, Spencer Ken	Florida	September 1967	Japan–Okinawa M.
Noble, Dora Annie*	Utah	February 1952	January 1954
Noda, Kazue*	Kanazawa	February 1956	April 1957
Noda, Yoshie*	Kanazawa	July 1957	January 1959
Noonchester, Michael Lee	California	January 1965	July 1967

Annex 10. Mormon Missionaries in the Japanese and Northern Far East Missions

Name (* female)	Home country, U.S. state, or Japan town	Month of arrival (+estimate)	Month of departure [2] (+estimate)
Norman, Vernal Garth	California	October 1956	October 1959
Norman, James Sidney	Utah	November 1961	May 1964
Norton, Harold E.	California	November 1949	December 1952
Norton, Kenneth Leroy	California	May 1962	October 1964
Norton, Donald Brion	California	June 1962	January 1965
Oakey, Russell W.	Idaho	April 1951	October 1953
O'Brien, John Dee	Idaho	June 1968	Japan M.
Ogden, Larry Filburn	Michigan	November 1961	May 1964
Ohumukini, Jr., Henry K.	Hawaii	July 1960	January 1963
Okabe, Gerald K.	Hawaii	July 1949	August 1952
Okahata, Meriyo*	California	November 1959	November 1961
Okauchi, Kooji[5]	Illinois	June 1948	February 1951
Okawa, Ruth Hisayo*	Hawaii	July 1961+	July 1963
Okawa, Marion S.*	Hawaii	March 1963	March 1965
Okawa, Faith Marie*	Hawaii	September 1963	September 1965
Okawa, Naomi Sue*	Hawaii	August 1966	August 1968
Okawa, Haruko*	Tokyo	August 1967	Japan M.
Okimoto, Bessie Yukiko*	Hawaii	October 1948	June 1950
Okura, Sanford Katsuji	Hawaii	June 1966	Japan M.
Oldfield, Louie Leopold	Australia	February 1968	Japan–Okinawa M.
Oldham, Hugh Lynn	Utah	April 1949	February 1952
Oldroyd, Mark Thomas	Utah	February 1958	September 1960
Oler, Douglas E.	Idaho	August 1968	Japan–Okinawa M.
Olsen, Joy McAllister*	Utah	May 1956	May 1958
Olsen, David Legrand	Utah	September 1960	March 1963
Olsen, Richard Reed	Idaho	February 1951	September 1953
Olson, Dallas Stanford	Hawaii	June 1962	December 1964
Olson, Wesley Sheldon	Idaho	November 1966	Japan M.
Omura, Yoichiro	Osaka	May 1953	December 1953
Oniki, Ben	Michigan	September 1953	August 1956
Ono, Kikuyo Eleanor*	Hawaii	April 1953	May 1955
Oppie, William Harry	Colorado	November 1949	November 1952
Orme, Larry Don	Idaho	April 1955	Korea D.
Orton, Kenneth J.	Utah	July 1958	January 1961
Osborn, Robert T.	Utah	July 1954	June 1957
Osborn, Bonner Douglas	Utah	December 1961	June 1964
Oshima, Eugene Torao	Hawaii	July 1960	January 1963
Ostergaard, Richard Floy	Utah	April 1966	Japan–Okinawa M.
Otake, Richard Susumu	Hawaii	March 1964	September 1966
Otsuka, Masaji	Yokohama	November 1952	September 1954
Ousbye, Donald Henry	California	November 1960	May 1963
Owens, Richard R.	Utah	October 1961	April 1964
Paalani, Aldous Kawailani	Hawaii	September 1965	February 1968
Pabst, Kathie*	Utah	March 1967	Japan–Okinawa M.
Pack, David Keith	Utah	July 1955	July 1958
Packer, Barlow Lamont	Utah	June 1960	December 1962
Packham, Michael Leroy	Idaho	November 1963	May 1966

Name (* female)	Home country, U.S. state, or Japan town	Month of arrival (+estimate)	Month of departure [2] (+estimate)
Page, Robert Dee	Utah	July 1961	January 1964
Palmer, Gary Melvin	Utah	September 1960	March 1963
Palmer, Arthur Arvin	Arizona	October 1960	April 1963
Parahi, Raiha June*	New Zealand	February 1963	February 1965
Parker, Frances*	Hawaii	April 1949	April 1951
Parkin, Robert Hill	Utah	December 1956	October 1959
Parkinson, Robert Hyrum	Idaho	August 1959	Korea D.
Parkinson, Randall L.	Utah	August 1968	Japan–Okinawa M.
Parrish, David F.	Utah	February 1951	February 1954
Parrish, Richard Udy	Utah	November 1960	Korea D.
Parton, Grant	Australia	October 1962	April 1965
Patterson, Kim William	Oregon	August 1968	Japan M.
Payne, Ila Marie*	Idaho	April 1960	May 1962
Peihopa, Thomas T.	New Zealand	February 1968	Japan–Okinawa M.
Perkins, George W.	Utah	October 1957	May 1960
Perkins, Jan Thomas	California	August 1965	February 1968
Perley Jr., Louis Lafayette	Colorado	March 1961	September 1963
Perry, III, William Oliver	Virginia	September 1965	March 1968
Peters, Heinie	Hawaii	July 1961	January 1964
Petersen, Eugene Gary	Utah	July 1961	October 1962
Petersen, Robert Dale	Idaho	November 1965	July 1967
Peterson, Dallas	Utah	June 1950	December 1952
Peterson IV, James M.	Texas	November 1961	May 1964
Peterson, Clifton Kent	Utah	March 1963	September 1965
Peterson, Dennis Roger	Utah	September 1964	March 1967
Peterson, Franklin Lawrence	Idaho	March 1966	Japan–Okinawa M.
Peterson, Forrest Brent	New Mexico	July 1966	Japan M.
Peterson, Bruce R.	Idaho	September 1966	Japan–Okinawa M.
Peterson, Steven J.	Utah	August 1968	Japan M.
Pexton, Ronald D.	Utah	October 1950	October 1953
Phillipps, Ray	Utah	October 1957	April 1960
Phillips, Douglas R.	Tokyo	November 1950	December 1953
Pierce, Larry Jack	Utah	November 1965	May 1968
Pincock, Lorin Dwight	Utah	December 1962	June 1965
Pokini, La Verla D. K.*	Hawaii	July 1955	July 1957
Pokipala, Allen Haulani	Hawaii	June 1963	December 1965
Pond, Nicholas Jensen	Utah	August 1965	February 1968
Pope, Karl Theodore	Utah	July 1957	January 1960
Poppleton, Gary Stennett	Utah	November 1965	May 1968
Porter, Larry Lamar	Idaho	December 1957	May 1960
Porter, Richard Gordon	Utah	December 1957+	July 1960
Porter, Rulon Nathan	Wyoming	January 1958	Korea D.
Porter, Gary Sargent	Idaho	March 1966	August 1968
Powell, Don Gayle	Idaho	March 1954	Korea D.
Powell, Richard R.[7]	Idaho	July 1967	Japan–Okinawa M.
Price, Harrison Theodore[5]	Utah	June 1948	January 1951
Price, Raymond Culver[5]	Utah	June 1948	April 1951

Annex 10. Mormon Missionaries in the Japanese and Northern Far East Missions 513

Name (* female)	Home country, U.S. state, or Japan town	Month of arrival (+estimate)	Month of departure [2] (+estimate)
Priddis, Robert Charles	California	July 1965	January 1968
Priest, Richard Harold	Idaho	July 1963	January 1966
Prisbrey, Keith Arlo	Utah	June 1965	December 1967
Przybyla, Michael John	California	June 1965	November 1967
Puha, Elizabeth*	Hawaii	July 1951	July 1953
Pule, Sarah Kekelaokalani*	Hawaii	July 1949	June 1951
Purdon, David John	Australia	July 1962	February 1965
Pusey, Eugene Harvey	Utah	February 1950	February 1953
Pyper, Richard L.	Utah	October 1967	Japan–Okinawa M.
Rampton, Kent Thomas	Utah	February 1963	August 1965
Randall, Steven K.	Utah	June 1968	Japan M.
Rasmussen, Dale W.	Idaho	July 1958	Korea D.
Rasmussen, John LeVar	Utah	March 1963	September 1965
Rasmussen, David John	Utah	May 1966	Japan–Okinawa M.
Ray Jr., Earnest Lee	Arizona	March 1960+	August 1962
Reed Jr., Cal Waddoups	Utah	October 1958	April 1961
Reese, Kenton Henry	Utah	October 1963	April 1966
Rhodes, Dennis L.	Utah	August 1968	Japan–Okinawa M.
Richards, Rex Alton	Utah	March 1961	September 1963
Richards, Steven Lee	Utah	June 1963	December 1965
Richards, Graham James	Australia	May 1965	November 1967
Richards, Steven C.	New Zealand	August 1968	Japan M.
Richins, Gerald Ward	Arizona	July 1963	January 1966
Riddle, Mark Alfred	Utah	July 1965	January 1968
Ridge, Robin W.	Utah	August 1967	Japan–Okinawa M.
Rima, William E.	Utah	October 1960	July 1961
Rimmasch, Dwight	Utah	August 1968	Japan–Okinawa M.
Riser, Scott Ward	Utah	November 1961	May 1964
Robbins, Jr., Burtis F.	Utah	February 1951	February 1954
Robertson, Hilton A.[3]	Utah	October 1953	November 1955
Robertson, Hazel M.*[4]	Utah	October 1953	November 1955
Robertson, Robert Douglas	Oregon	February 1954	February 1957
Robertson, David Franklin	Utah	January 1961	July 1963
Robertson, James W.	Arizona	February 1967	Japan M.
Rodgers, Steven Barlow	Utah	August 1962	March 1965
Romney Jr., Ianthus Barlow	Texas	March 1961	September 1963
Roper, Gary L.	Utah	June 1954	June 1957
Ross, Beverly Elaine*	Utah	September 1961	September 1963
Ross, Kenneth Richard	Utah	June 1968	Japan–Okinawa M.
Rowe, Glenn Neil	Washington	February 1968	Japan–Okinawa M.
Russell, Robert Allan	Utah	October 1963	March 1966
Rytting, Charles Brent	Utah	February 1961	February 196
Sabey, John Wayne	Utah	July 1960	January 1963
Sadler, Kent Joseph	Utah	May 1961	November 1963
Saito, Yuko*	Takasaki	January 1954	August 1955
Sakata, Kimiaki	Hawaii	October 1948	April 1951
Sakota, Kenneth Tadayoshi	Idaho	August 1966	Japan M.

Name (* female)	Home country, U.S. state, or Japan town	Month of arrival (+estimate)	Month of departure [2] (+estimate)
Sanborn, Rodney Roy	Hawaii	March 1962	September 1964
Sanders, Michael Ray Edwards	Utah	August 1965	February 1968
Sanderson, Eric M.	Utah	August 1968	Japan–Okinawa M.
Sasaki, Yaeko*	Sendai	June 1957	January 1959
Sasaki, Raymond Y.	Hawaii	August 1959	March 1962
Sato, Esther Nobuko*	Hawaii	July 1956	June 1958
Saunders, Robert Loughton	Utah	November 1960	Korea D.
Sawyer, David Archie	Wyoming	November 1962	May 1965
Schenck, Dee L.	Utah	July 1958	January 1961
Schroeder, Bryant Joseph	Utah	January 1963	July 1965
Schultz, Harry Sherman	California	July 1965	December 1967
Scott, Carey Brent	California	June 1962	December 1964
Scown, Paul Drew	Utah	August 1959	Korea D.
Seeley, Earl Joseph	Utah	March 1963	September 1965
Seeman, Hal Larry[6]	California	May 1963	November 1963
Sellers, Brian Lee	New Mexico	October 1960	Korea D.
Senior, Robert Lynn	Utah	September 1966	Japan M.
Shafer, Jack Allen	California	March 1964	September 1966
Shaum, Milton K.	Utah	October 1950	October 1953
Shelley, Douglas Lynn	Arizona	November 1966	August 1967
Shelley, Val Reid	Utah	August 1968	Japan M.
Shigoka, Yoshio	Takasaki	March 1957	March 1959
Shimabukuro, Sam K.	Hawaii	September 1954	September 1957
Shimada, Gary M.	Utah	July 1967	Japan–Okinawa M.
Shimazaki, Kazuko*	Asahikawa	August 1968	Japan–Okinawa M.
Shimbashi, Edward J.	Canada	April 1950	April 1952+
Shimizu, Masaru Tom	Utah	December 1959	January 1963
Shin, Paul Ho Bom	Utah	February 1957	September 1958
Shiozawa, George Kent	Idaho	July 1962	January 1965
Shipp, Robert Steele	Washington	October 1966	Japan–Okinawa M.
Shirai, Yaeko*	Shibata	April 1953	September 1954
Shirk, James Leslie[8]	Missouri	May 1961	November 1963
Shirota, Tomiko*	Hawaii	October 1948	June 1950
Shirota, Sumiko*	Hawaii	July 1951	July 1953
Shumate, Judith Marilyn*	Utah	June 1965	June 1967
Shumway, Jesse Fredrick	Arizona	February 1950	February 1953
Shumway, Norman David	California	November 1954	May 1958
Shumway, Larry Vee	Arizona	February 1955	February 1958
Shurtleff, Joseph Lynn	Utah	April 1966	Japan–Okinawa M.
Shurtz, Susan*	Utah	August 1968	Japan M.
Simard, III, Victor Louis	California	June 1963	December 1965
Simmons, William Don	Idaho	November 1955	November 1958
Simmons, Merlin	Idaho	January 1959	July 1961
Simmons, Roger Franklin	Illinois	March 1968	Japan M.
Simpson, Gilbert Herman	Idaho	September 1966	Japan M.
Skouson, Garth W.	Arizona	February 1951	February 1954
Slack, Robert A.	Utah	July 1958	December 1960

Annex 10. Mormon Missionaries in the Japanese and Northern Far East Missions   515

Name (* female)	Home country, U.S. state, or Japan town	Month of arrival (+estimate)	Month of departure [2] (+estimate)
Slack, Kenneth Rasmuson	Arizona	February 1967	Japan–Okinawa M.
Slade, Harold Dean	Utah	April 1954	May 1957
Slaugh, Burnell K.	Utah	June 1968	Japan–Okinawa M.
Smith, Richard Nelson	Utah	October 1950	October 1953
Smith, Carlos Dean	Idaho	December 1954	November 1957
Smith, Gary V.	Utah	September 1957+	April 1960
Smith, Boyd Francis	Idaho	July 1960	January 1963
Smith, James Wallace[8]	California	July 1961	December 1963
Smith, Carol Arvilla*	Utah	September 1961	September 1963
Smith, Edward	Hawaii	May 1962	November 1964
Smith, Kit Dean	Oregon	September 1962	March 1965
Smith, Paul Vernon	Utah	November 1962	May 1965
Smith, Thomas LaRon	Idaho	November 1962	May 1965
Smith, Lynn Edward	Utah	December 1962	June 1965
Smith, Jr., Wilford Emery	Utah	July 1964	January 1967
Smith, Jr., Arthur Vernon	Utah	May 1965	November 1967
Smith Jr., Albon Llewellyn	Idaho	June 1967	Japan M.
Smith, Stephen Barney	Utah	June 1967	Japan–Okinawa M.
Sonoda, George Hiroshi	Hawaii	November 1960	May 1963
Souza, Gertrude Keliikipi*	Hawaii	July 1951	July 1953
Spackman, Dennis Merlin	Idaho	May 1966	Japan–Okinawa M.
Sperry, Jr., Ralph B.	Utah	February 1950	February 1953
Spittal, Gary Edward	Colorado	September 1965	March 1968
Spotten, Gordon Paul	Utah	November 1960	May 1963
Sproat, William Gustaff	Hawaii	July 1949	January 1952
Sproat, Herbert Kamakaohua	Hawaii	May 1951	October 1953
Stallings, Lon B.	Utah	April 1950	April 1952
Stallings, Carol Anita*	Idaho	September 1961	September 1963
Staples, Max G.	Utah	June 1958	January 1961
Steele, Jerry Thomas	Utah	December 1957	May 1960
Steggell, Howard Don	Utah	September 1953	March 1956
Stephens, Blair Kenner	Utah	March 1960+	August 1962
Stephens, Kathleen*	Utah	July 1961	July 1963
Stephenson, Ralph Roger	Idaho	September 1961	March 1964
Stephenson, Treve R.	Utah	May 1968	Japan M.
Sterrett, Morris Ray	Oregon	November 1961	May 1964
Stevens, Lester Perry	California	November 1958	Korea D.
Stevens, Audrey*	Utah	April 1959	April 1961
Stevens, Thomas Robert	California	November 1965	April 1967
Stevens, Michael Brent	Idaho	February 1966	August 1968
Stewart, Dennis Owen	California	December 1962	June 1965
Stoddard, Linda Lee*	California	August 1967	Japan M.
Stone, Amy Louise*	Idaho	July 1963	July 1965
Stott, John Thomas	California	September 1965	March 1968
Stout, Robert T.	Idaho	April 1957	Korea D.
Strebe, David Albert	California	July 1957	Korea D.
Strode, Michael Ross	Ohio	November 1965	May 1968

Name (* female)	Home country, U.S. state, or Japan town	Month of arrival (+estimate)	Month of departure [2] (+estimate)
Su'a, Randolph Laumoli	Hawaii	January 1959	August 1961
Sudlow, Michael F.	California	October 1967	Japan–Okinawa M.
Summers, Wayne Wright	Utah	October 1956	October 1959
Sutton, Stanley B.	Idaho	December 1953	March 1955
Swenson, Robert A.	Utah	December 1949	April 1952
Swenson, Dale Gene	Utah	October 1950	October 1953
Taggart, Gregg B.	Utah	February 1968	Japan M.
Tahere Jr., Frank Manders	New Zealand	May 1962	November 1964
Takabe, Shigeko*	Osaka	December 1967	Japan M.
Takahashi, Henry T.	Canada	November 1957	May 1960
Takaki, Larry Susumu	Hawaii	December 1960	June 1963
Takane, Setsuko*	Muroran	July 1953	January 1955
Takano, Teruko*	Kofu	June 1967	Japan–Okinawa M.
Takara, Shinsei	Kyoto	July 1965	July 1967
Takeuchi, Katherine Kiyoko*	Hawaii	July 1949	April 1951
Takeuchi, Thomas T.	Hawaii	September 1952	August 1955
Takeuchi, Chizuru*	Nagoya	September 1963	March 1965
Talbot, James Edwin	Washington	February 1966	July 1968
Tam, Edna L. Y.*	Hawaii	Mary 1953	May 1955
Tamasaka, Thomas Kiyoshi	Hawaii	May 1960	December 1962
Tamura, Satoko*	Osaka	July 1965	January 1967
Tanaka, Teruo	Osaka	November 1952	November 1954
Tanaka, Nobuko*	Gunma	June 1963	December 1964
Tanaka, Frederick	Hawaii	January 1968	Japan–Okinawa M.
Tanner, Janet E.*	Alaska	February 1967	Japan M.
Tano, Melvin Masaru	Hawaii	January 1961	July 1963
Tasker, Thomas Leonard	Idaho	July 1965	January 1968
Tau'a, Irene*	Hawaii	February 1953	February 1955
Tau'a, Merriwell K.	Hawaii	June 1967	Japan–Okinawa M.
Taylor, James E.	Arizona	March 1951	January 1952
Taylor, Vearl H.	Idaho	June 1957	Korea D.
Taylor, Malcolm Dent	Utah	July 1958	January 1961
Taylor, David Whiteley	Oregon	November 1958	March 1960
Taylor, Charles Michael	Texas	July 1960	November 1960
Taylor, Denzel Eugene	Utah	July 1962	January 1965
Taylor, Randolph Paul	Idaho	October 1962	April 1965
Taylor, Melvin William	California	April 1963	October 1965
Telford, Ira Ralph	D. Columbia	November 1954	May 1958
Terazawa, Toshi*	Utah	August 1952	October 1954
Terry, Maeser Reginald	Utah	July 1956	August 1959
Thacker, Jr., John Weston	Arizona	August 1966	Japan–Okinawa M.
Thatcher, Lester Don	Oregon	November 1960	Korea D.
Thomas, Alan Reed	Idaho	March 1961	September 1963
Thompson, William Hoeft	Utah	April 1957+	October 1959
Thompson, Mitchell Dale	Washington	September 1966	Japan M.
Thompson, Merrill F.	Utah	August 1968	Japan–Okinawa M.
Tilby, Francis Louis	Nevada	May 1961	November 1963

Annex 10. Mormon Missionaries in the Japanese and Northern Far East Missions

Name (* female)	Home country, U.S. state, or Japan town	Month of arrival (+estimate)	Month of departure [2] (+estimate)
Till, Eugene Powell	Florida	January 1958	Korea D.
Tipton, Richard Alvin	Colorado	November 1965	May 1968
Todd, Ira Hatch	Utah	February 1950	February 1953
Tolley, Harold Dennis	Utah	June 1965	November 1967
Tolman, Jerald C.	Idaho	September 1960	March 1963
Toma, Rikuo	Naha	November 1965	November 1967
Tomlinson, Ian Ross	Canada	March 1968	Japan–Okinawa M.
Tong, Norman S. H. Kaletalii	Hawaii	January 1959	November 1961
Toyn, Richard L.	Utah	October 1953	October 1956
Tripp, Henry K. Joseph	Hawaii	November 1966	Japan–Okinawa M.
Troff, Arno William	Iowa	July 1961	December 1963
Tsukada, Keiko*	Tokyo	October 1963	April 1965
Tsuneda, Elaine Yoneko*	Hawaii	September 1965	September 1967
Tucker, Valdon Jay	Utah	March 1967	Japan M.
Tueller, Frank Eugene	Utah	November 1949	September 1952
Turley, Floyd Kemp	Arizona	November 1953	November 1956
Turner, Newell Reed	Utah	April 1955	May 1958
Tyler, Elton Ross	Arizona	June 1959	Korea D.
Uchiyama, Haruyuki	Tokyo	June 1967	Japan–Okinawa M.
Udall, Joseph Leon	Arizona	June 1954	June 1957
Ueda, Yoshiko*	Nagoya	September 1963	March 1965
Ueno, Hideo	Tokyo	June 1967	Japan–Okinawa M.
Umetsu, Chieko*	Sendai	January 1953	May 1954
Underwood, Glen S.	Utah	November 1958	May 1961
Ushio, David Evan	Utah	March 1965	August 1967
Uyehara, Alan M.	Hawaii	August 1963	February 1966
Van Dyke, Robert C.	Utah	July 1958	January 1961
Van Leuven, Clifford Ronald	Utah	Mary 1957	November 1959
Van Noy, LaDon	Wyoming	March 1956	March 1958+
Van Orden, Richard Dale	Illinois	September 1966	Japan–Okinawa M.
Van Twelves Jr., Wendell	Utah	June 1967	Japan–Okinawa M.
von Hungen, Erich Heinz Richardt	California	January 1965	August 1965
Wada, Mihoko*	Sapporo	June 1954	December 1955
Waddell, David Lynn	Idaho	November 1959	Korea D.
Wadsworth, Bryant Hinckley	Nevada	August 1962	March 1965
Waetford, James A.	New Zealand	July 1968	Japan–Okinawa M.
Waits, Robert Barton	Virginia	May 1965	November 1967
Walbeck, Douglas LaMar	Utah	October 1956	October 1959
Walker, Zona Evans*	California	December 1949	November 1951
Walker, Marvin Dahl	Idaho	October 1956	October 1959
Walker, Bobby Dean	North Carolina	August 1960	February 1963
Walker, Morris Glen	Canada	July 1963	January 1966
Walker, William Russell	Canada	June 1964	December 1966
Walker, Frank A.	Oregon	January 1965	July 1967
Walker, Ramsay Ralph	Canada	September 1965	March 1968
Walker, Judith Lavon*	New Mexico	February 1966	February 1968
Walley, Thomas Lavar	California	July 1965	January 1968

Name (* female)	Home country, U.S. state, or Japan town	Month of arrival (+estimate)	Month of departure [2] (+estimate)
Walpole, Kent Douglas	Utah	August 1966	Japan–Okinawa M.
Walther, Dale J.	Alaska	August 1968	Japan–Okinawa M.
Wanlass, John Wesley	Utah	July 1958	January 1961
Warnick, Frederick Merril	Utah	March 1961	September 1963
Watabe, Masahisa	Yokohama	June 1963	June 1965
Watabe, Masaji	Yokohama	June 1964	June 1966
Watanabe, Kan	Tokyo	March 1953	March 1955
Watanabe, Douglas T.	Utah	March 1962	September 1964
Watanabe Jr., George Noboru	Utah	January 1963	July 1965
Watanabe, Ken Charles	Hawaii	September 1965	March 1968
Weed, Thomas Mark	Delaware	June 1965	December 1967
Welch, John Charles	Wyoming	February 1954	February 1957
Welch, Theodore Franklin	California	September 1954	March 1958
Wells, Edward Jessie	California	October 1957	May 1960
West, Delwin Glen	Utah	August 1963	February 1966
West, Douglas L.	Utah	May 1966	Japan–Okinawa M.
Westbrook, John R.	Colorado	March 1967	Japan M.
Whipple, Charles Tyrell	Arizona	January 1961	July 1963
Whitaker, William O.	Utah	February 1956	March 1959
White, Rees Glover	Utah	January 1961	July 1963
Whitelock, MacArthur	Utah	July 1961	January 1964
Wiggins Jr., Ola W. Pete	Arkansas	March 1966	August 1968
Wilberg, Carolyn Sue*	Utah	July 1961	July 1963
Wilcox, Jerry Dean	Montana	October 1958	April 1961
Wilcox, Karla J.*	Georgia	July 1964	July 1966
Wilkins, Alita*	Idaho	August 1962	August 1964
Wilkinson, Harold Leroy	Utah	March 1961	September 1963
Willis, Kelland H.	Arizona	December 1953	November 1956
Wilson, Curtis Patrick	Wyoming	October 1961	April 1964
Wilson, Dennis William	Utah	February 1963	August 1965
Wilson, Lester J.	Idaho	September 1965	March 1968
Wilson, Saundra Sue*	Missouri	December 1966	Japan–Okinawa M.
Wilson, Stephen G.	Utah	February 1967	Japan–Okinawa M.
Wiscombe, Steven A.	California	June 1968	Japan M.
Wolsey, Marden Leroy[8]	Canada	October 1960	June 1963
Wolsey, Brian Laray	Canada	June 1965	September 1967
Wolters, Frederick Charles	Utah	January 1968+	Japan M.
Wood, Orion Howard	Utah	July 1957	February 1960
Woodbury, Steven C.	California	August 1967	Japan M.
Woolsey, Elvin Kenneth	California	February 1963	August 1963
Wooten, Charles Lee	California	October 1961	March 1964
Worthen, Joyce Camille*	Utah	November 1956	November 1958
Wright, Willis L.	Texas	January 1955	February 1958
Wright, Gary Hatch	California	July 1955	July 1958
Wright, Verla Dean*	Utah	July 1956	July 1958
Wynn, Jan Eugene	Oregon	July 1957	December 1959
Yafuso, Akira	Naha	August 1964	August 1966

Annex 10. Mormon Missionaries in the Japanese and Northern Far East Missions

Name (* female)	Home country, U.S. state, or Japan town	Month of arrival (+estimate)	Month of departure [2] (+estimate)
Yamada, Ikuko*	Sapporo	June 1954	December 1955
Yamada, Goro	Tokyo	December 1959	December 1961
Yamada, Hiroko*	Matsumoto	July 1963	July 1965
Yamada, Katsumaru	Gunma	August 1964	August 1966
Yamagata, Gene Hiroshi	Idaho	November 1957	May 1960
Yamashita, Mieko Margaret*	Hawaii	July 1958	July 1960
Yamashita, Yoriko*	Fukuoka	October 1963	October 1964
Yamashita, Wayne J.	Utah	November 1965	May 1968
Yamazato, Fumiko*	Naha	June 1966	December 1967
Yanagida, Takao	Nagoya	November 1966	Japan M.
Yanagisawa, Masataro	Sendai	November 1952	November 1954+
Yates, Pamela St. John*	Utah	December 1964	December 1966
Yonemori, Shirley Kazuko*	Hawaii	July 1959	August 1961
Yoshii, Kiyoshi	Hawaii	October 1948	January 1951
Yoshino, Yotaro	Tokyo	December 1951	October 1953+
Young, Ethel*	Hawaii	July 1953	August 1955
Young, Blake Morgan	Canada	June 1962	December 1964
Young, DeForrest Orval	California	June 1965	December 1967
Young, Melvin Spencer	Utah	June 1965	December 1967
Young, James Alden	Nevada	March 1966	April 1968
Young, Lowell Kent	Utah	June 1968	Japan M.
Zaugg, Rodney Paul[8]	Canada	October 1960	June 1963

[1] Excludes full-time missionaries on temporary assignment (at least three persons served in this capacity: Dorothy Taylor Curtis of Salt Lake City Utah, from August 1950 to May 1952, while her family lived in Tokyo; Miiko Kosaka Iwaasa of Sapporo for some months in 1952, while she waited for immigration clearance to join her husband in Canada; and Teruko Yamamoto of Kofu, from June to October 1964).
[2] Korea District, Japan Mission, or Japan–Okinawa Mission for those who moved to these units (their dates of departure are not noted).
[3] Mission president.
[4] Mission president's wife.
[5] Arrived from the Central Pacific Mission.
[6] Transferred to U.S. missions (including in Hawaii).
[7] Transferred from the Southern Far East Mission.
[8] Served as labor missionaries on assignment during part of their missions.
[9] Transferred from the Northern California Mission.
[10] Married couple.

Japanese and Northern Far East Missions, "Historical Records and Minutes," LDS Church Archives; Northern Far East Mission, "missionary release files," LDS Church Archives; Northern Far East Mission, *Success Messenger*, various issues; author's estimates.

Annex 11

Early American Labor Missionaries in Japan, 1962–69

Northern Far East Building Committee

	Names	Home	Arrival	Departure	Position
1	Melvin D. and Nondas Hales	Maywood, California	July 1962	September 1963	Area supervisor
2	Samuel Kaaumoana and Violet Doyle Kalama	Honolulu, Hawaii	July 1962	June 1964	Treasurer/assistant area supervisor
3	Lamar and Yoshie Walbeck	Provo, Utah	September 1963	November 1966	Treasurer
4	Rex Alton and Hildegard T. Cheney	San Gabriel, California	September 1963	July 1966	Area supervisor
5	Marvin Sudbury and Olive Rean Harding	Salt Lake City, Utah	July 1966	N.A.	Area supervisor

Building Supervisors

	Names	Home	Arrival	Departure	Building site	Remarks
1	Melvin R. (Bud) and Barbara Hales	La Puente, California	August 1962	November 1963	Tokyo West	Son of Melvin D.; completed work in record time
2	Clarence and Marjean Katwyk (Katwijk)	Salt Lake City, Utah	October 1962	April 1966	Tokyo North, Gunma, Yokohama	Left before Yokohama chapel was completed
3	Howard Theodore and Alice Pauline Gorringe	Midvale, Utah	February 1963	December 1963	Tokyo East (first phase)	Returned after completion of project
4	Kenji and Jean Akagi	Wahiawa, Hawaii	June 1963	N.A.	Electrical work in all Tokyo buildings	State licensed electrician
5	Theodore H. and Le Neve Willis	Laguna Beach, California	July 1963	September 1963	Naha (planned)	Worked on Tokyo East while waiting for building permit in Naha; reassigned to Salt Lake building office
6	Le Roy and Reta Mae Johnson	Yakima, Washington	July 1963	August 1965	Mission home addition	Left after completion of project
7	Walter Ray and Delta Johanna Chedister	California	March 1964	N.A.	Gunma, Sapporo	
8	Alden and Nita White	N.A.	April 1964	August 1965	Tokyo South	

	Names	Home	Arrival	Departure	Building site	Remarks
9	Jean Deith (J. D.) and Annabel M. Larson	Holladay, Utah	June 1964	December 1966	Naha, Gunma, Tokyo South	After completing work in Naha, moved to Gunma. After completing work in Gunma, moved to Tokyo South
10	Evan and Esther Larson	Utah	August 1964	N.A.	Abeno, Sapporo, Yokohama, Tokyo East (second phase), Naha, Okamachi	After completing work in Abeno in April 1966, moved to Yokohama to take over from Clarence Katwyk
11	Walter Ray and Delta Johanna Chedister	California	June 1969	N.A.	Asahikawa	Second time

Hildegard Anna Cheney, *Church Builders of the Far East, 1963–1966* (self-published, 1966); *Far East Construction News*.

Annex 12

Partial List of Locally Called Labor Missionaries in the Northern Far East Mission, 1962–68

Name	Home unit	Period (*estimate)	Building sites
Akama, Hiroshi	Sapporo	April 1968–N.A.	Okamachi
Amada, Katsushima	Gunma	April 1968–N.A.	Okamachi
Aoki, Kikuo	Tokyo Central	*March 1965–March 1967	Yokohama
Aoyagi, Koichi	Yokohama	October 1965–October 1967	N.A.
Aoyama, Tokuzo	Sapporo	*January 1965–N.A.	Mission home
Asanuma, Katsusuke	Nishinomiya	May 1963–N.A.	Tokyo North
Domae, Toshio	Yokohama	N.A.	Okamachi
Fukuda, Noriaki	Sapporo	April 1963–N.A.	Tokyo West or North; Abeno
Fukushima, Katsuaki	Niigata	September 1967–N.A.	Okamachi
Hanasawa	Kanazawa	N.A.	Okamachi
Hayashi, Takashi	Tokyo Central	January 1963–*January 1965	Tokyo West; Gunma
Higa, Kenneth Kosuke[1]	N. Far East Miss.	February 1963–March 1963	N.A.
Higuchi, Hiroshi	N.A.	N.A.	Gunma
Hoshino, Osamu	N.A.	N.A.–April 1966	N.A.
Hult, Merle Blythe[1]	N. Far East Miss.	October 1962–November 1962	N.A.
Igarashi	Sapporo	N.A.	Okamachi
Iida, Kazumi	Matsumoto	N.A.–October 1965	N.A.
Ikehata	Otaru	N.A.	Okamachi
Imai, Hirofumi	Fukuoka	N.A.–December 1966	N.A.
Inohara, Yukihiro	N.A.	February 1966–N.A.	N.A.
Isaito	Tokyo Central	February 1966–N.A.	N.A.
Ishii, Takashi	Sapporo	*January 1965–January 1967	Mission home; Gunma
Ishikawa, Zenjiro	Tokyo West	November 1962–*November 1964	Tokyo North; Gunma
Ishizaka, Koichi	Tokyo West	May 1964–N.A.	Mission home; Gunma
Itokazu, Tetsuo	Tokyo West	*late 1964–N.A.	N.A.
Jinno, Fusakimi	Sapporo	April 1966–N.A.	N.A.
Joga	N.A.	N.A.	Gunma
Kamijo, Katsuhiro	Tokyo East	January 1964–N.A.	N.A.
Kanda, Yasuo	Nishinomiya	N.A.–September 1967	N.A.
Kaneko, Hiroshi	Yokohama	April 1967–N.A.	Okamachi
Karatani, Shuroku	Kanazawa	April 1968–N.A.	Okamachi
Kawano, Masahiko	N.A.	N.A.	N.A.
Kikuchi, Yoshihiko	Muroran	N.A.	N.A.
Kimoto, Tadao	N.A.	N.A.	Tokyo South
Kobayashi, Katsuhiko	N.A.	N.A.–May 1966	N.A.
Kohagura, Sunao	Futenma	August 1963–N.A.	Tokyo East; Naha
Koizumi, Hironori[2]	Yokohama	November 1962–*November 1964	Tokyo West; Yokohama
Konami, Hirotsugu[3]	Abeno	April 1963–N.A.	Tokyo East; Gunma
Konomoto, Tadao	Hiroshima	October 1965–October 1967	N.A.
Kudo, Shunichi	Tokyo North	November 1962–*November 1964	Tokyo North; Gunma; Abeno
Laimana, Paul Kalei[4]	N. Far East Miss.	September 1962–January 1963	N.A.

Name	Home unit	Period (*estimate)	Building sites
Lee, Min Hyeong	Tokyo Central	June 1963–June 1965	N.A.
Makahi, Nonaina Hoopili[1]	N. Far East Miss.	October 1962–December 1962	N.A.
Matsumoto, Hiroshi	Kanazawa	July 1968–N.A.	N.A.
Matsushima, Retsui	Tokyo West	November 1962–*November 1964	Tokyo North
Matsuura, Hideaki	Fukuoka	February 1963–*February 1965	Tokyo West
Matsuura, Takayasu	N.A.	*late 1962/early 1963–N.A.	Tokyo West
Minamisawa, Teruyuki[5]	Tokyo West	December 1962–N.A.	Tokyo West
Miyagawa, Kiyoshi	Abeno	October 1963–October 1965	Tokyo West
Motohashi, Isao	Yokohama	N.A.	Okamachi
Murakami, Masahiro	N.A.	N.A.	Gunma; Sapporo
Murokawa	N.A.	N.A.	Gunma
Nakajima, Hatsuo	Nagoya	March 1967–N.A.	Okamachi
Nakata, Kazuhiko	N.A.	N.A.	Yokohama
Nara, Fujiya	Yokohama	November 1962–August 1963	Miss. living quarters (Tokyo)
Nara, Motoko	Yokohama	November 1962–August 1963	Miss. living quarters (Tokyo)
Niiyama, Yasuo	Yanai	*late 1962/early 1963–N.A.	Tokyo North
Nishimata, Yoshiaki	Nishimomiya	January 1965–N.A.	Mission home
Nishime, Tsutomu	Naha	N.A.	Gunma; Tokyo South
Nitta, Masanobu	Yokohama	August 1963–N.A.	Miss. living quarters (Tokyo)
Nitta, Fumie	Yokohama	August 1963–N.A.	Miss. living quarters (Tokyo)
Noma, Ryuichi	N.A.	N.A.	N.A.
Ochiai, Katsumi	Tokyo Central	September 1967–N.A.	Okamachi
Ogura, Masami	Asahikawa	June 1968–N.A.	N.A.
Ohashi, Masahiro	Tokyo North	November 1962–*November 1964	Tokyo North; Gunma; Abeno
Ozeki, Kanji	Okamachi	N.A.	Okamachi
Saito, Akira	Tokyo West	November 1962–*November 1964	Tokyo West, North, East; Yokohama; Misison home
Saito, Akira	N.A.	N.A.–August 1968	N.A.
Saito	Tokyo North	N.A.	Okamachi
Sasayama, Hiroshi	Kyoto	N.A.	Okamachi
Shibayama	N.A.	N.A.	N.A.
Shido, Hisato	N.A.	N.A.	Yokohama
Shimochi, Shoji	N.A.	N.A.	Gunma
Shirk, James Leslie[1]	N. Far East Miss.	June–November 1963	N.A.
Smith, James Wallace[1]	N. Far East Miss.	June–October 1963	N.A.
Sugie, Manabu	Okamachi	November 1967–N.A.	Okamachi
Tabata, Charles	Tokyo South	November 1962–*November 1964	Tokyo West
Taira, Takao	Futenma	June 1968–N.A.	N.A.
Takabayashi, Takahiro	Tokyo East	April 1966–N.A.	N.A.
Takamoto, Keiichi	Muroran	January 1963–*January 1965	Tokyo North
Takamoto, Shunichi	N.A.	N.A.	Tokyo North
Takara, Shinsei	N.A.	N.A.	Gunma
Takasugi, Yasuo	Sapporo	January 1964–N.A.	N.A.
Takayama, Shuji	Tokyo Central	N.A.	Gunma; Sapporo
Takeuchi, Koichi	Yanai	August 1968–N.A.	Short-term
Takeuchi, Takaichi	Hawaii	*early 1963–N.A.	Short-term (masonry work)
Takizawa, Koichi	N.A.	N.A.–May 1966	N.A.
Tanabe, Toyoharu	Okamachi	May 1963–N.A.	Tokyo North

Annex 12. Partial List of Locally-called Labor Missionaries

Name	Home unit	Period (*estimate)	Building sites
Tarumoto, Masahiro	Sannomiya	N.A.	N.A.
Tei, Toyoo	N.A.	*late 1962/early 1963–N.A.	Tokyo West
Tonoyama	N.A.	N.A.	N.A.
Toshi, Katsu	N.A.	N.A.–March 1966	N.A.
Tsubouchi, Kenji	N.A.	N.A.	Yokohama
Tsuchiya, Kazumi	Tokyo Central	October 1966–N.A.	Okamachi
Tsuchiya, Toshio	Okamachi	February 1966–January 1968	Okamachi
Tsukayama, Tasuke	Futenma	August 1963–N.A.	Tokyo East; Naha
Tsunoyama, Teruo	Abeno	*October 1964–October 1966	N.A.
Wakabayashi, Hajime	Tokyo Central	March 1967–N.A.	Okamachi
Wakabayashi, Masaru	N.A.	*late 1962/early 1963–N.A.	Tokyo West
Wolsey, Marden Leroy[1]	N. Far East Miss.	December 1962–June 1963	Tokyo North
Yamada, Toshiaki	Asahikawa	*late 1962/early 1963–N.A.	Tokyo West
Yokoyama, Tadashi	Otaru	May 1963–*May 1965	Yokohama; Sapporo
Yonezawa, Katsuyoshi	N.A.	N.A.–May 1966	N.A.
Yoshida, Jiro	Okamachi	March 1963–N.A.	Tokyo West or North; Gunma
Yoshida, Yukio	Asahikawa	June 1968–N.A.	N.A.
Yoshikawa, Toshio	Tokyo South	N.A.–December 1965	Yokohama
Zaugg, Rodney Paul[1]	N. Far East Miss.	March 1963–June 1963	Tokyo West

[1] Proselytizing missionary on temporary assignment.
[2] Alternative pronunciation is Yasuhiro.
[3] Alternative pronunciation is Keiji.
[4] He was likely a volunteer, not a formal missionary.
[5] Alternative pronunciation is Teruaki.

Northern Far East Mission, "Historical Records and Minutes," LDS Church Archives; Hildegard Anna Cheney, *Church Builders of the Far East, 1963–1966* (self-published, 1966); *Far East Construction News*; *Seito no Michi*, various issues.

Glossary of Mormon and Japanese Terms

apostle: a member of the Council (or Quorum) of the Twelve Apostles, the second highest governing body in the LDS Church after the First Presidency.

Aaronic priesthood: the lesser of the two priesthoods in the LDS Church, responsible for administering outward ordinances. See priesthood.

Articles of Faith: thirteen statements authored by Joseph Smith summarizing the fundamental beliefs or doctrines of Mormonism. They appear as part of the Pearl of Great Price.

baptism: an initiation ceremony in which a candidate for membership in the LDS Church is immersed in water and raised again, symbolizing the burial and resurrection of Jesus Christ. Baptism is followed by a confirmation ceremony in which the candidate is given the "gift of the Holy Ghost."

bishop: the ecclesiastical officer who presides over a ward.

branch: the smallest ecclesiastical unit, led by a branch president. These are the equivalent of wards in areas where a formal stake has not been organized. See stake; ward.

Choshu: the feudal domain (western portion of present-day Yamaguchi Prefecture) that played the leading role, along with Satsuma, in the overthrow of the Tokugawa shogunate in 1868.

chūgakkō: junior high (or middle) school in the postwar educational system and four or five-year secondary school in the prewar system; it is translated as junior high school in the postwar context and secondary school in the prewar context. Most prewar *chūgakkō* were converted to high schools in the postwar educational reform.

conference: a geographical area of church activity; the word was used in place of district during part of the prewar era. See also district; general conference.

daimyo: a vassal of the shogun who ruled one of the 250 or more domains or fiefdoms.

Diet: Japan's parliament. In prewar Japan, it consisted of the House of Peers (with hereditary or appointed members) and the popularly elected House of Representatives. The postwar constitution replaced the House of Peers with the popularly elected House of Councilors.

district: a geographical area of church activity, consisting of several branches, comparable to a stake when the church is fully established. See also conference.

Doctrine and Covenants: one of the standard works of the Mormon Church that contains revelations received by Joseph Smith and his successors.

domain: the English translation of the Japanese word *han*, which refers both to the fiefdom controlled by a daimyo and to its system of government that administered economic, military, and political affairs.

Edo: present-day Tokyo, from which the Tokugawa family ruled Japan from 1603 to 1868. This period is called the Edo or Tokugawa period.

elder: an office in the Melchizedek priesthood; also the title for anyone who is ordained to the Melchizedek priesthood, including a missionary and an apostle.

exaltation: the highest of the three degrees of glory that the Mormons believe characterize the after-life, enjoyed in the celestial kingdom. See telestial kingdom.

First Presidency: the highest governing body in the LDS Church, consisting of the president and two counselors.

Gan-nen-mono: the first group of 150 or so Japanese immigrants who left Japan in the first year of Meiji (1968) and worked as contractual laborers in Hawaii.

general authority: an ecclesiastical officer whose responsibility encompasses all geographical jurisdictions, including a member of the First Presidency or the Council of the Twelve Apostles. They are given a living allowance for their work, unlike local authorities who serve without pay.

general conference: a set of meetings held twice yearly, typically in April and October, in Salt Lake City, to conduct general business of the church and address sermons to the general membership.

genrō: a member of the inner circle of elder statesmen in prewar Japan who effectively monopolized political power. Numbering nine, all but one came from Satsuma or Choshu domains. They were a subset of the ruling class known as the Meiji oligarchy, which included members from other domains on the winning side of the Meiji revolution.

hatamoto: a direct vassal of the shogun who did not have his own domain but was a high-ranking official in the shogunate bureaucracy. See also daimyo.

Heian: the period (794–1192) in which the emperor ruled Japan from Kyoto, known as Heian-kyō, and when court culture flourished.

Issei: first-generation Japanese immigrants.

Jōdo Shinshū: the largest denomination of Pure Land Buddhism in Japan, the most prominent head temples of which are Nishi Honganji and Higashi Honganji. It teaches salvation in the pure land of heaven through faith in the power of Amida Buddha alone.

kanji: Chinese characters used in writing some Japanese words.

kōtō gakkō: high school in the postwar educational system and post-secondary school in the prewar system (not unlike junior college in the postwar system); it is translated as high school in the postwar context and higher school in the prewar context.

Lehi: the Book of Mormon prophet who brought his family from Jerusalem to America in the sixth century B.C.

Manifesto: the declaration made in October 1890 by the fourth church president, Wilford Woodruff, stating that the church no longer practiced polygamy.

Meiji: the period (January 1868–July 1912) that corresponds to the reign of the emperor posthumously named Meiji.

Melchizedek priesthood: the greater of the two priesthoods in the LDS Church, responsible for administering spiritual affairs. See priesthood.

mission: the geographical area presided over by a president in which missionary work is carried out by missionaries; also the service to which such missionaries are called to perform.

Mormon: the ancient American prophet after whom the Book of Mormon is named; the appellation by which believers in the Book of Mormon have been called.

Mutual Improvement Association (MIA): an auxiliary organization that was in place from the early days of the church until the postwar period, the purpose of which was to offer wholesome cultural, faith-building, and social opportunities for young men and women in the LDS Church.

Nisei: foreign-born children of Japanese immigrants; *Nisei* literally means second generation.

patriarch: one who gives a special blessing of guidance and comfort to members of his stake.

patriarchal blessing: the blessing given by a patriarch who is called in each stake.

Pearl of Great Price: one of the standard works of the Mormon Church containing the writings of Joseph Smith.

prefecture: the subdivision of Japan administered by a governor. The word was borrowed from French because in prewar Japan the governor (*prefect* in the French system) was appointed by the national government, not popularly elected. The number of prefectures has been forty-seven since the latter part of the nineteenth century.

Glossary of Mormon and Japanese Terms 529

priest: an office in the Aaronic priesthood, with authority to administer baptism and the sacrament. See baptism and sacrament.

priesthood: Mormon priesthood consists of two divisions, Aaronic and Melchizedek, and includes such offices as apostle, patriarch, elder, and priest. See apostle; patriarch; elder; and priest.

Primary [Association]: the auxiliary organization for children providing opportunities for religious instruction. Primary used to meet on a weekday but is now held as part of the Sunday program.

Relief Society: the auxiliary organization for women providing opportunities for personal growth and charitable service.

sacrament: the sacrament of the Lord's Supper, in which bread and water are partaken in remembrance of the body and blood of Jesus Christ.

sacrament meeting: the key Sunday worship service in which the sacrament is administered. See sacrament.

saint: the appellation by which Mormons sometimes call themselves in reference to the full name of the church (The Church of Jesus Christ of Latter-day Saints).

samurai: a warrior in medieval Japan, who during the Edo period of relative peace served as a civil servant for the administration of a fiefdom.

Satsuma: the feudal domain (roughly corresponding to present-day Kagoshima Prefecture) that played the leading role, along with Choshu, in the overthrow of the Tokugawa shogunate in 1868.

senmon gakkō: Literally, specialty school. It means post-secondary vocational school in the postwar educational system and post-secondary school of higher education in the prewar system. *Senmon gakkō* were under some conditions allowed to call themselves *daigaku* (university) in 1903, but the government did not regard them as such until the University Ordinance of 1918 allowed the establishment of private universities.

set apart: the term used to indicate the giving of a religious assignment to a member of the church. It is done by the "laying on of hands" (placing of hands on the head of the recipient) by a person who has the authority to confer the assignment.

shinbutsu shūgō: the syncretic religious tradition that developed in middle-age Japan between Shinto and Buddhism, incorporating elements of both.

Shinto: the indigenous religion of Japan that emerged in systematic form following the introduction of Buddhism from China.

shogun: the emperor's military general in name, who effectively ruled Japan. During the Edo period (1603–1868), the Tokugawa family held the right to the office. See shogunate.

shogunate: the English word meaning the office or government of a shogun. The Japanese equivalent is *bakufu*.

Showa: the period (December 1926–January 1989) that corresponds to the reign of the emperor posthumously named Showa.

stake: an ecclesiastical unit consisting of several wards and branches, presided over by a president and two counselors who constitute the stake presidency. The word stake comes from an Old Testament passage in the Book of Isaiah (54:2).

standard works: the Mormon canon of scripture, consisting of the Bible, the Book of Mormon, the Doctrine and Covenants, and the Pearl of Great Price.

Taisho: the period (July 1912–December 1926) that corresponds to the reign of the emperor posthumously named Taisho.

telestial kingdom: the lowest of the three degrees of glory believed by the Mormons to characterize the after-life. See also exaltation.

temple:	an edifice in which the most sacred religious rites are performed, including marriage, sealing of children to parents, and baptism for deceased ancestors.
tennō:	the Japanese word for emperor. Three emperors, posthumously named Meiji, Taisho, and Showa, reigned during the period covered by this book.
Tokugawa:	the name of the family who ruled Japan from its seat in Edo (present-day Tokyo), from 1603 to 1868. The period is equivalently called the Tokugawa or Edo period.
ward:	the ecclesiastical unit in a stake, presided over by a bishop and two counselors who constitute the bishopric. See bishop; stake.
Zion:	the word means, in addition to the land of Palestine, Utah and its vicinity and, more broadly, any place where a sufficient number of Mormons gather. A stake is often called a stake of Zion. See stake.

Bibliography

Abbreviations:

LDS Church Archives: Church Historical Department, Church of Jesus Christ of Latter-day Saints, Salt Lake City

BYU Archives: Special Collections and Manuscripts, Harold B. Lee Library, Brigham Young University, Provo, Utah

BYU–Hawaii Archives: University Archives, Brigham Young University–Hawaii, Laie, Hawaii

Books and Monographs:

Allen, James B., and Glen M. Leonard. *The Story of the Latter-day Saints*. Salt Lake City: Deseret Book, 1976.
Anesaki, Masaharu. *History of Japanese Religion*. London: Kegan Paul, Trench, Trubner & Co, 1930.
Aoyama Gakuin. *Aoyama Gakuin Ichiran*. Tokyo: Aoyama Gakuin, 1926.
Araragi, Shinzo. *Manshū Imin no Rekishi Shakaigaku*. Kyoto: Kōrosha, 1994.
Arrington, Leonard J. *Great Basin Kingdom: Economic History of the Latter-Day Saints, 1830–1900*. Cambridge, Massachusetts: Harvard University Press, 1958.
_____. *The Price of Prejudice: The Japanese–American Relocation Center in Utah during World War II*. Logan, Utah: Faculty Association, Utah State University, 1962.
_____. *Beet Sugar in the West: A History of the Utah–Idaho Sugar Company, 1891–1966*. Seattle: University of Washington Press, 1966.
_____. *History of Idaho*, vol. 2. Moscow, Idaho: University of Idaho Press and Boise, Idaho: Idaho State Historical Society, 1994.
Arrington, Leonard J., and Davis Bitton. *The Mormon Experience: A History of the Latter-day Saints*. New York: Alfred A. Knopf, 1979.
Aston, Willard A. *Teaching the Gospel with Prayer and Testimony*. Self-published, 1956.
Barnstone, Willis. *The Poetics of Translation: History, Theory, Practice*. New Haven: Yale University Press, 1993.
Barrows, John H., ed. *The World's Parliament of Religions*, vol. 1. Chicago: Parliament, 1893.
Beasley, W. G. *The Modern History of Japan*. London: Weidenfeld and Nicolson, 1963.
Bellah, Robert N. *Tokugawa Religion*. Glencoe, Illinois: Free Press, 1957.
Berger, Peter L. *The Sacred Canopy: Elements of a Sociological Theory of Religion*. Garden City, New York: Doubleday, 1967.
Brannen, Noah S. *Sōka Gakkai: Japan's Militant Buddhists*. Richmond, Virginia: John Knox Press, 1968.
Britsch, Lanier R. *Unto the Islands of the Sea: A History of the Latter-day Saints in the Pacific*. Salt Lake City: Deseret Book, 1986.
_____. *Moramona: The Mormons in Hawaii*. Laie, Hawaii: The Institute for Polynesian Studies, Brigham Young University, Hawaii, 1989.
Brooks, Juanita, ed. *On the Mormon Frontier: The Diary of Hosea Stout, 1844–1861*. Salt Lake City: University of Utah Press, 1964.
_____. *The Mountain Meadows Massacre*. Norman, Oklahoma: University of Oklahoma Press, 1970.
Brown, S. Kent, Donald Q. Cannon, and Richard H. Jackson, eds. *Historical Atlas of Mormonism*. New York: Simon and Schuster, 1994.
Brownlee, W. Elliot. *Dynamics of Ascent: A History of the American Economy*, second edition. New York: Alfred A. Knopf, 1979.
Bunkachō, ed. *Shūkyō Nenkan*. Tokyo: Bunkachō, 2015.

Cannon, Hugh J. *David O. McKay Around the World: An Apostolic Mission*. Provo, Utah: Spring Creek, 2005.
Cary, Otis. *A History of Christianity in Japan, Volume 1: Roman Catholic and Greek Orthodox Missions*. New York: Fleming H. Revell, 1909.
———. *A History of Christianity in Japan, Volume 2: Protestant Missions*. New York: Fleming H. Revell, 1909.
Cheney, Hildegard Anna. *Church Builders of the Far East, 1963–1966*. Self-published, 1966.
Chihō Jinji Chōsa Kai. *Kokutetsu Shi*. Takamatsu: Chihō Jinji Chōsa Kai, 1998.
Copeland, Luther E. *World Mission World Survival: The Challenge and Urgency of Global Missions Today*. Nashville, Tennessee: Broadman Press, 1985.
Dai-Nippon Jinmei Jisho Kankō Kai. *Shinban Dai-Nippon Jinmei Jisho*, vol. 2. Tokyo: Kōdansha, 1926.
———. *Dai-Nippon Jinmei Jisho*, vol. 1. Tokyo: Kōdansha, 1937.
Daniels, Roger, Sandra C. Taylor, and Harry H. L. Kitano, eds. *Japanese Americans: From Relocation to Redress*, revised edition. Seattle and London: University of Washington Press, 1991.
Dator, James Allen. *Sōka Gakkai, Builders of the Third Civilization: American and Japanese Members*. Seattle and London: University of Washington Press, 1969.
Davis, Winston. *Japanese Religion and Society: Paradigms of Structure and Change*. Albany, New York: State University of New York Press, 1992.
Dew, Sheri L. *Ezra Taft Benson: A Biography*. Salt Lake City: Deseret Book, 1987.
Dore, R. P. *Education in Tokugawa Japan*. Berkeley and Los Angeles: University of California Press, 1965.
Earhart, H. Byron. *Japanese Religion: Unity and Diversity*, fourth edition. Belmont, California: Wadsworth/Thomson, 2004.
Ebihara, Hachiro. *Nihon Ōji Shinbun Zasshi Shi*. Tokyo: Taiseidō, 1934.
Ebihara, Tsuyoshi. *Katogi Yasuji no Jinsei Techō*. Yokohama: self-published, 1977.
Eto, Jun. *Nihon Hondo Shinchū*. Tokyo: Kōdansha, 1982.
Fearey, Robert A. *The Occupation of Japan: Second Phase, 1948–50*. New York: Macmillan, 1950.
Fukuzawa Kenkyū Sentā. *Keiō Gijuku Nyūshachō*, vol. 4. Tokyo: Fukuzawa Kenkyū Sentā, 1986.
Gaimushō Tokubetsu Shiryōka, ed. *Nihon Senryō Jūyō Bunjo*, vol. 2, 3, 4. Tokyo: Nihon Tosho Sentā, 1949.
Gakushikai. *Kaiin Shimei Roku*. 1928.
———. *Kaiin Shimei Roku*. 1955.
Gibbons, Francis M. *Heber J. Grant: Man of Steel, Prophet of God*. Salt Lake City: Deseret Book, 1970.
———. *David O. McKay: Apostle to the World, Prophet of God*. Salt Lake City: Deseret Book, 1986.
Ginowan Kyōiku Iinkai. *Ginowan-shi Shi*. Ginowan, Okinawa: Ginowan Kyōiku Iinkai, 1994.
Goto, Yasuo Baron. *Children of Gan-nen-mono: The First-Year Men*. Honolulu: Bishop Museum Press, 1968.
Grew, Joseph C. *Ten Years in Japan*. New York: Simon and Schuster, 1944.
Gutjahr, Paul C. *The Book of Mormon: A Biography*. Princeton, New Jersey: Princeton University Press, 2012.
Haga, Shiro. *Nihon Kanri no Kikō to Seisaku*. Tokyo: Yūhikaku, 1951.
Hardacre, Helen. *Shinto and the State 1868–1988*. Princeton, New Jersey: Princeton University Press, 1989.
Henry, Matthew. *Commentary on the Bible*. Edited by L. F. Church. Grand Rapids, Michigan: Zondervan, 1961.
Hirao-chō. *Hirao-chō Shi*. Hirao, Yamaguchi: Hirao-chō, 1978.

Hisamatsu, Senichi, and Seiichi Yoshida, eds. *Kindai Nihon Bungaku Jiten*. Tokyo: Tōkyōdō Shuppan, 1954.
Hokkaidō-chō Keizaibu. *Hokkaidō Nōgyō Gaiyō*. Sapporo: Hokkaidō-chō Keizaibu, 1935.
Honolulu Star–Bulletin. *Men and Women of Hawaii*. Honolulu: Honolulu Star–Bulletin, 1954 and 1966.
Hosokawa, William K. *Nisei: The Quiet Americans*. New York: William Morrow and Company, 1969.
Hotta, Akio, and Tadashi Nishiguchi, eds. *Ōsaka Kawaguchi Kyoryūchi no Kenkyū*. Kyoto: Shibunkaku Shuppan, 1995.
Ichioka, Yuji. *The Issei: The World of the First Generation Japanese Immigrants, 1885–1924*. New York: The Free Press, 1988.
Iglehart, Charles W. *A Century of Protestant Christianity in Japan*. Rutland, Vermont and Tokyo: Charles E. Tuttle, 1959.
Ikimatsu, Keizo. *Taishōki no Shisō to Bunka*. Tokyo: Aoki Shoten, 1971.
Inoki, Takenori. *Gakkō to Kōjō: Nippon no Jinteki Shihon*. Tokyo: Yomiuri Shinbunha, 1996.
_____. *Keizai Seichō no Kajitsu 1955–1972*. Tokyo: Chūō Kōron Shinsha, 2000.
Ion, Hamish. *American Missionaries, Christian Oyatoi, and Japan, 1859–73*. Vancouver: University of British Columbia Press, 2009.
Irokawa, Daikichi. *The Culture of the Meiji Period*. Princeton, New Jersey: Princeton University Press, 1985.
Ishizuka, Hiromichi. *Tōkyō no Shakai Keizai Shi*. Tokyo: Kinokuniya Shoten, 1977.
Ishizuki, Minoru. *Kindai Nihon no Kaigai Ryūgaku Shi*. Kyoto: Mineruva Shobō, 1972.
Ito, Hirobumi. *Teikoku Kenpō Kōshitsu Tenpan Gikai*. Tokyo: Kokka Gakkai, 1889.
Iwata, Masakazu. *Ōkubo Toshimichi: The Bismarck of Japan*. Berkeley and Los Angeles: University of California Press, 1964.
Jamieson, Robert, A. R. Fausset, and David Brown. *Commentary Critical and Explanatory on the Old and New Testaments*. Hartford: S. S. Scranton & Co., 1871.
Jansen, Marius B. *The Making of Modern Japan*. Cambridge, Massachusetts and London: The Belknap Press of Harvard University Press, 2000.
Japanese Government, Bureau of Statistics. *Nihon no Chōki Tōkei Keiretsu*. Accessed 17 November 2015, http://www.stat.go.jp.
Japanese Government, Department of Education. *The Imperial Rescript on Education Translated into Chinese, English, French and German*. Tokyo: Japanese Government, Department of Education, 1909.
Japanese Government, Foreign Office, Division of Special Records, comp. *Documents Concerning the Allied Occupation and Control of Japan*, vol. 2. Tokyo: Japanese Government, Foreign Office, 1949.
Jenson, Andrew. *Latter-day Saint Biographical Encyclopedia*, vol. 1. Salt Lake City: Andrew Jenson History Company, 1901.
_____. *Latter-day Saint Biographical Encyclopedia*, vol. 4. Salt Lake City: Andrew Jensen Memorial Association, 1936.
Jiji Tsūshinsha. *Daihyōteki Jinbutsu oyobi Jigyō*. Tokyo: Jiji Tsūshinsha, 1913.
Jinja Shinpō Seikyō Kenkyūshitsu. *Kindai Jinja Shintōshi*. Tokyo: Jinja Shinpōsha, 1976.
Jinji Kōshinsho. *Zennihon Shinshi Roku*. Tokyo: Jinji Kōshinsho, 1950.
Jōetsu Kyōdo Kenkyū Kai, ed. *Shashinshū: Meiji-Taishō-Shōwa Takada Naoetsu*. Tokyo: Tosho Kankōkai, 1979.
Jones, Francis Clifford. *Extraterritoriality in Japan and the Diplomatic Relations Resulting in Its Abolition 1853–1899*. New Haven: Yale University Press, 1931.
Kahoku Shinpōsha. *Kahoku Shinpōsha Shōshi*. Sendai: Kahoku Shinpōsha, 1952.
_____. *Kahoku Shinpō no Hachijūnen*. Sendai: Kahoku Shinpōsha, 1977.
Kaikoku Hyakunen Kinen Bunka Jigyō Kai, ed. *Meiji Bunkashi*, vol. 6. Tokyo: Hara Shobō, 1979.

Kamata, Tadashi, and Torataro Yoneyama. *Dai Kango Rin*. Tokyo: Taishūkan Shoten, 1992.
Kamisaka, Fuyuko. *Obāchan no Yuta Nippō*. Tokyo: Bungei Shunjū, 1992.
Kansai Daigaku. *Kansai Daigaku Hyakunen Shi*. Osaka: Kansai Daigaku, 1987.
Katagiri, Kazuo. *Hirakareta Sakoku*. Tokyo: Kōdansha, 1997.
Katanuma, Seiji. *Kōda Rohan Kenkyū Josetsu*. Tokyo: Ōfūsha, 1978.
Katsunuma, Tomizo. *Kansho no Shiborikasu*. Honolulu: Katsunuma Kinen Shuppan Kōenkai, 1924.
Kawai, Kazuo. *Japan's American Interlude*. Chicago: University of Chicago Press, 1960.
Kawasoemachi-shi Hensan Iinkai. *Kawasoemachi Shi*. Saga: Sagashi Kyōiku Iinkai, 1979.
Keiō Gijuku. *Keiō Gijuku Hyakunenshi*, vol. 2. Tokyo: Keiō Gijuku, 1960.
Keishikai. "Ichishima-ke no Kankei Shiryō." Shibata, Niigata: Keishikai, 1991.
———. "Echigo no Kyodai Jinushi." Shibata, Niigata: Keishikai, not dated.
Kimura, Yukiko. *Issei: Japanese Immigrants in Hawaii*. Honolulu: University of Hawaii Press, 1988.
Kirisutokyō Shi Gakkai, ed. *Senjika no Kirisutokyō: Shūkyō Dantai Hō wo megutte*. Tokyo: Kyōbunkan, 2015.
Kishimoto, Hideo, ed. *Meiji Bunka Shi*, vol. 6. Tokyo: Hara Shobō, 1979.
Kitane, Yutaka, ed. *Nihon Shoki Shinbun Zenshū*, vol. 35–36. Tokyo: Perikansha, 1992.
Kodama, Kota, ed. *Zusetsu Nihon Bunka Shi Taikei, Volume 11: Meiji Jidai*. Tokyo: Shōgakukan, 1956.
———, ed. *Zusetsu Nihon Bunka Shi Taikei, Volume 12: Taishō Shōwa Jidai*. Tokyo: Shōgakukan, 1957.
Kōdansha. *Japan: An Illustrated Encyclopedia*. Tokyo: Kōdansha, 1993.
Kokuritsu Tenmon Dai, comp. *Rika Nenpyō*, vol. 88. Tokyo: Maruzen Shuppan, 2014.
Kōyūchōsakai, ed. *Teikoku Daigaku Shusshin Meikan*. Tokyo: Kōyūchōsakai, 1932.
Kudo, Eiichi. *Meijiki no Kirisutokyō*. Tokyo: Kyōbunkan, 1979.
Kume, Kunitake, comp. *Tokumei Zenken Taishi Beiō Kairan Jikki*. Tokyo: Iwanami Shoten, 1977 (English translation: *Japan Rising: The Iwakura Embassy to the USA and Europe 1871–1873*. Cambridge and New York: Cambridge University Press, 2009).
Kuno, Osamu, and Shunsuke Tsurumi. *Gendai Nihon no Shisō*. Tokyo: Iwanami Shoten, 1956.
Kuykendall, Ralph S. *The Hawaiian Kingdom, Volume II: 1854–1874 Twenty Critical Years*. Honolulu: University of Hawaii Press, 1953.
Kyōbashi Kyōkai, comp. *Kyōbashi Hanshō Ki*. Tokyo: Kyōbashi Kyōkai, 1912.
Lafeber, Walter. *The Clash: U.S.–Japanese Relations throughout History*. New York: W. W. Norton & Company, 1997.
Lanman, Charles. *The Japanese in America*. New York: University Publishing Company, 1872.
Le Gendre, General (Charles). *Progressive Japan, A Study of the Political and Social Needs of the Empire*. New York and Yokohama: C. Levy, 1878.
Ludlow, Daniel H., ed. *Encyclopedia of Mormonism*. New York: Macmillan, 1992.
Lyman, Edward Leo. *Political Deliverance: The Mormon Quest for Utah Statehood*. Urbana, Illinois: University of Illinois Press, 1986.
MacGillivray, Donald. *A Century of Protestant Missions in China (1807–1907)*. Shanghai: Christian Literature Society for China, 1907.
Mainichi Shinbunsha. *Mainichi Shinbun Shichijūnen*. Tokyo: Mainichi Shinbunsha, 1952.
Martin, Edwin M. *The Allied Occupation of Japan*. New York: American Institute of Pacific Relations, 1948.
Maruyama, Masao. *Nihon no Shisō*. Tokyo: Iwanami Shoten, 1961.
Masaoka, Mike Masaru, with Bill Hosokawa. *They Call Me Moses Masaoka: An American Saga*. New York: William Morrow and Company, 1987.
Matani, Ruikotsu. *Ningen Ruikotsu*. Kyoto: Chūgai Nippōsha, 1968.
Matsunaga, Yukei. *Mikkyō*. Tokyo: Iwanami Shoten, 1991.

Mauss, Armand L. *The Angel and the Beehive: The Mormon Struggle with Assimilation*. Urbana, Illinois: University of Illinois Press, 1994.

———. *All Abraham's Children: Changing Mormon Conceptions of Race and Lineage*. Urbana and Chicago: University of Illinois Press, 2003.

McKay, David O. *Gospel Ideals: Selections from the Discourses of David O. McKay*. Salt Lake City: Deseret Book, 1953.

Metraux, Daniel A. *The Soka Gakkai Revolution*. Lanham, Maryland: University Press of America, 1994.

Mitani, Taichiro. *Shinban Taishō Demokurashī Ron: Yoshino Sakuzō no Jidai*. Tokyo: Tōkyō Daigaku Shuppankai, 1995.

Miyagawa, Takayoshi, ed. *Rekidai Kokkai Giin Keireki Yōran*. Tokyo: Seiji Kōhō Sentā, 1990.

Miyagawa, Toru, and Kazuo Hijikata. *Jiyū Minken Shisō to Nihon no Roman Shugi*. Tokyo: Aoki Shoten, 1971.

Miyagawa, Yorinori. *Naoetsu Hanshō Ki*. Naoetsu: Muro Shobō, 1900.

Miyanaga, Takashi. *Amerika no Iwakura Shisetsudan*. Tokyo: Chikuma Shobō, 1992.

Miyazaki, Kentaro. *Kakure Kirishitan no Shinkō Sekai*. Tokyo: Tōkyō Daigaku Shuppankai, 1996.

Miyazaki, Toranosuke. *Waga Shin Fukuin*. Tokyo: Maekawa Bun-ei-kaku, 1904 (English translation: *My New Gospel*. Translated by Goro Takahashi. Tokyo: New Gospel Society Publishing House, 1910).

———. *Shinsei Kigen*. Kobe: Shinsei Kyōdan Kobe Shibu, 1925.

Moss, James R., R. Lanier Britsch, James R. Christianson, and Richard O. Cowan. *The International Church*. Provo, Utah: Brigham Young University Press, 1982.

Murakami, Shigeyoshi. *Nihon Hyakunen no Shūkyō*. Tokyo: Kōdansha, 1968.

Murayama, Tamotsu. *Shūsen no Koro*. Tokyo: Jiji Tsūshinsha, 1968.

Nagata, Ted, ed. *Japanese Americans in Utah*. Salt Lake City: JA Centennial Committee, 1996.

Nakamura, Yujiro. *Meiji Kokka no Aki to Shisō no Ketsujitsu*. Tokyo: Aoki Shoten, 1971.

Nakamura, Takafusa. *Meiji-Taishō-ki no Keizai*. Tokyo: Tōkyō Daigaku Shuppankai, 1985.

Naoetsu no Rekishi Henshū Iinkai, ed. *Naoetsu no Rekishi*. Naoetsu: Naoetsu Kyōiku Iinkai, 1971.

Naramoto, Tatsuya, ed. *Zusetsu Nihon Shomin Seikatsu Shi, vol. 7: Meiji Jidai*. Tokyo: Kawada Shobō Shinsha, 1962.

Naramoto, Tatsuya, ed. *Zusetsu Nihon Shomin Seikatsu Shi, vol. 8: Taishō Shōwa*. Tokyo: Kawada Shobō Shinsha, 1962.

Neilson, Reid L. *Early Mormon Missionary Activities in Japan, 1901–1924*. Salt Lake City: University of Utah Press, 2010.

Nibley, Hugh. *Lehi in the Desert and the World of the Jaredites*. Salt Lake City: Deseret Book, 1952.

Nietzsche, Friedrich W. *Also Sprach Zarathustra*. Translated by Choko Ikuta. Tokyo: Nippon Hyōronsha, 1935.

Nihon Keizai Shinbunsha Hyaku-sanjū-nen-shi Henshū Iinkai, ed. *Nihon Keizai Shinbunsha Hyaku-sanjū-nen Shi*. Tokyo: Nihon Keizai Shinbun, 2006.

Nihon Kindai Bungakukan, ed. *Nihon Kindai Bungaku Daijiten*. Tokyo: Kōdansha, 1977.

Nihon Kirisuto Kyōdan Shuppan Kyoku, ed. *Kirisutokyō Jinmei Jiten*. Tokyo: Nihon Kirisuto Kyōdan Shuppan Kyoku, 1986.

Nihon Rekishi Gakkai, comp. *Meiji Ishin Jinmei Jiten*. Tokyo: Yoshikawa Kōbun Kan, 1981.

Nihon Tensai Seitō Kabushiki Kaisha. *Nihon Tensai Seitō Shichijūnen Shōshi*. Tokyo: Nihon Tensai Seitō Kabushiki Kaisha, 1989.

Nihon Tosho Sentā. *Nihon Josei Jinmei Jiten*. Tokyo: Nihon Tosho Sentā, 1993.

Nippon Ginkō. *Nippon Ginkō Hyakunenshi*, vol. 5. Tokyo: Nippon Ginkō, 1985.

Nishi, Ian. *Japanese Foreign Policy 1869–1942: Kasumigaseki to Miyakezaka*. London and Boston: Routledge & Kegan Paul, 1977.

Nishida, Taketoshi. *Meiji Jidai no Shinbun to Zasshi*. Tokyo: Shibundō, 1961.

Nishikawa, Nagao, and Hideharu Matsumiya, eds. *Beiō Kairan Jikki wo Yomu*. Kyoto: Hōritsu Bunkasha, 1995.

Nitobe, Inazo. *Bushido: The Soul of Japan*, tenth edition. New York: G. P. Putnam's Sons, 1905.

———. *The Japanese Nation: Its Land, Its People, and Its Life, with Special Consideration to Its Relations with the United States*. New York: G. P. Putnam's Sons, 1912.

———. *Japanese Traits and Foreign Influences*. London: Kegan Paul, Trench, Trubner & Co., 1927.

———. *Nitobe Inazō Zenshū*, vol. 1. Tokyo: Kyōbunkan, 1969.

Nogami, Toyoichiro. *Honyaku Ron*. Tokyo: Iwanami Shoten, 1932.

Odagiri, Susumu, ed. *Nihon Kindai Bungaku Daijiten*, vol. 2. Tokyo: Kōdansha, 1977.

Odate Chūgakkō. *Akita Kenritsu Odate Chūgakkō Yōran*. Odate, Akita: Odate Chūgakkō, 1917.

Ohkawa, Kazushi, Nobukiyo Takamatsu, and Yuzo Yamamoto. *National Income*. Vol. 1 of *Estimates of Long-Term Economic Statistics of Japan Since 1868*, edited by Kazushi Ohkawa, Miyohei Shinohara, and Mataji Umemura. Tokyo: Tōyō Keizai Shinpōsha, 1974.

Okawa, Kazushi, Miyohei Shinohara, and Mataji Umemura, eds. *Chōki Keizai Tōkei*. Tokyo: Tōyō Keizai Shinpōsha, 1967.

Okazaki, Chieko N. *Aloha*. Salt Lake City: Deseret Book, 1995.

Okihiro, Gary Y. *Cane Fires: The Anti-Japanese Movement in Hawaii, 1865–1945*. Philadelphia: Temple University Press, 1991.

Ono, Hideo. *Nihon Shinbun Hattatsu Shi*. Osaka and Tokyo: Ōsaka Mainichi Shinbunsha and Tōkyō Nichinichi Shinbunsha, 1922.

———. *Nihon Shinbun Hattatsu Shi*. Tokyo: Itsuki Shobō, 1982.

———. *Shinbun no Rekishi*. Tokyo: Tōkyōdō Shuppan, 1961.

———. *Shinbun no Rekishi*, enlarged edition. Tokyo: Tōkyōdō Shuppan, 1970.

Oshiro, George. *Nitobe Inazō, Kokusai Shugi no Kaitakusha*. Tokyo: Chūō Daigaku Shuppanbu, 1992.

Ota, Hisayoshi. *Yokohama Enkakushi*. Tokyo: Tōyōsha, 1893.

Ota, Tamesaburo, ed. *Teikoku Chimei Jiten*. Tokyo: Sanseidō Shoten, 1912.

Raguet, Émile, trans. *Waga Shu Iezusu Kirisuto no Shinyaku Seisho*. Tokyo: Kōkyōkai, 1910.

Palmer, Spencer J. *The Church Encounters Asia*. Salt Lake City: Deseret Book, 1970.

Parker, F. Calvin. *The Southern Baptist Mission in Japan, 1889–1989*. Lanham, Maryland: University Press of America, 1991.

Parker Ranch Foundation Trust. "Parker Ranch Historic Homes." Kamuela, Hawaii: Parker Ranch Foundation Trust, not dated.

Saegusa, Hiroto, and Hiroo Torii. *Nihon Shūkyō Shisō Shi*. Tokyo: Mikasa Shobō, 1938.

Saito, Yoshifumi. *Honyaku no Sahō*. Tokyo: Tōkyō Daigaku Shuppankai, 2007.

Sakurai, Masashi. *Meiji Shūkyō Undō Shi*. Tokyo: Morimoto Shoten, 1932.

———. *Kinsei Nihon Shūkyō Shisō Shi*. Fukuoka: Tonshindō, 1944.

Sapporo Nōgakkō Gakugeikai, comp. *Sapporo Nōgaggō*. Tokyo: Shōkabō, 1898.

Sasaki, Sasabune (Shuichi). *Amerika Seikatsu*. Los Angeles: Taishūsha, 1937.

Sasaki, Sasabune. *Yokuryūjo Seikatsu Ki*. Los Angeles: Rafu Shoten, 1950.

Sato, Hideo, ed. *Kyōiku: Goshin-ei to Kyōiku Chokugo*, vol. 1. Tokyo: Misuzu Shobō, 1994.

Saturday Press. *The Shepherd Saint of Lanai, Priest of Melchisedec, President of the Isles of the Sea, Rich "Primacy" Revelations*. Honolulu: Thos. G. Thrum, 1882.

Scharffs, Gilbert W. *Mormonism in Germany: A History of the Church of Jesus Christ of Latter-day Saints in Germany between 1840 and 1970*. Salt Lake City: Deseret Book, 1970.

Serikawa, Hiromichi. *Kindaika no Bukkyō Shisō*. Tokyo: Daitō Shuppansha, 1989.

Shiga, Naoya. *Shiga Naoya Zenshū*, vol. 4. Tokyo: Iwanami Shoten, 1973.

Shimada, Hiromi. *Sōka Gakkai*. Tokyo: Shinchōsha, 2004.

Shimaoka, Hiroshi. *Hawai Imin no Rekishi*. Tokyo: Tosho Kankōkai, 1978.

Shimazono, Susumu. *Kokka Shintō to Nihonjin*. Tokyo: Iwanami Shoten, 2010.

Shimonaka, Kunihiko, comp. *Nihon Jinmei Daijiten*, vol. 1. Tokyo: Heibonsha, 1979.

Shiono, Kōshun. *Tenka no Daigimon Sōmake Dokusatsu Jiken*. Tokyo: Takajima Kiyoshichi, 1893.
Shōwa Joshi Daigaku Kindai Bungaku Kenkyū Shitsu. *Kindai Bungaku Kenkyū Sōsho*, vol. 39. Tokyo: Shōwa Joshi Daigaku Kindai Bungaku Kenkyū Shitsu, 1975.
Shunpokō Tsuishōkai. *Ito Hirobumi Den*, vol. 1. Tokyo: Tōseisha, 1940.
Sōmuchō Tōkeikyoku. *Nihon Tōkei Nenkan*, various issues.
Sonoda, Minoru, ed. *Shintō: Nihon no Minzoku Shūkyō*. Tokyo: Kōbundō, 1988.
Stark, Rodney and Roger Finke. *Acts of Faith: Explaining the Human Side of Religion*. Berkeley and Los Angeles: University of California Press, 2000.
Steiner, George. *After Babel: Aspects of Language and Translation*. London: Oxford University Press, 1975.
Sugimura, Sojinkan. *Hankyū Shūyū*. Tokyo: Yūrakusha, 1909.
Suzuki, Norihisa. *Meiji Shūkyō Shichō no Kenkyū, Shūkyōgaku Kotohajime*. Tokyo: Tōkyō Daigaku Shuppankai, 1979.
———. *Seisho no Nihongo*. Tokyo: Iwanami Shoten, 2006.
Takagi, Shinji. "From Recipient to Donor: Japan's Official Aid Flows, 1945 to 1990 and Beyond." *Princeton Essays in International Finance*, no. 196. Princeton, New Jersey: Department of Economics, Princeton University, 1995.
———. *Conquering the Fear of Freedom: Japanese Exchange Rate Policy since 1945*. Oxford: Oxford University Press, 2015.
Takahashi, Goro. *Hai Gitetsugaku Ron*. Tokyo: Minyūsha Shuppan, 1893.
———, trans. *Sei Fukuinsho, Jō*. Tokyo: Tenshu Kōkyōkai, 1895.
———, trans. *Sei Fukuinsho, Ge*. Tokyo: Tenshu Kōkyōkai, 1897.
———. *Morumonkyō to Morumonkyōto*. Tokyo: self-published, 1902.
———. *Sekai Sansei Ron*. Tokyo: Maekawa Bun-ei-kaku, 1903.
Takahashi, Kanji. *Imin no Chichi Katsunuma Tomizō Sensei*. Honolulu: Bunkichi Suda, 1953.
Takatori, Masao. *Shintō no Seiritsu*. Tokyo: Heibonsha, 1993.
Takemae, Eiji. *GHQ*. Tokyo: Iwanami Shoten, 1983.
Takemura, Tamio. *Haishō Undō*. Tokyo: Chūō Kōronsha, 1982.
Takenaka, Kenichi, ed. *Jinmei Jiten: Manshū ni Watatta Ichiman Nin*. Tokyo: Kōseisha, 2012.
Takeuchi, Hiroshi, ed. *Rainichi Seiyōjinmei Jiten*. Tokyo: Nichigai Associates, 1983.
Takeuchi, Kojiro. *Beikoku Seihokubu Nihon Imin Shi*. Seattle: Daihoku Nippōsha, 1929.
Tamamuro, Fumio. *Sōshiki to Danka*. Tokyo: Yoshikawa Kōbunsha, 1999.
Tamano, Kazushi. *Sōka Gakkai no Kenkyū*. Tokyo: Kōdansha, 2008.
Tamura, Yoshiro. *Japanese Buddhism: A Cultural History*. Tokyo: Kōsei Publishing, 2000.
Tate, Lucile C. *Boyd K. Packer: A Watchman on the Tower*. Salt Lake City: Bookcraft, 1995.
Tatsukawa, Shoji. *Byōki no Shakai Shi*. Tokyo: Nihon Hōsō Shuppan Kyōkai, 1971.
Teikoku Daigaku Shusshinroku Hensansho. *Teidai Shusshin Roku*. Tokyo: Teikoku Daigaku Shusshinroku Hensansho, 1922.
Teikoku Hoteru. *Teikoku Hoteru Hyakunenshi*. Tokyo: Teikoku Hoteru, 1990.
Thernstrom, Stephan, ed. *Harvard Encyclopedia of American Ethnic Groups*. Cambridge, Massachusetts: Harvard University Press, 1980.
Tōhoku Teikoku Daigaku. *Tōhoku Teikoku Daigaku Ichiran*. Sendai: Tōhoku Teikoku Daigaku, 1924 and 1925.
Tōkyō Daigaku. *Tōkyō Daigaku Hyakunen Shi*, vol. 1. Tokyo: Tōkyō Daigaku Shuppankai, 1984.
Tōkyō-shi, ed. *Tōkyō Annai*, vol. 1. Tokyo: Shōkabō, 1907.
———, ed. *Tōkyō-shi Chōmei Enkaku Shi*, vol. 1. Tokyo: Tōkyō-shi, 1938.
Tōkyō-to Chiyoda Kuyakusho, ed. *Chiyoda-ku Shi*. Tokyo: Tōkyō-to Chiyoda Kuyakusho, 1960.
Tōkyō-to Chūō Kuyakusho, ed. *Chūō-ku Shi*. Tokyo: Tōkyō-to Chūō Kuyakusho, 1958.
Toyoda, Minoru. *Shodai Sōri Itō Hirobumi*. Tokyo: Kōdansha, 1992.
Tōyō Keizai Shinpōsha. *Shōwa Kokuzei Sōran*, vol. 1. Tokyo: Tōyō Keizai Shinpōsha, 1991.

Tsunemitsu, Konen. *Nihon Bukkyō Tobei Shi*. Tokyo: Bukkyō Shuppankyoku, 1964.
Tsurumi, Shunsuke. *An Intellectual History of Wartime Japan 1931–1945*. London and New York: Routledge & Kegan Paul, 1986.
Tsūshinshashi Kankōkai. *Tsūshinsha Shi*. Tokyo: Tsūshinshashi Kankōkai, 1958.
Tsūshō Sangyōshō, ed. *Tsūshō Sangyō Seisaku Shi*, vol. 4. Tokyo: Tsūshō Sangyōshō, 1990.
Twine, Nanette. *Language and the Modern State: The Reform of Written Japanese*. New York: Routledge, 1991.
Uchida, Toru. *Morumonshū*. Tokyo: Bunmeidō, 1902.
———, comp. *The Light of Truth (The Life and Teachings of Buddha)*. Tokyo: Morie Honten, 1905.
Uchimura, Kanzo. *How I Became a Christian: Out of My Diary*. Tokyo: Keiseisha, 1906 (Japanese translation: *Yo wa Ikanishite Kirisuto Shinto to Narishika*. Translated by Saburo Ouchi. Tokyo: Kōdansha, 1971).
United Japanese Society of Hawaii, ed. *Hawai Nihonjin Imin Shi*, second edition with a Supplement. Honolulu: Hawai Hōchi, 1977.
United States Bureau of the Census. *Statistical Abstract of the United States: 1970*, ninety-first edition. Washington: United States Department of Commerce, 1970.
United States Department of Commerce. *Historical Statistics of the United States 1789–1945*. Washington: United States Department of Commerce, 1949.
Vine, William Edwy. *Vine's Concise Dictionary of the Bible*. Nashville: Thomas Nelson, 1997.
Vine, W. E., Merrill F. Unger, and William White Jr. *An Expository Dictionary of Biblical Words*. Nashville: Thomas Nelson, 1984.
Walker, Ronald W., Richard E. Turley Jr., and Glen M. Leonard. *Massacre at Mountain Meadows: An American Tragedy*. New York: Oxford University Press, 2008.
Walton, H. Dyke. *They Built With Faith*. Bountiful, Utah: Horizon Publishers, 1979.
Walz, Eric. *Nikkei in the Interior West: Japanese Immigration and Community Building 1882–1945*. Tucson, Arizona: University of Arizona Press, 2012.
Ward, Robert E., and Frank Joseph Shulman, eds. *The Allied Occupation of Japan, 1945–1952*. Chicago: American Library Association, 1974.
Waseda Daigaku Kōyūkai. *Kaiin Meibo*, 1965 edition. Tokyo: Waseda Daigaku Kōyūkai, 1966.
Waseda Daigaku Shakai Kagaku Kenkyūsho, ed. *Ōkuma Bunsho*, vol. 2. Tokyo: Waseda Daigaku Shakai Kagaku Kenkyūsho, 1959.
Watanabe, Minoru. *Kindai Nihon Kaigai Ryūgakusei Shi*, vol. 1. Tokyo: Kōdansha, 1977.
Williams, Justin, Sr. *Japan's Political Revolution under MacArthur: A Participant's Account*. Athens, Georgia: University of Georgia Press, 1979.
Yamamoto, Hideteru, ed. *Nihon Kirisuto Kyōkai Shi*. Tokyo: Nihon Kirisuto Kyōkai, 1928.
Yamamoto, Masahide. *Kindai Buntai Hassei no Shiteki Kenkyū*. Tokyo: Iwanami Shoten, 1965.
———. *Gembunitchi no Rekishi Kōsatsu*. Tokyo: Ōfūsha, 1971.
Yamamoto, Shigeru. *Jōyaku Kaisei Shi*. Tokyo: Takayama Shoin, 1943.
Yamashita, Soen. *Nippon Hawai Kōryū Shi*. Tokyo: Daitō Shuppansha, 1943.
———. *Gan-nen-mono no Omokage*. Tokyo: Nihon Hawai Kyōkai, 1968.
Yano Kōta Kinenkai. *Sūji de Miru Nihon no Hyakunen*, second edition. Tokyo: Kokuzeisha, 1981.
Yasuba, Yasukichi, and Takenori Inoki, eds. *Kōdo Seichō*. Tokyo: Iwanami Shoten, 1989.
Yasumaru, Yoshio. *Kamigami no Meiji Ishin*. Tokyo: Iwanami Shoten, 1979.
Yoshie, Akio. *Shinbutsu Shūgō*. Tokyo: Iwanami Shoten, 1996.
Yokohama Shiyakusho, ed. *Yokohama-shi Shikō Fuzokuhen*. Yokohama: Yokohama Shiyakusho, 1932.
Yoshida, Morio. *Nihon no Koto wa Naze Kūshū wo Manukareta Ka*. Tokyo: Asahi Shinbunsha, 2002.
Yoshimi, Kaneko. *Baishō no Shakaishi*. Tokyo: Yūzankaku Shuppan, 1984.
Yunojiri, Hatsutaro. *Katogi San Rōkyōdai*. Tokyo and Osaka: Denki-no-tomo-sha, 1932.

Bibliography

Book Chapters:

Akutagawa, Ryunosuke. "Sōgi Ki," 1916. In *Ryunosuke Akutagawa. Rashōmon, Hana, Imogayu.* Tokyo: Kadokawa Shoten, 1950.

Arrington, Leonard J. "Utah's Ambiguous Reception: The Relocated Japanese Americans." In *Japanese Americans: From Relocation to Redress*, revised edition, edited by R. Daniels, S. C. Taylor, and H. H. L. Kitano, 92–98. Seattle and London: University of Washington Press, 1991.

Cannon, Donald Q. "Angus M. Cannon: Pioneer, President, Patriarch." In *Supporting Saints: Life Stories of Nineteenth-Century Mormons*, edited by Donald Q. Cannon and David J. Whittaker, 369–401. Provo, Utah: Religious Studies Center, Brigham Young University, 1985.

Clement, Russell T. and Sheng-Luen Tsai. "East Wind to Hawaii: Contributions and History of Chinese and Japanese Mormons in Hawaii." In *Proceedings of the Second Annual Conference of the Mormon Pacific Historical Society*, 11–19. Laie, Hawaii: Brigham Young University–Hawaii, 1981.

Coox, Alvin D. "The Pacific War." In *The Cambridge History of Japan, vol. 6: The Twentieth Century*, edited by Peter Duus, 315–82. Cambridge and New York: Cambridge University Press, 1988.

Daniels, Roger. "The Forced Migrations of West Coast Japanese Americans, 1942–1946: A Quantitative Note." In *Japanese Americans: From Relocation to Redress*, revised edition, edited by R. Daniels, S. C. Taylor, and H. H. L. Kitano, 72–74. Seattle and London: University of Washington Press, 1991.

Dohi, Akio. "Kindai Tennōsei to Kirisutokyō." In *Kindai Tennōsei no Keisei to Kirisutokyō*, edited by Tomisaka Kirisutokyō Sentā, 239–345. Tokyo: Shinkyō Shuppansha, 1996.

———. "Kindai Tennōsei to Kirisutokyō." In *Taishō Demokurashī, Tennōsei, Kirisutokyō*, edited by Tomisaka Kirisutokyō Sentā, 288–328. Tokyo: Shinkyō Shuppansha, 2001.

Fukushima, Hirotaka. "Kaigai Kyōjō Shisatsu no Rekishiteki Igi." In *Rōnshu Nihon Bukkyōshi*, vol. 8, edited by E. Ikeda, 89–110. Tokyo: Yūzankan Shuppan, 1987.

Furuto, Sharlene B. C. L. "Japanese Saints in Hawaii and Japan: Values and Implications for Baptism." In *Proceedings of the Eleventh Annual Conference of the Mormon Pacific Historical Society*, 1–15. Laie, Hawaii: Brigham Young University–Hawaii, 1990.

Gessel, Van C. "Languages of the Lord: The Japanese Translations of the Book of Mormon." In *Taking the Gospel to the Japanese, 1901 to 2001*, edited by Reid L. Neilson and Van C. Gessel, 127–45. Provo, Utah: Brigham Young University Press, 2006.

Hahimoto, Tetsuya. "Toshika to Minshū Undō." In *Nihon Rekishi*, vol. 17, 303–49. Tokyo: Iwanami Shoten, 1976.

Hara, Makoto. "Shūkyō Dantai Hō no moto ni atta Senjika no Kirisutokyō." In *Senjika no Kirisutokyō: Shūkyō Dantai Hō wo megutte*, edited by Kirisutokyō Shi Gakkai, 13–26. Tokyo: Kyōbunkan, 2015.

Hiroi, Tatsutaro. "Kirisutokyō Kōyō." In *San Dai Shūkyō*, edited by Beiho Takashima, part 2 (1–58). Tokyo: Heigo Shuppansha, 1917.

Howes, John F. "Japanese Christians and American Missionaries." In *Changing Japanese Attitudes toward Modernization*, edited by Marius B. Jansen, 337–68. Princeton, New Jersey: Princeton University Press, 1965.

Ichida, Shinji, Oscar Misaka, Tats Misaka, and Raymond Uno. "J-Town Ogden." In *Japanese Americans in Utah*, edited by Ted Nagata, 36–39. Salt Lake City: JA Centennial Committee, 1996.

Ichiki, Shiro, "Ichiki Shirō Jijoden." In *Kagoshima-ken Shiryō: Chūgikō Shiryō*, vol. 7, edited by Kagoshima-ken Ishin Shiryō Hensan Sho, 901–1037. Kagoshima: Kagoshima-ken, 1980.

Ikeda, Eishun. "Kindaiteki Kaimei Shisō to Bukkyō." In *Rōnshu Nihon Bukkyō Shi*, vol. 8, edited by E. Ikeda, 1–65. Tokyo: Yūzankan Shuppan, 1987.
Imai, Hiroshi. "Meiji Ishin to Kyōiku." In *Kyōiku no Seido to Rekishi*, edited by Yoshiyuki Hirooka, 120–31. Kyoto: Mineruva Shobō, 2007.
———. "Kindai Kokka no Seiritsu to Kyōiku." In *Kyōiku no Seido to Rekishi*, edited by Yoshiyuki Hirooka, 132–42. Kyoto: Mineruva Shobō, 2007.
Kaino, Nobuo. "Nihon Kirisuto Kyōdan." In *Senjika no Kirisutokyō: Shūkyō Dantai Hō wo megutte*, edited by Kirisutokyō Shi Gakkai, 27–52. Tokyo: Kyōbunkan, 2015.
Kaminaka, Sanae. "Hōrinesu." In *Senjika no Kirisutokyō: Shūkyō Dantai Hō wo megutte*, edited by Kirisutokyō Shi Gakkai, 145–78. Tokyo: Kyōbunkan, 2015.
Kasai, Alice. "Wartime Years: Discrimination against Japanese-Americans during WWII." In *Japanese Americans in Utah*, edited by Ted Nagata, 138–41. Salt Lake City: JA Centennial Committee, 1996.
Kawagoe, Toshihiko. "Nōchi Kaikaku." In *Sengo Nihon no Keizai Kaikaku: Shijō to Seifu*, edited by Yutaka Kosai and Juro Teranishi. Tokyo: Tōkyō Daigaku Shuppankai, 1993.
Konishi, Jeanne Matsumiya. "The Tintic Mountains." In *Japanese Americans in Utah*, edited by Ted Nagata, 62–64. Salt Lake City: JA Centennial Committee, 1996.
Kurahashi, Katsuhito. "Taishō Demokurashī to Kagawa Toyohiko." In *Taishō Demokurashī, Tennōsei, Kirisutokyō*, edited by Tomisaka Kirisutokyo Sentā, 252–328. Tokyo: Shinkyō Shuppansha, 2001.
Le Gendre, Charles. "Ezochi Kaitaku ni Kansuru Ikensho," 18 July 1875. In *Ōkuma Bunsho*, vol. 2, compiled by Waseda Daigaku Shakai Kagaku Kenkyūsho, 9–27. Tokyo: Waseda Daigaku Shakai Kagaku Kenkyūsho, 1959.
Marumoto, Masaji. "'First Year' Immigrants to Hawaii and Eugene Van Reed." In *East across the Pacific: Historical and Sociological Studies of Japanese Immigration and Assimilation*, edited by Hilary Conroy and T. Scott Miyakawa, 5–39. Santa Barbara, California: American Bibliographical Center–Clio Press, 1972.
Matsuzawa, Hiroaki. "Kirisutokyō to Chishikijin." In *Nihon Rekishi*, vol. 16, 281–320. Tokyo: Iwanami Shoten, 1976.
Miyabe, Kingo. "Shōden." In Inazo Nitobe, *Nitobe Inazō Zenshū*, vol. 1, 427–45. Tokyo: Kyōbunkan, 1969.
Miyata, Noboru. "Hayari Shinbutsu to Zokushinkō." In *Edo Bukkyō*, edited by H. Nakamura, K. Kasahara, and H. Kaneoka, 183–221. Tokyo: Kōsei Shuppansha, 1972.
Miyoshi, Chiharu. "Katorikku Kyōkai (Nihon Tenshu Kōkyō Kyōdan)." In *Senjika no Kirisutokyō: Shūkyō Dantai Hō wo megutte*, edited by Kirisutokyō Shi Gakkai, 53–85. Tokyo: Kyōbunkan, 2015.
Mori, Ogai. "Kanzan Jittoku Engi," 1916. In Ogai Mori. *Abe Ichizoku, Maihime*. Tokyo: Shinchōsha, 1968.
Moriyasu, Haruko Terasawa. "Salt Lake's Nihonjin Machi." In *Japanese Americans in Utah*, edited by Ted Nagata, 29–31. Salt Lake City: JA Centennial Committee, 1996.
Moriyasu, Haruko Terasawa. "The Utah Nippo." In *Japanese Americans in Utah*, edited by Ted Nagata, 149–50. Salt Lake City: JA Centennial Committee, 1996.
Neilson, Reid L., and Laurie F. Maffly-Kipp. "Nineteenth-century Mormonism and the Pacific Basin Frontier: An Introduction." In *Proclamation to the People: Nineteenth-century Mormonism and the Pacific Basin Frontier*, edited by L. F. Maffly-Kipp and R. L. Neilson, 3–20. Salt Lake City: University of Utah Press, 2008.
Nish, Ian. Introduction to *Japan Rising: The Iwakura Embassy to the USA and Europe 1871–1873*, compiled by Kunitake Kume, xi–xxix. Cambridge and New York: Cambridge University Press, 2009.

Nitobe, Inazo. "Tōgyō Kairyō Ikensho," September 1901. In Inazo Itobe. *Nitobe Inazō Zenshū*, vol. 4, 169–226. Tokyo: Kyōbunkan, 1969.

Oe, Mitsuru. "Seikōkai." In *Senjika no Kirisutokyō: Shūkyō Dantai Hō wo megutte*, edited by Kirisutokyō Shi Gakkai, 115–43. Tokyo: Kyōbunkan, 2015.

Oguri, Junko, and Tetsuya Ohama. "Chika Shinkō: Sono Genryū to Jittai." In *Edo Bukkyō*, edited by H. Nakamura, K. Kasahara, and H. Kaneoka, 71–179. Tokyo: Kōsei Shuppansha, 1972.

Ouchi, Saburo. "Kaisetsu." In Kanzo Uchimura. *Yo wa Ikanishite Kirisuto Shinto to Narishika*, 236–51. Tokyo: Kōdansha, 1971.

———. "Nenpu." In Kanzo Uchimura. *Yo wa Ikanishite Kirisuto Shinto to Narishika*, 252–61. Tokyo: Kōdansha, 1971.

Papanikolas, Helen. "Northern Utah." In *Japanese Americans in Utah*, edited by Ted Nagata, 47–49. Salt Lake City: JA Centennial Committee, 1996.

Papanikolas, Helen Z., and Alice Kasai. "Japanese Life in Utah." In *The Peoples of Utah*, edited by H. Z. Papanikolas, 333–62. Salt Lake City: Utah State Historical Society, 1976.

Reid, David. "Internationalization in Japanese Religion." In *Religion in Japanese Culture: Where Living Traditions Meet a Changing World*, edited by Noriyoshi Tamaru and David Reid, 184–98. Tokyo: Kōdansha International, 1996.

Rochford, E. Burke Jr. "The Sociology of New Religious Movements." In *Religion and the Social Order, Volume 13: American Sociology of Religion: Histories*, edited by Anthony J. Blasi, 253–90. Boston: Brill Academic Publishers, 2007.

Sasaki, Sasabune. "Bafun Tetsugaku." In *Amerika Bungaku Shū*, edited by Isshin Yamasaki. Tokyo: Keigansha, 1937.

Sato, Tomi. "Dai Ichi Ward." In *Japanese Americans in Utah*, by Ted Nagata, 95–96. Salt Lake City: JA Centennial Committee, 1996.

Shiga, Naoya. "Kijin Dassai." In Naoya Shiga. *Shiga Naoya Zenshū*, vol. 4, 369–82. Tokyo: Iwanami Shoten, 1973.

Smith, Sarah Cox. "Translator or Translated? The Portrayal of the Church of Jesus Christ of Latter-day Saints in Print in Meiji Japan." In *Taking the Gospel to the Japanese, 1901 to 2001*, edited by R. L. Neilson and V. C. Gessel, 233–61. Provo, Utah: Brigham Young University Press, 2006.

Suzuki, Norihisa. "Kaisetsu." In *Fukkokuban Rikugō Zasshi*, vol. 12. Tokyo: Fuji Shuppan, 1988.

Takagi, Shinji. "Monks, Nationalists, and the Emperor: The Mormon Struggle in Japan, 1901–1924." In *Directions for Mormon Studies in the Twenty-First Century*, edited by Patrick Q. Mason, 49–71. Salt Lake City: University of Utah Press, 2016.

Tamamuro, Fumio, and Junko Oguri. "Bakuhan Taiseika no Bukkyō." In *Edo Bukkyō*, edited by H. Nakamura, K. Kasahara, and H. Kaneoka, 7–70. Tokyo: Kōsei Shuppansha, 1972.

Tamamuro, Fumio. "Bakuhan Taisei to Bukkyō." In *Ronshū Nihon Bukkyō Shi*, vol. 7, edited by F. Tamamura, 1–40. Tokyo: Yūzankaku, 1986.

Taniguchi, Nancy J. "Japanese in Carbon County." In *Japanese Americans in Utah*, edited by Ted Nagata, 60–62. Salt Lake City: JA Centennial Committee, 1996.

Thomas, Elbert D. "Elbert D. Thomas." In *Thirteen Americans: Their Spiritual Autobiographies*, edited by Louis Finkelstein, 129–58. New York: Harper & Brothers, 1953.

Ushio, Shake. "Early Farming." In *Japanese Americans in Utah*, edited by Ted Nagata, 79–81. Salt Lake City: JA Centennial Committee, 1996.

Ushioda, Sharlie C. "Man of Two Worlds: An Inquiry into the Value System of Inazo Nitobe (1862–1933)." In *East across the Pacific: Historical and Sociological Studies of Japanese Immigration and Assimilation*, edited by H. Conroy and T. S. Miyakawa, 187–210. Santa Barbara, California: American Bibliographical Center–Clio Press, 1972.

Van Wagoner, Richard S. *Mormon Polygamy: A History*. Salt Lake City: Signature Books, 1986.

Walker, Ronald W. "Heber J. Grant." In *The Presidents of the Church*, edited by L. J. Arrington, 211–48. Salt Lake City: Deseret Book, 1986.

Watanabe, Kan. "Japanese Baseball Fan Reaches Home." In *No More Strangers*, vol. 2, edited by Hartman and Connie Rector, 99–102. Salt Lake City: Bookcraft, 1973.

Yamamoto, Takeo. "Jinja eno Minzoku Shinkō." In *Edo Bukkyō*, edited by H. Nakamura, K. Kasahara, and H. Kaneoka, 223–45. Tokyo: Kōsei Shuppansha, 1972.

Yasumaru, Yoshio. "Rekishi no nakadeno Kattō to Mosaku." In *Kindaika to Dentō*, edited by Y. Yasumaru, 3–64. Tokyo: Shūjunsha, 1986.

———. "Tennōseika no Minshū to Shūkyō." *Nihon Rekishi*, vol. 16, 321–58. Tokyo: Iwanami Shoten, 1976.

Articles in LDS Church Periodicals:

"Activity in Japan Mission." *The Latter-day Saints' Millennial Star* 65 (1903): 363–66.

"Introducing the Gospel in Japan." *Improvement Era* 6 (1903): 708–14.

Anderson, Joseph. "When a Man is Called of God." *Instructor* 99 (1964): 302–4.

Andrus, Paul C. "Kanzen no Mama no Fukuinsho—Shinyaku Morumonkei wo Shuppansu." *Seito no Michi* 1 (June 1957): 1–2.

———. "Gisei wo Motomeru Sakebi." *Seito no Michi* 2 (December 1958): 8–9.

Brockbank, Bernard P. "The Mormon Pavilion at Expo '70." *Improvement Era* 74 (1970): 120–22.

Cannon, Hugh J. "The Land of China Dedicated." *Juvenile Instructor* 56 (1921): 115–17.

Clark, J. Reuben Jr. "The Outpost in Mid-Pacific." *Improvement Era* 38 (1935): 530–35.

Clissold, Edward L. "A Call to Japan." *Improvement Era* 52 (1948): 206–8, 243–45.

———. "Mission Head Reports Japanese Mission Baptisms." *Deseret News*, Church Section. 15 December 1948.

Cowley, Matthew. "The Language of Sincerity." *Improvement Era* 52 (1949): 715, 762.

Ensign, Horace S. "The Japanese Mission." *The Latter-day Saints' Millennial Star* 66 (1904): 337–40.

Fillmore, Wade W. "Shinden Projekuto." *Seito no Michi* 7 (1963): 672–73.

Fujiwara, Takeo. "Relationship between Shinto and Mormonism." *Improvement Era* 36 (1933): 654–55, 675–76.

Harris, Franklin S. "An International Science Congress: How the World Can Be Made a Paradise for Its Inhabitants." *Improvement Era* 30 (1927): 348–51.

Heal, Muriel Jenkins. "We Will Go: The Robertson Response." *Ensign* 12 (1982): 32–35.

Hinckley, Bryant S. "Hugh J. Cannon." *Improvement Era* 31 (1928): 453–56.

———. "Hugh J. Cannon." *Improvement Era* 35 (1931): 2–3.

Hinckley, Gordon B. "The Church in the Orient." *Improvement Era* 67 (1963): 167–70.

Inouye, Go. "Testimony of a Japanese Member of the Church." *Improvement Era* 21 (1918): 815–17.

Kikuchi, Yoshihiko. "Shu yo Ware wa Nani wo Nasubeki ka." *Seito no Michi* 9 (1965): 62–63.

Konno, Yukiko. "Fujiya Nara: Twice a Pioneer." *Ensign* 12 (1993): 31–33.

Kumagai, Tamano. "Letter from a Japanese Convert." *Juvenile Instructor* 53 (1918): 180.

Kurami, Mitsuo. "Nihon no Dendō Shoki no Kaishūsha Kumagai Tamano Shimai Jūnana Sai no Nikki ni miru Shinkō no Ibuki." *Seito no Michi* 27 (June 1985): local pages, 1–2.

McKay, David O. "Christmas in Tokyo." *Juvenile Instructor* 56 (1921): 113–15.

Nara, Fujiya. "Nihon Dendōbu no Kaiko." *Seito no Michi* 2 (1958): May, 31–32; June, 24–25; July, 27–28.

Price, Harrison T. "A Cup of Tea." *Improvement Era* 65 (1962): 160–61, 184, 186.

Sato, Tatsui. "Shinyaku Morumonkei no Shuppan ni saishite." *Seito no Michi* 1 (July 1957): 7–9.

———. "Shinyaku Morumonkei ni tsuite." *Seito no Michi* 1–2 (1957): August, 4–5; September, 7–8; October, 5–6; November, 5–6; December, 10–11; (1958) January, 13–14; February, 13–14.

———. "Watashi no Kaishū." *Seito no Michi* 2 (December 1958): 13–15.

Bibliography

———. "Nachie Tsune Shimai no Ato wo Tazunete." *Seito no Michi* 9 (1965): 508–10.
Smith, Joseph Fielding. "Report from the Far East Missions." *Improvement Era* 58 (1955): 917–18.
Smith, E. Wesley. "The First Japanese Convert to the Church." *Improvement Era* 23 (1919): 177.
Takagi, Tomigoro. "Nihon Dendōbu no Kaiko." *Seito no Michi* 2 (1958): August, 25–26; September, 23–25; October, 24–26; November, 29–31.
———. "Hikari wo Futatabi Uketa Koro." *Seito no Michi* 5 (1961): 23–26, 62–65, 126–27.
———. "Atarashii Sanbika wo Utaimashō." *Seito no Michi* 5 (1961): 380–81.
Taylor, Alma O. "Some Features of Japanese Life." *Improvement Era* 5 (1902): 448–55, 523–28.
———. "A Few Words from Japan." *Improvement Era* 12 (1909): 782–88.
———. "Japan, the Ideal Mission Field." *Improvement Era* 13 (1910): 779–85.
———. "Memories of Far-off Japan: President Grant's First Foreign Mission 1901 to 1903." *Improvement Era* 39 (1936): 690–91.
Yanagida, Toshiko. "Atarashii Sanbika ni Omou." *Seito no Michi* 5 (1961): 378–80.
Watabe, Masao. "Hawai Shinden Hōmon Ki." *Seito no Michi* 9 (1965): 449–57.
Widtsoe, John A. "The Japanese Mission in Action." *Improvement Era* 42 (1939): 88–89, 125.
Woodward, Ernest B. "Thrilling Experience of Four Mormon Missionaries in the Tokyo Disaster." *Improvement Era* 27 (1923): 126–33.

Articles in Other Periodicals:

Barney, Kevin L. "Poetic Diction and Parallel Word Pairs in the Book of Mormon." *Journal of Book of Mormon Studies* 4 (1995): 15–81.
Biggs, Barton M. "The Outraged Okinawans." *Harper's Magazine* 217 (December 1958): 56–60.
Bitton, Davis and Val Lambson. "Demographic Limits of Nineteenth-Century Mormon Polygyny." *Brigham Young University Studies Quarterly* 51 (2012): 7–26.
Brady, Frederick R. "Two Meiji Scholars Introduce the Mormons to Japan." *Brigham Young University Studies* 23 (1983): 167–78.
Britsch, Lanier R. "The Closing of the Early Japan Mission." *Brigham Young University Studies* 15 (1975): 171–90.
Brown, Hugh B. "Prophecies Regarding Japan." *Brigham Young University Studies* 10 (1970): 159–60.
Carter, Steve. "The Rise of the Nazi Dictatorship and Its Relationship with the Mormon Church in Germany, 1933–1939." *International Journal of Mormon Studies* 3 (2010): 56–89.
Caruthers, Sandra C. "Anodyne for Expansion: Meiji Japan, the Mormons, and Charles LeGendre." *Pacific Historical Review* 38 (May 1969): 129–39.
Conkling, Christopher J. "Members without a Church: Japanese Mormons in Japan from 1924 to 1948." *Brigham Young University Studies* 15 (1975): 191–214.
Dawson, Lorne L. "The Cultural Significance of New Religious Movements: The Case of Soka Gakkai." *Sociology of Religion* 62 (2001): 337–64.
Duke, James T. "The Literary Structure and Doctrinal Significance of Alma 13:1–9." *Journal of Book of Mormon Studies* 5 (1996): 103–18.
Fukumi, Hideo. "Nihon no Korera Ryūkō Shi (I)." *Kagaku* 47 (1977): 457–64.
Gao, Yu. "Kindai Nihon niokeru Kokka to Misshon Sukūru." *Tōkyō Daigaku Daigakuin Kyōikugaku Kiyō* 50 (2010): 35–43.
Gibney, Frank. "Okinawa: Forgotten Island." *Time* (28 November 1949): 24–25.
Hamasaki, Kazutoshi. "Nihon ni okeru Senjika no Bungakushatachi." *Nagasaki Daigaku Kyōyōbu Kiyō* 38 (1997): 63–86.
Hashimoto, Hideo, and William McPherson. "Rise and Decline of Sokagakkai: Japan and the United States." *Review of Religious Research* 17 (1976): 82–92.
Henderson, Jason, Brent Gloy, and Michael Boehlje. "Agriculture's Boom–Bust Cycles: Is This Time Different?" *Federal Reserve Bank of Kansas City Economic Review* (Fourth Quarter, 2011): 83–105.

Hiroi, Tatsutaro. "Dare ka Gyūba no tame ni Namida wo Sosogu mono zo." *Taiyō* 5 (1899): No. 17, 174–76; No. 18, 171–75.
Hiroi, Tatsutaro. "Dōbutsu Hogo Ron." *Chūō Kōron* 14 (December 1899): 7–14.
———. "Shingaku jō no Miketsu Mondai." *Rikugō Zasshi* 265 (1903): 17–29.
———. "Nyūkai no Ji." *Rikugō Zasshi* 284 (1904): 120–31.
Iannaccone, Laurence R. "Introduction to the Economics of Religion." *Journal of Economic Literature* 36 (1998): 1465–96.
Iseda, Tetsuji. "Meijiki Dōbutsu Aigo Undō no Dōkizuke wa Ikanaru Mono de atta ka." *Shakai to Rinri* 20 (2006): 139–53.
Ishida, Kazuo. "Shūkyō Kyōiku Kinshi no Shirei nitsutie." *Seisen Joshi Daigaku Kiyō* 8 (1961): 41–69.
Katanuma, Seiji. "The Church in Japan." *Brigham Young University Studies* 14 (1973): 16–28.
Kelly, Jason M. "Why Did Henry Stimson Spare Kyoto from the Bomb?: Confusion in Postwar Historiography." *Journal of American-East Asian Relations* 19 (2012): 183–203.
Kido, Jackie. "Hawaii's Ranching Dynasty: Parker Ranch." *Spirit of Hawaii* (July 1997): 8–12.
Kodama, Masaaki. "Imin Kaisha nitsuite no Ichi Kōsatsu." *Geibi Chihō Shi Kenkyū* 127 (1980): 12–25.
Komiya, Mayumi. "Taiheiyō Sensōka no Tekikokujin Yokuryū: Nihon Kokunai ni Zaijūshita Eibeikei Gaikokujin no Yokuryū nit suite." *Ochanomizu Shigaku* 43 (1999): 1–48.
Kunihara, Misako, and Rui Kohiyama. "Nihon Joshi Kirisutokyō Kyōikukai no Sōsetsu to Katsudō." *Kirisutokyō Gakkō Kyōiku Dōmei Hyakunenshi Kiyō* 7 (2009): 9–56.
Morino, Kenkichi. "Hokubei no Tankō Rōdō." *Amerika* 11 (1907): 8–9.
Murayama, Yuzo. "Contractors, Collusion, and Competition: Japanese Immigrant Railroad Laborers in the Pacific Northwest, 1898–1911." *Explorations in Economic History* 21 (1984): 290–305.
Masuta, Natsuko. "Terasawa Kuniko." *Sankei Shinbun*, 28 October 2001: 12; 29 October 2001: 13; 30 October 2001: 14; 31 October 2001: 13; 1 November 2001: 18.
Nakano, Jiro. "Sentaro Kawashima: Japanese Settlers of Waipio Valley." *Hawaii Herald*, 20 June 1986: 14–15.
Nara, Fujiya. Interview by Shinichi Yano. *Morumon Fōramu* 4 (1990): 26–36.
Oh, John Kie-chang. "The Nichiren Shoshu of America." *Review of Religious Research* 14 (1973): 169–77.
Ohata, Tokushiro. "Nihon ni okeru Gaikokujin Taigū no Hensen (2)." *Ajia Kenkyū* 15 (July 1968): 59–80.
Omori, Hideko. "Kirisutokyō Joshi Kyōikukai to Kirisutokyō Rengō Joshi Daigaku Undō." *Kirisutokyō Gakkō Kyōiku Dōmei Hyakunenshi Kiyō* 1 (2003): 1–33.
Onishi, Haruki. "Kirisutokyō Daigaku Setsuritsu Undō to Kyōiku Dōmei." *Kirisutokyō Gakkō Kyōiku Dōmei Hyakunenshi Kiyō* 1 (2003): 35–70.
Robinson, Greg. "The Great Unknown and the Unknown Great: Pioneering Nisei Writer and Physician, Yasuo Sasaki, Fought for Reproductive Freedom." *Nichi Bei Weekly* (18 October 2012).
Roper, Matthew. "Eyewitness Descriptions of Mesoamerican Swords." *Journal of Book of Mormon Studies* 5 (1996): 150–58.
Shinsato, Roy M. "The Gannen Mono: Great Expectations of the Earliest Japanese Immigrants of Hawaii." *Hawaii Historical Review* 1 (1965): 180–94.
Skousen, Royal. "The Original Language of the Book of Mormon: Upstate New York Dialect, King James English, or Hebrew?" *Journal of Book of Mormon Studies* 3 (1994): 28–38.
Smith, Elmer R. "The 'Japanese' in Utah." *Utah Humanities Review* 2 (1948): 129–44, 208–30.
Sperry, Sidney B. "The Book of Mormon as Translation English." *Journal of Book of Mormon Studies* 4 (1995): 109–17.
Steinberg, Rafael. "Our Unhappy Asia Bastion." *Washington Post* (3 May 1964): E2.

Stimson, Henry L. "The Decision to Use the Atomic Bomb." *Harper's Magazine* 194 (February 1947): 97–107.
Suzue, Eiichi. "Kirishitan Kinsei Kōsatsu Tekkyo Fukokugo no Kinkyō Seisaku." *Kirisutokyō Shigaku* 53 (1999): 83–102.
Takagi Shinji. "Tomizo and Tokujiro: The First Japanese Mormons." *Brigham Young University Studies* 39 (2000): 73–106.
———. "Mormons in the Press: Reactions to the 1901 Opening of the Japan Mission." *Brigham Young University Studies* 40 (2001): 141–75.
———. "The Eagle and the Scattered Flock: Church Beginnings in Occupied Japan, 1945–48." *Journal of Mormon History* 28 (2002): 104–38.
———. "Riding on the Eagle's Wings: The Japanese Mission under American Occupation, 1948–52." *Journal of Mormon History* 29 (2003): 200–232.
———. "Proclaiming the Way in Japanese: The 1909 Translation of the Book of Mormon." *Journal of the Book of Mormon and Other Restoration Scripture* 18 (2009): 18–37.
Takagi, Shinji, Mototsugu Shintani, and Tetsuro Okamoto. "Measuring the Economic Impact of Monetary Union: The Case of Okinawa." *Review of Economics and Statistics* 84 (2004): 858–67.
Takahashi, Goro. "Morumonkyō to Ramakyō." *Taiyō* 7 (October 1901): 21–25.
Tatsuyama, Gakujin. "Morumonshū Kitaru." *Taiyō* 7 (September 1901): 57–58.
Taylor, Leslie A. "The Word of God." *Journal of Book of Mormon Studies* 12 (2003): 52–63.
Thomas, E. D. "Netsuretsunaru Morumonkyō no Kyōri." *Seikō* 20 (1911): 185–92.
Toda, Tetsuko. "Misshon Bōdo to Hainichi Imin Hō." *Yamanachi Kenritsu Joshi Tanki Daigaku Kiyō* 38 (2005): 19–29.
Walker, Ronald W. "Strangers in a Strange Land: Heber J. Grant and the Opening of the Japanese Mission." *Journal of Mormon History* 13 (1986–87): 21–43.
Welch, John W. "Chiasmus in the Book of Mormon." *Brigham Young University Studies* 10 (1969): 69–84.
Yanagida, Toshiko. "Takagi Tomigoro ni tsuite." Interview by Jiro Numano. *Morumon Fōramu*, 6 (1991): 38–48.

Theses and Dissertations:

Boone, Joseph F. *The Roles of the Church of Jesus Christ of Latter-day Saints in Relation to the United States Military, 1900–1975*. PhD diss., Brigham Young University, 1975.
Brady, Frederick R. "The Japanese Reaction to Mormonism and the Translation of Mormon Scripture into Japanese." MA thesis, Sophia University, 1979.
Choi, Dong Sull. *A History of the Church of Jesus Christ of Latter-day Saints in Korea, 1950–1985*. PhD diss., Brigham Young University, 1990.
Fujiwara, Takeo. "The Political and Military Policies of the Tokugawa Shogunate." MA thesis, Brigham Young University, 1934.
Hoare, James Edward. *The Japanese Treaty Ports, 1868–1899: A Study of the Foreign Settlements*. PhD diss., University of London, 1970.
Maher, Richard Thomas. "For God and Country: Mormon Chaplains during World War II." MA thesis, Brigham Young University, 1975.
McGhie, Frank W. "The Life and Intrigues of Walter Murray Gibson." MS thesis, Brigham Young University, 1958.
Nelson, Terry G. "History of the Church of Jesus Christ of Latter-day Saints in Japan from 1948 to 1980." MA thesis, Brigham Young University, 1986.
Nichols, Murray L. "History of the Japan Mission of the Church of Jesus Christ of Latter-day Saints, 1901–1924." MA thesis, Brigham Young University, 1957.

Numano, Jiro. "The Japanese Translation of the Book of Mormon: A Study in the Theory and Practice of Translation." MA thesis, Brigham Young University, 1976.
Scharffs, Gilbert W. *History of the Church of Jesus Christ of Latter-day Saints in Germany between 1840 and 1968.* PhD diss., Brigham Young University, 1969.
Sousa, Esther Leonore Ferreira. "Walter Murray Gibson's Rise to Power in Hawaii." MA thesis, University of Hawaii, 1942.

Journals and Personal/Family Histories

(Copies in author's possession, unless otherwise noted):

Anonymous. "The Life of Sister Tsune Nachiye."
Andersen, Dwayne N. "Dwayne N. Andersen's Experience with the Japanese People." Not dated.
———. "The First Japanese Temple Excursion: Hawaii Temple, 1965." April 1982.
Andersen, Dwayne N. and Peggy H. Andersen. "History of the Northern Far East Mission (Japan and Okinawa), July 1962–August 1965." Not dated.
Andrus, Paul C. "Summary Report by Paul C. Andrus of His Term of Service as President of the Northern Far East Mission from December 9, 1955 to July 19, 1962." September 1975.
Atkin, Dennis H. Journal.
Bauman, Thomas E. "Personal History." Not dated.
Burton, David A. "Carl Christian Amussen." Prepared for the family reunion of the Ezra Taft Benson family, July 1978.
Clissold, Edward L. "Personal Experiences in the Life of Edward L. Clissold." Not dated.
Fairbourn, William R. Journal.
Featherstone, Joseph F. and Marie S. Journal. In possession of Dean R. Featherstone, Bountiful, Utah.
Grant, Heber J. "A Japanese Journal," compiled by Gordon A. Madsen. Provo, Utah: Americana Collection, Harold B. Lee Library, Brigham Young University.
Harris, Franklin Stewart. Journal, 1908–1954. Salt Lake City: LDS Church Archives.
Ivins, Grant Heber. Journal. Salt Lake City: Special Collections, J. Willard Marriott Library, University of Utah.
Jarvis, Gideon Stanford. Journal.
Jarvis, Zora Smith, comp. "Sketches from the Lives of Brigham Jarvis, Sr. and Mary Forsythe Jarvis." 1967.
Kamekona family records. In possession of Noelani Kamekona, Pearl City, Hawaii.
Kane, Joelle Segawa. "Gan-nen-mono." Not dated (a shorter version published in the *Hamakua Times*, June 1999).
Landgren, Leora F. "A Fairbourn Family History, 1927–1988." 1989.
McCune, George M. "A Tribute to Brother Tatsui Sato." June 1996.
Millward, Gene C. Journal, 24 October–17 December 1951.
Nelson, Maurine Larsen. "My Marriage." Not dated.
Nelson, Warren Richard. "Personal and Family Data." 1955.
Richins, James Alden. "The Life Story of Orlando Fowler, 1902–1923." June 1999.
Robertson, Hilton A. "The Autobiography and Daily Diary of Hilton A. Robertson." Salt Lake City: LDS Church Archives.
———. Journal. LDS Church Archives.
Shumway, Norman D. *Times and Seasons of Norman D. Shumway: An Autobiography.* 2009.
Stimpson, Joseph H. Journal. Provo, Utah: BYU Archives.
Stoker, John William. Journal. Salt Lake City: LDS Church Archives.
Takagi, Tomigoro. "Jijoden." Not dated.
Taylor, Alma O. Journal. BYU Archives. Also available electronically from the Harold B. Lee Library Digital Collections, under "Mormon Missionary Diaries."

Terazawa, Chiye and Toshi. Mission Papers, 1938–39, 1952–54. LDS Church Archives.
Woodland, Daniel P. Journal. In possession of John W. Welch, Provo, Utah.
Yanagida, Toshiko. "Ashiato." Not dated.
_____. "Takahashi Nikichi to Takagi Tomigoro." 15 March 1993.
Zitting, Dorothy K., and Barbara O. Kelsch. "The Life Story of Ludwig Koelsch (Louis A. Kelsch), 1856–1917." 1984.

Unpublished or Internet Sources:

Conkling, J. Christopher. "The Dark Ages: The L.D.S. Church and Japan from 1924 to 1948." Brigham Young University, December 1973.
Harris, Heidi. "Changing Racial Perceptions of the Japanese: LDS Rhetoric between 1901 and 1930." 23 August 2010. Accessed 18 November 2015, http://www.patheos.com/blogs/oneeternalround.
Schmalz, Charles L. "The Church in Japan 1905–1908, One Man's Mission." September 1994.
Smiley, Gene. "The U.S. Economy in the 1920s." EH.Net Encyclopedia of Economic and Business History (under "Economy, US, 1920"). Accessed 17 January 2016, https://eh.net/encyclopedia-2/.
Updike, Galen M. "The Iwakura Mission: The Mormons' First Encounter with Japan." Brigham Young University, April 1974.
Yoshinaga, Shinichi, comp. "Hirai Kinzo ni okeru Meiji Bukkyō no Kokusaika ni kansuru Shūkyōshi-Bunkashi-teki Kenkyū." Maizuru Kōtō Senmon Gakkō, 2007.
_____, comp. "Kindai Nihon ni okeru Chishikijin Shūkyō Undō no Gensetsu Kūkan." Maizuru Kōtō Senmon Gakkō, 2012.

Others (in author's possession):

List of attendees, Okamachi Branch, 2 December 1956. Prepared by Haruko Sakamoto, 3 December 1956.
Photocopy of a notice written by Yoshijiro Watanabe, Tazuko Watanabe, and Reiko Mochizuki. September 1935.
Photocopy of the cover page of Takeo Fujiwara's passport. 26 August 1927.
Photocopy of a resume prepared by Takeo Fujiwara. Circa 1934.
Photocopy of a passport application by Tamano Kumagai. 20 February 1928.
Photocopy of a prospectus signed by Genkichi Shiraishi, Torao Yamaide, Kentaro Mochizuki, Magoji Kitagawa, Koshi Nakagawa, Shimako Ishida, Fujiya Nara, Tsuruichi Katsura, Suketomo Nonogaki, and Tamano Kumagai. February 1930.

Correspondence:

Letters addressed to author:
Andersen, Dwayne N. 13 January 1996; 6 February 1997.
Andrus, Paul C. 10 January 1996.
Bauman, Thomas E. 11 December 1995.
Clawson, Philomena A. 11 February 1996; 12 March 1996.
Clissold, Richard L. 29 February 1996.
Davis, Reed. 4 January 1996.
Dodson, Joy, Missouri United Methodist Archives, Central Methodist College. E-mail. 5 June 1998.
Eliason, O. LeGrand. 21 September 1998.
Erickson, Einar C. 9 August 2014.
Fujiwara, Yoshiaki. 29 March 1998.
Ichiriki, Kazuo. 26 December 1997.

Iga, Mamoru. 15 June 1997
Ikegami, David T. 29 August 1998.
Inouye, Yukus. 3 November 1998.
Iwaasa, Jeaune. 16 January 1996.
Jensen, Wendell W. 26 February 1996.
Kalama, Samuel K. 28 February 1996.
Katanuma, Seiji. 25 November 1995.
Kitamura, Masataka. 23 November 1995.
Mauss, Armand L. 7 August 1999; email, 21 October 1999.
Moore, Ruth K. N. 3 January 1996.
Moriya, Kanji. E-mail. 9 October 2015.
Murakami, Ryoko. 9 November 1997.
Nanto, Dick K. E-mail. 19 November 1996.
Nichols, Murray L. 18 January 1996; 26 August 1996.
Nixon, Norton D. 10 December 1995; 17 January 1996.
Packer, Boyd K. 8 September 1995.
Price, Harrison Theodore. 27 November 1995; 29 December 1995.
Priday, Gene F., University Registrar, Brigham Young University. 31 October 1995.
Richards, C. Elliott. 7 November 1995; 16 November 1995; 7 December 1995.
Roberts, Clair L. 12 March 1997 (with a photocopy of the minutes of the baptismal service for Eugene Johnson).
Shimabukuro, Sam K. 28 November 1995.
Slover, Robert H. 8 September 1998.
Takeuchi, Thomas T. 20 February 1996.
Walz, Eric. 10 July 1998; 30 October 1998; E-mail, 24 November 1998; E-mail, 11 December 1998.
Yajima, Shigenori. 31 December 1995; 13 January 13 1996; 25 January 1996.
Yamada, Akitake. 30 May 1998; 23 June 1998.
Yamada, Tsugumi. 15 January 1997.
Yanagida, Toshiko. 19 March 1995; 2 November 1995; 9 November 1995.

Others (copies in author's possession):
Clissold, Edward L. Letter addressed to David O. McKay. 26 January 1942.
Dixon, W. Randall, Archivist, LDS Church Historical Department. Letter addressed to Marion D. Hanks. 11 January 1996.
Evans, Preston D. Letter addressed to Edward Clissold. 15 December 1945.
Fillmore, Wade. E-mail addressed to Bob and Marcia Sorenson. 5 December 2014.
Fujiwara, Takeo. Letter addressed to Tamano Kumagai. 27 October 1927.
_____. Letter addressed to Tamano Kumagai. 30 March 1935.
Kumagai, Tamano. Letter addressed to Hazel Robertson. 3 May 1939.
Nara, Fijiya. Letter addressed to Japanese members. July 1946.
Richards, C. Elliott. Letters addressed to Ray Hanks. 29 June 1946; 9 July 1946; 10 July 1946.
Sato, Tatsui. Letters addressed to Reed Davis. March 1946; 12 May 1946; 20 August 1947; 25 September 1948; 2 December 1949.
_____. Letters addressed to Thomas E. Bauman. 7 March 1949; 8 November 1950.
Taylor, Alma O. Letter addressed to Tamano Kumagai. 20 September 1926.

Personal Interviews:
L. Jerold Adams. Toyonaka, 28 October 1996.
Andrus, Paul C. Kaneohe, Hawaii, 1 February 1997.
Aki, Hiroshi. Telephone, November 1995.

Bibliography

Atkin, Dennis H. Kobe, 7 December 1995.
Davis, Reed. Telephone, 19 January 1996.
Fillmore, Wade W. Telephone, 2 December 2014.
Fujiwara, Yuko and Yoshiaki, nephew of Takeo Fujiwara. Sapporo, 3 March 1998.
Horiuchi, Russell N. and Aiko. Orem, Utah, 20 March 1996; 29 July 1996.
Igarashi, Amy. Telephone, 5 February 1996.
Ikegami, David Takeshi. Kobe, 30 June 1996; Tokyo, 5 September 1996.
Imai, Kazuo. Telephone, 9 January 1996; 27 January 1996; February 1996.
Inouye, Yukus and Betty. Telephone, 24 May 1998; Tokyo, 12 June 1998; 20 July 1998; 29 October 1998.
Jensen, Wendell W. Telephone, March 1996.
Kalama, Samuel K. Telephone, 29 February 1996.
Kamekona, Noelani Vera, granddaughter of Tokujiro Sato. Pearl City, Oahu, 7 February 1999.
Katayama, Tomio. Kobe, 31 December 1995.
Kikuchi, Yoshihiko. Tokyo. 29 November 1995; 23 February 1996; 24 April 1997.
Kawano, Emiko Teranishi. Kobe, 14 November 1995.
Komatsu, Adney Y. Telephone, April 1996.
Lactaoen, Leslie P. and Renee, then residents of the house built by Tokujiro Sato. Kukuihaele, Hawaii, 12 June 1999.
Matsushita, Yasuhiro. Kobe, October and December 1995.
Mizuno, Keiichi. Kobe, October 1995; November 1995; December 1995.
Murakami, Ryoko. Telephone, 11 November 1997; Sapporo, 2 March 1998.
Nagamine, Keisei. Tokyo, 24 March 1998.
Nakamura, Futazo, office chief, Keishikai. Toyouracho, Niigata, 10 March 1998.
Nakano, Masayuki. Telephone, December 1995.
Oldham, H. Lynn. Telephone, 13 January 1996.
Oppie, William H. Kobe, 18 December 1995.
Sakai, Kiyoshi. Telephone, December 1995.
Sagara, Kenichi. Telephone, December 1995.
Sakamoto, Haruko. Osaka, 24 November 1995.
Suzuki, George and June Stageberg, grandchildren of Tomizo Katsunuma. Honolulu, 1 February 1997.
Suzuki, Kiyomi Katsunuma, daughter of Tomizo Katsunuma. Honolulu, 1 February 1997.
Swenson, Robert A. Telephone, 25 January 1996; 28 January 1996; 30 January 1996.
Taise, Clara Toshiko, granddaughter of Tokujiro Sato. Naalehu, Hawaii, 7 February 1999.
Takeuchi, Thomas Tsutomu. Telephone, 22 February 1996.
Tanaka, Kenji. Telephone, September 1995; October 1995; Yokohama, 20 February 1996; Tokyo, 19 September 1996.
Todd, Ira H. Tokyo, 29 November 1995.
Toko, Albert Sato, grandson of Tokujiro Sato. Kamuela, Hawaii, 12 June 1999.
Watanabe, Kan. Tokyo, 18 April 1997.
Watanabe, Yaeko Shirai. Telephone, December 1996.
Watt, Ronald G. Salt Lake City, 19 March 1996.
Yajima, Shigenori. Tokyo, 19 September 1996.
Yamada, Akitake. Telephone, 27 March 1998.
Yanagida, Toshiko. Telephone, October 1995; November 1995; 11 January 1996; 8 March 1998.
Yano, Nobuyasu. Fukuoka, 5 January 1996.
Yasuda, Takuzo. Telephone, 21 February 1997.
Yoshizawa, Midori. Fukuoka, 29 December 1996.
Yoshizawa, Toshiro. Tokyo, 29 November 1995.

Archived Materials:

LDS Church Reports and Records:

Cannon, Hugh Jenne. "Around-the-World Travels of David O. McKay and Hugh J. Cannon." LDS Church Archives.

Central Pacific (Japanese) Mission. "Mission President's Reports, 1937–1949." BYU–Hawaii Archives.

Central Pacific Mission. "News of Happenings in the Mission Fields." 16 February 1947. BYU–Hawaii Archives.

Church of Jesus Christ of Latter-day Saints. "Census of Church Members, 1925 and 1930." LDS Church Archives.

_____. "Deceased Member Records, 1941–1988." LDS Church Archives.

_____. "Membership Records, Waipio Branch, Northern Hawaii District." LDS Church Archives.

Clissold, Edward L. "Missionary Work among the Japanese in the Hawaiian Islands," 1937. In Central Pacific (Japanese) Mission, "Mission President's Reports, 1937–1949." BYU–Hawaii Archives.

_____. "Acquiring a Mission Home in Japan, 1948." 5 December 1948. LDS Church Archives.

Fujiwara, Takeo. "Report on the Church Literary Books in Japanese at the Hawaiian Mission." Not dated (believed to be written in the first week of August 1934). LDS Church Archives.

_____. "The Official Records of the Church in Japan, 7 July–31 December 1934." LDS Church Archives.

_____. "The Official Report from the Japan Mission of the Church of Jesus Christ of Latter-day Saints, 1 January–30 April 1935." LDS Church Archives.

_____. "The Official Report from the Japan Mission of the Church of Jesus Christ of Latter-day Saints, 5 August 1935." LDS Church Archives.

Ivins, H. Grant. "List of Tracts in the Japan Mission, 1912." LDS Church Archives.

Japan Mission. "Historical Records and Minutes." LDS Church Archives.

_____. "Letterpress Copybooks, 1901–1923." LDS Church Archives.

Japanese Mission. "Historical Records and Minutes." LDS Church Archives.

_____. "List of ordained elders." Not dated. LDS Church Archives.

_____. "Missionary District Journal, November 1948–December 1949." LDS Church Archives.

_____. "Mission Highlights," monthly issues. BYU–Hawaii Archives.

_____. "Proselyting Area Histories, 1945–1952." LDS Church Archives.

Japanese/Northern Far East Mission. "Quarterly Historical Reports." LDS Church Archives.

Jenson, Andrew, comp. "History of the Japan Mission." 1934. In Japan Mission, "Historical Records and Minutes." LDS Church Archives.

Nara, Fujiya. "1945 nen niokeru Kaigō Hōkoku," January 1946. LDS Church Archives.

_____. "1946 nen niokeru Kaigō Hōkoku." January 1947. LDS Church Archives.

_____. "1946 nenchu niokeru Shūkai Hōkoku." January 1947. LDS Church Archives.

_____. "1947 nenchu niokeru Shūkai Hōkoku." July 1947. LDS Church Archives.

Nielsen, C. W. "Chaplain Corps of the US Navy, and the Church of Jesus Christ of Latter-day Saints." May 1952. LDS Church Archives.

Northern Far East Mission. "Mission President's Quarterly Summary." LDS Church Archives.

_____. "Presidents' Correspondence." LDS Church Archives.

_____. "Released Missionary Files." LDS Church Archives.

_____. "Manuscript History." LDS Church Archives.

Taylor, Alma O. "The History of the Japanese Translation of the Book of Mormon." Not dated. BYU Archives.

Bibliography

———. "Observations on Translation." Not dated. In "Alma O. Taylor Papers, 1904–1935." LDS Church Archives.

———. "Scrapbook, 1901–1924." LDS Church Archives.

Woodward, Ernest B. "Facts Concerning the Japan Mission from January 1, 1924 to the Close of the Mission in August 1924." 26 July 1949. LDS Church Archives.

Oral Histories:

Andrus, Paul C. Interview by R. Lanier Britsch. 1974. James Moyle Oral History Program. LDS Church Archives.

Christensen, Elwood L. Interview by R. Lanier Britsch. 1978. James Moyle Oral History Program. LDS Church Archives.

Christiansen, Horace A. Interview by Bruce Blumell. 1973. LDS Church Archives.

Clissold, Edward L. Interview by R. Lanier Britsch. 1976. James Moyle Oral History Program. LDS Church Archives.

Mauss, Vinal G. Interview by R. Lanier Britsch. 1975. James Moyle Oral History Program. LDS Church Archives.

Correspondence:

Andersen, Dwayne N. Letter addressed to Sister Davis. 29 July 1965. LDS Church Archives.

Andrus, Paul C. Letters addressed to Ho Jik Kim. 19 March 1956; 31 March 1956; 26 April 1956. In Northern Far East Mission. "Presidents' Correspondence." LDS Church Archives.

———. Letter addressed to Hilton A. Robertson. 29 May 1956. In Northern Far East Mission. "Presidents' Correspondence." LDS Church Archives.

———. Letter addressed to Koichi Takeuchi. 1 December 1956. In Northern Far East Mission. "Presidents' Correspondence." LDS Church Archives.

Clissold, Edward L. Letter addressed to the missionaries of the Central Pacific Mission. 15 May 1944. LDS Church Archives.

Ensign, Horace. Letter addressed to Samuel E. Woolley. 21 April 1902. In Japan Mission. "Letterpress Copybooks, 1901–23." LDS Church Archives.

First Presidency of the Church of Jesus Christ of Latter-day Saints. Letter addressed to Alma O. Taylor. 4 January 1908. In "Alma O. Taylor Papers, 1904–35." LDS Church Archives.

———. Letter addressed to Alma O. Taylor. 3 March 1908. In "Alma O. Taylor Papers, 1904–35." LDS Church Archives.

———. Letter addressed to Joseph H. Stimpson. 14 April 1919. LDS Church Archives.

———. Letter addressed to Alma O. Taylor. 2 April 1928. LDS Church Archives.

———. Letter addressed to Melvyn A. Weenig. 23 January 1946. LDS Church Archives.

———. Letter addressed to Melvyn A. Weenig. 7 February 1946. LDS Church Archives.

———. Letter addressed to Melvyn A. Weenig. 22 October 1947. LDS Church Archives.

———. Letter addressed to Edward L. Clissold. 23 April 1947. LDS Church Archives.

———. Letter addressed to Edward L. Clissold. 22 October 1947. LDS Church Archives.

Fujiwara, Takeo. Letter addressed to Alma O. Taylor. Not dated (believed to be written in early August 1934). LDS Church Archives.

———. Letter addressed to Alma O. Taylor. 14 August 1934. LDS Church Archives.

———. Letter addressed to Alma O. Taylor. 5 September 1935. In Japan Mission, "Miscellaneous Documents." LDS Church Archives.

Grant, Heber J. Letter addressed to Tatsutaro Hirai. 4 October 1901. In Japan Mission. "Letterpress Copybooks, 1901–1923." LDS Church Archives.

———. Letter addressed to N. Sumi. 9 April 1903. In Japan Mission. "Letterpress Copybooks, 1901–1923." LDS Church Archives.

———. Letter addressed to Alma O. Taylor. 14 March 1920. LDS Church Archives.

Harris, Franklin Steward. Letter addressed to Alma O. Taylor. 1 November 1926. In Alma O. Taylor Papers, 1904–1936." LDS Church Archives.

Hulet, Ray. Letter to Russell N. Horiuchi. 5 December 1947. LDS Church Archives.

———. Letters addressed to Edward L. Clissold. 19 and 20 February 1948. LDS Church Archives.

Ivie, Lloyd O. Letter addressed to the First Presidency. 9 August 1922. LDS Church Archives.

———. Letter addressed to Arthur Winter. 26 August 1922. LDS Church Archives.

Kumagai, Tamano, Takeo Yoshino, and Kenji Ono. Letter addressed to Alma O. Taylor. Not dated (circa February 1936). LDS Church Archives.

Mauss, Vinal G. Letter addressed to Ernest A. Nelson. 3 January 1952. LDS Church Archives.

McIvor, Kaufman & Yamamoto. Letter addressed to Vinal G. Mauss. 9 September 1952. LDS Church Archives.

McKay, David O. Letter addressed to Orson F. Whitney. 1 February 1921. LDS Church Archives.

Nara, Fujiya. Letter addressed to Alma O. Taylor. 10 June 1926. In "Alma O. Taylor Papers, 1904–1935." LDS Church Archives.

———. Letter addressed to Alma O. Taylor. 12 October 1927. In Japan Mission, "Miscellaneous Documents, 1901–1955." LDS Church Archives.

———. Letter addressed to the General Church Welfare Committee. 25 March 1947. LDS Church Archives.

Office of the Presiding Bishop of the Church of Jesus Christ of Latter-day Saints. Letter addressed to Vinal G. Mauss. 13 August 1952. LDS Church Archives.

Price, Harrison Theodore. Letter addressed to the Office of the Church Historian. 31 December 1956. LDS Church Archives.

Sato, Tatsui. Letter addressed to Harold B. Lee. Circa 1946. LDS Church Archives.

Stimpson, Joseph H. Letter addressed to the First Presidency, 28 November 1918. In Japan Mission, "Letterpress Copybooks, 1901–1923." LDS Church Archives.

Stimpson, Joseph H. Letter addressed to the First Presidency. 31 March 1919. In Japan Mission, "Letterpress Copybooks, 1901–1923." LDS Church Archives.

———. Letter addressed to the First Presidency. 18 March 1920. Japan Mission, "Letterpress Copybooks, 1901–1923." LDS Church Archives.

Taylor, Alma O. Letter addressed to Anthon Lund. 15 November 1904. In "Alma O. Taylor Papers." LDS Church Archives.

———. Letter addressed to the First Presidency. 27 September 1909. In Japan Mission, "Letterpress Copybooks, 1901–1923." LDS Church Archives.

———. Letter addressed to the First Presidency. 13 November 1909. In Japan Mission, "Letterpress Copybooks, 1901–1923." LDS Church Archives.

———. Letter addressed to Heber J. Grant. 27 January 1920. LDS Church Archives.

———. Letter addressed to Fujiya Nara. 25 January 1927. In "Alma O. Taylor Papers, 1904–1936." LDS Church Archives.

———. Letter addressed to the First Presidency. 31 March 1928. LDS Church Archives.

———. Letter addressed to the First Presidency. 3 April 1935. In "Alma O. Taylor Papers, 1904–1936." LDS Church Archives.

———. Letter addressed to Takeo Fujiwara. 14 April 1935. LDS Church Archives.

———. Letter addressed to Takeo Fujiwara. 10 September 1935. LDS Church Archives.

———. Letter addressed to the First Presidency. 14 March 1936. In "Alma O. Taylor Papers, 1904–1936." LDS Church Archives.

———. Letter addressed to Hilton A. Robertson. 27 February 1937. In "Alma O. Taylor Papers, 1904–1936." LDS Church Archives.

Thomas, Elbert D. Telegram addressed to Chojiro Kuriyama. 25 March 1935. LDS Church Archives.

———. Letter addressed to the First Presidency. 5 August 1950. LDS Church Archives.

Bibliography

Weenig, Melvyn A. Letter addressed to the First Presidency. 1 August 1946. LDS Church Archives.
―――. Letter addressed to Castle H. Murphy. 15 November 1946. LDS Church Archives.
―――. Letter addressed to the First Presidency. 3 July 1947. LDS Church Archives.

Periodicals, with their Depositories

Tokyo Newspapers:
Chūō Shinbun. Tokyo: National Diet Library.
Dokuritsu Shinbun. Tokyo: National Diet Library.
Hōchi Shinbun. Tokyo: National Diet Library.
Jiji Shinpō. Tokyo: National Diet Library.
Mainichi Shinbun. Tokyo: National Diet Library.
Miyako Shinbun. Tokyo: National Diet Library.
Niroku Shinpō. Tokyo: National Diet Library.
Tokyo Asahi Shinbun. Tokyo: National Diet Library.
Tokyo Nichinichi Shinbun. Tokyo: National Diet Library.
Yamato Shinbun. Tokyo: National Diet Library.
Yomiuri Shinbun. Tokyo: National Diet Library.
Yorozu Chōhō. Tokyo: National Diet Library.

Regional newspapers:
Akita Sakigake Shinpō. Tokyo: National Diet Library.
Chūgoku. Tokyo: National Diet Library.
Chūkyō Shinpō. Tokyo: National Diet Library.
Fukuoka Nichinichi Shinbun. Fukuoka: Fukuoka Municipal Library.
Hiroshima Kibi Nichinichi Shinbun. Tokyo: National Diet Library.
Hokkai Taimusu. Tokyo: National Diet Library.
Hokkoku Shinbun. Tokyo: National Diet Library.
Ise Shinbun. Tokyo: National Diet Library.
Iwate Nippō. Tokyo: National Diet Library.
Kahoku Shinpō. Sendai: Kahoku Shinpōsha.
Kobe Yūshin Nippō. Kobe: Kobe Municipal Library.
Kyōchū Nippō. Kofu: Yamanashi Prefectural Library.
Kyōgaku Hōchi. Kyoto: Ryūkoku University Library.
Kyoto Hinode Shinbun. Tokyo: National Diet Library.
Kyūshū Nichinichi Shinbun. Kumamoto: Kumamoto Prefectural Library.
Kyūshū Nippō. Fukuoka: Fukuoka Municipal Library.
Kyūshū Shinbun. Kumamoto: Kumamoto Prefectural Library.
Moji Shinpō. Kitakyushu: Kitakyushu Municipal Library.
Niigata Shinbun. Niigata: Niigata Prefectural Library.
Osaka Asahi Shinbun. Osaka: Osaka University Library.
Osaka Mainichi Shinbun. Osaka: Osaka University Library.
Ryūkyū Shinpō. Naha: Okinawa Prefectural Library.
Sanyō Shinpō. Tokyo: National Diet Library.
Shimotsuke Shinbun. Tokyo: National Diet Library.
Shin-Aichi. Tokyo: National Diet Library.
Shinano Mainichi Shinbun. Matsumoto: Matsumoto Municipal Library.
Shizuoka Minyū Shinbun. Tokyo: National Diet Library.
Tōhoku Nippō. Niigata: Niigata Prefectural Library.
Yamanashi Nichinichi Shinbun. Kofu: Yamanashi Prefectural Library.
Yonezawa Shinbun. Yamagata: Yamagata Prefectural Library.

Magazines and Other Periodicals:

Beikoku Bukkyō. Published by the Buddhist Mission, San Francisco. Kyoto: Ryūkoku University Library.

Chūō Kōron. Tokyo: Meiji Library, University of Tokyo.

Fujin Gahō. Tokyo: Ishikawa Takeyoshi Memorial Library.

Fujin Shinpō. Tokyo: National Diet Library.

Gokyō. Kyoto: Doshisha University Library.

Hattatsu. Published by the Japan Mission of the Church of Jesus Christ of Latter-day Saints. Copy of the first issue (May 1935) in author's possession.

Jogaku Sekai. Tokyo: National Diet Library.

Kanpō. Published by the Japanese Government. Osaka: Osaka University Library.

Kirisutokyō Sekai. Kyoto: Doshisha University Library.

Kyōiku Jikkenkai. Tokyo: Meiji Library, University of Tokyo.

Kyōkai Ichiran. Published by the Nishi Honganji Temple. Kyoto: Ryūkoku University Library.

LDS Messenger. Published by the Japanese Mission of the Church of Jesus Christ of Latter-day Saints. All issues, January 1950–May 1957, in author's possession.

Rikugō Zasshi. Kyoto: Doshisha University Library.

Seikō. Tokyo: National Diet Library.

Seito no Michi. Published by the Northern Far East Mission of the Church of Jesus Christ of Latter-day Saints. Issues, June 1957–August 1968. Available: www.ldschurch.jp.

Shinjin. Kyoto: Doshisha University Library.

Shuro. Published by the Japanese Mutual Improvement Association of the Church of Jesus Christ of Latter-day Saints. Copies of vol. 1, issues 1–2 and 4–10, vol. 2, issues 1–4 in author's possession.

Taiheiyō. Tokyo: National Diet Library.

Taiyō. Tokyo: National Diet Library.

Toki no Koe. Published by the Salvation Army. Tokyo: National Diet Library.

Zenbutsu Tsūshin. Published by Zen Nippon Bukkyōkai. Accessed, 18 November 2015, http://www.jbf.ne.jp

English-Language Publications:

Church News (prior to the 31 January 1953 issue, variously known as *Deseret News*, Church Section; *Church News*; or *Church Section*). LDS Church Archives.

Conference Report. Published by the Church of Jesus Christ of Latter-day Saints. LDS Church Archives.

Deseret Evening News. LDS Church Archives.

Eastern World. Yokohama: Yokohama Archives of History.

Japan Times. Tokyo: National Diet Library.

Japan Weekly Mail. Yokohama: Yokohama Archives of History.

Kobe Chronicle, weekly edition. Kobe: Kobe Municipal Library.

Missionary Messenger. Published by the Northern Far East Mission of the Church of Jesus Christ of Latter-day Saints. Issues October 1961–January 1962, in author's possession.

Service Messenger. Published by the Japan Mission of the Church of Jesus Christ of Latter-day Saints. Issue September 1968, in author's possession.

Success Messenger. Published by the Northern Far East Mission of the Church of Jesus Christ of Latter-day Saints. Issues February 1962–October 1963, December 1963–February 1964, May 1967 and January–August 1968, in author's possession.

Subject Index

A

Abeno (Osaka) Branch, 354, 367, 372, 382, 383, 391, 418, 419, 421, 422, 422n
"Address to the Great and Progressive Nation of Japan" (by Grant, 1901), 59, 59n, 63, 66
Agricultural College of Utah. *See* Utah State University
Agricultural Land Adjustment Law (1946), 358
agricultural land reform (1946–49), 340, 348, 358–60
Allied occupation of Japan. *See* American occupation of Japan
Amaterasu (Goddess of the Sun), 92n, 100, 100n. *See also* State Shinto
American occupation of Japan (1945–52), 13–14, 291. *See also* GHQ/SCAP
  administration of, 292, 304, 309
  aims and achievements, 293–94
  reverse course in policy of, 331, 333
Anglican–Episcopal Church of Japan. *See Nihon Seikō Kai*
Anglo–Japanese Alliance (1902), 231
Anglo–Japanese Friendship Treaty (1854), 448
Ansei treaties, 54, 54n, 99, 102
  extraterritoriality under, 36n, 54–56, 54n, 55n, 56n
  open ports and cities under, 35, 54n, 55, 55n, 99, 120
  revision of, 54, 55, 55n, 56, 105, 107, 443
Anti-Comintern Pact (1936), 233
anti-prostitution movement, 67–69, 115
Anti-Slavery Law (1872), 67
Articles of Faith, Japanese translation of, 59, 64–65, 86, 145, 157, 399–400
Asahi Shinbun (1940–), 78n, 388n. *See also Osaka Asahi Shinbun*; *Tokyo Asahi Shinbun*
Asahikawa
  postwar Mormon work in, 344, 348, 367, 367n, 372, 382t, 385, 390, 418t, 419, 422
  prewar Mormon work in, 141–42, 143t, 197, 198

Aston plan, introduction in Japan of, 412. *See also* Systematic Program for Teaching the Gospel

B

baptisms. *See* Mormon converts in Japan
Baptists, 1n, 56n, 229, 237, 240–241, 268, 318n, 445
"Batsujitsu Seito Iesu Kirisuto Kyōkai ni kansuru Kinkyū Rinkoku" (An Announcement concerning the Church of Jesus Christ of Latter-day Saints, by Grant, 1903), 147, 150t
Batsujitsu Seito Iesu Kirisuto Kyōkai Ryakushi (A Brief History of the Church of Jesus Christ of Latter-day Saints, by Anderson, 1907), 149, 155, 157, 175, 217, 401, 401n
believing blood. *See* Israel, blood of
Bible, Japanese translations of, 82n, 106, 106n, 126–27, 155, 171–72, 193, 400, 400n, 401–2
blood of Israel. *See* Israel, blood of
Book of Mormon, 2, 8, 54, 59, 64, 82, 84, 86, 145–47, 153, 242. *See also* Spaulding theory
  Japanese translations, 8, 12, 120, 129–33, 153–54, 158, 167–93, 222, 242, 272–73, 352, 395, 399–404
  accuracy of, 188–92, 406–7
  advertising of, 195–201
  quality, 178–84, 404–6
  Japanese translation and pronunciation of the term for, 65, 84, 155–56
Boso Peninsula (Chiba), prewar Mormon work in, 136–38, 137n
Brigham Young College (Logan), 21, 32, 228
Brigham Young University (BYU), 137, 249, 253–54, 297n, 312n, 352n, 393, 393n, 453–56, 456n, 464, 466
Brigham Young University–Hawaii. *See* Church College of Hawaii
Buddhism
  arrival and spread in Japan, 90–92

Edo, 95–98, 436
esoteric, 92, 92n
Meiji transformation, 101, 101n, 109–10, 115–16
persecution by Shinto fanatics, 99–100
See also Jōdo Shinshū; shinbutsu shūgō
Buddhist Churches of America, 84, 84n. *See also Jōdo Shinshū*
Buddhist Mission, 84, 84n, 288
building missionaries. *See* labor missionaries
Bukkyō Seito Dōshikai (Association of Buddhist Purists), 115–16
bungotai. *See* Japanese language, classical or literary style of

C

Central Pacific Mission (1944–50)
in conflict with Hawaiian Mission, 279–81, 280n
Japanese Mission renamed as, 275–77
merged with Hawaiian Mission, 277
preparation to resume work in Japan by, 315–19
Central Utah Relocation Center (Topaz), 288–89, 299–300
chapels. *See* Mormon meetinghouses in Japan
chaplains. *See* Mormon chaplains
Chiba, prewar Mormon work in, 136, 136n. *See also* Boso Peninsula
Chicago World Fair. *See* Columbian Exposition
China
early Mormon work in, 5, 211, 212n, 374
Japan's cultural borrowing from, 91, 104, 156
Japanese invasion of (1931), 234
China War (1937–45), 233, 235–36, 241–42. *See also* Sino-Japanese War (1894–95)
Chinese Exclusion Act (U.S., 1882), 18, 260, 260n
Chinese Mission (Hong Kong; San Francisco; Tokyo), 321, 321n, 349, 374
cholera, outbreak of, 448, 448n
chōnin, explained, 38
Choshu, feudal domain of, 4, 70n, 73n, 99, 107, 159, 166, 231, 260, 443n
Christianity
first arrival and early spread in Japan, 57, 93–94, 445
Meiji transformation, 114–16
persecution in Meiji Japan, 84, 109–13
second arrival, 102–5
spread in prewar Japan, 105–8, 206, 445, 446
suppression in Edo Japan, 94–96, 104n
war-time government control, 236–39
See also Roman Catholicism
Christians
hidden, 95–96, 102–4, 102n, 104n, 105
number in Japan of, 56n, 93, 93n, 107–8, 108n
Chūō Kōron (Central Review), 52, 52n, 76, 76n, 123n, 176, 195, 195n, 201, 404n
Church College of Hawaii (Brigham Young University–Hawaii), 428, 439
church correlation. *See* Church of Jesus Christ of Latter-day Saints, correlation movement
Church of England. *See Nihon Seikō Kai*
Church of Jesus Christ of Latter-day Saints
correlation movement, 8, 8n, 321, 425, 425n
establishment of, 2
First Presidency, 62, 122, 154, 163n, 182, 196, 198, 200, 210, 216–18, 223, 230, 242, 249, 251–53, 257, 257n, 258–59, 274–78, 280–81, 285, 296, 312, 315–16, 318, 319, 328, 336, 349, 351, 361n, 387, 390, 400n, 402–3, 415, 427, 459, 464, 466, 468
in interwar Germany, 230, 245, 245n
military units in Japan, 362, 362n
total membership in Japan, 1, 361–62, 438
church properties. *See* Mormon properties in Japan
Civil Information and Education Section (CIE), 292, 308–10, 319–20, 320n, 325, 328–30. *See also* GHQ/SCAP
Clover Beikaiwa Gakuin (Clover American Conversation Institute), 329, 330, 334, 350
Columbian Exposition (Chicago, 1893), 21n, 129. *See also* World's Parliament of Religions
Confucianism, 91, 98, 156
Constitution of Japan (1946), 293, 323–24
Constitution of the Empire of Japan. *See* Meiji Constitution
converts. *See* Mormon converts in Japan

D

Daiichi Branch (Salt Lake City), 266n
Daiichi Hotel (Tokyo), 282, 310–11, 320
Dainichi Nyorai (Cosmic Buddha), 92. *See also* Buddhism

Subject Index

Deshima, 95, 448n. *See also* Nagasaki
Diet, Imperial (prewar) or National (postwar), 19, 163, 231, 249, 357, 357n, 414, 458
districts. *See* Mormon districts in Japan
Doctrine and Covenants
   Japanese translation, 8, 146, 151, 153–54, 158, 223, 399, 402–3, 402n
   quality of, 407–9
Dodge plan, 333

E

E. D. Hashimoto Company, 262, 264
East Central District. *See* Mormon districts in Japan
Economic and Scientific Section (ESS), 292, 312. *See also* GHQ/SCAP
Edmunds Act (U.S., 1882), 3n
Edmunds–Tucker Act (U.S., 1887), 3
Edo, 4, 35–36, 39–41, 40n, 94, 96, 99. *See also* Tokyo
Edo period (1603–1868), explained, 11, 15
education, Japan's prewar system of, 133–34, 133n, 208, 301. *See also* nationalism in Japan
elders, Mormon
   organization in Japan of first quorum, 392
   quorums in Japan, 392, 392n, 429, 431
Emperor Meiji. *See* Meiji, Emperor
Emperor Showa. *See* Showa, Emperor
Emperor Taisho. *See* Taisho, Emperor
emperor worship. *See* State Shinto
Empress of India, 29, 29n, 51, 51n, 66
exchange controls, 326–27, 426, 426n–427n
Exclusion Act. *See* Johnson–Reed Act
Expo '70 (Osaka), 438, 439, 439n
extermination order (Missouri, 1838), 2
extraterritoriality. *See* Ansei treaties, extraterritoriality under

F

Far East Construction Office, 390, 417, 417n, 419n, 420. *See also* labor missionary program, Mormon
First Higher School, 112, 163, 165
First Presidency. *See* Church of Jesus Christ of Latter-day Saints, First Presidency of
first-year men. *See* Gan-nen-mono
Five-Power Treaty (1922), 231
foreign exchange controls. *See* exchange controls

Four-Power Treaty, with Britain, France, and the United States (1921), 231
Freedom and Popular Rights Movement, 19, 107, 110
Friends, Society of (Quakers), 163, 229
fukkō Shinto. *See* Shinto
fukoku kyōhei (enrich the state, strengthen the military), 4
Fukuoka
   opening of Mormon work in, 344–45, 357, 367
   postwar Mormon work in, 372, 373, 382t, 439n
   temporary suspension and reopening of Mormon work in, 368–70
Fukushima, opening of Mormon work in, 344, 373, 390n, 392n
Funakata. *See* Boso Peninsula
Futenma (Okinawa), 377–78, 384–85, 390, 390n, 426
   attempted building construction in, 389–90, 390n
   early Mormon work in, 372, 377–78, 426
   property purchase in, 381t, 384–85
futsūbun, 172, 172n, 192. *See also* Japanese language, classical or literary style of

G

gan-nen-mono (first-year men), 27, 27n, 34–38, 41–42, 45, 270. *See also* Japanese immigrants, in Hawaii
GDP (gross domestic product), 203, 397–99
gembunitchi movement in, 171–73. *See also* Japanese language, contemporary or colloquial style of
General Headquarters. *See* GHQ/SCAP
genrō, 107, 159, 205, 205n, 231
Germany. *See* Church of Jesus Christ of Latter-day Saints, in interwar Germany
GHQ/SCAP, 292–94, 304, 308–9, 311–12, 316, 324–25, 333, 348, 358, 383
Gibson trouble. *See* Walter Murray Gibson trouble
Ginowan (Okinawa). *See* Futenma
gold standard, 30n, 54, 154, 175, 177
go-on, 156. *See also* kan-on
goshin-ei, 111. *See also* State Shinto
Government of the Ryukyu Islands (GRI), 375–76
Grand Hotel (Yokohama), 51, 52, 63, 80

Great Kanto Earthquake (1923), 204, 213–15, 218, 223, 228, 243–44, 281, 465
Great Promulgation Campaign. *See taikyō senpu undō*
Guam, early Mormon work in, 345, 345n, 374
Gunma, Mormon work in, 352, 367, 372, 381t, 385, 418t, 419, 421. *See also* Maebashi; Takasaki
Gunma LDS Chorus (1952), 385

H

Hakodate, 141
  early Christian activity in, 102n
  treaty port, 54n, 99, 448, 448n
Harris Treaty. *See* Ansei treaties
Hattatsu (Progress), 256–57
Hawaii
  annexation to the United States, 24, 27, 270
  LDS Church among Japanese immigrants, 31–32, 272–81
  LDS Church in, 31, 272
  See also Japanese immigrants, in Hawaii
"Hawaii Calls" (1951), 385n. *See also* Mormon properties in Japan, fundraising for purchasing
Heian period, 129n, 170
hidden Christians (*kakure kirishitan*). *See* Christians, hidden
Hirao, early Mormon work in, 338, 340, 342, 342n, 356, 367–68, 371. *See also* Yanai
Hiroshima, Mormon work in, 141, 292, 338, 342, 344n, 356, 367–69, 372, 381t, 383, 384n, 391
Hiroshima Emigration Company, 20n, 22–23, 22n
Hojo. *See* Boso Peninsula
Hokkaido, island of, 68n, 102n, 159–60, 197n, 255, 434
  prewar Mormon work in, 140–41, 250
  sugar beet industry in, 164–65
  See also Asahikawa; Muroran; Otaru; Sapporo
Hokkaido Development Commission, 163–65, 163n
Hokkaido District. *See* Mormon districts in Japan
Holiness churches, 238–39, 242
honji suijaku theory, 92, 92n. *See also shinbutsu shūgō*
Hong Kong, Mormon work in, 5, 321n, 337, 374, 374n

honmatsu system, 96–97, 97n. *See also* Buddhism, Edo
House of Peers, 145, 163, 234, 357n–358n
House of Representatives, 19, 208, 327, 327n, 458
Household Register Law (1871), 42
Hōzanji Temple (Nara), 92
hyakushō, explained, 38
hymns. *See* Mormon publications in Japanese, hymnals
Hyogo. *See* Kobe

I

Ichishima land deal, 336, 340–41, 348–49, 357–60
Imado-gumi (group of immigrants), 41. *See also gan-nen-mono*
immigrants. *See* Japanese immigrants
Immigration Act. *See* Johnson–Reed Act
Imperial Hotel (Tokyo), 120n, 250, 251
Imperial Rescript on Education (1890), 111–13, 111n, 112n, 113n, 118, 127, 132, 207. *See also* State Shinto
Imperial University. *See* Tokyo Imperial University
International Buddhist Congress (San Francisco, 1915), 84, 84n
Ise, Grand Shrine of, 97–98, 100, 100n. *See also* Shinto; State Shinto; Tsu, city of
Israel, blood of, 54, 54n, 220–21, 221n
Issei, 263, 266–67, 266n, 285, 288, 299
Iwakura Embassy. *See* Iwakura Mission
Iwakura Mission, 105, 443–44
  visit to Salt Lake City of (1872), 5, 71, 71n, 159, 444–45

J

Japan
  dedication, for Mormon missionary work, 88, 120, 220
  demographic and social change in, 431–35
  industrialization and modernization of, 114, 203–4
  political developments in interwar period, 230–34
  population of, 9, 9t, 56, 88, 135–36, 219
  postwar economic recovery and high growth, 14, 397–98, 397n

Subject Index 559

religious and intellectual climate, 9–10, 10n, 12, 87–118, 234–39, 330–34
westernization policy of, 107, 110
Japan Advertiser, 57–59, 58n, 59n, 62, 197
Japan–British Exhibition (London, 1910), 467–68
Japan Central Mission. *See* Mormon missions in Japan
Japan East Mission. *See* Mormon missions in Japan
Japan–Hawaii Immigration Convention (1886), 18n, 451
Japan Herald, 57, 57n, 59–60, 59n, 61n, 62, 66–67, 69, 75
Japan Mail, 57, 57n, 59–60, 59n, 60n, 66–67, 69, 74
Japan Mission (1901–24)
    closing of, 216–18
        factors contributing to, 218–30
    "conference" structure established (1912), 142, 142n
    establishment of, 15, 51, 120–21
    locations of mission home, 135, 135n, 225
    opening and closing of areas for Mormon missionary work, 134–44
    presidents, 119
    proper name, 15n, 119n
Japan Mission (1968). *See* Mormon missions in Japan
Japan–Okinawa Mission. *See* Mormon missions in Japan
Japan Times, 57n, 60, 60n, 61, 216
Japan–United States Gentlemen's Agreement (1907), 24n, 215, 215n, 261
Japan–United States Security Treaty (1951), 346
Japan–United States Treaty of Commerce and Navigation (1911), 10n, 210
Japan–United States Treaty of Mutual Cooperation and Security (1960), 346
Japan West Mission. *See* Mormon missions in Japan
Japan Women's Christian Temperance Union (Nihon Kirisutokyō Fujin Kyōfū Kai, 1893), 68, 70
Japanese American Citizens League (JACL), 286n, 287, 288, 289
Japanese American Contracting Company (Nichibei Yōtatsusha), 20n
Japanese American Industrial Company (Nichibei Kangyōsha), 74n, 262

Japanese emigration. *See* Japanese immigrants
Japanese history, summarized, 3–4
Japanese immigrants
    in the continental United States, 15n, 260–62
        pattern of migration, 262–63
        phases of migration, 268–69
    in Hawaii, 22–25, 22n, 24n, 27, 34, 270–71. *See also gan-nen-mono*
    Americanization movement among, 271
    in Idaho and Utah, 263–65
    LDS Church among, 266–70, 272–81
Japanese immigration. *See* Japanese immigrants
Japanese language
    classical or literary style (*bungotai*), 170–73, 193n, 194–95, 401–2
    contemporary or colloquial style (*kōgotai*), 170–73, 171n, 194–95, 401–2. *See also gembunitchi* movement
Japanese Mission (Honolulu, 1937–44)
    establishment of, 31, 272–75
    renamed as Central Pacific Mission, 275–77
    trip to Japan by president of (1939), 281–84
Japanese Mission (Tokyo, 1948–55)
    "division structure" experimented in (1950–52), 344–46, 344n, 345n
    establishment of, 317–20, 324–25
    geographical enlargement, 345, 345n
    organization of first mission presidency, 343
    proper name, 15n, 119n
    setting up of mission home in, 326–28, 337–38
    See also Northern Far East Mission
Japheth theory, 221
Jehovah's Witnesses. *See* Watchtower Bible and Tract Society
Jiji Shinpō, 62–64, 63n, 67, 69n, 70, 72, 76, 80, 80n, 196, 200
Jōdo Shinshū (True Pure Land Buddhism), 65, 83–84, 93n, 100–101, 110n, 116, 125n, 174, 271. *See also* Nishi Honganji Temple
Johnson Act. *See* Quota Act
Johnson–Reed Act (U.S., 1924), 24n, 25, 215, 218, 228, 232, 243–44, 261
Juso (Osaka) Branch, 354, 367, 372n, 383, 387. *See also* Okamachi (Osaka) Branch

K

Kagoshima
    arrival of Francis Zavier in (1549), 93

visit by E. D. Thomas to (1911), 141
Kahoku Shinpō, 63, 174, 175, 197, 200
Kajima Construction Company, 326–28
Kalihi, Mormon meetinghouse, 31, 272–73, 277
Kanagawa. *See* Yokohama
Kanagawa, Treaty of, 54n, 99, 448n
Kanazawa, early Mormon work in, 342, 356, 367, 371–72, 382t, 434n. *See also* Komatsu
kan-on, 156. *See also* go-on
Kansei Gakuin, 174, 296–97, 296n, 305, 305n–306n
Kansho no Shiborikasu (Strained Lees of Sugarcane, by Katsunuma, 1924), 27
Kanto Earthquake. *See* Great Kanto Earthquake
Kinkikan (Tokyo), 116n, 129, 129n, 173
Kirisuto Iesu (Jesus the Christ, by Talmage, 1962), 424
Kitakyushu, 433, 433n
 early Mormon work in, 296, 373, 390n, 392n
Kobe
 postwar opening of Mormon work in, 354–55
 treaty port and foreign settlement, 55, 55n, 57n, 61n, 99, 142
 See also Sannomiya Branch
Kobe Chronicle, 57n, 61, 61n, 62
Kofu
 early postwar Mormon work in, 334–35, 339, 352–53, 367, 372, 381t, 391n
 prewar Mormon work in, 117, 131, 136, 140–42, 143t, 144, 158, 197–98, 209, 211–12, 226, 255–57
kōgotai. *See* Japanese language, contemporary or colloquial style
kokugaku (National Learning), 98–99, 126
Kokumin no Tomo, 108, 127
Kokura, 433n
 and Japan's first postwar baptism, 296
 See also Kitakyushu
kokutai (national structure), 99, 111, 118, 234, 239
Komatsu
 opening and closing of Mormon work, 336, 338–40, 342, 355–56, 371
 See also Kanazawa
Korea
 annexation by Japan, 70n, 90n
 beginning of Mormon work in, 363–65, 364n, 374, 374n, 375, 378–80
 See also Pusan; Seoul
Korean War, 300, 321, 321n, 331, 333, 343, 345, 345n, 361n, 367, 378, 393
Kukuihaele (Hawaii), 33–34, 43, 45, 45n, 47n
Kumamoto, early Mormon work in, 308, 373, 390n, 392n
Kumamoto Emigration Company, 23, 23n
Kushiki Miwaza (A Marvelous Work and a Wonder, by Richards, 2 volumes, 1963, 1964), 424
Kwantung Army, 232
Kyōgaku Hōchi, 65, 65n, 75–76, 84, 84n
Kyōiku to Shūkyō to no Shōtotsu (Conflict between Education and Religion, 1893), 112, 112n–113n, 127. *See also* Christianity, persecution in Meiji Japan
Kyoto
 as ancient imperial capital, 4, 36, 93, 99, 286–87, 286n, 371n
 closing and reopening of Mormon work in, 371–72, 371n, 382t
 opening of Mormon work in, 354–55
Kyushu, island of,
 as medieval center of Christian activity, 93–94, 93n
 tours by Mormon missionaries of, 141 (1911), 373 (1966)
 See also Fukuoka; Kitakyushu; Kokura; Kumamoto; Nagasaki

L

labor missionaries, Mormon
 calling in Japan of, 417–20, 523–25
 experiences in Japan, 420
 See also labor missionary program, Mormon; Mormon meetinghouses in Japan
labor missionary program, Mormon, 11, 398, 415, 415n
 construction of meetinghouses, 417–22, 423, 521–22
 introduction to Japan, 415–17
 See also Mormon meetinghouses in Japan
Laie (Hawaii), 8, 15n, 34, 34n, 272, 426, 428, 431, 451, 461, 462
Lanai (Hawaii), 33, 41–42, 450
Language Training Mission (Hawaii), 7, 438–39
Latter-day Saints, Japanese pronunciation of the term for, 155–56
LDS Church. *See* Church of Jesus Christ of Latter-day Saints

Subject Index

LDS Messenger, 384, 400–401, 422
League of Nations, 163–64, 231, 233, 253n, 459
Logan (Utah), 20–22, 228, 266, 298
London Naval Treaty (1930), 231, 233
lunar calendar, Japan's, explained, 17n, 35n, 444n

M

Maebashi, early Mormon work in, 352–53, 367, 372, 372n, 385. *See also* Gunma; Takasaki
Mainichi Shinbun (1886–1906), 62n, 63n, 65, 67, 67n, 68, 69n, 445, 445n
Mainichi Shinbun (1943–), 310, 327n, 388n, 462n, 469. *See also Osaka Mainichi Shinbun*; *Tokyo Nichinichi Shinbun*
Manchukuo, 232–33, 253
  recognition by Vatican, 238
Manchuria, 70, 115, 232, 232n, 236, 252–53, 253n, 255n, 256, 311–312, 329, 432n, 459, 459n, 464–65, 464n, 466n
Manchurian Incident (1932), 232, 253
Manifesto (1890), 3, 53, 53n, 59, 69–70
Matsumoto
  closing of Mormon work contemplated in, 371
  early Mormon work in, 353, 367, 372, 382t, 392n
Matsuyama, 141
McCarran–Walter Immigration and Nationality Act (U.S., 1952), 22n, 289
meetinghouses. *See* Mormon meetinghouses in Japan
Meiji, Emperor, 4, 17n, 36, 55, 90n, 111, 205–6, 387
  charter oath by, 4, 103
Meiji Constitution (1889), 19n, 53–54, 70n, 107, 110–12, 111n, 207–8, 234
  religious freedom under, 74, 77–78, 110, 118
Meiji period, 17, 17n, 35n, 90n, 99, 171
Meiji Restoration (1868), 4, 36, 55n, 70n, 90n, 99, 107, 159, 160
Meiji Shrine, 238, 387–88
Melody Men (1953), 385
Methodists, 31, 56n, 131, 174, 198, 237–38, 268, 301, 467
Metropole Hotel (Tokyo), 120, 120n, 126, 160–61
Mexican–American War (1946–48), 3, 146

MIA (Mutual Improvement Association), 211n, 249–51, 250n, 256, 294, 349, 349n, 352, 455–56, 464, 466
MIA group leader program, 294–95
minponshugi, 205. *See also* Taisho period, intellectual climate during
mission presidency, first organization in Japan, 343
missionaries. *See* Mormon missionaries
Mito, prewar Mormon work in, 143–44, 143n, 144n
Mito School, 98. *See also kokugaku*
Morioka
  postwar opening and closing of Mormon work, 344–45, 344n, 345n, 347
  prewar Mormon work, 117, 131, 141–42, 143t, 144, 197–98, 209n
Mormon, Book of. *See* Book of Mormon
Mormon chaplains, 295–96, 295n, 298, 300, 324, 378
Mormon converts in Japan
  characteristics of, 131–34, 133n, 391, 433–38
  numbers of, 14, 87, 89f, 120, 291, 331, 409, 413f
Mormon districts in Japan
  East Central (1958–), 372, 388, 392, 394, 416
  Central (1953–1958), 350, 367, 372
  Hokkaido (1953–), 347, 367, 372, 392
  Kyushu (1968–), 373
  Northern (1953–1958), 348, 367, 372
  Okinawa (1956–), 378, 392
  South Central (1953–1958), 353, 367, 372
  Southern (1953–1958), 356, 367, 368, 372
  West Central (1958–), 372–73, 391, 392–93
Mormon history, summarized, 2–3
Mormon meetinghouses in Japan.
  construction of, 417–21, 418t
  dedications of, 418t, 421–22
  See also labor missionaries, Mormon; labor missionary program, Mormon
Mormon missionaries in Japan
  number of, 9–10, 88–89, 120, 135–36, 331, 332f, 363, 364f, 366–67, 366f
  productivity of, 9, 88–89, 89n, 144, 334, compared to other missions (1920s), 219
  surge from 1957 in, 409–11, 410n, 410f
  under Taisho Democracy, 206–7, 207f

term of service, 6–7, 87–88, 221–22, 345, 345n, 365, 365t, 366, 439n
Mormon missions in Japan
Japan (1968–), 362–63, 363n, 395, 425, 438
Japan Central (1970–), 439
Japan East (1970–), 439, 439n
Japan Nagoya (1973–), 395
Japan West (1970–), 393, 439, 439n
Japan–Okinawa (1968–70), 278n, 363, 363n, 370n, 395, 425, 438, 439
See also Japan Mission (1901–24); Japanese Mission (Tokyo, 1948–55); Northern Far East Mission (1955–68)
Mormon properties in Japan
contemplated purchase in prewar period of, 10–11, 210, 210n
fundraising for purchasing, 385–86, 385n
postwar purchases of, 380–90, 381t–382t
See also Omotesando, property in
Mormon publications in Japanese
books, 149, 151, 153, 424
Book of Mormon (1909), 153–54, 167–93
hymnals, 151–53, 424–25, 465
standard works (1957), 402–9
texts and manuals, postwar, 424
tracts, prewar, 147–49, 150t
Mormon Tabernacle Choir, 152
Mormon temples, 2, 8–9, 85, 409
in Fukuoka, 338n
in Hawaii, 8, 16, 276–77, 308, 325, 461–62
trips by Japanese Mormons to, 9, 14, 397–98, 426–31, 456
in Salt Lake City, 86, 213, 254, 303, 303n, 318, 454
in Tokyo, 338, 388, 460
Mormon terminology, Japanese translation of, 155, 158. *See also* Articles of Faith, Japanese translation of; and sacrament prayers, Japanese translation of
Mormonism, explained, 2
Morrill Anti-Bigamy Act (U.S., 1862), 3n
Morumonkyō to Morumonkyōto (Mormonism and Mormons, by Takahashi, 1902), 126, 128, 144–47
"Morumonkyō to Ramakyō" (Mormonism and Lamaism, by Takahashi, 1901), 82, 126
Morumonshū (*The Mormon Sect*, by Uchida, 1902), 82, 83–86
Mountain Meadows Massacre (Utah, 1857), 65, 65n, 85

Muroran
and Asia's first Mormon chapel, 389
early Mormon work in, 344n, 348, 367, 372, 381t, 418t, 434n

N

Nagano, 136, 138–40, 143
Nagasaki
as medieval center of Christian activity, 94, 96
foreign settlement and treaty port, 54n, 99, 102, 105, 448
opening of postwar Mormon work, 373, 390n, 392n
visit by E. D. Thomas to (1911), 141
Nago. *See* Boso Peninsula
Nagoya
postwar Mormon work in, 336–37, 353–54, 367, 371–73, 381t, 386, 391, 434n
visit by J. H. Stimpson to (1917), 141n
visit by A. O. Taylor to (1907), 141
See also Narumi
Nagoya North Branch, 373
Naha (Okinawa)
opening of Mormon work in, 372, 378
property purchase and building construction in, 382t, 385, 390, 390n, 418t, 419–21
Nakaura. *See* Tenno
Nampa (Idaho), 20, 22, 263
Naoetsu, 136, 138–40
Nara Sunday group (Tokyo), 312–15, 319, 324–25, 334
Narumi
conversion to Mormonism of Tatsui Sato in, 297, 300–305
opening and closing of Mormon work in, 334–39, 353–54, 367, 371
postwar pre-mission Mormon work in, 306–7
See also Nagoya
National Anti-Prostitution League (1890), 68
National Christian Council, 237
National Learning. *See kokugaku*
national myth, Japan's
esoteric cult of, 207–8, 234, 234n
exoteric cult of, 207–8, 231, 234
See also nationalism in Japan
national seclusion, policy of (1639–1854), 95, 99
national structure. *See kokutai*

Subject Index

nationalism in Japan, 110–13, 116–18, 207–8. *See also* national myth, Japan's
nationalist reaction. *See* Christianity, persecution in Meiji Japan of
naturalization laws, United States, 22n, 261, 261n
Nauvoo (Illinois), 2, 85, 145
new religions. *See shinkō shūkyō*
Nihon Kirisuto Kyōdan (United Church of Christ in Japan), 237–39, 242
   bloc system (*busei*), 237, 239
   total membership in Japan, 1n
Nihon no Seito wa Utau (Japanese Saints Sing), 429. *See also* Project Temple
Nihon Seikō Kai (Anglican–Episcopal Church of Japan), 56n, 131, 137n, 148, 236, 238, 242, 456, 460
Niigata
   early Mormon work in, 344n, 349–50, 367, 367n, 371–72, 390n, 392n
   treaty port, 54n, 99
   See also Shibata; Tenno
Niitsu. *See* Niigata
Nipponjin (The Japanese), 109
Nippu Jiji, 26, 27, 27n, 32
Niroku Shinpō, 62, 63, 66, 73, 79–80, 79n
Nisei, 247, 264t, 265, 265n, 267n, 269–71, 277, 278n, 279, 285–86, 288–89, 311, 314, 330, 395
Nishi Honganji Temple, 83–84, 271. *See also Jōdo Shinshū*
Nishinomiya
   and Japan's early postwar baptisms, 296–98, 305, 305n–306n
   Mormon work in, 370–72, 382t, 383, 391
Northern Far East Mission (1955–68)
   divisions, 362–63, 364, 380, 438
   establishment of, 362, 373–75
   See also Japanese Mission (Tokyo, 1948–55)

O

occupation. *See* American occupation of Japan
OECD (Organization for Economic Cooperation and Development), 397
Ogden (Utah), 15, 20, 20n, 71, 228, 263–64, 268–69, 444
   J Town in, 264
Okamachi (Osaka) Branch, 372, 372n, 381t, 386–87, 391, 418t, 419–20, 422–23. *See also* Juso (Osaka) Branch

Okayama, early Mormon work in, 347n, 368–69, 372, 390n, 392n
Okinawa
   American administration of, 375–77
   early Mormon work in, 345, 345n, 374–75. *See also* Futenma; Naha
Omotesando (Tokyo), property in
   acquisition, 382t, 387
   disposition, 388–89, 398
organ theory (of the emperor's role), 205, 234
Organic Act (U.S., 1900), 270
Oriental Trading Company (Tōyō Bōeki Kaisha), 262
Osaka
   early postwar Mormon work in, 335, 339, 339n, 344, 354–55, 367, 370, 382t, 383, 386–87, 415, 431, 433, 434n, 438–39
   newspaper controversy on Mormonism in (1901), 76–79
   prewar Mormon work in, 136, 141–44, 143t, 158, 208–9, 213–14, 218, 223, 229, 242, 249–250, 255–59, 270, 282–83, 285
   treaty city, 54n, 57, 57n, 99, 120
   See also Abeno (Osaka) Branch; Juso (Osaka) Branch; Okamachi (Osaka) Branch
Osaka Asahi Shinbun, 62n, 63–65, 67n, 75–79, 78n, 80, 197, 200
Osaka Mainichi Shinbun, 63n, 64, 76–79, 78n, 242, 459
Otaru, Mormon work in, 344n, 348, 367, 372, 381t, 434n
Ōura Tenshudō, 102–3. *See also* Roman Catholicism; Twenty-Six Martyrs; Urakami Incident

P

Pacific Mission, 336, 336n
Pacific War (1941–45), 240, 278, 291, 376, 432
Patriotic League, 19–0, 22
Peace Preservation Law (1925), 234–35, 238–39
   impact, 234–39
Pearl Harbor, Japanese attack on (1941), 233, 240, 240n, 265n, 299
Pearl of Great Price, 2
   Japanese translation, 8, 399, 402–3
Peerage Act (1884), 70n
Philippines, opening of Mormon work in, 345, 345n, 374
picture brides, 24n, 25, 215n, 267

plural marriage. *See* polygamy, Mormon practice of
Plymouth Brethren, 208n, 238–39, 242
polyandry, 82
polygamy, Mormon practice of, 2–3, 3n, 53, 82, 86, 146, 161, 445
 discussion in the Japanese press, 63, 67, 69–70, 76
polygyny. *See* polygamy, Mormon practice of
Potsdam Declaration (1945), 292
Primary Association, 269
prisoners, exchange between Japan and the United States (1941, 1942), 240–41, 241n
Privy Council, 154
Project Temple (1963–65), 426–29
 assessment of, 430–31
Prostitute Liberalization Law (1872), 67, 68n
Protestantism. *See* Christianity
Pure Land Buddhism, 93n, 100, 110n. *See also Jōdo Shinshū*
Pusan (Korea), early Mormon work in, 378–80

Q

Quakers. *See* Friends, Society of
Quota Act (U.S., 1921), 261

R

Relief Society, 158, 278n, 394, 423, 426, 465
religion, economics and sociology of, 131–32, 131n, 436, 436n, 437n
religious freedom. *See* Meiji Constitution, religious freedom under
religious human capital. *See* religion, economics and sociology of
Religious Corporation Law (1951), 1n, 383, 384, 414, 414n
Religious Corporation Ordinance (1945), 293, 323, 327, 383–84
Religious Organization Law (1939), 141–42, 236–37, 293, 293n, 383–84, 414
Renmonkyō, 78, 78n
Rikugō Zasshi, 108, 125, 127, 127n, 198, 201
Rokki Jihō (Salt Lake City), 265
Roman Catholicism
 first arrival and spread in Japan, 93
 membership in Japan, 56n, 93, 93n, 106n
 second arrival and spread, 102, 114
 under Japan's militarism, 237–38, 237n, 240, 241n
 work among hidden Christians, 103–4, 104n, 106
 See also Christianity
Russian Orthodox Church, 56n, 102, 102n
Russo–Japanese War, 90n, 115, 117, 164, 197n
Ryukyu Islands. *See* Okinawa

S

sacrament prayers, Japanese translation of, 157, 399–400, 402
Salt Lake City
 early Japanese connections with, 20, 20n, 21, 159, 262, 26–70, 272
 Nihonjin Machi in, 263–65, 269
 See also Iwakura Mission
Salt Lake Valley Regional Mission, 266, 266n
Salvation Army, 68–69, 115, 236, 248
samurai, explained, 38
San Francisco Peace Treaty (1951), 13, 323–33, 346, 375
Sanjo, Mormon work in, 349, 350, 367, 371, 371n. *See also* Niigata
Sannomiya (Kobe) Branch, 355, 370, 370n, 372, 382t, 386, 391
Sapporo, 308, 334–35, 367, 383, 391, 419, 422, 434n, 439n, 455–57, 463
 prewar opening of Mormon work, 140–41
 postwar opening of Mormon work, 339, 347
 prewar Mormon work in, 136, 141–42, 144, 144n, 158, 209, 211, 213, 215, 218, 223, 249–50, 256, 283, 335
Sapporo Agricultural College, 108, 112, 149, 163, 165, 283
Sasebo, 372n
Satsuma, feudal domain of, 4, 99, 107, 159, 166, 231, 260, 443n
Satsuma Rebellion (1877), 18
Seagull miracle, 145, 145n
Seito no Michi, 371, 392, 403, 420, 422–25
Sekigahara, Battle of (1600), 94
Sendai
 early postwar Mormon work in, 334, 339–41, 350, 367, 372, 381t, 383
 prewar Mormon work in, 117, 136, 140–41, 143t, 144, 218
Seoul, 380
Seventh-day Adventists, 238, 242
Shibata, 338–42, 348–50, 367, 371. *See also* Niigata; Tenno

Subject Index

Shikoku, island of, 141, 373. *See also* Matsuyama; Takamatsu
Shimabara Rebellion (1637–38), 95–96
Shimoda, treaty port of, 54n, 99, 448n
shinbutsu bunri, 99–100
shinbutsu shūgō (Shinto–Buddhist syncretism), 90–92, 100. *See also honji suijaku* theory
Shinkō Kajō no Kenkyū (*Articles of Faith*, by Talmage, 1959), 401
shinkō shūkyō (new religions), 78n, 97, 132, 161, 437n, 436–37, 438
Shinshō Kōgi (*Articles of Faith*, by Talmage, 1915), 151, 153, 217, 273, 401
Shinto
   birth of, 90–91
   fukkō, 98–99
   Sect, 101, 121n, 206, 236
   Shrine, 101–2
   See also State Shinto
Shinto–Buddhist syncretism. *See shinbutsu shūgō*
Shinto–Confucian syncretism, 98
Shizuoka
   early postwar Mormon references, 336, 344
   prewar Mormon work in, 141–42, 197–98
shogun. *See* Tokugawa shogunate
Showa, Emperor, 28, 229
Showa period (1926–89), 229, 231
Shuro (Palm), 248–49, 251–52, 312, 464
Sino-Japanese War (1894–95), 54, 90n, 114–15, 117. *See also* China War (1937–45)
Sōgenji Temple, 419
Sōka Gakkai, 437, 437n. *See also shinkō shūkyō*
sonnō jōi (revere the emperor, expel the barbarians), 4, 99
Sophia University, 114. *See also* Roman Catholicism
South Manchurian Railway Company, 232, 253
Southern Baptists. *See* Baptists
Southern Far East Mission, 374
Spaulding theory (of the origin of the Book of Mormon), 64, 64n, 85, 145, 145n, 198, 198n
standard works, 2, 8, 153, 398–99, 402–3.
   See also Bible; Book of Mormon; Doctrine and Covenants; Pearl of Great Price
State Shinto, 98–102, 113, 237–38, 293, 432. *See also Amaterasu*; Imperial Rescript on Education; Shinto; Yasukuni Shrine
Supreme Commander for the Allied Powers. *See* GHQ/SCAP
Systematic Program for Teaching the Gospel (1961), 412–13. *See also* Aston plan, introduction in Japan of

T

taikyō senpu undō (Great Promulgation Campaign), 101
Taisho, Emperor, 28, 205–6
Taisho Democracy, 13, 204–6, 231–32, 234.
Taisho period (1912–26), 13, 203, 244
   intellectual climate during, 13, 204–5
Taiwan
   beginning of Mormon work in, 374
   Japan's colonial rule of, 162, 164, 235–36
Taiyō (Sun), 52, 52n, 76n, 81n, 123n, 126, 195, 195n, 201
Takamatsu, opening of Mormon work in, 373, 390n, 392n
Takasaki
   early Mormon work in, 334–35, 339, 339n, 351–52, 367, 372, 385
   property purchase in, 380, 381t, 384, 384n
   See also Gunma; Maebashi
Tateyama. *See* Boso Peninsula
Teaching the Gospel with Prayer and Testimony (Aston, 1956), 411–12. *See also* Systematic Program for Teaching the Gospel
temples. *See* Mormon temples
tenkō, 235, 235n. *See also* Peace Preservation Law, impact of
Tenno, 337–42, 339n, 348–49, 349n, 367. *See also* Ichishima land deal; Niigata; Shibata
Tenrikyō, 78, 78n
terauke system, 95–98. *See also* Buddhism, Edo; Christianity, suppression in Edo Japan
Tohoku, 23, 23n, 339, 344
   accent, 23, 26, 27
Tohoku Imperial University, 301, 379
Tokugawa shogunate, 4, 33, 35–36, 40, 54–55, 70n, 90n, 93–96, 98–99, 102–3, 108, 259–60, 282, 283, 443n
Tokyo
   and Japan's first Mormon baptisms, 121
   as Japan's new capital, 4, 99
   first Mormon missionaries' move to, 120–21
   postwar pre-mission Mormon work, 310–15
   postwar post-mission Mormon work, 326–28, 334–35, 342–43, 350–51

prewar Mormon work in, 117, 134–36, 142, 143t, 144, 208, 209–10, 218, 218n, 223, 223n, 225, 228, 249–51, 256, 282–83
treaty city and foreign settlement, 55, 57, 57n, 120, 120n
See also Japanese Mission (Tokyo, 1948–55); Tokyo, Mormon branches in
Tokyo, Mormon branches in
Aoyama (1949–1951), 342–43, 35–51
Ikebukuro (1950–1951), 343, 350–51, 391n
Meguro (1950–1951), 343, 351
Ogikubo (1949–1951), 330, 334, 339n, 342–43, 350–51, 391n
Tokyo Central (1956–), 370, 372, 381t, 382t, 387–88, 391, 416, 416n, 426
Tokyo East (1956–1957; 1962–), 370, 372, 372n, 382t, 389, 418t, 419, 421–2
Tokyo First (1951–1956), 343, 351, 367, 370
Tokyo North (1956–), 370, 372, 382t, 383, 390–91, 416–18, 418t, 420–22, 421n, 421t
Tokyo Second (1951–1956), 343, 351, 370
Tokyo South (1956–), 370, 372, 382t, 391, 393, 418–22, 418t
Tokyo West (1956–), 370, 372, 382t, 388, 391, 416, 417–21, 418t, 421n, 421t
Yukigaya (1949–1950), 342–43, 350–51, 391n
Tokyo Americans (a prewar amateur baseball team), 209
Tokyo Asahi Shinbun, 62, 69n, 72n, 75, 78, 84, 196, 200
Tokyo Imperial University, 18, 18n, 83, 109, 110n, 112, 127, 131–32, 163, 176, 234
Tokyo Nichinichi Shinbun, 63n, 73n, 75–76, 128n, 445, 459
Tokyo Stake (1970), 388, 395, 439, 439n
Tomioka, Mormon work in, 336, 352, 372n. *See also* Maebashi; Takasaki
Topaz. *See* Central Utah Relocation Center
Toyonaka. *See* Okamachi
transcontinental railroad, 3, 15, 15n, 19
translation committee (Tokyo), 399, 402–3
Treaty of Amity and Commerce. *See* Ansei treaties
Treaty of Peace and Amity. *See* Kanagawa, Treaty of
Treaty of Peace with Japan. *See* San Francisco Peace Treaty
Treaty of Portsmouth (1905), 232n

Treaty of Shimonoseki (1895), 164
treaty port journalism, 61–62
tripartite pact, with Germany and Italy (1940), 233
Tsu, city of, 197
Twenty-Six Martyrs, 94, 102, 103. *See also* Christianity, suppression in Edo Japan of; Ōura Tenshudō

U

Uchimura Incident (1891), 112, 112n, 127, 165. *See also* Christianity, persecution, in Meiji Japan of
Unequal Treaties. *See* Ansei treaties
Unitarian Association. *See* Unitarians
Unitarians, 58, 109, 109n, 114n, 116, 123, 124–25, 127n, 130, 173–74
United Church of Christ in Japan. *See* Nihon Kirisuto Kyōdan
Universal Manhood Suffrage Law (1924), 231
Universalists, 109, 114n, 176
University of Utah, 59, 148, 149n, 287–88, 297n, 308, 327n, 458
Urakami Christians. *See* Urakami Incident
Urakami Incident (1870), 102–3, 105. *See also* Christians, hidden
USCAR (United States Civil Administration of the Ryukyu Islands), 375–76, 376n, 420
Utah
1920s economic difficulties in, 226–28, 264
Japanese immigrant population in, 263–66, 264t
conversion to Mormonism, 266–70
statehood, 3, 53
Utah–Idaho Sugar Company, 74n, 162, 162n–163n, 262–63
Utah Nippō (Salt Lake City), 265, 265n, 267, 317, 458, 465
Utah State Agricultural College. *See* Utah State University
Utah State University, 16, 16n, 20, 21, 32, 267, 268, 287, 298, 299
Utah Sugar Company. *See* Utah–Idaho Sugar Company

W

"Wa ga Eikoku Kyōkai wo Satte Batsujitsu Seito Iesu Kirisuto Kyōkai ni Ireru Riyū" (My Reasons for Leaving the Church of England and Joining the Church of Jesus Christ of Latter-Day Saints, by Thomas, 1905), 148, 150t

Walter Murray Gibson trouble (1861–64), 33, 33n, 41, 44, 449–50

Watchtower Bible and Tract Society, 1n, 208n, 229–30, 230n, 235–36, 236n, 242

West Central District. *See* Mormon districts in Japan

Word of Wisdom, 8, 409, 457

World's Parliament of Religions (Chicago, 1893), 116, 129–30, 173–74

Y

Yamagata, Mormon work in, 141, 350, 367, 372, 382t, 389

Yamaguchi, prefecture of. *See* Hirao; Yanai

Yanai, Mormon work in, 340, 342, 356, 367–68, 371–72, 381t, 391, 434n. *See also* Hirao

Yasukuni Shrine, 101, 238. *See also* State Shinto

YMCA (Young Men's Christian Association), 115, 129, 209, 268

Yochomachi field house (Tokyo), 136. *See also* Japan Mission (1901–24)

Yokohama
  early days of LDS Japan Mission in, 29–30, 66–67, 88, 120–21, 220
  postwar opening of Mormon work in, 319, 325, 330, 351, 367, 372, 381t, 391, 394, 418t, 419, 421, 431
  treaty port and foreign settlement, 35–36, 52, 55, 55n, 57–58, 61n

Yorozu Chōhō, 62, 62n, 78n, 79n, 176n, 196, 196n, 199–200, 473, 476

Z

ZCMI (Zion's Cooperative Mercantile Institution), 146, 146n

Zion, 3, 152, 230

Name Index

A

Acheson, Dean G., 333
Akagi, Kenji, 329–30, 339, 339n, 340, 350–51, 353, 495, 521
Akashi, Junzo, 229–30, 236n
Akau, William, 342, 355–56, 495
Aki, Hiroshi, 368, 391, 485
Akimoto, Masanori, 74, 74n
Akutagawa, Ryunosuke, 161
Akya-Hutuktu, 82
Amakusa Shiro, 95
Amussen, Barbara, 31n
Amussen, Carl Christian, 21, 21n, 31n
An, Kyoko, 357, 494
Andersen, Dwayne N., 343, 352n, 361, 361n, 391n, 392–93, 416, 426, 428, 429–31, 435–36, 471, 495
Anderson, Edward H., 149, 155, 157, 401
Anderson, Ezra L., 87n, 477
Anderson, Clarence Leroy B., 377–78, 495
Anderson, James, 141, 148, 150t, 477
Andrade, Philomena, 385n, 496
Andrus, Frances. *See* Parker, Frances
Andrus, Paul C., 329–30, 339n, 344, 347, 351, 353, 361, 364, 364n, 367, 369–72, 370n, 372n, 375, 377n, 379, 380, 380n, 382t, 385–86, 385n, 386n, 388–92, 390n, 399, 402–3, 412–17, 416n, 427, 431, 456, 471, 496
Aoki, Kenjiro, 270
Aoki (Rev.), 125
Arai, Taki, 282, 480
Archibald, Reo S., 296n
Arnold, Mel, 302, 303
Arrington, Leonard, 268
Aston, Willard Allen, 411–12
Atkin, Dennis H., 332, 348, 350, 496
Aubrey, Kenneth L., 312–14

B

Ballard, Leon, 378
Bando, Kotaro, 248
Barton, Robert H., 142, 477
Bauman, Thomas E., 306–7
Bennion, Kenneth S., 401
Benson, Ezra T., 450
Benson, Ezra Taft, 21n, 295, 316, 418t, 439n
Benson, Flora Amussen, 21n, 31n
Bentley, Rondy, 373, 497
Berger, Peter, 132
Bills, Walter R., 266n, 362–63, 362n, 438
Bird, Ralph W., 377, 377n, 497
Bismarck, Otto von, 443
Black, Franklin S., 365, 497
Blake, Rowland S., 373, 497
Boggs, Lilburn, 2
Boud, John W., 295, 300
Bowles, Gilbert, 229
Boyack, Robert, 350, 497
Bradshaw, Howard W., 378
Bradshaw, James R., 363n, 497
Brinkley, F., 60, 60n
Britsch, Lanier, 223
Brooke, J. H. 59–60, 60n
Brooks, Harry B., 431
Brown, Hugh B., 294, 418t, 422, 422n
Brown, Samuel Robbins, 106, 126, 128
Brown, Victor, 425
Browning, Louese, 144, 218, 478
Browning, Wallace, 144, 218, 226, 478
Bryan, William Jennings, 22
Buchanan, James, 449
Bunce, William, 320
Burton, Harold W., 415
Bushman, Morris S., 278–79

C

Caine, Frederick A., 129, 136–38, 149, 150t, 151, 154, 167, 178, 193, 211, 221–22, 477
Cannon, Angus M., 70–72, 71n, 73
Cannon, George Q., 28–29, 71, 163n, 211, 444
Cannon, Hugh J., 211–12, 211n, 272
Carr, Gail E., 363, 380, 498
Carter, Paul S., 329–30, 339n, 498
Cary, Otis, 93, 93n
Chadwick, John, 140–41, 222, 477
Chedister, Walter R., 419, 521–22
Cheney, Rex Alton, 417, 521
Chiba, Yasubeiye, 132–33, 133n, 153, 479
Chinda, Sutemi, 19, 19n
Chosho, Hirotake, 163n
Christensen, Arva, 218, 478
Christensen, Elwood L., 214, 217n, 218, 250, 272, 274, 462, 478
Christensen, Kirk R., 296, 296n
Christensen, Max, 350, 498
Christopherson, Kenneth L., 373, 499
Cicero, 168
Clark, J. Reuben, 31, 274
Clark, William Smith, 108, 163, 163n
Clement, Russell, 461
Clissold, Edward Lavaun, 6, 16, 16n, 28–29, 28n, 31–32, 243, 272, 272n, 274–75, 276, 276n, 279–80, 308–11, 315–16, 318–21, 324–29, 331, 334–38, 338n, 339–42, 347–55, 371, 399, 427, 455–56, 458, 462, 469, 471, 499
Clissold, Irene Picknell, 308, 329–30, 351, 499
Copeland, Luther, 241
Cowley, Matthew, 280n, 332, 336–38, 338n, 340–41, 348, 359–60, 374n, 418t
Cramer, Lew W. M., 381t, 384
Curtis, Theodore E., 295
Cutler, Arthur, 161–62, 478
Cutler, Joseph Preston, 142, 477

D

DaBell, Robert S., 373, 499
Darley, Roy M., 295
Darwin, Charles, 109
Davies, Willaim, 227, 478
Davis, Reed, 302–3, 306
Detton, Richard Lee, 363, 379–80, 500
Dodge, Joseph, 333
Dougherty, Dennis Joseph, 238
Dozier, Edwin, 318n
Dulles, John Foster, 333
Dun, Edwin, 140
Duncan, Chapman, 5
Dunn, S. Howard, 415

E

Ebesu, Allan, 314
Eisenhower, Dwight D., 375n
Elkinton, Mary Patterson, 163
Ellis, William, 142, 477
Emmett, Henry Roland, 142, 477
Endo, Mine. *See* Katsunuma, Mine
Ensign, Horace S., 29n, 51, 66, 88, 119, 120–22, 129, 136–37, 148, 151, 471, 477
Erickson, Einar, 334–35, 334n, 338n
Esplin, Rulon, 144n, 218, 478
Evans, Preston D., 277, 312, 315

F

Fairbourn, William, 140–41, 477
Featherstone, Joseph, 129n, 136–37, 137n
Featherstone, Marie, 129n, 136–37, 137n
Ferguson, Hal G., 355, 500
Field, Harvey H., 296n
Fillmore, David P., 373, 500
Fillmore, Wade W., 428n, 500
Floyd, John, 278–79
Follett, Marvin, 345, 351, 501
Fowler, Orlando, 143–44, 144n, 222n, 223–24, 227n, 461n, 478
Fujimoto, Herbert Kenkichi, 277
Fujiwara, Ayumu, 453
Fujiwara, Mitsue, 399, 484
Fujiwara, Takeo, 221, 253–59, 266, 273–75, 282–85, 311, 347, 453–55, 456n, 457, 462n, 466–68, 482
Fujiwara, Yoshiaki, 453, 453n
Fujiwara, Yuko, 453
Fukuda, Masako, 357
Fukuda, Sumiko, 357

Name Index

Fukuzawa, Yukichi, 110
Fyans, J. Thomas, 425

G

Garrott, Max, 240, 241
Gehrig, Lou, 232
Gessel, Van C., 187, 192
Gibson, Walter Murray, 33, 33n, 41–42, 44, 449–51
Glover, Sylvia, 216, 218, 224, 478
Glover, William, 216, 218, 224, 478
Goble, Jonathan, 445
Godfrey, Lyman R., 412, 501
Gorringe, Howard Theodore (Ted), 350, 419, 502, 521
Goya, Kojin, 329, 330, 339, 339n, 342, 353, 356, 357, 502
Grant, Augusta, 51n, 122, 135, 477
Grant, Heber J., 5–6, 12, 28, 29, 29n, 30, 31, 51, 51n, 54, 56, 57, 58, 59, 60, 63, 66, 69, 69n, 72, 73n, 74, 75, 88, 119, 120, 121, 122, 123, 124, 125, 126, 128, 129, 130, 130n, 135, 136, 137, 138–40, 144, 150t, 158, 159, 160, 161, 162, 162n, 163n, 217, 220, 228, 230, 243, 244, 253, 254, 256, 274, 464, 471, 477
Green, Ray J., 296n
Greene, D. C., 106
Grew, Joseph C., 232n, 233, 233n, 234n, 286n
Griffith, Henry H., 381t, 384

H

Hadley, Darrell, 350, 502
Hales, Melvin D., 417, 521
Hales, Melvin R. (Bud), 417, 521
Hamada, Hisaichi, 214, 283, 284, 480
Hanks, Marion D., 418t, 421, 422, 422n
Hanks, Raymond E., 302, 303, 304, 305
Hansen, Peter Nelson, 343, 502
Hara, Kei (Takashi), 78, 78n, 205
Harding, Marvin S., 417, 521
Harris, Franklin Stewart, 249–51, 254, 256, 275, 453, 455, 456, 464, 466
Harris, Heidi, 54n, 220
Hayashi, Tadao, 391

Heaton, Herald Grant, 374
Hedges, Sanford, 136, 140, 150t, 477
Hepburn, James Curtis, 106
Herlin, Wayne R., 351, 503
Higa, Chiyoko, 277
Higa, Kenneth K., 417, 503, 523
Hill, Allen F., 373, 503
Hinckley, Gordon B., 88, 117, 387, 387n, 388, 389, 390n, 412, 415, 418t, 421, 422, 426n, 427
Hirai, Hirogoro, 129, 147–48, 150t, 154, 175–76, 176n, 177, 178, 178n, 192
Hirai, Kinzo, 116n, 128–30, 147, 148, 173
Hirata, Toshio, 354
Hiroi, Tatsutaro, 82, 83, 123–26, 137, 157, 159
Hisada, Susumu, 209, 257, 282–83, 335, 354, 482
Hoare, James, 62
Horace, 168
Hori, Susumu, 282, 357, 482
Horiuchi, Aiko Mori, 315
Horiuchi, Russell N., 311, 312, 313, 314, 315, 317, 321, 324, 439, 439n
Hotta, Hideji, 392, 485
Hotta, Uzuru, 355
Hult, Merle B., 417, 504
Hyde, Elizabeth, 271

I

Ibata, Motoyuki, 387
Ichiki, Shiro, 159–60
Ichishima, Noriatsu, 340, 341, 348, 348n, 349, 357–60
Iga, Mamoru, 296, 296n, 297, 297n, 298, 317, 354, 483
Igarashi, Amy, 344n, 504
Ikeda, Hayato, 375n
Ikegami, Kichitaro, 272, 272n, 274, 278
Ikuta, Choko (Hiroharu), 12, 114n, 131, 154, 170, 176–78, 178n, 187, 192, 193, 195n, 401
Imai, Kazuo, 387n, 391, 392, 465, 485
Imanaka, Elaine Sumiko, 277
Inoue, Enryo, 110n
Inoue, Tetsujiro, 112, 112n, 127

Inouye, Go, 208, 481
Inouye, Ronald N., 413, 504
Inouye, Yukus, 269
Ishikawa, Osamu, 373, 504
Ishikawa, Terutake, 256, 482
Ishikawa, Zenjiro, 418, 420, 523
Ishizaki, Masako, 277
Ishizuki, Minoru, 260
Isomura, Masayoshi, 373, 504
Ito, Hirobumi, 70–74, 70n, 205, 44–45
Ivie, Lloyd O., 87, 119, 142, 143n, 148–49, 150t, 152, 154, 154n, 209, 214n, 215, 221, 221n, 223–24, 224n, 226–27, 471, 477, 478
Ivins, Anthony W., 223, 250
Ivins, Heber Grant, 119, 149n, 151–52, 154, 161–62, 161n, 209, 223, 459, 471, 477
Iwaasa, Jeaune, 329–30, 339n, 347–48, 504
Iwakura, Tomomi, 5, 71, 105, 443–45
Iwata, Tomokazu, 329, 329n
Iwatsu, Koichi, 208, 481
Izumi, George, 277

J

Jarvis, Erastus, 136, 136n, 138, 138n, 447
Jarvis, G. Stanford, 447, 505
Jarvis, George, 5, 447–48
Jenkins, Ab, 288
Jenkins, Jane, 272
Jensen, A. Howard, 143–44, 478
Jensen, Jay C., 142, 275, 275n, 471, 477
Jensen, Nephi, 148, 150t
Jensen, Wendell W., 385, 505
Johnson, Eugene, 296, 296n
Johnson, Le Roy, 419, 521
Jones, James J. Jr, 412, 505

K

Kagahi, Soryu, 271
Kajiyama, Katsuhiro, 413, 505
Kakazu, Dwight M., 373, 505
Kalakaua (King), 44, 451
Kalama, Samuel, 341, 349, 385n, 417, 505, 521
Kamehameha (King) I, 43

Kamekona, Kalala Keliihananui, 33, 43, 44, 45n, 46–7, 49
Kametani, Florence, 277
Kamotani, Michiko, 356, 488
Kamotani, Miyako, 356, 488
Kaneko, Toichi, 208
Kanetsuna, Hideo, 348, 353, 505
Kano, Tessai, 467, 468
Kasuya, Yoshizo, 19
Katanuma, Seiji, 457
Katayama, Tomio, 355, 487
Kato, Kenzo, 132, 479
Katogi, Naochika, 17, 17n
Katogi, Shigenori, 19, 19n
Katogi, Shutaro, 20, 20n, 21n, 30, 268
Katsunuma, Mine, 19, 19n, 23, 29, 31–32, 48
Katsunuma, Tomizo, 11, 16–32, 47–48, 266–68, 272, 276–77, 281, 283, 285
Katsura, Kazuko, 283, 482
Katsura, Tsuru, 455, 482
Katsura, Tsuruichi, 213–14, 249n, 250, 253n, 256, 282–85, 335, 337, 354, 454–55, 466, 480
Katwyk, Clarence, 417, 419–20, 521
Kawai, Kosaburo (Suimei), 130–31, 152, 154, 178
Kawano, Suma, 267n, 481
Kawano, Tomosuke, 267n, 481
Kawasaki, Mitsuru, 368, 506
Kawashima, Sentaro, 45, 45n, 46n
Kelsch, Louis A., 51, 66, 69n, 88, 120, 121, 136–7, 477
Kennedy, John F., 375, 375n
Kido, Saburo, 287
Kido, Takayoshi, 443–44, 443n
Kikuchi, Saburo, 121, 131, 137
Kikuchi, Shizuo, 339n, 482
Kikuchi, Yoshiro, 208
Kim, Ho Jik, 378–79, 380
Kimball, Spencer W., 280n
Kimura, Shojiro, 282–83, 482
Kimura, Yukiko, 25
Kishi, Nobuhiko, 375n
Kishigami, Hide, 367–68, 491, 506
Kitagawa, Magoji, 253n, 483
Knapp, Arthur M., 58–59, 58n, 109

Name Index

Kobayashi, Takiji, 235
Kodama, Kotoe, 336, 399, 481
Koguro, Masako, 425
Koizumi, Hironori, 418, 523
Koji, Chiyo. *See* Shioki, Chiyo
Komatsu, Adney Y., 278, 361, 373, 394–95, 428, 471, 506
Komatsu, Judy, 394, 506
Koolau, Dorothy A., 385n, 506
Koroki, Yasuyuki Ernest, 277
Kudo, Shunichi, 418, 523
Kumagai, Tamano, 249n, 253n, 259, 283, 335, 337, 347, 455–57, 479
Kumagai, Yoshino, 283, 457, 457n, 482
Kuno, Osamu, 207, 208, 231
Kuribayashi, Norimitsu, 348
Kuriyama, Chojiro, 327, 327n, 328n, 336, 458–59, 481
Kuykendall, Ralph S., 451

L

Lafeber, Walter, 232
Laimana, Paul K., 417n, 506
Larson, Evan, 419, 522
Larson, Jean D., 419, 522
Lassig, Don Peter, 387, 507
Lee, David J., 37n
Lee, John D., 85
Lee, Young Bum, 364, 507
Le Gendre, Charles, 159–60, 160n
Lewis, James, 5
Lewis, Joseph E., 22
Lewis, R. M., 22
Lowe, George, 385n
Lund, Anthon H., 122n
Lundberg, Don C., 366, 403, 507
Lyman, Francis M., 122n
Lytton, A. G. R., 233

M

MacArthur, Douglas, 292, 294, 323, 330, 359, 393n
Madsen, Spencer D., 378, 379
Makahi, Nonaina H., 417, 508, 524
Makino, Tomisaburo, 37, 41–42, 42n
Markham, Ben S., 373, 508

Maruyama, Masao, 10n, 109n, 112n–13n, 234
Maruyama, Yoshinaga, 268
Masaoka, Mike Masaru, 269, 286–89
Masuda, Sachiko, 425, 484
Masukawa, Shigeo, 342, 355, 483
Matsuda, Ikuko Rose, 297–98, 317, 483
Matsukata, Masayoshi, 18
Matsumori, Minoru, 269
Matsumori, Tom, 269
Matsumoto, George (Joji), 269–70, 482
Matsumoto, Haruichi, 272
Matsumoto, Masao, 368, 490, 508
Matsumoto, Ochie, 272
Matsumoto, Otokichi, 272
Matsuoka, Tatsusaburo, 22
Matsushima, Retsui, 418, 524
Matsushita, Yasuhiro, 392, 425
Matsuura, Marye, 297
Matsuyama, Takayoshi, 106
Maughan, Peter Kent, 365, 508
Mauss, Armand L., 16n, 220, 321n
Mauss, Ethel Louise, 326, 508
Mauss, Vinal G., 218, 224, 228, 326, 332–34, 336, 342–45, 345n, 349–50, 356, 361, 374, 383–85, 391n, 399, 471, 478, 508
Maw, Herbert B., 288
McCune, George M., 301n, 305n, 373, 508
McDaniel, Wayne, 329–30, 339n, 341, 344, 349, 508
McKay, David O., 210–13, 217n, 223, 272, 279–80, 310, 315, 351, 374, 409, 423–24, 461, 468–69, 469n
McKinley, William Jr., 73n
Mendenhall, Wendell B., 415
Meng, Richard S., 373, 508
Merrill, William Paul, 318–19, 325, 330, 351, 354–55
Meurer, Dennis J., 373, 508
Mill, John Stuart, 109
Miller, James, 142, 477
Millward, Gene, 344n, 509
Mineta, Norman Y., 289
Minobe, Tatsukichi, 205, 234
Miyama, Kanichi, 268, 270–71
Miyamoto, Keijun, 271
Miyazaki, Toranosuke, 160–62

Mochizuki, Kentaro, 249, 253n, 312, 315, 336, 481
Mochizuki, Kyoko, 256, 482
Mochizuki, Reiko, 248, 256, 258, 282–83, 481
Moffit, Howard, 369, 509
Mogi, Seigo, 340
Moikeha, David H., 385, 509
Moore, John H., 297
Moore, Lewis H., 218, 456, 478
Mori, Aiko. *See* Horiuchi, Aiko
Mori, Arinori, 110
Mori, Betty Masako, 277
Mori, Hachiro, 116, 133, 133n, 153, 479
Mori, Ogai, 161
Mori, Shigeru, 297, 317–18
Moyle, Henry D., 387
Munk, Keith, 348, 510
Murakami, Toshiro, 331, 352, 352n, 367–68, 484, 510
Murayama, Tamotsu, 286n, 287
Murphy, Castle H., 31, 254, 272, 274, 276–81, 277n, 461–62, 471

N

Nachie, Ei, 256, 336, 354, 459–61, 479
Nachie, Tsune, 131, 152n, 256, 272, 274, 276, 459–62, 479
Nagamine, Kensei, 392, 420n
Nagao, Ei. *See* Nachie, Ei
Nagao, Yoshio, 459
Naito, Meisetsu, 26
Nakagawa, Koshi, 208, 208n, 249, 253n, 315, 334, 350, 482
Nakamura, Ayako, 377
Nakamura, Nobu, 377–78, 377n
Nakano, Lawrence Asao, 277
Nakano, Sayeko, 277
Nakano, Winifred Wakako, 277
Nakazawa, Hajime, 121, 128, 137, 152, 479
Namekawa, Hiroyuki, 154
Nanbu, Tatsusaburo, 131, 480
Napela, Harriet Panana, 43
Nara, Fujiya, 248–53, 255n, 256, 275, 284, 298, 311–15, 317, 324–25, 334, 336, 343, 348, 350, 391, 391n, 392n, 399–400, 418–19, 461–64, 464n, 469, 480, 524

Nara, Motoko, 255n, 298, 312–13, 315, 334, 336, 350, 418–19, 462, 463, 483, 524
Natsume, Soseki (Kinnosuke), 176, 176n
Neilson, Reid, 89, 89n, 243, 243n
Nelson, Daniel E., 329–30, 339n, 348, 353, 510
Nelson, Maurine, 299–300
Nelson, Warren Richard, 295–300, 303–5, 321, 324
Neslan, C. Clarence, 288
Nichols, Murray L., 124, 154n, 229, 243n, 329–30, 339n, 354–56, 354n, 356–57, 510
Nielsen, Ronald K., 364n, 510
Nishimura, Chieko. *See* Okazaki, Chieko N.
Nishiyama, Gen, 262
Nitobe, Inazo, 162–65
Nitta, Fumie, 419, 419n, 524
Nitta, Masanobu, 419, 419n, 524
Nixon, Norton, 302–3
Noguchi, Tomomitsu, 152, 480
Noguchi, Zenjiro, 392n, 400, 485
Noguchi, Zenshiro, 116n, 173–75, 174n
Nojima, Yukiko, 342, 355, 355n, 488
Nonogaki, Suketomo, 253n, 391n, 479
Nugent, Donald R., 319–20
Numano, Jiro, 404, 405, 425

O

Oakey, Russell W., 385, 511
Oda, Nobunaga, 93, 93n
Ogawa, Hisashi, 272
Ohashi, Ichitaro, 209, 282–83, 335, 354, 454, 481
Ohashi, Masahiro, 418, 524
Okabe, Gerald, 266n, 342, 355, 511
Okagi, Sonokichi, 277
Okagi, Tsukiyo, 277
Okano, Eitaro, 79–81
Okauchi, Kooji, 329–30, 339n, 350–52, 511
Okawa, James Morio, 277
Okazaki, Chieko N., 278n
Okazaki, Edward Y., 278n, 363, 438
Okimoto, Bessie Yukiko, 329–30, 339n, 342, 356, 511
Okimoto, Wallace Natsuo, 277
Okubo, Masatsuna, 106

Name Index

Okubo, Toshimichi, 159, 443–44, 443n
Okuma, Shigenobu, 28, 160
Olcott, Henry Steel, 173–74
Oldham, Lynn, 339–40, 344n, 345, 350, 353, 511
Olsen, Richard R., 385, 511
Oniki, Ben, 403, 511
Onishi, Rihei, 80n
Ono, Kenji, 283, 335, 347, 482
Oppie, William, 342, 356–57, 511
Orme, Larry D., 363, 511
Oshima, Kintaro, 149
Otsuka, Masaji, 391–92, 484, 511
Owada, Takeki, 130–31, 152
Oyama, Yoshiro, 131, 147, 479

P

Packer, Boyd K., 305
Parker, Arthur K., 274
Parker, Frances, 341, 349, 496, 512
Parker, John Palmer, 43
Parker, Samuel, 43–45, 45n
Perin, George L., 109
Perry, Matthew C., 4, 54n, 99
Peterson, Dallas, 353, 512
Peterson, Elmer G., 287
Peterson, Vadal E., 295, 298
Pexton, Ronald D., 385, 512
Powell, Don Gayle, 363, 379–80, 512
Prestige, Melvyn Shigeru, 277
Price, Harrison Theodore (Ted), 329–30, 338–39, 339n, 344, 353, 357, 512
Price, Raymond, 329–30, 339n, 344, 348, 351, 353, 512
Prior, Ann, 447
Pule, Sarah, 342, 356, 513
Pusey, Eugene Harvey, 340, 513
Puyi, 232

R

Reguet, Émile, 106, 400n
Richards, C. Elliott, 303–6
Richards, Franklin D., 447
Richards, Joseph Barrett, 297
Richards, LeGrand, 424
Rigdon, Sidney, 85
Roberts, Clair L., 296, 296n, 297

Robertson, Hazel, 213–14, 213n, 218, 275, 478, 513
Robertson, Hilton A., 6, 16n, 31–32, 119, 213–14, 213n, 214n, 216–19, 216n, 218n, 223n, 224–25, 224n, 227, 229, 242–43, 248–49, 252, 254, 256, 275–77, 279t, 281–85, 291–92, 296, 317–18, 321, 321n, 349, 361, 362n, 368–69, 370n, 374–75, 386, 409, 409n, 454–59, 462–69, 468n, 471, 478, 513
Roosevelt, Franklin D., 287, 299
Roosevelt, Theodore, 73n, 164, 261
Ruth, George Herman Jr. (Babe), 232, 232n

S

Sadachika (Prince), 25n
Sagara, Kenichi, 392
Saigo, Masagiku, 283, 336, 479
Sakai, Futa, 68n
Sakai, Kiyoshi, 425
Sakai, Ko, 315
Sakata, Kimiaki, 329–30, 339n, 353, 513
Sakuma, Komekichi, 41
Sakuma, Mitsuo, 456, 456n, 479
Sakuraba, Takeshiro. *See* Takahashi, Takeshiro
Sasaki, Shuichi, 267–68, 267n, 285
Sasaki, Takayuki, 445
Sato, Chiyo, 296, 297, 300–301, 305–6, 317, 483
Sato, Miyoshi, 298, 315, 334, 483
Sato, Morisaburo, 154, 256, 335, 337, 348, 351, 351n, 480
Sato, Tatsui, 193, 296–97, 300–307, 317, 324, 335–38, 351, 353, 393, 399–409, 413, 423–25, 427–29, 429n, 483
Sato, Tokujiro, 11, 16, 27n–28n, 32–49
Sato, Yasuo, 307, 483
Sato, Yuki, 357, 494
Savage, Spencer R., 315, 330
Scowcroft, James, 142, 477
Seda, Chiseko, 70
Seki, Hajime, 209
Seely, Justus B., 87n, 140, 477
Seelye, Julius Hawley, 165
Shaum, Milton, 348, 514
Shiga, Naoya, 468–69

Shimabukuro, Sam K., 377, 378, 385, 514
Shimaji, Mokurai, 101, 125n
Shimamura, Hogetsu, 208
Shimizu, Hachiro, 326–28, 326n–327n
Shimizu, Masaru T., 393, 514
Shimotoku, Yutaka, 334, 484
Shioki, Chiyo, 267n, 479
Shiono, Koshun, 152, 152n
Shirai, Joji, 154, 154n, 479
Shiraishi, Genkichi, 249, 253n, 310, 312–13, 315, 334, 336, 343, 343n, 350, 391n, 399, 479
Shirk, James L., 417, 514
Shirota, Tomiko, 329–30, 339n, 514
Shudo, Tamahiko, 391, 489
Shumway, Norman D., 366n, 412, 514
Skousen, Royal, 169–70
Slade, Harold D., 368, 515
Slover, Robert H., 379
Smith, Barbara McIsaac, 21n
Smith, Elias Wesley, 32–34, 38, 39n, 41, 43, 46–47, 47n, 325n
Smith, George Albert, 319, 321, 324, 326
Smith, James W., 417, 515, 524
Smith, Joseph, 2, 8, 64, 85, 145–47, 145n, 149, 151, 167, 170, 198, 198n, 424, 460
Smith, Joseph F., 33, 34n, 149, 450
Smith, Joseph Fielding, 373–74, 374n, 379, 402, 423–24, 440
Smith, Lucy Mack, 423–24, 424n
Smoot, Reed, 124, 287
Snow, Lorenzo, 69n, 72, 447, 450
Soga, Yasutaro, 25–27, 32
Soman, Masaichiro, 335, 347, 480
Sonoda, Alma, 314
Spaulding, Solomon, 64n, 145n, 198, 198n
Spear, Roy W., 277
Spencer, Herbert, 109
Sperry, Ralph, 349, 515
Sperry, Sidney, 169
Spinner, Wilfried, 109
Sproat, Herbert, 344n, 515
Sproat, William, 353, 515
Stapley, Delbert L., 370, 375
Steed, Walter, 142, 477
Steichen, Michel, 126–27
Stephens, Evan, 152

Stimpson, Joseph H., 87, 88n, 119, 130, 137n, 141–42, 141n, 152, 209, 210–12, 221–56, 454, 459, 468, 469n, 471, 477, 478
Stimson, Henry L., 286n
Stoker, John, 136, 140–41, 149, 150t, 157, 477
Stone, Walter S., 138
Stout, Hosea, 5
Stout, Robert T., 363n, 515
Suda, Suketomo. *See* Nonogaki, Suketomo
Sugawara, Tsutau, 22
Suzuki, Genta, 174, 174n, 175
Suzuki, Kiyomi Katsunuma, 24, 24n
Suzuki, Nami, 215, 281–83, 315, 336, 464–65, 479
Suzuki, Naruko, 283, 296, 482
Suzuki, Shozo, 391–92, 391n–92n, 394
Suzuki, Tsuneko, 283, 296, 482
Swenson, Robert, 357, 516

T

Tabata, Charles, 418, 524
Tai, Fude, 256, 479
Tajima, Kengo, 268
Takagi, Tomigoro, 152–53, 208, 249, 256, 282, 317, 336, 343, 343n, 348, 353–54, 391, 391n–92n, 394, 399–401, 403, 424–25, 458, 460, 465–66, 480
Takahashi, Goro, 82, 82n, 106, 106n, 112–13, 112n, 126–28, 144–47, 155, 157, 157n, 161
Takahashi, Nikichi, 465, 479
Takahashi, Takeshiro, 133, 133n, 151–52, 151n, 154, 479
Takamatsu (Prince), 326, 336
Takeuchi, Katherine, 341, 349, 516
Takeuchi, Koichi, 278, 342, 356, 371, 371n, 524
Takeuchi, Robert Makoto, 277
Takeuchi, Thomas Tsutomu, 277, 368–69, 516
Takizawa, Ryosaku, 208
Talmage, James E., 59n, 148, 150t, 151, 153, 157, 217, 273, 401, 424
Tamanaha, Kuniko, 377
Tanabe, Toyoharu, 420, 524

Tanaka, Kenji, 394–95, 431, 439
Tanaka, Kohei, 391, 484
Tanaka, Nobuko, 367, 516
Tanaka, Tadashichi, 20, 20n, 262
Taylor, Alma O., 12, 24n, 29–30, 51, 57, 58n, 60, 66, 70, 73–74, 80, 82n–83n, 88, 88n, 116–17, 119–23, 125–26, 129–30, 134, 136–37, 141–42, 147–49, 150t, 153–54, 157, 159–61, 165, 167, 170–78, 178n, 182, 187, 192–93, 195n, 196–98, 200–22, 249, 251–59, 255n, 273, 275, 285, 401, 457, 460, 464, 466–67, 468, 471, 477
Taylor, Elliot, 142, 477
Taylor, John, 34n
Taylor, Milton, 218, 224, 478
Telford, Ira R., 366n, 516
Teranishi, Akiko, 283, 482
Teranishi, Haruko, 283, 482
Teranishi, Michio, 283, 482
Teranishi, Muneharu, 208–9, 282–83, 481
Teranishi, Nagayo, 283, 482
Terasawa, Kuniko, 265n
Terasawa, Uneo, 265n
Terazawa, Chiye, 277
Terazawa, Toshi, 277n, 516
Thomas, Elbert D., 70, 119, 130, 130n, 141, 148–49, 150t, 154, 221–22, 256, 286, 286n, 287, 459, 471, 477
Thomas, Robert Moseley Bryce, 128, 148, 150t
Toko. *See* Sato, Tokujiro
Tokoyo, Katsumi, 132–33
Tokugawa, Hidetaka, 94
Tokugawa, Iemitsu, 95, 387
Tokugawa, Ieyasu, 93, 94
Tokunaga, Manshi, 174, 174n
Toyn, Richard, 368–69, 517
Toyotomi, H. (Rev.), 268
Toyotomi, Hideyoshi, 93, 94
Truman, Harry S., 286, 286n, 333
Tsai, Sheng-Luen, 461
Tsubouchi, Shoyo (Yujiro), 176–77, 176n
Tsukayama, Mike Kiyoshi, 313–14
Tsukiyama, Chomatsu, 32
Tsukuda, Tokuichi, 391
Tsurumi, Shunsuke, 207–8, 231, 234, 235n

U

Uchida, Toru, 82–86
Uchimura, Kanzo, 112–13, 112n, 165–66, 230
Ueno, Kagenori, 37, 41–42
Uenoyama, Kenjiro, 391
Updike, Galen M., 445
Ushio, Jim, 269
Ushio, Shigeki, 269
Uyehara, Alan M., 372n, 517
Uyetake, Wadsworth Shigeru, 306–7, 317

V

Van Reed, Eugene M., 35–37
Verbeck (Verbeek), Guido, 443

W

Waddoups, William M., 461
Walker, Zona, 344n, 517
Walz, Eric, 268–69
Wanlass, John W., 387, 518
Warner, Langdon, 286n
Watabe, Masahisa, 372n, 487, 518
Watabe, Masao, 350, 391n, 425, 426n, 427–28, 485
Watanabe, Kan, 355, 391–95, 425, 431, 439, 439n, 486, 518
Watanabe, Tazuko, 255, 258, 282–83, 310–12, 315, 336, 467, 469, 481
Watanabe, Yoshijiro, 254–55, 258–59, 282–84, 311, 466–69, 480
Weenig, Melvyn A., 277, 280–81, 280n, 315–19, 316n, 324, 325n, 328–29, 471
Welch, Theodore Franklin, 366n, 518
Whetten, E. Carling, 306, 307
White, Alden, 419, 521
Whitney, Orson F., 212, 212n
Widtsoe, John A., 28n, 31–32, 31n, 149, 149n, 228, 275
Willis, Theodore, 419, 521
Wilson, Joseph, 415
Wilson, Woodrow, 84, 84n
Wolfe, James, 288
Wolsey, Marden L., 417, 518, 525
Wood, James, 222
Woodland, Daniel P., 154, 477

Woodruff, Wilford, 3, 53n, 59, 162n–163n
Woodward, Ernest B., 215n, 218, 225, 243–44, 243n, 478
Woolley, Ralph E., 274, 276
Woolley, Samuel E., 29n, 33–34

X

Xavier, Francis, 93
Xuantong. *See* Puyi

Y

Yaginuma, Shuichi, 425
Yajima, Kajiko, 70
Yajima, Shigenori, 329, 329n, 334, 352, 484
Yamada, Goro, 393–94, 426, 519
Yamaguchi, Masuka, 443–45
Yamaide, Torao, 253n, 481
Yamamura, Yoichi, 391
Yamanaka, Kenjiro, 428–30, 430n
Yamane, Toshichi, 152, 152n
Yamashita, Tadashi, 209, 482
Yamauchi, Hiroo, 339n, 482
Yanagida, Tokichi, 391, 485
Yanagida, Toshiko, 153, 394, 424–25, 465, 484
Yanagisawa, Toshio, 391
Yano, Nobuyasu, 372n
Yokoi, Kentaro, 141n, 481
Yoneyama, Morizo, 257, 335, 479
Yoneyama, Muraji, 131, 256–58, 258n, 335, 352, 479
Yorihito (Prince), 21n
Yoshida, Morio, 286n
Yoshida, Shigeru, 359
Yoshii, Kiyoshi, 329–30, 339n, 354–55, 519
Yoshino, Sakuzo, 205
Yoshino, Takeo, 256, 259n, 481
Yoshino, Yotaro, 331, 352, 352n, 367–68, 393, 484, 519
Yoshizawa, Toshiro, 368
Young, Brigham, 2, 5, 20n, 86, 145, 146n, 444–45, 449–50
Young, Robert, 61, 61n
Youngberg, Al G., 384

Z

Zaugg, Rodney P., 417, 519, 525

Also available from
GREG KOFFORD BOOKS

For the Cause of Righteousness: A Global History of Blacks and Mormonism, 1830-2013

Russell W. Stevenson

Paperback, ISBN: 978-1-58958-529-4

**2015 Best Book Award,
Mormon History Association**

"In Russell Stevenson's *For the Cause of Righteousness: A Global History of Blacks and Mormonism*, he extends the story of Mormonism's long-standing priesthood ban to the broader history of the Church's interaction with blacks. In so doing he introduces both relevant atmospherics and important new context. These should inform all future discussions of this surprisingly enduring subject."
— Lester E. Bush, author of "Mormonism's Negro Doctrine: An Historical Overview"

"Russell Stevenson has produced a terrific compilation. Invaluable as a historical resource, and as a troubling morality tale. The array of documents compellingly reveals the tragedy and inconsistency of racial attitudes, policies, and doctrines in the LDS tradition, and the need for eternal vigilance in negotiating a faith that must never be unmoored from humaneness."
— Terryl L. Givens, author of *Parley P. Pratt: The Apostle Paul of Mormonism* and *By the Hand of Mormon: The American Scripture that Launched a New World Religion*

"You might wonder what a White man could possibly say to two Black women about Black Mormon history. Surprisingly a whole lot! As people who consider ourselves well informed in African-American Mormon History, we found a wealth of new information in *For the Cause of Righteousness*. Russell Stevenson's well-researched exploration of Blacks and Mormonism is an informative read, not just for those interested in Black history, but American history as well."
— Tamu Smith and Zandra Vranes (a.k.a. Sistas in Zion), authors, *Diary of Two Mad Black Mormons*

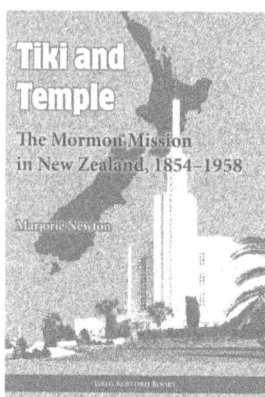

Tiki and Temple: The Mormon Mission in New Zealand, 1854–1958

Marjorie Newton

Paperback, ISBN: 978-1-58958-121-0

**2013 Best International Book Award,
Mormon History Association**

From the arrival of the first Mormon missionaries in New Zealand in 1854 until statehood and the dedication of the Hamilton New Zealand Temple in 1958, Tiki and Temple tells the enthralling story of Mormonism's encounter with the genuinely different but surprisingly harmonious Maori culture.

Mormon interest in the Maori can be documented to 1832, soon after Joseph Smith organized the Church of Jesus Christ of Latter-day Saints in America. Under his successor Brigham Young, Mormon missionaries arrived in New Zealand in 1854, but another three decades passed before they began sustained proselytising among the Maori people—living in Maori pa, eating eels and potatoes with their fingers from communal dishes, learning to speak the language, and establishing schools. They grew to love—and were loved by—their Maori converts, whose numbers mushroomed until by 1898, when the Australasian Mission was divided, the New Zealand Mission was ten times larger than the parent Australian Mission.

The New Zealand Mission of the Mormon Church was virtually two missions—one to the English-speaking immigrants and their descendants, and one to the tangata whenua—"people of the land." The difficulties this dichotomy caused, as both leaders and converts struggled with cultural differences and their isolation from Church headquarters, make a fascinating story. Drawing on hitherto untapped sources, including missionary journals and letters and government documents, this absorbing book is the fullest narrative available of Mormonism's flourishing in New Zealand.

Although written primarily for a Latter-day Saint audience, this book fills a gap for anyone interested in an accurate and coherent account of the growth of Mormonism in New Zealand.

Mormon and Maori

Marjorie Newton

Paperback, ISBN: 978-1-58958-639-0

2015 Best International Book Award,
Mormon History Association

Praise for *The Liberal Soul*:

"*Mormon and Maori* is the result of a labor of love that reflects not years but decades of diligent research. Indeed, in combination with Newton's earlier Tiki and Temple, it constitutes the most detailed discussion in print of the fascinating 160-year saga of accommodation and adjustment between Maori culture and Mormonism. Unflinchingly honest yet unfailingly compassionate, *Mormon and Maori* is a must-read for anyone interested in the extraordinary history of the LDS experience in New Zealand."
— Grant Underwood, Professor of History, Brigham Young University

"*Mormon and Maori* offers a substantial historical account that structures and organizes *te iwi* Māori's (The Māori people's) often complex relationship and attachment to an American religion. In this respect Newton's work should be considered groundbreaking."
— Gina Colvin, *Journal of Mormon History*

From Above and Below: The Mormon Embrace of Revolution, 1840–1940

Craig Livingston

Paperback, ISBN: 978-1-58958-621-5

2014 Best International Book Award, Mormon History Association

Praise for *From Above and Below*:

"In this engaging study, Craig Livingston examines Mormon responses to political revolutions across the globe from the 1840s to the 1930s. Latter-day Saints saw utopian possibilities in revolutions from the European tumults of 1848 to the Mexican Revolution. Highlighting the often radical anti-capitalist and anti-imperialist rhetoric of Mormon leaders, Livingston demonstrates how Latter-day Saints interpreted revolutions through their unique theology and millennialism."
--Matthew J. Grow, author of *Liberty to the Downtrodden: Thomas L. Kane, Romantic Reformer*

"Craig Livingston's landmark book demonstrates how 21st-century Mormonism's arch-conservatism was preceded by its pro-revolutionary worldview that was dominant from the 1830s to the 1930s. Shown by current opinion-polling to be the most politically conservative religious group in the United States, contemporary Mormons are unaware that leaders of the LDS Church once praised radical liberalism and violent revolutionaries. By this pre-1936 Mormon view, 'The people would reduce privilege and exploitation in the crucible of revolution, then reforge society in a spiritual union of peace' before the Coming of Christ and His Millennium. With profound research in Mormon sources and in academic studies about various social revolutions and political upheavals, Livingston provides a nuanced examination of this little-known dimension of LDS thought which tenuously balanced pro-revolutionary enthusiasms with anti-mob sentiments."
--D. Michael Quinn, author of *Elder Statesman: A Biography of J. Reuben Clark*

Mormonism in Transition: A History of the Latter-day Saints, 1890–1930, 3rd ed.

Thomas G. Alexander

Paperback, ISBN: 978-1-58958-188-3

More than two decades after its original publication, Thomas G. Alexander's Mormonism in Transition still engages audiences with its insightful study of the pivotal, early years of the Churcah of Jesus Christ of Latter-day Saints. Serving as a vital read for both students and scholars of American religious and social history, Alexander's book explains and charts the Church's transformation over this 40-year period of both religious and American history.

For those familiar with the LDS Church in modern times, it is impossible to study Mormonism in Transition without pondering the enormous amount of changes the Church has been through since 1890. For those new to the study of Mormonism, this book will give them a clear understanding the challenges the Church went through to go from a persecuted and scorned society to the rapidly growing, respected community it is today.

Praise for Mormonism in Transition:

"A must read for any serious student of this 'peculiar people' and Western history." – STANLEY B. KIMBALL, *Journal of the West*

"Will be required reading for all historians of Mormonism for some time to come." – WILLIAM D. RUSSELL, *Journal of American History*

"This is by far the most important book on this crucial period in LDS history." – JAN SHIPPS, author of *Mormonism: The Story of a New Religious Tradition*

"A work of careful and prodigious scholarship." – LEONARD J. ARRINGTON, author of *Brigham Young: American Moses*

"Clearly fills a tremendous void in the history of Mormonism." – Klaus J. Hansen, author of *Mormonism and the American Experience*

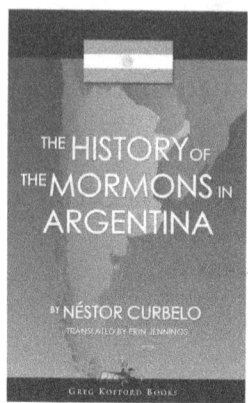

The History of Mormons in Argentina

Néstor Curbelo

English, ISBN: 978-1-58958-052-7

Originally published in Spanish, Curbelo's The History of the Mormons in Argentina is a groundbreaking book detailing the growth of the Church in this Latin American country.

Through numerous interviews and access to other primary resources, Curbelo has constructed a timeline, and then documents the story of the Church's growth. Starting with a brief discussion of Parley P. Pratt's assignment to preside over the Pacific and South American regions, continuing on with the translation of the scriptures into Spanish, the opening of the first missions in South America, and the building of temples, the book provides a survey history of the Church in Argentina. This book will be of interest not only to history buffs but also to thousands of past, present, and future missionaries.

Translated by Erin Jennings

Joseph Smith's Polygamy, 3 Vols.

Brian Hales

Hardcover
Volume 1: History 978-1-58958-189-0
Volume 2: History 978-1-58958-548-5
Volume 3: Theology 978-1-58958-190-6

Perhaps the least understood part of Joseph Smith's life and teachings is his introduction of polygamy to the Saints in Nauvoo. Because of the persecution he knew it would bring, Joseph said little about it publicly and only taught it to his closest and most trusted friends and associates before his martyrdom.

In this three-volume work, Brian C. Hales provides the most comprehensive faithful examination of this much misunderstood period in LDS Church history. Drawing for the first time on every known account, Hales helps us understand the history and teachings surrounding this secretive practice and also addresses and corrects many of the numerous allegations and misrepresentations concerning it. Hales further discusses how polygamy was practiced during this time and why so many of the early Saints were willing to participate in it.

Joseph Smith's Polygamy is an essential resource in understanding this challenging and misunderstood practice of early Mormonism.

Praise for *Joseph Smith's Polygamy*:

"Brian Hales wants to face up to every question, every problem, every fear about plural marriage. His answers may not satisfy everyone, but he gives readers the relevant sources where answers, if they exist, are to be found. There has never been a more thorough examination of the polygamy idea."
—Richard L. Bushman, author of *Joseph Smith: Rough Stone Rolling*

"Hales's massive and well documented three volume examination of the history and theology of Mormon plural marriage, as introduced and practiced during the life of Joseph Smith, will now be the standard against which all other treatments of this important subject will be measured." —Danel W. Bachman, author of "A Study of the Mormon Practice of Plural Marriage before the Death of Joseph Smith"

The End of the World, Plan B: A Guide for the Future

Charles Shirō Inouye

Paperback, ISBN: 978-1-58958-755-7

Praise for *End of the World, Plan B*:

"Mormonism needs Inouye's voice. We need, in general, voices that are a bit less Ayn Rand and a bit more Siddhartha Gautama. Inouye reminds us that justice is not enough and that obedience is not the currency of salvation. He urges us to recognize the limits of the law, to see that, severed from a willingness to compassionately suffer with the world's imperfection and evanescence, our righteous hunger for balancing life's books will destroy us all."
— Adam S. Miller, author of *Rube Goldberg Machines: Essays in Mormon Theology* and *Letters to a Young Mormon*

"Drawing on Christian, Buddhist, Daoist, and other modes of thought, Charles Inouye shows how an attitude of hope can arise from a narrative of doom. The End of the World, Plan B is not simply a rethinking of the end of our world, but is a meditation on the possibility of compassionate self-transformation. In a world that looks to the just punishment of the wicked, Inouye shows how sorrow, which comes from the demands of justice, can create peace, forgiveness, and love."
— Michael D.K. Ing, Assistant Professor, Department of Religious Studies, Indiana University

"For years I've hoped to see a book that related Mormonism to the great spiritual traditions beyond Christianity and Judaism. Charles Inouye has done this in one of the best Mormon devotional books I've ever read. His Mormon reading of the fourfold path of the Bodhisattva offers a beautiful eschatology of the end/purpose of the world as the revelation of compassion. I hope the book is read widely."
— James M. McLachlan, co-editor of *Discourses in Mormon Theology: Philosophical and Theological Possibilities*

William B. Smith: In the Shadow of a Prophet

Kyle R. Walker

Paperback, ISBN: 978-1-58958-503-4

Younger brother of Joseph Smith, a member of the Quorum of the Twelve Apostles, and Church Patriarch for a time, William Smith had tumultuous yet devoted relationships with Joseph, his fellow members of the Twelve, and the LDS and RLDS (Community of Christ) churches. Walker's imposing biography examines not only William's complex life in detail, but also sheds additional light on the family dynamics of Joseph and Lucy Mack Smith, as well as the turbulent intersections between the LDS and RLDS churches. *William B. Smith: In the Shadow of a Prophet* is a vital contribution to Mormon history in both the LDS and RLDS traditions.

Praise for *William B. Smith*:

"Bullseye! Kyle Walker's biography of Joseph Smith Jr.'s lesser known younger brother William is right on target. It weaves a narrative that is searching, balanced, and comprehensive. Walker puts this former Mormon apostle solidly within a Smith family setting, and he hits the mark for anyone interested in Joseph Smith and his family. Walker's biography will become essential reading on leadership dynamics within Mormonism after Joseph Smith's death." — Mark Staker, author *Hearken, O Ye People: The Historical Setting of Joseph Smith's Ohio Revelations*

"This perceptive biography on William, the last remaining Smith brother, provides a thorough timeline of his life's journey and elucidates how his insatiable discontent eventually tempered the once irascible young man into a seasoned patriarch loved by those who knew him." — Erin B. Metcalfe, president (2014–15) John Whitmer Historical Association

"I suspect that this comprehensive treatment will serve as the definitive biography for years to come; it will certainly be difficult to improve upon." — Joe Steve Swick III, Association for Mormon Letters

Hearken, O Ye People: The Historical Setting of Joseph Smith's Ohio Revelations

Mark Lyman Staker

Hardcover, ISBN: 978-1-58958-113-5

2010 Best Book Award - John Whitmer Historical Association
2011 Best Book Award - Mormon History Association

More of Mormonism's canonized revelations originated in or near Kirtland than any other place. Yet many of the events connected with those revelations and their 1830s historical context have faded over time. Mark Staker reconstructs the cultural experiences by which Kirtland's Latter-day Saints made sense of the revelations Joseph Smith pronounced. This volume rebuilds that exciting decade using clues from numerous archives, privately held records, museum collections, and even the soil where early members planted corn and homes. From this vast array of sources he shapes a detailed narrative of weather, religious backgrounds, dialect differences, race relations, theological discussions, food preparation, frontier violence, astronomical phenomena, and myriad daily customs of nineteenth-century life. The result is a "from the ground up" experience that today's Latter-day Saints can all but walk into and touch.

Praise for *Hearken O Ye People*:

"I am not aware of a more deeply researched and richly contextualized study of any period of Mormon church history than Mark Staker's study of Mormons in Ohio. We learn about everything from the details of Alexander Campbell's views on priesthood authority to the road conditions and weather on the four Lamanite missionaries' journey from New York to Ohio. All the Ohio revelations and even the First Vision are made to pulse with new meaning. This book sets a new standard of in-depth research in Latter-day Saint history."
        -Richard Bushman, author of *Joseph Smith: Rough Stone Rolling*

"To be well-informed, any student of Latter-day Saint history and doctrine must now be acquainted with the remarkable research of Mark Staker on the important history of the church in the Kirtland, Ohio, area."
        -Neal A. Maxwell Institute, Brigham Young University

www.ingramcontent.com/pod-product-compliance
Lightning Source LLC
Chambersburg PA
CBHW052052300426
44117CB00013B/2096